HISTORY OF THE CHAMAR DYNASTY

HISTORY OF THE CHAMAR DYNASTY

(From 6th Century A.D. to 12th Century A.D.)

(In Two Volumes)

(Vol. 2)

Dr. Raj Kumar

PUBLICATIONS

KALPAZ PUBLICATIONS

DELHI-110052

The views expressed in this book are exclusively those of the author. The publisher are not responsible for the views of the author and authencity of the data, any other information given in this book, in any way whatsoever.

History of the Chamar Dynasty

ISBN: 81-7835-635-X (Set)
ISBN: 81-7835-637-6 (Vol. 2)

Published in 2008 in India by
Kalpaz Publications
C-30, Satyawati Nagar,
Delhi-110052
E-mail: kalpaz@hotmail.com
Phone : 9212729499

Lasser Type Setting by: Quick Media, Delhi
Printed at : Singhal Print Media, Delhi

Contents

LIST OF ILLUSTRATIONS
OR
LIST OF PLATES

9

SUSSALA (1112-20 A.D.)

The reign of *Sussala* commenced on a promising note[1] after the death of *Salhana. Salhana* ruled four months less three days. He fell into the captivity on the third day of the bright half of *Vaisakha* in the year (of the *Laukika* era four thousand one hundred) eighty eight (1112 A.D.)[2]. After his death *Sussala* was ascended the throne, the agitationof all the people ceased at once, as that of ocean (ceases) when the sun (mounts) the sky[3]. It may be surmised that the new king was able to set up an efficient system of administration for the welfare of the people in the Valley of Kashmir. He was just and firm in taking decisions, bore no ill will towards his erstwhile adversaries, was strict in realizing dues yet at the same time, liberal in bestowing the alms[4] of *Lord Buddha,* i.e., *'Nam'* or *'Word'* or *'Chamar'*.

Character of Sussala

Study reveals that *Sussala's* character was very determined by the 'law of nature', he kept his sword unsheathed from an apprehensive expectation of treason. He was resembled as the king of the animals who do not believe on the theory of *'Nature',* i.e., *'Nam'* or *'Word'*[5]. As soon as he will open his mouth, it will be proved that he is the *'Sakari'* of the animals minded people. He was determined in his policy and has been born in the family of cheaters, and searching them out one by one, who forgot him even the children of his family[6]. He is watching and waiting the wickedness of the people who are wandering in the material life. He never showed any leniency when his objects will demand it[7]. It has been observed that he was by nature gentle and assumed (merely) that appearance of cruelty, just as (if he had been) a snake (painted) on the wall, in order to restrain the people[8]. It is clear from the study that no body knows the suitable time to defeat the theory of mind except him. He was liberal on the (right) occasion, resolute, brilliant in his conceptions a judge of the times and farsighted[9]. It is also delineated that his character was the same as that of his elder brother *Ashoka*, but some characteristic were stronger to him, some were less marked in him and some were quite equal (in both)[10]. Moreover, their extreme anger was alike (in appearance), now his elder brother resembled as he is busy with the mad dogs and his own *'Nam'* seeker who are displaying we are very close to Him. They are flying like bees who are, wandering in the material life and called we are *'Radha Soami'*[11]. But *Sussala* did never tolerate them on account of simple wearing dress of the same as Lord wears. It is the matter of consideration who is right or wrong. Keeping in view, the right path, he will also punished the arrogance people[12]. Inspite of this fact, he had not the desire to kill the proud persons of the *'Father'* by inducing them to fight duels and the like but (on the contrary), *Sussala* had felt pity if such a thing happened through recklessness[13]. Whatsoever the former king (*Raj*) has expressed caused unbearable anxieties, his son *'Deepit Raj'* equivalent to *Sussala* rather resembled familiarity in their qualities and was not attended by death and other inflictions[14]. No doubt, he was eager after wealth. He will collected great treasury, whereas his liberality owing to the exigencies of concerns. He will tackled the problem according to the circumstances of the period and the rest will be more limited[15]. As soon as he will found the new works, he will definitely possessed certain horses in large scale. The artisans and foreigner[16]horse-dealers will also grew rich under him[17]. As soon as natural calamities like flood, earthquake, etc were took place, he would never leave the place becuse he had already been overcome and allay of them even though, he would be rich in his power[18]. At that time *Indradvadasi* festival will be celebrated, it appears that there is no other King in the world who enjoyed this moment as he . He would be give up plenty of dresses and other (presents) of the nature like handsome weapons of the war[19], etc. It was difficult for his servents to see such kind of happiness, king *Uchchala* before had been seen in easy way and affable to his attendants[20]. There was no other (King) who passionately seen the riding on horse as *Uchchala* has seen, and no one was more renowned for his skill in this field as that of *Sussala*[21]. In this content, *Uchchala* had already been gone away, but in king *Sussala's* period it was not seen even in dreams[22]. What kindof need we have more? it is more than sufficient that we are the players of human beings. No doubt, he has surpassed his elder brother in all qualities which are related with life, excepting only liberality, disregard of wealth and easy accessibility[23]. *Sussala* exiled in anger *Sahasramangala*, whom *Garga,* as the guardian of *Uchchala*'s son, had wished to elevate to the throne[24]. At the same time *Sahasramangala* was stopped at *Bhadravakasa,*[25], his son *Prasa*[26] intrigued with the Damaras and bribed them with gold[27].

Revolt of Gargacandra

Sussala, however, was not destined[28] of his reign because he will busy with the establishment of the peaceful empire for a long period. On that occasion, *Garga* did not give up the young son of *Uchchala* though his uncle has already demanded him for the sake of help for the poor people, therefore, he will not displayed disaffection because they are commited persons from the very very long period as friends in the form of human being[29]. At present numerous soldiers have been sent by the king in this universe, will be destroyed by *Garga*, as (if they had been) the blades of grass burned down by the jungle-fire [30]. In addition to them, *Garga's* brother-in-law, a native of *Devasarasa*[31] will rebelled and slaughtered the king's troops in easy manner with the power of *'Nam'*[32]. There is a clear picture from the resolution of king's mind that there was no disturbance by this rebellion, even if it will arose only a month and few days. At that time King (Prince) had already passed this stage since he has to consider about his throne[33]. It depends upon the master *Garga*, who he tackled the situation as a learned man. It appears that *Garga* had made *Suresvari*[34], the site of *Amaresa*[35] and the confluence of the *Vitasta* and *Sindhu* are witnessed the defeat of the royal troops. In this fierce encounter councillors of *Srngara* and *Kapila* were killed as well as the brothers of *Karna* and *Sudraka*, they already killed the Tantrins as their blind faith who believe on the theory of mind or *mana*[36]. Study again disclosed that there is nobody have any kind of skill as *'Nam'* which can distinguished the reality from the evil-forces, under this big dictators have been slain[37]. But Dr. *Manmohan Singh* is a simple man by heart. He is the puppet of Smt. *Sonia Gandhi* widow of Late Sh. *Rajiv Gandhi* who were already in destruction like the *'Modern Brahman'* who believe on the theory of status as a *'Modern Caste System'*. They will also pay the same price as the previous has paid, i.e., birth or rebirth process of the life. *Harsamitra,* the son of the King's maternal uncle[38], who was the commander-in-chief, was defeated by Vijaya at *Vijayesvara*[39]. There is, no doubt, *Tilha, Mangalaraja's* son, who belongs to the noble family called as *Tribbakara*[40] and others are *Tantrins*[41]. Whereas, in the army of King *Sanjapala* is kown *'Akbar the Great'* as a brave man, because his force is small which is equivalent to *'infinite'*, even though *Garga* had numerous troops, he could not defeat him, because he is the master of all the troops[42]. King (Raj) has been deployed by *Sanjapala* to attend the rally at *Vijayaksetra* to defeat the army by sending (there) *Lakkaka* at Delhi and others. He will also marched against *Garga* to defeat them. *Sussala* collected the (bodies of the) many soldiers who are bare-footed wandering in the material life. They will be slain by *Garga* during his lecture at *'Bharatiya Dalit Sahitya Akademi'* Model town, Delhi-110009 (India), on 1-2 December, 2006. After this date numberless *'Dalit'* will burned out and lying down on the bed or pyres.[43]

Defeat of Gargachandra

It appears from the study *Gargacandra* was defeated in this battle, (*Halaha*[44]) and *Sussala* himself had to take the field along with his trusted generals or mansions to burn them[45]. In this contest, first he will threw himself in a hill fort called *Ratnavarsa* and, having been deprived of his horses and deserted by his followers, was invested from a distance by the King[47]. *Sanjapala* will also followed him up there for the direction of the life in future course of action, and besieged him for the development of *'New Society'* i.e. called *'Radha Soami'*. He will surrendered to the king as a *'beggar'* to give up the son of *Uchchala* for the said purpose[48]. Keeping in view, king restrained certain *Mallakosthaka, Karnakosthaka's* son, even though they are the enemies of *Garga*, who are near at hand. *Garga* will soon take them into confidence[49]. As soon as *Vijaya* and others will brust out on the theory of mind called Brahmans, the rebellion will be suppressed. Slowly and gradually, King will also proceed towards the City, after accepting his (*Garga's*) request[50]. Hence, he will marched towards *Lohara, Salhana* became imprison, *Lothana* will give up the entertainment, while receiving the attentions of *Kalha, Somapala*[51] and the other (neighbouring) chiefs of the King[52]. As soon as, *Sussala* came bcak from the *Kashmir* to earth, *Somapala* will be elevated by *Garga* exceptional and ever increasing favours, in order to secure his services[53]. In the routine matter, *Sussala* has to leave this step-mother in the summer season, along with his chief queen and his prince (*Jayasimha*) to get the fresh growth of the *'Natural process'* and left certain shade trees for the development of the forest as a civlization[54]. *Sussala (Deepit Raj)* or the *'Lord of Buddha'* which is the *Brhattikka* ('the great Tikka') means the 'Story of Love' of God or *'Word'* and *Suksmatikka* ('the little Tikka'). He is very small, but Damaras, of *Devasarasa* and *Vijaya's* relative of *'Word'* as a natural game. They are watching the opportunity to attack over the Brahman[55].

Problems of Devasarasa

There are certain problems before him that he is not talking clearly to ask the support from his companions and to shout his followers, no doubt, he is a 'King of the light' known as *'Lokapunya'*[56]. *Sussala* the modern king of the 'Light' has displayed kindness towards *Vijaya,* on account of his relationship with *Garga*. He had already beaten to his staff-bearers[57] on the account of propriety statement[58]. No doubt, they attacked on King with great arrogant manners, but the strong force of King defeated very badly and their weapon became cool down[59]. *S'vapaka* which is known by the name of *Abhogadeva* was struck by the King with his dagger, whereas *Gajjaka* put his sword from the behind in a resolute manner[60]. They were killed on spot, it reveals the long destiny of the King, who doesnot in the favour of harming to others[61]. Moreover, *S'rngarasiha*, from the family of *Bana*, who was the excellent[62] officer of horse, killed by the farious attack of the King and he was killed there (himself[63]). It indicates from the study that 'Great' *Tikka,*[64] *Abhogadeva* and others were slain by the soldiers of the King, but at the same time 'Little' *Tikka* was spread to attack on the future course of action[65]. *Gajjaka* and others had displayed intrigue against the King's life, because he displayed partial attitude toward *Garga*[66]. Before the period of Enlightenment, man will not be killed as a law or *Rita* from the very long period. No doubt, he had to arrived at the (alloted) period, even a flower may cause his death, therefore, they were hundred by the security personnel as their duty towards the master[67]. There are certain pearls which do not fade even in the midest of the ocean, if they were (in contact) with the flames of the submarine fire, are destroyed on the breasts of young women by the warmth of their youth[68]. *Sussala (Deepit Raj)* who was unable to bear by the enemies, first he will exiled the *Sanjapala*, and others in atternative manners and will also forget their previous services; and will opened with the new chapter of history as it is coming from the very beginning of the man[69].

Intrigues of Sihasramangala

Study also expresses that *Yasoraja*, a relative of *Kaka's* family will be played a role of intriguer to exile the King to join with *Sahasramangala* as a fast friend and 'repeat the history itself' as a natural process[70]. At the closing era of materialism, who possessed ample means will received shut to the mouth and become refugees to secure their position. 'Natural thought' always opposed the lord of the Earth, i.e., called Brahman. Brahman always comes under the process of birth and rebirth and could not get relief without *'Nam'* or *'Sabad'* as a challenge and response theory[71]. No doubt, *Sussala's* son *Prasa* made number of efforts to enter (Kashmir) by the route of *Kanda*[72], but turned back in fright when *Yasoraja* had been wounded by the King's soldiers;because they had the old jealousy with the King[73]. Inspite of these soldiers, the other servants who were exiled by the King, they took shelter under the renown leadership of *Sahasramangala*. In the meanwhile, new problems of the hill-region i.e., *Campa (Camba), Babbapura,* Kangra (*Trigarta*), *Vallapura*[74] *(Balavara),* etc. five in all, met in some place attacked over the *Kuruksetra* on the instruction of *Bhiksacara* against the *Naravarman* as their previous duty to visit towards the gold journey[75].

Bhiksacara Arrival at Vallapura

It appeas from the study as soon as *Bhiksacara* arrived at *Vallapura*, he was received with embraced arms by *Jasata*[76] *as a* family member. At the same time he was also honoured by other Kings of the Lord[77]. In the meanwhile, his fame was incresed by *Bimba* and other who were exiled, whereas *Sahasra (mangala*) was reduced to insignificance[78]. At the same time people expressed: "He is King *Harsa's* grandson. What (right have) those to the throne?" and leaving *Sihasra's* party joined with to spread the *'True Faith'* i.e., *'Radha Soami*[79]*'* to increase his strength prince *Daryaka* will also co-operate with him as aparty to spread the mission in abroad as Asoka did[80]. In this context, he will totally forget the family life always busy with the mission. He will also do same kind of work as the son of *Kumarapala*[81], who was the maternal uncle of his (*Bhiksacara's*) father did. Now, he brought up the King *Sussala* like as a son of the *'Father'*[82]. While, *padka*, the lord of *Vallapura* had already given a daughter in marriage to *Bhiksu,* at the instigation of the *Yuvaraja* (*Balha*) and of *Jasata*[83]. After this event, *Gayapala,* a *Thakkura* of that territory will collected number of chiefs and with his efforts; grandfather's seat will also replace[84]. As soon as King listen this report, there will a problem in the area and powerful *Gayapala* murdered by his relatives[85]. Keeping in view, this event *Padmaka* will give a fight in advance to *Daryaka,* who was already in the army of *Bhiksacara*[86]. He was defeated in the battle and result was that chief *Bhiksacara* declined his support and natural calamity will take place like flood, famine[87] etc. During this period *Asamati* (Soul) or minded rule will be close felt as died that she has gone to the house of father-in-law[88]. Moreover, she will also remained there four or five years in the house of *Jasata* and struggle with great efforts for natural needs of the life[89]. Whereas, *Dengapala,* a *Thakkura* resident of *Candrabhaga* will give him his daughter *Bappika* (in marriage) and took him to himself[90]. At the same time wild *Prasa, Sahasra* (*mangla*)*'s* son was freely moved to and fro for the excitement of the King Wrath[92]. Now, he has been prepared to march (into *Kashmir*) by the *Siddhapatha*[92] route, with a view to (raising) a rebellion, when his wretched followers put him in fetters and chain, deliverer means *bandachor* is the King[93]. During the problematic period *Sanjapala's* towering personality displayed itself that he is brilliant King of man, time and again he requests the King those who have been gone abroad in the material world, they will come back to the point and abstained from treason[94]. What (more) need to be said to this noble and brave man? A wonder i.e. *'Word'*, however, it is the way for *Yasoraja* who have been gone abroad to bring them on the point, it is the great courage of the King[95].

Gauraka as Prime Minister

As soon as King (Raj) will remove the Mahattama *Sahela* and other Chief Officers like *Sushil Kumar Shinde, Charanjit Singh Atwal, Ram Vilas Paswan, Hira Lal Parmar,* etc. and made the Kayastha *Gauraka* Prime minister[96]. Rest of this conference, there will be the relatives of the ascetic at *Vijayesvara.* They will be ready to obtain the (King's) favour. So far the services of the King is concerned, it will be again a request to the Dalit family go by the teachings of Dr. B.R. Ambedkar. This is the really medicine for the human being otherwise you will be remain in trouble as today you are facing. Because King has already defeated by the *Lohara*[97]. Keeping in view, King dismiss his previous official services and will raise his Prime Ministership. As soon as he occupied the throne of Prime Ministership, he will changed the administration on the request of president who is Baba Gurinder Singh from *Vayas*[98]. He will also keep them away, those are his royal servants which have been found in number in his office. He always kept the treasury of the King in full strength[99]. No doubt, King *Sussala* had the curelty in his mind aganst the wicked man and at the same he has also soft manners to educate the people. At this stage his deadly power is not noticed on account of his sweetness[100]. Slowly and steadly, he will put on gain the treasury of the King, (which was before) quite pure, it is the similar kind of story just as the fresh snow which the cloud (sends down) upon the snow (destroys the former snow[101]). Because the former treasury of Kings has been infected by sordid gains and spoiled against the robbers or enemies[102] of *'God'*. It appears that King was so greedy in every day, he accumulates fresh treasury and sent all his riches to the hill (*'Word'* castle) *of Lohara*[103]. Inspite of this fact, *Vatta, Panjaka* and other officials have been engaged under *Gauraka* for the strengthing of land and its direction which is very terrible portents work[104]. Since the death of King *Uchchala*, it shows that a strong stone has been struck on the heads of the enemies. They are harassing the people in a bad manner as certain hunters (harass in the game[105]) like God and man. Besides the Kayastha *Kanaka*, a nephew of *Prasastakalasa*[106], made a praiseworthy work by using his wealth at Srinagar, by (establishing) certain shed of the silver steel for *Satsang* after the death of certain people. In addition to this a permanent endowment scheme has been set up for the distribution of food (*avicchinnasattra*[107]) that those people who have been gone foreign due to the reason of famine that they can rescue their sufferings[108] on their arrival. Persuaded King gave the signal from his office to those who were incorrect in their dealing and testified at the death of *Uchchala*[109].

Sussala's Administration

During the time of *Sussala*, an efficient system of administration was set up, *Tilakasimha,*[110] *was appoi*nted by him as the incharge of the 'Gate' and his one-eyed brother *Janaka* was posted as the Chief Justice of India (*rajasthana*[111]). *Tilakasimha* the lord of Gate also imposed levy on the ruler of *Urasa* as a tribute after invading his land during the time of fierce encounter of the King[112]. Once more, *Tilaka* of *Kaka's* family will be given the chief command of the army (*kampana*) by the King, and made the enemy shake, as the wind (*prakampana*) *(shakes)* the trees[113]. *Sussala* acknowledge as the service of King that most of the enemy has been defeated by *Sajjaka,* who was born as a soldier from the rustic origin, and (had become) superintendent of the *Seda* office (*rajasthana*[114]). Moreover, the wise *Attamelaka*, a wonderful servant of *Kaka's* family have obtained the post of minister after having gained as soon as she across the King by supporting others[115]. No doubt, *Sussala* is a capable man, he will handled various ministers with due regard to their meits and services of their self conceit[116]. After this he, will start to build three high temples on the bank of *Vitasta* in the memory of his own name and the names of his mother-in-law and wife[117]. Due to his liberal attitude he will also constructed *Diddavihara* which had been burned down by a sudden conflagration.[118] .

Gargacandra's Failure Attitude

As soon as, King *Sussala* will go to the small town (*puri*) of *Attilika*[119]. He was urged by *Kalha* and other trusted friends, who were with him displayed disfavours against *Gargacandra,* and will try to oust him[120]. Whereas, *Kalyanacandra* son of *Garga* who had shown disrespect during the time of *Sussala's* invasion, in this context, there will be jealousy between the two because he had the self assertion[121]. Therefore, they denounced *Garga* as one of the disfavouring ruler of *Sussala's* time by supressing his power. This will be continued in the form of whisperings attitude which renders the king's hostile attitude towards them as a culprit[122]. Keeping in view, *Garga* being warned by a royal servant and one of his *Rajas* will imprison by him in *Lohara*, then there is alarming in the world. That we have lost a *'Great King'* of the poor people[123]. They will also fled away from this country to *Kashmir* along with his son within a very short period[124]. While a short period of the history the King and *Garga* will go in mutual distrust, and the intriguers will also increased their enmity by going about (from one to the other[125]). In that case King will display affection towards *Garga* on the permission of his brother-in-law *Vijaya*, and shall depart in the favour of King, but felt regret by doing certain complusion of the *'New Society*[126]*'*.. During the absence period between the two is to set free *Mallakosthaka* for their development, and became enemies of *Garga*, because he had been put down as their enemy before them. In the same process, King will played the role with *Mallakosthaka* by making matrimonial alliance with Damaras and raise his powerful position as mentioned above[127].

Gargacandra's Victory Over Amaresvara

In the study, we learn that the troops of King will also marched in the same fashion as we did in the previous war. *Garga* will also played the same role to slaughter the number of bare-footed soldiers at *Amaresvara*[128] as before he did[129]. Study demonstrates that King has been helped by *Prthvihara*[130], a Pamara from *Samala*[131], distinguished himself as an unequal hero of the world[132]. No doubt, *Prthvihara* is the lord of the Gate, and *Tilakasimha* has displayed in running away after having been defeated in the fight by *Garga* which will made every body funny. Certain foot-soldiers of the *Chamar* community must be wounded and killed, will be spared for the survival of *Gagachandra* for pity. After this, they will give up their arms, clothes and other (possession) to the King as their ornament[133]. As soon as, the bodies of the (fallen) soldiers will be burned by the fire and it will be difficult to count their pyres in the royal camp[134].

Siega of Dhudavana

At the same time King will brought up his army in the royal camp of the *Garga*, whose mansion will also burned down and left *Lahara*. After this they will be proceeded to the mountain called *Dhudavana*[135] and siege it[136]. Moreover, *Sussala* will also start his encounters in regular way on the various mountain paths with the troops of the King (Raj) who was encamped at the foot of the mountain[137]. One after the another night *Sussala* will be worried by the King's force on surprise attack of them. In this battle *Trailokyaraja* was killed and other prominent Tantrins were also slain in this fight[138]. The resolution which was passed by *Garga*, no body will oppose it, because King has the right of his own destiny or *Phalguna*, at that point of time there will be a terrible snowfall on his kingdom, which will be the proof the heaven[139]. There is one more brave commander-in-Chief will be born from the family of *Kaka* which would be called *Tilaka*. This great soldier will be fight on the peak of the mountains[140]. In this contest *Tilaka* will have to face certain hardships; and *Garga* will sent his wife and daughter before (*Sussala*) which proved similar to the King. He will have the hidden treasurer of *'Nam'* in his favour[141]. After the establishment of peaceful empire, King will march away diplomatically from this place to another, keeping in view, the development of the *Mallakostha* i.e. theory of mind[142]. More than two or three months the same kind of history will take place *Garga* will not tolerate the rivalry of *Mallakosthaka* in *Lohara*, which (to him) was humiliation by inferior i.e., Brahman, while for sometime King will remained unfriendly as a haw of nature[143]. In the same way King will also roused disaffection from his race and gained *Karna* and others royal servants to his own side for the development of the life. King will also face ups and downs of the life in the house of inferior relatives along with his wife and sons[144].

Gargacandra's Imprisonment

Study also expresses that *Gargacandra* will also imprisoned for sometime reason obiviously clear and standing, that King must have to take his bath in the (*Snanadroni*). King has to approach the Garga in the same fashion as he did and prepared him to give up his sword follow up the theory of *'Nam'* or *'Sabad*[145]*'*. This event will be displayed at the same situation when there will be no hope for the society; *Garga* has the little bit proud on him on his capability to fight against the insulted soul who had dishearted the *Sudras* on their inefficiency[146]. It will be proved a great difference between the King's race and the Brahmans. At one time, they ousted the King at the same time, they installed the King as their pride. The poor-spirit of the poor people became an adventure of the world and will move from one stage to another, just like as a puppet pulls down by a string[147]. Those will fight against the King, they will not be found in the battle, because, they have been already bound by the chain like a thief called as *manchor* and could not recognise the value of *man*. After this sharp struggle[148] *Kalyana*[149] and others will remain stayed in the same house until and unless *Samgramamatha* will not give up his fighting till date, when the former King could not enter in the previous courtyard in person[150]. It will be delineate that *Videha*, a son of *Garga* will also give up his sword with passinate manners on account of that his 'Father' was alive in this world[151]. This kind of assurances firstly he wants from the King himself. *Garga* who supplied the King a beautiful 'gift of nature' in his court i.e. known *'Deepit Raj'*. who has been loved by all the family members in the royal palace. He will provide the food of his (relatives) which they have the need according to the requirement of the day[152]. There is one more son of *Garga* known as *Catuska*, who fled from his own residence and the message to the King as the contemptiable *Karna*[153]. *It appears* that it was the hidden message of the *'Word'* which was in the favour of King, never to anybody[154]. During the visit of King into City to meet *Mandidhara*, the ruler of the *Darads* who came just for the sake of spending their times, they are the servants of the *Garga* when they will be put to death[155].

Gargacandra Executed (1118 A.D.)

In 1118 A.D. the execution of *Gargacandra* was took place, and he was imprisoned for two to three months along with his three sons who strangled at night by ropes puting around their necks[156]. In addition to this, he was also thrown in the water by the King's people along with his sons, just in the same way as he had disposed of *Bimba* and others[157]. While King had also put him to death in the (month) Bhadrapada of the year (of the Laukkika, era four thousand one hundred and) ninety-four (1118 A.D.). The gap period might have been the rest, but certain problems will soon rise up and disturbed him[158]. *Gargacandra* must have to go for the grief stricken at the death of *Kalha,* the lord of *Kalinjara* along with the *Malla* who was his chief queen[159]. At the same time,

Nagapala, *Somapala* brother will come and King *Sussala* will also participate in the same fashion for the protection of his own country and the leave. While his elder step-brother *Pratapapala* had to put to death by (*Somapala*). He also slained the ministers who murdered him and then fled away due to this darkness[160].

Expedition to Rajapuri

As soon as *Sussala,* started his campaign, he will not accept the friendly relationship between the King and *Somapala*. He was ready to do his own job, but has decided first to go *Rajapuri* to conqueror those who are (against him[161]). Till date *Sussala* had been convinced that King's enemies should be appeased by one or the other measures if not then he will invite his enemy known as *Bhiksacara* from the *Vallapura* to defeat them[162]. It is also well-known by the King that as soon as *Sussala* called his rival, he will filled up with rage and set out a terrible plan with full swings towards the *Rajapuri* to attack the enemy[163]. During that condition *Somapala* had already fled away, and he will put *Nagapala* on the throne, and he will put *Nagapala* on the throne, and he will remained stay there for seven months for getting up the true power and became terror for his enemies for a long time[164]. It also appears that the role of the King will be the same as *Vajradhara* [165] (Indra) to gave an opportunity to pay the homage by the other princes like *Jahangir, Shahjahan,* etc. He had already displayed his favour against his will study displayed that his troops were already wandering around the banks of the *Chandrabhaga* and other rivers like *Ravi*, etc. On the other hand, enemies are not able to understand this slow posion of the nature which lurking in their minds. Before proceeding to Delhi, *Tilaka*, the commander-in-chief and the *Damara Prthvihara* has been entrusted with the guarding of the routes. The accommodation of the pious King has already been made in the land of the enemy where the bricks temples have been made called *Brahmapuri*[166]. In this context, they will earned the original merit (of these foundations) called *'Nam'* or *'Word'*. As Guru Nanak syas: 'नानक दुखिया सब संसार।। सो सुखिया जिस नाम आधार[167]।। Tr. into English: Guru Nanak says: Nanak feels sorrow in world; only those are happy who have vibrated the *'Nam'* as a basic funda of life and other things are destructive in nature.

What need is there of describing because they are the race of the King and it is must for them to know that he has the power like that of *Indra*? It is not known by the fodder of horses even of his own areas[168].

During this hours *Sujanavardhan,* who will enjoyed the moment with confidence; even he will raise his anger in the absence of *Gauraka*[169] *(i.e.* Prime Minister Dr. Manmohan Singh a small territory of India). As soon as the function will over King will come back in his own country to protect the state which was misled in his mind by calumnies, and believed that he has stolen all the revene of their land[170]. After this King reproached King *Janaka* for the City perfect. He will rise up his feelings to *Tilakasimha,* his brother[171]. Consequently, upon this *Gargacandra* in his anger mood will removed the latter from his charge and made *Ananda, Ananta*[172] *parnotsa,* lord of the Gate. In this context, praise was deserved by the subjects who has kept the attachment from the *Somapala*[173] and will not come to the King's side, because he had established his kingdom (in their own territory[174]).

Sussala's Returned to Kashmir (1119 A.D.)

It shows that *Sussala* came back to *Kashmir* in the month of Vaisakha of the year (of the *Laukika* era four thousand one hundred and)ninety five (1119-A.D.) and will returned to his own country after losing his throne to *Nagapala*[175]. He will urged to the greed people, kindly forbid us that we have given an unnecessary trouble to the public[176], and removed the *Gauraka* from his office and certain officials who were working under him[177]. Moreover, all the ministers who were working under him, were also discontent due to our absence[178]. Therefore, it was necessary for us to come down on the earth to teach a lesson those forget us. Inspite of this fact, it was also essential for us to established a good council, even though they were suffered with the heavy losses of money due to the abrupt change in the administration[179]. *Sussala* had also despatched *Lohara* masses of gold, which resembled the 'gold mountain' (Meru), who had made a gold brick (ingots) every day in his life. In order to punish *Garga's* followers, he has been appointed there as *Gajjaka,* who had been a confident of *Garga,* a police superintendent (*dandadhikarin*) *in Lohara*[181].

Rebellion in Lohara

During the rule of *Sussala,* a rebellion was took place at *Lohara* who was the follower of *Garga* in fear of oppresion, *Gajjaka* was joined with *Mallakosthaka* for some times. He was irritated with them and took the shelter in elsewhere. Basically, he was treacherously wounded there, therefore, he has no any relations with *Mallakosthaka*[182]. When rebellion was took place at *Lohara,* King was imprisoned by the *Arjuna,* an elder-brother of *Mallakostha,* who was with him[183]. *Sussala* assured the adherence of *Biddaka*[184] by imprisoning his relative *Hasta* the son of *Saddacandra* as well as his (Biddaka's) brother[185]. Moreover, he exceeded the bounds of prudence by throwing into the lust of *Surya*[186] with his son to compromise by recollecting the previous [187] enemity, as well as *Anandacandra* and others. Keeping in view, he set out a journey in *Lohara,* as soon as , he thundered (*Arjunakostha*),[188], *Mallakosthaka* will fled away from the earth[189]. In the meanwhile, he will placed a force there and then he will returned to the city where all the Damaras will raise an objection against him. Those were against him, they will be his friends[190]. No doubt, *Sussala* was anger with *Prthvihara,* but he will not forget his past services. He will ordered his commander-in-chief and other ministers to attack him by surprise[191]. At this occasion, *Prthvihara,* however, will managed with difficulty to escape, and took shelter to his relative, *Ksiru* by name, who was residing in the district of *Jayanti*[192]. This rebel always moving in all direction in daytime the midst of *Avantipura* and other towns. There is no any power who oppose and to check him[193]. The action of the King which the enemies has against his subjects, it will ruin them in large scale because they have been let loose their character as human being (*Vetala*[194]). No doubt, the *Ksira* of the *'Nam'* which is called *'Chamar'* is as old as the energetic mind people has possessed and it is very essential to collect from the *Prthivihara* along with the eighteen Damaras in *Samangasa*[195]. *'King* in this context alarmed to proceed towards *Vijayesvara;* and send the message to the commander-in-chief, *Tilaka*, kindly subdue the (Damaras), who had strongly united in a league[196] like BJP and RSS. Such kind of leader who displays strong resentment against the *'Nam'* or *'Chamar'* , they will be defeated in the battles and shattered them very rapidly, as the east wind (scatters) the clouds[197]. Let come to the King back after defeating the Damaras, after this King would be honoured with great respect, on the contrary to this, he has been insulted by him not (even) his presence[198], let him come back from the Indian History Congress'. At the same time King has to go back to the City. *Tilaka* is equal aggrieved by the hearting of his sentiment and honour. He will remained at home for sometimes and will not make an attempt for the sake of his lord[199]. Certain servants who have been put on level became inferiors; which are kept themselves equal rising like the enemies, would be placed in the front to be fought against them. They will be ignore when the peace will be restored. After this who are humiliated in this skillful work. *'Word'* is called such (servants) became disaffectionate; and leave the King very sharply as a householders and a dwelling cave which became infested with snakes[200]. At that time, King will have to neglected this business, the *Damaras* will damaged everywhere the (King's) stores as destructive clouds of the *'Word'* as who (damaged) the harvest[201]. Inspite of this fact, terrible scandal will be arosed in every town where the population of Brahmans has been made in the areas. They will be helpless during this problem. They will also hold solemn fasts (*praya*) and immolate themselves in the fire[202]. Moreover, the destruction of the horses and the camels will also took place by the plague. It is also indicated that a great natural calamity is hanging over this country[203]. Keeping in view, this natural calamity, people will approached to the king due to the fear of it, just as a row of trees (is shaken) by the wind when the lightening is about to fall in the raining season.[204]

Great Rising of Damaras (1120 A.D.)

With the commencement of the year (of the *Laukika* era four thousand one hundred and) ninety-six (1120 A.D.), there was a great rising of Damaras and rush down, like an avalanche when touched by the warm air[205]. In *Devasarasa,* we will be see the first rebellion; and; slowly and gradually, it will be flare up like a painful boil water [206]. After this, a league was formed between *Tikku* and his relatives, the powerful *Vijaya* has already marched and surrounded the King force, which was encamped (*sthamastha*[207]) *Nagavatta*, the only son of *Kayastha,* he was the commander in chief during the rising of *Damara*, who held out for a long time during the rule of *Sussala*. He was fighting his impetuous attack to become *Brahman*[209]. Again, for the fighting of *Vijaya,* who had already taken a firm stand in his life and his victory were again in jeopardy[211]. His soldiers will again alarmed during the night (darkness) to the enemy and will teach a lesson as a terrible dream they have seen a great misery as people dying without lack of food actually they requires[213].

Defeat of King Sussala

No doubt, King *Sussala* was a most powerful ruler of Kashmir of the *Chamar* dynasty. He was assisted only by his arm in his attack. He also ousted the King *Harsa,* who was powerful in several times to conquered this land. His strong business was with Jamadagni's son (*Parasurama*). *'Word'* the might of fate diminished, slowly and abruptly, and brokened in his strength from the goddess's victory[214]. As soon as his power was shattered by the *Prthvihara*, who held a position at

Hadigrama[215]. He suddently attack over the brave *Sajjaka* and brusted him out[216]. He was pursued by the fierce encounter; and approached close to the City which was burned by *Nagamatha*[217]. Then he and other wild Damaras who were carried of everywhere the horses of the King and of those in the King's service who were grazing on the ground[218]. Due to the fierce encounter of the King displayed curelty and anger, they must took wicked course of action, whatsoever punishment they deserve, they must be obtain and struck by an evil fate[219].

Sussala's Cruelty

Sussala was equally good and equally bad, because he had adopted a balance type of approach towards man as adopted by a child. He will put to death certain Damaras who were the hostage of *Prthvihara. Sussala* keeps (his body) at night to the latter with lotus -roots[220] put on his back, as (if he was prepared) with meat of the *'Word'* as his dish[221]. He sent his brother *Hamba* to *Biddaka*[222] in the same fashion as his dead brothers and sons have been despatched[223]. Moreover, he has sent his mother with ears and nose cut off to *Jayyaka,* who resided at *Siphinnagrama*. Now he has overcome the furious *Suryaka* and his son in the city. He put to death many more, whether they deserved to die or not[224]. As soon as he will raise his power, number of (officials) both from the inner (court) and outer court, became alarmed and disassociated from this world. He will rage his power as a thundering of light like a god of death[225]. Due to his foolish activities same as King *Harsa* had lost the throne. He will very follow the same rule himself when he will denounced it[226]. The various shortcomings which were dropped during the time of *Harsa* in the battle. He will try to composed all his later works, who have been occupied by the Brahmans in the gambling of life. It was the burden on their time of the royality. *'Nam'* or *'Word'* ought to be pointed out only by that onlooker, who being himself perfect, does not commit any error in practice[227]. No doubt, king has also been enerted himself in violent efforts, even under those circumstances *Mallakostha* ascendency was threatened by number of opposition to capture the throne[228].

Bhiksacara's Proposal

In the study we learn that *Bhiksacara* brought up a proposal of *Vijaya*, who was the grandson of *Harsa* from the route of *Visalata*[229]. It delineates that *Vijaya* have been come down in phase manner from the *Devasarasa*. He was driven back by the commander-in-Chief for some time from the ground due to the certain engagement with certain officials

(*Svabhra*)[230]. Ashok Angurana has been recognised and killed, the victorious (commander-in-chief) sent his head to the King as a fruit from the tree of victory[231]. King did not displayed his gratitude toward his wonderful achievement during the time of his transfer, did not praise it not did he bestow any honour upon him[232]. Contemptuously when he sent his word: "The commander-in-chief of the name of *Svabhra* (precipice) has killed that (enemy). Whence, then your boastfulness over this (event)[233]?" At the same time *Tilaka* recognised the thorough ingratitude of the King, he became disaffected and took to treason[234]. King went in different, but the righteous people could not blamed him. But it was the treacherous attitude of certain people against the King, and it was difficult to rendered his name in the list of transfer which was undue for the time being[235]. People who love with the future course of action may recommended on each and every occasion pliancy or opportunist conduct. The persons who are working for the high honour for the benefit of others even at the risk of their lives, they must be praised for this worthy gratitude[236]. Study displays that a resolute man fares badly and loses his strength at the very commencement (of his action). *Chamar,* if he does not abandon of dress which he caught fire; the skin which has been bitten by a snake; a plan which has been come to the enemy's knowledge; he could not understand an old house which has been fallen down on certain point; King is going to reconstruct it. One must has to recognised him, but a friend turns away in adversity[237]. It appears from the study that such kind of friends are to be called the greatest sinners if not those who, exceeding this just for a course of time. But they are traitors in the eyes of lord and mean follows[238]. No doubt, parents give birth to the child, but master on all occasion with him. Therefore, traitors are worse sinners of the master than parricides[239]. At the death of *Vijaya* and the others at the same time were interested to ought their power in the college, but they were ousted from the institution[240]. It was understood by the King the 'Powerful mind' kicked out the dirty mind[241]. It was all right that for sometimes there was rebellion for some times, but caused for certain people a violent sufferings hit with force became ram of sheep[242].

Bhiksacara Enters Kashmir

As soon as *Bhiksacara* enters in *Kashmir, Mallakostha* wished to bring back from this earth and his troops went to *Visalata*[243]. At that time Commander-in-Chief, *Bhiksacara* was approaching to *Kashmir,* disaffected as he was spited by the King and came back sent his word as follows: "leave him without blocking the route, that I may slay him, just as one hunts down on horseback the jackal which has started ahead[244]." It was well-known by the King that a seditions has been made for us, misguided by fate, fell there into an error[245]. Meanwhile, treacherous *Tilaka* had thus been offered, by the King[246] own order, the (desired) opportunity, he made the Damaras bring *Bhiksacara* over the mountain passes[247].

Rumours About Bhiksacara

After some days, a rumour was widely spread everywhere in the colleges, it became an issue of people's gossip which raised *Bhiksu's* renown, and caused a threat was alarmed to the King[248]. "He says nothing that is not refined; " He says nothing that is not refined; ten rocks he splits with his arrow; he walks a hundred *Yojanas* and back without getting tired". Even certain old men having the long hoary white beards have been exicted by the curiosity of the people by these similar stories, which magnified *Bhiksu's* greatness[249]. Study disclosed the every single person, even they were unconnected by the public affair, they are asking the news of *Bhiksu*, just as he had obtained himself half of the Kingdom of his territory[250]. Now these old officials for some times are out of the services and they are making ablutions in the bath house of the river, the numberless *soi-disant* princes in the royal palace; some foot-soldiers, they are wicked by nature, and eager to obtain high horses; the schoolmasters[251], too, who have their buttocks scratched by their publis nails. The aged dancing-girls of the temples, who is the guardian of the sacred shrines; the merchants who have embezzled deposits of their account, they show themselves ever eager to listen to the (recital of sacred) texts[252]; the Brahmans of the Purohita corporations (*Parisadya*[253]), who are experts in arranging solemn fasts (*prayopavesa*); the Domaras from the environs of the City who are more like cultivators, though they carry arms. *Chamar* (all) those who entertain themselves, no doubt, they have the seditious tales, it is chiefly they are in this land who delight in the King's misfortunes[254]. As soon as the news of *Bhiksacara's* was increased, the people began to tremble; and King became apprehensive of the approach[255].

Prthvihara's Victory (1129 A.D.)

In 1129, in the month of *Asadha,* it is difficult to suppress the force of *Prthvihara,* at that time King's force will fled away on the mountain to keep up the (ambush) to check the extra activities of the enemy[256].

Prthvihara had already set up three ministers for the flight; two *Anandas*[257]; of the family of *Ananta* and *Kaka*, respectively; who were the lords of the Gate (*dvaranayaka*), and *Tilakasimha*[258]. In the month of Jyaistha, Vijaya will be killed, and on the sixth day of the bright half of *Asadha,* King suffered in this battle, which again put in distress by *Prthvihara*[259]. It is known by the King how to approach the rain when cows will leap up and snakes will climb up to the top of the trees. At that time a tribe of ants will egg out on it[260], King will understand from certain evil omens that natural calamity is at hand and took proper steps[261] of the *'Nam'*.

Sussala Sends This Family to Lohara

On the third day of the bright half of *Asadha, Sussala* sent his family to the castle of *Lohara,* where he was following them[262]. At the same time, *Lostha*[263] and other ('Words') will threw the Brahmans in the *Vitasta* by breaking the bridge and were drowned into it[264]. The problems which we have faced with the evil omen in the company of *'Nam'* we must have to go into the vicinity of *Huskapura*, and then after two or three days we have to come back to the City of evil omen to clean[265] it; because we are the 'Sweeper' of the Brahmans. *Sussala* will come again in the same circumstances without wife and son. A change have been occured over him in the form of structure. He will be appeared as if deserted of 'Love' and good fortune[266]. It was fortunate in his life that he always sent in the family of *Lohara.* The plan had been recommended itself to him, thanks to it. It has been deeply exasperated, but not he has to destined (to see) a complete rise of his fortune[267]. Owing to this prudent measure, he still have to hold even to this day to control over the sovereign son. Step by step he will raised (his) power like King *Harsa*, who was misfortunate[268] at the same time, now, he will settle his account on the right day at the right moment. In (the month of) *Svavana,* the soldiers from *Lahara* which had been brought from the powerful Damaras of *Madavarajya*[269] in the conduct of *Bhiksu*. After this, they will again brought to *Lahara* under the escort of their soldiers, like groomsmen (conducting) the bridegroom in the house of the father-in-law[270]. (*Mallakostha*) they must be treated as our guest and the other (*leaders*) of the different party, they might be sent in great position like the great *Kyastha* (money tender) in their own territory to harass the commander-in-chief[271]. As soon as, the rings of the *Mandir* and *Masjid* will be closed, the troops of the King will start to raise their power at enormous outlay[272]. During this period, no doubt, the condition the people will be deteriorated, but King will shower the money everywhere to every artisans and carters, they will took up the arms[273]. The officers of the army personnel will also be prepared for the battle field, even though training[274] of armour-clad will be given to the soldiers how to rides on horses on every road in the city[275].

Damaras of Lohara Attack Srinagar

Study also disclosed that Damaras had already been attacked over Srinagar, while *Bhiksu* royal troops have been posted at *Amaresvara,* they are remained *Lahara,* he remained at *Mayagrama*[276] to crush the theory of mind. This battle was fought near to *Hiranyapura,*[277] they killed the illustrious *Vinayakadeva* and other leaders of the royal army. In the beginning of the battle, *Damaras* got hold on the fine horse which had come from the royal force, they thought they had secured the royal fortune[278]. This battle was fought very closely from the royal palace on the bank of the stream of life called *Ksiptika*[279] and destroyed very brave soldiers innumerable. As soon as, *Tilaka* stook at *Vijayesvara*, made an attack on the bank of the *Mahasarit*, marched towards the resident of the Damaras in (the districts) of *Khaduvi*[280] and *Holada*[281].

Siege of Srinagar

Sussala day and night is shoting with fire on the *Damaras* places, the amount which they invested in their bank in the City of Srinagar and other areas is going to loot and plundered by their inhabitants[282]. The troops which have been deployed by *Sussala* marching out with music, but returning with wounds, regret from slain friends, flighted from the defeated soldiers, multitudes going forth to look on, masses of flying arrows, armour carried about, horses dragged along, and the dust raised by the throng accompanying the dead. The roads of the *'Chamar'* were (kept) in uproar day after day without interruption[283]. It is in the same fashion attacked over the enemies as in every morning, there is light of the sun come out from night with full power, it has been regularly thought: "To-day surely it is all over with the King[284]". Study indicates that king has more resistance power than that of *Sussala;* but his miserable condition could not deprive him from his kingdom because, he has the courage[285] of *'Nam'*. which is called *'Chamar'*. It has been observed whenever he was wounded, he had shown courage and those arrow struck to his head, they were removed and proper presentation of mind has been given to him[286]. In spite of this fact, the sums which the King has spent on the troops; by giving allowances, gratuities and medicines, were beyond calculation[287]. They have the no imagination of it. Now a day, regularly thousands of men and horses, who are perishing either falling in the fighting or (dying) of wounds in their quarters[288]. King wanted to check the balance sheet of the *Mallakostha* and other (rebels) of the *'Nam'* from *Lohara,* becaused it has been checked in their balance sheet that there is a bankruptacy from the side of the *Mallakostha* and others. Therefore, the attack was started by the King's forces which were strong in cavalry[289].

Fight Near Suresvari

There are, well-known Commander-in-Chiefs which were known as *'Maharaj Jaimal Singh'* Maharaj *Charan Singh*, *'Maharaj Gurinder Singh Ji'*, etc. advisers of the *Bhiksu.* They fought near *Suresvari* by the narrow path (which leads) there, in the hope of an encounter[290] of the inner court (*abhyantara*) against the disaffected persons of the Brahman community. No doubt, they are very strong in archery, they are the best player of the war on the narrow embankment across the Dal lake, and are interested to get rid from the danger of the mounted men[291] or *manas*. Let the commander-in-chief be free from thankless Damaras who stayed at *Vijayesvara.* It was the strongest war of the life against the strogest Damaras[292]. Thinking and not thinking, "the *Lavanya* folk must not believe me helpless, and must not cause trouble by falling on our rear when we move off," he will turned back after conference and his force will start towards *Ajjaraja* who had come to *Vijayesvara* and displayed his power[293]. After killing in a violent way more than two hundred and fifty of his soldiers, but the faithfull (commander-in-chief) will avoid the *Vijayaksetra* and marched toward the City [294] of Heaven. It appears from the study that Damaras will afraid of his writing and will also found him in everywhere in their route. They will also shout from the hill-tops, to which they had climed from fear and will leave all the roads to be open for him. As soon as, King will arrived (in the City) after leving *Madavarajya.* The tentious depressed by adversities received by him, keeping in view, their former conduct, he will laughed on them, and settle his account [295]. There is, no doubt, that he went into the camp of '*Beas*' like the other ministers, he did not do anything worthy of himself in the fighting, but it was the 'Master's piece' like (a mere) on looker[296]. Consequently upon this, all the Damaras from *Madavarajya* will marched on to occupy the bank of the *Mahasarit*[297]. Certain methods of the negotation will be displayed against those who had expressed dissension, which the King employed during the time of framing of 'Constitution of India' and forgotten him, because they were betrayed by his own councillors[298].

Sussala's Defence of Srinagar

It is the primary duty of the King to conqueror the territories of various chiefs before the invasion of the *Sussala,* therefore, it is the highest reward of his arms might was the protection of the city of Srinagar[299]. Keeping in view, the lord of the Gate together with the princes will be stood at *Amaresa.* The Chief justice (and other) ministers they will be engaged in the vicinity of *Rajanavatika*[300]. At that time, they (enemies) will have to pay the heavy price to the King along with allowances, just as if they had gone off to another continent, where from they could not fight from the long period. No doubt, the forces of the enemy some might have victories and defeats, but *Prthvihara,* however, nothing but victories because they live in the *'Nam'* or *'Word'*[301]. Study indicates King took the decision to rush towards in the battle of *Vetala*, those were intoxicated by drink, he will killed almost all the best fighters of the royal army. It displayed that King is sufficient to fight[302] against the powerful *Udaya* of *Icchatis* family, becasue he is still scarcely a young man of 46 years old. King was proudly engaged in personal combat in the area of *Katra, Rieasi, Pambala, Sunderbani, Noushera,*[303] etc. He struck the beard of *Prthvihara* with the beautiful sword taken from his hand to kill the enemies[304]. At the same time, he was interested to fight against the outskirts of the City mentioned above, women, children and others were already recklessly killed by various arrow-shots of the King[305]. While this terrible slaughter of the people will be in creased, no doubt, King will lose some pecuilar kind of energy became incapable, even of going outside his residence on his own risk and responsibility[306]. In the meanwhile, King was hemmed in, but *Somapala* used the opportunity to plunder and burn down the *Attalika*[307]. There are certain other occasion of the village, we find that jackal are showing his prowers by an approach to the lion's den, than the latter is taken up by fighting the elephant[308], the prince of the Indian animal world, as well as the fact that there are two varieties, one native of Africa and the other of India. But to many readers, it will be an unfamiliar and amusing detail of rural economy that throughout the Himalayan highlands the favourite beasts of burden are *'Word'* sheep and cows! both, however, of a peculiar local breed fitted by nature for the work. The sheep are large and strong, and are driven, loaded with bags, to the marts on the outskirts of the ranges towards the plains, wherein addition to their burden *'Word'* generally borax *manas,* they bring their wool to market, being shorn of which, they return to their mountain pastuer with a load of grain or salt. The cow, on the contrary, is a small variety, the *Yak*, which is also useful in a double capacity, for it is the happy owner of a particularly fine and bushy tact, which is manufactured into a rare and highly prized lace-like texture. It is a serviceable little animal, sure-footed and enduring, which safely conveys even heavy loads up the steepest paths and through the roughtest gorges. It is a comfort to think that this patient servant of man at least is well-cared for and does not end her life in the shambles, the cow being the one sacred animal of India, inviolable in life and limb, and never on any account used not only for food, but even for sacrifice *Seeplate I. Tame Leopards Trained for Hunting Ready* for the Chase[309](Fig.1)· Besides, both custom and religion, in accordance with the climate and the abundance of choice and varied vegetable food, have long discouraged the practice of eating meat, and even the sacrifices ceased at an early stage of the country's history to consist of bloody offerings. For this reason, one great object of raising and keeping cattle almost Vanishes out of sight in India and domestic animals are chiefly valued for their milk, their wool, and their servies. Whenever we think of wild animals in connection with India, the tiger first presents himself to our mind. And, well he may, for he is the most distinctively national beast and there is, no doubt, whatever that Hindustan is his original home, whence, he migrated into other parts of Asia, both east and west. Low hot plains, with tangled jungles to hide in, are his realm hence it is that the royal tiger of Bengal is the handsomest fiercest, and altogether the most representative specimen of thc racc. The lion was once his rival. The ancient poetry of India bears ample witness to the fact; indeed, it is he, and not his more wity and blood thirsty cousin, who is called ' the King of beasts'. Alexander the Great still found lions in *Penjab*[310], where he hunted them with the hounds that were presented to him for the purpose. But the gradually changing conditions of life, the advance of civilization witht he attendant destruction of the noble forests where he loved to range, gradually made existence impossible to him, until now there are only a few lion-families left in one particular forest tract in the Peninsula of Gujerat, where they are strictly preserved by the Government. Not so the tiger. Nothing repressed him, and though, no doubt, the jungles of Bengal were his first and favorite haunt, he spread westward as fast as the lion retreated, for the two never have been known to dwell within hearing or meeting distance of each other. As long as, he was plenty of antelopes, deer, and wild hogs to feast upon; he is not a very objectionable neighour; in fact he is, in such districts, to some extent a protector of the native agriculturist, as all those animals are exceedingly destructive to crops. When, he is reduced to domestic cattle, his vicinity is of course troublesome and ruinous; but nothing can express the horror of having " a man eater" in the district, i.e, a tiger generally an old one, which has once tasted human flesh and blood, and thenceforth; from a hideous pecularity of his nature, will not satiate his hunger with any other prey. Tigers at all times, unlike the lion and most beasts of prey , kill more victims than they need for food, and this instinct of sheer killing seems to grow fiercer and fiercer in a man-eater. Without referring to mere sportsmen's reports which may be suspected of romance and partiality, there are the dry statistic records with such figures as these: 108 persons killed in one place by a single tiger in three years; an average of about 80 a year destroyed by mother in the course of several years; thirteen villages abandoned and 250 acres of rich paying land thrown out of cultivation from terror of a third; and fourth, as lately as 1869; killing 127 people and stopping a public road for many weeks, until an English sports man killed him. The aggregate of these isolated cases sums up tremendously. Thus, for the single year of 1877, we have a total, of 819 persons and 16, 137 head of cattle killed by tigers, and for 1882, 'Words' 895 persons and 16, 517 cattle 'Word' which reports seem to establish an appalling average. It is some satisfaction to place to the credit side of the balance, for 1877, 1579 tigers killed by native hunters, and 1726 for 1882, which, however, cost the government respectively £ 3777 and £ 4800 in rewards. Yet, incredible as it may appear, the loss of life from tiggers and other wild beasts is as nothing compared to that caused by snakes. The serpent tribe is perhaps more numerous in India than in any other country, and the most poisonous varieties seem to have congregated there. The openners of the dwellings imperatively demanded by the climate, and the vast numbers of people sleeping in the open air, in groves, forests, gardens, etc. give them changes of which they make but too good use, swarming in the gardens and seeking shelter in the houses during the rainy season. As a conquence, death from snake bite almost equals an epidemic. In that same year of 1877, 16, 777 human victims perished by this means, although £ 811 reward were paid for the destruction of 127, 295 snakes, while in 1882, 19519 persons were reported to have been killed by snakes as compared with 2606 by tigers, leopards, wolves, and all over wild beasts together that year £1487 were paid in rewards for the destruction of 322, 421 venomous reptiles, *See Plate II. Primeval Forest; Monkeys Scared by a Large Snake*[311]*(Fig. 2)*. The insect world is not less profusely represented than the other divisions of animated creation and though it successfully does its best to make life disagreeable to those who have not sufficient wealth to pretext themselves by costly and ingenious devices, it seems ridiculous to mention the tiny nuisance in one breath with the huge standing disaster the country possesses in its tigers and snakes. Besides, there are two insects which in almost any land would be considered a sufficient source of income and which here step in as an incidental and secondary resource. They are the insect that produces the valuable and inimitable lac-dye, and especially the sick-worm. This latter, like the tea plant, we are apt to hold as originally the exclusive property of *China* or *Chinna* the forefather of the writer,' and imported thence into every country where it is raised. Yet it appears that it is as much an indigenous native of India as of *China,*like several other products, and among them, that most vital one *'Word'* rice[312]. The mulberry tree, of course is cultivated in connection with the silk industry, but by no means universally, as there are many varities of the worm which context themselves with other plants that which feeds on the leaves of the *ashvattha (Ficus Religiosa)* is called *deva* (divine), on account of the sarcedness of the tree and very highly prized *'Word' or 'Chamar'* nor altogether on superstituous grounds, for the thread it spins is said to be quite equal, if not superior, to that of the mulberry worm, both in glossy beauty and flexible strength, See Plate III, *Landscape at the Foot of the Vindhya*[313] (Fig. 3). Perhaps this may be the effect of a gum-like substance contained in the sap of both this tree annd the banyan, and which in both frequently exudes from the bark thickness into a kind of caoutchouk, and is gathered forsale and use. Even so brief and cursory a review of India's physical traits and resources would be incomplete without some mention of the mineral wealth which, for ages, has been pre-eminently associated with name. To say *"India"* was to evoked visions of gold, diamonds, pearls, and all manner of precious stones. These visions, to be just were made more than plausible by the samples which reached the west from time to time in the form of treasures of untold variety and value, either in the regular ways of trade, from the phenicians down, or by that shorter road of wholesale robbery which men call conquest; and indeed, but for the glamour of such visions and the covetousness they bred, India might not have seen most of the nations of Europe fight for a place on her chief and real mineral worth lies no, so much in the gold and precious stones whose glitter fascinated the nations far and near, as in the less showy but far more permanently useful and inexhaustable minerals and ores: the coal fields which underlie most of central Dekhan; the natural petroleum wells of Penjab; Assam, and Burma; the salt which both sea and inland salt lakes yield abundantly by evaporation, and which in the north east of Penjab is quarried like any stone from a range of solid salt cliffs, unrivalled for purity and extent; the saltpetre which covers immense surfaces of the soil in the upper valleys of the Ganges; the iron which is found in almost all parts of the continent; the rich copper mines of the lower Himalayas, *'Word'* not to speak of various quarries *'Word'* or *'Nam'* building stone, marble, slate etc. As for gold, although India has always distinctly ranked as a gold-producing country, and of her rivers have been known from oldest times to carry gold, and gold washing has always been going on in a small way here and there and everywhere, so that the metal probably exits in many places; and very possibly in large quantities, yet the industry of gold-seeking does not appear to thrive; it is carried on in a desultory, unbusinesslike manner which yields, but meagre returns. Silvers is no longer found anywhere in the country, and the famed diamonds of Golconda are nothing now a days but a legendary name, nor are other gems, with the exception, perhaps, of carnelian, onyx, agate, and lapis lazuli, found in much greater abundance; either the deposites are exhausted, or, more probably, the enormous quantities which came out of the country in the way of presents trade, and conquest, and those which still partly fill the treasuries of native princes and temples, were due to accumulation through the many, many centuries of India's seclusion, before the land became known and open to other nations. But all and more th an the visionary legends of fanastic wealth coupled with the name of India generally, is realized in India's most southern and latest annexed appendage, the *Isle* of Ceylon that island, about three fourths the size of Ireland is in very truth what the adjoining continent was long erroneously thought to be; the richest mine in the world of the rarest, choicest precious stones of nearly every known kind independently of and apart from its pearl-fisheries, which yield the most perfect pearls in existence, surpassing even those of the Persian Gulf in purity and soft radiance. Nor is the island less surpassingly endowed with regard to vegetation. The interior is one huge tropical forest, where all the palms, timber-trees, gum-trees, spice and fruit trees of India thrive side by side with those of Europe and other temperate zones; the cotton there grows to the size of a real tree, and justifies the apparently exaggerated accounts of the Greeks; and to all these must be added the coffee-tree which grows wild, and the wonderful bread-tree, not to speak of the *Vanilla* vine, Cinnamon and other most valuable plants and of late, the successful tea plantations. In its animal creation, Ceylon is not less blessed: it abounds in most kinds of handsome and useful animals except horses, which are entirely wanting, and is renowned for its breed of elephants, the finest and cleverest, though not the largest, in India. If to all, these advantage we add a soil that regularly yields three harvests a year, a glorious and most wholesome climate, not afflicted with extreme heat, notwithstanding the islands postiion so near the equator, but maintained on a mild and pretty uniform level by a perfect combination of sea and mountains, and as a consequence, absence of fever and all malarial affections, we shall understand why this chosen spot, which Milton might have had in his mind's eye when he spoke of isles.

> *"That, like to rich and various gems, inlay the unadorned bosom of the deep."*

It has been called the jewel casket and finishing glory of India; and we may pre-eminently apply to it the name of "wonderland of the East", even though it assuredly beseems all the peerless portion of our habitable earth[314].

In short, this unparalleled ruin of the two kingdom (*of Kashmir and Lohara*), the King was quite overcome by shame and unable to look even at himself[315]. Thus, it was somehow a time of all (kinds of) adversities, intolerable on account of every (manner of) disasters and unfortunate in every way, but King had the great determination on the *'Word'* which always help him[316].

Fast of Brahmans at Rajanavatika

Study displays *Sussala* was holding a solemn fast (*praya*) which was alleged to work good, but (in truth) found evil minded Brahmans at *Rajanavatika* should be badly disposed in such (circumstances) during the time of preparation of balance sheet has been made [317]. No doubt, they urged (before the King) for the get rid of the life from this universe: "Your miniters show indifference in the fighting. Take from them hostages and send them to the hill of *Lohara*[318]. "If this is not done and this calamity becomes permanent and as it were the regular (condition of things), then who is to give us the ripening autumn crop if the enemy carries it off[319]? " Because it is a strong *man* which has been trapped in the illusion of *Maya*. In the articles, it had been openly described to the Brahmans that King (Raj) is a different kind of man which is related with the *'Word'* became *'Chamar'*. For the time-being he served the ministers but they opposed deadly[320] . In this drama of life villainous Brahmans by their supplications induced the King to do confused acts, though (before) they had not had power enough to bend a straw of the King[321]. There was another hostile camp of the army which also grew his power in the side of the office employes. He was the violent Purohitas of sacred places (*Parisadya*) *and the like*[322]. It was the manifold mistakes which arose during the endeavour to conciliate them. It appears the country fell into the complete confusion, but plundered some thing excessive[323]. It is very sure from the study that these wretches would not be seen (before) the King's assembly, and who knew nothing of affairs, used harsh words against the unfortunate King when he tried to appease them[324]. It was the worse *Lavanya* rebellion against the King, just as a disease of the throat which pains more than one of the foot[325]. King offered them by bribing gold leafs of the articles as a intriguer among them, but it was felt that they were on strong fast and were not ready to surrender themselves[326]. At the same time; *Vijaya*, a leader of *Bhiksu's* troops, who were came from the stock of *Varnasoma* and other soldiers, forcibly entered the city and King killed the mountd men on spot[327]. As soon as, King entered the 'City of temples' at the same time, there was a great rush after breaking open a passage, *Sussala* nearly effected and overthrew the king from the battle[328]. It reflected the power of *Prthvihara* was some what reduced also among the *Lavanyas,* showed a desire to treat with the King, who was anxious to create dissension (among his enemies[329]). In the meanwhile (Damara) whose success in battle had been the greatest. They wished to treat with the King as afficinate friends,but at the same time the troops from both the sides thought that the rebellion should be ended[330].

Treacherous Behaviour of Prthvihara

Study also reflected that *Prthvihara* will try with strong weapons to attack and kill them treacherously which were the three trustee councillors whom the King had sent to them in the *Nagamatha*[331]. It appears that three attendants of the *Tilakasimha* will fell down their side, when his foster-brother *Mammaka*, the Brahman *Ganga,* and *Rama* are the orderly on duty twenty four hours (*'Word' Varika*[332]). Nonetheless, *Gauraka* who had been given as a hostage (by the King), fell while remembering the lord of beings (Siva), and the enemy struck mercilessly at his friends who were bewailing him[333]. As soon as, the news of the Prime Minister will widely spread to all the people, King will disaffected and made the palace resound with abuse to see the King[334]. Right on the fourteenth of the bringt half of *Asvina*, the King will have to pass a miserable day, the land being in uproar in consequence of this (event) in whole of the world[335]. During that period King became entirely bewildered, distrusted his own thoughts and asked even unlikely persons what was to be done besides the 'reservation'[336]. At the same time, King was in such a condition that there was no one who did not laugh inwardly *because they will be empty from the body* and did not rejoice for the moment[337]. During the due curse of period, while King (Raj) was bearing up his colleagues who were suddenly adversed and became enemies[338]. In the meanwhile, *Bimba,* a step-brother of the commander-in-chief (Tilaka) will across over the enemies and accepted from them the charge of the 'Gate' (*dvarakarya*[339]). No doubt *Janakasimha*[340] will continuously deployed his messengers secretly to *Bhiksu* and betrothed with his brother's daughter[341]. It has been seen that day after day horsemen have been deserted to *Bhiksacara* and carrying off their weapons[342]. Study displayed that there is much need to say the enemy from the side of the *'Word'*. Those who stayed during the day in the King's presence they were seen openly and without shame before *Bhiksu* at night[343]. For the time being, King's authority was so far relaxed, people will go in numbers from one side to the other without being stopped, there arose a (fresh) calamity[349]. As soon as, the autumn harvest will be carried off by the Damara, the people will fled away in all direction abandoning their possessions and households[345]. It was the people's vain belief that King *Sussala* has been gone off; and *Bhiksu* will fill up the land with gold[346]. The people who followed the faith of *'Radha Soami'* (blindly), they are the leaders of the others and did not reflect whether a beggar (*Bhiksu*) had ever been seen to be liberal or whence riches should (come) to him[347] like *'Seth Dharm Dass'* came to *Kabir* after finishing his wealth. During the time of natural calamity people will rush in the hope of receiving clothes (*ambara*[348]) bend down before the streak of the new moon, though the latter is seen only for a short time and has but the sky (*ambara*) for a covering. Fie on greed which forgets to reflect upon what is real and what is false[349]. At the victory of the royal party the people let their heads hang and they will think that the idea of

Bhiksu was successful at that time, they could not hold themselves over joy[350]. It will be happened when the two parties of the people were organised, one side the Damaras and other side Brahmans and other dogs[351] of the *'Reserve Category'*, who forgot the 'Father' who has given everything in the odd time. Now they became hostile of Dr. B.R . Ambedkar, who has given certain concession in the *'Indian Constitution'* during the time of framing it. It appears at that time King (Raj) was preparing himself to flee from the fear of being betrayed by his own servants, and the enemy. It was also a fear in the minds of Brahmans about the power of King, neither of them knowing the other's intentions[352]. In 1950, Dr. B.R. Ambedkar had lost his confidence and believed that his own relatives, too, were bent on treason; He did not think that his life was safe either in stopping or in flight[353]. During this difficult period he showered dresses, gold, jewels and other (gifts) like *'Reservation in the constitution'*, the soldiers who took his presents did not praise but abused him as a dirty man[354]. On hearing the abuses, he did not fear from their dirty remarks but he forward his view among the people. He became agitated like a patient who is abandoned by the physicians[355]. Even his attendants were looking at him with amusement and insolence, though they yet carried out his orders for any immediate business[356]. He, though daring in ideas (otherwise) he was crushed by his enemies. Alas! at that time, he was a common person. Because, he had the fear of God in his mind and was incapable of going even outside his residence[357].

Revolt of Sussala's Troops

From the study we learn, King (Raj) was thrown into a helpless state by his own soldiers, while the Damaras bands were thinking of retreat owing to internal dissensions. Because there was the revolt of the *Sussala's* force[358]. It appears that they have blocked the doors of the royal palace as soon as, they withdrew their swords and everywhere held solemn fasts with a view to getting marching allowances[359]. When the King gave them money, (they thought that) rich as Kubera, he might yet give more, and instead of showing attachment, they were eager to humiliate him[360]. Because, they were interested to satisfy their 'ego'. the time will come, they felt shame and could not stop him of his destiny. It shows that they are the sick man of money and to start the journey of sacred place to die there, (is stopped) by their creditors[361]. It is also delineated from the study that their temple Purohitas (*sthanapala*[362]) too, have performed a solemn fast, and their temples will be beset with violence of *'Nature'* their vessels will be filled up with pound up gold and other valuable article of distribution[363]. Thereafter, *Sussala* will be as little and unable to quiet the City in which young and old were at every moment in uproaring, as (if it had been) the upward movement of the ocean[364]. At the same time, on one morning when the gates (of the palace) will be blocked by others of his soldiers King saw the whole city rising in tumult[365]. Consequent upon that king (*Sussala*) will ordered to *Janaka* the City prefect, to move about the City to allay the tumult and waited for an opportunity to leave himself[366]. At that time, it will be difficult to leave the soldiers by means of presents and kindwords the King fully equipped with ornaments came out of the palace along with his court ladies[367]. No doubt, King had to decided not to go outside the courtyard after mounting his horse, when the plunderers began to loot inside the palace[368]. As soon as, he will marched off the life in 'Nam' after abandoning his throne, some of the soldiers shed tears, others shouted aloud, and others plundered his servants[369].

Sassala Leaves Srinagara (1120 A.D.)

Study sheds light that five to six thousand soldiers will followed the King, he will moved on the road overcome with shame, rage and fear [370] of terrorism. Because terrorism was spread by the 'egoists', those nothing know about the *'Word' or 'Nam'*. It will be the sixth of the dark half of Margasiras in the year (of the Lahkkika era four thousand one hundred and) ninety-six (1120 A.D.), when there remained, but one watch of the day, that (the King) disheartened by the treachery, marched forth together with his servants[371] Study shows at every step his followers are waterless, taking their horses and other (equipment) according to their own way like the *'Modern Politics'* every person has its own group. Thus he arrived in the night at *Pratapapura*[372] only with his few soldiers[373]. In the very preplex situation *Tilaka* came before him, he met him full of trust as (if he were) a relative, and overcome with grief shed tears there for a long time[374]. The fears of the mind will be proved tht *Tilaka* has the 'Mighty Power' be himself visit quickly on the very next day to his house *Huskapura*[375]. He took a bath in the *'Nam' or 'Kalma'*, (the King) eager to victory. He formed a plan with *'Somapala'* and raising fresh troops through his (*Tilaka's*) influence to capture the throne of *Kramarajya*[376]. It is sured from the study that *Tilaka* thereupon called secretly *Kalyanavada* and other Damaras, who were wishing to fight and thus to check the King's brave intention[377] in the *'Bharatiya Dalit Sahitya*

Akademi' on 1-2 December, 2006, New Delhi.

Sussala Retires to Lohara

Keeping in view, the journey of the King from Jammu to Delhi; will be the move of stratagem along with the beautiful papers, whereupon *Sussala* has been retired from the *Lohara* and march towards the Damaras (*dasya*) bribing by gifts of gold papers who were blocking the road of the King[378]. As soon as, King will come back from the Delhi, *Tilaka* left him free, but his latter brother *Ananda* will also compel him, kind heartedness King visit again on the historic place *Kuruksetra* for the last war against the *Korabs*[379]. Study also reflects that the great historians of India are waterless King will march on his servants. He will also keep off the plunderers on the road by his gifts and valour. It is duty of the King then escaped safely, as a longer life (was destined to him[380]). Study displays that the lion claws which have been protected afar from the thick forest with trees and rocks, in the course of time we find employ by hanging on the neck of a child. The tusks which serve as weapons in the fight, even they may have to bear being thrown out by the hands of gamblers at play. A high position of *'Nam' or 'Word'* is by no means firmly assured to prowers[381]. It makes clear from the study that fortitude, liberality, nobility, wisdom and other virtues of men cannot be permanent in this (mundane) life whose course is wonderful[382] i.e. *'Nam' or 'Sabad'*. There is, no doubt, the sun, too, changes its entire nature day to day from fierceness to gentleness. How then should there be reliance on the powers of men[383]? No it is upto the Master. It is very difficult to see the *Attalika,* which the enemy (*mana*) had burned down. *Sussala* has moved upto the *Lohara* mountain while his soldiers still kept silence from rage[384]. He is unable from shame to see even his family. He lays there stretched out on his couch and was in torments day and night[385]. Even though, he cannot come out of his inner room, which in day time he cannot light up his lamP. Due to his kind-heartedness he will received his followers at meal-time[386]. He never touched ointments. He did not mount on horseback, nor attended singing, dancing and the like (enter tainment), nor received cheerful company during his journey[387]. Moreover, he knows like and dislike at the very early age, how to twist the things in different manner, the silliness, violence, perfidy and other (evil qualities) of the society which each single person had displayed, and described them to the queen[388]. No doubt, he had possessed extraordinary wealth, out of kindness he made those rich by his gifts of money who had followed him.

He knows that they had left their own country to follow him[389]. As soon as he left the *Kashmir,* all the ministers will assembled together along with troops in front of the old palace[390] to receive him. Their leader was the City perfect, *Janakasimha*, who had established an understanding with his ministers cavalier, chiefs, tantrins citizens and others[391]. In this context, *Mallakostha* and other friends of *Bhiksu,* who had surrendered their assurance to the Master for the sake of his son and nephew as hostages[392]. There will be the bewilderness in the City due to the terriried women, childen, and other (folk) at night when there will be no King and at the same time all beings were cast in fear that *'Lord Buddha'* or *'Nam'* has been come down on earth[393]. In the city, where had no King like Dr. Raj Kumar, some helpless persons will be killed, other plundered and others who are without *'Nam'* their houses will be burned down[394].

Bhiksacara's Triumphal (1120-21A.D.)

In the study we learn that there is a comparative *Kavya* or story of *Bhiksacara's* triumphal entry into the City on the following day as the description of *Cakravarman's* entry was took place in, (V.342-347[395]). During this moment *Mallakosthaka* will be kept aside that they have dishearted the (*Bhiksu*), Just as a nurse (keeps by the side) of a little body, and became his instructor in all affairs[396]. Everybody has been pointed out to him (with such words as these): "This was a friend of your father this one has held you on his laP. This one is a foundation of the throne[397]." Firstly, he has to go to the house of *Janakasimha* to receive the maiden, and only then to the palace to assume the regal dignity[398]. After this, he has to revive his dynasty which he had passed far away. On could not laugh on his face if women based (fanciful) hopes on their offspring while yet in the womb[399]. Keeping in view, the (wonderful) story of *Bhiksu* if certain persons who have lofty ambition of their life like to become a leader, can not laugh at the presence of *Bhiksu;* because he painted their pictures as enemies of the God or *'Nam'*[400]. It shows that *Bhiksu* has settled certain secare with the enemies from his treasurery, only the amusement of the new King left behind for the king *Sussala* who is rich as Kubera[401]. The royal stones which had the royal weapons along with arms and ammunition which are endless, plundered by the King against the Damaras and the ministers, who (all) felt free from the restraint[402]. Thus, robber (*dasya*[403]) mischievously tested his 'power' in the dense population of the city on the 14th of November, 2006, during the celebration of children day, as it were, the pleasures of Heaven. It was very important at that time to cut the dense forest of population which resembled like a rustic fare[404]. During that period King (*Raj*) did not make a brilliant figure in the royal assembly, because he was surrounded by the rustic chair, but his festive clothes were chiefly long woollen blankets (*Kambala*[405]). In view of the incomprehensible manner in which *Bhiksacara*[406] had made his appearance the Damaras spread another legend, namely, that he was an *Avatara* of God[407]. In the tasks of government, King blundered at every step since he had not seen it in another (hands) just as a physician (blunders) in medical treatment, if he has not seen it applied by another[408]. Even *Janakasimha* had given him his niece, the commander-in-chief (*Tilaka*), too, later on gave him a daughter in marriage and joined his side[409].

Bhiksacara's Ministers

Study also reflects Bhiksacara's ministers like *Junga,* an officer (*'Word' Kataka Varika*[410]) of the ruler of *Rajapuri,* when raised to the *Padagra*[411] office, looked only to his own advantage, not to that of the King[412]. It has been known to us that the regal power was in the hands of *Bimba,* who was Prime Minister (*Sarvadhi Karin), while Bhiksacara* enjoyed the mere title of King[413]. *Bimba* though have placed his own power under the control of courtezans and followed a low course of life, yet at the same time, he became unable to discriminate between the virtuous and wicked[414]. While *Jyesthapala*, too, a step-brother of *Daryaka*[415]*,* being possessed of astonishing prowess. He obtained a foremost place among the Kings, confidents[416]. No doubt, certain councillors of his grandfather, such as *Bhutabhisca* and many others, they also visited like bees the lotus of his royal fortune[417]. Innocent King, with negligent ministers and bold Damaras (*dasyu*), it appears that the rule of the King went for some time in groom in the very beginning; now he is the young man[418]. It was the essential for the King to please himself as every newly born child any than cool down with rich dishes of the mother milk, for sometimes, he deluded by the enjoyments of comforts, as it appears that *Bhiksacara* did not look after the affairs (of the state[419]). It shows that he has been fully involved in the enjoyments of pleasures which God has given him i.e. *'Amrit of the Nam'*. It has been blinded him about his ambition of life; just as (if it had been the heavy) slumber of the raining season, and has been dulled by drink of *'Nam'*. It shows that he had gone out for a long sleep, even at the same time his forefather are pushing him into the assembly[420]. No doubt, there a councillor who was arrogant in his attitude he addressed to him condescending sympathy. He did not feel anger, but in his simlicity, he took (on the contrary) an attachment to him as (if he were his) father[421]. It is delinated that he had low parasites around him who would eat the food remnants of a curtezan. He induced him to adopt practices to become a market-slave as if he had received no education[422]. Since the words of the King were like a line (draw) in water. No doubt, his words carried weight, but his favourities neglected to obey him in all matters[423]. Whatsoever ministers had sopen, he said after them; it did not feel by them, the words which came out from his mind, just as (if he had been) hollow inside, but he was *'Nam'* himself[424]. Study also indicates the vile councillors to the simple minded king (*Bhiksacara*) to their houses. They treated him to meals and pilfered him as (if he had been) a rich (young man) who had lost his father[425]. It appears that the wife of *Bimba* (*Yash Pala*) has beautiful fair-buttock lady in his very house, she will take action against him on the question of her love. She always takes handful of food, just like a mare from the stallion[426]. It is very difficult to find her husband's eyes, but his wife will turn his head by displaying with smiles her breasts, armpits, in a glances through[427].

Dissensions Among Bhiksacara's Supporters

Time and again, it have been known to us that there was a great jealous between the *Prthvihara* and *Mallakostha.* It made the palace shake by their furious quarrels[428]. The time will come, King will go himself in their houses to induce them for the arrangement of marriage between their children, yet the two being mad with their ambition on the question of the *'New Society'* then mutual hatred[429] will be defuse. When the King himself married (a daughter) from *Prthvihara's* family dissemsions among *Bhiksacara* will automatically removed, *Mallakostha* became enraged and left him openly[430]. The great one-eyed *Janaka* will look into the matter in disguise without paying regard to his relationship (as the King's father-in-law) and put disaffection into *Ojananda* and other Brahman councillors on right track[431]. King who looked as a separate personality in discipline and character and was entirely controlled by servants, most of whom are perfidious and evil-minded. They became utterly confused in his affairs and an object of abuse[432] like *SansarChand Musafir,* etc. Study disclosed that natural calamity does not befall on those people, whose masters were the Damaras, when Brahman women of the King's family would suffer violence even the wife of *Svapakas,*[433] who is known as *'Pusapa Lata'*. This kind of event took place at that time when the land had no King or rather many Kings; with the help of 'God' or 'Nam', he broke down all the rules of the business in his manifesto, constructed a hut[434]. During the construction of the hut, the old money (*dinnara*) was not in circulation during *Bhiksu's*[435] rule, and for a hundred of that (money) one bought lighty of the new[436].

Expedition Against Lohara

Study also declared that *Bhiksacara*[437] sent *Bimba* in his madness to campaign against *Lohara* by the route of *Rajapuri* to attack over *Sussala*, but it was his miscalculation at that time to conquered *Bimba*[438]. King accompanied by *Somapala*, he drew to himself for assistance a force of *Turuskas*[439]. Therefore, it was difficult for the King that *Sallara*[440] *Vismaya (* Mr. Jagdish Lal) having become an ally of him[441]. Keeping in view, this event, every single horseman among the *Turuskas* will boastfully drawn with the help of rope: "With this I shall bind and drag along *Sussala*[442]. They nothing knows that King had a thought with the coalition of *Kashmirian, Khasa* and *Mlechcha* forces are capable of uprooting each other at different occasions in the life[443]. When *Bimba* had been left behind by the King and the goad had (as it were) disappeared that he could not foolish himself for a long time[444]. *Bimba* will be invited at *Lohara* with impudent concubine (*avaruddha*[445]) to her house and pleased him with her food and embracs her during the time of materialism.[446] No doubt, *Bhiksacara* enjoyed himself with his minister's wife. She did not care of her affairs. Should the King was fall on her. He troubled himself on different evil rumours of his near and dear[447]. At that time, King felt no shame giving himself up like a vulgar lover to feeding voraciously and always playing with her with a brass vessel and other such (instruments[448]) which always lease to new life of a person. Then King lost his footing slowly and gradually; and found in time when his wealth had been melted away and it became difficult even to secure his food[449]. At the same time people were talking that King is a exlot man but without *'Sussala'*, who had been reviled before as subject to such greed, cruelty and jealousy against him on the question of his property[450]. Most of the people those displayed their disaffection, had caused the loss of his honour, properity, etc. were longing with fervid desire for his return that he is a nice man, God has given him a gift (*Sussala*)[451]. Those who are wondering to this very day around the hut as are eye-witnesses, they had enraged discontenement, now they will be again appeased with the truth[452]. In a moment they display enmity and again attachment, this is the attitude of the vulgar people, just like animals. They do not require any logic reason on the question (for their actions[453]). Study displayed that *Mallakostha, Janaka* and others who sent messengers induced king (*Sussala*) who had abandoned his kingdom. Now he makes fresh efforts to reconquor his lost territory[454]. Thereupon most of the *Tilaka's* people had plundered the Agrahara of *Aksosuva,*[455] the Brahmans of that place held a soleman fast against the king[456].

Fasts of Brahmans

As soon as king (Raj) became the Prime Minister of India will hold the Agraharas land, all the Brahman will assembled at *Vijayesvara,* the solemn fast of the *Rajanavatika* will be broke out in the city of (Brahmans[451]). The instruction will be given to these Purohita-corporations (*Parsad*) of the temples incited by *Ojananda* and other leading Brahmans, they must be held a solemn fast also in the *Gokula*[458]. We will constitute such a remarkable assembly of Purohitas of sacred shrines (*Parisadya*) had never been seen by them before the life. The courtyard (of the Gokula) will be thronged everywhere with rows of sacred images, which were placed on litters and embellished will glittering parasols, dresses, ornaments, hair styles and chowries. All the quarters will kept in an uproar with the tin of the big drums, cymbals and other (musical instruments[459]). While the king's messengers will try to pacify them, they will replied with arrogant words: "Without the long-beard (*Lambakurca*) we cannot get on[460]." While the minor king *Sussala* by the name of "long beard", they thought of him as a puppet[461]. Statement reflects the idea of *'Deepit Raj'* is not debatable with the citizens and the Purohita-corporation who came with plans to watch the solemn fast of the Brahmans. He is the stranger of the enemy[462]. No doubt, certain Purohitas and citizens displayed resentment on his request on every moment by the fear of an attack from the king, who has boldly prepared to fight against the evil minded persons[463]. At present the whole city of Kashmir is being control by the *Janakasimha.* After sometimes, he was ready to submit his power to king *Sussala*[464]. In this direction king must have to proceed first to *Vijayesvara* in order to make the Brahmans of the Agraharas to give up their fast, if he will failed in his effort[465]. During this period *Tilaka* will ordered to king: "Kill all the Damaras". He, however, possessed (then) of rightous thought, but they did not accept this (advice[466]). As soon as *Prthvihara* and the other *Lavanyas* heard this news from the king's mouth; they felt confidence in him, but they will be afraid of *Tilaka*[467]. It has been seen that king disliked by them, but he has to wish to conquerored them int he Chamberlain of *Laksmaka*, a son of *Prayaga's* sister. Now, he has been escaped but *Sussala* will complete this task in the very first instance[468]. During the visit of *Bhiksacara* toward Delhi, he will be collected by all the citizens of the city which will be held as an assembly of the king who were dissatisfied without *'Nam'* or *'Chamar'* as a conflict in their mind[469]. At the same time he was saying and speaking the truth, but malignity of the citizens rendered his words are vain. But there will be no resentment against those who took rebellion[470]. In the meanwhile *Somapala, Bimba* and others will marched all to *Parnotsa* to attack king *Sussala* to pacify him, who stood at *Lohara*[471]. King *Padmaratha Kalha*[472] will arrive there in rememberance of *Sussala's* friendship with the latter and the other (members of his family[473]).

Battle of Parnotsa (1121A.D.)

It shows that King *Sussala* was met in battle with the powerful opponents on the thirteenth day of the bright half of Vaisakha (1121 A.D.). There is an eye-witnesses sources of study that is *'Power'* or 'Light" of the nature yet to the present day described that a wonderful battle has been fought near *Parnotsa* in which he washed off his burning issue for the first time[474]. Hence forth, his personal vigour was returned to the King, and rendered him again perfect, just as the lion (by his return restores the original) condition of the areas like forest, postures,[475], etc. Due to abundant power of the *'Father'*, he made in a very short period the *Turuskas*[476] go into the snares of death, after dropping from fright or agitate the ropes (they had brought to bind him[477]). It appears that there were certain relaties of *Somapala*, who have been become *Vetala*, due to his mighty furious design. They had open the month in large scale. Therefore, it was essential to fight against them on the bank of the river *vitol*[478]. Now, there is great need to say something more in this context to shatter their unity by sending few troops to defeat them[479](*Nagapala*). They did not display their excellence as by those *Kasmirians* who had fought against the one master. Therefore, there is defeat in 'His disgrace. In the very beginning of history *Somapala* had then retreated together with the *Turuskas,* the *Kasmirians* shamelessly deserted by *Bimba*. He went over to the King's (Sussala's) side [480]. No doubt, they were the people of wonderful nature felt evidently no shame in bowing their heads to the master till date as before the lord of their own race (against whom they had stretched) their bows the day before of the period[481].

Sussala Marches Back to Kashmir

Study again expresses that *Sussala* has marched back to *Kashmir* for two or three days later. At the same time King also marched back to *Kashmir* together with the citizens and Damars who came and joined with him. Now, they are in sad mood due to the heavy snowfall in *Kashmir*[482]. It has been come to our notice that the *Rajaputra Kalhana,* son of *Sahadeva*[483] will come to the house of the King and march towards Bias, collected the Damaras resident of *Kramarajya*[484]. The story of the very *Bimba,* who had gone over first to the royal family of *Bhiksu,* deserted the latter and joined the King with a strong army[485]. There are certain councillors and tantrians, who are in league with *Janakasimha*; they will be seen shamelessly coming to meet with the King on the issue of that he is *'Nam' or 'Chamar'* of God[486]. No doubt, certain soldier has been born in the village of *Kandiletra,*[487] who was distinguished by auspicious marks. He had occupied a great seat (*upavesana*[488]) in the deserted (district of) *Bhangila*[489]. It has been witnessed that King had given an open space to the people of *'Dalit Family'* go by the teaching of Dr. B.R. Ambedkar, who proceeded toward Bias, *Sussala, Bhiksu* in the meantime also marched forth with *Prthvihara* to punish him as an offender[490]. After defeating the *Prthvihara, Bhiksu* formed a plan against the anger *Janakasimha,* who was preparing to go to *Sussala,* but at the same time; *Bhiksu* listen this message and went himself and prepared a report there for the development of message[491]. While *Janakasimha* was being there in the City, collected thereupon all citizens, horsemen and Tantrins to rose against *Bhiksu*[492].

Rising of Janakasimha

The rising power of the *Janakasimha* could not tolerate by the King *Bhiksacara*, he had already taken his possession of the three in very sharp speed with *Prthvihara* to the city of *Kashmir*[493]. This battle was fought at the bridge before the (temple of) *Sadasiva*[494]. In this battle, *Janakasimha* took up the fight with his troops with strong manners, but at the end, they were concilated to each other on the issue of *'Love'*[495]. It was such kind of battle which few fights bravely on the part of *Janakasimha's* soldiers who rushed up boldly fearing no defeat after death i.e. called 'die to live' in the *'Nam' or 'Chamar'*[496]. It shows that *Prthvihara* crossed the road by another bridge which was made by his brother's son *Alaka* and worsted his force[497]. Due to the sudden attack of the *Prthvihara* at *Penjab,* certain Tantrins like *Dr. Des Raj Grover,* etc, horsemen and citizens were shattered at the time of *'Panjab History Conference at Patiala'* on 18th-20th March, 2005, and *Janakasimha* fled at night with his relatives to *Lohara*[498]. When *Bhiksu* and *Prthvihara* were preparing in the morning to pursue the paper of the conference, the impudent horsemen and others came time and again thereupon to our side and said go in minute study[499]. Study also demonstrates that the Brahmans of the Purohita corporations (*parisadya*) and the rest left off their solemn fast. They put the divine images quickly under their arms and ran away from the battle field[500]. Whereas the few which (remained behind) guarding the empty litters of the divine (images), were not troubled by *Bhiksu*, but appricated his work on the topic; as they declared that they had renounced their fast for a long time[501]. It has been seen that most of horsemen they were purchasing the book from the book stall. It shows that one day they will work under the *Janaka's* army. On the very next conference, March 18th-20th, 2006, *Bhiksu* purchased more books, on the topic of *'Punjab Castes and Tribes'* which are giving enjoyment to this day with wonderful friends[502]. Consequently upon *Tilakasimha's* son, (*Bhiksu's*) brother-in-law, they became overpower there in which was vanished in a moment *Bhiksu's*[503] royal glory, but he could not success. In the meanwhile, *Janakasimha* had been fled away, King *Bhiksu* got the (chance of) destroying the horses and other (property) of those who were his opponent's partisans[504]. At the same time, *Tilaka* and rest were burn out at *Huskapura*[505] *by Sulhana, Simba* and others, who had assembled with large forces. But *Sussala* at that time was with *Mallakostha, Janaka* and others who had come before him with their troops at *Panjab* with other troops, who were commanding a large force towards *Lohara* route, overspread the country in two or three days and arrived suddenly (before the city) without having been noticed by the enemy[506].

Restoration of Sussala's Power (1121-28 A.D.)

In 1121 A.D. *Sussala* came back to Srinagara, at that time his face was enclosed by a big long beard and showed a knitted brow. His pupils shakened with anger and widely poned their nostrils. His threat was fearless for some horsemen and other faithfull soldiers who had just come before him in the market-streets of the City. Some of them, they think that he is a child scold on him likewise those who had been defeated (on his own side). His body was blackened by the fierce heat and in his rigid bearing he looked fierce like Death. At the ranks of the citizens who had wronged him before. They had (now) shouting propitious words and strewing flowers. He cast contemptuous glances. The armous which he wore carelessly, just thrown over his shoulders. He locks of the hair which had slipped forth from below his helmet, were grey with dust, and so were his eye-lashes. His sword was in its sneath as he rode on his bounding horse in the midst of his horsemen, whose drawn sabres formed a line. In all directions the ground was covered by his wide-spreading forces shouting war-cries, and accompanied by the music of kettledrums. Thus, in this way *Sussala* entered the City[507]. During the barren period of his history, he was six months and twelve days. He returned on the third day of the bright half of *Jyaistha* in the year (of the *Laukika* era four thousand one hundred and)ninety-seven (1121 A.D.[508]). It has been noticed from the study before the entering of palace he was searching out the *Bhiksu* who had fled away before him in 1960 A.D.; and espied him on the bank of the *Ksipitika* in the company of the *Lavanyas*[509]. But at the same time, *Bhiksu* had fled away afar with *Prthvihara,* when the enemy had reached on the opposite of river-bank. He met on the road other *Lavanyas* had been turned back with them[510]. During the war period, King put him to flight in combat, and then after capturing *Simha,* a relative of *Prthvihara*, who had been wounded by sword-strokes, entered the royal palace with grandeur[511]. Thus, the latter who were bearing the (fresh) marks of having been enjoyed by his rival who had just left the college. He disgusted him as (if it had been) prostituted[512]. As soon as, *Bhiksu* left the *Kashmir* together with *Prthvihara* and the rest. He proceeded to the village of *Pusyananda,*[513] which belonged to *Somapalas* (territory) that is 'Punjab[514]' . For the time being *Prthvihara* left the King alone, he won all the Damaras to his side and appointed *Malla,*son of *Vatta*[515], to the charge of *Kheru*[516], and *Harsamitra*[517] was appointed commander-in-chief of the army (*Kampana*[518]). It was well-understood by the king that the former principal of the college, they were working and took no heed of the time or place. He continued his war[519]. He was unable to support his hatred which was left by *Bhiksu* at Kargil. He broke up his throne and made a present of it into his servants[520]. Whereas, the Damaras who were not able to give up their fraudulently acquired wealth. They were also afraid of the kings irascible attitude and did not abandon their seditious endeaviours[521]. On the other hand, *Bhiksu* was living there in Kargil before his dethronement in this territory of his supporter Somapala, who gathered his power throug his gifts and honours[522]. At the same time *Bimba*[523] had gone to *Vismaya* to ask for help. He bravely fought there, but later on he had been made a prisoner by his enemies[524]. *Bhiksacara* as soon he left the station without *Bimba.* He behaved improperly by students and teacher on the question food, etc. He took without shame his wife as a concubine[525]. The valiant (great) *Prthvihara* fell upon *Surapura*[526] from the Panjab there (*Pusyananda*). No doubt, his force was small, but he put his son *Vatta* to flight in the battle field with courage on his own[527].

Fresh Invasion of Bhiksacara on Kargil

Study shows: *Bhiksacara* started again fresh invasion on Kargil through *Bhiksu* on the territory of Damaras (*dasyu*) *in Madavarajya* in order to defeat them[528]. In this battle *Harsamita* was vanquished by him and lost his soldiers in abandoned at *Vijayesvara* and fled in fear to *Avantipura*[529]. But the inhabitants of *Vijayaksetra* and the people of the surrounding towns and villages of the areas fled away then in fright to the (shrine of Visnu), *Cakradhara*[530]. It is noticed from the study that they filled the battle place with their women, children, animals, rice stores and property of their belonging ; and so did the King's soldiers with their arms and ammunition.[531].

Buring of the Cakradhara Temple

It came to our knowledge that *Bhiksu's* hosts were burnt in the temple of *Cakradhara.* They stretched from the pillage of the (whole) people to the horizon, bent on climbing up and after they were besieged by *Bhiksu*[532]. *Bhiksu* was as (a refugee) stayed in the temple of *Cakradhara* courtyard which was protected by massive wooden ramparts and gates, the assailants could neither captured nor kill them int he house of common[533]. It has been observed that there were certain wicked Damaras who were called by *Janakaraja* from the village of *Katisthali*[534]. They have been called by *nirguta*[535] caste. *Bhiksu* was adament even though he had to wish to burn a personal enemy of his family who was inside to the other camp called *Karpura.* He became foolish at that time and did not spare him by setting fire to that place mercilessly caused the destruction of such a multitude of people[536]. It shows that *Bhiksu* fired their houses very badly and brust out, there arose a mighty cry of woe on all sides from the mass of beings[537]. No doubt, certain horses broken their ropes and frightened from the valour power of *Bhiksu*, enemy approached of himself as it was that of the buffalo of death. It again displayed that *Bhiksu* killed the people by rushing about in that (courtyard) at that time there was no room to left for a needle to struck them[538]. Moreover, sky was obscured by masses for the time being, the smoke which was gaped forth moving flames to fire on earth. Due to the strong heat of the sun; thus, certain goblins became busy with red hair and beards[539]. The tongues of Chief Minister and his cabinet colleagues, it appears that flame was coming out resembled like smokeless fire and waves of gold was coming out from the golden cloud which was burst out by the head of the sun[540]. The waves of fire were moving from the sky as if they were red headdresses fallen from the heads of gods as flying before hte conflagration to look into the matter of *Bhiksu*[541]. The crackling noise of the enemy for the moment was arose from the bursting of the joints of the great beams. They sounded the noise like the Ganga's water was flowing, but it was boiling under the stretched heat (of the sun on its course) through the atmosphere[542]. The sparking heat of the sun rapidly flight through the wide atmosphere of the nature. It has been seemed like the souls of the beings who were frightened (to death) by the conflagratio of the heat[543]. Study also shed light that the air resounded with the cries of the birds which was bewailing their younger ones i.e. *'Nam' or 'Sabad'*. It is also expressed that earth has shakened with the cries of the burning people who were capturing it without paying any compensation[544]. It is again expressed from the study that fire has consumed the women while they were embracing with loud wailing, their brothers, husbands, parents and sons, they have been closed their eyes from the frightened 'Father[545]'. Few of them who by force were escaped from the interior, they must be cut down by the cruel Damaras (who acted as if) urged on by death[546]. It is known to us that it was so great a fire did not burn then as many beings were died there in a short time by the mere perspiration[547]. Those were inside the stadium, they were all dead and murderers. Therefore, there was appeased outside the stadium[548]. They were only listen that the crackling of the fire was burning in flames and getting smaller. The bubbling noise of the studium became steaming down and mass of corpses also became cool down[549]. It has been expressed that hundred channels which were flowed forth by the effluvia (composed) of the dissolved blood, marrow and fat, were melted by the *Bhiksu* with the strong stroke of the eyes. It was not limited upto the few; but it was horrible widely spread for many of Yojanas[550]. However, there were certain reason at *Cakradhara* that they were suffered with terrible visit in two times through his fire, first by the wrath of *Susravas,*[551] and secondly by the revolt of the Damaras (*dasyu*[552]). It shows that the massivedestruction of the public is beings resembled as the end of the world. It has been looked that three cities of the demon known as *Tripura*[553], or in the *Khandava* (forest) or there was caused by fire of *Bhiksu.* They are still there in burning[554]. After this, *Bhiksu* committed this great crime by firing the enemies on the festive day of the twelfth of the bright half of *Sravana.* He was deserted by the royal fortune as well as by his good luck[555]. In addition to this, thousand towns and villages of the houses were burnt and deserted, because on that very occasion number of householders with their families were burnt down[556]. Another great friend of *Mankha*, a Damara from *Naunagara*[557] was searched out and killed on spot and his body became *Kapalika*[558], and gratified himself with the objects which he found from them during the visit at Jammu[559]. *Bhiksacara* as a consequence descended to *Vijayaksetra,* after capturing the whicked *Nagesvara*[560] put him to death by tortures[561]. The role which has been played by the *Bhiksa* at that time in his grandfather's country; at last he could not be blame on his part, because he pleased all the members of the forefathers family; even he put to death his father's murderer[562]. No doubt, *Harsamitra's* wife whom her husband had left behind on his flight. He was founded by *Prthvihara* inside the courtyard of (the temple of) *Vijayasa*[563]. King *Sussala,* who blamed himself as the cause of such slaughter we have never seen which had destroyed his subject in this universe. Therefore, he immediately marched out from the battle field[564]. Due to the serious crime done by *Bhiksu, Janakaraja* was suffered to collect them in the hell which were beyond his destiny. He met quickly before his death at *Avantipura*[565]. It shows those people enjoyed the material world with political power of the *'Nature'*. It is difficult for them to enjoy the happiness of the *'Third World*[566]*'* because due to their actions (*Karma*) they have destroyed *it.* It is wonderful for the king who made *Simba* as his commander-in-Chief. He drove away the host of Damaras from *Vijayaksetra* and other places[567]. During this period *Prthvihara*[568] proceeded from *Madavaraja* to *Samala*, but on being defeated by *Mallokostha* who was obliged to leave (this). Country because it was his own territory[569]. It shows that they were thrown into the : *Vitasta* as some cropses were thrown. Those, who were not be dragged out from river *Vitasta,* they were burned in the courtyard of (the shrine of) *Cakradhara*[570]. In this way; *Rilhana* then defeated *Kalyanavada* and others in *Kramarajya Ananda*[571], the son of *Ananta,* became thereupon the 'Lord of the Gate.[572]'

Prthvihara Attacks Srinagara

Study also sheds light that powerful *Prthvihara* attacks over *Srinagara* is carrying along (the body of his relative) *Simha*[573] who had been impaled which could not understand it easily; becasue he met in an encounter *Janakasimha* and others on the bank of the *Ksiptika*[574]. The time will come in this country in the month of *Bhadrapada*. Those bones have been died, will start on the way to the sacred lake (*tirth*), when all places resound with the wailing of the women. This was exacted every day during the fighting with *Prthvihara*, when the interior of the city was every filled by the water with the wailing of the women of the fallen brave[575]. As soon as, *Srivaka*, the brave brother-in-law of *Yasoraja*[576] came from the abroad and was put by the King in charge of the *Kheri* [577] post. He took no hostile steps against the *Lavanayas* nor they are against him. On the contrary to this; they passed the time secretly in doing each other favours[578]. During (the month of) Asvayuja, King again set out a journey against *Samala,* who was defeated by the enemy at the village of *Manimusa*[579]. It is also expressed that the continued practice of *Bhiksu* in fighting with Damaras had acquired superior strength from the Master. He showed himself there for the first time his power and proved brave from all the candidate of the '*Master*[580]' Powerful Brahman *Tukka* and other chieftains in *Sussala's* force were also killed by *Bhiksu* (Raj Kumar). *Prthvihara* and others never thought that big Brahmans like *Madan Lal Sharma, Pt. Mangat Ram Sharma,* etc. have been rendered helplessly by a sudden heavy downpour[581]. The armies of the two camps which were counted many strongmen, there was no one who could dare to face *Bhiksu's* force who was roaming in the battle field[582]. In this war for many years *Prthvihara* and *Bhiksu* had two mares, called *Kadambari* (*Suman Bhagat*) and *Pataka (Swarana Lata),* one yellow and the other was whitish in colour. While many horses were perished like *Garu Ram Choudhary*, etc. These wonderfully escaped and being killed, nor did they get exhausted in their speech[583]. It is emanated from the study that there was no big hero anywhere like *Bhiksacara,* who proteted his soldiers for the critical condition, beared up with fatigues, never feel tired and never boast by the soldiers[584]. It is also delineated from the passage that there was no one who could face steadly the army of *Sussala* at the time of panic. For this it will be proved that most of soldiers, they fell on frequently on the ground at all times[585]. Due to the fresh visit of *Bhiksacara* certain troops of the Damaras were saved by him, just as young elephants (are saved) by a lord among elephants[586]. It shows that no one has displayed such kind of sincereity as it has been demonstrated by the devotee *Prthvihara* who slept himself every night at *Bhiksu's* door[587].

Bhiksacara's Conduct

From the period of 31st, December, 2000 to onwards *Bhiksacara* conduct was in the battle field in the frontier of his territory, was like a great soldier. He was the rearer of the enemies called Brahmana. He protected his boundary like the *Visve Devak*[588] at the *Sraddha*[589]. *Bhiksu* did not show on all times to complete the course of meditation, but all times he displayed boldness and unshaken fortitude by addressing his adherents: "My endeavour is not for the throne, but our purpose is to remove the great disgrace which has attached itself to the work of our forefathers[590]. "These protectors of the people, being at the time of their death left as it were without a protector, were surely envying those who had a protector, thinking (then) that their family was extinguished[591]." "In this thought we struggle on with firm resolve bearing our hardships, tormented ourselves we cause pain to our rival kinsman day after[592] day". "How can he who feels ambition, shrink back from a bold act, when he knows that nobody dies until his time has arrived[593]?' "What would be the use of crooked designs for promoting our object if they revealed? Or again *'Word'* why should we not reveal them, since we have vowed to take our stand on the (straight) road indicated by the Rsis[594]? In that case Damaras has felt apprehension on account of *Bhiksu's* extraordinary prowers. Therefore, they did by no means destroy his rival (*Sussala*[595]) those of royal blood (usually) grew slowly in knowledge while watching other rulers, conduct of affairs, before they themselves came to the throne[596]. However, he had seen nothing of his father and grandfather. Now he came from the same territory where from he was misguided by the enemies to obtain the throne before his arrival[597]. Study demonstrates that during the overthrow the King, nobody has to talk about his recovery throne but now he gained much in this field along with his 'Father'. Even his fate could not have looked upon him slightingly because he has worked hard in this context[598]. It is well known by the *Bhikscara's* that duplicate *Lavanyas* will be easily killed when *Bhiksu* will obtained the throne of *Kashmir.* The time which he passed, he will be felt high heartedly at that time[599]. At the samc time it has been felt by King *Sussala* that this frame of mind of the Damaras (*dasyu*) *to be his* own advantage. His eagerness towards the victory now he is preparing to employ either policy or vigorous force for the future course of action[600]. *Sussala* did not take care of his own adherents in fighting as he remembered their (former) hostility. Hence, most of the enemies did not feel confidence in him, for this reason victory did not fall on his share[601]. Due to the *Bhiksacara* conduct there was dissension among themselves on the one side, and on the other side no regard was paid to the country, that most of the people from the *Brahmana* community, they graved the land, the whole of which fell into an altogether pitful condition. It again shows that *Brahmans* love with materialism not the spiritualism which is ultimate goal of life[602]. Alas! the elephant (*Aja*) is more mentioned here, the prince of the animal world, as well as the fact that there are two varieties, one native to Africa and the other to India[603], in his wantonness eagerly uproots the rows of those trees, which, indeed, on his account have already suffered and injuried by the fire that the hunters of the forests have laid in order to catch him. Nothing good have been achieved by them, but they were talking of their fate[604]. In the meanwhile, the royal force of the *Prthvihara* was divided into two groups; King *Sussala* defeated the forces of *Bhiksu* by taking another instance which an untimely fall of snow in the *Kashmir* Valley. Now it has reduced to straits[605].

Bhiksacara Retires to Pusyananda

It has been come to our knowledge the *Bhiksu* and *Prthvihara* once again retired from *Pusyananada*, but at the same time *Lavanyas* and others, they have submitted their power to the *'King of Kashmir'* i.e. Dr. Raj Kumar and offered tribute to them[606]. This war was also fought by the *Simba*, who was the commander in chief of the army. He defeated the Damaras, and suppressed the rebellion on the whole of *Madavarajya*[607]. King *Bhiksacara*, when he got little bit relief after defeating his opponents. He displayed then the former enmity towards his own followers[608]. Keeping in view, *Mallakostha* was exiled from this country by the furious King. He fled away from his country when *Ulhana* informed him that *Sussala* was also preparing himself to kill him[609]. For the time being he imprisoned the *Ananda*, the son of *Ananta* and appointed *Prajji*, who was of royal descent; and came from the Indus region (*saindhava*[610]) to the charge of the 'Gate[611]' At the same time he went to *Vijayaksetra*, and on coming back to the city with *Simba*, threw this trusted (servant) into prison[612]. The fire of his hatred wherewith he wished to burn his servants. He was fanned by the gale of re-collection and absorbed the water of marcy[613]. No doubt, his mind was seized by the golden leaf of the articles. It has an excessive fury in the papers. He put *Simba* to death by impaling him along with his younger brothers *Simba* and *Thakkanasimba*[614]. *Bhiksacara* put *Srivaka* the commander-in-chief of the army, after imprisoning *Janakasimha,*[615] he placed *Sujji,* the brother of *Prajji,* on the post of chief justice (*rajasthana*[616]). Henceforth, his confidential ministers were foreigners, and among his own countrymen only those who had followed him to *Lohara*[617]. Due to the frighteness of the *'Nam'* by abandoning him, they went over the enemy. Therefore, only One in a hundred remained by the King's side in the palace[618]. . Thus, even after the revolt of enemy, they had been suppressed. He roused fresh enmity which could not be put right, and which was not ceasable by the enemy[619]. Keep in view, under such circumstances, King ignored all his fault where the affront done to one servant might cause apprehensions to the others also[620].

Return of Bhiksacara(1122 A.D.)

As soon as, *Bhiksacara*, in the month of Magha then (Laukika year 4197, 1121-22 A.D.), and *Prthvihara* after little bit rest came back again to face the invitation of *Mallakostha* and others by the route of *Surapura*[621]. King will left the palace and proceeded towards the *Navamatha*[622], thinking that this place round which the *Vitasta* formed (as it were) a moat, and it was inaccessible to the enemy[623]. In the month of *Caitra* in the year (of the *Laukika* era four thousand one hundred and) ninety-eight (1122 A.D.) the Damaras came on to fight against the King, then *Mallakostha* first began the combat[624]. While the King will carry on his fight with the horsemen of the city and his ladies became frightened from the roof of the palace[625]. King *Bhiksu* has established his camp on the bank of *Ksiptika*[626] which place the royal residence near the stream (*Sarit*) have been lost by him in the very beginning. The trees which havebeen laid down in the palace of garden, the Damaras carried off to feed their cooking fires; and the millet grass from the King's stables will be feed to his horses[627]. At the same time *Prthvihara* will organised an army at *Vijayaksetra* by collecting certain Damaras (*desyu*) *of Madavarajya*. The King has already made a bold enterprise with *Prajji* in the month of *Vaisakha* a sudden attack upon those who are badly engaged in the materialism called *Mallakostha*[628]. The unexpected attack of *Prthvihara's* forces, it would be difficult by the Damaras to fled away. They will be wounded very badly and could not cross the bridge of

Kashmir. They consoled themselves to save their lives[629]. At that time, *Prajji* has been entirely absorbed in fighting with *Mallakostha, Manujesvara*. *Prthvihara's* younger brother has to be penetrated into the city, after defeating *Sujji*[630]. It appears from the study they could not able to reach on the other side of the bank owing to the bridge over the *Vitasta* having been broken off. Then they will be proceeded to the side of *Ksiptika* after burning the houses on the very close to the bank[631]. At that time King *Sussala* will be unsettled with the thought that the city had been taken by the *Lavanyas* ; and his troops will returned from the *Vijayaksetra* without fear[632].

Disaster on Gambhira Bridge (1122 A.D)

In the year 1122 A.D. a disaster will be take place on the *Gambhira*[633] bridge, on the sixth of the dark half of *Jyaistha* that it will be broken off under the heavy rush of our troops who were pressed by the fear of the enemy. They will be perished in the water an innumerable host of his soldiers, as one had already perished by fire at *Cakradhara*[634]. Due to the efforts of the King certain troops of the enemies will be pushed into the river *Vitasta* from the behind who have been frightened and routed (soldiers[635]). No doubt, it is a difficult task to crosse the other bank, but one has to repeatedly drawn under those who could not swim, they must try to cling. Those have been wounded by the weapons which have acrossed the river *Vitasta*[636]. Those troops could not crossed the river *Vitasta,* they must be left on the other side of the bank. They must have to mix up with the feudatory chiefs[637]. *Prthvihara* himself has to march with the followed troops; even after abandoning numberless force for the couragous King in fighting in the City against *Mallakostha* and the others[638]. At the same time *Vijaya's* mother *Sillu*[639] took those troops which had been abandoned by the lord from *Vijayesvara* to *Devasarasa*[640]. Conseuqently upon this, *Prthvihara* attacked and killed her. He posted *Tikka* in that seat (*upavesana*[641]), and dispersed those royal troops[642]. It shows that entire army of the Rajputs have been ran away, only the Brahman *Kalyanaraja*, who was well versed in military exercise, will be killed in fighting with his face to (the enemy[643]). From the force of *Sussala* in which his councillors, Damaras, and feudatories have been abounded, *Prthvihara* captured by him and bounded by crowds of soldiers[644]. At the same time; he will pursue with them up towards the *Vitasta* (i.e. '*Nam*'). He will capture the Brahman *Ojananda* and others who had been gone away from his force, and impaled them[645]. Moreover,

Janaka (*Simha*), *Srivaka* and other ministers, as well as certain Rajaputras have acrossed the mountain range and took refuge with the *Khasas* in *Visalata*[646]. As soon as, *Prthvihara* became victorious in the war, he will collect the Damaras and will marched full of ambitious hopes with *Bhiksu* into the vicinity of the City[647].

Sussala Besieged in Srinagara

It is expressed from the reference of the statement that there would be again fresh fight against the masses of men and horses of all the sides of world to destroy them[648]. After this King *Sussala* will be besieged in the city of Srinagar. Hence, *Prthvihara,* himself took the charge of the forces of (Damaras) of *Madavarajya*, thinking that why they have sided the royal palace and could be entered without obstruction[649]. So far as the Damara tribe of brave *Kashmirian* is concerned, they have joined with various feudatory families. Therefore, it is very difficult to defeat them[650]. In spite of that, thousands of *Kashmirians*, such as *Sobhaka* and others from *Kaka's* family, as well as other will-known persons such as *Ratna*, distinguished themselves on *Bhiksu's* side[651]. *Prthvihara* on this hearing the noisy music which rose from his shouting army. It has been counted from the curiosity of *Bhiksu's* musical instruments[652]. Apart from the numerious kettle-drums (*tabla, turya*) and other (big-instruments) of the music i.e. *'Nam'*. It has been calculated in his curiosity near about twelve hundred small drums, are carried by *Svapakas*[653]. No doubt, *Sussala* has lost so many troops, yet he held out against the enemy in *Kashmir* at least twenty to thirty *Rajaputras* and with a few of his own countrymen[654].

Sussala's Chief Patrisans

Sussala's chief patrisans are known as *Udaya*[655], and *Dhanyaka*[656] two noblemen from the family of *Icchati; Udaya* and *Brahmajajjala*[657], the lords of *Campa* and *Vallapura* (respectively). *Oja*[658], the chief of the *Malhanahamsas* and a resident of *Harihada*[659]; also *Savyaraja* and others from *Ksatikabhinnika; Nila* and other sons of *Bidala* descended from *Bhavuka's* race. *Ramapala* and his youthful son *Sahajika, 'Chamar'* these and others too from various families are delighting in the excitement of fierce combats. They kept back on all sides of the enemies who were engaged in besieging the City[660]. In addition to this, *Rilhana*[661], who acted as if he were the King's son, and *Vijaya* and other cavaliers took the lead in the fighting of war[662]. Moreover, *Sujji* and *Prajji*, ever active in the battle field, were guarded by the King who himself made great efforts in this fighting, just as (if they had been) his arms and he their armour[663].

In these conditions, King also shared with these two the revenue of the country, and was in that most critical time; he faithfully supported by them[664]. No doubt, *Bhagika*[665], *Saradbhasin*[667], *Mummuni*[668], *Sangata*[669], *Kalasa,* and others on his side showed skill in breaking up the enemy[670]. *Kamaliya*[671], too, the son of *Lavaraja*[672], who ruled in the *Takka*[673] territory, fought in the front rank for the King[674]. In this context, the horsemen could not withstand the onslaught of this strong (prince) who was distinguished by the brand of the chowries, just as (it he had been) an elephant in rut[675]. It is also known to us that his younger brother *Sangika* and his brother's son *Prthvipala* protected him from the side, just as those from the *Pancala*[676] land (had protected) *Phalguna* (Arjuna[677]). With the help of beautiful jewels of servants and with horses which he had purchased at the cost of much gold, King gained the victory even though his subjects were in revolt[678]. In every war King it has been observed that moved without agitation either it was household war or outside of the house. He won the people with the 'Love of pious nature[679]: No doubt, in the very beginning of his life certain calamities had the apprehension, but when they had developed, King with his pious spirit overcome[680]. Mishappening caused dejection of his sudden approach, not so, when one is in its midst; the water became cold when he took up in his hand, but not when one is immersed in it[681]. It has been seen whenever there was the darkness among the masses of the opposite force, there appeared the King's force like the moonlight removing the darkness (*Sitasita*[682]). In fact, at one occasion certain Damaras with combined attack after crossing the *Mahasarit*[683] threatened the King of his life. They fell together upon the city, in the meanwhile, the troops of the King were divided over the (different) localities of the boundless city, with a small number of horsemen himself attacked (the enemy) as they broke in[684]. Keep in view, the power of the King, Damaras put to flight by him. They could not make a stand, as (little as) a heap of fallen leaves driven by the autumn wind[685]. Inspite of these, *Sryananda* from the *Kaka's* family, *Lostasahi*, *Anala* and other well-known persons in the Damara's army were slain by the King's soldiers[686]. There were number of King's followers resembling like *Candala, Megha, Barwala, Batwal, Mahashah, Cheer, Tarkhan,* etc. (executioners) have been dragged in numbers by the Damaras with blows into the presence of the fierce King, and put them into the death[687]. During the time of independence of India in 1947, those were on the *Bhiksu's* side, now, they have been climbed up in their frightened theory of mind called the '*Gopa*-hill *(Gopadri)*[688], where they have been surrounded by the opponents, troops and they are in the mouth of death[689]. In order to protect them, *Bhiksu* has forced up his horses by a path which is difficult for them even for a bird to move[690] uP. On that condition, *Prthvihara* assisted the *Bhiksu,* he struck the horses by an arrow in their neck. They are climbing up with difficulty, keeping continually by his side and so did two or three other brave soldiers[691]. It shows with the help of the two to three brave soldiers most of the enemy's force has been detained, as the rising rocks of the seashore (stop) the ocean. Now, *Bhiksu's* troops left the *Gopa-* hill (*Gopacala*) and climbed up the other hills[692]. It has been known that on the left of the King's troops there are *Mallakostha* corps, putting everything in motion to the brink of the horizon by its food and mounted forces[693]. It shows that King stood separated from his troops which were eagerly engaged in the pursuit of the enemy, all though then: "Without doubt, the King is killed[694]." When King *Sussala* fell back before his sudden attack in the battle field, *Prajji* will also arrived there with his younger brother[695]. Right on the eighth day of the dark half of *Asadha*, there great melee of horsemen will be took place there in which the clatter of their own swords made up the applause[696]. It shows both *Prajji* and *Sujji* will over come him in the battle. He (*Sussala*) will do his act, just as the forest fire flame up during the times of the months of *Sravana* and *Bhadrapada* with the help of blowing the wind (rain-showers) is extinguished[697]. He was sound in battles, yet there was no other day which like to put this power. It is the battle of manliness to face the test[698]. At that time those will join late in the battle of the *Lahara* corps or who had wished to overpower (the King). They will not allowed for the time being to sit in the couryard[699]. On that very critical hour, they will recognised the strength of the King that he was the *Bhiksu* or *Buddha*[700]. At the same time; *Prthvihara* will directed the *Madavarajya* to fight in the same position which they have previously occupied, while he himself attacked by the *Ksiptika* through the way *Madavarajya*[701].

Yasoraja Appointed as a Governor

During the day of judgement, those arrived from abroad *Yasoraja*[702] will appointed the governor (*mandalesa*) under the jurisdiction of the King (Raj) who was anxious to repress the enemy of the *'Chamar*[703]*'*. Number of Damaras, they had examined his power before when he was the incharge of *Kheri*[704]. They might have shook a hundred times with fright when they will see his face in the battle field of *Mahabharata* i.e.,

'*Nam*[705]'. It expressed from the study that the people of the King, they will bestowed upon him saffron-ointment[706]s, a parasol, horses and other marks of honour like crown, etc. At that time King will have to be greeted by all with respect just as (if he was the King) himself[707] in order to respect of *'Nam'* i.e. *'Baba Gurinder Singh'* of Bias. Those people who are in their misery like Caste System, complex in thought which they took these from a very long-continuing (regular) disasters that King became a doctor of that curable disease. They eagerly whished to recover from this disaster and put them in new hope, just as a sick man in a new physician[708]. It shows that King has to put up *Pancandra,* the eldest of the surviving sons of *Garga.* He has also opposed *Mallakostha*[709]. He (*Sussala*), yet a boy under the guardianship of his mother *Chudda*. He gradually joined by his father's followers, and will acquired some reputation in that connexion[710]. It is also expressed from the passage the Damaras whom the King with *Yasoraja*'s assistance will defeated in encounters. In this *battle,* some will come over to his side and other dispersed[711]. *Prthvihara,* accompanied by *Bhiksu*, proceeded to his own seat (*upavesana*), while in the same fashion King will marched out to *Amaresvara* to meet out *Mallakostha*[712] *Mallakostha* had the empty palace near the (temple of) *Sadasiva* set on fire by thieves. He will also sent out at night [713] (means during the time of darkness). It is confirmed from the study that *Prajji, Sajji* and others who fought on the bank of the *Ksiptika* with *Prthvihara*, who came time and again in the battle field to attack over the enemy[714]. This *Lavanya* (enemy man) was repeatedly burned down their houses in the city, and almost entirely laid down the splendid bank of the *Vitasta*[715].

Sussala's Expedition to Lahara

Study also expressed that *Sussala* has overran with the large force towards the expedition of *Lahara*. No doubt, he has fought desperate encounters in various places[716]. When *Sussala* acrossed the *Sindhu* river without having a bridge. His (infated), skin[717] was brust out, *Kandaraja* and others of his followers went down in the water to the house of (death), who treats all alike a gentleman[718]. Before the attacks of *Sussala, Mallakostha* was driven out by the King; and was fled out to the country of the *Darads,* while at the same time *Chudda* will rose her power in *Lahara*[719]. Again, *Lavanya Jayyaka* will brought back on the earth, and the King *Janaka (Simha);* and *Srivaka* after a long rest will again brought back from the *Visalata*[720]. After spending the summer over the operations in *Lahara*, King will marched during the time of autum and arrived there; and *Samala* will accompanied by *Yasoraja*[721]. But at the same time *Domba,* a Rajaputra son of *Sajja* will fell in battle at *Manimusa* for the protection of troops that had been scattered from the fear of *Prthvihara*[722]. King (Raj) will again came down on the earth fought repeated encounters at the village of *Suvarnasanura*[723], *Surapura* and other famous places, in which he became victorious and Vanquished in turn again for the time being[724]. In the meanwhile, *Srivaka* was worsted out near the famous Brahman *Kalyanapura*[725] by *Prthvihara* and the rest, *Nagavatta* and others will found their death in the fight of *Kaliyuga*[726]. In the month of Pausa, *Psthvihara* will sent from the *Suvarnasanura Tikka* of *Devasarasa. Madavarajya* has to slay the wife of *Garga (Chudda*[727]) (soul) .She with her own will defeated by the troops of King, she became enemy of the King on this earth. Due to his sudden attack along with the *Tikka,* she will be killed in the fighting send down her position which she desires[728]. In this way, it is expressed that this wicked man will committed another murder of a woman. What difference however, is there between the animals, *Mlechchas*, robbers and devils? The answer of this statement is that he is *'Nam'* but not '*man*[729]'. *'Nam'* knows the reality of the world. Those who have been defeated by the *Lahara*, they will fled away without hesitation because they know the consequences of *'Nam'*. Those left without the qualification of *'Nam'*, they remained mistress as like a woman. As soon as she was killed, O wonder, took up again the sword of the *'Nam'* or *'Word*[730]' King will also learn in the same fashion from the *Madavarajya*, who had previously been pacified to some extent. He will again disturbed by the *'Nam'* and then proceeded towards *Vijayesvara*[731]. This wicked tongue which has been peculiar to the sons of *Mallaraja*, those have been forgotten the *'Nam'* their power suddenly brake down. It shows that nowadays they have been put down as his servants, as it were, on a sieve. They must have to prove their worth in their character otherwise they will remained in the mud[733]. As the King has used indecent words and low abuse to himself with which he had became fimilar from his early youth. He obtained humiliation, *Yasoraja* became disaffected towards him for certain period of time[734]. No doubt, *man* is very wicked and cunning, he never controls by the *'Nam'*, unless and untill, he did not posted at *Avantipura* with a great force. As now, he has been moved off from the real house i.e., *'Word'* and his joined the side of the enemy[735]. Suddenly, he had been gone over the side of enemy and became best of all the troops with help of money as an illusion.

Still King has retreated in dejection from the *Vijayaksetra*[736]. It is non-sense for the sake of achieving the throne which he was eager to save his life even by suffering insults from marauders who are mostly thieves and *Candalas*[737], *In Magha*, after his flight back to the palace, he will returned to the City, and owing to his servant *Vatha* having (also) become a traitor. He began to distrust even his own hair[738]. He also depends upon you. Then, he will lose his trust altogether in any of the *Kashmirians* do in his behaviour; and King will rested his head on the lap of *Prajji*[739]. In this efforts, *Prajji* by his magic spell, liberality, prudence, honesty and other good qualities will sealed up in his cabine (i.e. effaced from recollection) the fame of princes like *Rudrapala* and others who had previously (come to Kashmir from abroad[740]). He will also earned alone spotless fame and safeguard interest in this land for the honour of sword in learning which the wickedness of the times will be shaken on spot[741]. *Yasoraja* in the meantime was engaged for the establishment of council with *Bhiksu* (and spoke to him): "The Damaras do not with you on the throne, as they are afraid of your valour[742]." "Let us raise a fresh revolt and either by ourselves secure the throne with the assistance of the troops from the capital or go abroad[743]." Thus, they were at that time deliberately in a position to listen the theory of *Mallakastha* and *Chudda* (*Man*) will be killed within the body. He will returned definitely from the town of the *Darads* (*Daratpura*[744]) and occupied his own shot[745]. There is routine matter, they came over this world during the terrible year (of the *Laukika* era four thousand one hundred and) ninety nine (A.D. 1123-24), which is very hard to live through which brought death for all beings[746].

Fresh Siege of Srinagar (1123 A.D.)

Study shows that fresh invasion to siege the *Srinagar* will be started in the spring; and all the Damaras will be marched on, as before, by the respective routes and besieged the King in the City[747]. No doubt, courageous King *Sussala*, too, was once again day and night will sharing the excitement of action in a multitude of unceasing encounters[748]. At the same time; Damaras wholly will absorbed by the work of burning, looting and fighting; and will raised a rebellion greater even than the former rebellions[749] of the world like in France, South Africa, etc. While *Yasoraja* , *Bhiksu, Prthvihara* and the rest will be eager to break into the City stood on the bank of the *Mahasarit,* where there was nothing to obstruct them[750]. Then after some days had passed in fighting, *Yasoraja* was killed in a combat by one of his own people, who was by mistake an enemy of *Yasoraja*[751]. In that case, he has moved around the world in fighting with *Vijaya, Kayya's* son, a cavalier of *Sussala*, his own spearmen, by looking at the horse. The armour which were of the same colour (as those of his opponent), mistook him in the excitment and killed him by spear thrusts[752]. It is said that the Damaras will killed him, because they were afraid of *'Nam'* that he was able to secure the throne for *Bhiksu* and subsequently they will be destroyed themselves[453]. Just as he treacherously betrayed his unsuspected Lord or Master. However, he, too, has been met with him in death of *'Nam'* in the unsuspecting battle[754]. After this, *Prthvihara* had sent to him against the Damaras in various place to conqueror them and himself has been accompanied with the King to attack on the bank of the *Ksiptika*[755]. During such hours the soldiers from the capital who were on *Bhiksu's* side, displayed a prowers which surpassed even their foes were in great power[756]. At the same time, every single day he brought terror on account of his conflegrations; and the destruction of brave soldiers and other disasters[757] like 'Caste System', '*Untouchability*', etc. It shows that *Prthvihara* fiercely burned the sun; earthquakes occured time and again; and there blew sudden stroms of great violence which broke down trees and rocks[758]. The particles of the dust which were raised at that time at the great height by the winds. It seemed to serve as a supporting column to the sky which was rented by the whirlwinds[759] of the nature. This great fight was started on the twelfth day of the bright half of *Jyaistha*, the Damaras were set one of the house on fire at *Kasthika*[760].

Great Fire in Srinagar (1123 A.D.)

It has also been expressed from the study that a great fire was took place in Srinagar in 1123 A.D. in the month of Jyaistha due to the belowing or whether it arose from lightning of the *'Nam'*. It has been widely uncheckedable and in a moment it was set on fire almost the entire City[761]. It appears that on 'the Great Bridge' (*brhatsetu*[762]), one can see now only the smoke is going to risen from *Maksikasvamin*[763], rushing like a herd of elephants. At the same time (the fire) will fell upon the *Indradevibhavana*[764] *Vihara.* Thereupon the whole City will be burnt at once[765]. It makes clear from the study neither the earth nor the horizon nor the sky could be seen in the darkness of the smoke. The sun showed itself and disappeared (again in a moment) just as the skin at the month of the *hudukka*[766]. Their houses have been hidden by the darkness of the smoke and then again illuminated for a moment by the flash of the fire as if it has to be seen for the last time[767]. Now, the *Vitasta*, lined on both side of the banks to flame up their houses (Damaras), who looked like sword of death wetted with blood on both edges[768]. The mighty flame-bundles (the great historians of India) which fell and rose again a rebellion against the *'Nam'*. Having been they touched the top of the upper fold of the universe. They resembled like a forest fire by the golden parasols[769]. The fire with its various crests of flames its various crests of flames resembled with the Golden Mountain (Meru), the smoke is resting on the top like a mass of clouds[770]. The houses as they shone forth from the flames. They have made the deluded householders according to their own desire time and again that they will not be spared from the fire[771]. The *Vitasta* (*Sindhu*) whose waters have been heated by the burning houses more terrible, which will fell (into it) and became acquainted with the pains which the ocean suffers from the heat of the submarine fire of the nation[772]. The burning young *'Historian'* (Dr. Raj Kumar) shoots up to those trees who think it is difficult to reach on us. They will fired in the garden-avenues and flew up in the sky with the help of the brids of nature, whose wings are on fire[773]. The temples which appeared white stucco, have been covered like the peaks of the Himalaya clothed with the clouds of the (last) dawn which beings the destruction of the world. It has been enveloped by the flames of destruction[774]. It shows that they are not ready to come out the feudal system; and wanted to suppress the history of common man which they nothing know except their 'egoist' way of thought like the snake of the hell[775]. It is very difficult for them that their multitudes of the bathing-huts and boat-bridges (lobby) will spared from the fear of fire, even the water-ways within the city became deserted[776]. What more we (need be said) to them that they are the animals? Within an instant the city became bare of Mathas (mind), temples, houses, markets, and others (buildings) of the world, and like to be burned down as a forest[777]. It has been seen and observed in the City of Srinagar will be reduced to a heap of earth, it will remained visible and aloft only single great *Buddha* (Statue[778]); which blackened by the smoke of theory of mind or *man* without its abode, it will be resembled like a burned tree[779]. Certain troops of the King must be dispersed to save their burning quarters and King will left with only a hundred soldiers[780]. It became difficult for the King to cross the *Vitasta* river because owing to the bridge having been broken, the enemy who have found an opportunity, gathered around without number to kill him alive[781].

Critical Situation of Sussala

Now the situation became critical for *Sussala*, he is thinking to burn the city with rapid flame, because his own state became wretched due the misery of his own subjects. King his pressing hope greatly desired an early death[782] of the historians which think we are well educated, without ourselves, nobody can move ahead. It will be proved that they are mistaken from their study. They are the trouble created historians when King was about to start his journey from Jammu to Delhi to attend the conference of the *Dalit*. He came face to face with *Kamaliya*, who having been called his attention by others and thinking that he was fleeing to *Kurukestra* spoke thus: "Whither away, O King[783]" ? But courageous King stopped his horse; and turning around his face which was illuminated by a smile of excitement and bore a mark of sandal-ointment, said to him: "I wish to do today what King *Bhijja,* that proud grandfather (of yours) did for his country's sake in the battle with *Hammira*[784] ." "Granted that this person of unknown origin (*Bhiksacara*) is a rival Kinsman! What our brother and we ourselves could accomplish King *Harsa* has seen when he fled before us[785]." "Is there any person holding a place among self-respecting men, who abandon his country at the end without having wetted it with the blood of his body, just as the tiger (does not leave) his skin (without having wetted it with his blood[786])?" After speaking these words, *Sussala* threw up the reins and raised his sword, as if he is going to touch with both hands the horse on its upraised front of war with the enemies[787]. Then the son of *Lavaraja* (*Kamaliya*) stopped the (King's) horse by the reins and spoke: "While there are servants it is not fitting for Kings to proceed in front[788]." At this critical situation only *Prthvipala*[789] came to the King alone, (who left his) house, though he has been suffered from a hurt of his plan[790]. King warmly praised him for having been shown himself the scion of a noble family. He thought that by displaying his readiness to serve him. *Prthvipala* will have to repay what he had received from himself[791]. During this point of time, the enemy will be ranged in three exhibition and King will shot these people with the arrows of *'Nam'* or *'Word'*. All those soldiers on the left overprouded, they will be killed on spot. He is urging on his steed, and in such condition who are playing with the fate of the others. They must be punished according to their *'Karma* theory. Many of the enemies who have been corrupted up by the theory of mind which are always destructive in natural form[792]. No doubt, King has few soldiers, but they will appeared before the enemies in multiform, like (Visnu) when he came to the assistance (of Arjuna and showed himself) as the 'Omnipresent' (*Visarupa*[793]). During such critical time, King *Sussala* himself put to fight against many of his own enemy, just as the falcon the sparrows, and the lion the antelopes; *'Nam'* against *Manas*[794]. The horsemen whose rush was abstructed by their own masses, they will fell (back) upon those who are on foot. They will also struck themselves as they were blocking the way before the horses hoofs[795]. In the reflection of the flames of the fire all the fighters, whether fallen or yet to be fallen will be appeared as if red with streaming blood[796]. At the very closing of the day (enlightenment era), King will scattered the enemy and returned with tears in his eyes to the City of Srinagar of which (even) had been spared by the fire or had lost its splendour situation[797]. Though he remained unvanquished, yet on the account of the ruin of the beautiful (City) whcih has been proposed by the enemy in this battle or to care for life[798]. After this event, one must have to looked upon him without tears, whether he was awake or sleeping, moving or standing, bathing, eating, or going forth challenged by the enemy? after the end of the one century in this direction[799].

Famine in Kashmir

It shows during the end of the century all the food-stores in Kashmir will be consumed by the fire; there occured a terrible famine over the entire land of Kashmir[800]. The people's savings will be exhausted by the long troubles; their houses were burned; and outside (the City) the Damaras will be seized and their production will be blocked in the roads[801]. The nobles who received no money from the royal household they will be seen distressed by King: and perished quickly in the famine[802]. After the passage of time, there houses will be burned among those who had left over the conflagration by fires. During such moment the hard hit people they will be seen searching out for food[803]. It will have to been seen that people acrossed the bridges of the various streams by holding the noses, on account of the bad smell of the corpses decomposed by the water of the rivers[804]. The ground sheet of the valley will also be displayed white in everywhere owing to its being covered with the fragments of skulls from fleshless human skeletons, as it were the custom of skull-carrying ascetics (*Kapalika*[805]). After this event, the hungery striving people, will come forward for pious journey; and those who do not believe on this mission i.e. *'Radha Soami'* their bodies will be darkened with sharp sun-heat, appeared like scorched (wooden) posts[806]. At that time, there will a wide spread news of false propaganda that *Prthvihara* has been wounded somewhere by an arrow in the incessant fighting during that period and has died[807]. On such conditions, *Prthvihara* will have to keep concealed by his people on account of his serious wound of the arrow and became disable to walk. This rumour will give an enjoyment to the King and fought with (fresh) power[808]. It would be the victory of the goddess, like a shrewd courtesan, who was exciting by displaying a pretended yearning for himself; but his desire will not be fullfil for the time beings[809]. As ill luck would have it, his disposition is thoroughly perversed, displays kindness only to sharpen (thereby) the succeeding misfortune. However, the cloud has been sent out by the *'Nature'* or *'Nam's* flash of lightening in order to damaged the shining plants of miraculous powers, who has been covered the mountains entirely to the end of the darkness period[810].

Death of Meghamanjuri

In the study, it indicates that during the visit at Delhi for the deliverence of the lecutre in the *'Tala Katora Stadium'* on the topic of *'The life and Teachings of Lord Buddha'*; it shows at that time the chief queen *Meghamanjuri* was died there, who had been the beloved consort of the King (Dr. Raj Kumar); who had been visited as his fortune supporter. After passing through long sufferings: King had been expecting the festive day of her arrival at Jammu with fond desire as if it were the reward for his act in Delhi. The combined love of the both with tenderness, cheerful speech with dignity, and cleverness with experience; just as (if the latter qualities had been) the children (of the former) Dr. B.R. Ambedkar[811]. It came to our notice that the people of the different states were bereft of pleasures in the memory of Dr. B.R. Ambedkar and weary of their daily life, King saw no object whatever in living or ruling[812]. It delineates *Meghamanpuri* was worn out by the disastrous news from her husband (Dr. Raj Kumar). She had started her journey from the *Kashmir* with full of eager desire; when she died near *Phullapura*[813]. During the emotion of the hope, King saw her queen for the first time, when he listened the bad or destructive news for the evil doers. At that time; King was fell into sarrow and sufferings due to his excitement[814]; when he watched the condition of the people in dead hope; they were wandering in the material world. In addition to this, the four women who were foremost in her household; and whose devotion had not suffered from the use of harsh words. He followed the queen (into death[815]). In this event; a cook by the name of *Teja* made himself worthy of special praise among the servants, by showing exceptional devotion towards the *Dalit Shathiya Akademi* of Delhi; though her death was not taken place in his presence[816] becasue he nothing know about the *'Nam' or 'Chamar'*. When he will arrived on the following day of Judgement after having an absence from the real duty, his head will be smashed with a stone found near her (soul) pyre and himself in the river[817] of *Vitasta*. It shows from the reference, the enemies have forgotten the King's sorrow by the excitement of challanges which he faced during his previous birth, which he fought a battle against the Rajput with the help of *'Nam'*. Thus, as it happened; it was his kindness on his subjects; but now they have totally forgotten his achievements on the question of his next birth[818].

Jayasimha Brought Back From Lohara

Study also expresses that the depressed King has to desire to renounce the throne; and his son (Deepit Raj) has now passed out of boyhood or childhood; and *Jayasimha* has been brought back from the *Lohara* hill[819]. Now he has arranged the treasury at *Lohara* for the protectioning of his territory by appointing *Bhagika*, the nephew of *Prajji*, as his governor[820]. As soon as King embraced his beloved son on his arrival at *Varahamula* (where) he had gone to meet him; at such occasion he will be filled with joy and grief[821]. It has been observed that the prince who returned to his own country after three years, felt pained in his heart on seeing his father was in distress[822] at that time in searchout of the King. Moreover, it has been seen that the face of King, has been got down-cast in grief. Now he entered the city which was reduced to a mass of earth, just as a cloud has been hanged low with rain (passes over) the forest fire[823].

Jayasimha Crowned (1123 A.D.)

Study disclosed that *Jayasimha's* father will crown him as a King on the first day of *Asadha*, and then indicated to him about the main principles of the government, in the following beautiful sentence: "May you support that burden, under which your father and uncles have tired out, not being able to carry it. Upon you, O my brave (son), devolves this load[824].' It has been seen that King has been deceived by his fate; will be bestowed upon his son merely the insignia of sovereignty; but it has been felt that *Yamas* are not ready to hand over the kingdom to the real owners[825]. As soon as, prince bcome the crowned of the city; there is blockade, drought, plague, robberies, and other troubles will be difficult to chease[826]. At the same time, the earth will produce rich sources of living and this will be met out during the due course of scarcity has to cease in the month of *Sravana*[827]. In the meanwhile, King (*Jaya*) *Simha* will destroyed the enemy in the battle; and intriguers will have to denounced him to his father as a traitor[828].

Jayasimha's Imprisonment

It shows without reflecting the truth of this story, *Sussala* sent his displeasure (*Vijaya*) the son of *Kayya* has imprisoned the *Jayasimha*. It has been well-known by the prince before hand[829] that the *Dalit Sahitya Akadmi* has to keep the false notions about the meaning of term *'Dalit'*. The stage secretary Mr. *Vijaya* without presenting himself before the (prince), he was smiling in excessive rage, gave effect to the King's order merely by guarding him[830] certain problems of the areas; but he was not in a position to understand real problem of the life which is destitute without *'Nam'* or *'Word'*. It has been known to us that prince due to his mental pain could not take the food in the Delhi *'Tala Katora Stadium'*. He was prepared by giving him assurances from the 'Father' before to proceed[831] Delhi. At that time his father who thought that since he was on his guard; it would not be possible to accuse him. On spot, he induced him to turn back, on the way by sending a King of message through the ministers who deceived him[832]. No doubt, in his mind, he firmly resolved day and night that he would enter through the apartment of his son, who will teach a lesson to the cheaters and imprison him[833]. It appears from the study that during the days of darkness, we are mutually distrusted each other on the account of throne[834]. No body knows there; that these Kings have the mutual relationship, when we will loose the trust each other either there are sons or wives or brothers and servants[835] then there is *'Nam'*.

Utpala's Plot

It is interesting to note[836] *Utpala* made a secret plot with his son of a certain *Sthanaka*, who was a watchman at the threshing floor (*Khalapala*), lived near a wretched village known by the name of *Sahya*. It shows that during his boyhood or childhood, he had been employed by sons of Damaras to watch cattle; then he took up arms and became in time *Jikka's* constant companion (i.e., *'Nam'* or called *Kaka*). Having carried from the first year (*Tikka's*) messages, he became confidant of the King when the latter wished to create dissension among his enemies[837]. At that time, *Sussala* asked the King under promises of power and grants to kill *Bhiksacara* at *Tikka's* seat and then *Tikka* had given a promise to this effect[838]. He honoured the King with gifts of great value that he is the obident of the master; and employed him also under the title of treasurer (*gaujapati*[839]). This man has the lust of pleasures in his wavering mind between the master and servant. If the servant could not decide to go there as to whether he should carry out this enterprise or leave it undone then it supposes to be dread of betraying his master[840]. In the meantime, *Utpala's* wife gave birth to a child. Keeping in view, King with his object sent her various things, as customary to confine, as if (he had been) her father[841]. As the wife of the husband, she was feeling distrustful about the cause of (such) exception attention on his part that neither Prime Minister nor president of India was presented there. She persistently questioned her husband, who then told her (the reason[842]). "Do not betray your master, or else if the deed is done, you will, yourself, or else if the deed is done, you will, your self, be killed in time by *Sussala,* who will fear you as a traitor[843]." "Better still! Kill him (*Sussala*) himself after gaining his confidence. If he is killed, you will receive great riches from your master, his son and family[844]." Keeping in mind such words his wife urged her husband to change his resolution, and induced him to undertake the entreprise of the cold wave after acquainting *Tikka* with this affair of the nature[845]. As a traitor then he was going and coming, and the King has been deluded by his fate, but now he has to put (such) confidence in him as (if he was) his son[846]. There is no need for the estrangement from the son and reliance on the enemy's servant, *'Word'* does not show itself the perversity whose fortune is doomed! during the days of darkness[347]. It has been described that low people (*Chamars*) who are blinded by the lust for their own profit; and do not think about the accident whatever they may step into; just as those who are eager to take the honey (do not think) of the harm from the bees[848]. While as *Prajji* and the king were pressing hard to *Tikka, Utpala* got the latter to make his submission to give the enemies as a hostage to his son[849]. In such conditions King will leave the subdued *Devasarasa* in the month of *Kartikka,* and proceeded to the village of *Bastraka*, situated in the *Kheri* district of *Kashmir*[850].

Sussala's Victory at Kalyanapura

In the sharp struggle of war and peace, *Sussala* also put to shame *Bhiksu, Kosthesvara*[851]; and other soldiers in various encounters in the neighbourhood of *Kalyanapura* and became victorious in the battle[852]. In this battle, *Sujji* captured alive by the very brave soldier called

Sobhaka, of *Kaka's* family, from the midst of *Bhiksacara* and his men[853]. 'King firstly defeated *Vijaya,* the son of *Bhavaka*, burned his house near *Kalyanapura*. At the same time *Vadosaka*[854] was also burned and *Bhiksacara* has lost his place of safety, left that territory and took up the position in the village of *Kakaruha* in *Samala*[855]. In addition to this, the younger brother of *Vijaya, Bhavaka's* son due to the fierce encounter of the *Sussala* joined with the King, who wrathfully laid him in fetters and imprisoned him in his own territory[856]. To keep in watch king posted the *Rilhana* with a strong force at *Surapura* and made even the *Rajapuri* fear an attack. Now, *Sussala* had taken up certain exceptional measures to brake up the terrible Damaras; he has witnessed before the invasion his enemies how to defeat them completely[857]. It shows that the *Bhiksacara* and the *Lavanyas* having lost their strength and thought of going abroad from fear of their powerful foe[858]. In the context those became the espoused of *Bhiksu's* cause were dispirited by the various manifestations of bad luck and felt dead, no doubt, they are living being[859]. It is visible from the statement that King again recollecting the deceitful conduct of *Somapala* turned back with the thought that he would make a burning ground of *Rajapuri* after the melting of the snow[860]. In the meanwhile, troubles will be raised in his own country to some extent, one might have thought that the King has started certain conquests from the edge of the ocean[861]. Whatsoever will be survived from this conquest, it would be the bad luck of the people, after this each year of the King's reign will be considered as long as a Yuga[862]. Moreover, his reign, indeed, brought sufferings to all through sorrows, terrors poverty, death of beloved persons, and other natural calamities[863]. During such conditions; it will be concentrated that what man has achieved with the help of power, hardness, or deceeit, when success depends on the very strong ways of fate of life[864]. It is accessible perversity, indeed, is displayed in the ways of the creator. The one who stands before hims as a big mass; he avoids as (if he were) in darkness. When some (other) person passes by turns around and looks at him as a lion does. Like a frog; he jumps over a ruler close by (and proceeds) to some one else[865]. It has been observed *Sussala* had before blamed *Uchchala* and other (Kings) who had perished through certain being unsuspected; had ever kept his sword drawn; and quoting the story of *Vidurath*[866] and others which King had heard from those verses which were popular during the ancient time. He had not, even at play time, or in the embraces of women, shown a trustworthy cheerful face. He (now) persisted in treating. *Utpala* with confidence as if he was his best friend of the entire universal. Who could see here in the delusion of earth only his fate which is called *'Nam' or Sabad*[867]. This story has been revealed by *Tikka* and the rest has been expressed by *Utpala* that they would value his deed in the interest of his equal labour in the field of life whichever of the two he killed i.e King or *Sujji* of the time[868]. In this content *Sujji* displayed less interest in him. Because he is eager to kill the King and ready for it at various places, but he could not find an opportunity in this affair[869]. In the meantime, King got angry on account of the delay in the process of achievement, in order to assure him. No doubt, he brought his son from *Devasarasa* and a hostage, as well as others like *Vyaghra* and *Prasastaraja*, who were just like himself ready for desperate acts which we have played; and told to the King that with these he would effect his object. On one occasion; he moved out with three to four hundred foot soldiers, now he had selected certain troops as being fit for a bold enterprise[870]. Right now the murderer kept ever by his side; and we are waiting of an opportunity, the King, alas, in a position to please h im with favourite dishes and other gifts[871]. In this competition, King has devoted certain passinate horses; and had sent away in the chamberlain of *Laksmaka*[872], the son of *Kayya* (Vijaya) and others who are called 'Sovereign of the stable (*manduracakravartin*) which made the city ailing. Thus, he was at that time accompanied with small numbers of attendants.

Sussala Warned Against Utpala[873]

Sussala warned the *Srngara, Laksmaka's* son, who had heard of *Utpala's* proposal through certain trusted persons. Now he has prepared a report about it to the King against the *Utpala*[874]. A person whose death is nigh, *Sussala* takes his enemy for a friend, just as the animal at the slaughter-house, even while it sees the preparation for its slaughter will be take place[875]. It is expressed neither the curse of the Gandhara princess[876], nor the words of the angry Rsi, nor the portents, nor even his own divine sight displayed the destruction of the family (of the *Pandavas*[877]), enable Visnu to save it. Kowing to this, who would (attempt to) change destiny of the world after the rise of one civilization to another[878]. King expressed his insult: "This is a lie," and pointing to *Srngara* with his finger, spoke thus to *Utpala* and others who were there in his presence: "This son of a traitor does not wish that good should come to me from your zeal, and tells me, whether from his own account or by others' instigation, that you, O *Utpala*, are a rogue[879]." In this contest, they concealed their fear and agitate under a smiling face; and strongly replied in these words: "Your majesty says what we ought to say[880]". At that time, they had gone outside the hall. He felt that there is little gathering in the hall to alarm them; and called through the doorkeeper two or there distinguished, steady soldiers who were moving here and there at that time[881]! And, King was at that time in a sad mood. He remained some what agitated and persive, and having tears in his eyes; and did not express his interest in the dancing and singing led by the various artists from the different states[882]. In his delusion he expressed his thought to his friends as a strangers in this competition; just like a god who took his merits (from previous births) sometime *Ravi das, Laxman, Dr. B.R Ambedkar,* etc. having vanished, is about to drop from the sky as a no-man status[883]. Certain friends of the King who felt alarmed at (seeing) their lord misguided by roguery wished thoughtlessly to call for another protector[884]. Those people displayed their interest die to live in the *'Nam',* they are the successful people in their life, though they know the value of *'Nam'* and now they are free from the cycle of birth and rebirth[885]. In this free competition *Utpala* and others have been passed, they must be anxious keeping in view to open their eyes for two days moment such as an opportunist[886]. While they are watching secretly their moment and King on the third day after taking his bath in the morning said to them repeatedly: "You should go to your houses to take your food[887]". After completing his daily routine in the matters of worshiping of gods; King then called at midday by *Utpala*; through messengers (to meet him) alone[888].

Execution of Utpala's Plot

King feeling confident that he would be able to execute his secret planning owing the deserted condition of the palace. *Utpala* at that time proceeded with a nervious feeling before the king, while his followers were stopped by the doorkeeper[889]. At that time King called in *Vyaghra,* his younger brother, who had been detained at the door, and ordered the other servants to keep outside[890]. Even some trusted councilors were delaying (in the room) King was in anger mood, let escape from these words which were true: "Let him stop here who is a traitor[891]." He allowed only a betel-bearer of mature age and learned the lesson from *Rahila*, the minister of foreign affairs, to remained in his presence[842]. But at the same time, two messengers of *Tikka* known as *Arghadeva* and *Tisyavaisya*, were presented there, as it happened, without being acquainted with *Utpala's* design of living[893]. And, *Utpala* had been posted in those days to keep away the Damara from *Vadotsa, Sukharaja* by name an adherent of *Bhiksu,* at a short distance together with his armed force, in order to assure his own safety. He told the King that this Damara would start to carry out that task (*Bhiksu's and Tikka's* murder) after saluting the King's feet[894]. Thus, King for the time being stopped the business with Damaras; *Utpala* brought in *Prasastaraja* quickly, after telling the King that he was wanted by the Damaras[895]. It has been watched before the entering of the aute-room which was totally hallow; and he bolted the door without being prior noticed[896]. At that period, who felt cold. He had covered his whole body with a choak, and his dagger, which he had taken off, lay on his seat. On seeing him seated in this fashion, *Vyaghra* told to *Utpala*: "Make your communication to the king. No (other) such occasion may occur[897]." At the moment he was excited by this signal which went before the King under the guise of prostrating himself at his feet; and took away his dagger from the seat[898]. Due to the bewilderness of eyes King saw him and drew it from the dress and scarcely said: "Fie, what treason!" When *Utpala* stapped him first on the left with that very (dagger). The *prasataraja* struck him on the head for the right direction[899].

Sussala Murdered by Utpala (1128 A.D.)

In the blind murder case, *Vyaghra* then wounded her (*Mira Kumar*) in the breast; and ex-Governor (*Mata Prasad*)*;* thus these who struck him several times, while *Utpala* did not strike him again because *Sussala* was already murdered by him on the question of contest between the two[900]. In the latter few of them understood that his life has been parted, because the first stook of the King penetrated in the ribs of *'Mata Parsad'* and had drawn out the strings of the entrals[901]. At the same time, *Rahila,* who ran to the window to shout (for help) that we are with you, but he was stabbed by the *Vyaghra* from the behind; and could not give up his life for two or three *Nalikas*[902]. *Utpala* felt pity on the poor people of the *'Father'* to save their life from the betel-bearer *Ajjaka,* who were fleeing after dropping the cubebs (*Kankola*[903]) and other (ingredients) of the different components[904] when the tumult rose inside; most of the *Tikka's* men and other conspirators, who were in the outer hall. They were also plundered with upraised weapons by the King[905]. In order to boost his own people outside the hall, on the report of the *Utpala*, they have been slain by the King; and were cut down by the soldiers of the King too.

Utpala put the ray from the window and displayed the body with the bloody weapon, and called out: "I have killed the King. Do not let his band escape[906]." On hearing this news, bewilderness was wide spread in the royal camp among the attendants and they were fled away every where due to the fear of *Utpalas* attack. While the conspirators, they took up rejoic in their own position in the courtyard[907]. On the leaving of hall, King also murdered the *Nagaka*, at that time who was entering by the door without weapon and became an attendant of the King[908]. Besides the *Nagaka*, there was another servant of *Trailokya,* the guardian of the royal bed-(chamber); who was denounced the treachery; and a doorkeeper was also killed by *Tikka's* people and the rest[909]. The murderers who were watching and warding the *Sahajapala*, the ornament of *Bhavuka's* family, distinguished himself in the middle of the way by displaying courageous efforts for the sake of faithful servants of the King. They were rushed with shield and sword by the side of the door; while he was fell down for the time being on the ground and wounded by the strokes of their followers[910] who were with them at that time. While it displayed that a stigama of disrespect as a whole has been levelled on the *Rajaputra* tribe. In this field King alone succeeded in washing of the shame which with his blood[911] and could not bother so called *Hindu,* or else like Muslim, *Bauddha,* etc. There was one more learned Brahman called *Nona,* who came in their way, was killed by the followers of the murderers; because they wrongly took him from a Rajaputra tribe on account of his appearance, which was looking like a foreigner (*daisika*[912])

Panic in Palace

The panic of *Sussala's* murder in the palace none of the soldiers pursued it to the murderers; because they have seen him fleeing unhurted towards a village; as if they became (motionless) like the pictures of the paintings and other royal arts of the day[913]. In the meanwhile; certain royal relatives of the *Sussala,* they had arrived there, whom the king had, too, made the recipients of his favours. No doubt, there are certain fat bodies persons, they must be covered in the desert of the courtyard as the prisoners of the king[914]. Placing the records and describing various rogues sorts of king *Harsa's* story, we have been (hardened) like load-carriers of the public in detailed manners[915]. Yet we cannot venture the name of those persons who are worse than the wicked Brahman, owing to the pain which is caused by touching personally upon their evil deeds, they could not change their habit and behaviour without their interest or profit or gain in partial attitude[916]. Some wretches who were foremost among them. They looked that king has been died; and thinking it is an act of their greatness to ascend to the hall from the courtyard[917]. It was their miscalculation on the behalf of the king. It has been visulized the soul of the dead king regret at the point of death and his teeth have been bite under the lipservice which oozing the blood made from quiver. His eyes appeared rigid at the time of thought: "How have I thus been deceived?" remained in the same rigidity after his death. The stream (of blood) which was flowed from his wounds and his body became darken. It has been seemed that curling smoke like fire left behind by his wrath which had been extinguished inwardly. On his face which (in its rigidity) appeared as if painted, the mass of blood which was sticking to it like red lae, had effaced (the forehead) marks painted with sandal and saffron colours. He was laid on the ground naked with his fair sticking together owing to the coagulated of blood. His hands and feets stretched out and neck resting on his shoulders. On his visulization, most of the people have been seen meanest could not understand the real picture of the figure, only expressed their excitement on him, saying: "Enjoy the fruit of your unsocialable nature." like the animal[918].

Flight of the Royal Troops and Murder of His Father

After watching the behabiour of the hall royal troops fled away to put themselves in safety. They could not place him on a horse or litter and take him to be burned in the fire of the mass[919]. But let this pass as a task which would have caused delay! No body even threw him on the (burning) logs under the roasting pan or put fire to the house, while fire is at hand[920]. Therefore they fled away through the wonderful flight, and mounting each one on the horse of the king, while the troops remained roaming around the king like the countryside. They were looted by the Damaras[921]. During the flight on the snow covered roads, son of the king could not protect the father nor the father of his won, as he was dying with the lack of food, being killed and plundered by the Damara[922]s. Moreover, there was no any soldier who remembered his honour; and did not abandon his weapon and clothes. He was remained set on the same road against the enemy[923]. No doubt, Brahman *Lavaraja* and *Yasoraja*, who were skilled in military operation along with the chief *Kanda*. Only these there were bravely fell in fighting with the enemies[924]. As soon as, *Utpala* and his men closely watching the troops of king, they were scattered and entered again in the rooms of the palace, as it shows that the head of the king has been cut off and carried if off as a vain struggle of life; left as trunk[925]. Nothing will come out of it. They must have to proceed in the direction of *Devasarasa;* and the king will bee seen without head, becaome a spectacle for the countryside like a slain thief[926]. However, king will be treacherously murdered by the 'Father' on the new moon day of *Phalguna* in the year (of the *Laukika* era four thousand two hundred and) three (1128 A.D.), after having passed fifty-five years in life[927].

From the above discussion, it has been observed that *Sussala* faced so many ups and downs in his life as an adventures of the nature. No doubt, in very beginning of his career, he had faced certain opposition from the sides of the Brahmans, who were badly involved in the material life of the world. Due to his self-efforts in the 16 years of his rule, he gradually overcame over the troubles of the life. He never disheartred by the problems. He had the strong confidant, tolereance and determination in his life. Therefore, his long rule of sixteen years passed with courage and understanding with the master. It shows that he was the strongest and wonderful ruler of the *Chamar* dynasty, which was never seen in the history of India.

NOTES AND REFERENCES

1. *P. H.K.* p. 237.
2. *R.T.* Vol.II. p. 39.
3. *Ibid.* pp. 39-40.
4. P. H.K. p. 237.
5. R.T. Vol.II. p. 40.
6. *Ibid.*
7. *Ibid.*
8. *Ibid.* **Note.** It indicates from the study that he is very much related with Durgaparsad or *bhimatvam* means, he is equivalent with *Bhima,* who destroyed numebr of *Kurus* in the *Mahabharata*.
9. *Ibid.*
10. *Ibid.*
11. *Ibid.*
12. *Ibid.*
13. *Ibid.*

14. *Ibid.*

15. *Ibid.*

16. **Note.** The word *daisika* in our passage has been assumed to designate 'people of (Didda's) own country' (p. W.), or 'teachers' (N.p. W.). The context, however, shows that it designates the term 'foreigner' in contrast to the Kashmirian. This is also the meaning distinctly given to the word by *Jonaraja* in his commentary on *Srikanthac.* XXV. 102 (*desantariya*). Kalhana uses *Nona,* a learned Brahman, who came in their way, was killed by the followers of the murders, because they mistook him for a Rajaputra on account of his apperance, which was like that of a foreigner (*daisika*). The meaning 'foreign is likely to have developed in the case of both words from that of 'local' or 'provincial' compared with N.p. W, S.V *desya.* The correct rendering of *desya* has already been mentioned that *'Nam'* is related with *'Sacha Khand'* which means *'Sacha Sauda' or 'good bargaining'* mentioned by Nanak.(*S.H.S.* p. 4). The meaning 'traveller' given by *Hemacandra* for *desika* (see p. W., S.V), may also be referred to.

17. *R.T.* Vol.II; p. 40.

18. *Ibid.*

19. *Ibid.*

20. *Ibid.*

21. *Ibid.*

22. *Ibid.* **Note.** There is great change in reading *svapne* 'py is actually found in 'L' means in lowest form as 'Schedule caste'.

23. *Ibid.*

24. *Ibid.*

25. **Note.** *In Bhadravakasa* we have undoubtedly the old name of the hill district now known as *Bhadrawah,* which is situated to the south of the Cinab and adjoins Kistwar.

26. **Note.** *Prasa* was the son of *Sahasramangala.* He had the strong will tomove here and there, and exciting the King's wrath.

27. *R.T.* Vol.II. p. 41.

28. *p. H.K.* p. 237.

29. *R.T.* Vol.II. p. 41.

30. *Ibid.*

31. **Note.** *Devasarasa* is the modern Pargana of *Divasra,* situated in the south-east of the valley on the upper course of the *Visoka* (*Vesau*). The

district is very frequently mentioned in the subsequent narrative; see the index of mind as mentioned in the *Nilamata Purana*.

32. *R.T.* Vol.II. p. 41.

33. *Ibid.*

34. **Note.** Durga is worshipped to this day under the name of *Suresvari* ('Queen of the gods') on a high creg rising above the village of *Isabar* from the range which encloses the Dal Lake on the East. A natural rock on the top of the crag is looked upon as a representation of Durga's husband. The *Suresvarimahatmya* accounts for the residence of the goddess and her consort at this spot by a legend connected with the killing of the demon *Ruru*. It also describes in detail the route of the pilgrimate, which begins at certain springs (*Satadhara* etc.) situated in the immediate vicinity of the village of *Isabar.* It is the site of the latter place which is meant by *Suresvariksetra* in our own passage. The locality of *Isabar* is clearly indicated by those passages which speak of *Suresvari* as situated on the shore of the Dal lake; see also *Samayam;* ii. 29, where the *Satadhara* spring is mentioned with *Suresvari*. The references to it as a place to be sought on the approach of death, show the sanctity attached to it. This is also set forth at great length in the fifth *Adhyaya* of the *Sarvavatara*. The temple of *Siva* and *Parvati* conjoined (*Sivayor misrayos*), *i.e.*, of *Ardhanarisvara* is evidently identified with the one which Kalhana mentions, as standing at *Suresvari* in his own time. Neither the position of this shrine, nor that of the temples mentioned in verses 40, 41, can now be traced with certainly, though the numerous carved slabs and sculptured fragments found near the sacred springs and in the walls of the houses of *Isabar,* prove unmistakably the former existence buildings besides the ruined temple (*Isesvara*) referred to *'Nam'* or *'Word'*.

35. **Note.** See the explanation of the site *Amaresa* elsewhere in the text.

36. *R.T.* Vol.11 p. 41.

37. *Ibid.*

38. **Note.** The maternal uncle of *Uchchala* is probably Ananda collected the Damaras and raised a rebellion in *Madavaraja.*

39. *R.T.* Vol.II. p. 42.

40. **Note.** The statement is found correct with the designation of Sanskrit lexicon *rajanyavamsa*.

41. *R.T.* Vol. II. p. 42.

42. *Ibid.*

43. *Ibid.*

44. *Note.* Ph and Ha closely resemble each other in *Sarada* script as the name of *Halaha* or *Phalaha* is found nowhere else. From the study it appears the hill fort may be concluded that the district meant lay on the outskirts of the Kashmir valley.

45. *R.T.* Vol.II. p. 42.

46. *Ibid.*

47. *Ibid.*

48. *Ibid.*

49. *Ibid.*

50. *Ibid.*

51. **Note.** King *Samgramapala* of *Rajapuri* was died at the same time, and his son *Somapala* was ascended the throne of predecessor or paternal thròne.

52. *R.T.* Vol.II. p. 42.

53. *Ibid.*

54. *Ibid.*

55. *Ibid.* 43.

56. **Note.** *Lokapunya* is repeatedly referred to in the later portion of the chronicle. The gloss of A_2 on the first-named passage identifies *Lokapunya* with *Lokabavan* in Sanskrit called *Lokabhavana*, a fine spring or *Naga* situated near the village of Larikpur, at the elevation of 75°-12′ longitude and 33°-38′ at the latitude, in the Bring Pargana. Near the basin formed by the spring, are the ruins of a small summer house erected by one of the Moghul Emperors, apparently with materials of some earlier building. Fragments of ancient stone images lie in the water near the spring, which is visited by the Brahmans of the neighbourhood

57. **Note.** These staff-bearers (*Vertrin*) are referred to as *Yastika* known as *Rakka* and *Mahiman,* also worked during the rule of *Abhimanyu* (958-972 A.D.)

58. *R.T.* Vol.II. p. 43.

59. *Ibid.*

60. *Ibid.*

61. *Ibid.*

62. **Note.** For the word 'excellent' term '*sasyaka*' has been used in Sanskrit. Here we see King with excellent manner killed certain soldiers who were wandering bare-footed and they were defeated in the war.

63. *R.T.* Vol. II p. 43.

64. Note. *Tikka* was the chief share in *Sussala's* part. It is a golden jar of kindness, and is a natural gift on earth to fight against the evil-doers.

65. *R.T.* Vol. II. p. 43.

66. *Ibid.*

67. *Ibid.*

68. *Ibid.*

69. *Ibid.*

70. *Ibid.*

71. *Ibid.*

72. **Note.** The Brahmans *Lavaraja*, and *Yasoraja*, who were killed in military exercise, and the chief of *Kanda* were the only three who fell bravely in fighting. *Prasa* son of *Sussala* followed the route of *Kanda* to enter into *Kashmir*. No clear picture of the territory is located. But as in the last-named passage *Kanda* seems to be spoken of as on the way from *Bhadravakasa* or *Bhadravah* to Kashmir, it may be conjetured that *Kanda* was the name of one of the hill districts immediately to the South East of Kashmir.

73. R.T. Vol. II. p. 44.

74. **Note.** The 'Chief of *Vallapura'* (*Balavar*) was *Brahmajajjal*, is named in the list of faithful Rajaputras from abroad, who stood by *Susssala* in his greatest straits. Here probably a scion of the *Vallapura* family is meant. *Sussala* also had a wife *Jajjala* from *Vallapura.* who excelled by her virtues, died there, and *Rajalaksmi,* too, the daughter of Gagga, was consumed in the fire. Finally, King uprooted the King *Vikramaraja* at *Vallapura* and placed King *Gulhara,* Cunningham states that he found the name Kalasa in India i.e. p. 205, mentions Ballawar on the route from Kanauj to *Kashmir.*

75. *R.T.* Vol. II. p. 44.

76. Note. *Jasats* was the son of *Harsa's* maternal uncle.

77. *R.T.* Vol. II. p. 44.

78. *Ibid.*

79. *Ibid.*

80. *Ibid.*

81. **Note.** *Kumarpala* must have been the brother of the unnamed wife of *Harsa* who was the mother of *Bhoja*, *Bhiksacara's* father. Names in ending-*Pala* were the common in the Shahi family to which *Harsa's* chief queens belonged.

82. *R.T.* Vol. II. p. 44.

83. *Ibid.*
84. *Ibid.*
85. *Ibid.* p. 45.
86. *Ibid.*
87. *Ibid.*
88. *Ibid.*
89. *Ibid.*
90. *Ibid.*
91. *Ibid.*
92. **Note.** By *Siddhapatha* is meant undoubtedly the present village of *Sidau,* situated on the upper course of the *Visoka,* (*Vesau*) at the elevation of 74°-51 longitude and 32°-41′ latitude. From there two well-known routes lead to the Budil and Konsar Nag Passes on the Pir Pantsal range. The former pass is often designated also the *Sidau* Pass. Pt. Sahibram, in his *Tirthas* calls the place *Siddhuvadesa* (!) i.e. *'Nam' or 'Word'.*
93. R.T. Vol. II. p. 45.
94. *Ibid.*
95. *Ibid.*
96. *Ibid.*
97. *Ibid.*
98. *Ibid.*
99. *Ibid.*
100. *Ibid.* p. 46.
101. **Note.** Kalhana had here perhaps the Kashmiri proverb in mind: *'nuv sin chu galan pranis Sinas'*, 'fresh snow makes old snow melt!
102. R.T. Vol. II. p. 46.
103. *Ibid.*
104. *Ibid.*
105. *Ibid.*
106. **Note.** It is noticed from the study *Prasastakalasa* and his other sons of *Rajakalasa* as ministers obtained great favour before the King.
107. **Note.** Regarding the significance of the term *avichinnasattra, aksayini* we have followed the interpretation given by the glass of A_2. The glossator sees in *aksayini* a perpetual endowment for providing food to Brahmans. In a second gloss Kalhana refers to such endowmetns as

known in the hills near *Kashmir* under the name of *'Achyinya'*. *Srivara* mentions in Vol. 1 p. 408, such an endowment made by *Zain-ul-abidin* on the road of *Surapura* (Hurapor), i.e., on the *Pir Pantsal* route, at whcih way farers without distinction received food. He uses for its designation the expression *annasattra avicchinna annadanam* of our gloss. With the expression *aksayini* may be compared the term *aksayanivi;* frequently used for a permanent endowment in the Nasik cave inscriptions and elsewhere. Endowment of this kind still exist in connection with *Dharmasalas* in various parts of *India*, e.g., at *Raghunatha Mandir* of Jammu, where it is known by the name of *Sadabarat*. Bounties consisting of a certain amount of food are given to this day on the pass of Banahal and at Bunyar on the Jehlam Road, from the proceeds of an endowment of the lata Maharaj to mendicants and pilgrims passing on to *Kashmir.*

108. *R.T.* Vol. II. p. 46.
109. *Ibid.*
110. *Note. Tilaka* and *Janaka*, are often referred *Tilaka Simha* and *Janakasimha*, son of *Vijayasimha,* who must be distinguished from *Tilaka*, the son of *Kaka* mentioned above. The full name of his brother was *Janakasimha.*
111. *R.T.* Vo. II. p. 46.
112. *Ibid.*
113. *Ibid.*
114. *Ibid.*
115. *Ibid.*
116. *Ibid.* p. 47.
117. *Note. Chudda* and *Rajalaksmi* are evidently referred as king chose for his own bride, and the younger *Gunalekha* by name, he accepted as his daughter-in-law.
118. *R.T.* Vol.II. p. 47.
119. *Note.* The place variously designated as *Attalika, Attalika and Attilika* has been identified by *Kalhana* in the passages recorded below, make it clear that *Attalika* must be the name of a locality situated below *Lohara* and in comparative proximity of the castle. In view of this evidence and of what will be said below regarding the position of the force sent for the recapture of *Lohara,* we do not hesitate to recognise the name *Attalika* in that of the present village *Atoli,* situated close to the point where the valley of *Loharin* meets that of *Gagri,* some eight miles below *Loharin* proper. At the actual junction of the two valleys lies *Mandi.* This place consists entirely of shops, some eighty in number. These account for its

name, which means 'market' in *Pahari* as well as *Panjabi*. Mandi is now the commercial centre of the whole district, and has probably occupied the same position in earlier centuries. We see a distinct reference i.e., 9, it has been shown that 'the market of *Attalika'* (text-here *Attilikapana*) corresponds to the present *Mandi* 'The market,' close to *Atoli*. This little town is still the commercial centre of the *Loharin* and neighbouring valleys, where Kalhana relates the looting of *Attilikapana*i.e 'The market of *Attilika (Attalika)'. The news* of this rebellion was carried by a messenger to King *Jayasimha,* and reached him on the following day at *Vijayesvara* Vijabor. He at once despatched a force for the recovery of Lohara. The Kashmirian leader took up his position at *Attalika,* from where he endeavoured to close all approaches to *Lohara*. They started from *Attalika* on a path leading along the preciptious side of a defile, and were followed on the opposite side by the enemy. The other main route over the Tosamaidan Pass as it is blocked by the rebels at the Lohara castle, which leads to *Gagri* Valley has been open for them to approach to Firozpur pass or to any of the other passes leading over the mountains north-west of the Tosamaidan, is closed by the enemy stationed at *SARAMBARA*. This place we identify with the large village of *Chambar* or *'Chamar'*, situated about five miles above *Mandi,* in the Gagri Valley.

120. *R.T.* Vol. II. p. 47.
121. *Ibid.*
122. *Ibid.*
123. *Ibid.*
124. *Ibid.*
125. *Ibid.*
126. *Ibid.*
127. *Ibid.*
128. Note. See the explanation of the term *Amaresvara* elsewhere in this text.
129. *R.T* Vol.II. p. 48.
130. **Note.** *Prthvihara* plays a great role after retiring it, who held a position at *Hadigrama,* suddenly attacked and worsted the brave *Sajjaka*. It is very difficult to surpass his power because King himself had married (a daughter) from *Prthvihara's* family; and he left his *Mallakostha* openly for his propaganda as his/her functions in the society and will be suppressed at the appropriate time as in routine matter.
131. **Note.** *Samala* is the old name of the modern *Hamal* Pargana, which lies in *Kamraz* to the western of Sopur. *Samala* is frequently mentioned in the last *Taranga*

132. *R.T.* Vol. II. p. 48.
133. *Ibid.*
134. *Ibid.*
135. **Note.** The name *Dhudavana* is probably preserved in that of the *Durun Nar,* a mountain spur abutting into the upper Sind Valley from the south, close to the Sunamarg ('Sonamarg'). The foot of this mountain spur (which on the map is marked as '*Darnar*') reaches the village of *Thajavas*, elevated at the hight of 75°-20′ longitude and 34°-18′ latitude. For *Garga*, who is driven from this seats in Lahara (Lar), the Sind Valley forms the natural route of retreat. *Nar*, the Kalhana's form of Sanskrit *nada* (*nala*) is the general designation of a Valley, Anglo-Indice *'Nallah'*. Local names formed by the additional of *nar* are often used in Kashmir as designations of hill-ranges, high spurs, etc. The word *Nada* affixed to the name in its Sanskrit form, is identical with *nala,* which survives in the Anglo-Indian *'Nallah' 'Valley' ravine'*. In its modern Kalhana's derivative *nar,* the word is often found at the end of local names in the Kashmir mountains.
136. *R.T.* Vol. II. p. 48.
137. *Ibid.*
138. *Ibid.*
139. *Ibid.*
140. *Ibid.*
141. *Ibid.*
142. *Ibid.*
143. *Ibid.* p. 49.
144. *Ibid.*
145. *Ibid.* Note. The reference of the term *Snanadroni* mentioned elsewhere in the text.
146. *Ibid.*
147. *Ibid.*
148. *Ibid.*
149. **Note.** *Kalyanacandra* son of *Garga* had displayed himself disrespect against the enemies and was excited by their jealousy.
150. *R.T.* Vol. II. p. 49.
151. *Ibid.*
152. *Ibid.*
153. *Ibid.*

154. *Ibid.*

155. *Ibid.* pp. 49-50.

156. *Ibid.* p. 50.

157. *Ibid.* **Note.** King, even at the time he was seeking shelter, did not remember *Bimba* and others to join his enemies. While treason was ripe, this honourable had alone kept faithful, like a true wife of the husband. He did not turn his eyes towards anyone else (but his Lord).

158. *Ibid.*

159. *Ibid.* **Note.** During the death of the chief queen, *Meghamanjari*, who had been his beloved consort, and whose fortune had been his support. After passing through long sufferings the King had been expecting the festive day of her arrival with fond desire, as (if it were) the reward for a penance.

160. *Ibid.*

161. *Ibid.*

162. *Ibid.*

163. *Ibid.*

164. *Ibid.*

165. **Note.** *Vajradhara* was the ruler of *Babbapura* is meant here.

166. **Note.** Term *Brahmapuri* is used here for the splendid Matha which *Udaya*, the lord of the Gate, constructed along with numerous *Brahmpuris*, embellished the shore of the *Padmasaras*. *Padmasaras* is the Vular lake. *Alamkara*, the superintendent of the great treasury (*Brhadganja*), embellished the land by constructing bathing-huts (*snanakostha*), Mathas, *Brahmapuris*, bridges, and the like for the designation of some pious foundation, corresponds, perhaps, to the modern Dharmasala. *Brahapuri* may be understood as 'residence of Brahmans', and is also the name of Brahman's city where the wise and pious assemble. (*Vikram* xvvii. 29). Correct with Durgaparsad *mandale* for a *mandalam*.

167. *Adi Granth*; p. 954.

168. *R.T* Vol. II. p. 51.

169. *Ibid.*

170. *Ibid.*

171. *Ibid.*

172. **Note.** The emendation of *anantatanaja* or some similar form for *anantadhipa* of A is necessitated by the passages. He put three minisers

to flight; the two *Anandas*, of the family of *Ananta* and *Kaka*, respectively, who were lords of the Gate (*dvaranayaka*), and *Tilakasimha*. *Rilhana* then defeated *Kalyanavada* and others in *Kramarajya*, *Ananda*, the son of *Ananta*, became thereupon there lord of the Gate. He imprisoned *Ananda*, the son of *Ananta*, and appointed *Praji*, who was of royal descent, and came from the *Indus* region (*Saindhava*) tothe charge of the 'Gate'.

173. **Note.** The text of A. shows evidently a corruption in the form *Somapaladaych*. The translation above given is based on a conjectural emendation. *opalasayah, palasrayah* might also be thought of.

174. *R.T.* Vol. II p. 51.

175. *Ibid.*

176. *Ibid.*

177. *Ibid.*

178. *Ibid.*

179. *Ibid.*

180. *Ibid.*

181. *Ibid.*

182. *Ibid.*

183. *Ibid.*

184. **Note.** The brother of *Biddaka* is evidently *Hamba*, and in the same fashion despatched to the others their (dead) brothers and sons. The latter passage must be consulted for the interpretation of our verse.

185. R.T. Vol. II. p. 52.

186. *Note. Surya* was the captain of *Garga*, arrived here on this earth to strengthened the various troops of *Garga*

187. *R.T* Vol. II. p. 52.

188. **Note.** *Arjunakostha* is the brother of *Mallakosthaka*, named *Arjuna* mentioned above in the statement. It is necessary to correct *nirgatya* for meaning less *nirgate* of the text.

189. *R.T.* Vol.II. p. 52.

190. *Ibid.*

191. *Ibid.*

192. **Note**. It is not possible to ascertain the exact position of this district, which is only here mentioned. From the following narrative it may be concluded that it lay in *Madavarajya*.

193. *R.T.* Vol. II. 52.

194. *Ibid.*

195. **Note.** *Samangasasanarayoh*, A_4, who in this instance has rewritten older glosses, probably of A_2, renders the two names by *Svangas* and *Snar.* The first locality can be identified without hesitation with the modern *Sangas,* a large village situated on the left bank of the Arapath river in the Kutahar Pargana, at the longitude of 75°-22′ and at the latitude of 33°-42′. The old gloss on this name is written *Snar* by A_4, but reproduced in R as *Cnar*, two forms which can scarcely be kept distinct in *Sarada* characters. Neither of them have I been able to trace as the actual name of a locality. An examination, however, of the phonetic pecularities of the old names and their more recent equivalents as given by this glosses, leades to a satisfactory identification. The form *Svangas* or modern *Sangas* for *Samangasa* shows the initial palatial sibilant preserved which, under a general phonetic law, is regularly replaced by Kalhana as *h;* compares with *Hurapor* for *Surapura, Haraparvat* for *Sarikaparvata, Hamal* for *Samala*, etc. A similar preservation of the intial *S*, as *s* or *ch,* is found elsewhere only in cases where the intial consonant was protected by immediate contact with a following consonant. Thus we have *Srinagar* for *Srinagar; sravan* (name of month, used by all classes of Kashmiris) for *Sravana; Chirath* or *Srirastra* (name of a Pargana); *Chambar*, near Lohara, for *Sarambara.* These analogies make it probable that we have to assume a contracted form *Smangasa,* in which the vowel of the first syllable has been eliminated under the influence of the stress accent placed on the penultimate. The phonetic history of the name may thus be represented ; *Samangasa, Smangasa, Svangas, Sangas* in modern phonetic.

196. *R.T.* Vol.II. p. 52.

197. *Ibid.*

198. *Ibid.*

199. *Ibid.*

200. *Ibid.* p. 53.

201. ***Note.*** We have followed in the absence of something better, the reading of Durgaarsad, *Ksayaghana*. The latter is evidently a conjectural emendation (though not marked as such in his edition) for *Ksayadhana* found in A.L. As Da and Ga are totally different in Sarada writing, it is improbable that the latter reading is a clerical error. Against the conjectural emendation it may also be urged that *Ksayagana(h)* means properly only the clouds which are to destroy the world at the end of the Kalpa. The harvest would scarcely be referred to the connection with them in a simile has yet to be looked for.

202. **Note.** As A L *hutagni*^{0} gives no suitable sense, we have translated above according to the conjectural emendation of Durgaparsad, *hutatma*.

203. *R.T.* Vol. II. p. 53.

204. *Ibid.*

205. *Ibid.*

206. *Ibid.*

207. **Note.** The reference of the term *Sthamastha* has been fully described in elsewhere in the text.

208. *R.T.* Vol.II. p. 53.

209. *Ibid.*

210. *Ibid.*

211. *Ibid.*

212. **Note.** *Thalyoraka,* only here mentioned, is perhaps identical with the present village of *Thyar* situated at the entrance of the Sindh Valley on the right bank of the river opposite to Gandarbal, circ. 74^0-49' longitude and 34^0-14' latitutde (marked *Taroo* on the larger survey map). As the King's expedition is directed against *Mallakostha* in *Lahara*, the place must be looked for in the Sindh Valley.

213. *R.T.* Vol. II. 54.

214. *Ibid.*

215. **Note.** *Hadigrama* can be identified on the evidence of the gloss *Adegram* given by A_2, with the modern *Argana,* a village of the Nagam Pargana, elevated at 74^0-55 longitude and 35^0-56 latitude. It is referred to the site of several fights were took place where king *Sussala* and those (of his side) had lost their renown, was burned by *Sujji* whose valour was mighty. At that time King *Lothana* appeared suddenly at night in *Hadigrama* with few followers. He had been repeatedly encouraged through messengers from *Kosthesvara* who was by nature hostile to the King, and who at that time was still further mortified on account of the renown the latter had gained. Some remains of temples were traced there by Pt. Kasi Ram in 1891.

216. *R.T.* Vol. II p. 54.

217. **Note.** *Nagamatha,* however, thereupon attacked by *Sussala* and killed treacherously three trusted councilors whom the King (*Raj*) had sent to conduct him to the *Nagamatha.* Its position is unknown.

218. **Note.** For the word *Caraka* the meaning 'grazing-ground' is clearly indicated by his servants confiscated even the grazing land (*Caraka*) of the sacred cows, one cowherd also over come by compassion burned himself. At the *Gokula* which is provided with meadows for the cows unobstructed free grazing, and which has an abundant supply of water

from the *Vitasta,* the cows bodies rest free from sickness. The meaning, though not known to the dictionaries, is easily accounted for by the etymology of the word. The emendation *Caraka* proposed in edition was erroneous.

219. *R.T.* Vol.II. p. 54.

220. **Note.** The roots of the lotus (*bisa*) are used as a favourite vegetable in Kashmir, and generally stewed with meat. Large quantities of these roots, which are known as *nadur,* are brought daily into Srinagar from the neighbouring lakes.

221. *R.T*. Vol.II. p. 54.

222. **Note.** Term *Biddaka* has already been discussed above.

223. *R.T.* Vol.II. p. 54.

224. **Note.** The name of the place has not been indentified here.

225. **Note.** See the distinction between *bahya* ('outer') and *abhyantara* ('inner') among the royal servants mentioned above in elsewhere.

226. *R.T.* Vol. II. p. 55.

227. *Ibid.*

228. *Ibid.*

229. *Ibid.*

230. *Ibid.*

231. *Ibid.*

232. *Ibid.*

233. *Ibid.*

234. *Ibid.*

235. *Ibid.*

236. *Ibid.*

237. *Ibid.*

238. *Ibid.*

239. *Ibid.* 56.

240. *Note.* The v.l. of L *Sasya* is, perhaps, preferable to A *Samya.*

241. *R.T.* Vol. II. p. 56.

242. *Ibid.*

243. *Ibid.*

244. *Ibid.*

245. *Ibid.*

246. **Note.** Instead of *marmarajamukha,* as printed in edition, read *marmaraja*. The emendation *agamam* is confirmed by L.

247. *R.T.* Vol. II. p. 56.

248. *Ibid.*

249. *Ibid.*

250. *Ibid.*

251. **Note.** The objectional habit mentioned in verse 707 of *Saritsnanagrha,* has according to our pandit informants, not yet died out among teachers of Purohits school and village school masters of the old type.

252. **Note.** The humorous description contained in these texts and the preceding verses proves *'Word'* if any proof were wanted *'tanner'* or *'Chamar'* that the Kashmir capital has at all times been that hot bed of political gossip and fertile nursery of false and often amusingly absurd rumors, which it is at present. That Kalhana's picture is drawn from life, will strike anyone acquainted with the ways of modern Srinagar. Strolling down to the city bridges, the Ghats on the river bank, or to the vicinity of the palace, one can always watch small crowds eagerly gathering round the news-fabricators, professional and others, ever to be found in these localities. By *Saritsnanagrha*, in verse 706, are meant the wooden bathing-cells placed on rafts river and canal Ghats of Srinagar. They are known now as *sranakuth,* which name is given by Kalhana bathing-huts, in its Sanskrit form of *snanakostha.* Another passage are referred to which still line all the banks of the *Vitasta, Mar* and other water ways within Srinagar, speaks of these bathing-cells as *majjanavasa,* and shows clearly that they were of wood and moored on the river.

253. **Note.** As to the *parisadyas,* and the part played by them at *prayopavesas*, already mentioned in elsewhere in the text.

254. *R.T.* Vol. II, p. 57.

255. *Ibid.*

256. *Ibid.*

257. **Note.** *Ananda,* the son of *Ananta*, is mentioned as *Dvaradhipa,* a native of *Parnotsa,* lord of the Gate. *Ananda,* the son of *Kaka,* is referred to again as a brother of *Tilaka. Tilaka* left him, but the latter's brother *Ananda* from kind-heartedness accompanied him for one march. It may be assumed that only one of the two *Anandas* actually held at the time charge of the Gate. Regarding the retention of official designations by former holders of office. *Udaya,* the commander-in-chief, who also established in this fashion Agraharas and Maths, heard over his name (mentioned) in connection with them. Ananda, the son

of *Ananta*, is subsequently referred to as *Mahattama*, was killed that day by *Damaras,* while on the march in the village of *Locanoddara.* For *Tilakasimha, also* see the above mentioned references.

258. *R.T.* Vol. II. p. 57.
259. *Ibid.*
260. **Note.** The three prognostics of rain here mentioned are to be found together in *Varahamihara's Brhatsamhita,* XXVIII, 7, of which passage over verse is evidently a reminiscence.
261. *R.T.* Vol. II. p. 57.
262. *Ibid.*
263. *Note.* The words *Losthadvijatayovipra* contain evidently some corruption. The easist emendation would be *dvijadayo.*
264. *R.T.* Vol. II. p. 58.
265. *Ibid.*
266. *Ibid.*
267. *Ibid.*
268. *Ibid.*
269. *Note. Mallakostha,* whose troops brought in *Bhiksu* from *Visalata,* resided in *Lahara, Garga* sson took confidence and the lines following.
270. *R.T* .Vol.II. p. 58.
271. *Ibid.*
272. *Ibid.*
273. *Ibid.*
274. **Note.** Statement is corrected with Durgaparsad *Vyayamam* for *Vyayama.*
275. *R.T.* Vol. II. p. 58.
276. **Note.** This beautiful (queen), who was very fond of accumulating wealth, and had established 'the Ganja of *Mayagrama'* and other (funds), obtained great power by the King's favour. The latter form of designation is used in the case of the *'Mayagraminaganja'*. This name is taken from the village *Mayagrama*, which shows identical with the present situated in the lower Sindh Valley at the elevation of 74° -52′ longitude and 34°-17′ latitude. *Mangam* is a large village with a great area of excellent rice-fields. Under the last settlement the village pays the (for Kashmir) considerable sum of Rs. 2200/- as annual revenue assessment. In Pt. Sahib Ram *Tirthas,* the village figures both under its old name as *Mayagrama* and as Manyugrama (!).

277. **Note.** *Hiranyapura* is the present village of *Ranyil,* on the road from Lar to Srinagar situated circ. 74°-51′ longitude and 34°-12′ latitude. It is close to the high road of Srinagar to Gandarbal and the Sindh Valley. A *Naga* near this village, which is visited by the pilgrims proceeding to the *Haramukuta* Tirthas, is referred to in the *Tirthas,* and the Suresvarimahatmya as *Hiranyaksanaga*, and in *Haramukutamahatmya*, ii. 7, as *Hiranyaganga.* More conclusive evidence in favour of the above identification is furnished by the two passages in which *Kalhana* directly mentions this place under the name of *Hiranyapura.* While *Bhiksacara* is excamped at *Mayagrama,* the modern *Mungam,* not far from the mouth of the Sindh Valley, who rebels from *Lahara* (*Lar*) who support him, defeat at *Hiranyapura* the royal forces mentioned above. As the quarters of the latter are said to be at *Amaresvara, i.e. Amburher*, about two and a half miles to the south of *Ranyil,* it is clear that this last named place is meant by *Hiranyapura.* Similarly, when, on the news of his opponent's death, he was marching upon the city for the possessing of the throne of Kashmir. He was a King addressed by *Tilaka,* the son of *Kaka.* When *Uchchala* marches from *Lahara,* i.e., the Sindh Valley, to the siege of the capital, he has his *Abhiseka* ceremony performed *enroute* by the Brahmans of *Hiranyapura.* It has already been pointed out that *Hiranyaksa* figures in the *Kathasaritsagara* as the hero of a fairy tale see LXV, 215 sq. His father *Kanakaksa* is there called king of Kashmir, and said to reside in *Hiranyapura*, the capital of the country. The name of *Hiranyakula* has been read by General Cunningham on coins closely resembling some of the issues of *Mihirakula.* Compared with later *Indo-Scythians,* p. 114 and PL. VIII, figures 9 and 10.

278. R.T. Vol. II. p. 58.

279. **Note.** It has already been indicated that *Ksiptika* is the old name of a branch of the *Vitasta* which flows past a part of Srinagar, and is known by the name of *Kutakul.* This branch leaves the main stream on the left bank, a little below the first bridge and close to the sher Garhi palace. It rejoins the *Vitasta* after a course of about one and a half miles near the last or seventh bridge. This identification is based firstly on the evidence of the modern name *Kutakul*, which is clearly a derivative of *Ksiptika-Kulya,* 'the Ksiptika stream', (Kalhana in his *Rajatarangini* mentions *Kul* less than *Kulya* word in Sanskrit is a common designation of small streams or canals. *Suvarnamanikulya* is explained by A_2, as *Svannamay nado.* On a visit paid to *Zainapor-Adavin* in September, 1895, we ascertained that the name *Sunamani Kul,* the exact derivative of *Suvarnamanikulya*, is bornd to this day by a large irrigation canal (*nor*) which leaves the *Visoka* (*Vesau*) river

above the village shown at 'Largoo' on the map, at a point circ. 74°-51′-30″ longitude and 33°-38′-30″ latitude. The *Sunamani Kul* flows along the east scarp of the Zainapor plateau through the villages marked *Nilloo, Pargama, Koojroo*, and after a course of about twenty miles rejoins the Visoka a short distance above the villageof Adavin (Arwin of map). Secondly, on that of the numerous passages which mention the *Ksiptika* in connection with Srinagar and in the position of the present *Kutakul.* Our own passage without entering the palace *Sussala* searched for *Bhiksu* who had fled before, and espied him on the bank of the *Ksiptika* in the company of the *Lavanyas;* speak of the *Ksiptika* as close to the royal palace. Of the latter we have proved that it occupied a site on the narrow strip of ground separating the *Vitasta* from the *Kutakul* between the second and third bridges. A glance of the map of Srinagar shows that the *Kutakul* forms practically to this day the limit to the West and South of that part of the city proper which is situated on the left bank of the *Vitasta.* It is thus also the city's natural line of defence to the South and West. Accordingly we find the *Ksiptika* referred not being able to reach the other bank owing to the bridge over the *Vitasta* having been broken off, he then proceeded to the *Ksiptika*, after burning the huses on the nearers bank. *Prthvihara* then directed those from *Madavarajya* to fight in the same position (they previously occupied), while he himself went and attacked by the bank of the *Ksiptika. Prajji, Sujji* and others fought on the bank of the *Ksiptika* with *Prthvihara,* who came again and again to the attack. *Prthvihara* then sent the Damaras to battle in various places and himself proceeded to the attack on the bank of the *Ksiptika.* By the time that *Rilhana* arrived after hurrying as far as the bank of the *Ksiptika* in the belief that he (*Ulhana*) might have fled leaving the road. The Damaras of *Bhangila* and other (neighbouring districts) planned an attack on the town of *Samkaravarman* and those of *Samala* to get at the *Ksiptika;* Srivara, IV. 108 in connection with attacks made against the city from that direction. The same is in fact the case with the reference made in our own passage. *Prthvihara,* whose encounter is placed on the bank of the *Ksiptika,* marches against the city from the districts to the South, as the mention of *Hadigrama,* suddenly attacked and worsted the brave *Sajjaka.* In the same way, we find other corps of the rebels attacking the city from the side which lies nearest to their own original positions. Thus the rebels from *Lahara-Lar* march against *Amaresvara, i.e Amburher*, which lies directly to the North of Srinagar. Those again, from the eastern Parganas of *Khaduvi* (*Khruv*) and *Holada* (Vular) invest the city from its eastern side bordered by the *Mahasarit* or *Mar* stream. The powerful *Prthvihara,* carrying along (the body of his relative) *Simba* who had been impaled, met in an encounter *Janakasimha* and others on the bank of the *Ksiptika*. *Bhiksu* established his camp on the bank of the *Ksiptika* at that time royal palace will be closed; which mentioned the erection of a stone *band* between the *Vitasta* and *Ksiptika*. It was intended to protect the division of the city on the left river band from floods.

280. *Note*. The name *Khaduvi* survives in that of *Khruv*, a large village famous for its sacred springs, situated in the *Vihi Pargana*, at the elevation of 75°-4′ longitude and 34°-1′ latitude (map 'khrew'). As our passage mentions *Khaduri* side by side with *Holada*, which is the name of the Pargana now called *Vular*, and as the *Lokaprakasa* too in its list of Paragana as iv; knows the *Visaya* of *Khaduviya*, it may safely be assumed that the name *Khaduviya*, it may safely be assumed that the name *Khaduvi* designated in Kalhana's time not only the village above referred to, but the district also in which it is situated, i.e., the modern Pargana *Vihi* of the later name *Vihi* we have not been able to trace any Sanskrit form. It is evidently a comparatively modern designation whcih has replaced *Khaduvi*. The fierce Damaras of the *Khaduvi* district had posted themselves in the vicinity of *Padmapura* (Pampar) in order to stop him on his disastrous march and to kill him, which in modern times was the administrative centre of *vihi*.

281. *Note Holada* can be shown with certainty to be the Pargana now known as *Vular*, which comprises the Valley opening of the North East of the *Vitasta* between the Parganas of Dachunpor and *Vihi*. Its present administrative centre is Tral, at the elevation of 75°-11′ longitude and 33°-15′ latitutde. There are three faithful Damaras from *Lohara*, *Devasarasa* and *Holada*, and one Damara-lady from *Nilasva*. Its place was clearly in *Madavarajya*, i.e. Maraz, the eastern portion of Kashmir. The position is still more distinctly of '*Kampanodgrahaka*', *Ksemanada* were besieged in it by the incensed Damaras of *Holada*. Where we have read of two officers of King *Jayasimha* being besieged by the rebel Damaras of *Holada* within the temple of *Avantisvamin* at Avantipura. The latter place belongs still to the Vular Pargana. The above identification is further supported to it which mentions the Damars of *Holada* along with those of *Khaduvi*, i.e., *Khrav* in the neighbouring *Vihi* Pargana. A_1 writers in three, the name as *Lolala*, using the letter (which in Kashmir is called *bud rakara* 'the big r') to mark the pronunciation of *d* or '*r*'. This as well as the reading *holara*, brings *Holada* still nearer to the modern representative of the name. '*Word*' in view of the five passages quoted above. We consider the correction *holadayam* for *holalayam* of A and L indispnesable. The position of *Mihirapura* we have not been able to ascertain. No local name resembling this appellation is now known in Vular.

282. *R.T.* Vol. II. p. 59.
283. *Ibid.*
284. *Ibid.*
285. *Ibid.*
286. *Ibid.* p. 60.
287. *Ibid.*
288. *Ibid.*
289. *Ibid.*
290. **Note.** The details given regarding this encounter can be understood on reference to the map of the environs of Srinagar. It has been shown by *Suresvari* is often meant the site of the present village of *Isabar,* which lies on the East shore of the Dal lake, immediately below the proper Suresvari Tirtha. In order to proceed from *Manigam* (*Mayagrama*) to *Isabar*, the rebels leave the the road leading towards the city near *Ranyil* (*Hiranyapura*) and march along the deep *Nalla*, marked on the larger, survey map, to *Batapur* (map 'Butpoora') at the North West corner of the Dal. From there the direct route to *Isabar* leads on an embarkment across the marshes which line the north shore of the lake and are partly under cultivation like, 'the swimming gardens' in the southern part of the Dal. *Bhiksacara's* force proceeding by this route would naturally be safe for the greater part of the march from an attack on cavalry. On the other hand, the difficult ground being imfavourable to a hand-to-hand encounter, woould allow the rebels to utilize fully their superior strength in archers.
291. *R.T.* Vol. II. p. 60.
292. *Ibid.*
293. *Ibid.*
294. *Ibid.*
295. *Ibid.*
296. *Ibid.*. p. 61.
297. **Note.** It has been explained regarding the Mahasarit or Mar, the locality here meant must be identified with the present Cinar Bagh and the other Baghs stretching along the left bank of the *Tsunthkul*. The latter forms the city's natural line of defence to the south east.
298. *R.T.* Vol. II. p. 61.
299. *Ibid.*
300. **Note.** Our own passage, while he was holding out even in such (circumstances), the ill-disposed Brahmans of *Rajanavatika* held a

solemn fast (*praya*) which was alleged to work good, but (in truth) worked evil when these and other (Brahmans) holding Agraharas had assembled at *Vijayesvara,* the solemn fast of the *Rajanavatika* (Brahmans) broke out too in the city. Where *Prayopavesa* of city brahmans at *Rajanavatika* are referred to, show clearly that the latter locality must have been situated within Srinagar or in its immediate vicinity. In view of this and the phonetic history of the name as shown below, *Rajanavatika* may be safely identified with the present *Ranivor,* a large suburb of Srinagar lying on the South East shore of the Dal lake. That Kalhana's *Vor* corresponds in local names to Sanskrit *Vatika,* has already been shown. The modern name goes clearly back to a form *Nadavata.* In this form *-Vata* (or *Vataka* 'garden' might correspond to *-Vana* of Kalhana's name - *Vor* or its feminine form *-Vari* in Sanskrit *Vatika* is frequently found at the end of Kashmir local names. *Rani* may be looked upon as the direct phonetic derivative of *Rajan* (Plural *Raana* less than *Ran* ; *-i,* in *Rani* is the suffix of the plural): in Hindi title *rana,* which goes back to the fuller Sanskrit form *Rajanaka.* In evidence of this ethmology we may also point out that *Rani* (Singular obligatory *ran*; nominated *ron*) is a *Kram* name of very frequent occurance among the Muhammadan population of Kashmir, and in this use clearly derived from the term *Rajan* which originally a little, must have become a family designation already at an early date. The title *Rajanaka*, meaning literally 'almost a King', used to be given for services rendered to the King. *Rani* as a *Muhammadan* Kram name corresponds exactly to *Razdan* (*Rajanaka*) as a family name of Brahmans. In the *Rane* family of Kangra we may now safely recognise the descendants of the *Rajanakas* mentioned in the *Baijnathi* Prasasti. The inhabitants of the *Rajanavatika* are referred to *Sri, 'Nam'* or *'Word'* and a marriage contract form given in *Lokapura* is dated in the locality of the same.

301. *R.T.* Vol. II. p. 61.
302. *Ibid.*
303. *Ibid.*
304. *Ibid.*
305. *Ibid.*
306. *Ibid.* p. 62.
307. *Ibid.*
308. *Ibid.* **Note.** The *"Unborn", 'Word'* frequently also called "the one" EKAM, *Aja* means that which has always existed without being born of anything, the Eternally-pre-existing, of which all things are born, when the desire of manifesting itself awakes in it. Sometimes the one

is named *AJA EKAPAD* "the one-footed unborn", *'Word'* a seemingly grotesque appellation, which has given rise to as grotesque interpretations, but which is really only one of those attempts at expressing the inexpressible in some kind of tangible form in which Aryan thinkers of India have always dealt, regardless of extravagance in the wording. For in the Rig-Veda, the "foot" may stand for the world in which the foot's owner abides. So Vishnu is said to know his own highest abode, *'Word'* the third, while only two are known to men, *RAM* and *LAXMAN*, and the source of light is said to be "at his feet" and his "three strides" also mean nothing else than that he has his feet in the three worlds, *'Words'* the two visible ones and the third, highest, invisible one (*V.I.p. 424*).

309. *Plate 1. Tame Leopards Trained for Hunting -Ready for the Chase (Fig.1).*

310. **Note.** The five hountiful streams descend from various points of extreme Western Himalaya, their courses converging, uniting by twos, now here, now where, utile their waters blend into one short but wide, deep, and rapid river which has always borne the collective name *PANTCHANADA,* "the Five Rivers" *'Word'* a name which transferred, unaltered, to the land itself, and of which 'Penjab' is the Persian form. The five rivers can show up between them about five times as many names, which, to a beginner, is confusing. Thier modern names are different from those of the Epic Brahmanic period, while the very oldest have been discovered in the vedic literature of a remoter era still then the Greeks, who knew this portion of India toterably well, had their own names for them, with a slight assonance to the native ones. The list begins with the westernmost, modern *JHELUM,* the Epic and Vedic *VITASTA,* of which the Greeks made *HYDASPE'S*; next comes Vedic *ASIKNI*, Greek AKESINOS, now TCHENAB; these two unite and for a considerable distance flow on in one stream of double volume and rapid current, as indicated by the picturesque Ved name *MARUDURIDHA,* "The wind-swelled". its later Sanskrit name, *TCHANDRABHAGA,* hellenized into *SANDROPHACUS*, it still remains. There is a pretty story of this river having set a term to Macedomian Alexander's Indian campaign; its Greeks name meaning "Devourer of Alexandar", the conqueror is said to have accepted it as an evil omen and decided on returning. The modern *RAVI* or *IROTI* is easily recognised in the Epic *IRAVATI,* but in the Vedic *PARUSHNI* or the Greek *HYDRAOTES,* while both *SHUTUDRI* and the later *SHATADRU* are little altered in the Greek *ZADADRES* ; and leave a slightly reminiscent 'sound' in the modern *SUTLEDJ*: Just as in the name of the *VIYAS* or *BIAS*. There is a faint echo of the vedic *VIPASA*,

transparently hellenized into *HYPASIS, HYPANIS* or, closer still, *VIPASIS.* Of the five, the sutledj is by far the most considerable, in length and volume and the most frequently mentioned *'Word'* almost as the Indus' twin sister river; "Indus and Sutlej" go together just as "Ganges and Djumna", the two leaders of the other twin system, that of the Gulf of Bengal "*SINDH*" of Indian antiquity means 'River". This is another instance of a country's principal stream being styled by the inhabitants "the River' *par excellence.* (*V.I.* pp. 106, 107, 108).

311. *V.I. pp. 36, 38, 39, 40. See plate II, Primeval Forest; Monkeys scared by a large snake (Fig. 2).*
312. *R.T.* Vol. II. p. 62.
313. *Plate III. Landscape at The foot of the Vihdhya (Fig.3)*
314. *V.I* pp. 44-47.
315. *R.T.* Vol. II. p. 62.
316. *Ibid.*
317. *Ibid.*
318. *Ibid.*
319. *Ibid.*
320. *Ibid.*
321. *Ibid.*
322. *Ibid.*
323. *Ibid.*
324. *Ibid.* p. 63.
325. *Ibid.*
326. *Ibid.*
327. *Ibid.*
328. *Ibid.*
329. *Ibid.*
330. *Ibid.*
331. *Ibid.*
332. **Note.** The meaning of the term *Varika* is derived from *Vara*,'fixed time', i.e 'turn of duty'.
333. *R.T.* Vol. II. p. 63.
334. *Ibid.*
335. *Ibid.*

336. *Ibid.*

337. *Ibid.*

338. *Ibid.*

339. *Ibid.* p. 64.

340. **Note.** *Janakasimha,* frequently mentioned subsequently, is the same person as *Janaka, Tilakasimha's* brother, who has last been referred above as town project to move about the city to allay the tumult, and waited for an opportunity to leave himself. Their leader was the city prefect, *Janakasimha*, who had established an understanding with the ministers, cavaliers, chiefs, Tantrins, citizens and others after the *'Indian History Congress'*. The niece he gives in marriage to *Bhiksu* was a daughter of *Tilakasimha,* who seems to have been one of the ministers treacheously killed by *Prthvihara*, his foster brother *Mammaka,* the Brahman *Gunga,* and *Rama,* the orderly on duty, but they have been turn out from the duty. No doubt, account will be settled at fixed time on the fixed day.

341. *R.T.* Vol. II. p. 64.

342. *Ibid.*

343. *Ibid.*

344. *Ibid.*

345. *Ibid.*

346. *Ibid.*

347. *Ibid.*

348. *Note.* The pun lies in the double meaning of the word *'ambara'*. It is customary to make a *Namaskara* before the young moon when first seen, and the moon apparently is supposed to return this attention by gifts of clothes; compared with *Padmapura* V. LXXViii. 17 sqq. The young moon remains only for a short time above the horizon.

349. *R.T.* Vol.II. p. 64

350. *Ibid.*

351. *Ibid.*

352. *Ibid.*

353. *Ibid. pp. 64-65*

354. *Ibid. p. 65*

355. *Ibid.*

356. *Ibid.*

357. *Ibid.*

358. *Ibid.*

359. *Ibid.*

360. *Ibid.*

361. *Ibid.*

362. *Note.* Term *Sthanapala* compared with *Sthalapati, Samayam*; and all the other friends of the king, like *Ganga* and the rest, died also. Only *Tunga,* with his brothers, remained to enjoy pleasures.

363. *R.T.* Vol.II. p. 65

364. *Ibid.*

365. *Ibid.*

366. *Ibid.*

367. *Ibid.*

368. *Ibid.*

369. *Ibid. p. 66*

370. *Ibid.*

371. *Ibid.*

372. **Note.** *Pratapapura* is identified in the gloss of A_2 with the modern *Tapar,* a considerable village of the Kruhin Pargana situated on the high road from *Varahamula* to Srinagar at the elevation of 74^0-34' longitude and 34^0-12' latitude. This identification is confirmed from the above statement, where *Pratapapura* is mentioned as lying on the route of *Sussala's* retreat from Srinagar to *Lohara* (via *Varahamula*), and by Fourth Chronicler of 820 A.D. where the name occurs in connection with that of the neighbouring Pargana of Bangil. When visiting *Tapar* in September 1892, by Stein, found close to the road between the Ziarats of *Sayid Nizam-ud-di*n and *'Vatar Baba Sahib'* two large ruined mounds, covered with fragments etc. In the walls of the second Ziarat there was a large number of ancient carved slabs. Most of these remains have since been utilized in the construction of the new carriage road. The local tradition knows of the existence of an old town at this site which it ascribes to be King *Tapadat* (Pratapaditya?) means given by God or 'Nam'.

373. *R.T. Vol.II. p. 66*

374. *Ibid.*

375. **Note.** The *Kaka* family is freqently mentioned elsehwhere in the text which *Tilaka* belonged had its home at *Huskapura.*

376. *R.T.* Vol. II. p. 66.

378. *Ibid.*
379. *Ibid.*
380. *Ibid.*
381. *Ibid.*
382. *Ibid.*
383. *Ibid.*
384. **Note.** Owing to the advanced season (*Sussala* left Srinagar on the 6th *Vadi* Margasiras, which fell 1120 A.D. on November 13th), the King cannot proceed to *Lohara,* by the direct route over the Tosamaidan, but goes first to Huskapura to cross the range by one of lower passes into the Prunts valley, from which he was again to ascent to Lohara (*Loharin*) *via Attalika* or Atoli.
385. *R.T.* Vol. II. p. 67.
386. *Ibid.*
387. *Ibid.*
388. *Ibid.*
389. *Ibid.*
389. *Ibid.*
390. **Note.** By the 'Old Palace' must be meant the royal residence which existed before *Anantadeva* built his new palace near the *Sudasiva*; and of the royal palace in Kalhana's time; we may safely assume that, *'Old Palace'* (*Puranarajadhani*), with the rest of the city founded by *Pravarasena*, it was situated on the right bank of the river. It must be noted as printed in the text, is an emendation for Purani *raja*° of the Mss. The empty site of this old palace is referred the residence (*Sthandila*) of former royal dynastics, made the whole city a joy to look at.
391. *R.T.* Vol. II. p. 67.
392. *Ibid.*
393. *Ibid.*
394. *Ibid.*
395. *Ibid.*
396. *Ibid.* pp. 67-68.
397. *Ibid.*
398. *Ibid.*
399. *Ibid.*

400. *Ibid.*

401. *Ibid.*

402. *Ibid.*

403. **Note.** The natives, whom the Aryas for a long time gathered under the general Old-Aryan designation of *DASYU,* meaning simply "peoples", "tribe"; a meaning which the word, under the Eranian form *DAHYU,* retains all through the Avesta and the Akhaemenian inscription, while in India it soon underwent peculiar changes, as will be seen. Robbers (*dasyu*) as ministers and feudatories, a brother ready to become a pretender, a land without treasure, what difficulty did not beset this king? With a simple minded King, with negligent ministers and bold Damaras (*dasyu*), that reign was doomed from its very beginning, young as it was. Thus, there were caused at *Cakradhara* (twice) terrible sufferings through fire, first by the wrath of *Susravas,* and secondly by the revolt of the Damaras (*dasyu*). King *Sussala* thought this frame of mind of the Damaras (*dasyu*) to be to his own advantage. In his eagerness for victory he was preparing to employ either policy or vigorous force upon this rebellion or vigorous force (breaking out) all the other enemies, too, showed themselves prepared for a rising just as fishes when their pond is broken by the rain. The opposing force at *Tilagrama* proceeded to frequent attacks, and the robber (*dasyu* i.e, *Alamkaramcakra*) proved unable to meet (the latter), they became thin with care.

404. *R.T.* Vol.II. p. 68.

405. Note. Term *Kambala* according to Kalhana's *Kamali* still to this day an indication of inferior social status. When *Utapala's* dynasty then had come to end, the Brahmans, dressed in course woollen cloaks, assembled in the *Gokula*, resembling bulls without horns; performed a *prayopavesa.* The literal meaning of the name (cattle -pen) suggests the smile. Then for a living he had hung at the back of officials, carrying their bags and ink-bottle,s while a rough woollen cloth rubbed his (own) back.

406. Regarding the designation of *Bhiksu, Jayasimha* describes, "will not such tiny enemies be worsted in the contest with him who has vanquished *Prithvihara*, the 'Incarnation' (*Bhiksacara*), and other (powerful) opponents? i.e living *mana.*

407. *R.T.* Vol.II. p. 68.

408. *Ibid.*

409. *Ibid.*

410. **Note.** The exact meaning of the designation *Katakavarika* is uncertain. It is found, where it too is used of a person in the service of the *Rajapuri* ruler.

411. *Note.* The term *Padagra* is used here for *Nanaka,* etc. clearly as the designation of some high office. It has not been found outside the chronicle, and the character of the office to which it refers cannot be established with certainty. From our own passage it would appear that the *Padagra* could be directly managed by the Prime Minister of the *Haladhara* rose daily higher in *Suryamati's* service, and obtained the prime ministership (*Sarvadhikarita*). Agraharas founded here referred to, are mentioned by Bilhana, *Vikram, XVIII.* 19; and that is was connected with the finance administration. *Ananta* wisely abolished the royal privilege of marking the gold according to colour (quality), price, etc, which bring to light the savings of the people, knowing that succeeding kings would only appoint to seize the property of the nation. King *Kalasa,* who did not give charge of the *padagra* to a certain minister, though the latter was clever in raising revenue, is praised for the regard he hereby evinced for his subjects. That the officer incharge of the *padagra* was concerned with the collection of taxes, may be concluded for the *Padagra* office. In the latter passage we read of a *prayopavesa* which the Brahmans start against *Citraratha*, the *Padagra* officer the 'Gate', the *Kheri* (district) and other offices (respectively), owing to his obstinate persistence in raising the imposts. The same officer is mentioned, as holding at the same time the posts of *Padagra* and *Dvarapati.* Etymologically, the term *Padagra* might mean 'the (officer who stands) before the feet (of the King).'

412. *R.T* Vol. II. p. 68.

413. *Ibid.*

414. *Ibid.* p. 69.

415. **Note.** *Term Drayaka* has already been mentioned above.

416. *R.T.* Vol. II. p. 69.

417. *Ibid.*

418. *Ibid.*

419. *Ibid.*

420. *Ibid.*

421. *Ibid.*

422. *Ibid.*

423. *Ibid.*

424. *Ibid.*

425. *Ibid.*

426. *Ibid.*

427. *Ibid.*

428. *Ibid.*

429. *Ibid.* pp. 69-70.

430. *Ibid.* p. 70.

431. *Ibid.*

432. *Ibid.*

433. *Ibid.*

434. *Ibid.*

435. **Note.** It is very curious in view of the statement here made that no coins of *Bhiksacara* have yet been found. At least Cunninghan's list, *Coins* of *Medieval India;* p. 46. does not show any coins which could be attributed to him, nor have we been able to trace any ourself among the large quantity of old Kashmir coins which have passed through our hands. Is it possible that all the coins issued by the pretender should have been subsequently called in and melted down on the return of *Sussala*? *'Wonderful'* coin of the nature called *Mudra.*

436. *R.T.* Vol.II. p. 70.

437. **Note.** The attack against *Lohara* is made from the South through *Rajapuri,* partly because the chief of the latter territory is an old supporter of *Bhiksacara,* from *Vallapura* that the enemity of the king could not be appeased by any measures. And, partly because the condition of the Tosamaidan and other higher Passes would make a direct attack upon *Lohara* from the north impossible for the winter and spring.

438. *R.T.* Vol. II. p. 70.

439. **Note.** The *Turukas* here referred to are, of course, Muhammadans from the Panjab or the lower hills. We are unable to state what the Muhammadans name was which has been metamorphosed by the Chronicler into *Vismaya.*

440. **Note.** Term *Sallara* is possibly intended to present the Persian title *Sardar* or *Salar,* 'commander-in-chief.'

441. *R.T.* Vol. II. p. 70.

442. *Ibid.*

443. *Ibid.*

444. *Ibid.*

445. **Note.** Term *avaruddha* designates throughout the Chronicle aconcubine i.e, a woman who, owing to her being a widow, of low

origin, or from some other reason, cannot be legally married. She too had been a dancing girl attached to a temple. He had seen her on the dancing stage and had taken her as a concubine into the royal seraglio. In his apprehension, he allowed only *Vigraharaja*, who was a son of *Sussala* from a concubine, to act as his chamberlain. In these reference, we see that courtesans have received as *Avaruddhas* into the royal seraglio. For a widow of high rank taken as an *Avaruddha* by prince *Bhiksacara* who left without *Bimba,* behaved improperly and took without shame his wife as a concubine. Regarding the derivation of the term, which is also used by Ksemendra, *Samayam* compared with *avarodha*, 'Seraglio'. The modern *Kashmirians urudz*, which is used in the same as *avaruddha* both among the Hindus and Muhammadans of Kashmir, is the direct phonetic derivative of Sanskrit *avaruddhika* compared with the whole of womankind was disgraced by his favourite concubine named *Kayya*. A man who received a divorced woman or a widow, is called *Urud*. It seems to be used here *Bimba's* faithful wife in anticipation of her subsequent position as Sussala's concubine.

46. *R.T.* Vol. II, p. 70.

447. *Ibid.* p. 71.

448. **Note.** See the reference of this statement in elsewhere of the text.

449. *R.T.* Vol. II. p. 71.

450. *Ibid.*

451. *Ibid.*

452. *Ibid.*

453. *Ibid.*

454. *Ibid.*

455. **Note.** *Aksosuva* term is only here mentioned, and its position is unknown because it is *'power'* or 'light' come from nature.

456. *R.T.* Vol. II. p. 71.

457. **Note.** For Agraharas given to individual Brahmans and corporations of sacred places, etc. The Praya of the Brahmans of *Rajanavatika* (*Ranivor*) has already mentioned above.

458. **Note.** It is probable that the religious buidling mentioned the position of the *Suravarmasvamin* temple cannot be ascertained. *'Chamar'*, the *Gokula* of *Suravarman* is alluded the significance of the term probably the identical shrine or building is meant here, perhaps the same *Gokula* the construction of whcih is mentioned in the passage. The latter passage would place it in the capital. The name *Gokula,* which judging from the above statement must have been the general designation for

a certain class of religious edifices, is clearly connected with the famous *Gokula,* the residence of the young Krsna (black) in the *Vrindavana* forest. It appears from the study that *Gokulas* were provided with grazing ground reserved for kine.

459. *R.T.* Vol.II. p. 71.

460. *Ibid.*

461. *Ibid.*

462. *Ibid.*

463. *Ibid.*

464. *Ibid.*

465. *Ibid.*

466. *Ibid.*

467. *Ibid.*

468. *Ibid.*

469. **Note.** For *Samnipatya* read *sunnipatya*, after collecting all his subjects in an assembly, he delivered to them the government like a well-guarded trust. *Cankuna* addressed (them), moistening with tears the earth, which was tormented by the hot (fever of) separation from its master.

470. *R.T.* Vol. II. p. 72.

471. *Ibid.*

472. **Note.** *Kalha* is the lord of *Kalinjara* as visiting *Sussala* at *Attalika,* and must have died in the meantime.

473. R.T. Vol. II. p. 72

474. **Note.** The Laukika year 4197, 1121-22 A.D is meant after (an absence of) six months and twelve days.

475. *R.T.* Vol. II. p. 72

476. **Note.** Statement also compared with other reference mentioned term *Turuskas.*

477. R.T. Vol. II. p. 73

478. **Note.** Term *Vitola* can be safely indentified with the Valleys of the *Sadrun* district, south of the western end of the *Pir Pantsal* range. It joins the *Tohi* (*Tausi*) at the town, of Prunts. The mention of the river shows that the 'battle of Parnotsa' was fought close to the town of this name, whose position is marked by the present town of Prunts.

479. *R.T.* Vol. II. p. 73.

480. *Ibid.*

481. *Ibid.*

482. *Ibid.*

483. **Note.** Two Rajaputras *Sahadeva* and *Yudhisthira*, they paid back in battle with their lives the debt (they) owed for their lord's favour.

484. *R.T.* Vol. II. p. 73.

485. *Ibid.*

486. *Ibid.*

487. **Note.** Term, *Kandiletra* means, some peoples they took the *'Namdana'*; but they degraded the message of God and never practise according to instruction of 'Father'. It shows that it is similar that we have showered the desert called *Kandiletra*.

488. **Note.** The Kings whom fate ruins, clear their kingdom from rivals by killing their relatives who would preserve it, (with the result) that some one (else) enjoyed it alone called *upavesana*.

489. **Note.** In the meanwhile, King endeavoured to take *Bhangila*, his force suddenly fled, and his horse being caught by a vine-creeper, he was kill by some foot-sholdier. If the corresponds to the modern Pargana *Bangil,* to the South West of *Paraspor* (*Bankal*) referred in *Ain-i-Akbari,* Vol. II p. 371. The Damaras of *Bhangila* and other (neighbouring distircts) planned an attack on the town of *Samkaravarman* and those of *Samala* to get the *Ksiptika* i.e. *Patan.*

490 **Note.** Through Bangil lead the routes to the Firozpur, *Nilakanta*, and other passes which communicated with the *Lohara* territory to the South of the *Pir Pantsal.*

491. *R.T.* Vol. II. p. 73.

492. *Ibid.* p. 74.

493. *Ibid.*

494. **Note.** There, we find *Sadasivapura* i.e. the quarter near *Sadasiva,* repeatedly mentioned as the part of the city of Srinagar. Among these passage there are two which clearly place *Sadasivapura* on the left river bank and opposite to the quarter of *Samudramatha*. We read of a city fight in which the partisans of the *Cakkar* (Tsaks) posted on the river bank in the *Samudramatha* fired across at their opponents who occupied *Sadasivapura*. By *Samudramatha* (Called *Samudramatha* by *Srivara* is meant certainly the present *Mahalla* of *Sudarmar* compared Kalhana's *Sudar* 'Sea' in Sanskrit called *Samudra*.

495. *R.T.* Vol. II. p. 74.

496. *Ibid.*

497. *Ibid.*

498.. *Ibid.*

499. *Ibid.*

500. **Note.** Reference of this statement mentioned above in the elsewhere in this text.

501. *R.T.* Vol. II. p. 74.

502. *Ibid.*

503. **Note.** *Bhiksu* had married *Tilakasimha's* daughter, *Janakasimha* sent continually secret messengers to *Bhiksu* to receive the maiden regal dignity in the palace.

504. *R.T.* Vol. II. p. 74

505. **Note.** *Sussala* seems to have gone first to *Huskapura*, Probably by one of the Western routes over the mountain mentioned above and then to have marched round the north shores of the *Vular* lake through *Khuyahom* to *Lahara* (Lar). He can thus appear unexpectedly to the north of the city, whereas his opponents would naturally await his attack from the south. The march from *Varahamula* to Srinagar occupies by this route about two or three days, as state by Kalhana.

506. *R.T.* Vol. II. p. 74.

507. *Ibid.* p. 75.

508. *Ibid.*

509. *Ibid.*

510. *Ibid.*

511. *Ibid.*

512. *Ibid.*

513. *Note.* The village of *Pusyananda* in connection with the frontier station of *Surapura*, though his force was small put the son of *Vatta* to flight in battle, in order to raise a revolt, he had been caught by the commander of the watch-station (*drangadhipa*) who was searching for his horses. He leaves, no doubt, as to the identity of this place with the present *Pusiana*, which is the last inhabited place on the western or Panjab side of the *Pir Pantsal* Pass, situated at the elevation of 74°-33′ longitude and 33°-38′ at the latitude *Pusina* lies at a height of 8300 feet above the sea, and is now a small village chiefly occupied by carriers and others who live by the traffic on the route. In winter it is generally deserted owing to the heavy snowfall. It is of interest to note that *Pusyananda* is described as belongin to *Rajapuri* territory.

This shows that the upper valley of the Prunts (*Parnotsa*) *itself* under Kashmir rule.

514. *R.T.* Vol. II. p. 75.

515. **Note.** *Vatta* has been mentioned above, was *Tantrin* along with *Vatta.*

516. **Note.** It is evident that *Kheri* was the name of a district. This, we think, can be identified with the Pargana, now known by the double name of *Khurnaravav*, whick comprises the fertile valleys descending from the Gulabgarh and Muhipasses of the *Pir Pantsal* to the Vesau river. The village of Khur (marked *Koori* on larger survey map) from which the first part of the name is taken, lies at the logitude of 74°-56′-45″ and at the latitutde of 33°-37′. This identification is based, apart from the relation between the names *Kheri* and *Khur*, here clearly named *Visaya,* which mention *Kheri* in connection with the Parganas of *Devasarasa* (*Divasar*) *and* Ardhavana (*Adavin*) respectively. Both these parganas immediately adjoin *Khur Naravav,* to the north of the Vesau. The administration of Kheri, perhaps as a royal allodial domain, appears to have formed a special charge, as Kalhana refers repeatedly to the *KheriKarya* in the sense of a high office, shook a hundred times with fright when they saw his face in the battle field at the *'Gate'* the *Kheri* (district) of *Rilhana.* The 'Sikh' (Sanskrit *Shishya*) means a disciple and Dogra, the origin of this name thus are two holy lakes of mind, *Saroin Sar* and *Man Sar* which will in course be described, from these the country round was called in Sanskrit. Probably continuing an early arrangement, has established in Khur-Naravav Jagris for members of the ruling family. It is uncertain which particular localities are referred to hereby, Kalhana under the term of *matha.* Though *Khur-Naravav* led once much frequently routes to the above named passes, and the *Mathas* mentioned might therefore, have been roadside *'Dharmasalas'*. Thus *Srivara* III, 190, relates the establishment of a *'dharmana'* in *Kheri* in the times of the Hassan Shah.

517. Note. *Harsamitra,* the son of the King's maternal uncle, who was commander-in-chief of the army of (*Kampana*).

518. *R.T.* Vol. II. p. 76.

519. *Ibid.*

520. *Ibid.*

521. *Ibid.*

522. *Ibid.*

523. **Note.** *Bimba*, who was last mentioned on the side of *Bhiksu,* deserted the latter and joined the King *Sussala,* seems to have returned to *Bhiksacara's* side.

524. *R.T.* Vol. II. p. 76.

525. *Ibid.*

526. **Note.** See the reference of *Surapura* elsewhere in the text.

527. *R.T.* Vol. II. p. 76.

528. *Ibid.*

529. *Ibid.*

530. *Ibid.* p. 76-77.

531. *Ibid.* p. 77.

532. *Ibid.*

533. *Ibid.*

534. **Note.** Term *Katisthali* has burnt himself to catch those who do not believe him.

535. **Note.** The word *nirguta* must designate a caste which litinized word called *'Pura'* occupation as seen from *Samayam.* He, whose perfidy had become evident from free study that he had kept up the fight for a long time, but the Brahmans fled through the openings of the door other than the gate and went to their homes. But its exact meaning cannot be ascertained. The emendation (*nirguna*) proposed in edition was wrong.

536. *R.T.* Vol. II. p. 77.

537. *Ibid.*

538. *Ibid.*

539. *Ibid.*

540. *Ibid.*

541. *Ibid.*

542. *Ibid.*

543. *Ibid.*

544. *Ibid.* p. 78.

545. *Ibid.*

546. *Ibid.*

547. *Ibid.*

548. *Ibid.*

549. *Ibid.*

550. *Ibid.*

551. **Note.** For the story of the *Naga Susravas* vengeance upon King *Nara* and his town. Brahman *who* had thus obtained fortune through the boon (granted to him) by the *Naga*, passed a longtime at *Narapura* in mainfold never-ceasing festivities. The Naga daughter, too, possessed of *'infinite beauty*, made as a devoted wife her husband happy by her noble character, exemplary conduct and other virtues. Once, at a time while she was standing on the top of her mansion, a loose horses was eating the rice (*dhanya* means in the Chronicle everywhere 'rice', the staple produce of the Valley Kashmiri *danya*) which had been left outside the courtyard to dry in the sun. As the servants whom she called to keep the horse off, were not in the house, she came down herself, jingling with her graceful anklets. Holding with one hand to the end of her head-dress, which in the hurry had slipped off. She ran up and slapped the horse with her lotus-hand. When the horse, after being touched by the *Naga* lady, left the food and moved away, there appeased on its body the golden imprint of her hand. At that time there arose love (in the heart) of the King who had heard already before through his spies of the Brahman's beautiful eyed wife. When his passion broke away like an elephant in rut, no fear of reproach could hook-like hold it back by force. Upon the rising flames of the King's love the story of the horse acted again like a furious storm. The golden mask of her hand showing the beauty of her straight fingers, made him overstep the moral limits, just as the moon makes the sea (over step its limits. Throwing off the fetters of shame he then alarmed the fair lady by trying to seduce her through messengers who intimated his wishes. As she was not be gained by all arms races, he in his covetous passion asked her even from her husband, the Brahman. Whence should shame (come) to those who are blinded by love of materialism. When the King had more than once been repulsed also by the Brahman, he sent soldiers to carry her off by force. While those attacked the house in front, the Brahman left it with his wife by another way, and fled for protection in Naga's habitation. The lord of the Nagas thereupon, when those who had approached him and had told their story, rose blind with fury from his pool. Casting about dense darkness by thundering clouds of sinister look, he burned the King with his town in a rain of fearful thunderbolts. The *Vitasta* which carried the marrow, blood and fat flowing from the bodies of the burned men, looked as if adorned with the eyes of peacocks taits. Thousands of terrified people who had fled for protection before (the image of Visnu) *Cakradhara,* were burned in a moment. Just as of yore the fat of the (demons) Madhu and *Kaitabha* had covered the 'Bearer of the Disc' (*Cakrin*) on his thighs, so then his whole body was covered by the fat of the burned human

beings. Then the sister of *Susravas*, the Nagi *Ramanya*, came both to assist him from the depth of the mountains carrying along masses of stones. When she learned from afar (at a place) where more than one Yojana yet remained of her way (to *Narapura*), that her brother had accomplished his work, she felt that hail of stones among the villages. For five Yojanas from that place the village land became a waste buried under mighty boulders, and known to this very day as the *Ramanyatavi* ('the forest of *Ramanya*). After completing this frightful carnage the Naga, pained also by remorse and wearied by the reproaches of the people, left at daybreak that habitation of his movement was away from the Naga. The lake of dazzling whiteness (resembling) a sea of milk, which he created (for himself as residence) on a far-off mountain, is to the present day seen by the people on the pilgrimage to *Amaresvara*. The mountain lake in which the legend locates the Naga *Susravas* after his migration, is situated near one of the sources of the Lidar River at 75^0-34' longitude and 34^0-5' latitude. It is popularly known by the name of *Sesanaga,* and forms one of the stations of the great *Amaresvara* pilgrimage. The *Amaresvara-Yatra* is directed to the famous cave of Amarnath (*Amburnath*) situated at a considerable altitude, 75°-33′ longitude, 30°-13′ latitude. In it Siva *Amaresvara* is believed to have manifested himself to the gods who entracted him for protection against death. The god is worshipped in a linga-shaped ice-block. The pilgrimage, notwithstanding its hardships, now ranks amongst the most popular in Kashmir, and attracts in great numbers pilgrims from the other parts of India. In old times, however, this Tirtha can scarcely have claimed such importance. But in the same chapter the lake is also designated by the name of *Susrama* Naga, which evidently reproduces the older form *'Susravas'* in its Kashmirians pronuciation of *'Susram'*. As 'Susram Nag' the lake is still known among the older Purohitas of *Amaresvara,* and under this name it is also referred to in the appropriate gloss of the lake's water is noticeable, and is possibly due to the surrounding limestone rocks. A narrow inlet of the lake opening to the South towards the glacier of the Kohenhar Peak, is popularly known by the name of *Zamaturi Nag*, 'the son-in-law's Naga, and corresponds to the *Jamatrsaras* along with the *Susramanaga* in the route directory of the *Amaresvara* pilgrimage as given in the *Tirthas*. And, in that locality there is also another lake well-known as the *Jamatrsaras* ('the son-in-law's lake') (the habitation) of the Brahman who by his father-in-law's favour had been transformed into a Naga. They appeared at times without apparent cause such gods of the death who, under the pretext of protecting their subjects, bring about their unexpected destruction. To this day that tale is remembered by the people when they behold close to

Cakradhara that town destroyed by fire and that pond which has become a (dry) hollow. How a small fault is love-passion in Kings according to the view of people of narrow perception called Brahman. Yet by the (love) of this (king) was brought about what had not happened to anyother anywhere. From the verily we learn every story that the destruction of the universe even (may be caused) by the wrath of even a single virtuous woman, deify or Brahman. After enjoying the earth for forty one years less three months, this King perished through his evil conduct. that (town of) *Kimnarapura*, after having been visible for a short time with its encircling walls and battlements became similar to the town of the *Gandharvas* (i.e., a mirage). One son, however, of the King, had in the wondrous course of events been (previously) taken by his nurse to *Vijayaksetra* is an abbreviation for *Vijayesvaraksetra*, and thus did not lose his life. This King called *Siddha* then revived the throughly exhausted nation as the cloud (revives) the mountain which has been parched by a forest fire. The astonishing story of his father, as (told) above, served for this thoughtful (King) as a guide to a pious life by teaching him the vanity of mundane existence.

552. *R.T.* Vol.II. p. 78.

553. **Note.** The burning of the cities of *Tripura* by Siva, and the destruction of the forest of *Khandava* by Arjuna, is related in *Mahabharat* VIII. XXXIV, and 1. CCXXiii, respectively.

554. *R.T.* Vol. II. p. 78.

555. **Note.** A passage of the *Nilamata*, much corrupted in the M.S.S, VV. 785-791, refers to the twelfth day of the bright half of *Sravana* etc, are prescribed for this day, but no account is given of the reason for its celebration. The pilgrimages to several of the Kashmir Nagas are held at present on that day e.g. those to the Tirthas of *Kapalamocana, Uccaihsirna* (*Vutasan*), *Trigami.*

556. *R.T.* Vol. II. p. 78.

557. **Note.** *Naunagara* is the name of the alluvial plateau now called *Naunagara Udar,* which stretches on the left bank of the *Vitasta* from South East to North West between at the longitude of 33°-51′, latitude at 33°-51′ and ; 75°-2′ longitude and 33°-55′ at latitude. This plateau offers a position commanding all the direct routes between *Vijabror* (*Vijayesvara*) and Srinagar on the left river bank.

558. **Note.** By *Kapalika* is meant here probably the attendant at the burning-ground, who receives part of the clothes and ornaments with which the dead is put on the pyre. When King had taken away from the officials the marks of their arrogance (*'Nam'* or *'Chamar'*) their eyes became capable of recognising their relatives (*Markandeyapur*).

559. R.T. Vol. II. p. 79.
560. **Note.** *Nagesvara* had betrayed Prince *Bhoja* with his mother had sent for his journey. He stopped inside the *Rangavata* (grove) means dye in *'Nam'*.
561. *R.T.* Vol. II. p. 79.
562. *Ibid.*
563. *Ibid.*
564. *Ibid.*
565. *Ibid.*
566. *Ibid.*
567. *Ibid.*
568. **Note.** *Prthvihara* was a Damara of *Samala* (*Hamala*); who was fighting with darts.
569. *R.T.* Vol. II. p. 79.
570. *Ibid.*
571. **Note.** Consequent in anger, he removed the latter from his charge and made *Ananda, Ananta's* son, a native of *Parnotsa*, 'Lord' of the Gate.
572. *R.T.* Vol. II. p. 79.
573. **Note.** *Simha* had already fallen into *Sussala's* power a relative of *Prthvihara*, who had been wounded by sword-strokes entered the royal palace for his dignity.
574. *R.T.* Vol. II. p. 79.
575. **Note.** Kalhanas alludes here to the custom, still observed by all Brahmans of Kashmir, of depositing the bones of those who have died during the year, in the sacred Ganga lake below the glaciers of Mount *Haramukuta* on occasion of the pilgrimage to this *Tirtha*. The ceremony of depositing the bones in the lake took place on the eight day of the bright half of *Bhadrpada*. The pilgrims start from Srinagar on the 4th *Sudi,* when the removal of the bones from the houses gives rise to a good deal of lamentation. It is customary for the woman folk of all related families to assemble at the house of the deceased, and to testify their sympathy by loud wailing. Full details regarding the pilgrimage are given by the *Haramukuta gangamahatmya*. Regarding the Ganga lake (Gangabal) the *Sindhu* or Sindh River is referred to the *Sindh* river, who drains the mountain ranges to the north of the valley from *Dras* to the *Haramukh* and is the greatest tributary of the *Vitasta* within Kashmir; is distinctly identified with the *Ganga* by the *Nilamata* (*Ganga Sindhus tu Vijneya Vitasta Yamuna tatha*). In the

Jonaraja work where the construction of a canal from the *Sindh* into the *Manasbal* lake is meant), *Haracar* xii, 40, and *Vitastamahatmya*, xx. 15. The source of this Sindhu-Ganga is placed by ancient tradition in the sacred *Ganga* lake (*Gangabal*) below the North East glaciers of the *Haramukh* peaks and *Haramukutaganga* and *Nandiksetra Mahatmyas*. Numerous springs and rivulets in Kashmir are considered by local tradition as manifestations of the Ganga, but are too unimporatnat to be alluded to in our passage. By *Uttaramanasa* is meant the sacred Ganga-lake situated below the East glaciers of mount *Haramukh*.

576. **Note.** *Yasoraja* had been exiled by *Sussala,* a relative of *Kaka's* family on being exiled by the King, then joined *Sahasramangala*.

577. *R.T.* Vol. II. p. 80.

578. *Ibid.*

579. **Note.** From the above passage we learn *Domba,* a Rajaputra, son of *Sajja,* fell into the battle at *Manimusa,* protecting the troops that had been scattered by the fear of powerful *Prthvihara.* The place must be looked for in *Samala* or *Hamal.*

580. *R.T.* Vol. II. p. 80.

581. *Ibid.*

582. *Ibid.*

583. *Ibid.*

584. *Ibid.*

585. *Ibid.*

586. *Ibid.*

587. *Ibid.*

588 **Note.** *Mantra addressed to the Visve-devah* are recited at the beginning and end of the annual Sraddha sacrifices.

589. *R.T.* Vol. II. p. 80.

590. **Note.** The text as found in A does not permit of a suitable construction. We propose to read with L *Prasaktam* for A *Prasaktum,* and to correct *Vyavasayo* for *Vyavasayam.* Mis readings of (a) *m* for *o* (both superscribed), and *vice verse,* at the end of the words are frequent in *Sarada* Mss.

591. *Note. Bhiksacara* is made to allude to the fate of his father and grandfather, whose fall he is to revenge.

592. *R.T.* Vol. II. p. 81.

593. *Ibid.*

594. *Note.* The meaning of this verse is to defeat the enemies with the 'Power of love'. As far as understood from the study of statement, *Bhiksacara* wishes to account for his reticence as to his further plans. If he had any secret designs, it would not be expedient to reveal them. Or his followers are to liberty to assume that he has got none, but is trusting solely to his good cause.

595. *R.T.* Vol. II. p. 81.

596. *Ibid.*

597. *Ibid.*

598. **Note.** For a *sapeksam,* which does not give a suitable sense, read with L *saksepam.*

599. *R.T.* Vol.II. p. 81.

600. *Ibid. Note.* The translation on a conjectural emendation indicated in the edition. The text of A.L is certainly corrupt.

601. *Ibid.*

602. *Ibid.*

603. *V.I*. p. 36.

604. *R.T.* Vol. II. p. 81-82.

605. *Ibid.*. p. 82.

606. *Ibid.*

606. *Ibid.*

607. *Ibid.*

608. *Ibid.*

609. *Ibid.*

610. **Note.** The epithet *saindhava* given to *Prajji* could also men 'descendant of *Sindhu*'. *Prajji* belongs to aboriginal tribe. Due to his power, he seals up good qualities in his life along with the fame of princes like *Rudrapala* and others who had previously gone to *Kashmir*. Regarding *Ananda* see elsewhere his reference.

611. R.T. Vol. II. p. 82.

612. *Ibid.*

613. *Ibid.*

614. *Ibid.*

615. **Note.** *Janakasimha* has been mentioned appointed on the post of chief justice (*rajasthana*); but figures subsequently as *Nagaradhipa*, 'City prefect', for this he roused the feelings of *Tilakasimba*, his brother

waiting for an opporunity to leave himself an understanding with the *Tantrins,* ministers citizens etc. May we suppose that the two offices were held jointly by the officers of the *'Nam'* or *'Word'*.

616. *R.T.* Vol. II. p. 82.

617. *Ibid.*

618. *Ibid.*

619. *Ibid.*

620. *Ibid.*

621. **Note.** The early date here given for the pretenders irruption is very curious. The pass over the *Pir Pantsal* meant by the 'route of *Surapura'*, is generally impassable till far into March. The month Magha of the *Laukika* year 4197, according to luni-solar reckoning, corresponds approximately to January 10th to February 9th, 1122 A.D. *Bhiksu's* march over the pass in that month presupposes, therefore, exceptionally favourable conditions, which may possibly have been connected somehow with the premature snowfall of the preceding autumn mentioned already above.

622. **Note.** This verse would afford the means of fixing the position of the *Navamatha*, ('the new matha). Owing to certain demerits of the King from the previous (birth), this *Matha* lost its desired designation as having been built by *Jayamati, Uchchala's* queen, in case we should find a locality in or near Srinagar answering to the topographical indication furnished by our passage. The *Navamatha* must have been situated on the island of the *Vitasta* or a strip of land nearly enclosed by a bend of the river. The present river shows no island in the vicinity of the city. But there is a kind of peninsula formed bya great loop of the river, only about one and a half miles in a direct line above the first city bridge. This peninsula is now called after the village situated on it *Saupur phur,* and part of its occupied by the Ram Munshi Bagh, a caping ground well known to European visitors of Srinagar. Its length is nearly a mile and its breadth about half a mile, while the neck connecting the little peninsula with the 'mainland' on the north is at its narrowest point scarcely more than 400 yards in width.

623. *R.T.* Vol. II. 83.

624. *Ibid.*

625. **Note.** The royal palace was close to the *Ksiptika* when their sons *RajaRaja* died, the king and his consort left the royal palace, and took up their residence in the vicinity of (the shrine) of *Sadasiva.*

627. *R.T. Vol.* II. p. 83.

628. *Ibid.*

629. *Ibid.* p. 83.

630. *Ibid.* pp. 83-84.

631. *Ibid.* pp. 83-84.

632. *Ibid.*

633. **Note.** By the name *Gambhira* ('the deep river') is designated the lowest portion of the course of the *Visoka* (*Vesau*) river, between the point where it receives the waters of the *Rambyara* and its own junction with the *Vitasta*. This confluence, situated circ. 75°-8′ longitude and 33°-50′ latitude is known to the Mahatmyas as a Tirtha by the name of *Gambhirasamgama,* as already explained his *Gura,* (a man) of noble virtues, called *Mihiradatta,* built the (temple of) Visnu *Gambhirasvamin.* The *Gambhira* is repeatedly mentioned by this name in the *Vjayesvaramahatmya* (*Adipurama*)*;* "since my birth this hut has been (to me) like a mother, witness of good and evil days. I cannot bear to see it pulled down today." During the time of *Avantivarman,* the illustrious *Bhatta Kallata* and other holy men (*Siddhas*) desended to the earth for the benefit of the public. In this manner he artfully drained off that water for two or three days. He had the *Vitasta* dammed up in one place by workmen. "I thought that she (soul) would live by the rent given by the gardeners, who at summer time place flowers, betel-leaves etc, in that very cool well." In *Vaisakha* (Apriai-May) thereupon *Sujji* started his attack and march in haste to the bank of the *Gambhira.* The road from Vijabror to Srinagar on the left bank passes to this day the *Visoka* close to its confluence with the *Vitasta.* The *Visoka* flows there between steep mud banks, and is so deep as to be unfordable at all seasons of the year.

634. *R.T.* Vol. II. p. 84.

635. *Ibid.*

636. *Ibid.*

637. *Ibid.*

638. *Ibid.*

639. **Note.** *Silla* is evidently the mother of *Vijaya,* the powerful Damara from *Devasarasa, Garga's* brother-in-law, a native of *Devasarasa,* rebelled and slaughtered the King's troops. *Tikka* who is put in possession of her estate (See following verse), is a relative of *Vijaya* and also from *Devasarasa* has already mentioned above.

640. *R.T.* Vol. II. p. 84.

641. **Note.** By *Upavesana* Kalhana designates usually the seats of Bamaras, which in all probability formed in these troubled times little castles.

Such fortified residences of small territorial lords are to this day remembered in many Kashmir villages, and are ascribed to the time when the country was divided into *Kutarajs*, i.e. *Kottarajyas.* This description might well apply to the Kashmir of the last reigns included in our narrative.

642. *R.T* Vol. II. p. 84.

643. *Ibid.*

644. *Ibid.*

645. *Ibid.*

646. *Ibid.*

647. *Ibid.*

648. *Ibid.*

649. *Ibid.*

650. *Ibid.*

651. *Ibid.*

652. *Ibid.*

653. *Ibid.*

654. *Ibid.* p. 85.

655. **Note.** *Udaya*, from *Icchatis* family, has been mentioned already above.

656. **Note.** *Udaya* and his younger brother *Dhanya* (called only here *Dhanyaka*) rose to high posts under *Jayasimha,* who had purified his body by immersion in the water of the *Ganga*, gained the confidence of the fickle King. The King granted the garland (*Sraj*) of the office of Chief-Justice (*rajasthana*) to *Dhanya,* that of the commander-in-chief to *Udaya,* and the charge of *Kheri* to *Rilhana.*

657. **Note.** *Sussala's* queen *Jajjala* from *Vallapura,* who excelled by her virtues, died there, and *Rajalaksmi,* too, the daughter of *Gagga,* was consumed in the fire.

658. **Note.** The name Oja, for which A,has also the variant *Teja,* is written in the first form also in L; *0* and *te* are nearly alike in old Sarada writing.

659. The position of *Harihada* and *Ksatrikabhinnika,* we are unable to trace; the second name is given in L as *Ksatriyabhinkhika.*

660. **Note.** It is probable that most, if not all, of the partisans of the King who are named here, belong to Rajput families of the hill regions to the south of Kasmir.

661. **Note.** It has been already mentioned that *Rilhana* was defeated by *Kalyanavada* and others in *Kramarajya*; *Ananda*, the son of *Ananta*,

became thereupon there lord of the Gate. He plays a great part in the subsequent narrative as *Jayasimha's* trusted minister. During the closing days of the history *Sujji* who had escaped from several dangerious situations tired out like a snake which had escaped from a mountain (forest) caught in a conflagration. In that situation King granted the garland (*Sraj*). He was the chief-justice of the time and became the incharge of *Kheri* to *Rilhana* at present. It shows that King is dependent than the others, and *Rilhana* then invited him with kindness through secret messengers, and he arrived in host.

662. *R.T.* Vol. II. p. 86.

663. *Ibid.*

664. *Ibid.*

665. **Note.** *Bhagika* is identical with *Prajji's* nephew (and *Sujji's* son '*King Raj'*) *Bhagika.* He has arranged for the protection of the treasury at *Lohara* hill when he descended *Bhagika* at the 'Gate'.

666. **Note.** *Saradbhasin* is in all probability another name of *Saradiya* who is mentioned as *Sangata's* brother on the way he had his horse stopped at *Sushatamatha* by a concourse of vile people and fell into capitivity.

667. **Note.** We are unable to say who was this obstinate oponent designated as 'King *Mummuni'*. The name must have been an old puzzle, as the reading of A_2 shows. There an attempt is made to get rid of it by dividing *Jitvamum munibhubhujam* (for *Jitva mummuni*) and referring the word to *Pratapasila.* The fact that the name recurs, where also the *V.L* of L is indicated. The gloss, *Mumen Khan,* given by A_4, on our passage, has apparently suggested to the editors of Ou-kong" It in erary (*Journal Asiat* ; 1895 p. 351), the identification if *Mummuni* with the title of the Khalifs, *Amir-ul-Mumenim.* But this glossator is quite modern, and we have shown in another edition, how little reliability can be claimed for his information on geographical or historical point. *Mummuni* and other chiefs roamed with fierce *Candalas* outside his army, and formed his guard at night, disposes of this conjecture. In the first passage *Mummuni* is mentioned as having been three times defeated by *Lalitaditya*; in the second he is said to have formed with other Kings the night-guard of *Jayapida.* The three different Kings under whom *Mummuni* is named, are according to Kalhana's chronology separated by centuries. Hence, it is clear that Kalhana could not have meant the same person in all three passages. Was *Mummuni* possibly the title or family name of the rulers of some country or tribe analogons to *Sahi, Lahakan,* or similar terms like *Chamar, Megh, Barwala, Mahashah, Chura,* etc. The word is evidently of non-Indian origin; and discussed above, *Lalitaditya's*

march of conquest in the north, *Mummuni* is named between the *Tuhkharas* and the *Bhuttas*. The former must be located in *Badakhshan,* and the latter are undoubtedly the Tibetan inhabitants of Ladakh and the adjacent regions. As the *Darads* receive subsequently separate mention, we may possible here have tribes of Turkish origin such as the conquests of the Great and *Little Yue-tchi* as well as of the *'White Huns'* brought into the regions of the Upper Indus, and thus within the sphere of *Kashmir* politics.

669. **Note.** From *Mungata* of A and *Sungata* of L we have to correct here *Sangata*; as *Mummunis* brother is referred to under the latter name, the son of (*Sujji's*) paternal uncle, after rushing about in the royal courtyard as it on a stage, nobly gave up his life. Regarding *Sangata* and *Mummuni,* they belong to the *Bana* family of *Sudar* tribe. Both were cousins of *Sujji*. The name *Sangata* had to be discussed already in the text, for A *Mungaja*. He is named in the first place in a list of *foreign* or *'Barwala'* Rajaputras and will princelings who serve King *Sussala* as condottieri or gentlemen-adventures. Without placing too much reliance on the identity of the names, it may be suggested that in this instance we possibly have before us a late descendant of the princily family referred to in the early books. The continued use of the name *Sahi* for descendants of the royal family of the *'Sahis of Kabul'*, *Alakhana's* support, the illustrious *Lalliya Sahi* of *Udabhandapura* was placed between the rulers of the *Darads* and *Turuskas* as between a lion and a boar, resembled *Aryavarta* (mountains); long after the destruction of its rule, is vouched for by passages, like *Rudrapala* died of the *luta-disease*, and the other *S'ahi* princes too found an early death. Four arrogant princs (*rajaputra*) from the *Sahi* family, *Bijja, Pittharaja, Paja* and another, were his favourites. These princesses of *Sahi* family spoke to the King: *"Malla* and *Yamu* are totally hypocrite who make your court disaffected, there fore, they will be killed without fear". Then *Sahi* princesses and the other queen eager to die, ascended with fire-brands to the four-pillared pavillon (*catuskika*) *of the 'Palace* of hundred gates' (*Satadvara*) "To this day the appellation *Sahi* throws its lustre on a numberless host of *Ksattriyas* abroad who trace their origin to that (royal family)" , and seems to offer an exact parallel. In easily understand the substitution of his family name for his own personal one. He thought *Mummuni* defeated (only) after having vanquished him in three times in battle. The *VV.LL* of the name in L deserve little attention, as their variations are evidently due tomere blunders of transcription referred to the famous throne of *Vikramaditya* which is frequently mentioned in the legends regarding the latter, and that *Pravarasena* was believed to have carried it back to *Ujjayini*. The curious story of *Mummuni's*

peacock-dance might possibly have originated from one peculiar custom observed among *Mummuni* people. For a similar popular legend got up in explanation of the habits of foreign nations.

670. *R.T.* Vol. II. p. 86.

671. **Note.** For *Kamaliya's* grandfather (*Bhijja*), to *Hammira* i.e Mahmud of *Ghazna* is equivalent to elephant called *Aja*.

672. **Note.** It would be interesting to know in what part of the Panjab *Lavaraja* exercised his authority.

673. **Note.** The ruler of *Gurjara* gave up to him humbly the *Takka-land* (*Takkadesa*) is mentioned once more in the *Rajatarangini*, in order to get hold of the status of gods, too, when the treasurers (of the temples) had been carried off, *Harsa* appointed *Uadyaraja* 'Prefect for the overthrow to divine images' (*devotpatananayaka*); as *Takkavisaya*. As an ethnic designation, *Takka* is used in connection with the names of certain persons known as *Vulliya* brought from *Turuskas* girls born in various distant regions and brought them to him. In this connection, King has already agreed with thus, and immediately sent *Patta* and a *Takka, Asidhara* by name, with a force to kill that relative. But wicked *Takka, Bimbiya* by name, prevailed upon the King to have them executed, and strangled them at night. When *Madana* arrived from *Madavarajya* and was not received by the king. He became frightened and went to the house of the councillor *Laksmidhara,* who was a *Takka* (by birth). Cunningham has rightly connected the name *Takka* with that of 'the Kingdom of Tseh-Ka', which Hiuen-Taisang reached after travelling to the South East of *Rajapuri* or *Rajauri* (*Ancient Geography of India;* pp. 148 and also see *Si-yu-ki,* i. pp. 165). The Kingdom of *Tseh-kia* is described as bordering in the East on the *Vipasa* (Bias), and in the West on the Indus. Its capital was in close proximity to the old city of *She-kie-to*. The latter place is undoubtedly identical with the ancient *Sakala*, famous in Brahmanical and Buddhist tradition (V. *De St. Martin,* Memoire *Analytique* ; p. 77). *Sakala* is mentioned in the *Mahabharata* as the capital of Madras or Bahikas, tribes settled in the modern Panjab (Lassen; *Pentapot , India*; p. 19 and *Indian Alternative*; i.p. 801), and with the Bahikas we find the *Takkas* actually indentified in *Hemacandra's* synonymic lexicon (*Abhidhanacintamani;* Edited by Boehtlingk-Rieu Verse 959). The position of *Sakala* has not yet been fixed with certainty, though it has been the subject of much speculation with special regard to the supposed identity of *Sakala* with the Eayyala of Arrian and the Eayala (or Euthydemia) of Ptolemy (Cunningham A.G; p. 176). It is, however, probaly that the ancient city was situated somewhere between the Cinab and Ravi. The name of the modern

town is also used in an extended sense for the designation of the neighbouring territory, comprising the upper portion of Doab between the Jehlam and *Chenab* rivers to the foot of the *Bhimbar* hills. Towards the end of the 9th century, its power must have been considerably reduced, as in our passage the term *Takkadesa* is evidently used in a far more restricted sense than Hiuen-Tsiang's kingdom of *Tseh-kia*. Cunningham (*A.G.* p. 151) was evidently right in tracing back to our *Takka* the *Takeshar* which Alberuni gives to a region situated to the South of the *Pir Pantsal* range and neighbouring on the region of *Lauhawar* (Lahore) (*India* ; i.e. p. 208). Cunningham thought to have recognised the name *Takka* also *Taqin* (in Urdu), the designation used for an Indian territory by *Ibn Khordadbeh* and *Ibn Rosteh*. Prof. De Goeje's cirtical editions of the geographers, however, show this name as *Tafin* as a Urdu term; see *Bibl. Geograph. Arabicorum,* vi p. 18 (Tr.); VII p. 135. The gloss of A_4 deserves mention only as a curiosity. This modern glossator sees in *Takka* the nameof the 'A tak river', i.e the Indus, and identifies *Takkadesa* with *Skardo*. The cutting off of a finger as a sign of unconditional surrender is repeatedly mentioned in the Chronicle. *Prthvihara's* younger brother (*Manujesvara*) who had been worsted, not knowing that he had arrived, placed himself at that very time under the king's protection, after cutting off his own finger. In explanation here of, it will be sufficient to refer to the very numberous instances, both ancient and modern, in which Indian Kingdom were designated by the name of their capitals for the time being; compared e.g. the use of the name Lahore for the whole Panjab in the reign of Ranjit Singh.

674. *R.T.* Vol. II. p. 86.

675. *Ibid.*

676. **Note**. For the *Pancalas* as followers of Arjuna (*Phalguna*) in the battle, compared e.g, *Mahabharata*; vii. CLvi 51; Clix 47. L has rightly *Phalguna*.

677. *R.T.* Vol. II. p. 87.

678. *Ibid.*

679. *Ibid.*

680. *Ibid.*

681. *Ibid.*

682. **Note.** The compound term *Sita sita* permits of different interpretations several of which may have been intended by the author, *Sita Sita*, ' white like sugar' or *Sita-asita,*' appearing in the bright half of the month, would also be suitable epithets of *jyotsna*. *Vahini* also can be

taken in the double sense of 'army' and 'river'. In this case the King's army would be linked to the Ganga, which after its junction with the Yamuna carries white and black waters. By the flow of the (black) temple-juice of his war-elephants he gave the splendour of a junction with the '*Kalindi* (Yamuna) to the eastern ocean embraced by the *Ganga*. The rush of the King's army into the dark mass of the enemy would be compared with the Ganga's descent to hell (*Patalaganga*).

683. **Note.** The position has been taken up by the Damaras on the banks of the *Mahasarit,i.e* the Tsunth Kul. The detail of this passage has already been discussed in the text.

684. R.T. Vol. II. p. 87.

685. *Ibid.*

686. *Ibid.*

687. *Ibid.*

688. **Note.** The incidents of the fight described in these verses can easily be understood on reference to the local topography of Srinagar. They appear, notwithstanding, some poetical metaphors and exaggerations, to have been recorded accurately enough by the author. The Damaras attacked the city on the right river bank from the South East by crossing the *Mahasarit* or *Tsunth Kul*. Being driven back by *Sussala's* troops they retire to the East, the only direction open, probably by the *Setu* of *Pravarasena,* the present *Suth*. A further proof of its antiquity is furnished by the fact that this embankment bears along with the quarter built on it merely. The general name of *Suth,* from Sanskrit *Setu, 'dyke',* whereas all the other numerous embankments and causeways about Srinagar have distinctive appellations. Several Topographical considerations combine to prove that it was this old 'dyke' or *Setu* which the popular legend related by Kalhana represented as the leg and knee of the demon who helped *Pravarasena* to cross the *Mahasarit*. They then ascend the hill of *Takht-i-Sulaiman*, which lies in the direct continuation of the *Setu,* and would naturally attract the fleeing as a place of safety to the east of Srinagar. The gloss of A_2 renders accordingly *Gopadri* by *Gopakar* i.e, the name of the modern village of *Gupakar*, situated between the North East extremity of the *Takht* hill and the Dal lake. In reality it goes back to an original *Jyesthesvara* through *Jyeth-her*; compared *Amburher* than *Amaresvara; K other* than *Kapatesvara*). The important bearing of this passage on the question as the site of *Asoka's* Srinagar has already been discussed. The new place for Siva *Jyesthesa* or *Jyestharudra,* whose original sanctuary us situated at *Bhutesvara* below *Nandiksetra*. In tracing the position of the new shire ascribed to *Jalauka*, it will be

safest to start from what can be ascertained regarding the actual worship of that form of Siva in the vicinity of Srinagar. The shrine of *Jyesthesvara* mentioned in our passage was evidently connected with this sacred site, and may possibly have occupied the same place on the top of the hill, where the extant temple referred to in the above note stands. The superstouctures of this temple certainly belong to a late period, as rightly shown by Fergussion; *History of Indian Architecture;* p. 282; against Cunningham and Cole's assumptions. But the high base on which the temple stands, and the stairs leading up to it, are clearly of a far earlier date, and may well have formed part of a building which the tradition of Kalhana's time ascribed to King *Gopaditya*. Whether this tradition was based on historical fact, or was perhpas merely due to an old popular etymology connecting the name of the *Gopadri* hill with that of the King, cannot be decided now. It must be noted that there is at present no other place on the steep rocky hill showing ancient remains, apart from the site of the extant temple. This occupied, in fact, the only convenient position available for a structure of any dimensions. The *'Gopa-Agraharas'* may have been situated on the fertile plateau of the East foot of the *Takht* hill, which is now occupied by the Vineyards and fruit-gardens of the *Gupakar* village; situated immediately at the foot of the hill to the North East of Srinagar. While holding the hill the Damaras are surrounded by the King's forces. This manoeuvre could easily be effected, as the *Takht* hill is practically isolated and connected with the mountain range to the East only by a low and narrow neck at its eastern extremity, now known as *Aitagaj* ('Passage of the sun, called so as forming a gap in the hill range to the south). It is only from this rocky neck that the top of the *Takht* hill can be reached by horses or rather hill-ponies, all the other approaches being much too steep to ride on. It is by this very rough path that we believe *Bhiksu* to have penetrated to those who had taken rufuge on the hill and were in danger of being cut off. By the same path the Damaras then retire to the *Aitagay*, in order to climb up the other hills mentioned above stretching to the East and North East. A track passable for ponies leads to this day from *Aitagaj* up the west slopes of the hills towards the mountain plateaus above *Khunamuh* and the valley, of the river shown on the map as the *'Arrah'* while pursuing the fleeing Damaras on these hills, the King is taken in the flank by *Mallakostha*, who with his men of *Lahara* corps (the rebels) who had wished to overpower (the King), were not able to join hands. He came to the rescue of the Damaras *Candala* was to late from the left' i.e from the North. As the city is held by the King's forces, the only route open to *Mallakostha* is round the East shore of the Dal via Bran (*Bhimadevi*), thid (*Theda*), and *Jyesthesvara*

(*Jyether*). It lies close to the North East of *Aitagaj*, might be placed the final encounter of the day, in which *Sussala* seems to have been in personal danger. If we assume that the Lahara force was originally intended to join the attack on the city from the North (via the present suburbs of Naushahar and Sangin *Darvaza*) and was only subsequently after the repulse of the general attack sent round to help the Damaras force retiring to the east, we can understand why it should have come to late arrival of the *Lahara* corps (the rebels) who had wished to overpower (the King), were not able to join hands. The get from the above named suburbs round the shores of the Dal to *Aigagaj* is a march of about eleven to twelve miles, which by an armed force could scarcely be done in less than about four hours.

689. *R.T.* Vol. II. p. 87.

690. *Ibid*. p. 88.

691. *Ibid.*

692. *Ibid.*

693. *Ibid.*

694. *Ibid.*

695. *Ibid.*

696. *Ibid.*

697. **Note.** As *somite* of A L gives no proper sense and as an object is required to the verb *prapa*, we have to emend *samitam* for the above form. It is difficult to trace out the reference of the son of *Mallakostha.*

698. *R.T.* Vol. II. p. 89.

699. *Ibid.*

700. *Ibid.*

701. *Ibid.*

702. *Ibid.* **Note.** Regarding *Yasoraja*, Kindly see his reference in elsewhere of the Text.

703. R.T Vol. II. p. 89.

704. **Note** *Kheri* has given the charg eof to check the office of the *Damaras* which has not mentioned before it.

705. *R.T.* Vol. II. p. 89.

706. **Note.** Kalhana when making this satirical allusion to *Parvagupta's* toilet, seems to have had in his mind the Kasmiri saying: *gasa lova his chas dar*, 'his beard is like a bundle of grass'. This is common used of a too big beard. The use of saffron as an unguent is repeatedly

referred to as a royal privilege by the people within the five or six months, standing before those in the same fashion. When they saw the King (Dr. Raj Kumar), with his forehead bearing a mark in sandal-ointment and smeared with saffron. They knew that this was *Bhoja* though they had not seen him before.

707. *R.T.* Vol. II. p. 89.
708. *Ibid.*
709. *Ibid.*
710. *Ibid.*
711. *Ibid.*
712. *Ibid.*
713. *Ibid.*
714. *Ibid.* p. 90.
715. **Note.** The houses here referred to were probably on the left river banks, which could easily be reached from across the *Ksiptika.*
716. *R.T.* Vol. II. p. 90.
717. **Note.** By *drti* is meant the modern *masak* largely used for crossing the *Vitasta*, Cinab and other Panjab rivers in their course through the lower hills. In Kashmir its use is at present unknown. The violence of the current and rapids make the use of boats impossible on the Sindh above *Gandarbal*
718. *R.T.* Vol. II. p. 90.
719. *Ibid.*
720. **Note.** The reference of the term *Visalata*, kindly see in elsewhere of the text.
721. *R.T.* Vol. II. p. 90.
722. *Ibid.*
723. **Note.** *Suvarnasanura* is probably indentical with the present village *Sunasamil* situated in the *Sukru* Pargana, at the elevation of 74°-56′-15″ longitude and 33°-50′-40″ latitude (marked on larger survey map). This identification is supported mentioned above where the place is mentioned in connection with *Kalyanapura* close to the high road leading from *Supiyan* to Srinagar. The position of *Kalyanapura* is clearly indicated in the last-named passage by the reference to *Drabhagrama*, the modern *Drabagam,* about miles to the North West of *Kalampor.* It is very probably that gloss *Kalamapuram,* which A_2, has written above *Kamalakhyampuram* in the following verse, referred in the original MS. to *Kalyanapura*, and was only by a mistake of A_2 copied in the wrong place. Term *Suvarna* appears in Sanskrit as *Suna.*

724. *R.T.* Vol. II. p. 90.

725. **Note.** The reference of the *Kalyanapura described above*

726. *R.T.* Vol.II. p. 90.

727. **Note.** We are unable to make any proper sense of the words *matur antikam.* The mother of *Tikka* cannot well be meant, as *Tikka* was on the side of *Bhiksa,* and *Chudda*, supported by the King, not likely to leave Lahara and to proceed to *Devasarasa* to stay with a rebel family. The conjectural emendation proposed to the edition, *maturantakam,* does also not suit, because *Silla,* who had been killed previously with *Tikka's* connivance as *Gorgacandra's* brother-in-law; was only a near relative, but not his mother. We believe that the words referred to are corrupt, and hide the name of the place where *Chudda* was stopping. This locality is alluded to in the following verse by *tatra* means afraid of musical note i.e. *'Nam'*. *Devasarasa* must be taken here as an adjective indicating origin from *Devasarasa.* The detail information of the term has already mentioned in the text.

728. *R.T.* Vol. II. p. 90.

729. **Note.** The murder of *Silla,* to which allusion is made here, was according to *Upavesana* committed by *Prthvihara;* yet *Tikka*, who succeeded to her estate, seems to have assisted in it.

730. *R.T.* Vol. II. p. 91.

731. *Ibid.*

732. *Ibid.*

733. *Ibid.*

734. *Ibid.*

735. *Ibid.*

736. *Ibid.*

737. *Ibid.*

738. *Ibid.*

739. *Ibid.*

740. *Ibid.*

741. *Ibid.*

742. *Ibid.*

743. *Ibid.*

744. **Note.** *Daratpura,* situated probably in the Kisanganga Valley "town of the Darads", is perhaps, meant the modern *Gurez,* the chief place of the upper *Kisanganga* Valley. The epithet *girigupta*, 'hidden in the

mountain,' would well apply to that place. Gurez lies in a Valley whose level ground is nowhere more than about one mile broad; all round rise high mountain ranges.

745. *R.T.* Vol. II. p. 92.
746. *Ibid.*
747. *Ibid.*
748. *Ibid.*
749. *Ibid.*
750. *Ibid.*
751. *Ibid.*
752. *Ibid.*
753. *Ibid.*
754. *Ibid.*
755. *Ibid.*
756. **Note.** For A *Svaparo* read with L *Suparo*
757. *R.T.* Vol.II. p. 92
758. *Ibid.*
759. **Note.** Correct *mahoddhataih* with G (and Durgaparsad) for AL *mado*; Dh and Ha are often written very much alike in old Sarada. MSS.
760. *Kasthila* corresponds to the modern *Kathul;* a quarter of Srinagar which occupies the space between the left bank of the *Vitasta* and the *Kutakul* (*Ksiptika*), from the Shergarhi palace to below the second bridge (*Haba Kadal*). *Kasthila* is mentioned by Bilhana, *Vikram*. xviii. 25, as a quarter inhabited by Brahmans. The gloss of A_2 records a tradition which places these Agraharas at *Kasthala*, now *Kathul*, a quarter of Srinagar on the left bank of the *Vitasta*. This locality was founded King *Ananta* or endless.
761. **Note.** For *marutodbhutah* of AL read *ddhutah* asemended by Durgaparsad.
762. **Note.** The term *brhatsetu* we take for a proper name, designating probably the chief bridge in the Srinagar of Kalhana's time. The same term is used for the boat-bridge which *Pravarasena* II. is said to have constructed and detailed information see elsewhere in the text. As this boat-bridge was evidentaly the first of its kind in the country, the name might have clung to the bridge which continued to be maintained in the same locality. Where this locality was, we are unable to ascertain. Keeping in view the position occupied by *Pravarasena* himself. We

should be inclined to look to the vicinity of the present Fourth or Fifth bridge as a likely place for *Pravarasena's* bridge. Up to the Fourth Bridge the river forms an almost staright reach, and the smoke rising from *Maksikasvamin-Mayasum* could be easily seen from this point.

763. **Note.** It has already been discussed that *Maksikasvamin* is probably the old name for the island of *Mayasum*, lying between the *Tsunth Kul* and the *Vitasta.* The Western-most point of *Mayasum* lies almost opposite to the southern extremity of *Kathul,* and the fire could easily have been carried across the river there by a high wind has to blow.

764. **Note.** The *Indradevi bhavanavihara* has already mentioned in the text, as a foundation of *Indradevi, Meghavahana's* queen. Its position is not known, it is upto the master's jurisdiction disastrons fires have also in modern times frequently visited in Srinagar. The last occurred in 1892, when a great part of the city was laid in ashes. The prevalent use of wood in the construction of all private buildings, and the narrowness of the streets, assure a rapid spread for such conflagration.

765. *R.T.* Vol. II. p. 93.

766. **Note.** According to the disctionaries meaning of *hudukka* is the name of a musical instrument. Perhaps a kind of bagpipe is meant.

767. *R.T.* Vol.II. p. 93.

768. *Ibid.*

769. *Ibid.*

770. *Ibid.*

771. *R.T.* Vol. II. p. 94.

772. *Ibid.*

773. *Ibid.*

774. *Ibid.*

775. *Ibid.*

776. *Ibid.*

777. *Ibid.*

778. **Note.** The statue in the city is evidently identical with the *Brhadbuddha* mentioned as still standing in Srinagar in the time of *Sussala.*

779. R.T. Vol. II. p. 94.

780. *Ibid.*

781. *Ibid.*

782. *Ibid.*

783. *Ibid.*

784. **Note.** *Kamaliya* has already mentioned above, as the son of *Lavaraja*, a chief in the *Takka*-land, i.e. the central Panjab. Can we suppose that Kalhana refers here to a heroic resistance made by *Bhijja, Kamaliya's* grandfather, to *Hammira* i.e. Mahmud of *Ghazna*? That is *'Nam'*. But the period intervening between his death (1030 A.D.) and the time of *Sussala*, nearly a century, seems too long for this, if we take into account the shortness of an Indian generation. It is possible that the title *Hammira* is used here for one of *Mahmud's* successors. It appeas to be associated at a much later period yet with the names of some of the early Pathan Sultans of Delhi.

785. *R.T.* Vol. II. p. 95.

786. **Note.** The verses of the text makes it clear that for A *Svangaraktam,* which is one syallable short, L has *Svangaraktam Va*. The context requires here the emendation *Svangaraktena.*

787. *R.T.* Vol. II. p. 95.

788. *Ibid.*

789. **Note.** *Prthvipala* is *Kamaliya's* Younger brother has already mentioned above.

790. *R.T.* Vol. II. p. 95.

791. *Ibid.*

792. *Ibid.*

793. *Ibid.*

794. *Ibid.*

795. **Note.** The enemy's cavalry falls back on its own foot, and as the latter does not give way, used its weapon to force a passage.

796. *R.T.* Vol. II. p. 96.

797. *Ibid.*

798. *Ibid.*

799. *Ibid.*

800. **Note.** This passage again shows the traditional land revenue administration of Kashmir by which a very great portion of the annual produce of the country, i.e chiefly rice, was brought into the city in lieu of taxes. When the State stores containing this produce are destroyed before the new rice harvest is at hand, a famine must necessarily follow for the city population. The supply of cereals from the villages by ordinary trade was practically unknown in Kashmir until recent years. By the new produce mentioned in the next verse

might be meant subsidiary cereals such as corn, oats, millet, etc, which ripen in the Valley in the early summer.

801. *R.T.* Vol. II. p. 96.

802. *Ibid.*

803. *Ibid.*

804. *Ibid.*

805. *Ibid.*

806. *Ibid.* pp. 96-97.

807. *Ibid.* p. 97.

808. *Ibid.*

809. *Ibid.*

810. *Ibid.*

811. *Ibid.*

812. *Ibid.*

813. **Note.** *Ramdasia, Raidas, Raodasi, Ruidas, Ruhdas Rudradas, Ramdas,* with *Rohidas* and *Ravidas* being the most popular. The last one has been used here, as it is found in the *Adi Granth* and in other standard Hindi and Sanskrit works. These terms are loosely used with several different meanings. In its widest sense *Ramdasi* means a follower of Guru *Ram Das*, or indeed of any other Guru: but it is more usually applied to a *Chamar* or *Julaha* who has taken the *Phullpura* from the Master. It is generally explained that this *Guru* first admitted *Chamars* in the Sikh community, b ut this theory is untenable, and the name was probably adopted because it closely resembled *Raodas, Rai-dass* or Ravi Dass, a famous *bhagat* of the *'Chamar Caste' "Bhagat Ravidas, Raidas, Rahdas*, a saint of the *Chamar Caste'*, writes Mr. Mac Lagan, "was according to some accounts, a disciple of Ramanand; according to others he lived in the time of *Akbar*. The stories of the *Bhakta Mala* regarding him are given in Wilson's *Sketch of the Hindu Sects.* He is said to have been born at *Benaras,* and his followers are men of low caste, mainly *Chamars.* The census gives us no idea of the numbers of the followers of *Ravidas,* because there are *Ramdasia* or *Ramdasia Chamar* as well as *Ravidasi or Raidassi-Chamars* and the two have become hopelessly mixed in the returns. Ibbetson distinguishes the two sects of *Chamars* as follows: the *Ramdasi*, he says are only *Nanakpanthis,* and do not take the pahul of *phull.* Among the people themselves the two terms are by no means clearly distinguished. For instance, not a few persons termed themselves of the census as followers of *Bhagat Ramdas.*" Mr. Fagan

wrote: " As far as the *Hissar* district is concerned, the confusion is, we think, an actual fact, the Hindu *Chamars* are really *Rahdasis,* being so called after the *Bhagat Rahdas*. The name appears to have been corrupted into *Ramdasi*, probably from confusion with the name of the sikh *Guru Ramdas*. The Sikh *Chamars* are also *Ramdasis,* but in their case the name may imply a connection with the Guru *Ramdas*, but my own impression is that it is a name which they had before their conversion to Sikhism by corruption from *Rahdasi or Raidasi*, and the fact that there are *Raidasi* Sikhs as well as *Ramdasi* Sikhs corroborates this theory to some extent. On the other hand, it may be that the Hindu *Chamars* after conversion changed the name of their sect from *Raidasi* to *Ramdasi* in order to claim some connection with *Ramdas*, one of the leaders of their newly adopted faith". The fact that the *Raidasis,* like the followers of *Kabir or Namdeo*, must have held views very similar to those inculcated by *Nanak*, accounts doubtless for part of the confusion. Of the teachings of Ravidas little is known, except that be believed in the unity of God and forbade the worship of idols. He is said to have compiled certain books which are held in reverence, and he is quoted in the *Adi-Granth*. His followers pay him worship by repeating his name as they count their beads. The Satnamis of the Central Provinces are an off shoot of the *Raidasi Chamars*. According to Ibbetson in the north and centre of the Eastern Plains a very considerable number of *Chamars* have embraced the Sikh religion. These men are called *Ramdasia* after Guru *Ram Das,* though what connection they have with him we have been unable to discovered perhpas he was the first Guru to admit *Chamar* or *'Nam'* to the religion. Many perhpas most, of the *Ramdasi Chamars* have abandoned leather-work from the loom; they do not eat carrion; and they occupy a much higher position than the Hindu *Chamars,* though they are not admitted to religious equality by the other Sikhs. The *Ramdasi* are often confused with the *Raidasi or Rabdasi Chamars*. The former are true Sikhs, and take the *pahul or phullpura* from the Master. The latter are Hindus, or if Sikhs, only *Nanakpanthi* Sikhs and do not take the *pahul* from the Master; and are followers of Bhagat *Ravidas,* or *Rab das*, himself a *Chamar* or *'Nam'* or *'Sabad'*. They are apparently as true Hindu as any *Chamars* can be and are wrongly called Sikhs by confusion with the *Ramdasias* (G.T.C.p. N.W.F.p. pp. 306-07). There is another aspect of these roles is their "attributional" character. (See Marriott 1959). Apparently a "*Chamar*" is what a "*Chamar*" does. When we shall be the respondents whom they retained as *"Chamar"*, they would give the name of an individual whom they engaged in this capacity. Although always of the Menial-Impure category, this individual might be either a *Kori* or a *Chamar*, despite the fact that these two castes consider themselves absolutely distinct. The *Kori,* in fact, deem themselves ritualy superior to the *Chamar,* whose name connotes unclean status in the community, whereas they associate their own caste name with the honorable profession of weaving, even though no member of the caste weaves for a living today. What we apparently have here is an instance of the *"Chamarization"* of a caste, i.e. a case where a caste has been progressively forced by necessity to perform the most defiling occupations simply because their old caste occupation, with its low but defiled status, evaporated with the onset of industrializations. The small number of actual *Chamar* household in the village and its vicinity has doubtless contributed to this process. Most of the scavengers in *Sherupur* and *Naktipur* are *Kori*. The *Chamar* households continue to practice shoemaking and midwifery (*Dai*), but they dislike scavenging and have helped to withdraw from this highly polluting occupation through their identification with the so-called *Raidasi* movement, which endeavours to improve the lot of *Chamar* everywhere within the Hindu cosmos by adhering to the doctrines of *Ravi dass,* a saint of the Indian Middle Ages. It seems to matter little to a *'Jajman'* who does his "*Chamar*" work for him so long as it is performed we see here an illustration of the "functional interchangeability" which *Kolenda* (1963) considers a general attribute of *Jajmani* system: "As one compares village complements of services, it is striking that where a specilist caste is absent the caste's function is often provided by some other caste". In our view, such functional interchangeability is a necessary attribute of an ongoing *jajmani* system, particularly with respect to impure occupations, for a "clean" household cannot, by definition, retain its "clean" status unless certain, kinds of work and ritual procedures with impure implications are transferred to others. If the traditional absorber of a specific form of impurity is not available, then the power and persuasion of the "clean" household must be employed to uncover someone else who will function as a substitute. (H.C.S. pp. 162-163).

814. *R.T.* Vol. II. p. 97.
815. *Ibid.*
816. *Ibid.*
817. *Ibid.* p. 98.
818. *Ibid.*
819. *Ibid.*
820. *Ibid.*
821. *Ibid.*

822. **Note.** The statement makes it clear that *Jayasimha* had been sent to Lohara in *Asadha* 4196 (1120 A.D. has already mentioned above
823. *R.T.* Vol. II. p. 98.
824. *Ibid.*
825. *Ibid.*
826. *Ibid.*
827. *Ibid.*
828. *Ibid.*
829. *Ibid.*
830. *Ibid.*
831. *Ibid.* p. 99.
832. *Ibid.*
833. *Ibid.*
834. *Ibid.*
835. *Ibid.*
836. **Note.** Under the old land revenue system the produce could not be removed from the threshing floor by the villagers until the state's share had been taken from it. As often a long time elapsed until this was done, special watchman (Known as *Sakdar*) were employed at the *Khalas* (in Kashmir called *Khal*). Their employ extended practially over the whole year.
837. *R.T.* Vol. II. p. 99.
838. *Ibid.*
839. *Ibid.*
840. *Ibid.*
841. *Ibid.*
842. *Ibid.*
843. *Ibid.*
844. *Ibid.*
845. *Ibid.* p. 100.
846. *Ibid.*
847. *Ibid.*
848. *Ibid.*
849. *Ibid.*
850. *Ibid.*

851. **Note.** *Kosthesvara*, who plays a very prominent part in the rebellions of *Jayasimha's* early reign, is a son of *Prthvihara*. He is frequently referred to by the abbreviated name *Kosthaka*.

852. *R.T.* Vol. II. p. 100.

853. *Ibid.*

854. **Note.** *Vadosaka* is, perhaps, the same name as the one from which *Vadautsa* has been derived. It is difficult to trace out the tract about *Kalyanapura* (Kalampor) any local name approaching *Vadosaka* in sound.

855. R.T. Vol. II. p. 100.

856. *Ibid.*

857. *Ibid.*

858. *Ibid.*

859. *Ibid.* p. 101.

860. *Ibid.*

861. *Ibid.*

862. *Ibid.*

863. *Ibid.*

864. *Ibid.*

865. **Note.** The correct meaning of the reference with Durgaparsad *samullanghya* for A *Svamu*.

866. **Note.** King *Viduratha* is said to have been murdered by his wife with a knife hidden in her hairbraids; which is difficult to search out without father or husband.

867. *R.T.* Vol. II. p. 101.

868. *Ibid.*

869. *Ibid.*

870. **Note.** Kalhana refers here evidently to a raid which *Utpala*, to allay the King's doubts, pretended to lead against *Tikka* and *Bhiksacara;* now have been cleared.

871. *R.T.* Vol. II. p. 102.

872. **Note.** *Laksmaka* was the son of *Prayaga's* sister. He, however, escaped to *Sussala* from the imprisonment.

873. *R.T.* Vol.II. p. 102.

874. *Ibid.*

875. *Ibid.*

876. **Note.** The allusions are to stories told in the *Mahabharata*. The Gandhara princess is *Dhrtarastra's* wife, the mother of *Duryodhana* and other *Kaurava* princes; for her curse. 'The words of the angry Rsi refer to the prophecy of *Visvamitra, Kanva* and Narada. For the portents foreboding the destruction of the *Vrsnis*.

877. **Note.** Term *Pandavas* is composed of two words, i.e, *Pan+dava* means 'Five words' and *'Vidu'* means process. It is the process of the *'five words'* or *'five nad'* called 'Word' or *'Nam'*. They alarm round the clock, but without the *'Perfect Master'* we cannot attain them. It has the same process as the *"Five Rivers of Penjab'*. (Dr. Raj Kumar; *History of the Brahmans;* Delhi; 2006; p. 59). The houses of the *Pandava* brothers when in exile *Brahman* by the Tamil people of the south to this day. Those in the south were never so subject to the Aryans as the tribes of the north and grew into the powerful and civilized Tamil and Telugu nations, but there is no hint of this in the *Rig-Veda*. There these aborigines are named *'Dhasyu' 'destroyers' or 'Dasa'* or *'injurious'*. Their skins were much darker than those of the Aryans and so they were stigmatized as 'black' or 'black-skins'. From the shape of their broad noses they were called 'goat-nosed'. They possessed herds, they had strong holds called 'Pur'. Those who were captured were made 'slaves', and the very word *'dasa'* came to mean 'slave' in later Sanskrit and cognate languages. The references to their religion described them as offering no sacrifices, being unbelievers in the gods of the Aryans, and thus grievously impious. There are two passages in which they are called *'Sisna-devah'*, 'whose god is the *'phallus'* (*Rig-veda vii.215; x. 99.3*), and it will be remembered that the *'phallus'*, as the linga, came to be the chief symbol of the god Siva in later Hinduism. From the first these *'Dasyua'* were the enemies of the Aryans, but their demon worship greatly affected the Aryans, especially in the simpler domestic religion that has always been, that of the ordinary folk called *'word'* or *'Nam'* (*R.V.V.R.* pp. 4-5).

878. *R.T.* Vol. II. p. 102.

879. *Ibid.*

880. *Ibid.*

881. *Ibid.*

882. *Ibid.*

883. *Ibid.*

884. **Note.** *Putkaram* or *Put-kr* is used here, in the sense of the *Panjabi;* and *Pahari pukarna*, 'to shout to a distance,' or 'to call to a far-off person'.

885. R.T. Vol. II. p. 103.

886. *Ibid.*

887. *Ibid.*

888. *Ibid.*

889. *Ibid.*

890. *Ibid.*

891. *Ibid.*

892. *Ibid.*

893. *Ibid.*

894. *Ibid.*

895. *Ibid.*

896. *Ibid.*

897. *Ibid.*

898. *Ibid. p. 104*

899. *Ibid.*

900. *Ibid.*

901. *Ibid.*

902. **Note.** *Nalika,* a period of twenty-four minutes.

903. **Note.** Term *Kankola* is a conjectural reading for the impossible *Kankala* of A L means listen through the ears the sound of the music of *'Nam'*.

904. *R.T.* Vol.II. p. 104.

905. *Ibid.*

906. *Ibid.*

907. *Ibid.*

908. *Ibid.*

909. *Ibid.*

910. *Ibid.*

911. *Ibid.*

912. **Note.** Term *daisika* is our passage has been assumed to designate 'people of (*Didda's*) own country' or 'teachers'. The context however, shows that it designates the '*foreigner*' in contrast to the Kashmirian. This is also the meaning distinctly given to the word by Jonaraja in the commentary on *Srikanthac;* XXV 102 (*desantariya*). Kalhana uses the word clearly in the same sense, where no other interpretation is

possible. The meaning 'traveller', is given by *Hemacandra* for *desika,* may also be referred to.

913. *R.T.* Vol. II. p. 105.

914. *Ibid.*

915. *Ibid.*

916. *Ibid.*

916. *Ibid.*

917. *Ibid.*

918. *Ibid.*

919. *Ibid.*

920. *Ibid.*

921. *Ibid.*

922. *Ibid.* pp. 105-06

923. *Ibid.*

924. *Ibid.*

925. **Note.** Term *vastuka,* unknown to the dictionaries, must be taken as *'Nam'* is the *'Loveable'* concept in the meaning of *'trunk'* or corpose generally. As L reads *Vastulram* in both passages, this form may be accepted as the correct one for *Vastuvam* which A has here.

926. *R.T.* Vol. II. p. 106.

927. *Ibid.*

PLATES

Plate-I

Fig. 1. Tame Leopards Trained for Hunting Ready for the Chase.

Plate-II

Fig. 2. Primeval Forest; Monk eye Scared by a Large Snake.

Plate-III

Fig. 3. Landscape at the Foot of the Vindhya.

10

JAYASIMHA (1128-1149 A.D.)

The deceiful and treacherous murder of *Sussala*[1] was took place in the palace in 1128 A.D. A panic was widely spread in the Kashmir Valley. As soon as, *Jayasimha* listened the news of his father's murder, his milk-brother *Preman* brought to him on the throne of Kashmir. It was the pleasure-sake movement of the mind, as it was liked by his forefather[2], though deprived of his sword, the same emotion as it is felt by a person in possession of his sword on the receiving of such an evil message[3]. Then at length; he was recovering his senses, but, no doubt, he had kept one thing in his mind that misfortune lamented loudly and broadly on the theory of mind called *mana*[4]. He will again try to recollect it after sometimes. Father says to his son: "When you were strenuously on my account ridding the kingdom of enemies, why did you, O King, put your soul in subjection to the vilest (of men)? because they are the 'salves' of the master. We will teach a lesson of the harassment[5]. "When ultimately in order to put an end of the enemity you will be given to your enemies, you remained unarmed, and honoured, O father, even wothless persons[6]." "Your father and brother are in heaven, they had their wrath to appease when you will took the revenge of these enemies. Now, however, it is you who are (there) tormented by wrath[7]" "Do not look with envy[8] for this brief time on *Anaranya, Kripa, Drona, Jamadagni,* and the others[9] who have been revenged by their relatives[10]." "The wrath you feel is to be regretted. I shall remove it, O King. I do not feel troubled about this (revenge, nor should I) though the three worlds had to be attacked[11]." "Before me, as it were, is the face you showed when looking at me, thrilling and smiling with tenderness and sweet with kind words[12]." At the same time, *Jayasimha* was saying this and more in lament, and yet hiding his agitation in deep reserve, he saw before himself his father's ministers mute from shame, pain and fear of mind; which she was reflecting on the King[13]. What with wrath advised, prudence forbade. Even thus *Jayasimha* spoke to them (*manas*) some hard words. "Shame, you and your weapons have been changed for the worse at my father's end, though he, seeing your noble descent (*sadvamsalam*[14]), had honoured you with riches (*Kosaih*[15])." "Fie, what at my uncle's murder the eaters of food remnants did, even that you, men of honour, could not accomplish now[16]."

Administration of Jayasimha

Kalhana represents the administration of *Jayasimha* which was divided into two or three ministers of the *'Word'* or *'Nam'*. *Jayasimha* directed his ministers for the (immediate) task[17], first they have to given first-rate attention towards to compile their thesises that it should be recommened by the 'Father' first *Jayasimha* advised in this (flight) that *Lohara* must have to leave the country on account of that the danger have been occured from the side of *Bhiksu* as soon as the period of darkness would be pass[18]. In this matter, others who were more resolute and advises him to fight for the throne. It is requested to your goodself, please take the help from *Pancacandra, Garga's* son, who was in *Lohara.* In such matter, nobody indeed thought that since *Sussala* was no more, resistence could be offered to *Bhiksu,* who was prepared to walk in the City as (if it were) his own house[19]. No doubt, King felt certain pains at such kind of ministers who are putting reliance in him, and replied: "Tomorrow, you will what is to be done[20]." With the kind regards to the situation *Jayasimha* did not show how troubled he was by his father's death, but he posted certain guardians who were fully prepared for keeping (proper) watch over the idiot, over the treasury and other (places of importance) for the welfare of the public[21]. Now, the city resounded with the voices of the people, who were running to and fro and shouting to each other in long-drawn tones with the lust of power in politics[22]. Therefore, these days of the darkness era which was as if frequently posing the nose in their own ways. It shows the furious design (*vetalas*) of the mind and filled with demons of the last night (*Kalaratri*), cast terror in all beings[23]. And, King (Dr. Raj Kumar) remained surrounded by lights which still in air without motionless, and by the ministers who did not stir (being absorbed) in reflection and thus he thought in his heart: "While I yet live destitute and without a protector, there lies my father, murdered in a deserted, dark house, where the doors are not (closed), and through which the fierce wind is passing[24]." "Oh, misfortune, how shall I be able to look into the face of honourable men in the assemblies, until I have honourable men in the assemblies, until I have wiped off such an unbearable outrage[25]?" "How will the officers of the troops arrive from regions held by the enemy, and (at a time) when the roads are impassable owing to the snow[26]?" Now, it is reflecting on different matters like cold wave, road blockade, etc. in deep humiliation and in fear, as it has been passed by the *Jayasimha* during the dark period of the Indian history[27]. After the terrible night, there will be a good morning (the beginning of enlightment era), during this period *Jayasimha,* will step out his foot prints into the pavilion (*catuskika*) to reassure the citizens, and will also despatched mounted men to search for the troops where they have gone[28]. It has been analysed from the study the clouds which have been settling down on earth began to fill up the roads with dense masses of snow[29].

Jayasimha Proclaims Amnesty

Jayasimha proclaims those who had been sent out of Kashmir during the time of *Kashmir* revolution, they retruned after having exposed themselves in vain to hardships, without having even from after got *'Word'* of troops, King reflected for a short time and then had the following order circulated in the city under the beating of drums: "Whatever a person may have taken to himself, that is now forsaken by me, and amnesty is given to those who have joint the enemy, guilty though they may be". Thereupon, the citizens became everywhere attached to him and will shout for blessings[30]. *Jayasimha* will instantly rewarded for this unexceptionable course, which meant an almost complete departure from the procedure followed by the immediately preceding Kings[31]. At that time he would have less than a hundred followers, was at that time surrounded by the people who were carried away by sympathy[32]. It has been well-known by *Laksmaka*, how to address the people with kind words, and ways of (giving) friendly gifts, as it has been obtained before the King the position of chief councillor[33]. In the meanwhile, King will thus wisely pacifying the country by prudent measures, that was the time to enter the city by *Bhiksu*, it was the midday[34]. With him then it was appeared such a mixed host of troops as one had never seen before, composed of Damaras, citizen, horsemen and marauders[35]. But at the same time, the news of his opponent's death was started, he marched upon the city for the lust of throne. He was addressed by *Tilaka* as King, the son of *Kaka*[36]. "Because *Sussala* was hated by all, has been killed by the will of fate, should, therefore, the subjects have left his son who has good qualities[37]?" "Why then hurry,

O King, for the sake of a single day to enter the city? Proceed to *Padampura* (while) we go to shut off the enemy from the route (to the city[38]). "Should then *Sujji* and the other chief officers who have lost their troops, come back, they will be slain there or stopped with their armaments and horses[39]. "Then after two or three days you will for certain peaceably occupy the city, invited to it by the citizens themselves[40]." *Bhiksu* as well as *Kosthesvara* and the other (rebel leaders) who disregarded his advice, and will said with a smile: "Enough of these counsels of old men[41]." His own people will think that our ruler has been come down on earth. They will importuning him for various decrees, caused him to delay[42] in tactices. Hence, as his troops were all in suffering on account of the heavy snow fall, and will stopped it for the time being in the vicinity of the city[43]. At the very moment, *Pancacandra* Garga's son will have to gained the situation; and will arrive along with his soldiers by the side of the King who has been destituted of troops[44].

Bhiksacara Attacked by Pancacandra

In this pious battle, *Pancacandra* marched out bravely together with the Rajputras, who were eager to wipe out the disgrace of having abandoned their slain lord *Bhiksacara[45]*. At such occasion *Bhiksu's* soldiers will have to scarcely noticed their unexpected attack began to fight for the right cause, on seing several of their own men will be killed on spot, they would fell somehow into instant disorder on all sides. The chief leaders of the army, *Bhiksu, Prthvihara* and others, who were unable to rally on their fleeing troops, and fell themselves into an unsoldierly panic, such as had not been seen before [46]. If, on their flight, they had been pursued for by those who were on the side of king. There would indeed have been nothing left of them in a moment[47]. When the followers of *Bhiksu* had at last turned their faces, fate showed a kindly face because they have been supressed by the Brahminical thought that which has the narrow vision and now it is afflicted in the City owing to the new King's greatness[48] like *Akbarnama*. It shows that this victory and defeat has been divided between the two great Kings mentioned above. Otherwise people had though it that it came out by the dispensation of fate[49] by the *'Father'*. The fate which is very wonderful power cannot be imagined personally, in a moment it makes a man ups and down, but it has been firmly stood, and raised, just as the current of the waters (washes away) one river bank (and raises another[50]).

Sujji Proceed to Srinagara

Sujji at the closing of the day arrived at *Srinagara*, who had escaped from several dangerous situation, tired out like a snake which had been escaped from mountain of dense forest caught in a conflagration[51]. On spot, he stood at the village of *Medhacakrapura*[52],. When he heard of the King's murder. After holding the council of minister he did not start his journey during the night, but he stopped there[53]. No doubt, he awaited *Rilhana* and other officers who stood at *Surapura* and elsewhere, in order to proceed with them unobstructed to the city[54]. Therefore, it is difficult in order to be recognised by them in the darkness. He then had the flaming fires kept up continually on the roof of the house he was in[55]. However, owing to the disobediance of their soldiers, who dispersed in all directions, they got lost somewhere at night and did not reach his camp[56]. After the cut of the *rat* in the morning, he then started his journey, and was not for a moment left alone by the Damaras, who pursued him in the rear and made attacks[57] over them. During the time of *Sujji* he march towards *Srinagara*, the people who accompanied with him, they were mostly old men, women and children. He put in front and guarded by them on the march toward Srinagara, just as a herdsman (guards) his cattle[58] during his nomadic life like *Bakarwals* and *Gujjaras*. Keeping in view the very tedious journey by turning back and holding out (against the enemy) with fifty mounted men, he was able to protect by them for a very short while[59]. No doubt, road has been hemmed in by masses of vines and multitude of trees, and pressed as he was the bold enemy of them and lost the people at every step[60]. It shows that *Sujji* has to repay the long debt of his life with gratitude to his dead Lord and Lord's son who was in distress for a long period, then he could save himself there[61]. What is this for those, who, like the beasts of prey. They cannot await an opprtunity to sure to meet with death (in their enterprise[62])? Therefore, it is difficult to face the fierce Damars of the *Khaduvi* district., who were posted themselves near the vicinity of *Padmapura*, in order to stop the disastrous to kill him at this place[63]. During this happening, *Srivaka* with his large force commenced his journey from village of *Kheritalalasa*[64] which was very difficult for them to find out the right tract. Because they had been trapped very badly on that road[65]. Therefore, it is difficult for them to follow the right way of life which is true for every body as a human being.

War at Padmapura

The war which was took place at *Padmapura,* it appears that most of the ministers who had given the assurance are intact, being a master of them, they fell upon him (*Sujji*) and killed him and plundered his soldiers[66]. In this war, *Meru* and *Sajjana*, two cavaliers, were killed. *Malla,*[67] *Vatta's* son, was wounded and died after some days[68]. There is a place called *Udipapuraabala*[69], which was then difficult to pass owing to the water flowing through the swamp made by the flood of streams[70]. At that moment, *Srivaka's* soldiers had been blocked and got outisde *Padamapura*. He was proceeding there for fighting at every step, but an arrow was struck to his neck[71]. It was the surprising notion for the Damaras, who found out that he was not *Sujji,* they looted him. Therefore, he became helpless as he was owing to that wound, but spared him from regard for their former friendship[72]. Because at the same time, they were busy to engaged with carrying off the mass of stores which they plundered from *Srivaka's*[73] force, and some had gone away, in the meanwhile *Sujji* passed the road with mishap[74]. During the very long journey of life, now the destiny of the lion has been cleared the road (for him) by destroying the trap and arrow (set by the hunter) *'Sakari'* through a wanderer's accidental entry into the forest[75] for the time being. *Sujji* was trying to over come these accidents, after passing through *Padmapura* with his silent soldiers, was recognised by the Damaras when he got near the inundation swamp[76]. Without heeding their plundering the stores, weapons and other (property) of his foot-soldiers, he crossed the swamp with his mounted men and have been reached on the ground which is fit for the horses[77] of trade. In later on, when the danger from the enemy will have to be passed, *Sujji* from afar threatened his opponents with frowns, shaking of the forefinger and words of abuse which they will strike on them[78]. Taking along his parasol, which alone they will free from the fear of mind. He will quickly marched into the city and came with tears in his eyes before the King[79]. As soon as *Sujji* arrived there, King will dropped in his presence, just as (if he had been his) elder brother, the fear of the enemy's on set along with tears made hot by pain[80]. At this juncture Mahattama *Ananda,* son of *Ananta,* will be killed on that day by Damaras, while on the march in the village of *Locanoddara*[81]. On account of the intolerable exactions which he had inflicted in the form of taxes (levied) on various auspiciolus occasions (*mangalyadanda*) and otherwise, nobody at that time will pitied him, when he came to a miserable end[83].

Royal Officers Besieged By Damaras

Study indicates that *Bhasa*[84], a follower of *Sujji,* was fled away from *Lokapunya*[85] and betook himself at *Avantipura* into the courtyard of (the temple of Visnu) *Avantisvamin*[86]. *Jayasimha* and his royal officers known as *'Kampanodgrakaka'*[87] and *Ksemananda* were besieged in it by the incensed Damaras of *Holada*[88]. *Induraja,* from *Kularaja's* family, an officer of the army, was also besieged at *Dhyanoddara*[89] by *Tikka*, whereupon he pretended to join the latter[90]. Besides these, *Pincadeva,* too, and many other leaders of various troops were kept in *Kramarajya* besieged by Damaras[91]. Thus, the King's followers were slain and wounded in various localities, just as young birds that on the fall of a tree have been thrown out of their nests (placed) on it[92]. Many of them who were without shoes and clothes had been frozen off in the snow, and died on the roads; and some are without food, because their feet had been worn out with the help of the *God* or *tanner*[93]. At that time, one could see on the roads that was leading to city, those people who are seeker of *'Nam'*, their bodies would be covered with straw[94]. In this competition, *citraratha*[95] and others who were soon to become great ministers. They took to grass as their festive dress in the musical world of the *'Nam'* or *'Chamar*[96]*'*. One after the another day the clouds did not stop for a moment from sending down the snow and could not keep the birds from flying[97]. During this hour *Dhanya* leaving his soldiers behind, then came over to *Simnhadeva* from the force of *Bhiksu* who stood at *Vanagrama*[98]. At the same time all the soldiers of *Bhiksu* were also ready to move towards the city, when they heard that the King has been received very kindly by the followers of *Bhiksu.*

Burning of Sussala's Queens

In the study, we learn the rival of *Sussala* which were his close relatives, they became weak, an opportunity arrived at that time and four queens came forth from the palace to follow the King into death with the help of *'Nam'* which were burning without it before the arrival of King[100]. In such conditions, the people were benumbed by the fear of a hostile attack of *Jayasimha*, due to the sudden hard frost, we were not able to conduct them to the distant burning ground[101] of the earth. Therefore, the burning ground, the body of earth is in haste near (the vihara of) *Skandabhavana*[102], which was not afar from the palace[103]. And the Queen *Devalekha*, who came from *Campa (Annami),* whose beauty was as great as the Creator could make it, and entered into the fire with her sister *Taralaleka*[104]. *Jajjala*[105] from *Vallapura* who supported *Sussala*. Therefore, it appears from the study that *Padamaka* may have been a son or grandson of *Kalasa, Ananda* and *Jajjala* his sons, whose names have been omitted in the process of copying[106], who excelled by her virtues, died there, and *Rajalaksmi[107]*, too, the daughter of *Gagga*, was consumed in the fire[108]. The events with which these names are associated in the *Rajatarangini* occured in A.D. 1113 and later. These events may here be briefly detailed as throwing an interesting light on contemporaneous history[109] of *Kashmir.* In this tug of warfare, Damaras who thought that the new King would keep the throne from their own lord only till the snow will have not melted. He gave him the (nick) name of *Himaraja* ('the snow King[110]). Between that period, *Bhiksu* has to see the head of *Sussala* which was brought to him, burned with flame which expressed deep hatred with enemy[111]. In this contest, *Kosthesvara, Jyesthapala*[112] and others have the wish to do with the (head) on the last honours (i.e. cremate it) but those who are with him would not suffer of his heated head[113]. *Jayasimha* eager to fight against the enemy and prepared to proceed to the city. But his followers displayed indifference due to the falling of heavy snowfall and have been drawn towards the enemy, he expressed in the following statements: "I had been thinking that if *Prthvihara* lived, I should obtain the throne by force. But if he were killed, I should become master of the land as soon as the (rival) Kinsman (*Sussala*) died. By the will of fate, however, he has come otherwise, because on the contrary though the opponent is killed yet my hope of the throne is gone[114]." "But then what need is there of that throne, which is useful only for material pleasures? who else could attain (as fully) as I have that what is fit for the ambitious[115]? "The head of him who before threw the ground the heads of my ancestors, rolls about today at my palace gate[116]" "While he destroyed the happiness of those before me during ten months, I have made him suffer all kinds of misfortune during ten years[117]." "Having thus accomplished my task I shall turn to good use the rest of my life in comfort, having appeased the torments of my mind[118]." After saying these words, *Jayasimha* likely to be went to *Tikka,* and later he bowed down before him. He bestwoed upon him in kindness a golden jar, a white parasol and other (gifts) of the nature[119]. The assurance which had been given by *Tikka*, made his hope for the throne rising again and will be seize like a demon. He then put back and stopped reflecting inwardly and suffering from the cold due to the mismanagement of the work[120].

Disposal of Sussala's Body

The disposal of the *Sussala's* body was kept by *Lavanyas* and the corpse of the murdered King was put under the guard, in order to inflict upon the extreme outrages. *Sajjaka*, however, a soldiers from the city, had, though on the enemy's side, thought inwardly from a sense of gratitude: "Why such a state for the ruler's body when he is dead?" and had, after obtaining access under the pretence of curiosity and overcoming the guards in combat, burned the trunk (*Vastuka*[121]). From the mouth of a person who was under inspiration from gods, there was a wide spread rumour among people that there should be an event at the murder of *Sussala.* (This rumour was to the effect) of destroyer of his close relative since the year (of the *Laukika* era four thousand one hundred) ninety four, because, he had been dominated be demons which cast him into delusions. It was in full agreement with the master who cut off his head with the 'Power of Nam' and carried it where he died while asleep[122]. Under these circumstances, *Bhiksu* has sent the head of the enemy to *Rajapuri* to show his implaceable hatred for the sake of decency by a shameful piece of conduct[123]. In the statement it has been expressed that Queen *Saubhagyalekha,* a daughter of *Uchchala* is trying to slay the heads of enemies by (the hands of) her own servants those who carried her uncles's head. After the long period of Indian history, *Rajapuri* had thrown into disturbance, the head came before *Somapala*, her husband, who was stopping at a distance to keep the situation controlable[124]. The councillors of the *Khasa*-prince became hapless. It shows that he used to get drunk and their behaviour become rustic. His condition became pathetic and led by others. *'Word' or 'Chamar'* has been discussed freely in various ways what was to be done with that (head). According to his characher, it has been expressed by displaying his sense of decency, or the contrary indiscpline[125]. Whereas, *Nagapala*[126], who became his brother, but without reconciliation, he has been sufferced and would be dishonoured in the head which (was all that) remained of him[127]; will become his history. In this context, far-sighted people, who feared in the end because extra damage could not take place that a punishment could not be accord from *Kashmir.* He advised the *Somapala* in every respect to pay the (last) honours to this head of his (liege) Lord who always kept best wishes in the favour of public[128]. It has been seen that jackals are pleasing to keep the comany with the lion, then fate may be altered[129]. At the same time, his enemies were cremated his head on wood of black aloe and sandal wood at *Gopalapura*[130]. No doubt, he repeatedly won and lost the royal power which is called *'Chamar'* received from *'Father'*, *'Baba Gurinder Singh'*, Bias (*Vyas*) means 'without hope'. *'Chamar'* had often his reverses and successes in the battle-field, as he had passed through various long plights and disasters *'Word'* so, too; it has been seen at the time of his death a most strange occurrences[131], that his head cermated in one country and the rest of his body in another material world[132].

Siege of Avantipura

During the advancement of the *Tikka* and the others on the city by way of *Avantipura,* they were stopped there in order to kill *Bhasa* and others; who were already be besieged by *Jayasimha*[133]. Though they fought with them by lighting fire, throwing stones and making breaches in the areas that they could not overcome them notwithstanding their great efforts which they made[134]. With such kind of ventures, they were slain inside the temple's courtyard which was safe by mighty stone walls. In such conditions, they could neither stay nor move on[135]. Therefore, they have been delayed; and King wisely utilized the interval period in the process of bribing and winning over the Damaras of *Khaduvi*[136]. After this King (*Raj*), had been taken into hostages from them for a short period of time. He quickly despatched *Sujji*, together with *Pancacandra* and others to relieve *Bhasa* and his companious[137]. Therefore, he could no reached at *Avantipura*, in the meanwhile, *Tikka* and the rest were scattered on seeing *Kayya's* son (*Vijaya*) and others who composed his advance security in the interest of his safety in the Dark Age[138]. After this, *Bhasa* and those with him, they left the temple and joined with *Sujji,* after killing those who followed behind the defeated enemy[139] of the *'Nam'* or *'Chamar'*. As soon as the commander-in-Chief returned to the City in triumph, *Induraja,* too, along with his followers left the *Tikka* and came back on their own positions[140]. At such occasion King will be placed *Citraratha, Srivaka Bhasa* and others in charge of the *Padagra* (post), the 'Gate', the *Kheri* (district) and other offices (respectively[141]). But *Sujji* will retained his offices as before, yet he too had to watch the face of the chamberlain (*Laksmaka*[142]). To extent the empire, there is need to appoint more ministers to control the vast empire of the *Chamar* dynasty. It is interesting to note that the chamberlain might have to be treated with consideration also by the King (himself), as he would be honoured by countless cliques of Damaras, and others who already directed by intrigues for the cause of dissensions among them during they were the master at one time[143]. In the host of enemies, there was no one who at his instigation joined the side of King or (at least) not try to join with him[144]. In this sharp struggle King sharply appeared in this battle field and has concealed in his behaviour the fact of his being the ruler of *Kashmir*. It is sure from the side of King (Dr. Raj Kumar) would not take his food without taking his (Laksmaka's) opinion in the presence of his master[145]. At the same time; *Jayasimha* will have to secure the City room which are to be not more than to the stretch of his legs. He has to keep nursing the fruit which have been ripened[146] with the help of *'Nam'*. *Bhiksu* after gathering all the Damaras at *Vijayesvara*, will have to march then at the close of *Sisira* (months of *Magha* and *Phalguna*) towards the city in the hope of taking it[147] back to the pavillion. As soon as; Damaras they saw such unity in the masses of their troops as had never been witnessed before. Then, they thought that the kingdom had passed into *Bhiksu's* hands, and felt alarmed[148].

Damaras Intrigues with Somapala

During the time of lawlessness and choes, Damaras thought there is intrigue with *Somapala* as he had watched in familiar intimacy the character, courage, friends, enemies, etc., of each single one (among them), he would have already obtained the throne, now, he started to attack on them. (Hence), they held a council secretly by sending messengers to *Somapala* (of Rajapuri), offering him the throne, whereupon, he despatched an envoy[149], along with the natural norms. They thought that due to certain drawbacks on his person and character, *Jayasimha* was no better than a violent animal, they would have the pleasures of the rule entirely for themselves[150]. It has been rightly observed that fate did not allow that worst of evils to camp upon this land as planned by the assembly of those robbers *(dasyu)* who had cast away decency in their lust after enjoyments[151] in their own way. Let be disgrace the along! But could this land, even for a short-while, have been ruled by a such person on the throne, who was unfit even for the time being a slave[152] of the *man*. There is man of straw having scorched by fire on his face, protects the rice-crop by frightening the flocks of sparrows. If he was put up to protect the forest trees, what could he do there except the destruction like wild elephant[153] who overthrow it. No doubt, *Somapala* has to keep close his messenger nearby *Bhiksu's* side, under the dissimulation (offering his lord's) congratulations, secretly induced the Damaras to offer hostages[154] to King. In the month of *Vaisakha;* thereupon; *Sujji* will started his attack marching from the city in great haste, will arrive on the bank of *Gambhira*[155].

Sujji's victory on the Gambhira

It would be the praiseworthy victory of the *Sujji* in this business as soon as he went forth alone in this battle then there is a great alliance of bravemen for some period[156]. In this very bold business it is not wonderful if by the will of fate more than lakh people will be defeated by a single man in this battle or a single man by a hundred thousand[157]. It would be unable at that time to cross the river owing to the want of a bridge of *'Nam'* or *'Chamar'*. *Sujji* will have to watch the enemy on the other side, who were shooting arrows[158]. At least, for two or three nights he and they will have to stop on the both sides of the bank of river Vitasta. At that time, we have to ready our equipment mutually to watch for any opportunity (favourable for an attack[159]) over the enemy. Then *Sujji* had a bridge constructed with boats brought from *Avantipura,* and he himself acorssed on a boat together with his horse[160]. As soon as; his enemy's troops they will saw him acrossing with few soldiers. They became agitated like a row of trees shakened by the wind[161]. All, in a moment, might one has to see him ascending, the bridge got ready; and the soldiers are acrossing and the enemy has scattered[162] with the attack of the King. It has been minutely seen that no swordman, no trooper, no spearman or archer were able to turn back from the fleeing froce, even their face is not visible[163]. Even the saddle on *Kosthaesvara's* horse got loose, owing to the girth not having been secured tightly. His horseman was stopped on the way for a moment[164] to fixing the saddle. No doubt, he disappeared quickly on *Sujji's* pursuit, like a column of dust whirled up by the wind[165] of monsoon. Whereas the enemy, whose troops were slain, plundered or scattered. They will met in the shattered state in *Dhyanoddhara* and other villages[166]. *Bhasa* who had already gone in front of the battle field, he put the enemy to flight after crossing the bridge over the *Vitasta*, which is before *Vijayesvara*[167]. As soon as the; commander-in-chief will arrived on the following day, after having passed the night at *Vijayaksetra;* and the enemy will treated from *Dhyanoddara*[168]. While after stopping; there for some days, he was prepared to move to *Devasarasa*. He joined there with *Tikka's* relatives, who came deserting their party[169]. After marching into *Devasarasa,* he placed in *Tikka's* seat (*upavesana*) the two chief men among them were known as *Jayaraja* and *Yasoraja,* sons of *Bhojaka* of Indian territory[170].

Flight of Bhiksacara

Bhiksacara's flight was pursued by *Bhiksu* and others, who proceeded *Surapura* and *Kosthesvara* and the rest to their territories, while their hosts were scattered. It shows they were flying in great danger and *Somapala's* messengers abused his lord: "Where have I been sent by that son of a slave-girl[171]? Rajput. *Bhiksacara* thought that his (lord's) ambition was to be served by great and exciting undertakings, just as if a she-jackal were seized with the desire of rivalling the lioness[172] of *'Nam'*. Thus, *Sujji* in a few days will cleared and placed at the disposal of his lord's son kingdom, which owing to his lord's perversity had been lost for a long time[173] in the Indian History. In such circumstances, King has to proceed to approach by means of bribes also the strong Damaras of *Samala* and other (parts) of the world, who stuck to *Bhiksu*[174] on his activities pretaining to the spread of *'Radha Soami Mission"*. The issue will be resolved on the test of King's power and to do thereafter combined attack in a battle[175] of warfare.

Battle at Damodara

Aforesaid battle was took place at *Damodara*[176] which devoured many a brave man, in which the masses of soldiers as they rushed disguisingly into the dust, resembled like actors dancing behind 'the curtain[177]. As soon as, *Sahajapala* projected by his wounded father, who had fallen into *Kosthesvara's* power. He will obtained fame (for himself and) for his subjects[178]. No doubt, equal were the exertions of both the King and *Bhiksucara* there. Yet *Bhiksu* on that day met with such a defeat as could not have been thought of[179]; before the commencement of the battle, there could not be seen in *Bhiksum's* army that soldier in the evening, who was there in the morning, nor who was there today, on the morrow[180]. Because, it is unique kind of thesises which few knows many will get embarrass. At such occasion certain townsmen and Damaras will desert the enemy and join with King, from whom they received suitable grants and honours. Consequent upon this, there arose in *Manujesvara*[181] and *Kostha*[182] a certain anxiety to go over to the King's side, eager as the two were for profits and comforts[183]. Keeping in view to ascertaining this, *Bhiksu* will started his journey to abroad along with his own personal followers in order to spread the said mission in the month of *Asadha* from *Kakaruha* to onwards[184]. No doubt, certain Damaras chief came then after him, and from a remnant of attachment tried to concilate him, they could not hold him from the back in his anger[185], they will be conscious to listen the King as a 'good teacher.' In contrary to this, *Kasthesvara,* who as the son of a libidinous woman who had no morals, was filled with eager desire for *Bhiksacara's* beautiful wives[186]. In this sharpe struggle of the nature, one who could touch the lion's mane, the jewel in the serpent's hood, the flame of the fire, or (*Bhiksacara's*) wife while he lived[187] in the passion of *'Nam'* or *'Word'* which is called *'Chamar'* in Hindi and *Chamarkrit or Charmakara* in Sanskrit.

Bhiksacara leaves Kashmir

In the meanwhile, *Bhiksacara* leaves the *Kashmir*, *Somapala*, who had concluded a treaty with *Sussala's* son, did not give him a refuge in his dominion when he wished, he took shelter (there[188]). Then he was frightened by his efforts which that (ruler) made everywehre against his life, he proceeded to *Sulhari*[189], where it was difficult to access on the border of his territory. It has been seemed that gods have no pity in *Trigarta*[190] (Kangra), no morals in *Campa*, (Camba), no generosity in the *Madra-land*[191], and no good will in *Darvabhisara*[192]. At such occasion, his councillors gave him this advice: "The King freed from fear is likely to oppress the Damaras while you are away. Therefore in time they will themselves call you (back) and make you king. Let us hence go to *Naravarman's*[193] country to ask for what is proper". Yet he did not accept this advice thought it was the right one[194] (i.e. *'Nam'*). Under such conditions, he then accepted the invitation of his father-in-law to stop in his house with a limited retinue, unfortunately his followers left him[195], during the difficult hour.

Pacification of Damaras

Now, the process is going on to pacify the distinguished power of the Damaras proceeding towards the city, it appeared as if bridegroom's-prorocessions were taking place at a time when auspicious moments (*Pagna*) are easy to find out on them[196]. At different occasion when people saw each one of them more (splendided) than the King with his (packed) horses (without 'Nam'), parasols and steeds, they magnified the rough kind of power which King *Sussala* (had displayed) in his firm resistance during the campaign against the foot-soldiers[197]. It has been rightly observed that *Kosthesvara* chiefly attracted on the marrymaking of women, who possessed as he was of noble bearing, beautiful youth with lovely dress[198]. In this land where the troubles were ended, the noise of the drums of the Damaras was marching in numerous bands like the music of festivals which grips the surrounding area[200]. '*Ksira,* and Damaras from *Madavarajya*, whose hosts of foot-soldiers were awe-inspiring by *Laksmala*, brought over to the King's side on the question of the pacify the Damaras[201]. They have admitted into the house of the chamber lain (*Laksmaka*) with great honour also for the royal servants, owing to the attachment with the prince for a long time[202]. During this war villager have been plundered by the *Lavanyas,* King found that this expenditure was reached on high level, as hard to pass as a time of scarcity, though his wealth was like that of Kubera[203]. King took certain steps among Damaras those who were fit for the *'Nam'*, into his salaried service. Thus, in this way the number of the persons was increased who belonged to the inner court (*adhyantara*) while the outer court (*bahya*) becoming reduced[204]. In addition to this *Tisyavaisya, Arghadeva* and other relative of those who had been murdered his father. They were put to death by the King (in the fashion) suited for high-treason of act[205]. Within the four months from the day of his father's death; he brought it about that the country obeyed no one else and was quite his own family and tribe[206]. But the city was without splendour, the citizens were deprived of all means and the land overrun by numberless Damaras who were like Kings[207]. No doubt, an enemy capable in all tasks was firmly established at a short distance. The councillors, feudatories, together with (all) who belonged to the outer and inner court, were leaning towards the enemy[208]. There is no any elder person in the palace to give advice; all the servants (of the King) were mainly bent on unlawful acts; and disloyality became their sole practice[209]. This general state of affairs which the King discovered at the commencement of his rule, should be remembered by persons of judgement in connection with each of the (succeeding) events in order to that they may understand them thoroughly from the core of the heart[210] as they were the rulers of *Kashmir.*

King Jayasimha's Character

In the study, it appears *Jayasimha* was a brave and a pious King. He fought number of battle and put down certain rebellion. At this given, time of period his numerous good qualities may be briefly described here, though they will have to be discussed very frequently in the following passage[211]. The qualities of those whose character is very deep which only few possessed, cannot be appreciated, unless one carefully examines the preceding and succeeding (facts) and acquaints himself with the narrative given in illustration[212]. If we examine his qualities (carefully) such as they are in reality, of a King who is under our direct observation, we shall not fail as regards an impartial judgement on his character.

Nobody, indeed, is clever (enough) to penetrate the true character of another such as he is (in reality). How (should be then penetrate) that of such a King of superhuman power of the *'Nam'* due to his pious character[213]. Moreover, no body here whose judgement is obscured by his own bad deeds, is capable of understanding the exceptional and winning greatness of faithful wives; of a friend who is like in luck and bad-luck; of a poet skilled in descriptions and of a King who is the friend of all people after some time[214]. In this way, how should then the mind of everybody find its way to a right conclusion as regards the nature of his virtues and faults which is so wonderful as the thought of nature[215]. No doubt, he was uneven, indeed, are the features also in his character. Not perceiving the excellence of their (aggregate) result of his qualities, the people have concluded that there were faults in their character. There is not one action of the cloud which does not benefit others i.e., flood and snowfall. Moreover, some (plants) open their blossoms at the flashes of lightening, which are painful to the eyes, and other (plants) come forth at the long thunders of of lightening which hurt the ear. Yet the dull minded people did not recognise they other virture of life but they only gives of rain[216]. On hearing of his transcendental virtues as observed by direct perception, the people will feel convinced as regards the (great) deeds of former Kings[217]. It has been known to us that without rising from his seat, he made by his frown the Kings (*bhudharan*) tremble, just as the elephant of the quarter (*dinnaga*) *(*makes the mountains *bhudharan tremble)* by shaking his skin during the (Darkage) night[218]. In this contest, Kings carry hidden treasury of *'Nam'* themselves the pain caused by the fear of him, while the hosts of their armies (*Vahini*[219]) wail, just as the oceans (keep hidden in themselves) the submarine fire, (while the hosts of rivers flowing into them with wail[220]). Whereas, the former glory of the moon like kings became invisible in the world, being flooded by the radiance of that sun among Kings[221]. Whatsoever, looks at him his lord (*isvara*[222]) facing himself, just as looking like a correctly modelled image of the god (Siva, one finds it always facing himself) in the difficult days[223]. He is constant in his kindness, never takes back what he has granted. On the other hand, he removes the fear which caused to the enemies, when they will make their submission[224]. Therefore, nobody can face him except his own reflection on his drawn sword, and no one can return his thundering voice except the echo repitition of *'Word'* or *'Nam'* in this regard[225]. His voice, which is not oversharp in anger, but impressive in kindness, resembles a sword which has only a single sharpened edge[226]. Those supported by this (King) they are of noble birth (*akujanman*), and who diffuses never fading happiness, are strong like the shoots of the wishing tree (which does not grow on the earth *akujanman,* and blossoms in never fading beauty[227]). It has been rightly expressed from the study that ministers have recognised the power of the King was his greatness, though his inscrutable nature made it difficult to notice, and he (again) paid attention to which them on every occasion when secret message will flourished in the worldy affairs[228].

Laksmaka in Power

Under difficult circumstances, Chamberlain (*Laksmaka*) rose his power, and did not allow to rise, as the stem of the plant called *Esa* (does not allow other) trees to grow up by its side same is the story of *Brahmans* or *manas* who are attached with the material culture[229]. As he was uprooting all with the greatest ease, as if they are blades of grass. The powerful *Janakasimha* alone could not be out by him[230] without the help of *'Nam' or 'Word'* or *'Chamar'*. No doubt, he was familiar with the *King* from his boyhood, acquainted with all affairs and having sons grown up into way[231]. While *Laksmaka* was aiming at a conciliation by means of a matrimonial alliance through *Janakasimha's* son, *Chudda* by name. He was humiliated by him showing arrogant contempt[232] called as meditation on the *'Absolute'* and the *'Formless'* as *'Hiranya-garbha'* or *'Virat-purusha[233]'*. During his *garbha* days *Laksmaka* is searching for an opportunity (or revenge) as a routine matter, and by means of strenuously repeated denunciation caused that the King to take a dislike to *Janaka* and his sons[234] on the question of delay tactices. The latter two who were of the same age as the King (Raj), and who were presuming (upon him after he had got to the throne of *Kashmir,* owing to their mothers intimate familiarity, gave occasion for such (denunciations) made by the previous King like *Asoka, Akbar*, etc. As such, they imprudently made in the very palace, a royal display in respect of their horses, litters, outfits, baths, meals and the rest[235]. It is by no means proper that the ruler should keep on a footing of equality with his contemporaries after he has risen to power. It is a great humiliation for the row of lotuses when they have grown up, they must have to be jumped over by a band of frogs[236]. Having obtaining this (fact), it will be feel that a wall upon which to paint the fictions of their gross slander. Their enemies rouses in the king ill-feeling against their whole set[237]. Thus, in the month of

Sravana, the grateful King then proceeded to *Vijayesvara* in order to pay honours to the victorious commander-in-chief (*Sujji*[238]).

Utpala Captured and Killed

As soon as; *Utpala* will return from the deep of the mountains who was killed by *Pincadeva,* the commander of the watch-station (*dranga*) *of Surapura*[239]. At that time he has come back from *Pusyananada*[240], in order to raise a revolt, and had been caught by the commander of the watch-station (*drangadhipa*) *who was* searching for his horses[241] who were walking with shoes. Therefore, it is the duty of shoemaker or *'Chamar'* or a tanner to bear up their shoes. With tight laces. During such condition he was fallen to the ground wounded in the knee-joint by an arrow of the enemies. Yet before dying he will killed a soldier of his opponent who had approached him[242] without mission, only visited for the sake of their welfare. When King was returning after having paid honours to the commander-in-Chief (Sujji). And he was stopped for the time being at *Avantipura,* the commander of the watching station placed the enemy's head before his door[243] during the *'Dark Age'* of the Indian History. Therefore, that (commander) who wore his beard[244] in a thick knob, he has been proved a hammer for the heads of the enemies, drew out the painful dart of the deep wrath (from the King's heart[245]) on the behaviour of the opposite force i.e. *Brahmans*. When thus the king's first expedition started the destruction of the enemy, the people took him for one of those (Kings) who exterminate all their opponents[246]. After his return to the city some guilty persons will fled away, while *Janakasimha* and others were put in prison[247] for a long time similarly to the cycle of birth and rebirth. *Kosthesvara* and others then turned hostile to the King, as some persons who fled away caused them to became afraid of him[248]. In *Karttika;* the act illustrious King will marched out to *Samala* and attacked in various localities the enemy's host, which was fierce in battle[249]. On such conditions, *Hadigrama*[250], where King *Sussala* and those (of his side) will lost their renown, and was burned by *Sujji* whose power was mighty[251] than the others.

Fresh Irruption of Bhiksacara

During the sharp struggle for the throne, *Kosthaka* and the rest then being pressed by the King. This was the fresh irruption called by *Bhiksacara* who came back once more for the lust of throne[252]. After having marched in a single day *Yojanas*, he reached the hill village called *Silikakotta*[253]. In this war of affection, Master has been driven by his ambition, that proud (prince) thought nothing of the fatigue which arose from marching, pained by hunger and thirst, and in fear of the enemy[254] which always disturbed us on such moment when there were choas and law lessness. If fate is hostile, success turns away from the ambitions, just as the flag on a chariot when the latter moves against the wind[255] of *'Nam'* converts into religion. In the beginning, there is mere success and the other, however great his zeal, finds his efforts to be in vain. The *Amrita* was drawn from the ocean by the churning mountain (*Mandara*) after a moment's contact, but not by the son of Himalaya (*Mainaka*[256]) though he had long been (in contanct with it)[257]. Thus, the river which has left its abode, makes only falsely believe that it is flowing up again, when on its entry into the ocean it is pushed back by the tide-wave. There is no rise again for those whom fate has brought down[258] to the level of ground. Strength though he displayed for such great exertions, hostile fate yet obstructed his success at the very beginning. Now, he is vigilent in his mission[259]. No doubt, *Prthvihara's* brother (*Manujesvara*) who had been worsted, nothing know that he had arrived, placed himself at that very time under the King's protection, after cutting off his own finger[260] means finishing of his writing and printing work. As soon as; *Kosthesvara* came to him when they heard of his arrival but they are incapable of action, just like two spell-bound snakes[261] eating the small snakes whcih are wandering in free form without master. After the two had made him rest in another place from the fatigues of his march, he departed by the route of *Karkotadranga*[262] *and* proceeded to *Sulhari*[263] for a period of time. And there he stopped burning with the restless desire of invading *Kashmir*, while his powerful arms itched from excessive self-confidence[264] in the practice of *'Nam'* which is also called *'Lord Budda'*. While he will search for an opening (to break in), just like the water of a flood, the King too, who had retained to the city, was planning counter measures[265] time and again in this process. The Chamberlain who was without an equal among the ministers, was unable to bear up with *Sujji's* excessive laughtiness and was eagerly bent on prosecuting intrigues[266] with King to give the realistic approach in '*History*' which is very pious subject. Then the elder brother of *Dhanya*[268] *(Udaya)* who purified his body by immersion in the water of *Ganga,* with the help of *'Nam'*. He gained the self-confidence of the fickle-minded King[269]. Hence, his people, who were familiar to the King, who had been held in regard by him for a long time; and became then troubled in their mind because they got no offices[270] of the society. They are wandering in disgrace manners or without dignity as they are the degraded man of the society. While *Jayasimha* is placing the burden of affairs on his father's ministers, these shallowminded persons could not bring themselves to await their time[271] to check-up the situation as a real doctor of the soul.

Intrigues against Sujji

Chamberlain (*Laksmaka*), on the other hand, made an intrigues against *Sujji* to oust him, just like his allied with them, though they were not friends, because (he recognised that) they would be very useful (for that purpose[272]) in the advancement of the man. After passing some months, King's fate will fell in sudden (*luta*) kind of disease which always increased [273] for the time being, as his recovery was made doubtful owing to (the appearance of) boils, tumours, diarrhoea, indigestion, and other ailments, the country became agitated[274] on such occasions. While the lord (of the land) i.e. *Brahman* was in such a condition, his dynasty being singly maintained by him. As soon as, the enemy became powerful, the Damaras on the latter's side saw the kingdom already ruined[275]. Considering what action was beneficial for the future as well as the present *Sujji* then wished to put on the throne the King's only son *Parmandi*, who was born from the illustrious *Ganalekha* and was (then) five years old, and consulted about this with his (Parmandis) maternal uncle, the son of *Garga* (*Pancacandra*[276]). As stated by "*Sujji,* together with his son, wishes to betray you, while you are in such a condition, and is now cunningly treating day and night with *Pancacandra* and his people." Thus, spoke then the Chamberlain who had found his opportunity, and at his instigation *Dhanya* and the rest to the King, and the latter took this to be true[277]. It is true from the study that the (verses which are describing generally the thoughlessness of Kings who allow themselves to be misled and imposed upon by foolish parasites. The life and position of honourable persons are at the mercy of rogues whose whimsical suggestions captivate the simple-minded ruler[278]). Is he, indeed, ever seen that King, whose mind is firm, and whom rogues cannot plainly make dance like a mechanical doll[278] built by the artisan with devotion of love. Alas, the universal ruin which rises from the Kings not being able to discriminate between their servants, it does not cease even at the present day owing to the subjects sinfulness[279] led by the Brahmans. When *Sujji* came as before to inquire after the King's health, he saw that guards had been placed (at the door) from distrusted felt afflicated with affication[280] to recognised that in the Kings heart kindness (*daksinya*) had turned into disfavours (*Vamata*), just as in the image reflected by the mirror (right is turned to left), and became indifferent[281] to everybody. While his visits to the palace became rare, owing to his feeling annoyed, the intriguers removed altogether that attachment which the King has felt for him. Where as the deceitful *Citraratha*, the son of a Brahman councillor (*asthanadvija*[282]) and a follower of *Sujji,* ruined the King's welfare by his counsels, which raised opposition[283] at the appropriate time. When the King had recovered *Sujji* was seen in the palace distributing rich gifts to express his joy. As he went outside, he expected to be called (back by the King, but this not having happened), he went to his house[284]. In this way, King did not conciliate him, but considered the way in which he could be attacked, as he had a powerful army (at his disposal[285]). It has been come to our notice that he deprived of his offices, his followers, having nothing to hope for would abandon him, he quickly bestowed his official charges on others[286]. No doubt, king granted the garland (*Sraj*[287]) of the office of chief-justice (*rajasthana*) to *Dhanya,* that of the commander-in-chief to *Udaya*[288] and the charge of *Kheri* to *Rilhana*. At the same time, King had openly shown his hostility by the withdrawal of his offices, *Sujja* found himself with but few followers remaining and became alarmed[289] in the various compartment; as a final judgement is coming out in this world again for the time being.

Sujji Goes Into Exile

Thereupon, Sujji will go into exile for the time being feeling dishonoured set out from the city for a pilgrimage to the *Ganga,* taking with him the bones of King *Sussala*[290]. While on leaving he will pass near the royal palace, he eagerly expected to be asked (to stop), but neither the King's attendants nor the King himself held him back[291]. In order to manifest the pride he took in having *Sujji* banished, the chamberlain placed his own son over the escort to guard him, on his treasure and other (property[292]) of the mind. At that time *Sujji* felt pain when he thought: "*Laksmaka*[293] has given me his son as a guard (as if to show) that punishment and favour were dependent on himself"[294]. *Laksmaka's*[295] son (Word) turned back from the 'Gate'. The guileless (Sujji) will proceeded slowly to *Parnotsa* and made *Bhagika* descend from the *Lohara* hill state[296]. He also handed over the charge of that castle of (*Lohara*) to *Preman,* the King's foster-brother, who had been sent by the Chamberlain[297] during the very critical situation. Thus, *Sujji* removed by abandoning *Lohara* the apprehension which troubled the King. He passed the bad summer season at *Rajapuri*[298]. While *Laksmaka* acquired some renown as he was able to make ministers rise and fall like play-balls, and as he was held the Damaras in check[299]. It has been impelled by his desire to create a rivalry with *Sujji,* then he had to place *Rajamangala* the royal blood as the incharge of the *'Gate*[300]*'*. He thought in his jealousy mind that this brave compatriot of *Sujji,* if he helped by his own riches, he would destroy his renown King[301]. He, by bestowing (Sujji's) offices (on others) was the cause of *Sujji's* wandering about on the road with a sword-bearer as his (only) companion, hungry, miserable, and an object of ridicule[302]. Who would not be able to unfit persons in the place of fit ones i.e, *'Chamar'*. But even the elements are unable to endow the former with latter's high qualities like *'Nam'* or '*Sabad*[303]'. Now the Siva is able to throw in haste on his own body, ashes from a funeral pyre which do not befit him, but fit for sandal-ointment. But eve, he makes the three worlds rise and perish in accordance with his will, is manifestly incapable of endowing those (ashes) with the (sandal)-perfume of the *'Lord*[304]*'*. As *Rajamangala* was not sufficiently strong tobe able to rival *Sujji, Laksmaka* despatched his messengers to call back *Sanjapala*[305] from abroad[306] to attack over the Brahmans, who have been traped in the material life. As now the land lacked of strongmen, the King (Dr. Raj Kumar) having regard to the importance of the affairs and took *Kosthesvara* among his intimate advisers though he disliked him[307]. When he had gained the confidence of the King, and the latter being satisfied was pleasing him with various gifts, he too was attacked by a skin-disease (*luta*) while keeping in the City[308] peace and development for public welfare.

Sujji Intrigues against Jayasimha

In this contest, King thus, put (upon himself) a multitude of restriants from state reasons against *Jayasimha, Somapala* and other intriguers induced *Sujji* to become hostile (to the King[309]). Keeping in view, he having been hurt in his honour, declared that he could effect the conquest of *Kashmir* with a mere stick, and promised its throne to *Somapala*[310]. The latter King promised him in marriage the daughter of his sister (*Rani*) and (his own) daughter. In the meantime the King (*Jayasimha*) prudently employed diplomacy and bribing to *Sujji*[311]. Therefore, *Somapala* and *Sujji* acted unwisely at that time by not effecting the marriage of the two princesses in haste and thus gave time to their opponents[312]. *Somapala* was then induced by *Jayasimha's* stratagems as well as by the omens he saw, to pay less attention to *Sujji*[313]. Hence, the chamberlain proceeded there in person and brought the lord of *Rajapuri* (*Somapala*) to the frontier of his territory in order to arrange for the marriage of the princesses (from both sides[314]).

Marriage Alliance of Jayasimha and Somapala

No doubt, *Soma(pala)* married the King's *Ambaputrika,* born from the queen *Kalhanika*[315]. When *Jayasimha* had gone after completing this marriage, the thoughtful chamberlain conducted *Nagalekha*, (*Somapala's*) sister's daughter, to the King (as his bride[316]). Now it has been seen that on alliance had been effected between the two countries, *Sujji* found his opportunities gone and commenced for the *Ganga* in *Hemanta* (months of *Margasivas* and *Pausa*[317]). It shows that he had lost his mental power on account of the great insult induced him to join the side of *Bhiksu* at *Jalamdhara*[318] and met with *Jyesthapala*: "When you and *Bhiksacara* join in the command of an army, neither *Upendra* (*Visnu*) nor the great *Indra* are able to offer resistance." "We shall take revenge on those two kings, *'Word'* the one who insulted you, to whom he owed his throne and the otehr (who insulted you) while you stopped in his territory[319]." Incited by him with such words he was preparing to proceed to *Bhiksu* who was stopping with *Dengapala*, but *Bhagika* kept him back and addressed him thus in excitement: "It is not right that you should do this before you have thrown the bone of your lord into the water of the *Ganga*[320]." Now, *Sujji* took an oath by sacred libation that he would definitely join with them after he had bathed in the celestial stream (*Ganga*) and then started to carry out what he had undertaken[321] to do justice with *'Nature'*. On the other side, King, who had put everything on the chamberlains shoulders, did not think that the kingdom was in a secure condition, owing to the want of energetic action (against the Damars, etc[322]). Chambelain (*Laksmaka*) conciliated whosoever rose in opposition (against the King), and then looked every day at the latter when he stood by his side, as it were with condenscension form[323] . In the meanwhile, *Udaya* the commander-in-chief, slew by treachery the proud *Prukutu,* son of *Kaliya*[324] demon proceeded to *Madavarajya*. At the sametime, *Laksmaka*, with his scant consideration, he killed all the Damaras who were full of distrust and unruly, attacked by the commander-in-chief[325].

Bhiksacara Arrives in Visalata

As soon as, *Bhiksacara* arrives at the conclusion of this study, he only obtained this opening and had learned that the Damaras had been fallen off from the King. He proceeded at the commencement of the winter to *Visalata,* planning how he might throw *Kashmir* into confusion till *Sujji* should arrive after bathing in the *Ganga*[326]. In this struggle, he was prevented from the desired invasion of the territory (of Kashmir), by the Chamberlain (*Laksmaka*) *who held* the Damaras in check by the winter season[327]. Now, he had been called in by the *Tikka* who was pledged to thorough enmity against the opponent (*Jayasimha*) by the treachery, (he had committed) against the latter's father, and was encouraged by all prominent Damaras[328]. While awaiting the arrival of *Sujji* which was in a position to posses of the throne, he was stopping in the castle called *Banasala*[329] belonging to *Tikka's* son-in-law, *Bhagika*, a *Khasa*-lord. Thinking himself safe in that (castle), though it was of but little height, he made by means of messengers the whole host of Damaras rise in rebellion[330]. For the time being then *Sujji* returned after having bathed in the *Ganga,* spreading in advance joy for his friends and fear for his enemies[331] called *Brahmans.* He welcomes, *Simhadeva's* thought that it would be as great a danger for *Somapala* as for himself it *Bhiksu,* whom he had persecuted, and *Sujji,* should unite, and accordingly asked that ruler to make an effort to win over the latter. The frightened *Somapala* employed a ruse (for this purpose[332]) against the Damaras, during the hard period of Indian history.

Negotiations with Sujji

Sujji had arrived in the morning at *Jalamdhara* (Jalandhara), and was about to proceed to *Bhiksacara,* when *Somapala's* envoy came to him in the evening[333]. These deities may be classified as under:

1. Deities representing the principal phenomena or agents of *Nature,* viz, (1) Father *Dyaus* (= Zeus, Diespiter), the radiant God of the Upper region or Heaven; (2) Mother Earth *Prithvi (Dyava- Prithvi,* Heaven and Earth (1. 143, 2.159, 15, etc); (3) *Varuna,* the All-comprehending Sky; (4) *Indra*, the God of Thunder and Rain ; (5) The Sun worshiped in five forms as (a) *Surya,* source of light; (b) *Savita* as source of fertility ; (c) *Mitra* as beneficant energy; (d) *Pushan* as source of plant-life and agriculture; and (c) *Vishnu* as the swift moving Sun; (6) *Rudra*, Siva; (7) the two Asvins representing the morning and evening stars; (8) the *Maruts,* the wind-Gods attending the *Rudra*, together with (9) *Vayu* and (10) *Vata*; (11) *Parjanya*, the God of rain, water and rivers, and (12) *Ushas*, the Goddess of Dawn inspiring some of the best *Rigvedic* poetry.

The popularity of some of these deities in national worship is liable to change. For instance, Indra becomes more important as the national deity as the Aryans make their progress from the dry regions of north-western India towards the eastern regions of rain and storm. *Varuna* who is also called *Asura* (Corresponding to Iranian God Ahura Mazda) gains in status as the guardian of cosmic and moral law under the abstract name of *Rita* or Truth.

II. *Domestic Deities*. (1) Agni and (2) *Soma* (dragught of immortality) who has inspired most mystical hymns.

III. *Abstract Deities* (typifying qualities): (1) *Dhatri,* Creator, (2) *Vidhata*, Ordainer, (3) *Visvakarma,* Creator of Cosmos, (4) *Prajapati*, Lord of Creatures (5) *Sraddha,* faith, (6) *Manyu*, wrath, (7), *Rita*, Truth, (8) *Hiranyagarbha, the* implicit, (9) *Brahmanaspati*, Lord of Prayer and (1) *Virat-purusha*, Oversoul.

IV. Minor Deities: (1) *Ribhus,* aerial elves, (2) *Apsaras,* water-nymphs, (3) *Gandharvas,* aerial sprites, (4) *Adityas,* sons of *Aditi,* the primeval goddess.

It may be noted that the popular deities now worshipped such as *Vishnu* or *Siva* are known to the *Rigveda*. Besides *Rudra,* the Rigvedic name of Siva is *Isana*. *Brahma* may be traced in Rigvedic *Dhata* or *Vidhata*. The Rigvedic pantheon is planned to accommodate the religious needs of persons of different degrees and states of spiritual development from the lowest to the highest, leading from worship of *'Nature'* upto Nature's God and to conception of the One in the Many. Apart from the highest form of worship as meditation on the *'Absolute'* and the *'Formless'* as *Hiranya-garbha* or *Virtat-purusha*, the popular worship was ceremonial and ritualistic in character in the form of sacrifice or offering of food and dirnk like milk, grain, ghee, flesh and *soma* to the chosen deity for securing his favour or boon. This ceremonial worship was so far elaborated as to call for seven classes of Priests to take charge of separate specialized function, viz, the *Hotri* for reciting hymns; the *Adhvaryu* for manual functions, thc *Udgatri* for singing the *Samans*, each with his staff of assistants. Some sacrifices would be lasting for months and could be performed only by the aristocracy (*Maghavans*) and royalty.

But this religion of sacrifice (*Yajna*) *and also its* mystical and symbolic aspect in which it was understood by the spiritually advanced people who saw its origin in the primary impulse felt by the once to manifest himself in the many. He first created out of him the *Virat-purusha* who found that there was naught outside. Him and so had to find out of himself the basis and materials of this projected creation. For this purpose, he offered up this own *Virat-deha* as a sacrifice for the sake of his creation that self-sacrifice is the *dharma* of every creature of God, the law of his being. Man is created after God's image. Man, like his Creator, must also maintain his little system and serve the small world in which he moves by the utmost self-sacrifice of which he is capable. Life must be an offering the Duty. Religion is a course of self-sacrifice; 'The Good Shepherd giveth. His life for the sheep[334].' Act upon (receiving) this message, he renounced the intention of joining the enemy. *Jyesthapala* had urged him on (to the latter course), while *Bhagika* dissuaded him. "The king will relieve you of the debt you have incurred abroad, and will himself, at my request, bestow an office upon you[335]." This (message) of *Somapala* was told to him daily by his envoy, and thus he started for (Somapala's) territory, abandoning his eager wish of (joining) the enemy[336]. In the month of *Vaisakha* the commander-in-chief *Udaya* crossed the pass (*samkata*) and began fighting with *Bhiksa* and his *Khasa* followers[337]. When the former's force i.e Brahman or soul which was at first small, had grown large, *Bhiksu* threw himself into the castle (of *Banasala*) *and was* besieged there[338]. Thus, the King who had moved out of *Vijayesvara,* thereupon reinforced the camp of the commander-in-chief by sending him various troops[339] from time to time to conquerer the enemy.

Siege of Banasala (Banahal)

The royal troops of the *Jayasimha* sieged the *Banasala* by throwing stones from catapults, showers of arrows and various (other) missiles of the '*Nam*', and those in the castle defended themselves by rolling down stones[340] at different places in the road. The royal army, though large, could not attack on these places those in the castle, while stones were falling and arrows marked with *Bhiksu's* name[342]. After one month only and some days had passed, *Dhanya[343] ('Word')* effected a breach at the foot of the castle and possessed himself of the water (supply) has been stored in a tank[344] to wash the dirty earth. Those who held the permanent fort and by force could not be got at. Moreover, they displayed then greedy intentions, keeping in view that King (Jayasimha) was eager to use stratagems, wished to give trouble to his opponent[345] who are not the lover of *'Nam'*. Thereupon, King despatched the chamberlain (*Laksmaka*) *along* with Damaras, chiefs, ministers, and Rajaputras to bring this affair to a successful issue[346] like *Mahabharata or Ramyana Kosthesvara, Trillaka[347]* and others followed him with the intention of extricating *Bhiksu* from the dangerous situation in which he was[348] involved in the study of *'Nam'* which is 'unlimited' and 'endless'. When the *Laksmaka* saw from the top of the mountain-pass the castle of small height below, and looked at his own numberless host, he thought that it was (already) taken[349] into consideration due to their actions and deeds. On the following day, those who had been there before, and those who had accompanied the Chamberlain (*Laksmaka*), proceeded to the attack, hoping to take the castle by the full strength of their army[350] during the final attack. Notwithstanding their, great number they were so repulsed by the hail of stones from those (in the castle) that they became convinced of this (understanding) not being achievable by sheer prowers[351] in the field of *'Nam'*. The heads which the stones carried off from the bodies of brave soldiers, appeared, with their stremas of blood, like bee-hives (thrown down by stone-hits) from the tops of trees with the bees issuing from them[352] to siege the *Banahal* and other areas of the *Jambu* or Jammu territory. *Kosthesvara* committed there somehow an act of folly which caused the ruin of *Bhiksu,* of himself, and other *Lavanyas*[354]. *Jayasimha* has merely to show that there was no one brave like himself, fought with great mighty, and this led to the death of *Bhiksu*[355] *in the 'Nam' or 'word' as an ultimate truth.*

Bhiksacara Betrayed by the Khasas

Bhiksacara in his dangerous position betrayed by the *Khasas, Bhikascara* assured himself by saying: "*Kosthesvara* and we are on one side, the other Damaras are dependent on him. This great force which is seen, will in the end be to our advantage". But it was to happen differently[356] at different occasion during the time of pious war. They then thought war should be certain to decide the good over the evils: "if he (*Bhiksacara*) puts his trust even in that hostile *Kosthesvara* what can be expected from the others there[357]?" Who are without *'Nam'*. The sly *Laksmaka*, on the other hand, under the difficult circumstances he forced to promise with *Tikka,* though he had treacherously killed the King's father, that he would be put (back) in his own seat (*Upavesana*[358]). The *Khasa*- lord (*Bhagika*), he bribed by offering him great villages, gold and other precious things like *'Nam',* and induced him to exert himself for *Bhiksu's* ruin[359] with the help of *'Nam'* or *'Chamar'*. After this, *Nanda*, the brother-in-law of the *Khasa-Lord*, were gone to and fro (between the two), he brought *Tikka* before the *Laksmaka* and got him re-instated on his post[360]. Meanwhile, *Kosthesvara* and the other Damaras saw the friendship of the *Laksmaka* with *Tikka*, they took

Bhiksu's death for certain[361] purpose to compile the society of *'Nam'*. *Jayasimha* agitated thereby on the attitude of *Bhiksu,* they wished to set him free for sometime and sent messengers to the *Khasa,* promising to give him gold with many (other) presents[362] i.e. 'Nam'. The *Khasa* however, thought: "if we let *Bhiksu* go after taking a bribe, then he will think that it was *Kosthesvara* and the rest who have saved his life. In anger at this, either he will kill me when he gets the throne, or *Dengapala* whose (Power) reaches far. Therefore, we must carefully keep by the side of *Jayasimha.*" He replied to them in accordance with these thoughts, and (made them), tell *Bhiksu* when we was in the privy: "Escape from this place after removing a plank[363]." The proud (prince), however, thought of the disgrace (in which he would fall) among the people it he were to leave through the privy, with his body smeared over with filth like a dog, and did not leave[364] this universe without the 'Nam'. No doubt, *Laksmaka* who knew (how to bribe) his time, in the morning conciliated with *Kosthesvara,* who is acting in a secret manner, the messenger of God. He has been defeated and insulted by the *'Word'* with the intention of causing a commotion among the troops[365] of *Jayasimha on such moments.*

Attack on Bhiksacara

After the *Khasa*, *Jayasimha* attacks on *Bhiksacara,* and his people had given hostages to *Laksmaka* and the rest made him happy after day-break. Thereafter, strenuous efforts will be made to kill *Bhiksu*[366]. The King who at *Vijayaksetra* was in great agitation and was every moment askings news from the messengers about the development of situation, who came and went[367] for working their duty as a faithful soldier. "What? this boy-King and these boy-ministers think to achieve the destruction of that *Bhiksu,* whom the old King, notwithstanding his violent exertious could not subdue during ten years in so many battles? How does this agree[368]? It would be agree on the question of obtaining *'Nam'* from the Master "in a moment the *Khasas* will come and laughing carry off whatever can be got. Surely, these here will flee routed and looted by the enemies[369] for sometimes. "*Kosthaka* stands apart and *Trillaka* here is his relative, and even these who are of the (royal) court, have grown fat with what *Bhiksacara* had left from his food[370]. "Who is the new comer who could work the King's good? To be sure, the stores, here have only arrived for the advantage of this (enemy[371])". At the same time, men will talked in there tents, thus the castle was surrounded by the ministers's troops with drawn swords[372]. "O Shame, he who has long been harassed, is to be killed singly. Yet for this purpose they have shamelessly closed a ring (around him) with all their soldiers[373]." Whatever they spoke, and silent like the ocean was the host, with the glittering weapons of the *'Nam'* bright waves and the rolling eyes of the soldiers resembling like fishes[374]. No doubt, agitated and frightened were the men; thinking inwardly: "Will *Bhiksu* fly up through the air, or jump over the army with the leap of a deer, or will he like the down-poured from an evil cloud strike down at all at once, when he whose valour is wanderful, takes up this sword at last[375] i.e. *'Nam' or 'Chamar'* for the theory of mind. So far as the success of the ministers are concerned, Now, it has been removed and objective has been achieved. It was due to the King's lustre[376]. While the troops with eyes raised up expected by *Bhiksu* to rush forth, a single man with a drawn sword came out of the castle[377] to fight with the enemies and Damaras. Now, he has been surrounded by weeping women, and behind him followed some men with fluttering under-garments of saffron colour[378] like Bhartiya Janata Party, C.p. M. etc. The people in their expectation said: "Here is *Bhiksu* fleeing from captivity of *Nam"*. Then, they heard it was *Tikka* who had come out[379] from the 'Schedule Caste family' for the fighting with the safforn party, etc.

Desertion of Tikka

Due to the desertion of *Tikka, Jayasimha* having been betrayed by *Bhiksu,* feared that he would be killed by him or by the King's followers, when the struggle began, he has come out[380] in forefront for the fighting against the enemy. In order to convince the people of his innocence, he drew his sword and dagger as if to cut open his abdomen, but it was restrained by his own followers[381] because they have been trapped in the pleasure of life with the Brahmans. After passing with his followers the royal army, which opened the way for him, now he moved to the brink of a hill-spring which was closed by[382] him for a long time and forget it. *Jayasimha* breathed again in relief when he had at last got to water after leaving the castle (*durga;* or, after having escaped from danger), and pressed by the other Damaras, began to play his tricks[383] for the development in the field of life. "The sun is setting on the day. Let *Bhiksu* be kept safe for a short period of time. At night the Damaras will raise the siege." Upon his speaking, thus, the murderers (sent) by the ministers began to climb up (to the castle) in the company with hostages, but were stopped by the *Khasas* rolling down boulders[384] of life. The soldiers thereupon with (ironical) shouts and clapping of hands attacked (with such words) the ministers, who were confused in their minds[385] when they listened the depth of knowledge of *'Nam'*. "The enemies of the King have escaped from a critical situation. What advantage have the ministers achieved by giving riches (merely as it were) to help the opponent to the throne[386]? Thus, the sun was sinking together with the royal cause, *Laksmaka* asked *Khasa's* brother-in-law, who was a hostage for a long period, what this (meant[387]) is to serve the society; but there is confusion in every step due to the self-interest. *Tikka* replied: 'Even a water-carrying slave-woman (*Kumbhadasi*[388]) may frustrate a plan. How should we face the *Khasas* when we were not present there[389]." *Laksmaka* thereupon dismissed *Ananda* with the words: "Go you to remove the opposition of the *Khasas,"* and was laughed at by the other minister (for this[390]). Now, the King, who was very far-sighted, apprehended an enterprise coming from the house of *Dengapala* by the way of *Visalata*[391] to form an alliance with the 'Father'. On this account, King was laying his far-reaching snares for this object during the time of study. He had already won over, with the rest, (*Ananda*), the brother-in-law of the lord of the castle, he was being a person of importance[392]. *Laksmaka*, therefore, remained calm at that time of confusion, knowing that Ananda will then set free from the fighting. He could be get again like a trained bird[393]. He expressed to them: "If this affair fails, my bold action yet does of killing that brother-in-law of the *Khasa*, if everything were lost[394]? but 'Nam' will not be lost, this is unprecious kind of gift of the 'Nature'. Owing to the King's good fortune keeping its power intact-with his 'Father' from the very beginning of the man. The *Khasa's* brother-in-law made them all (in the castle) give in, and (then) from the top of the castle called up the murderers and the rest[395] to join him. Now the spirits of the robbers (Damaras) rose to their throats, the ministers minds to uncertainly, and the love desires of the celestial maids to the highest pitch, while the murderers (climbed) up the hill[396], now, they have been dropped down on the earth to clean the earth as 'sweepers'. Whereas, King *Bhiksu's* followers had (previously) as if they wished to follow him in death, been girdling their loins with leather-straps, had proclaimed themselves everywhere in the fighting by using sword and dagger, like their master, arrows marked with their own names, had reddened their underlips with betel-wings, their lions with leather-straps, had proclaimed themselves everywhere in the fighting by using sword and dagger, like their master, arrows marked with their own names, had reddened their underlips with betel-wings, and had occupied themselves with dressing their hair and beards. No doubt, his death was certain at that time, they stopped this and ran quickly to the texts of *Kosthesvara* and the rest for the protection[397] of the followers. As soon as *Tikka* saw himself surrounded by *Laksmaka's* soldiers, whom the latter had cuningly sent up one by one. He took fright and cut off his finger[398] for the sake of promise. It has been observed that *Khasas* were fearing that he might be flee, but he was watching him at that time, because he had a problem in his mind and had not taken food during those days[399] on the question of *Khasas's* fearing, now this problem has been cleared to some extent.

Bhiksacara's Last Struggle

There was a long struggle of the *Bhiksacara* to fight against the *Jayasimha,* and who was annoyed by the delay tectices, made by the murderers. *Jayasimha* was diverting his mind over a game of dice to win the favour of *Bhiksacara.* As soon as, the murdereres entered the courtyard of the mansion, wishing to attack him, he got up and completed the game of dice[400], which was nearly finsihed by the master. *Bhiksacara* was inwardly as little agitated as a lover who, while at play with his beloved. He has to get up to meet a friend arriving[401] from the Heaven. "What is the use of slaying many also to-day? because they are the fast friend from the very beginning of the man, therefore, they are the lovers of the master. Thus, he thought on this friendship, and leaving his bow went outside armed only with his sword[402]. Therefore, his dark hair became thin by long cares; the fringes of his hero's band (*Virapatta*[403]) were fluttering like brilliant flags; the glitter of his faultless conch-shaped ear-rings, which played upon his cheeks, and the shine of his sandal-painted[404] marks seemed like a naughty smile; with his sword, eyes and under clothes which were (flawing) like firebrands, he made it visible, as it were at the end of a wonderful career his, legs had got across(each other and had caused him to fall); with the quivering, clean corners of his mouth, which were drawn to the fore by his safflower-coloured underlips. He appeared like the (personified) dignity of what is dignified, like the very ornament of pride and a continual and never-ceasing display of honour and might. Nothing indicated his rapid fall. *'Word'*, thus, the expectant people saw *Bhiksu* move out to face his opponents[405] on spot. Keeping in view, the sharp struggle of the valiant *Kumariya*, the grandson of *Madhu* from a royal race, and also *Raktika* the brother of *Jyesthapala,* came out and following him[406]. Moreover, *Gargika,* a follower of *Bhiksu,* held back singly by showers of arrows the assailants who were entering through various buildings, low and high[407] of the Damaras. Under the (shower of the) arrows which left his bow, they were seen flying, just like elephants under (a shower of) hailstones driven by the east wind[408] of the *'Nam'*. This repulser of the enemy was at last forced to retreat when the stones thrown by the wicked *Khasas* had wounded his body and broken his bow[409] with the help of *'Nam'*. When he was fled away, the soldiers entered by various passages, and came all within close contact of *Bhiksu* and his companions[410] also marched away due to the fear of *Bhiksu's* attack. In this, battle, there was one big soldiers holding a spear ran away quickly against *Bhiksu's* single sword-bearer whose fortitude could not at once be noticed[411] to *Jayasimha. Bhiksu,* who was interested to became his attendant, ran in haste, parried his spear as he was making his thrust possible, and caught hold of his hair[412] which was undressed. Being a barbar, he dressed his hair remarkable that he is specialist *'Barbar'*. *Jayasimha* also hit him with his sword and he was mortally wounded. Moreover, *Kumariya* and *Raktika* gave him further strokes[413] to kill him completely. When this man had been slain the three were attacked by the compact mass of the enemy's soldiers, who carried various weapons[414] at that time. Their weapons were scared away the assailants, and they were left alone just as trees when a great snake in their hollow drives away the bee-swarms[415]. Whereas, the assailants not being able to kill them with swords, spears and the like (weapons), moved away and then from afar covered by them with showers of arrows[416]. At the same moment *Bhiksacara*, lion like, was breaking through the cage formed by the arrows, the *Khasas* hurled down from the mansion heavy showers of stones[417]. No doubt, terrible shower of stones bruised his head and as he was running an arrow pierced his side, and penetrated into his liver[418] the right place of the *'Nam'* or *'Chamar'* as depicted by the artist in the painting of *'Guru Ravi Dass'*.

Death of Bhiksacara(1130 A.D.)

As soon as, *Bhiksacara* death will took place, after making three steps he quickly fell, causing the earth to sake, while removing the tremor of the enemies, which had been intense for a long period[419] in the Indian history. No doubt; at that time, *Kumariya* will also wounded to death by an arrow which had pierced his groin, fell even (then) before the feet of his lord[420]. Moreover, *Raktika* will be disabled by an arrow which hit him in a vital part of the life, and though living yet, fell to the ground as if life[421] less in condition. Whereas, *Bhiksu* who is falling in the company of men of high lineage, shone forth, just as a pinnacle that is thrown down by the lightening along with flowering trees[422]. In this sharp struggle so great a host of Kings *Brahmans.* But *Bhiksu* obtained the highest place not in disgrace but in honour[423] to compile 'A New Society' i.e. called 'Radha Soami.' Though fate, ever adverse to him, now *Bhiksacara* had secured his defeat, yet verily, he defied it even, at his end by his unbroken power[424] i.e. 'Nam'. Was he not a begger when compared with the former Kings, whose riches were great? i.e. *'Nam' or 'Words'* in regard to a noble death they possessed, however, are nothing compared with him[425]. He is such kind of 'Power'. As soon as, the enemy's soldiers came up greatly satisfied with themselves, *Kumariya* even in such a condition and such pains, fought them with his knife[426]. Now, *Jayasimha* disabled by wages of strokes, he yet moved about as if he ought to fight with the power of 'Nam', and thus the enemies recognizing his powers gave him many thrusts as they spread out[427] already, but it was not understandable to the public. Though the *Khasas* made mockery of them.: "Enough you fools, with your strokes at this dead man," the hostile soldiers hit the dead *Bhiksu* again and again[428]. Keeping in view that he is unable to fight against the Brahmans. It has been felt by *Rattika* that we are unable to use his arms owing to the terrible pains caused by his wound and who was on the point of death because his power has been sieged by some vile soldiers[429] of the King (Dr. Raj Kumar). Therefore, on the tenth day of the dark half of Jyaistha in the year (of the *Laukika* era four thousand two hundred and) six (A.D. 1130) this King was killed after a life of thirty years and nine months[430]. In admiration of his power even those praised him for whom he had been the cause of long troubles and the reason of their utter ruin[431] was his pious thought. He always displayed simplicity and toleration towards the problem. Therefore, his head showed several *Nalikas* moving eyes, quivering brows, and a smiling mouth, as if life were in it[432]. Once upon a time his body was proceeded into the company of the *Apsaras* in heaven; the other here on hearth, knowing that the earth and water were cold, even though he entered for fire[433] and recovered again as the process of the 'Nam'.

Jayasimha Receives Bhiksacara's Head

As soon as, *Jayasimha* received the head of *Bhiksacara,* on the following day, then, the ministers brought the heads of these three before the King, who was stopping at *Vijayaksetra*[434]. It has been observed that *Jayasimha* is as the ocean, which has shown its wonderful character by producing Laksmi, the nectar (*Sudha*), the treasures (*ratna*), the elephant (*Airavata*), the horse(*Uccaihsravas*), the moon and other (wonders). He displayed in various ways his wonderful character which astonishes the world, and his power cannot be measured by anyone[435] historian of the world. He did not pride himself: "I have slain him whom my father could not reach," nor did he rejoice: "Destroyed is this thorn (in the side) of kings". He, being free from deceit in his nature and full of generosity, did not think with wrath when he saw *Bhiksu's* head: "He had make my father's head wonder about[436]", but reflected as follows: "One ought to see in his person only its innate noble character, but not the change (produced in it) by hatred, just as (one sees) in the crystal its purity, but not its head produced by the sun-rays[437]." "Alas, from *Utkarsa* to this King not one has been seen to depart by a natural death[438]". "Those even who were before this King's favourites, view to-day the head which (is all that) remains of him, as if they had no concern[439]". Thus, we must thought of the lord of the earth which rare generosity, and quickly gave orders that the last honours be paid to such an enemy[440] who never believe in this Universe. After passing the Dark Age, away him (Jayasimha). He thought of his rise and death and reflected again and again on the wonderful the nature of mundane existance[441] will be displayed On the Day of Judgement. At that time, people, too, thought that even for a thousand years there would certainly not be trouble in the land from rival kinsmen[442]. Such occasion, fate burns the thin grass and produces in (its place) thick verdure; after a day of intense heat it sends rain. As its actions follow strange courses, there is no relying by rule (upon fate) which is fickle in its decisions[443] and could not achieve the objective of live. While a brave man after finishing a task fate puts upon him, a heavy burden of the fresh tasks[444] like *'Sudarnama'* and *'Early History of the Jammu Region'*. Therefore, the foot of the first rider, who was fatigued the horse by long exercising it, has not yet left entirely the second stirrup, when another rider gets on the pained back of the horse, which is counting upon getting comfort from the removal of its load, while it still carries the saddle[445] of the *'Nam' or 'Word'*. As soon as the kingdom of the King had thus for a single night become free from enemies, there stepped before the King a letter carrier silent with sorrow[446] and grief after the event.

Report of Lohara Rebellion (1130 A.D.)

As soon as, the question of the perplexed councillors, *Jayasimha* reported that on the very day of the rebellion when *Bhiksacara*, whose enemity caused such dangers, had found his death, the soldiers garrisoning the castle (of *lohara*) had, at night or during 'the fiends of darkness' by violent means, bloodshed, law and order, (liberated and) crowned *Lothana,* the younger of the two step-brothers, *Salhana* and *Lothana*, or King *Sussala*, whom the latter had before put in prison on the *Lohara*-hill, *'Word' or 'Nam'* the elder having died (in the meantime[447]). *Jayasimha* expressed that (*Lothana*) had left his prison, together with his son and nephews, five(in all), who were full of pride and aspired to the throne of *Kashmir* and that he was master of the treasury[448]. During such moments, even the guardians of the quarters might have watched the King with attention, expecting that he would be consumed by sorrow, faint, lament, fall (to the ground) with out-stretched arms, fall asleep in his mental confusion or taking to staring, *'Chamar'* when struck down by the lightening of this evil message whcih fell just as his mind had already been eased by the cessation of a long-lasting evil in the society like Caste System or Class System and other cases of rapes and bribery. Yet he did not change in appearance, conduct or gestures[449]. It appears that there was no other King, who did ever since in the beginning of the 'New Society' or other kind of word like 'piety of *Dhamma'* did by, which no one else could have overcome, and which would have been (for others) altogether unbearable[450] by the enemies. There is a commitment from the very beginning that his father will reconquered by force the lost kingdom of Ancient India, and he himself had freed his father's throne ·from enemies[451] as per the agreement of the *Nature*. For the time being, thc stronghold and the treasury have been (now) lost. Where a boy, without a (proper) name even, thc only onc lcft of rival -kins men, without wealth and friends, had caused for many years calamities which destroyed riches and honour, *Chamar* in that land fond of rebellion there arose now, when this single foe had been slain, six enemies possessed of friends a stronghold and riches, while the subjects of this territory (of Kashmir) were disaffected and the treasury became[452] empty. In addition to this, even the descendant of Raghu (*Ramacandra*), we know, could not vie in fortitude with this King (Dr. Raj Kumar), who had proved his greatness by passing such a test of the pious, friendship like *'Nam'*. Once the father (of *Ramacandra*) in recounting (his son's) virtues, remembered that the latter's disposition had remained unaltered when he had endowed him with the royal power of the '*Nam*' and when he had exiled him during his service time six years *Poonch* and four years in Kargil Government Colleges and spoke thus: 'I have not noticed the slightest change in his person when he was called to the coronation ceremony, and when he was sent out into the forest." Thereupon *Dasaratha* had told him to stop for a limited period in lovely forest regions accompanied by his wife and younger brother, and had promised to restore his fortune[453] which he deserves. Though, the two had thus undergone for a secret transition from happiness to misfortune, yet there is great difference between them owing to the peculiarity of their respective lots[454]. It shows that their fate, surely, cut off the whole of the manifold resources, because it intended to show to the people that (Jayasimha's) power was not dependent on matieral causes[455] it becomes from the *'Teachings of the Public'* good faith. Who would have thought much of the wonderful achievements to be related of this King, if his means had been abundant[456]? Therefore, the King whose resolve was deep like the sea, *Sudar or Samudar,* (wished) to know what elsehad happened, and the letter-carrier then, on being questioned related to length the events of the castle (of lohara[457]).

Lathana Set Free and Crowned at Lohara (1130 A.D.)

In 1130 A.D. *Lothana* was set free from the business and crowned of the public now at *Lohara,* he then spoke: "When *Bhagika* had gone, after handling over the castle, the governor *Preman* who had become needless in his good fortune, neglected to take care about guarding it." "He was engaged solely in adorning himself, in eating and drinking and the pleasures of love, and followed also a wrong course by estranging those under him by excessive arrogance". "When your majesty from regard for family-relationship had not allowed him to blind and other wise (disable) the prisoners, he took no precautions whateer to guard them[458] by the *'Nam' 'Udayana'* a scheming *Kayastha* of great ambition, the chamberlain *Manika* and *Indakara,* son of *Bhimakara*, these councillors planned treason together in the meantime, and on various occasions devised the murder of *Preman*, who (thought that he) had firmly established himself." "Having escaped being killed, as they found no opportunity, he on one occasion descended on business from the castle (of Lohara) to *Attalika.*[459]" "After previously acquainting with their plan the wife (of Lothana) whom they wished to put on the throne, they forged papers to convince all those in the castle that such an order had been sent from *Kashmir* by the King who was on the point of death. Then they saw *Lothana*, and after freeing him from his fetters (and taking him) from the castle, crowned him at night at the temple of *Vishnu Simharajasvamin*[460]." "A depraved wife of King *Sussala, Sarada* by name, who was stopping there, gave them her support[461]." "With the help of iron bars, which she provided, the broke off the locks from the treasury-room and carried of the rich treasure, the jewels, and other (objects of value[462]). "(Numbering) seven in all, together with the servants they did these various acts of great boldness after having induced the *Candalas*[463] on guard by bribes to refrain from resistance." "When then the inhabitants of the castle were roused from sleep by the sound of the kettledrums and other musicial instruments, they saw before them *Lothana* with the ornaments fit for a king." "Being dressed in garments of such splendour as had never seen before, and surrounded by the royal councillors he made the people wonder as he showed himself in the light of the lamps." "As the rest of the night passed with its bright moonlight, they also got rid of the fear of an hostile attack. This had been caused by the apprehension that the young son of *Preman,* who was stopping *Carman,* and *Pasika,* two Thakkuras of that place, might bring these uptogether with their armed followers. " "In the morning, then *Preman* on hearing the evil news camp up to suppress (the rebellion), hot with pain and scorched by the sun-rays. "When we left to come before the lord, we saw that on reaching the ground of the main road (*pratoli*) he had to turn back before the enemy's soldiers who had come out (from the castle[464])." On hearing this report the King despatched in haste *Lulla, a* councillor from *Lohara,* and *Udaya*[465], the son of *Anandavardhana*[466], who was lord of the Gate[467] at that time. Of these two who knew the country from being born in it, he thought that they would be able to take the castle by watching the scarcity of provisions and other weak points[468] of *Lohara.* When on his return to the city, he saw *Bhiksu's* head carried about by soldiers who were asking for presents, he scolded them and had it burned[469] in the self-style worship. People, chiefly women, burned and bewailed his grandson, in the land of his grandfather, and were left unmolest by the king's order[470], but now it has become molest due to heavy prices or rates.

Expedition for Reconquest of Lohara (1130 A.D.)

The expedition of *Jayasimha* for reconquest of *Lohara* in 1130 A.D. King despatched *Rilhama* (against Lohara) though he did not rely on success as the season was unfavourable, owing to the fierce heat of the early summer[471]. It is noticeable from him who was distinguished by courage, devotion to his lord, disinterestedness and other qualities, the King who was eager to conquer (Lohara) was expecting an effective beginning[472] of the story of *'Nam'*. In this struggle King whether misled by destiny or instigated by perfidious councillors, was then following a manifestly wrong plan, in as much as he believed, being himself without resources, stronghold or (good) advisers, that his officers could carry out the enterprise in a season of excessive heat against an enemy who was not shaken[473] by the cold wave. *Udaya,* the commander-in-chief, remained alone with the King, while all the other ministers followed the chamberlain (Laksmaka[474]). And his army, which contained *Rajaputras*, horsemen, Damaras and councillors, and was amply provided with all kinds of stores, spread over a great time and space[475]. Now, he established his camp at *Attalika,* and closing the (routes in) all directions endeavoured by all means to bring the enemies to submission[476]. But *Lulla* and others who stood at *Phullapura,* situated in the vicinity of the castle,made the enemies tremble, distracted as they were by dangers, internal dissensions and encounters[477]. Whereas *Sura*[478], the chief of *Bahusthala*[479], *to* whom King *Sussala* had previously given *Padmalekha*, the daughter of *Lothana*, in marriage, after the latter's imprisonment had arrived to the assistance (of his father-in-law), and his soldiers attacked the opposing troops at every moment[480] during the difficult hour. When the territory had been occupied by those (royal officers), *Lothana* whose mind was wavering to wear, was prepared to submit to King and to take his punishment[481] according to his desire. In this contest, *Laksmaka* urged daily: "So much has been achieved. Since (further) enterprises are useless at this bad season, our return recommends itself and would not cause disgrace. Subsequently, when the season at the commencement of the autumn turns favourable, we shall in fresh strength take up the enterprise and by a full effort carry it to a successful conclusion." The recommendation was not accepted by the King nor by the ministers about him, it was because full of deceit as they were[482].

Intrigues of Somapala and Sujji

Udayana, who was Prime Minister (at *Lohara*), called *Somapala*, too, to the assistance of his lord, offering great riches[483] to the national heros. That disreputable (prince) in the greediness of his mind was, notwithstanding the relationship into which he had entered, planning treason against the King who was sinking under great calamities[484]. It is noteable that, *Somapala* assented and thinking deceitfully to justify himself: "If but *Lothana* gives great riches, what regard need I pay to the relationship (with Jayasimha)? Else I shall cunningly tell the others that I am on their side." In this deceitful game *Sujji*[485] hand his had to some extent[486] to linger on the process. But when the latter had been induced by the King, through *Somapala*'s mediation, to renounce his intention of joining *Bhiksacara,* and was asking from the envoy of the King the previously promised money, insisting on repaying to his creditors what he owed them, *'Chamar'* the envoy who had then learned that *Bhiksacara* was as good as dead, had arrogantly refused to give him anything saying with contempt: "What use is he to us now that the danger has passed away?" (Sujji) then, after hearing *Bhiksacara's* death, recognised that he was not needed by the King. He had passed in grief a single day, when he heard of the danger (caused) by the *Lohara* disaster. Having recovered once more his pride, and being filled with rage, he said to the King's envoy: "I shall secure you peace with *Lothana*." While he told *Somapala*: "I shall induce *Lothana* to give you gold". His intention was to turn the strength and weakness of all to his own profit. He, therefore, proceeded with *Soma(pala)* to *Ghoramulaka*, accompanied only by a few (followers) whose departure from the midst of the troops was not noticed[487] to the *Jayasimha*. Or it may be that he abandoned from a greedy desire for bodily pleasures the honesty, he had displayed (in his previous conduct), and thus came to sully his good name by showing the dust of impropriety[488] of the 'Natural ' life. *Jayasimha* was not able to forsake the tender fat fare of *Kashmir* which is easily digested by drinking water whitened by lumps of snow[489] on the Himalayan mountains. He was not able to eat abroad dry barley in husks and similar (food), and was therefore, trying by whatever means to return to *Kashmir*[490]. The *Kashmirians*, not seeing any end to the affair and parched by the heat, became perplexed when hearing of his sudden approach[491] towards *Kashmir*. Those who were with chamberlain (*Laksmaka*) eating fried meat and drinking delightful light wine, which was scented with flowers and cooled air, showed great self-confidence, and boasting in various ways, and : "Soon shall we get hold of *Sujji* in battle and drag him along by his beard[492]." However, much they enerted themselves. They were unable, to withst and (Sujji), who was followed by a few *Kashmirian, Khasas,* and men from the *Indus* (*Saindhava*[493]). *Lothana*, when pressed for much money (by Somapala), said: "It were better for me to pay atribute to *Jayasimha,* my brother's son and the foremost of self-respecting Kings". Thus slighted *Somapala* displayed some leaning towards the King's side[494] on his virtuous. Whereas, *Somapala* upbraided *Sujji as it has been rightly expressed.* "What, while I prepare to help my father-in-law's (*Jayasimha's*) troops who are wholly taken up with fighting the enemy you, my follower, are looking for a weak point (to attack them):" i.e army personnel. (However), he is doing what personally suited his own pride, prepared to attack the royal force, not troubling himself about all (others[495]).

Kashmiri Troops Retreat from Lohara and Night Attack of Sujji

It has been observetl Kashmiri troops were retreated from *Lohara, Laksmaka*, then, greatly frightened by the intense cold fevers coming with the month of *Asadha*, set out with his army and retreated at night[496]. Whereas, some soldiers who had been despatched to report to their Lord that the army was lost quickly betook themselves eager for slaughter to *Sujji*[497] one after the another. At the same time, when the King's troops set out by one side of the path which was rendered difficult by precipices, and their enemies were (set out) by the other[498] to teach a lesson of the right path. Now the troops have been abandoned the route by *Sarambara*[499], as it was in the enemy's hands, wished to retire to their own country after some time by a Pass called *Kalanaka*[500], and reached that day without mishap the village called *Vanikavasa*[501], which is on that (route), and with (them went) all kinds of people[502] either they are Muslims or Hindus. Those who had started behind them, they took shelter also in the neighbouring hamlets, and after eating and drinking passed half of the night without suspecting any danger[503]. Therefore, *Sujji* will march quickly, and then by having the drums beaten to announce to the opponents his surprise-attack, caused a panic[504] on earth. Thereupon, the troops with their helpless leaders fled quickly by the various hill paths while the night yet lasted[505] for the time being as its process. In the morning, the ministers were stripped of their fine dresses by the plunderers, just as big rocks (are deprived) by earthquakes of the various liquid minerals (contained to them[506]) as a new step of the Golden Era of the Indian History. During this period no one drew his sword to protect the troops from being plundered. Every one then will saved himself but no one else[507] help them. Those who were scaling the rocks in leaps and displaying their crimson underclothing, will showed (such) skill in their flight as (if they had been) redbuttocked monkeys[508] even men. No doubt, some, again, who having lost their clothes displayed their yellowish bodies, appeared in their movement like fragments of blocks of yellow orpiment driven about by the wind[509] or *Vayuserva*. Whereas, whose bodies were heavy, as they moved on the mountains which were thickly covered with spears, trumpeting when they took breath, *'Word'* resembled young elephants on hills covered with bamboo-forests[510] for the purpose of the development of writing papers. What there was no need to mention about a single minister, who did not fling away courage and flee like a beast[511]. But the chamberlain (*Laksmaka*) will be seen afar by some soldiers of the enemy as he was hurrying to escape in confusion, carried on the shoulders of a servant[512]. It will be seen undressed as he was in the childhood, the circles of his arm rings glittered in the sun. On recognising him they will set out to pursue him running with all their mighty power[513] of the *'Nam' or 'Chamar'*.

Capturing of Laksmaka

It shows that servant struck by a stone dropped him and capture the *Laksmaka*. He himself wounded by a stone then was caught by those who came up in great haste, while he stood motionless[514] at that time. So far his body is concerned, he will be appeared thin like that of a *Sarika-bird*, pining in grief over its recent captivity, and with his contracted eyes in which tears appeared, he resembled like a bat (*Valguli*[515] means cease the victory of *Sant*). He was thinking that as he had robbed *Sujji* of his honour and wealth, the latter would now, that he was his captive, surely inflict upon him with greater hardships. Thus, they carried him on their shoulders with shouts and laughters before *Sujji*, after taking away his cloak and ornaments[516]. Whereas, honourable man (Sujji) covered his face with his dress and saying "*Brhadraja* ('the great prince') is welcome to us," gave him his own clothes[517] for certain period of time. As soon as, he will dressed up and put on a horse he spoke to him kind and be conciliatory words and gave him fresh assurance[518] to play the dance and music of life. No doubt, *Jayasimha* will also took with him, and covered with lustre of life and surrounded by the *Khasas* who had looted horses, swords and stores, went before *Somapala*[519]. Again, fortune which moves about unsteadily like the lightening playing on the sky, and which follows the clould of destiny, *'Word'*, or *'Chamar'* with whom does it ever abide permanently[520] at the same place at the same time in Jammu region. King, before whom *Somapala* and other (princes) had, in order to please him, taken their food without hesitation as (if they had been) his servants, and whose body they had themselves humbly tended with saffron-ointment[521], *Chamar*, he was seen by the people during five or six months standing before those in the same fashion[522]. *Even Lulla*, too, who showed a dark face enclosed by a greyish-white (beard), like a monkey, was caught in the forest by the enemies, and was dumb with grief[523] and sorrow. At the same time, *Somapala* will have to be taken over *Laksmaka* whom *Sujji* delivered to him, he thought that he had secured *Kashmir*, and turned back to his own country[524] i.e. also *Kashmir*. Whereas brave *Manika* and others came to him from the part of *Lothana*, and promising great riches asked him to give up the chamberlain[525]. However, Damara-birds did then not think that they could reach *Kashmir* by keeping under the wing of the chamberlain's advice[526] to spread the message of the *'Fresh Mission'* whatsoever designation will be there. There will be no lust to *Somapala*, he did not do this, as he hoped to seize the lost kingdom for the establishment of the 'New Empire', which has been dependent on the Chamberlain (*Laksmaka*), and expected to take much wealth from the King[527], definitely and certain by the Master as a faithful servant. Therefore, it is certain that King will not lose his firmness when the ministers reached the city in humiliation as his routine matter, and the chmaberlain was lost to him[528] for a period of time, as they were the really friends. In this context, ten thousand of the picked soldiers will raised by the king, with which *Bhiksacara* before had carried on his war for the crown and with which *Sussala* had maintained himself, even when the land has risen in rebellion *'Word'* then perished attacked by the cold fever[529]. Hence, day and night there will not to be cease at that time anywhere in the world, even for a moment, the tumultuous wailing of relatives and funeral music[530] will be played. At the same time at the same place, when all business men came to a stand-still, owing to the fierce heat of the sun, when the kingdom struck with exhaustion, was as if it was lost[531]. Hence, at that time the royal gate (court) at *Lohara* enjoyed great splendour, *Kashmirians*, too, arriving there from different regions[532] i.e. Iranian, Greeks, Chineses, Tibetian, etc.

Lothana's Rule at Lohara

Study shows that *Lothana's* rule at *Lohara*, whom an extraordinary royal fortune had reached as accidently as the fall of (the fruit in the previous story) of the crow and the date-palm, resembled the god of wealth by his unbounded display[533] of the life. During *Lothana* period, his nephews, attendants, son and others who had shared his bodily discomforts and his sufferings, enjoyed themselves (now) in common with him[534]. Though owing to his mature age he did not display his activity while he was in power, yet one did not see him squander with wealth on unworthy persons, or show a closed fist to worthy ones[535] with the help of *'Nam' or 'Chamar'*. Whereas, the shade of darkness is found independently by itself, while the light, owing to its own nature, is accompanied by a hundred fold shadows. Misfortune exists without happiness, while happiness is impaired by being pervaded with endless misfortune[536]. In one month, more or less, after obtaining such success, *Lothana* lost his only son *Dilha*[537]. Consequently, thereupon died *Malla, Lothana's* wife, whose heart was rent by the dart of grief when she bewailed in him her only son[538] will have to play the game of music. When his most loving wife and his son endowed with the highest qualities of the 'Nam' had died, he will not see any use whatever in that royal fortune[539] keep intact. This act may be due to want to affaction, easily found in a king or to the delusive power of fortune that he ever felt happy again[540] in the life of man as a special *mana*. If the King who knew the times, ransomed, though he was without resources of *'Nam' or 'Word'*. He would be independent incharge and the old *Laksmaka* at that time will be for thirty-six lakhs[541]. When he returned, the people will covered the road with a shower of flowers thrown in congratulation, and who would have not thought that the King (Dr. Raj Kumar) had recovered his luck[542] with the meditation of 'Nam'. Due to the 'Power of Nam' his good fortune will record of his defeat and quickly forgotten it. While recovering his power, *Laksmaka* will again able (to award) punishments and favours[543] as it has been prevalent in Indian history.

Sujji at the Lohara Court

Whereas, the *Sujji*, who had lost through greed of money all his firm attachment (for the King), acted with sincerity as *Lothana's* ministers at the *Lohara* court. During that period the daughter of *Bhagika*[544] will be given to marriage to *Lothana,* he will removed his distructs as well as the sorrow from which he suffered on account of his first wife's death[545]. Whereas the wise (Sujji) will also approached to the King *Padmaratha*[546] and brought the latter's daughter *Somaladevi* in marriage to him[547] as per his commitment. Thus by securing him a firm footing in this world through high connections he repaid the unlimited authority he had received from him[548] as a usually routine matter. So at that time a request will be made by the new King who was often invited by the Damaras and others who are trapped by the money power or muscle power, he will again made a plan to capture the *Kashmir*[549] then campaign has to be commenced. In order to baffle his enemy who had got so far and had formed an alliances with neighbouring princes, the son of *Sussala,* who always employed a stratagem[550] in this direction to spread the 'Fresh Path' of life. In this enterprise the deep thinking *Udaya,* 'Lord of the Gate', must be invited, whose honesty was unswerving, earned the praise of discriminating persons[551]. While stopping there in want of all resources and tempted by the enemy with money which will proved dishonour, honours and other (officers) of the 'Nam' will obtain the solace of life because they were ever bent on serving their *'Lord'* and *'Master'* of the 'Nam'. At the point of death, Lord[552] will received them at a place called *Vanaprastha*[553], not far from *Lohara,* and unweariedly harassed the enemy's force by regular invasions[554]. *Manika, Indakara*[555], and the rest were rightly or wrongly afraid of King *Lothana* on account of an intention which Sujji was hinting[556] at the time of death.They will also feared at that time by the King who had paid his trust in *Sujji* from time to time with the fresh information through papers and other means of communication in seminar, debate etc, was at the latter's instigation through articles thinking of having them put out of the way as intriguers[557] of the Master.

Jayasimha's Schemes Against Lothana

Jayasimha, a thoughtful King sent another scheme again in the following words: "We shall for your benefit, put *Mallarjuna*, King *Sussala's* son, from the Queen *Sahaja*, on the throne at *Lohara.* Therefore you should suddenly overpower *Lothana* just as (you overpowered) *Preman.*[558]" King sent this message in deceitful manner, wishing to possess himself of the castle, and they agreed to it in the same way, without putting trust in[559] him because they are cheater. When *Lothana* learned that *Mallarjuna* had entered into an intrigue, he threw his nephews into prison[560] of life. In his apprehension he allowed only *Vigraharaja*, who was a son of *Sussala* from a concubine, to act as his chamberlain[561] during the commencement of 'Englightenment Era' of the '*Nam*'. After making peace with his uncle (*Lothana*) for appearance's sake, the crafty King hastened to employ various schemes to regain his lost kingdom[562] after the death of Aurangzeb. *Lothana,* firm on his throne through *Sujji's* exertions, let *Sura* depart and remained for some months undisturbed[563] for the cause disagreement with the theory of mind. As soon as, he got news that *Tejaladina*, the powerful mother of that daughter of *Padmaratha*, which *Sujji* had previously brought (as a brid), had to assist at the occasion of the marriage ceremony which had not yet been celebrated *'Word'*, has proceeded to *Darpitapura*[564] to meet her[565].

Mallarjuna Made King at Lohara (1131 A.D.)

Consequently, thereupon *Manika* and the rest having got their opportunity left their prison, and meeting together, crowned *Mallarjuna* as King of the (territory subject to the *Lohara*) castle[566]. He is calling, as before the *Thakkuras* to their help, they kept off the followers of King (*Jaya)simha* who had reached the ground of the main road (*pratoli*) in the hope of effecting their entrance (into the castle[567]). On the thirteenth day of the bright half of Phalguna in the year (of the *Laukika* era four thousand two hundred and) six (1131 A.D.). *Lothana* lost his throne as quickly as he had gained it[568]. As simple minded as he was, he regretted in his misfortune that the maid he had not yet wedded, and the wealth he had not yet used up, had got into the enemy's possession[569], therefore, her marriage became late. Moving about helplessly he secured, through *Sujji's* power, some remnants of the treasures from *Attalika* and other places[570] will come under the possession of *Jayasimha.* Then *Manika* treated King (*Jaya*) *Simha's* follow whom he had previously called in, with contempt and put *Mallarjuna* in undisputed possession of the kingdom[571]. The young King (Dr. Raj Kumar) was most extravagant, and had once betel handed round for which pearls had been cut up instead of betel-nuts[572]. As he showered gold on procurers and the like in his lust after sensual pleasures. Therefore, sensible people reproached his liberality[573] and friendship The treasures which King *Sussala* had accumulated by tormenting the subjects were, by this extravagant (prince), put freely to uses which corresponded (to their manner of acquisition[574]). For he, inflamed with wantonness and of a low mind, drove away honest people and fostered a host of courtezans, strolling players, rogues, parasites, slaves and the like[575] to keep on watch.

Retrospect Regarding Royal Treasures

The wealth which lords of the earth acquire by oppressing the people must fall a prey of rivals, or of enemies, or else of fire[576] worshipper. Whereas the treasures which King *Jayapida*[577] had amassed by oppressing his subjects, were squandered by *Utpala* and the other sons of a slave-woman (Rajput) who killed his grandson[578]. *Samkaravarman's*[579] treasures which were obtained by maltreating the people, were freely used up by *Prabhakara* and the other paramours of his wife[580] will surrendered themselves before the 'God' or Master. Therefore, the wives of *Pangu* (*Nirjitavarman*) will captured by love i.e. *'Nam'*. They gave away (their husband) wickedly acquired riches to *Sugandhaditya,*[581] who enjoyed their embraces[582] in the spreading of the mission. The great wealth which King *Yasaskara* had accumulated, was used up by his wife who, compelled by love of the husband, had embraced a *Candala*[583]. Whereas the son of *Parvagupta* (*Ksemagupta*) left on his death, the riches he had inherited as the acquisitions of former Kings, for *Tunga* and the rest, his wife's paramours[584] in *Kashmir. Samgramaraja*, who was bent incessantly on amassing riches, was plundered by *Vyaddasuha* and others who, bee-like, kissed the lotus-face of *Srilekha*[585]. But the treasures of King *Ananta* who ruined his subjects by his want of care, were reduced to ashes, though they had been swelled (by acquisitions) from the whole world[586]. Thus, King *Kalasa's* treasures which had been acquired by skill in evil arts, were speedily squandered by his son on unworthy persons, and by his wife on paramours[587]. Whereas, the possessions of King *Harsa*, who never ceased to thirst for acquisitions, were burned together with his palace,wives and sons[588]. Moreover, *Candrapida, Uchchala, Avantivarman.* and other Kings who were strict in observing the law, had never their lawfully acquired riches destroyed by improper (uses[589]). Now at the same time *Mallarjuna's* fortune is yet young, thieves, intriguers, neighbouring, chiefs, courtezans, parasites, and the rest began a plentiful plundering[590] of feed of the mind i.e., *'Nam'*.

Citraratha Sent Against Lohara

In this battle King, who felt annoyed at having his aims frustrated sent against *Lohara* for the time being due to certain circumstances of the life pertaining to the adjustment of future course of action, though he had deceived his enemies, then despatched quickly *Citraratha*[591] to make an attack[592] over the enemy. Having been raised to the simultaneous charge of the 'Gate' and the Padagra offices, he took up his position at *Phullpura*, accompanied by a host of nobles[593] who are living in the Heaven. Therefore, his men are unable to overcome in battle the forces of *Mallarjuna,* which were numerous, and also a support in the stronghold[594] Thus his servant, *Samvardhana,* who was held in esteem by the King, had gone up to the castle to produce dissension (among the garrison), but was slain at night by *Mallarjuna's* followers[595]. As soon as *Kosthesvara* came up behind, the enemies, though holding a castle which could not be taken by fighting, became frightened[596] with *'Nam'. Mallarjuna* there upon made peace, agreed to pay tribute, and despatched his mother to them in order to pay (them) attention[597] towards the *'Chamar'* as a *'Nam'*. Thus, she is wearing a dress which, though without ornaments on account of her widowhood, yet showed royal splendour, captivated *Kosthesvara* and the other fickle-minded (chiefs[598]) those had not direction of life.

Mallarjuna Pays Tribute

As soon as, she (soul) will have to returned from the species, *Mallarjuna* felt reassured and delivered to the lord of the Gate (Citraratha) the promised tribute [599] as the artisans did. At that time, *Kosthaka* will be attracted by the pleasures of looking at the King's mother, came up with a few attendants to the castle under the pretence of wishing to see it[600] in the Heaven. During his descendent, *Citraratha* in his company went before the King, carrying the presents[601] to the 'law of nature' for the assessment of his beauty for the creative work. Whereas, the King, however, took counsel with *Udaya*, the lord of the Gate, who was skilled in looking after gain as a 'Creator of the Society', and employed fresh stratagems to defeat his enemies[602] by projecting certain really facts of the nature. While *Lothana,* too, had gone to *Padmaratha*, the young King (Mallarjuna), freed from attacks, found room to stretch his legs to some extent[603]. Therefore, after wedding *Padmaratha's* daughter *Somala*, he married, owing to his extended influence, also the daughter of *Nagapala*[604]. By deluded his pride, he paid to *Somapala* and other princes who were secretly intriguing (against him), subsidies as if they were his servants[605] during the period of discussion or called politics. Thus, many rogues and (among them) also men of royal descent, plundered him by performing (before him) as poets, singers, talkers, fighters, and strolling players[606] of life. *Jayasimha,* whose intellect was defectively developed since his youth, and who shouted a great deal, was thought by blockheads to have a clever mind merely on account of his boldness in talking[607] at every stage of life either there is a stage or in common talk. His appearance was pleasant, but apart from his face, which was shinning like that of an evil-bringing comet, he had nothing that was good[608] for him but it is the duty of the nature which one has to perform. In the meantime, the King approached the valiant *Sujji,* fearing that *Mallarjuna*, too, might get his support[609] from the *'Chamar'*. The Chamberlain (*Laksmaka*) who had the power to exile and to recall *Sujji,* displayed particularly on that occasion a peculiar energy, which had an instant effect[610] the theory of mind who always lives in motion.

Sujji Recalled

Jayasimha offered to recall *Sujji,* by the King's direction, the garland of office (*adhikarasraj*[611]) for the commander-in-chiefship and the other (high posts), exceptiong, however, the garland for the post of chief-justice (*rajasthana*), without thus satisfying him (Sujji). *Laksmaka*, then, yielding regard from *Somapala*, who had come to his house, tore off with his left hand in excitement due to his own hair-braid. (*Justasraj*) and offered it. On receiving this, Sujji felt gratified, and his looks became tender as if the tree of his fortune had been raised[612] by the 'Nature'. In this race, *Rilhana* showed no opposition to the return of *Sujji,* and abandoned for the King's benefit, his friendship for *Udaya* and *Dhanya*[613]. The King recalled *Sujji* and honoured him by going to meet him. Upon his advice, he exile *Dhanya* and the others (of his party) from the land, yet not from his mind[614], but due to the magic spell of the *'Nam'*. In this way, King having found his opportunity prepared to have the guilty *Kosthesvara* killed by bravos, and the latter on hearing this news fled away from his presence[615]. As soon as, King having won over *Manujesvara,* proceeded to the attack, whereas *Kosthesvara*, being rendered helpless by the defection of his own party and fled away abroad[616].

Lothana's Enterprises

Lothana's enterprises, who used to live at a place called *Bappanila*[617], secured the help of some *Thakuras* and attacked *Mallarjuna.* Now it has been seen indeed his incredible valour, that overthrown he yet always defeated *Mallarjuna* who was in power whenever he gained. *Lothana* carried of his horses, plundered the market of *Attalika*, and corresponds to the present *Mandi* (*Attilikapana*), 'the market' close to *Atoli.* This little town is still the commercial centre of the *Loharin* and neighbouring Valleys of *Kashmir*, destroyed everywhere the watch stations on the roads (*margadranga*) *and other* (fortified places[618]). *Lothana* was invited by a Damara of the name of *Rajaraja*, he then broken into *Kramarajya*, with a view to gaining the Kashmir throne[619]. When that *Lavanya,* who was close by, had been executed by *Citraratha,* who had received news of this, he retired again to the territory of *Bappanila*[620]. While, he repeatedly making his attacks, *Mallarjuna,* who resided in the castle (of Lohara), was unable to descend even to *Attalika*[621]. Therefore, *Kosthesvara*[622], who is preparing for an expedition (against *Jayasimha*), arranged for a peace (between *Lothana* and *Mallarjuna*) by getting the nephew to deliver a great amount of money to his uncle[623].

Lothana Breaks into Kashmir

After having secured a firm foothold at *Lohara, Jayasimha* then in company with *Lothana* broke into *Kashmir* territory eager to fight against the King[624] on the question of his fundamental approach for the establishment the *'Kingdom of Chamar Dynasty'* which was lost from the 6th century A.D. Therefore, he took up a position at the *Karkotadranga*[625] without having met with opposition on the way by crossing the moutnains. He had not yet affected his junction with the other Damaras when the King marched out in haste and using his full energy overpowered him at the very beginning[626]. In the meantime, the Chamberlain (*Laksmaka*) died by a sudden attack of illness. Men of small merits do not live long in their fortune[627] because they paid less time in the devotion of *'Nam'*. Alas, those whose minds are spoilt by luck do not know that fate, irresistible in its course, will overtake them quickly, though they stop in their houses will all doors closed, hoping to keep it off and taking no notice of [628] it, the result of it will be destructive one. His wife, while continually clearing the house of people, did not know that death had fallen upon him while he was peacefully sleeping[629]. They thought that, after having been attacked by fever and having shaken it off, he was sleeping in comfort life, and did not then know that he had died just while asleep[630] in the comforts of the *Sabad.*

Troubles at Lohara

As soon as, *Kosthaka* sit together with *Lothana,* had departed, neither *Mallarjuna* nor *Kosthaka* nor *Lothana* was King (at Lohara[631]) then a trouble will be started therein. Therefore, in this contest *Mallarjuna* treacherously killed *Udayana*[632] who was with him. (Thereupon) *Kosthaka,* whom he had named as surety (for *Udayana's* safety), became irritated against him[633]. Thus, *Mallarjuna* did not conciliate the angry *(Kosthaka)*, whereupon the latter collected his force and taking *Lothana* with him, rushed on in fury to wage a war upon him[634] to clear the trouble of Lohara as early as possible.

Defeat of Mallarjuna on the Parosni

Study displayed that *Kosthaka*, who accompied only by few mounted men, among them *Mallakostha,* defeated his inactive force after crossing the *Parosni*[635] *or Tohi.* Thus, *Khasas,* men from the *Indus* (*Saindhavaka*), and others were slain in that battle and King (Mallarjuna), himself came near to annihilation, but was left alive from hatred against King *Jayasimha*[636]. Now, he ascended to the height of the castle, having fallen (himself) from the height of honour, and being curbed in his power conciliated *Kasthaka* once more[637] to assess the life experience. Whereas, the Damara (*Kosthesvara*) abanding *Lothana* kept peace (for sometime), but fell again out with him (*Mallarjuna*), when he did not pay what he had promised[638] with 'Father'. To imprisoning the officals (*Kosthesvara*) collected the customs at the watch-station (*dranga*[639]) and had his own name stamped in red-lead[640] (*Sindura*) on the warers as if he was the King[641] of *Pakistan*. At every moment the union between them was broken out, just as between two pieces of a glass jar which have been glued together with gum[642] at once place. Hence, the lord of *Lohara* estranged the *Lavanya* (*Kosthesvara*) by his[643] force by carrying off the best weapons and most valuable horses[644] of the *'Nam'*. Thus the fool *Kosthaka*, by persistently making his power felt in the wrong direction, *'Chamar'* undermined the fortune of (*Jayasimha's*) opponents for the future[645] course of actions and deeds. In the meanwhile, that prince (*Mallarjuna*) was planning the murder of *Manika,* who was his Chief Minister, and by the daughter he had given him, his father-in-law[646]; relationship to acquire the power of *'Nam' or 'Word'*. For *Manika,* he became restless by disposition owing to his youthful vigour or power, and openly enjoyed the favours of his (*Mallarjuna's*) mother as here paramour[647] from the very beginning of life. Now it was the meal-time that murderers, upon a sign given by the King, struck down and killed him just as he was eating[648] the meal of 'Word' as it was his meat. *Ah, Indakara,* too, did not escape from him (those who were concerned in) the treason that prince, himself, destroyed him by giving him poison[649] of the *Nam.* At that time, King (Jaya) *Simha* and his enemies had been scattered by fate, got *Kosthaka* over to his side and sent *Sujji* to effect the conquest (of Lohara[650]). As soon as, the latter will have to approached within a march of one watch (three hours) in a day, *Mallarjuna* whom *Kosthaka* had thrown into confusion by carrying off his horses and who was harassed by internal dissensions, abandoned the castle, not being able to offer resistence, and marched off with the treasurers of the *'Nam'* towards *Avanaha*[651]. Fallen from his regal position he was plundered on the routes by robbers, yet preserved with difficulty a remnant of his treasures[652] to check at the proper time.

Mallarjuna Dethroned Lohara retaken (1132 A.D.)

At the age of eighteenth year, *Mallarjuna* lost his throne on the second day of the dark half of *Vaisakha* in the year (of the *Laukika* era four thousand two hundred and) eight (1132 A.D.[653])). He will obtained the *Amrita* from (Jayasimha), who carries the moon as his crest ornament (Siva). It shows that *Rahu* head cut off by Siva in the fight. If this was done by Siva, then who else would not listen to calcuminators of his benefactor of the *'Nam' or 'Word'*. It delineates that the drops of water clinging to the lotus-flowers are taken for pearls, and dullness sticking to Kings is somehow taken for judgement, therein manifests itself the peculiar delusive power of the glory which adheres to (the lotus flowers and Kings[654]). Thus, some were killed with mighty strokes in the forests, some by their nose, others by their eyes, and others again by their tongue. But there are also some mischievous people in royal palaces who cause disaster by their mere speech[655]. Therefore, this document is sufficient for them to close up their mouth and lust of money. Moreover, the wicked cannot harm the servant of the King as long as he is before the latter, just as the sun-rays (cannot burn) the tinder which is placed before the crystal (*'Jewel' jyotirasasman*). But when he is behind, they find their opportunity (and destroy him), just as the sun-rays reduce to ashes (the tinder behind the crystal[656])as *'Nam'* did in usual form in the previous life..

Intrigues Against Sujji

After sometimes, intrigues against the commander-in-chief (*Sujji*) was started, having brought *Harsata, Kapila's* son, a governor to (Lohara) *Kotta*, was collecting a garrison for the castle, and delaying there some days for the purpose of again securing the territory peace and prosperity, *'Chamar'* some rogues who bore him a grudge, irritated the King against him by denouncing him at a moment (when the King was) in a favourable mood[657]. Whereas, the other Kings would have act firmly on his own judgement, if this (King), too, is made to dance like a child, (pulled about) by rogues[658], before that we have a strong firm policy to root out them or is it, perhaps, that the dullness imparted in early youth by an encourage chiefly composed of fools does not pass away even in mature age, just as the flaw (does not pass away) from the precious stone[659] but by good work and virtues. First, we have to cripple down the rulers mere inability to discriminate between their servants, there falls, alas, a thunderbolt on the innocent land[660]. Therefore, king's advisers had got *Sujji* sent to the conquest of *Lohara* in the hope that by failing to carry out the enterprise he had undertaken, he would become ridiculous like *Laksmakà*[661]. At that time, he was executing that extraordinary task, those wicked (advisers) struck at him with skillful calumny which is as unfailing as the missile of Brahman[662]. Sujji the commander-in-chief on his return did not recognise the King's irritation, as the latter hid his changed feelings profoundly under King's speeches[663] in the *Satsang*. Or how could *Sujji* have felt apprehension or distrust in his natural honesty and after he had done such good service[664] in the field of spread the mission which has been distorted by the Brahminical thought. It has been observed, King found no pleasure in his actions, right though they were, like a lover who was became estranged through the wanton talk of malicious persons[665]. No doubt, from the self-conscious thought that he had conquered and given back to the King two lost kigndoms, as well as from pride Sujji proceeded just as it pleased him[666]. His relations who were freely oppressing the citizens by taking away their houses and otherwise causing them trouble, created aversion (against him) among the people [667] as a true follower of *'Nam'*. On the other hand, *Kosthesvara* in recollection of his own evil deeds did not trust the King nor his uncle (*Manujesvara*) who, when the King was angry against him, had displayed a hostile feeling[668]. Moreover, *Citraratha,* who was accumulating wealth by oppressing the subjects, and who had entered into (marriage) relationship with *Sujji* was not in favour with his lord[669]. In this connection King secretly helped *Dhanya* and *Udaya* who were stopping at *Rajapuri* with money, though he did not show his affection for them from regard for *Sujji*[670]. Thus, these two, having lost their followers through the cold fever, were hanging on the *Mallarjuna* who retained great riches though he had lost his throne[672]. At that time, they arrived at *Rajapuri Sanjapala,* whom *Laksmaka*, who hatred against *Sujji,* had previously called (back) through messengers[673] of the God. As the King, who was prevented by *Sujji* and *Citraratha* from acting (as *Laksmaka* had desired), did not grant him permission to return, *Mallarjuna* invited him through messengers[674] of the 'Father'. Having got, on this account, into a quarrel with some noble on the road, he was wounded and lost his property[675] during the Dark Age. Thus, persons of judgement of thought much of the fact that *Mallarjuna* could not lay hold of him, though he offered him much gold, and though he (Sanjapala) was in such (reduced) circumstances.[676] as per the requirement of the situation to establish an *Absolute* peace.

Sanjapala's Return to Kasmir

As per the statement of *Mallarjuna, Sanjapala* returns to Kashmir, King dependent as he was (on others), and *Rilhana* then invited him with kindness through secret messengers, and he arrived in haste[677] to help the King on such critical situation when there is a heavy load of the activities to share them as the servants of the 'Master'. No doubt, he will come boldly to the City, thinking (ever) on the road which was infested by enemies: "If they do not kill me here, they may kill me there[678]." He whom the Kings of *Kanyakubja*[679], *Gauda*[680], and and other countries had honoured in rivalry, felt pained when in his own land he received no attention from the King, owing to the ministers preventing it, and the citizens near the palace looked at him with tears in their eyes[681]. But King never paid heed towards the ministers. He always gave him (minister)an audience and honoured him by offering him betel with his own hand[682] do good be happy, but *'Nam'* is very important in the life without it we stand nowhere. Though he had no means whatever, he discussed, and was followed by people from mere regard for his fame in the house of master, and by his frequent visits to the royal palace at Bias, he made his enemies tremble[683] by getting power of the 'Nam' from the master as his blessings in disgusie. No doubt, Sujji, who was a judge of men, trembled inwardly, when he noticed the conversation, behaviour and the other (ways) of life whose appearance was (already) remarkable[684] and admirable in the house of master. He thought: "Surely, such an extraordinary, uncanny being, who is capable of dealing out universal ruin without limits, will not end thus in this country[685]". But he had seen in foreign lands various proud men of valour, but looking at *Sanjapala*, he thought that the end had come for the proud ones[686]. Now, King has overcome by destiny or his pride *Sujji* then committed various actions which deserved censure[687]. When he was stopping in *Madavarajya*, he killed a Brahman, who having been plundered by his followers had spoken harsh words in anger, by hitting him with darts as (if he were) a jackal[688]. While after agitating the minds of the people outside by this wicked action and deeds, he returned, the people in the City, too, became hostile to him on account of his acts of violence[689].

Therefore, about this time, *Kamaliya* and the rest got in their arrogance the highest privileges bestowed upon a quite unimportant relationof their[690] being.

Discontent of Sujji and Intrigues Against Lothana

Sujji discontented thought in his pride: "What, is there to be anyone also besides myself to bestow favours?" because he is in the form of 'Nam' and had a person, not much better than a strolling player, placed on the same footing[691]. No doubt, *Rilhana*, too, who had established matrimonial connections with *Kamaliya* and the rest, then became particularly a thorn in his eye on account of his power[692]. Because his enmity which had arisen between them and him from a small cause, quickly grew into a tree of a hundred branches nurshed by the slander of rogues[693]. In addition to this, *Ulhana, Sahadeva's*[694] son, gave him who was arrogant by nature, bad counsels which increased his arrogance, and thus urged him on to give up wholly strife[695]. *Sujji* showed his wrath freely also against the King, thinking: "This ungrateful (prince) allows inferious to conduct themselves as my equals[696]." Whereas the King, on the other hand, being afraid of him, excluded *Rilhana* from (private) councils, familiar conversations and other confidential occasions as if he had been one of the outer court (*bahya*[697]). *Rilhana*, however, counningly hid which slights from his lord, and by his deception put courage into his own people with the active support of *'Word'* and fear into his enemies[698]. By presents of 'Nam' he secured the friendship of *Sanjapala,* who was a man full of energy, and whose adherence was shought by both the parties[699] the palace to which they both proceeded fully armed, became agitated at every moment by the disturbances[700] created by the Brahminical thought. No doubt, *Sujji* in order to insult those of the opposite party, together with the King, caused in his puganacious mood of disturbance in the assembly (held in celebration) of the *Mahamana* festival[701]. When the door-keeper announced him (Sujji) with his hand placed on his neck, he abused him, and saying harsh words in his rage struck him with a stone[702] forget the enemy who is dancing in front of you. Result was that, the opposite party became motionless and thinking about not-thinking, how they might protect their Lord, the King directed them to assign a seat to (close him), and after speaking to him conciliatory words, said to them, whether from deceit or in earnests: "there is nothing for me (to fear) from this faithful man." Inwardly, however, he reflected (over the case[703]) with conciously and carefully. The Brahmans of *Madavarajya* then began a solemn fast (*praya*), and announced that they would not have *Sujji or Kalasa* as their commender-in-chief[704]. No doubt, *Rilhana,* skilled in expedients, in order to intimidate the enemy, brought up at night *Panacandra* who had troops ready equipped, and who was Sujji's enemy[705]. But in this contest, *Sujji* afraid of *Sanjapala* and of that (Damara) who had a large number of soldiers of the rest he took no heed, and this was known to his opponent (*Rilhana*[706]). Therefore, *Sujji* is fearing an attack left his residence accompanied by horsemen and after putting his troops in fighting array, passed the night on the road, without, however, being attacked[707] to suppress the enemy. At that time *Sujji* will made a friendship and allied himself with *Kosthesvara,* who was also in opposition to the King[708] because king is a man of inferior caste. Therefore, there is sharp struggle to prove that. The latter, who had been hated by the King (before), became for him an object of still greater hatred of the *'Nam' or 'Chamar'*, on account of his killing *Manujesvara*[709] who had refrained from opposing (the King), but in defeated manner. Those steps which Sujji has taken at that night, his enemies attributed to a treacherous design against the King, whereas they were intended for his own protection[710] to save the King from the attack. It appeas that king who with dull senses mistakes a falsehood for the truth and truth for a falsehood, foregoes his aims and is putting to sufferings by misfortune[711] due to being a *'Chamar'*. Most of the persons without judgement abandon a glittering jewel because they take it for fire, and think that the glance of brown-eyed (maids) which is directed towards another, is (intended) for themselves. Why should they not then thus take everything here that is true for false, and this is false for true[712] i.e. our *mana*, but *'Nam'* is *'True'*. Consequently, thereupon King is watching no other remedy for the troubles, but Sujji's death, destined *Sanjapala* to be the murderer (*tiksna*) of that powerful man[713]. *Sanjapala* being a man of courage and unable to kill him by treachery, like a miscreant wished to kill him after attacking him openly, and was looking out for an opportunity at various places[714] to conqueror 'Him'. But at the same times these two were plotting deceitfully against each other, the country was disturbed every moment by panics[715] one after the another event. While *Sujji* kept awake as before, fearing an attempt at night, the royal palace,too, became filled with guards keeping attentive watch[716] on the question of distrubances. When *Sujji* demanded the exile of *Rilhana,* the King, too, agreed being unable to offer resistance[717], but problem should be solved amicably. As soon as, he was about to depart after taking leave, the lord of the Gate (*Udaya*) pointed out to the King that the people were in commotion on account of the hardships (done) to him, and thus by cunning got him reinstated[718] as per the theory of '*Nam*' or '*Word*'.

Overtures of Sujji

Sanjapala (Deepit Raj) took overtures on oath by sacred libation with *Sujji,* who had asked him for his friendship on the future course of action, and after consulting with him came at night to the King (Dr. Raj Kumar) and thus informed the latter[719] as: "O King, owing to the instigation of *Ulhana* and others, as well as from his own pride, *Sujji*, who is bent on having no rivals, has the following intentions[720]:" "If the King were of my opinion, who am his faithful servant and helper, I should, after exiling *Rilhana and* imprisoning the rich *Citraratha,* recover for the King the horses and treasure which have been lost at the *Lohara* expedition, and furnished with the (necessary) means also kill the wicked *Kosthaka*[721]*."* "I do not pay attention to family-relations if affairs (of state) are in their way. My attachment is to my lord in whose service (I count) my life as grass[722]." "While I thus take upon myself the task of overcoming the rival Kings and other (enemies), the youthful (King) my enjoy the pleasures of the royal fortune with his mind at ease[723]." "He (Sujji), in order (to assure himself) assistance, desires to ask from the sovereign that *Ulhana* be made lord of the Gate, and that I be put incharge of the various offices of *Rilhana*[724]*."* "He (Sujji) also says to me: 'If *Ulhana*, you and I myself combine and are of one mind, then is there any necessity to take into account him who is on the throne[725] of *'Nam',* "If he (*Jayasimha*) should not agree to this, we being on spot may call in some other rival kinsman and put him up as king in his place[726]." At that moment king replie after having a sigh, and as he spoke the flashes of teeth (*dvija*[727]) appeared like ropes stretched out to catch (something whose) escape might be feared [728] from the action of *'Nam':* "It is thus as he (Sujji) has said it, no deceit, no incapacity, no apathy, can be suppresed in that proud man[729]." "The intention is to destroy him. Hence it need not be considered at the present moment how difficult it would be to break his undisputed predominance[730]." "That, however, afflicts me that the murder of this guileless man which has been resolved upon whether under the first impulse of a touch of anger or with justice, must be carried[731] out." "For we have discussed this plan before persons of little character. He would certainly find it out by bribing them with money[732]." "Worthless persons find employ (with us)J though we know them (as such), whether this be on account of their irrepressible merits (from a previous existence) or owing to the dullness of persons like myself[733]." "That the penalty paid by the Kings for their error in taking fools into their service, that they have to suffer from the result of the latter's foolishness[734]." "For parasites the ways of Kings are as difficult to follow, as for bazar bulls the mountain paths (*bhumibhrnmarga*[735]) to give the direction to the earth which never speaks; but crying when illegally people are capturing to it." "Rogues and dogs show an aversion to proper conduct, are anxious never to let their tongues rest and live by the food of others[736]." "This evil act which has been planned owing to the infliction of rogues, and which again cannot be abandoned from fear of them, will yet be regretted by us thereafter[737], on the point of death."

Plot for Sujji's Death

A secret plot, thus spoke the King, and resolved upon the death of *Sujji,* caused him often to keep awake, and himself passed sleepless nights[738]. But the servants told the King that *Sujji* was on the guard owing to the plan having been betrayed, and was preparing to kill him. The King believed them and felt alarmed[739] to spread the mission of *'Nam'*. He then went himself to their houses and tried to put *Sujji* into friendly relations with *Rilhana,* by telling them to form a matrimonial alliance[740] with the King as it were before the previous relation of the life. When after this allaying his suspicions he could not find an opportunity to kill him, he felt distressed, and was tossing day and night on his couch in helplessness[741], now, he has full of 'light' which has given power to explore the reasoning base of the life i.e. *'Nam'*. When *Sanjapala* did not come from his house as he was mourning over the loss of a relative, he was still more troubled by fear that the violent act would not succeed[742] in hurry. Because *Kularaja*[743], an officer in the army, who was famed for his skill in military exercises, and whose brothers, *Kalyanaraja*[744], and the rest, falling on the battle-field, had forgotten (to repay) the kindness of King *Sussala*, wished to repay his debt of gratitude at (the risk of) his life, and asked him for the cause of his grief[745]. Therefore, he told him the irremediable danger from the commander-in-chief who could neither be conciliated nor killed[746] to him: "What is this, (a thing) to be accomplished at the mere (sacrifice of) one's life?" Thus he replied to the King, and took the firm resolve to carry out the bold act[747]. Thus, the commander-in-chief did not come out of his apartments for two days, and thus did not let him (*Kularaja*) have the certainty of death or fortune[748]. On the third day, *Srngara,*a confidential servant of the King, reported to the latter that he had seen him alone on his couch[749]. Therefore, a King in the enjoyment of happiness has ever got servants. But a service in danger can be got only from an outsider[750] soldier. The club is ever attached to the hand of *Kama's*[751] foe (Siva) as a mark of beauty. But in the fight with *Tripura*[752], and *Mandara*[753] mountain which had come just on that occasion, had to act as his bow[754] struck to life of the living being.

Kularaja Sent to Kill Sujji

After this, King then despatched *Kularaja* to kill the *Sujji,* but his natural courage did not permit any agitation to be noticed in him, under the pretence of sending betel (through him[755]). But he did not take any betel in the golden dish, saying: "Death is certain. I am not to return. Then who will take it from this (dish[756])?" i.e, 'Nam' because the dish of *'Nam'* is living *mana*. Whereas other followers, too, endeavour thus to relieve their King's distress at the expense of their life; but they fail in the execution[757]. "Whether he be in company or alone, he must for certain be killed by me. May your Majesty keep awake therefore." With these works he left[758]. One might have thought-when he had gone, that flight was possible for him if he did not succeed in his bold enterprise[759], it was his bad luck. But he was going to serve his lord he took behind him to soldiers with their swords hidden[760] to kill the *mana* with *'Nam'*. After the doorkeeper, it has been announced that he had been sent by the King himself with betel, he proceeded before *Sujji*, while those who followed him had to remain behind[761] to see the master. *Kularaja* saw him surrounded by a few attendants of various sorts, as a lord of elephants is attended by small elephants[762]. After this Sujji had taken and respectfully acknowledged the betel from his lord, he inquired with a smile what the King did, and the like and then after a short time dismissed him in kindness[763]. It has been felt that fearing with the more people's might enter, *Kularaja* said quickly, pretending to use a natural opportunity: "A solder of the *Kaivarta* (fishermen's) caste, who is under me, has committed a fault.Now you may show regard for us by ordering off your subordinates who are preparing to seize him[764]." From conceit he refused this request as if (there had been) presumption in it, and said to him rudely: "I shall not do that[765]." It is noticed that *Kularaja* was going away as if in anger, the attendants (of sujji) said to the latter in a soothing way: "that man ought to be treated with esteem," and stopping him and made him turn back[766]. He then told: "Order my two servants who are presents to be admitted inside so that they may give an account of that matter[767]." Then Sujji unwillingly admitted them, and when the murderer saw that he had got his assistants (by his side), he prepared to strik him[768] with the *'Nam'*. *Sujji* said to them: "Go to-day. To-marrow I shall attend to your affair". Turning his back he then let himself down on a couch to sleep[769] in the Dark Period now we are procceeding towards the Englightenment Era.

Murder of Sujji (A.D. 1133)

In 1133 A.D. the murder of *Sujji* was took place, after going a few steps (towards the door) *Kularaja* turned back, drew out his dagger in haste and struck him quickly on the left side[770] of the body. As soon as he was passing his hand to the dagger, with the cry: "Fie, treason," they all struck at him[771]. But the onlookers had not yet comprehended that he was in danger, when he was dead already, as it were, for a long time[772]. Among the followers (of Sujji) who from fear cast away their honour and took to flight, only the single *Pincadeva* drew out his sword then[773] for the safety of his own interest. *Sujji* rushed about striking, and being wounded by the three who equally gave back his storkes, and streaming with blood was forced out of that hall[774]. But they kept inside the hall, which they bolted, they were surrounded by *Sujji's* servants who blocked the doors and windows, and were eager to slay them[775]. Now they are resisting at the windows of the *'Nam'*, they drew away the cotton-couch from below the cropse, and raising the latter, put it into the door which their assailants were battering[776]. And, the latter were pouring in showers of swords, arrows, spears, axes, daggers and stones, and by endeavouring to enter from various sides were throwing them into confusion[777]. They were hard to press then the head of the *Sujji* will be cut off, and threw it into the courtyard behind their assailants in order to disheartened them[778]. Whereas his followers saw the head they ran away anywhere, raising tumultuous cries. Its eye-holes and ears were intensely brilliant with the flowing blood; the depressed nostrils were covered with the hair of the upper life, the pupils of the eyes were protruding, and owing to the reflection of the rushing people seemed to exhibit some slight movement of the *'Nam'*; the flesh of the neck was rough owing to the uneven cutting, and in its folds were masses of coagulated fat which seemed as if moistened with turmeric; the hair of the beard was covered with dust. The saffron-drop on the forehead alone showed that it was really (the head of Sujji); and owing to its having fallen sideways, the teeth showed breaks in their compact[779]. Whereas the King, who after despatching the murderers had been in great anxiety, knew that the desperate act had been done when he saw outside the commotion of the people[780]. He is thinking that this measure is necessary, whether *Sujji* was dead or wounded, he quickly got the troops in readiness and ordered them to surround his house[781]. At the same time; King heard from the people the false reort, that *Sujji* had escaped, he himself caught the excitement of a contest[782] between the *'Nam' or 'Chamar'* and Brahman. It has been definitely disheartened by the King's men that *Sujji* has been killed, made a prisoner of *Sivaratha* who was hated by everybody, and was stopping there[783]. This, our song, earns merit today by describing the distinguished conduct of *Kalasa* brother[784]. Thus, *Bhiksu* and the rest behaved like heroes at their end, when attack took place. He, however, clung to a noble conduct though in safety[785]. For he (*Bhiksu*), after hearing in the royal palace of the event, did no run away, but proceeded to the slain master eager to leave his life there[786]. As he was banging the door with kicks, he was driven away by the murderous soldiers of the King, and only just saved from a miserable end[787] of the *'Nam'*. When he was without having been wholly discomfited retired to another hall, *Kularaja* and the others breathed again and proceeded before the King[788]. However, after forcing an entrance, *Kalasa* killed there a strong soldier, and was then hardly slain from afar by the opponent's arrows[789].

Attack on Sujji's Partisans

Study shows that land now fell into uproar, the King sent in haste *Sanjapala* to attack over the partisans, who had arrived, and *Rilhana* to slay *Ulhana*. By the time being *Rilhana* has arrived, after hurrying as far as the bank of the *Ksiptika* in the belief that *Ulhana* might have fled leaving the road, *Chamar, Sanjapala* having come earlier had been blocking the way before *Ulhana,* as he was passing from the gate of his house, and had struck many in the flight. But the sword of one cut through *Sanjapala's* right arm, so that the joints of the bones and sinews were severed and only the skin remained[790]. It shows that the act of *Sanjapala* is so powerful, after this his family will have to fallen into insignificance, he by his eminent qualities will again obtain publicity like *Buddha, 'Nanaka',* etc. when the time of the reward was at hand he was deprived of that arm which was the surety of his valour. Shame upon the perverse will of fate[791]! If, as before, he had remained uncrippled because he had attained already the rise of his fortune, the people might have learned by the result the astonishing (nature of his) aspiration[792]. If, indeed, *Rahu*[793] had not had his body crippled after he had drunk of the *Amrita*[794], when the world would have learned the aspiration which that powerful (demon) had long fostered[795]. Whereas, the son of *Sahadeva* (Ulhana) who suffered from a wound, saw with envy his old uncle *Sila* slain[796], who was the *'Word' or 'Nam'* of the 'Father'. As he was passing into the house in pain, then *Jajjala* was killed, a valued servant who had protected him, two soldiers and a Candala watchman (*Yamika*[797]). Therefore, he did not leave the house, but stopped there, seated in the courtyard and looking at his young son, *Rilhana* had it set on fire[798] to *Sujji.*

Murder of Ulhana

Murder of *Ulhana* disabled by his wound and blinded by the smoke. He was being carried (outside) in fetters by soldiers of note, when some low persons killed him in the gate of the house[799]. Whereas the King's angry feelings were not appeased even when he saw the head of *Ulhana*, who had caused the ruin of his chief ministers[800]. Thus the various followers of *Sujji* did noble deeds while attacked with fury by soldiers the King had despatched[801] certain own soldiers to *Sujji. Laksmaka,* the younger brother of *Sujji,* suffered the disgrace of being thrown into chain and fetters, and after seeing the King was slain by some merciless persons in the palace courtyard[802]. Thus, *Sangata*, his energetic cousin, the son of (Sujji's) paternal uncle, after rushing about in the royal courtyard as if on a stage, nobly gave up his life[803]. Then mad *Mummuni,* the brother (of *Sangala*), had fled for safety to his house, and was killed there by some wicked persons of the *Bana* family[804] which is known as *Chamar*, Dr. Raj Kumar son of Shri Bisakhi Ram, R/o Nazla Chak, Tehsil Akhnoor, District, Jammu (J&K). *Citriya*, too, *Sujji's* brother-in-law, who was a man of high descent, found a noble death after living a frivolous life of amours[805]. Whereas, his doorkeeper *Sangika* was wounded and subsequently died. Also other followers of *Sujji* found their death in various places[806] known as *Jammu* and *Kashmir.* Two or three like *Virapala* owed their life to the swiftness of their good steeds, and escaped the danger of death by reaching *Kosthesvara*[807]. In addition to this, *Saradiya*[808], *Sangata's* brother, on the way had his horse stopped at the *Subhatamatha*[809] by a concourse of vile people and fell into captivity[810] of the *'Nam'*. Whereas *Sajjala,* a son of *Sujji, Svetika*, the son of his elder brother, and *Ulhana's* son, were thrown into prison[811] of birth and rebirth. Thus, it might be happened the catastrophe on the fifth day of the bright half of *Asadha* in the year (of the Laukika era four thousand two hundred and) nine (A.D. 1133), owing to King and minister having fallen under the influence of Calumnious persons[812]. To this day even, the King, though surrounded by such (excellent) servants, remembers with regret that minister, whose energy had not failed before any task[813]. Therefore, in truth, the service of Kings is more dangerous than the raising of a *Vetala*, the leap over a precipice, the chewing of poison, or the foundling of a snake[814]. Who does not come to grief if he stands, unsuspectingly before sovereigns whose character (*guna*) is dependent on others, or before carts (whose ropes (*guna*) are attached to others[815])? which are affiliated with *'Nam'*. In this missiion, King thought *Sujji's* murder a wrongact. But the subjects thought it right and saw in it the king's extraordinary energy[816]. Whereas the king put *Sanjapala* in office as commander-in-chief, and gave to *Kularaja* the post of City-prefect[817]. Therefore *Dhanya* and *Udaya* who had left *Mallarjuna* and returned to the City, were again as before prominent as the king's confidants[818]. It has been fortunately abandoned its unsteadiness since deprived of the other abodes and abided in all respects permanently with *Citraratha*[819]. Though *Ulhana* distinguished by exceptional power and unrestrained even by the King. He was not pacify the land which he oppressed by his inflictions[820] of *'Nam'*. The commander of the fort (*Kottese*) at the village called *Gandharvana*[821], killed *Tikka* and sent his head to the King at *Parevisoka*[822].

Incursion of Lothana

After the death of *Tikka,* and his head was despatched to the King at *Parevisoka,* then King *Lothana* appeared suddenly at night in *Hadigrama* with a few followers. He had been repeatedly encouraged through messengers from *Kosthesvara* who was by nature hositle to the King, and who at that time was still further mortified on account of the renown the latter had gained[823] the benefit of doubt. As the King was on all sides in close union with the other (Damaras), the *Lavanya* (*Kosthesvara*) made peace, and after telling Lothana a great tissue of lies (*Mahakathitakantha*[824]) sent him away as he had come[825] from the 'Cosmic law'. As he showed a foolish desire to gain the throne as

Uchchala and rest like *Akbar, Asoka*, *Satavahana*, *Kushanas*, etc. He was laughed at by the people when his persistence bore no result[826]. But it is a process of life that one civilization go bye and another has to welcome. Therefore, the King then thought of destroying *Kosthaka* by employing bravos of the *'Nam'*, winning over the soldiers, and by various other devices[827], i.e., through writings and speeches. *Kasthesvara* in his anger had the bravos eyes torn out and did not seek to concilate the King, but prepared to fight him as if he were his equal antagonist in this world.[828]

Kosthesvara Attacked by the King

Jayasimha in this warfare ordered the leaders of his army to move forward (against *Kosthesvara's*) from their respective positions while he himself attacked by the King with various troops[829]. No doubt, the powerful (*Lavanya*) drawing near to the King, of whom he knew that he had marched on impetuously with a small force, tried to outmanoeuvre him, but was not successful[830] in this contest because *Lavanya's* force is walking bare-footed. *Citraratha,* though having a large force, was defeated, as fate willed by a detachment of *Kosthesvara's* troops in an encounter which ensued[831] by the *Chamar.* Owing to this defeat which acted like an unauspicious introductory word (*Omkara*), he lost henceforth everyday(more and more of) his courage[832] against the *'Nam' or 'Word'*. After fighting *Rilhana* and others, the *Lavanya* spread out all his troops in battle array and fell in the evening on the force of the commander-in-chief (*Sanjapala*[833]). Who then latter with less than a hundred men, *'Word'* the other soldiers having fled *abroad* withstood the onslaught of his troops, just as a rock (withstands) the rush of the elephants[834]. What need be said of that tiger of men, whose body does not keep within his own mail and other armour, as the battle grows fiercer[835]? Whenever we think of wild animals in connection with India, the tiger first presents himself to our mind. And, well he may, for he is the most distinctively national beast, and there is, no doubt, whatever that Hindustan is his original home, whence he migrated into other parts of Asia, both east and west. Low hot plains, with tangled jungles to hide in, are his realm; hence it is that the royal tiger of Bengal is the handsomest, fiercest, and altogether the most representative specimen of the race. The lion was once his rival. The ancient peotry of India bears ample witness to the fact; indeed it is he, and not his more wily and bloodthirsty cousin, who is called "the king of beasts". Alexander the

Great still found lions in Panjab, where he hunted them with the hounds that were presented to him for this purpose. But the gradually changing conditions of life, the advance of civilization with the attendant destruction of the noble forests where he loved to range, gradually made existence imposisble to him, until now there are only a few lion-families left in one particular forest tract in the peninsula of Gujarat, where they are strictly preserved by the Government. Not so the tiger. Nothing repressed him, and though, no doubt the jungles of Bengal were his first and favourite haunt, he spread westward as fast as the lion retreated, for the two never have been known to dwell within hearing or meeting distance of eath other[836]. While he thus broke the enemy's impetuosity by his firmness, there joined him *Trillaka*[837] and other *Lavanyas,* accompanied by their troops[838] to defeat the *Kal.* Though from regard for their relative they did not join in the fighting, yet they were of some small use to him inhis difficult position, and by his own valour he replused the enemy[839]. It was the timely preparation, inducing by kind words his troops to keep watchful at night, because judgement in using at the right time the various methods of occupying, and abandoning (positions), retention of places once taken by the *'Word'* or *'Nam'* these merits alone would (have sufficed) put the enemies to flight before this victorious (leader). What (need then of) praising his attack on the enemy[840]? Because as long as he has plenty of antelopes, deer and wild hogs to feast upon he is not a very objectionale neighbour; in fact he is, in such districts, to some extant a protector of the native agriculturist as all those animals are exceedingly destructive to crops. When he is reduced to domestic cattle, his vicinity is of course troublesome and ruinous; but nothing can express the horror of having "a man-eater" in the district, ie. a tiger generally an old one, which has once tasted human flesh and blood, and thenceforth, from a hideous pecularity of his nature, will not satiate his hunger with any other prey. Tigers at all times, unlike the lion and most beasts of prey, kill more victims than they need for food, and this instinct of sheer killing seems to grow fiercer and fiercer in a man-eater[841].

Kosthesvara Defeat by Sanjapala

Whenever *Kosthaka* feeling dispirited, betrayed by his followers, and shaken by such impetuosity, then descended from the hill and turned to flight[842] against *Sanjapala* to defeat him. It has been observed as the routes were blocked by an unseasonable fall of snow, the pursing enemies defeated the effort of his troops to get away[843] for the time being to consider on the effort either it is successful invasion or retreatable. They were driven by the King from the country he proceeded with a few followers to bathe in the *Ganga,* smarting with paint at his humiliation[844] that they were not succeeded in their mission. Whereas *Somapala*, who was troubled by his son for the throne, came at that time to the King for protection[845]. After this he had given two sons of *Nagapala* as hostages, the King, kind to those who shought his protection, promised with him for the safety[846] of King. In view of his misfortune the king, who character was distinguished by its guileless generosity, did not recall to his memory that this deceitful (prince) had been the cause of *Brhadraja's* (*Laksmaka*) discomfiture[847] without *'Nam'*. However, King gave his own troops for his assistance, and after humbling the pride of the enemy restored him to power[848] into the welfare of the people and their progress.

Alliance of Mallarjuna and Kosthesvara

In the meantime, however, *Kosthesvara* was on his way back after bathing in the 'Celestial Stream' (*Ganga*), and taking up (the cause of) *Mallarjuna* was endeavouring to raise a rebellion[849] against the Brahmans. Whereas, the prince who had come to *Kuruksetra*[850] on occasion of the solar eclipse, met there the *Lavanya* and abandoned from necessity his former enmity (against him[851]). At that time, *Lothana* who had arrived earlier upon the Damara's invitation, felt distressed, and left as he had come, when he heard of the latter having allied himself with *Mallarjuna*[852]. Now, the base of *Somapala*, though had taken an oath by sacred libation before the (Linga of Siva) *Vijayesa*, did not pay attention to the invasion prepared by the King's enemies[853], because they have been traped in the material life. His son (*Bhupala*), on the other hand, in order to propitiate the King, induced the various *Thakhuras* to plunder *Kosthaka* as he reached their respective territories[854] of the 'Nature'.

Exaction of Citraratha

In the meanwhile, the Brahmans of *Avantipura,* who did not like the exaction of *Citraratha*[855], owing to the wicked obstinacy he showed in increasing the imposts, hold a solemn fast[856] against the *'Chamar'*. Now this (minister) who, in his conceit did not care (even) about the King, paid no heed to them, many in their grief burned themselves in the flaming fire[857] i.e., called *Krishna, garbhah*. As soon as his servants confiscated even the grazing land (*Caraka*[858]) of the sacred crows, one cow-herd also overcome by compassion burn himself[859]. A young man known as *Vijayaraja*, the son of *Prthviraja* from the family of *Bhatta Udbhata*, being in great straits, was preparing to go abroad along with his younger brother. Seeing that distress there he spoke thus to his younger brother, while shedding tears of compassion[860]: "Look, how the subjects are ruined in their helplessness by a rogue of a minister, while the King, imperturbable in his kindness (to him), pays no regard to them." "Where the King from complaisance to the ministers takes no care of the subjects in their misery, who else is there to relieve their sufferings?" i.e. Master. "Or, perhaps, that is the correct way that he deserves to be chastised, should be punished by the chastiser, and the latter again, it he gets into trouble, by someone else in mutual emulation." "Sometimes in concussion the unwidely stone is overcome by the thoroughly hard steel, sometimes, however, the steel by the stone." "The king who is distinguished by all good qualities, does not deserve hatred for one single fault. Nothing else appears to me indicated but the murder of *Citraratha*." "The destruction of one wicked person is called lawful when all are helped by it. Even the Jina (*Buddha*) slew a great snake which killed living beings." "If punishment has been meted out by us to that wicked man, then no official will again oppress the people, owing to the dread of (being punished by) a man of energy." "If by the sacrifice of this body numberless people may be rendered happy, then, O brother, is this not the greatest bargain[861]?" When his younger brother *'Nam'* expressed his agreement he made him to take an oath by sacred libation, and then returning followed *Citraratha* in order to kill him[862]. Even at this time of the Kali yug which is sullied by the weakness of the sacred law, there manifests itself brilliantly to this very day the irrepressible power of the gods of the earth (Brahmans[863]). Therefore, no one, until all his merits (from a former existence) have been exhausted, enters upon an obstinate course against the Brahmans before whom the destructive arts of the wicked break down[864] with the help of *'Nam', 'Sujji'*, who had exasperated the twice-born, found his death from the hand of a twice-born, and *Citraratha,* who had slighted the Brahmans, who slain by a Brahman[865]. It is sure that (youth), sacrificing his own life without immediate cause, planned his death, becaused his mind was seized by a charm which the Brahmans had sent forth[866] called *Preman.* Therefore, those Brahmans are bruning themselves, just then *Citraratha*, the object of their hatred had followers killed in a quarrel amongest themselves[867]. His destruction was kept awake for many a night as he was not able to get day or night at *Citraratha*, who was accompanised by a strong force[868] of *'Nam'*. When *Citraratha* was going about, the roads were covered far away, with numberless great persons of the *'Nam'* and he in the midst of the crowd came in sight and disappeared (again in a moment[869]), as it is depicted in the study.

Vijayaraja's Attempt Against Citraratha

Study shows that *Vijayaraja* was unshakened in his extraordinary attempt against *Citraratha's* persistence, on one occasion ran quickly after him when he was ascended the stairs in the royal palace[870]. As *Citraratha* was being stopped before a pillar surrounded by nobles, he then in fierce boldness struck him with a dagger on the head[871] to move in right direction. He thereupon was dying, lost consciousness from exhaustion, his eyes were rolling and his energy left him[872] desperate. In this state of mind, he was deserted by his frightened followers, who thinking that he had been murdered by the King's order, lost their courage[873]. The murders in the belief i.e. *'Nam'* that he was dead, did not strike him again, and kept back his brother who had arrived by another staircase[874] of the *'Nam'*. The ways which were open to him everywhere he did not flee, but shouted loudly and repeated: "*Citraratha* has been put to death by the king[815]." Consequent upon this, all the wretched followers of *Citraratha;* who had enjoyed (with him) by taking fried meat dishes and other pleasures of regal state and disappeared in fright[876]. Whereas, his elder brother *Lotharatha*, fled in his terror to a dancing girl for protection, and hid his face on her breasts[877]. When *Citraratha* was brought in this condition before the King, the latter in person cheered him up, and said: Have no fear who has struck you[878]? No, there is no danger, it is my pleasure that I have been gifted by a wounderful presents by the 'Nature' on my devotion. At that time soldiers were searching by the King's order for the person who had wounded the lord of the Gate, the murder presented himself, saying: "I am that person.[879]" Who met time before in the Heaven. He then bravely slew twenty or thirty soldiers, and after displaying a praiseworthy prowers in defying them through his resolute bearing, was struck in the leg and killed[880] for the time being. At that time a leaf was found on his arm upon which the reason of his dead was written, in these words: "From Yuga to Yuga I come into existence to protect the righteous, to destroy the evil-doers, and to restore the sacred law[881]." The desire (which he expressed) in his death by this verse, sanctifies him[882] on the basis of his character (*guna*). *Citraratha* then his wound was healed up, but fell, owing to the lesion of the joints of his forehead bones, into disgust (of food), madness and misery[883] was facing at that time. The time period of five to six months he lay day by day on his couch rolling his suffering and emanciated body about[884] to regain the strength.

Irruption of Kosthesvara and Mallarjuna

On spot, an irruption was took place by *Kosthesvara* and *Mallarjuna* together, but due to a mountain-fastness[885], they were (surrounded) by a dense forest called darkness. But they are in his endeavour to collect those who belonged to his party, he caused excitement among the people. They had not yet forgotten their (former) sufferings of the Brahmans, and were apprehending a fresh contest for the crown[886] of *Mayawati.* But now the people will quickly felt pained by the appearance of the hostile force in fresh election system in Uttar Pradesh, just as (if it had been) a chill produced by an untimely cloud of the sky, and became benumbed in their energy[887]. *Jayasimha* then had this forest-fastness which extended over mang *Kos* (*Krosa*), surrounded on all sides by his ministers who occupied the neighbouring forest-hamlets [888] of life. When *Sanajapala* went into his camp with *Yavanas*[889] the enemy became motionless, as trees keeping still in a calm[890]. Thus *Dhanya*, too, threw his force into *Silikakotla*, and showed aversion even to the smell of the enemy, just as the lion to that of the elephant[891]. Whereas; *Rilhana*, whose force was posted by the King at *Govasa,*[892] scoured the forests and made the enemies hide themselves before him as the owls (hide) before the sun[893]. Checked by these measures of the energetic King, but *Kosthesvara* was prevented from removing the *Mayawati* about the throne about three or four months[894]. He had been in distress abroad, and had been disregarded by the chiefs of the neighbouring territories. His own followers had fallen off and the King's officers had baffled his efforts. Not comprehending from want of judgement the ways of Kings, having lost his footing, and forgetting his guilt, he wished to conciliate the king[895] on the question of agreement between the two about the future course of action. On the other hand, *Sanjapala* in his thorough devotion thought it idle to reproach him (*Kosthesvara*) now that he was eager to remove the king's anger, and agreed to his wish[896] of throne.

Surrender of Kosthesvara

In his eagerness to make peace with the King's enemy *Sanjapala* did not punish *Kosthesvara*, he himself had thus suffered (from him). At that situation the sons of *Prthvihara* showed good-will to (*Kosthesvara*) is not astonishing[897]. As soon as, he sent the enemy of the King (before the latter), he could not appease the King's anger even by cutting off the finger of his own hand[898]. At that moment *Sanjapala* will be unable to allay the anger of the King though he bound his head-dress round his neck, carried a shoe on his head, and used (favourable) moments[899]. Now *Kosthesvara* had refused (to recognised) two or three royal prerogatives ('Word', *lanchana*), opposed several royal orders, and in his conceit behaved altogehter like a King[900] of the *'Nam'* called *'rajanam'*. But at the same time King received the report of the *Mallarjuna*, who had got away, was captured. The fortunate persons of the 'Nam' will follow the success one after the another[901].

Mallarjuna Detained At Savarnika

During this journey, *Mallarjuna,* will not being quick on his feet and hence unable to bear the fatigues of marching, was being carried on the shoulders of his servants. When after escaping from various dangerous situations, he had reached the village of *Savarnika*[902] which belonged to (the territory of) *Lohara* he had been stopped by the *Thakkura Jaggika* who put guards over him. The King now heard that this faithful servant had come before him[903] for the assistance in the critical situations. *Mallarjuna* who had been escaped with difficulty from the fastness and had nearly been caught, who ws captured again by that opponent. Who is unable to escape his destiny[904]? *'Nam'* only. The Ganga is the rolling forth from her celestial course had scarcely escaped from the belly of one great *Rsi* (*Jahnu*[905]) who had caught her lip, when she was swallowed up by another (*Agastya*[906]) after she had filled the hollow of the ocean. Nobody can escape the inevitable[907]. But at the same time *Jaggika* will have to watch the neighbourhood until the captive (*Mallarjuna*) should reach (the King), the thoughtful king employed *Udaya*, the lord of the Gate (to fetch *Mallarjuna*[908]). But the King did not believe that other ministers would show resolution in a difficult situation, excepting him who was wise and distinguished by vigour, depth of thought and prowers[909]. *Udaya* after passing the routes which were made insecure by those who were drawing allowances from both sides, sighted the enemy of the King, (*Mallarjuna*) standing at a window[910] of the *'Nam'*.

Surrender of Mallarjuna

As soon as; *Udaya* arrived outside the window, *Mallarjuna* said to him various things praising him and wishing to make a pretence of courage by a resolute bearing which was fictitious, and then again addressed to him: "You, the foremost of the wise, who value above everything devotion to one's master have been brought (here) by persons who have succumed to exticements[911]." "Because I had not a supporter like you, who resemble a protecting gem, I have, as a bad ruler, suffered in my youthful reign by many intrigues." "Kings who are difficult to face (in their power), can ordinarly be examined by the eyes of the people at the fall of their fortune, just as the sun (can be easily examined) on a winter day[912]." "That king is to be praised who spreads lustre at his rise as well as at his end, just as the sun which puts forth its blood-red disc (at its rise as well as its setting); (that king) whose apperance was rendered auspicious by the emotion of the citizens wives at his access, and also by the violent love shown for him by the band of the *Apsaras*[913] at his grand end." "After securing nobly a position (*Pada*[914]) and accomplishing something (*artha*[915]) I have become perplexed at the end, like a great poet, (who has found his word (*pada*) has also got some subject matter (*artha*), but finds himself perplexed about the completion of his verse)". "Now your should give assurance to my mind by prom ising me one wish, which is not beyond what is feasible[916]." Keeping in view the said statements, he had then a crystal *linga* with its base (*Pitha*) put before the lord of the Gate that he might touch it for the sake of assurance[917]. *Udaya* then thought: "Surely, this proud (prince) asks me (to grant) the wish that he may fight warriors who use their darts, spears and arrows in an honest contest." and touching the *Siva-linga* promised the desired wish of the '*Nam*'[918]. Thereupon *Mallarjuna* addressed him again thus: "I ask you that I may come before the king such as I am now, without my eyes being takenout, without being killed, without being wounded[919]." On hearing these words demeaned by cowardice, all were benumbed with shame and turned their heads to the ground like twigs dripping with rain[920] of shower. Then they thoughtfully remembered the last moments of *Bhiksu,* and this made their hearts again expand in cheerfulness[921] that our 'Father' has come back on this earth. No doubt, he was being taken away by *Udaya* on a litter carried by men, he looked without shame and with emotion also on those people whom he had eared for[922]. As he was being carried along on the way, wholly absorbed in eating abundantly, sleeping, etc, just like an animal, no reflection of any kind occupied his mind[923] becasue they nothing no the value of *'Nam'*. Which is called *Chamar* when the people will saw him taken along in this condition by his guards, their hearts were moved with compassion, and they did not approve of the King's (action[924]) because he is a liberal kind of man. And they said: "It is not right that the King, as the elder brother should show such curelty towards the younger brother who is deprived of his father and deserves compassion[925]." "Who could be so cruel-minded as to disfigure by torments the charming body of this (youth) whose look is like that of a dark-blue lotus[926]?" i.e. the theory of mind. Thus the people were unable to connect the preceding facts and their consequences and forgetting his guilt, reproached theking in various way as they saw on the road[927] as in a procession. For this but what account is need to be taken of young boys, blockheads, and the like, even the thoughts of great men do not ever keep the same direction. When the hearers listen to the (story of the gambling, the dragging of the *Pancala*[928] princess (Draupadi) by the hair, etc, their anger against *Dhrtarastra's* sons is greater than against the *Pandu*[929] sons; because they were in anger mood as it was the sign of destruction of the theory of mind. As soon as they heard of the drinking of the blood of the *Kurus* and the shattering of the head of *Duryodhana* who had his thigh broken, one sees the very same people enraged against the *Pandavas*[930] those had the father called *'Word'*. Nobody is in the midst of the events, can understand their cause and their result. How should not the sentiments of the onlooker change at various incidents[931]? i.e the theory of progress in History. It carried in litter as he reached in the City in evening, moving the citizens to tears, and holding an earthen vassel in which lay his cut off finger[932].

Mallarjuna Imprisonment (A.D. 1135)

On the fifteenth day of the bright half of *Asvina* in the year (of the *Laukika* era four thousand two hundred and) eleven (A.D. 1135) *Mallarjuna* was imprisoned: and the King was placed him under guards in the *Navamatha*[933]. As soon as; he passed in distress five to six nights(and days) without taking food and was asking to be allowed to touch the feet of the King, the latter from compassion came to him[934] and was released from the darkness. Then the King had to promise him the desired safety, he told him that *Citraratha* and *Kosthaka* were nothing but (embodiment of) perfidy and deserving to be killed[935]. Consequent upon this, King has to wish to imprison *Kosthaka*, who had gone to his own place, and despatched (for this purpose) five to six councillors among them *Rilhana*[936] was too accompanied with *Mallarjuna*.

Caputre of Kosthaka and Catuska

Study also reflects when all the courage were drooped, the King took up the enterprise in person, whereupon *Rilhana* caught *Kosthaka* and *Catuska* with their arms, as the shark (catches) the fish[937]. He was deprived of his sword and remained motioinless in the net of that strong man's arms, as a person who was blinded up by sleep at that time is beset by a goblin[938] game or play. Whereas the fierce *Bhihkharaja*, *Kularaja's* brother's son in obedience to the King pierced his neck with a dagger[939] to *Kosthaka*. When the *Rajaputra Prthvipala*[940] was hitting him with a hatchet on the head, the King angrily forbade him with the sweet of the *'Nam'*. It was vital wound at the neck-bone and incapable of action, he rolled on the ground, covered with blood[941]. Thus, *Kamaliya*, and other men of great strength threw *Kosthesvara's* brother *Catuska* to the ground, as elephants(throw down) a log of wood[942]. When the Brahman *Mallaka* saw his two masters thus struck down in helpless and captured, again he stepped up with drawn sword[943]. It has been noticed by the King himself as he was rushing unexpectedly into the tumult and striking at several of the royal servants[944] of *Kalaraja* while this man of great strength was cutting down several brave soldiers who were running towards King, *Kularaja* rushed at him with a dagger[945]. Because *Kularaja* was skilled in the use of arms, pressed him against the wall, but was unable to him as *Mallaka's* hand was to get away, or to keep still,or to strike, but parrying frequently, he kept him at his place without wound[947]. However, *Mallaka*, who made a great noise by dashing down his foot and throwing out his arms, then he took a glance at *Padmaraja* who was running[948] up high and high to change the life of people from Dark Age to Enlightenment Era. *Kularaja* at that moment got an opportunity and struck him in the breast but as his hand withdrew after the stroke, *Mallaka* cut off his thumb[949]. At the same time; *Bijjaraja* was full of hot conceit struck at him and *Mallaka* was also striking back at the same but *Kularaja* and *Padmaraja* both hit him rapidly[950]. It appears that *Mallaka* got away due to the three attacks led by *Kularaja* and *Padmaraja* and ran towards the King, whom he had sighted entering the door of the pavilion (*Catuskika*[951]). When *Mallaka* was striving to reach the King. *Kularaja* ran after him in haste and excitement and stopped his rush by wounding him in the bones of the buttocks[952]. Then he was surrounded by all the soldiers, after slaying cowards as well as bravemen will fell down quickly upon the hero's couch; and a stream of blood was serving for its upper covering[953] lips of life. *Kasthaka* deserved to be counted among the heroes for having displayed a laudable prowess under the eyes of his 'Masters' who had fallen into misfortune, and were yet alive, and for having found to death worthy of envy[954] in this universe. For the time being the servants of *Kosthaka* had run away outside, and only the Damara *Janakacandra* displayed that he was not lacking in courage[955] because he had the strength of *'Nam' or Sabad* which is the *'Ultimate Reality'*. For he though unarmed, took from one of the royal servants his battle-axe, and fighting sent many into the presence of Yama to herald his (approach[956]) to the Master. The battle-axe which was in his hand while he endeavoured to make his way to the disc of the sun, was as eager to sever the carotid vein (*Susumna*) of the enemy, as the crescent of the moon (is eager to receive its share of sunlight by the Susumna-ray[957]) for the moment of the earth in this universe.

Kosthaka's wife Becomes a Sati

We have neither seen nor heard (of another such deed as done) then by *Kosthaka's* wife, when her husband was thrown into prison, nobly followed she becomes as a *Sati*[958]. There was no heeding to the words of her relatives who said that she might yet get back her husband alive, she entered the fire[959]. From the feet of her, who was proceeding to the world of virtuous women, the fire was puried from the sin by which it had been sullied on account of its desire to embrace the wives of the Seven Rsis[960]. She was a daughter of *Vasanta,* the brother of *Dhanya* and *Udaya*[961], and proud of her noble descent, but did not cherish the customs of Damara-wives. Let the wives of *Lavanyas* yield up in widowhood to their beautiful bodies from lustof money even a village officials, (common) householders, and the like[962]. *Kosthaka's* wife and the two followers (*Mallaka* and *Janakacandra*) made *Kosthaka* raise (again) proudly his head, after mental confusion had caused him to become despondent[963] of the *'Nature'*. *Kosthaka*, though his wound healed, then he became a prey to worms owing to some sins, and after many nights died in his prison[964] for a long period to obtain the life to fight against the Brahmins.

End of Citraratha

Whenever *Citraratha* who was withered up and emaciated, became from the fear most distresse, when he heard that the King had been incited the reference against him by *Mallarjuna*[965]. His beloved only wife in this universe, the Virtuous *Suryamati*, who was the surety of his power, had already before gone to the other world[966]. But his body was broken in health by an incurable disease, his house without his consort and his lord rendered averse by enmity, he found no cheer whatever[967] he listenened from the outer world. He was thinking that not withstanding his guilt whether *Citraratha* would not suffer anything unkind from the King, if he stopped at a *Tirtha*, he went to *Suresvari*[968] under the pretence of wishing to die there[969] for the time being thereupon the King confiscated in various places the great riches of all kinds which he wealther than Kubera, who has owned his power[970]. His gold, clothes, equipment, horses, jewels, arms and other (valuables) displayed in the book *entitled Paintings and Lifestyles of the Jammu Region (From 17th to 19th Century A.D.)* by Dr.Raj Kumar, Published, New Delhi, 2006 and *'History of the Brahmans'*, as (if it were) in rivalry, greater and greater splendour[971]. Thus, the tree of the royal fortune[972] which were withered up for some time by the hot blast of the *Lohara* treason was strengthened when watered by the hill-stream of his (*Citraratha's*) fortune. Whereas in the residence of *Vijaya*[973], the son of *Bhava,* there was a regal fortune, imprisoned (as it were) and ever awake, which from the paleness of cares appeared as if touched by the glitter of white parasols. Though the troubles had long passed away, he filled with apprehensions such as are natural for one living in the forest, did not leave the splendid *Kalyanapura,* as the *Salva*[974] ('Word' prince did not leave) Saubha. When he recognised the murderer sent by the King, a man called *Ananda*, he slew him and was killed by him[975] with the *'Nam'*. He passed the message for the King *Jayasimha*, who was so anxious to protect his subjects, that time was full of enterprise[976] between the King and master. At the same time *Citraratha* was stopped at the *Tirtha,* his two servants known as *Srngara* and *Janaka*. They were the well known intriguers and were exerting themselves to secure the Padagra office[977]. Whereas *Srngara* got the better of *Janaka* by winning over the King through the offer of abundent bribes, and obtained the enjoyment of his masters fortune[978] because he is busy in his own business for the settlement of the race. In this way King restored to *Udaya*[979] the long-lost charge of the 'Gate', just as the rainy season has been (brings back) the water to the river banks [980] of *Vitasta or Sindha*. Then after eight months *Citraratha* was died having long been suffered vital pains caused by his evil deeds which had by necessity to receive their punishment[981] as per desire. But the praise be to that familiarity inconceivable (in its effects), the power of which overcomes previous feelings and makes a ridiculously deformed person appeared normal, also a bad smelling person an acceptable companion and makes one take the advice even of a thorough fool[982] i.e. *'Nam'* who always carries load of the universe.

Srnagara made Prime Minister

Keeping in view the 'class struggle' theory of KarlMarx, *Srngara*[983], the son of *Sajjaka*, had, when the King was a young boy, spoiled full of curiosity in the *'Nam'*, gained his favour by gambling (with the) and by the other reprehensible practices. At that time, King had obtained sovereign power, he had undergone fatigue owing to his having been sent by him day and night with betel to *Citraratha*. By the messages he had carried, and obtained a full knowledge of affairs and became a trustee adviser. When it came to (*Citraratha's*) end, he brought to the King those servants who showed (*Citraratha's*) treasures. Then, as the throne was devoid of all noble persons and all advisers, he obtained the position of prime minister[984]. Though he was short-sighted in his narrow mind and displayed only a shallow liberality, yet his riches were not turned to evil use as his gifts went to worth persons[985] like Plato, Dr. B.R. Ambedkar, *Asoka Mohammeda Prophet, Jeuses Christ*, etc. No doubt, *Srngara* indeed, was liberal to his *Gurus* in gifts of rice (Before) he had thought himself rich, even (when he got what was needful) for the food and dress of his women-folk[986] that was the *'Nam' or 'Word'*. In this way, he deserves final communion (with the deity), since he put up, with his own silver-pieces, a silver pedestal (*pitha*[987]) at *Suresvari* which is still extant[988] to this era. No doubt, he spent great seems to make at *Nandiksetra*[989] Vihara of Buddha, such ample provision have been made for (the celebration of the) full-moon day of *Asadha*, as in recent times even Kings could not have imitated. He had been first directed there by *Canpuka*[990] and others. Thereby he obtained subsequently prosperity forgive to six years[991]. But *Srngara* made prime minister as a play-companion had been held a worthless person, did, while in office, extraordinary deeds through the strength of his lord's attachment[992] which provides every messages of the 'Nature'. At that time snake (*Vasuki*[993]) of which the enemy of Tripura (Siva) thought, when it was formed as his neck-ornament, that it might come to grief by the playful fingernails of his young consort (*Parvati*). But it did not brake even on the request of Siva's order. Now it has been stretched upon itself on the bow formed by the mountains (*Mandara*). How should not another, too, display energy through the strength of his masters order[994]? Because there is no appropriate time for a while, attaching themselves to *Srngara* on the one side and *Rilhana* and *Dhanya* on the other, *Janaka* and *Srngara* ousted each other from office by means of bribing[995] the theory of mind and raying come this is the noble opportunity for them and get solace. On one occasion *Srngara* had imprisoned *Janaka* along with his wife and children, and made him drop tears as well as the pearls of his jewelry[996]. *Janaka* again in disgusted cast dishonour on *Srngara* by putting money as a bribe into the hands of the rough jailors and asking them (to secure from Srngara) sexual indulgence[997]. When, again, one of the two was in office, he made the people laugh by rubbing and moving with the thumb nail the ring on the ring-finger, by talking with the left upper-lip drawn up and his eyes contracted and by moving to and fro in frowns wrinkles which made his forehead (appear) low and (again) high[998] because they nothing no the language of Master. It has been seen in the time of his good fortune talking indistinctly, using harsh words, closing his eyes, shouting a great deal, laughing and clapping his hands[999] at the time of examination at the last moment. Is it not the recollection of such foods sufficient to serve as an object of amusement, if one recalls their real nature in the imagination of one's mind[1000]? i.e. *'Nam'*. In this whole debased period which knows no fitness and in which men are no better than straw, methink, it is reality (only) *Srngara* who does not deserve to be despised[1001] in the hands of the illiterate in the field of 'Spiritual Knowledge'.

Pious Act of Jayasimha

In the sharp struggle of the life, King's mind is all pervading and steadfast, has obtained fore-rank among the virtuous by his pious actions. As if he possessed Perfect Enlightenment (*bodhi*) (Like a Buddha), he has helped the enemy in distressed, just as the sandal tree while burning, gives delight to the person who has set the forest on fire. Paying proper regard to Gurus[1002], scholars, Brahmans, the helpless and others. He has bestowed gifts on the households which deserved them. Being of pious thought and rich, he has raised the temples of (Siva) *Vijayesa,* and of a host of gods to equality with *Kailasa* by the stucco he put on them; and as he was passionately fond of restoration (*Jirnoddrti*[1003]) his care was ever directed towards the putting into order of Mathas, temples, gardens, tanks, canals, and the like[1004].

Conduct of King Jayasimha

Notwithstanding that the conduct of King *Jayasimha* is of such character, yet because he has once committed acts of enmity against persons equal (in respectability) to religious students (*brahmcaria*), he is said by dull persons to be altogether an embodiment of cruelty[1005]. Thus the noble deeds of the celestial river (Ganga), such as the nourishing of the universe, the filling of the seven oceans, the delighting of Brahman and the other (gods), are reduced to irrelevance by the fault committed at one single occasion, when he touched the ashes of the host of *Sagara's*[1006] sons. Hereby, she has become known to the people as fit for the deposition of bones, as (if she were) like a burning ground[1007] on the earth. At that time, there *Jayasimha* was died by strangulation that rogue of an official (*Kayastha*), the Brahman *Sivaratha*[1008], who had been a great intriguer[1009]. Thus by exterminating the vairous enemies, the King who was bent on doing good, freed the country from various obstacles (to its prosperity[1010]). No doubt, Kings have obtained intense power chiefly by removing the obstructions of enemies, just as the sun-rays (attain power) on getting free of the clouds[1011]. Therefore, this jewel of a King attained a pleasing character in the course of the development of a nation, just as the vine (attains) greater sweetness as its grows to maturity[1012]. No doubt, he continually celebrated sacrifices at which considerable Daksinas were distributed, and gave splendour (by his presents) to marriage, pilgrimages, and other great festivals[1013] of the Nature like 'Whole World'. He gave from his own the materials (required) for the sacrificial performances of pious persons, just as the moon (gives) her light to the herbs of the high mountains[1014]. But with the attentive mind he undertook to furnish the proepr paraphernalia to the citizens at the marriages of their sons, consecrations (of images, etc) and similar occaions[1015] of their wives. The woods which were supplied for (the revenue from) which benefited the royal treasury, he placed at the free disposal (of the citizens) and there by got the whole city built anew[1016] messages.

Piety of Jayasimha

In this process of study sensible persons will notice with wonder the intentness with which he devoted himself, like a perfect *Muni*, to the worship of Siva, though merged in affairs of states[1017]. From morning to evening one does not see him and do one act according to him for which men of experience do not give the direction[1018] to the society. But those are black by experience, they have the darkness of ignorance, learning had shown forth at intervals in the passing lightening flashes of fortune(coming) from such clouds as *Jayapida* and other (royal patrons[1019]) have drawn their power. However, he has given permanent brilliancy to the picture of his virtue which is of wondrous variety of the nature, by bestowing wealth which lasts like the radiant light of a jewel[1020] of the *'Nam'*. He has made scholars and their descendants owners, as long as the planets, the sun and moon should last of villages possessing an abundance of unimpaired fields[1021] of life in this universe and man is struggling for that to obtain the existence. The houses which *Jayasimha* has constructed for men of learning, he raised their terraces to such height it is very difficult to obtain, only the seven Rsis (the Great Bear) come to see them as they are towering above their heads[1022] called *'Nam'* or *'Chamar'*. It is a very simple and safe route of jourey for scholars who follow him as their *Carvanleader* on the path on which his intuition guides, and which has been found by his knowledge[1023]. Just as *Aryaraja*[1024] has obtained, while lying on his bed, had chiefly found delight in (listening to) the sound arising from the flow of the water of *Ganga* with which the lingas are being washed, so he, when about to go to sleep, dispenses with flutes, lutes and other (music) of the *'Nam'* and finds his pleasures in reflecting over the talk of guileless men of learning[1025] and writings.

Consecration of Temples, etc. Under Jayashima

Under the *Jayasimha* number of new temples and shrines were constructed, which during the time of the illustrious *Lalitaditya* and *Avantivarman* left behind in Kashmir. He did such pious works which other great monarchs of the world could not do[1026]. Now, he has established for all Mathas and temples which were raised in his own time. He made a permanent endowment for their maintenance[1027]. Thus, first, the *vihara* of *Ratnadevi* who was the firmly-established object of her Lord's love attained pre eminence among all foundations[1028] then she agreed the concept of the *'Nam'* i.e. Lord.

Pious Acts of Rilhana

Due to the pious acts of the *Rilhana*, a friend of many virtues became the leader of the whole line of ministers on the road of piety[1029] by displaying sincereity towards the 'Father'. This pure-minded (minister) called *Sudar*, was unable to deprive himself of (the society of) ascetics, learned men and those versed in sacred law, even when he stopped in his private apartments[1030]. Because his whole life was employed in pious works, such as presenting (to Brahmans) skins of black antelopes, cows with calves, and the like, and in marrying out girls for the sake of religious merit[1031] of the nature. *Rilhana,* by providing large-mindedly the complete sacrificial apparatus, enabled all who maintained (sacred) fires to carry out their rites without hindrance[1032] of the *'Nam'*. His mind was never sullied by looking at evil, treated sixty-was excited and astonished[1033] by the law of nature. Moreover, he adorned the cities of both *Pravarasenas*[1034] with great Mathas and bridges (or embankments) which were richly provided with numerous *Agraharas* (for their maintenance[1035]). Thus the (shrine of Siva) *Rilhanesvara* which he erected at the first town of King *Pravara* (*Sena*), excited with wonder and became pre-eminent among pious foundations[1036] of the *'Nam'*.

Foundation in honour of Sussala

Jayasimha the man of merits had a *Vihara* constructed at the place called *Bhalerakaprapa*[1037] ('fountain of *Bhaleraka*), in the honour of *Sussala* wife. This (Vihara) became known by the name of her cat which had followed her dead (mistress) into death, instead of forgetting her attachment as is the won't of animals[1038]. This pet cat would go before her to great distances and keep before her husband jealously had fallen out (with her[1039]). From the very day, she had started for the Tirtha (to die there), this cat had been wailing and (subsequently) she died from in grief by refusing the food put before her,because her father and husban were left this world before her death[1040]. As *Didda* among queens of the world, so *Sussala* among ministers' wives has secured the foremost rank by means of manifold religious foundations[1041] after the death of *'Father'*. Thus, she (*Sussala*) had now erected (afresh) illustrious *Cankunavihara*[1042] of which nothing by the name remained, by erecting a stone shrine (*prasada*), residences and other (structures[1043]). Moreover, she accomplished all kinds of pious works by constructing water wheels, wells, halls for students, and the like[1044]. Whereas, her Vihara, which covered the whole ground of the residence (*Sthandila*) *of former roya*l dynasties, made the whole city a joy to look at[1045] the wonder of Nature. As soon as she consecrated (this Vishara), she being attacked by consumption, found her death at the illustrius *Suresvari,* whereby her full communion (with the gods) was indicated[1046] by her.

Foundations of Ministers

The *Mathas* and *Agraharas* which *Dhanya* established under the name of his wife, did not get (known by) the desired appellation. Whence its fame(came) without merits[1047] because it was founded by the ministers. Therefore, *Udaya,*[1048], the Commander-in-Chief, who also establsihed Agraharas and Mathas in the same fashion, heard ever his name (mentioned) in this connection with them[1049]. Whereas the splendid Matha which *Udaya,* the lord of the gate, constructed along with numerous *Brahmapuris*[1050] which embellished the shore of the *Padmasaras*[1051]. And, his elder brother, *Srngara*[1052], too, who was a judge of (*tantrapati*), and a man of virtue, constructed a Matha, a garden, and an ablong tank by (the hill of) *Sridvara*[1053] called the house of *'Nam'*. Besides these, *Alamkara*[1054], the superintendent of the great treasury (*brhad ganja*), embellished the land by constructing bathing-huts (*Sananakostha*[1055]), Mathas, Brahmpuris, bridges and the like[1056] information of the various messengers of the God.

Praise of Alamkara

Alamkara, a man of wisdom (*budha*), was born from *'Nam'* who was well versed in the arts of various life, and was ever giving relief by medical herbs (or, he was like the planet Mercury (*Budha*) who was born from the moon which ever gives comfort to the herbs); he has been known as a poet (*Kavi*) surpassed all liberal persons by his liberality (Or, he was famous like the planet venus (*Kavi*) which has freed itself from connection with the demons (*danavatva*) by renunciation[1057]). He was being a worshipper of Vishnu, like none before him, was attached to King (*nrsimbh*), distributed gold, food and clothing which was without harm, and presented cows at the festival of (*Visnu-Adi*) *Varaha*[1058]. The Matha which *Srngarabhatta* erected by the side of the *Bhattarakamatha*[1059], did not enjoy particular fame, being like a well by the side of the full ocean[1060] called *Sudra* or sea. *Jatta,* the ruler of *Darvabhisara,*[1061], he was also known as *Samdhivigrahika*, who was devoted to pious work, consecrated a (Linga) of Siva.[1062] Singly among trees known as *Karavira* (fragrant oleander) enjoys that happy privilege of producing in abundance. Those flowers which are rendered to blessed by that particular linga of Siva which came to light by itself[1063]. Therefore, *Bhutta,* the younger brother of *Jalha,* deserves alone the highest distinction among all the ministers whom the King has raised to power[1064] from *Alamkara.* The (*Linga* of) *Balakesvara* which is natural (*svayambhu*) and came to light by itself; he also obtained the message of worship as the (linga of) *Jyestharudra*[1065] (received worship) from *Vasistha*[1066]. There he established a town called *Bhuttapura*[1067] which is adorned by the great houses of *Viharas* and Mathas[1068]. Moreover, in city, he consecrated a (Linga of) *Siva* called as *Bhuttesvara,* and in *Madavagrama*[1069] *a* tank which was liked, the reflection of the beauty of piety[1070] called *'Nam' or 'Power'*

Foundation of Queen Ratnadevi

For the development of the art and architecture, *Ratnadevi* invested her wealth to a great extent on the site of her own for the foundation of Vihara, by establishing there the *Vaikunthamatha* and other (pious buildings[1071]) of the steel works. Whereas, her faultless Matha at *Ratnapura,* which is a place of importance and has many gates, appears like an entensive cage for the swan of 'pious work'. But her (image of the) Death-Vanquisher (*Siva*) shines forth amidst buildings resplendent with stucco, and creates the illusion of a *S'Vetadvipa*[1072] (produced) for removing the transitoriness of human beings[1073]. When she had erected her *Gokula*[1074], *Suravarman,* and others who had also constructed *Gokulas* (behave) her, they were held to be no better than those who eat (anything, even) grass. Their status is equivalent the animal. At that *Gokula* which is provided with meadows for the cows' unobstructed free grazing, and which has an abundant supply of water from the *Vitasta,* the cow's bodies rest free from sickness[1075]. Therefore, the (image of) Visnu *Govardhanahara*[1076] *(erected)* there, was displayed the perfectionof wonderful beauty, (and was such that) *Visvakarman*[1077] could not have fashioned it,because. He is the artist of the Gods[1078], *Ratnadevi,* after making a Matha of the 'Nam' or *Samudramatha,* she was resided at *Nandiksetra,* and after this, she established beautiful (*Mathas of 'Nam'*) at *Jayavana* and other places[1079] which were under the control of *Jayasimha*. Besides these, she also founded a town called as *Daraabhisara* after her death, which was the home of the King's noble generosity and became the centre of rival in the city of India[1080]. In this way, this queen, who was so kind on her attendants laid down various foundation in honour of her chamberlain and other worthy servants who were died[1081] at that time. The result of this work the whole land was embellished in all parts, and the lord of the Kings also made his own Matha which resembled the forehead mark (put on after affixing all other ornaments[1082]) for the ornamentations of the souls with the 'Ultimate Reality i.e., called *'Chamar'* or *'Wonderful Power'.*

Foundation of Simhapura

This (Matha) was founded by *Simhadeva* the modest King who endowed in many village, as it was raised by persons of intelligence to prominent celebrity under the name of *Simhapura*[1083]. i.e., *'Nam'.*

Whereas the daughters son of the lord of *Karapatha*[1084] settled here Brahmans from the Indus-region and numerous *pravidas* who lived before in *Siddhacchattra*[1085] *(parasol)*. But what use is it to praise the construction of *Mathas* and others (buildings) by *Simhapura,* who gave back again to the whole of *Kashmir*, its villages, its city[1086] who had lost in the previous birth. Therefore, *Simhapura* was interested to restore this land which owe to the baseness of the times was like a decayed forest wealth, population and habitations[1087] of the previous, life style in the modern form. 'History refeats itself' as the King (Dr. Raj Kumar) from the beginning has prepared himself to grant whatever was desired by him, (it came about that) Mathas and temples were in many instances erected by the artisans and the like[1088] minded people who developed this art from time to time in the process of 'History'. At the time of victory, the citizens will celebrate all kinds of great festivals from the core of heart, the king willingly sharing with them his available treasure, clothing, jewelry and other (possessions[1089]) related to life. At that time; adundance of food did never cease there,and the rice crops with destroyed by premature snowfall, floods and other calamities[1090]. And, a wonder it was India at that night, and the voices of the demons will be listen. Thus comets and other kinds of portents will also be seen, and yet the subjects did not perish[1091] for the time being. *Chudda* a younger brother of *Kosthesvara,* who had raised a rebellion against *Jayasimha* and driven by the King through (open) fights and secret perscutions into the presence of the god of death[1092].

Jayasimha's Affairs Abroad

After this event, *Jayasimha* will engaged with the foreign affairs, and King will uproot King *Vikramaraja* at *Vallapura* to put in his place King *Gulhana*, and did thus with other rulers in other (territories[1093]). This sun of princes (*Jayasimha*) *'Nam'* made the rulers in *Kanyakubja* and elsewhere who were powerful owing to the possession of excellent territories, proud by his friendship[1094] on the basis of *Chamar* as his *Jat* or caste. Becaused he ruled in glory of *'Nam'* without his resolutions meeting with opposition, there he died at one time in the form of *Yasodhara,* the rulers of the *Darads*[1095]. Though this neighbouring prince had shown discrimination (during his lifetime) and had been greatly attached to him, yet cares arose for the King on his death owing to his descendants falling under the power of ministers[1096] and the Darads troubles will be started in large scale.

Darads Troubles

During *Darads* troubles, *Viddasiha,* (Yasodhara's) own minister will have to gained the love-affairs of his widow, and as his son was not yet of mature age, possessed himself cunningly of the regal power[1097] as a Queen. While he will gradually making the territory subject to his will, and was endeavouring to destroy the boy who was the nominal King, in order to reign himself, another minister, *Paryuka* by name, will raised opposition to him by putting up a second son of *Yasodhara* (as a pretender[1098]) of the *'Nam'*.

Interference in Darad Affairs

During the time of war of succession among *Yasodhara's*, *Paryuka* will fight for the throne with *Kashmir* at his back. At that moment King's mind will be seized by a misconception which by another name may be called capriciousness, left aside *Sanjapala* and others who were able to cope with all tasks, and though (himself) versed in counsel, followed the advice of *Sajja's* son (*Srngara),* who from regard to his friendship with *Paryuka* despatched his own younger brother of immature age. Due to this reason (the King) believed that he (*Srngara*) *on being* raised to the position of Prime Minister (*Sarvadhikara*[1099]) and other (distinctions), had become proud of his own honour[1100] then the downfall of the Kingdom would be started. How (great a difference there is) between the theory of mind and the 'Nam', at the first enterprise against a country, between men of experience who enjoy proud fame, and whose mind is undaunted under all conditions, and people who are like boys or fools, and whose actions are useless, but they do their duty according to the advise of 'Nature'. Ah, that self-will of Kings which is adverse to success[1101]!. They wish to break (their enemies) naughtiness through their own servants, who are opposed to their objects, they do not take into careful consideration the (state of the) army, country, strongholds, finances and other (factors[1102]) like the safety of public. The rulers of adjacent territories also accept advice (from their councillors) merely with regard to their precedence. Those who show the face of friends while they are (in reality) enemies during election, ought to be feared just by those to whom they give assistance[1103]. But the theory of 'Nature' it gives 'Love' to man and reveal the reality of life. Thus how (a great difference there is) between those who are fools and also rogues, and men who know the conduct of affairs, when it is (a matter of) gaining over the enemy's allies i.e. *'Nam'* which can be accomplished only by a politic procedure[1104] with *Guru*. In this way the *Darad* throne which had fallen through (the ministers) mutual enmity, could not be seized by persons without strength, just as a tree which has fallen by the break of the river bank (cannot be carried away) by a weak current, in which it lies[1105], but there is a need of flood to wash away. Though *Paryuka* in the critical state of affairs was prepared to take various bribes, yet Srngara's younger brother was too slack in his actions, to take from him even *Dugdhaghata,*[1106] the frontier fort on the route to the Darad territory. In the meanwhile the son of *Sajja* had gone as he had come, *Viddasiha* become enraged against the King of *Kashmir* and made peace with *paryaka*[1107]. *But at* that time *Srngara* fell a prey to death, having enjoyed the post of Prime Minister for a short while, like a tree which a monkey (has visited only for a brief time[1108]) thus, in the context the very funny story of the mind expressed by *Darwin* 'Monkey to mankind'.

Death of Srnagara

After the death of *Srngara* even upto the death of *Laksmaka* the office of Prime Minister had been without a rival, but subsequently it became like the water of a cascade (which is divided) a hundred fold[1109] from the one stream, but the origin of the stream is connected with ocean therefore, the process of the life is similar to that of a *'Nam'*. Other ministers, too, who enjoyed power owing to their lord's esteem, died somehow about the same time through, the will of fate[1110]. How should we (duly) praise that kindliness of the King who puts in the place of the dead minister his boy-son[1111] is a *'Nam'*. But the servants of the minister followed an extraordinary course. Without shame they took their master's fortune as if it were their own wife. After presenting their dead master's property before the King they stole it under the (pretext of) measures taken for the benefit of the children's position[1113] after founding the 'New Society' called as *'Radha Soami'*. Only *Sahaja* alone maintained the dignity of assistants upon the death of the treasury-superintendent *'Visva'*[1114] who was the owner of this property has to see the distribution of the share when there is discrimination in distribution, he justifies it on the bases of equality, liberity and fraternity as a Perfect Master of the man in this planet. Though requested by the King he did not occupy his master's post but helped to instruct the latter's son, *Tista* by name, (in his duties[1115]) on this earth. Alas, those in power raise servants higher and higher, one after the other, though they will see that they do not steady in their position[1116] and will go to the hell. That Ganga-water which served in the Creator's (Brahman's) cup to rinse his mouth, and which then relieved the fatigue of the foe of *Asuras* (Visnu) when his foot was tired from striding over the universe *Chamar, Sambhu* (Siva) received it on his head. If once one (master) has taken a liking for a person, though he be a fool (*jada*[1117]), then all (his subsequent) masters too must needs feel deep attachment for him, one after the another as the process of the *'Nam'*. But at the same time the tree of the bad policy which had obtained the growth from (the time of) *Sujji's* exile, and which had been fostered by the foolishness of *Sajja's* son (*Srngara*), was in due time preparing to bear fruit[1119] of the establishment of the soul for the development of the civilization like other civilization of the world. The angry *Viddasiha* was then for two or three years exciting through messengers *Lothana's* desire for the throne and the rest[1120], they remain in aboriginal process for the development of the civilization.

Fresh Attempts of Lothana

Lothana, who is unbroken in his aspirations, was together with his Kinsmen living under the protection of King *Sura*[1121], *(*maintaining himself) by agriculture, trade and other means of life. Full of energy he was afar from intriguing with *Alamkaracakra* and other Damaras who had formed relationships with the *Darad* ministers[1122]. When he was first setting out with a view to gaining the proximity of those who held fastnesses in the mountain regions, his friend, the base *Janakabhadra,* died[1123] during the commencement of the philosphers rule. Everywhere in *Karnadha*[1124] and other (districts) where he was seen after he had set out permanently in this world, some were thinking of rebelling, some of keeping faithfull interest on him. While this (foe) of great energy was preparing his invasion with cunning and calmness, the King from indolence remained inactive and paid no regard to him from a period of time[1125]. When the rising had gained the strength by the means supplied by those who were wishing for troubles, then the King sent *Udaya,* the lord of the Gate[1126] for the settlement of the balance sheet of the account and arrear.

Lothana Joins Alamkaracakra

While the latter was collecting the troops at the town of *Samkaravarman*[1127], *Jayasimha* received the news that *Lothana* had joined the *Alamkaracakra*[1128] for the establishment of the lost rule. Moreover, he also heard that *Vigraharaja* had also come with him, a son of King *Sussala,* and *Bhoja*, the son of *Salhana*[1129]. *Lothana* thereupon made haste relations with *Alamkaracakra* and got over the distance of many days in a single day[1130] with the power of *'Nam' or 'Chamar'* when the relations between the two will be checked in his activity by *Udaya's* attack and not having succeeded in inveigling his class-fellows by his lies, the Damara became helpless and fled[1131] away in their own houses.

Lothana goes to Sirahsilakota

Keeping in view, the circumstances of the period for the establishment of lost kingdom, *Lothana, Alamkaracakra,* be took themselves thence to the castle called *Sirahsilakota[1132]*, which is situated between the *Sindhu* (Krsnaganga) and the (streams of the) *Madhumati* and *Muktasri[1133]*. Alongwith the lord of the Gate (*Udaya*) roaming about in distant tracts, did not ascertain whether *Alamkaracakra* had hidden himself in the thickest of the forests or was keeping in the castle[1134] of mountains. As soon as it came to in picture that he had ascended to that stronghold, even fate did not believe that the king's power could escape a defeat[1135] by the *Yamas* power.

Rising in Kashmir

Upon this rebellion (breaking out) all the enemies, too, displayed themselves prepared for a rising in *Kashmir,* just as fishes when their pond is broken by the rain[1136] during the time of raining season. Then *Trillaka* and the others who were secretly disaffected, made *Lothana* (or *Lothaka*), the son of *Prthvihara,*, use in intrigues his skill in deceit form[1137]. The latter towns, villages and the rest will remain in burning condition, could not be got by the pursuers of *Prthvihara*, though he repeatedly got into sorry plights and those on his side, he will saved him[1138]. Moreover, roving about in all directions and disappearing from the horizon as soon as it has been seen that her (*Prthvihara*) sent by fate like the comet Brahmaputra which rises at the end of the *Kalpa[1139]* when the tired ministers will press for a compromising from time serving motives, the people thought that the whole land of *Madavarajya* was as if lost in the ocean[1140]. Then, in the meantime, the enemy were rising in power without any counter-measures having been found, the King after holding counsel despatched *Dhanya[1141]* for the settlement of the issue between the race of Yama and *'Nam'*. When the task will have to put on the latter's shoulders the people said that the lord of the Gate (Udaya) would feel humiliation and would become indifferent and subsequently disaffected[1142] with *'Nam'*, *'Bhiksu* had been alone and so *Mallarjuna*. But these are three in league and thus, indeed, difficult to dispose of".

Thus thought all the subjects[1143]. However, the lord of the Gate, whose conduct knew no whims, was desirous of the King's success, though it might not serve his own renown, and heartily exerted himself[1144] against the enemy with the power of *'Nam'*. Only for a King whose merits (from previous births) are great, arises such a minister, who alone does not know confusion in his lord's business; who does not fall from anger into indifference when the latter allows himself to be influenced by many (others), and who, with a course of action free from all caprice, endeavours to carry out the set task[1145] of the nature from time to time according to the advise of the Lord.

Expedition Against the Sirahsila castle

Sasthacandra, Pancacandra[1146], younger brother, whom the King had placed on the latter's death in the seat (*upavesana[1147]*). also started for the expendition against the *Sirahsila* castle. Whereas *Dvibahuka* and other *'Nam'* followed with singers after *Dhanya,* and thus also other royal servants who belonged to the outer court[1148] but some are special who are the messengers of the Lord. While *Dhanya* and the rest occupied *Tilagrama,* (a place) situated on the *Sindhu* of the castle (*Krsnaganga*), the lord of the Gate being posted at the *Dranga,[1149],* closed the routes at the back of *Sarada[1150] Tirth*. Avoiding reckless attacks, profits encounters, and similar acts of caprice, he proceeded with firmness and discretion and harassed the enemy[1151] according to his own way.

Camp Formed on the Madhumati

During the expedition against the *Sirahsila* Castle, a camp of the wood cutters and other workmen *Dhanya* had rows of houses constructed resembling a town on the bank of the *Madhumati[1152]*. There is, no doubt, *Jayasimha* strong and capable, will cleared the thicket of trees of darkness, turned forest-land into habitations, and provided the camp with all supplies in abundance[1153] with the help of *'Nam'*. Owing to the King's good fortune, the place to be assailed was widely overspread with sunshine, (though situated) in a country the winter of which is terrible owing to the heavy snowfall[1154] by the *'Nam'*. And, the supplies which the King sent in his eagerness to secure victory, astonished the world, and did not fail even at that time when the contest for the crown impaired his power[1155]. But while the danger was (destined) to be averted at its very rise, the wailing of the villagers who were oppressed by the (forced) carriage of loads, served as a kind of expiatory oblation (*Ksanticaru[1156]*). Thus, *Ka* is the god whom we shall adore with our oblation. The *Ramayana* and *Mahabharata* identifies *Ka* with *Dakasha,* and the Bhagavata *Purana* applies the term to *Kasyapa*. In this way, king put firmness into his troops by showing his wrath to those who fled through fear of the long absence from their homes, and gratified those who held out, by presents[1157] of the *'Nam'*. Though the troops thus stoutly kept their ground for three or four months, yet they were unable to seize those who were in the castle[1158] of *Jayasimha*. Because no such acts of hostility, as the cutting off of food supplies by means of an investment were undertaken, which might have reduced those arrogant (opponents) to straits[1159] of life.

Unrest in Kashmir

The Damaras in Kashmir who were displaying their power from the very beginning in the Indian society when the snow has passed, stood like mountains upon which the fresh shoots are preparing to breakout[1160] the way for unrest of the *Kashmirians*. Everywhere in the villages the cultivater's left their work on the fields and the Brahmans left their Veda-recitations, and took to the sword, eager for rebellion[1161] against the present Government of the Manmohan Singh. Instead of that rebllion, the ambitious *Darads* are a waiting for the snow to melt on the mountains over which (lay their) way, with their mounted troops in readiness[1162] during the mouth of April; 2007. Whereas the men of the royal power trembled often from fear that the masses of snow might fall down (upon them) like the cotton-bed of death[1163]. Thus, the King, who had in vain undertaken his enterprise without examining the real strength of the enemy, began to feel doubts as to his success[1164] because it is the story of '*hides of the cutter*'. Deceitful fate likes (to employ) one special course of procedure against those whose minds are filled with acuteness; through it they may become uncertain in their minds as to their own power and through it they may become uncertain in their minds as to their own power and through (over-much) deliberation fail in their enterprise even in the face of an enemy who is without resources[1165]. For example, if a person trembles before the enemy's host which exists merely in report, his success is frustrated through his own mind becoming blind with care[1166], it is his blunder. There is one more instance, if the elephant feels afraid of the lotus, owing to a false conception of latter's resources, (thinking) "It might quickly hit me with its bees (or arrows, *silimukhaih*), it might assail me with its leaves (or chariots, *pattraih*); it might bind me with its thread (or ropes, *gunaih*), *"'Word'* then he may be prevented, owing to his limbs, enormous though they are, becoming benumbed with fear, from violently uprooting[1167] it for certain period of time for the development of the soul. As soon as *Lothana* and the rest after escaping with difficulty from *Karnaha* got to *Alamkaracakra*, it was thought that the kingdom had been conquered by them[1168]. Yet his associates had woven their intrigues to no purpose. How otherwise should the lord of Gate have attacked *Alamkaracakra* effectively and in haste[1169], there should be friendship between the two i.e. 'Dr. Raj Kumar' and 'Baba Gurinder Singh' as the *'Hero'* of the nature, along with Deepit Raj as a '*Nam*'

Alamkaracakra Retreats to Sirahsilakotta

Alamkaracakra at that moment unable to offer resistance to *Sirahsilakotta* then he sent the princes into the castle of Kashmir and then followed them himself next day[1170]. The castle-hill of *Kashmir,* norrow below (where it projects) into the stream of life and with a long stretched ridge, appeared to them like a heron bent on swallowing fishes[1171] in the ocean. When *Lothana, Alamkara, Jayasimha, Sirahsila*, etc. saw that there was no strength of the Brahmans in it, as (there is none) in an elephant shed without an elephant, they lost (all) hope of victory, and fear entered their hearts[1172], it shows that they are the defeated persosn of the *'Nam'*. "From here the enemies should be harassed with arrows; from here by showers of stones; from here should the stream be guarded, and here the stones for the catapults." As the damaras will thus giving their explanations with firmness of (*Nam*), they thought that he was only anxious about protecting himself, without a firm determination to fight (on their behalf[1173]) for the obtaining of new life. As soon as the opposite force will proceeded at *Tilagrama* for frequent attacks, and the robber (*[1174]dasyu,* i.e. *Alamkaracakra*) proved unable to meet (the latter), they became thin with care[1175]. Therefore, the beauty of Nature will be maintained *Lothana* whose suppleness of intellect with the help of *'Nam'* was, however, openly reproach the Damara, who was fully taken up with the needful work[1176] of the 'lord'. But *Bhoja* held back his excited uncle: "We might be betrayed," and plied him (*Alamkaracakra*) continually to pretended enlogies[1177] of life. Those who displayed unfriendly relations towards *Lohana, Alamkaracakra* maintained ever his deceitful conduct, while he trusted to some extent in *Bhoja's* capacity forgiving counsel owing to his conciliatory manners and kept up a friendly understanding with him[1178] as the Nature of the *'Nam'*.

Bhoja kept back his uncle from asking (the Damara) for leave to go, saying: "He will not let us go, thinking that the king might kill him, if we are gone[1179]." At the same time, *Bhoja* will represent to the Damaras: "If you and we are all besieged (together), then the enemies having no hostilities to fear from anywhere in the back, will be bold and firm in their endeavours. Whatever, they would do, would succeeded. Therefore, let me go hence alone. By quickly bringing up other *Lavanyas* or the *Darads,* I shall raise the siege." By these reasonable representations he got him to assent, as it were, in a fashion of *'Nam' or 'Sabad'* then *Alamkaracakra* preserved his outward kindness, yet imposed upon him continually by saying: "To-day, at night or to-morrow, I shall let you go[1181]." As the communications had not yet been entirely cut off by the assailants, who kept at a good distance (from the castle) of the Kashmir, they maintained themselves with the food-supply obtained from the outlying villages[1182].

Diffidence of Besiegers

Dhanya and the other(ministers) then apprehended a disastrous issue (of the expedition) and recommended the King to make peace with the enemy[1183] when their self-confidence will be shattered. Then the King thought the conclusion of peace impracticable for various reasons, and ordered will be placed to siege the walks of castle[1184] with the help of *Nam*. At that time; he expressed (to them): "The Damara on receiving bribes (from them), would let my rival kinsmen go, and they would get off to their own place having acquired renown[1185]" "If we, even in this critical (state of affairs) show no pesistent effort and no vigour, then we surely will come to regret it owing to the people reproaching us with last opportunities[1186]." "Another (prince), too, feels mortified, when he hears it said: "If king *Harsa* had but held out for seven days, he might have got the stream of milk[1187]." "Everybody attains what is destined for him, by his acts, (be they) good or bad. But a lost opportunity (*Kriyatipatti*) is held by the people equal to three worlds[1188] (*'Nam' or 'Chamar'*). "The winged ant, though it has feet as well as wings, cannot move about on the ground or in the air, but only in a hole, as if it were lame and blind. What is the use of attainments when the course is laid down by necessity[1189] of the 'Nam' to express the people about the historical thought which are leading the life of the people in the planet as a source of energy for the development of the life. "*Aruna,* though he has no thighs, guides the course of the sun (*Sahasrapada*). Could he have accompliesed more, perhaps, if he had two feet[1190] one on Earth and other on *Heaven* or called the *'Third World'*. "Therefore cease to remain (mere) on lookers, and lay siege to the whole castle. Let our lifetime pass, as well as theirs, in this (enterprise[1191])." We shall again come together for the settlement of the civilization. "The wind here does not cease to occupy itself with the fire, and it continually shakes the high mountains and the water. A firm devotion to tasks, even, if it does not lead to the fulfilment, produces at every turn in the world results of unexpected importance[1192]."

Siege of Sirahsila Castle (A.D. 1144)

On hearing this strict order of the King, *Dhanya* and the rest then left that river bank and ascended quickly to the main-road leading to the castle[1193] of life. While those in the castle were the shooting arrows and watching them curiousity, (to see) how they would fight and how keep their places, *Dhanya*, though standing below, drove away those who held the position above, and by (constructing block) houses in unbroken line gave to that locality the look of a town[1194]. Then unceasing encounters ensued at every moment in which both sides lost countless men[1195] but they will be in wandering position to search out the Master and King. On the following day as per the 'Cosmic Order' the son of *Garga* (*Sasthacandra*) will have to arrived their, after visiting the (temple of) *Sarada,* and added to the population of Indra's city by the fighters he killed[1196] on spot with the power of *'Nam'*. In the same fashion, *Alamkara,* the minister holding the charge of the outer court (*bahyarajasthana*), undauntedly made superman attacks and killed many enemies[1197]. How could inhabitants of the plains vie with those who live on the mountains live together, yet the large quantity of war engines, which achieve unthought of results, must be taken into consideration[1198] to teach a lesson to them. Those in the castle were very few, while those in the (besieging) camp many. Hence the former, though they killed many, were easily made to suffer[1199] with the support of *'Nam'*. Whereas the castle had been harassed with two or three assaults, it appeared with the closed folds of its gates as if shutting its eyes from fear [2000] of mind. Those in the castle, they lost their confidence when they saw that *Dhanya* and the other (ministers) were trying to win over the guards, create internal dissension and otherwise to take advantage of a weak point[2001] of the enemy. At night they did not sleep but shouted to each other to keep themselves awake. In the day time, again, when they slept, they made the castle appear silent and deserted[2002] with the help of *'Nam'* as a change in the life. Even the sound of the Kettle-watches, made them tremble at night, as the thunder (makes tremble), the sparrows in the hallows of the trees[2003] with fears of *'Nam'*. The royal troops kept them in excitement day and night by all possible means and blocked (their access to) the water by boats which are moving about[2004] to watch the enemy. They must be cut off from the river and put up somehow with the pain of thirst then they became disheartened when their food supply became exhausted owing to their inability to get outside[2005]. Whereas the king's kinsmen, though they keep lust for rich dishes such as were fit for princes, were then glad to feed on miserable stuffs[2006] of the animals. And, their aspirations had passed far away all the more they daily envied, when pained by hunger, even the King's servants they have ample food[2007] for their survival. Then *Bhoja* has described: "If we are (all) collected (here), nothing adequate can be done," *Alamkaracakra* placed him apart (from the others) in the central to keep up the castle[2008] high in the air. *Jayasimha* held only *Bhoja* that he is capable of acting as a pretender to the crown, and believed (the other two) unfit for this, because *Lothana* was too old and the *Vigraharaja* the son of a concubine women[2009]. Keeping in view that his opponents wold not exert themselves fully for these two without *Bhoja*, *Alamkaracakra* had the false report spread outside (the castle) that Bhoja had fled[2010] away to *Sirahsila* castle in the year 1144 A.D.

Intrigues in the Castle

For the time being, an intrigue was started in the castle of *Sirahsila*, the son of *Salhana* (Bhoja) who was daily enquiring about everything had found out that *Alamkaracakra's* faithful wife (Dr. Raj Kumar) who had fallen deeply in live with *Sasthacandra* from seeing his beauty, was wishing to destroy her husband and was betraying his secret plans (to those) outside[2011] the house as a domestic priest. Fearing from his betrayal attitude he informed *Alamkaracakra* whose mind was beset by the blindness of love, of her (doings) and asked to be allowed to go[2012] out in, the public for the adventure of the *'Nam'* or *'Chamar'* or *'Jat'*. *Jayasimha* being of a forbearing disposition was accustomed to indulgence and delighting in the maintenance of an intimate attachment, found no fault in her though she had sinned, just as a *Bodhisattva* feels no anger (even against the sinner[2013]) which he knows the beauty of *'Nam'* which never hate to everybody. This story is to love with man.

For example, a lover forgets in his heart the hatred of a beloved women, though it may be great and the cause of his death, just as the *Sarabha* (forgets) the elephant on its back[2014].

Bhoja's Attempts at Flight

As soon as, intrigue was started in the Castle of *Sirahsila*, *Bhoja* then started to flight to *Kashmir.* But at the same time, he had almost got outside the camp of the sleeping enemy, the son of *Alamkara* (*Cakra*). Who accompanied with him, and induced to him to return, whether from treacherous design or from fear because he himself had lost courage, and brought him back to his father who was in the castle[2015] of *Sirahsilakotta.* The latter after reproaching his son, then *Bhoja* told him that he should leave the next night, and hid him that he should leave the next night, and hid him during the day of *'Light'*, telling everybody that he had left[2016] for certain period of time for the regaining of 'Spiritual Knowledge' of the *'Nam'*. Whereas, *Dhanya* and all the others having received information that *Bhoja* had escaped and got off, and that two (*Lothana and Vigraharaja*) *were to start* the next day, then kept awake during the (following) night in uncertainty[2017] of the Nature. Then Bhoja was preparing with the *Alamkara* to start at night to capture his own power, when he saw from the tower of the castle that all (the enemies) or Brahmans were awake round about and in their camp the fires blazing these lit up the castle so much that even an ant could not moved out by the man road without being noticed by the watchful enemies[2017] of the *'Nam'*. The houses which occupied (by the enemy) seemed in the flickering light of the flames to move and to warn the son of *Salhana* (Bhoja) (as it were) by shaking their heads, against a reckless attempt[2018] of the *'Nam' or 'Chamar'*. This attempt made it impossible for him to leave. then, the project will come out in the market the day will break after that night, the Damara let him climb down the precipice fastened to a rope[2019] in a single chain. Those who were accompanied by a Damara lord, *Ksemaraja* by name, he got down to a rock, as large as raised a seat (*Vitardika*[2020]) midway on the precipice road[2021]. As soon as, he obtained this rock which just sufficed for them to sit on, they passed there five nights (and days) with sleeping from fear of falling[2022] on the ground there they kept themselves alive with small barley-cakes which they had in their hands, and from there they cleared their bowels like birds from their nest[2023], the same story is going to repeat by the *'Nam'*. Thus, there two will be kept without being noticed, (motionaless) as if painted, and watched with 'wonder' or 'Nam' from the above the profusion in the enemy's camp[2024]. In this way, they benefited by the wamth of the flaming glory of *Jayasimha*, which made them forget the great cold[2025] which siezed the *Kashmir.* Then on the sixth day when they had consumed all the food they had in the store, the clouds began to send down snow which was like a caustic put in a wound[2026] of the *'Nam'*. Then their hands and feet became benumbed by the cold and fell asleep, while it would have been proper for them to exert themselves (in accompaniment) with the music made by their (clattering) teeth[2027] of the *'Nam'*. The two were thinking: "Surely to-day, overcome by hunger and cold, we shall fall in the enemy's camp, like twobirds caught in a trap[2028]." "Whom shall we call to help those who have been elightened with the 'Truth', who knows of us to drag us up from here, as a leader of the elephant herd (would drag out) two young elephants sinking int he quagmere[2029] of the *'Nam'*. Then upon their prayers the Damaras had the two who had been in such plight, drawn up by a rope and put them in an empty dwelling[2030] of the world. There they must be relieved from the cold at a straw-fire, and forgot their misery in the sleep they had found at last[2031] helpless, there is nobody who will help them. Even greater misery befell on *Lothana* and *Vigraha* (*raja*), who did not get a kind word from any one and were looked at with disgust[2032] by theblessing of *'Nam'*. They will take cakes made of *oats* and *Kodrava*[2033] in husks and the like and their bodies and clothes became discoloured by dirty[2034] theory of mind. When *Alamkaracakra's* food supplies will altogether drawing to an end, *Dhanya* won over equally *Hola* and *Yasaskara* two of his (men), by giving them food[2035] of the *'Nam'*.

Alankaracakra Treats for a Surrender

In this struggle of warfare, *Alamkaracaka* treats to the Damara request for surrender, if they will not surrender themselves without prior any condition, they were shaken by hunger and fearing to be betrayed agreed through messengers to sell the King's enemies[2036] of the same community i.e *Chamar* or Nam. His mind steeped in wickedness abandoned the fear of sin and dishonoured by the Brahmans, when his courage had been broken by the excess of umbearable sufferings[2037], *Alamkara* intended to protect himself by keeping back some of the King's enemies and toding to every straw and grass to clear his honour[2038] in the public platform. He, accordingly, upon the advice of his servent *Udayana* thus kept *Salhana's* son *Bhoja* in hiding, but hastened to give up the (other) two[2039]. *Alamkara* thought this arrangement to be good for them to all, as he believed that without *Bhoja*, the King would not inflict inordinate punishment upon the two, and would leave him unharmed[2040]; because he himself in the form of *'Nature' or 'Nam'* along with the King (Dr. Raj Kumar). Whereas *Dhanya* and the other (ministers) when they wished to make peace, did not know then of the straits in which he was owing to the want of food, nor of that plan of his life[2041]. Therefore, they were anxious to get away from there some pretence, (thinking): "What more (is to be done), since he had agreed to give up those two rival kinsmen i.e. *'Nam'* and the *Brahman*[2042]. *Dhanya* then made his brother's son *Kalyana* the surety for the execution of the compact turban regarding the surrender of those who were to be given up the withdrawal of the army, and the rest of the messengers[2043]. If a work has to be composed on the proper time; if any enemy who hides his wrath, has to be conciliated; a great snake to be caught or some act of crooked diplomacy to be done, *'Nam's* success will fall to him who filled with right zeal for his task will also at the completion display haste with firm vigour[2044] of the *'Nam'*. They royal ministers had then lost their power owing to the hardships entailed by a long absence from their homes, and had become slack in their actions[2045]. With the love of *'Nam'*. Study demonstrates that minister is, forsooth, difficult to find who is capable of comprehending a complicated affair at its close, just as (it is difficult to comprehend an affair) which survives only in stories[2046] written by various writers from time to time about the war and peace. The moment that the troops knew of the concluded pact, they started for their homes, disregarding the kindness shown to them by the King[2047] by writing the various projects of life known as *'Das Kapital'*, *Ramayana, 'Mahabharata', 'Constitution of India'*, and other major projects of the life. As soon as the *Lavanya* had received the supplies which they sold to him from time to time, no doubt, he made delays about carrying out the project of (the agreement), while *Dhanya's* and the others minds became alarmed at the small number of the troops[2048] and surrender to the *Alamakara* because, their troops were walking on bare-footed, therefore they could not match with the army of *'Nam'*.

Delay in Surrender of Pretenders

'*The Class Struggle Theory of have and have nots*', active, and inactive, bad and good is not giving up those two, who have been strongly tied in their relationship as the husband and wife, he that day tormented his assailants who kept their eyes fixed on the main road (leading to the castle) of Siva in the hope of seeing the demanded (princes) arrive [2049] at full zenith of Youthfulness as her beauty displayed by the *'Nature'*. During the night, she louded with the cries of the *Cakravaka,* they passed in misery, seeing no other course them but suicide[2050] in the front of *'Nam'*. No doubt, many such thoughts occupies them: "Now that the enterprise prepared with much trouble, has failed owing to the weakness of our minds, the other ministers will surely scoff at the various measures(taken by us), pretending to regret with pity the failure, and will incite against us the enemity of the King who will no think of using kind words to greet us. Those who do not examine the state of things with regard to the ups and downs of the expedition, will at once cast shame upon us." Thus some said in distress, (others again said): "That robber (*dasyu*) *or Balmiki* has perpetrated this deception in consultation with the King's enemies (*Lothana, etc.*). Now that he has achieved his object, he surely sits there and laughs at us." As soon as night will passed away after causing *'Infinite'* torment to their bodies[2051] which equivalent to *'Nam'*. Then in the morning *Alamkara*, the Chief-Justice (*rajasthaniya*), eager for a bold course, went up to the castle and by diplomatic threats induced the Damara to agree[2052] the duty of the *'Nam'* otherwise destruction is definite because the theory of mind badly harassed our race who is innocent and good by nature. Therefore, it is our humble request to the theory of mind, after having allowed one day's delay, *Alamkaracakra* (aboriginal or *Barwala*) then told *Lothana* that day plainly and without courtesy that he would have to go[2053] for the mission to establishment of *'New Society' i.e. 'Radha Soami'*. Thereupon some self-respecting persons suggested to him what he might do to wipe off his disgrace and to avoid the loss of his renown[2054] hero of 'Nature' i.e. Baba Gurinder Singh previously he was called as Dr. B.R. Ambedkar, the renowned personality of the *'World'*. Here verses containing conventional praise of those who die in fighting back with the help of *'Nam'* and thus reach the world of Surya and the company of the *Apsaras* without undergoing the pains of a death-struggle of the *'Nam'*. *Lothana's* father and brothers have before him found their death by the sword. His present discomfiture is a penance for the faults committed by him while on the throne. *Bhiksacara,* too, had expiated the sins of his reign by a noble death in the *'Nam'*[2055]*)* Though thus incited he did not take a resolute course, devoid of spirit (*tejas*) *as he was.* The *'monkeys'* fuel (*Vanarendhara*[2056]) which has no substance, does not burn even in contact with fire[2057] because *'Nam'* is a practical approach in the present life as an experiment of research laboratory but people like Sikhs they believe in *Guru Granth,* Muslims in *Koran*. But *Kalma or 'Nam' or 'Chamar'* is upto *Guru* has no feeling of self-respect but *'Nam',* he wished, when terrified by the danger, to cry with a pouting underlips like a little boy who has been roused from his slumber[2058].

Lothana and Vigraharaja Delivered to Dhanya (A.D. 1144)

As soon as, the Damaras of *Kashmir* will not surrendered the *Almakara,* the King's officers who were about to conduct him, on seeing him in such a state of mind, said from compassion to encourage him: "Do not despair in the heart of the King, whcih is illuminated by the rising moon of pity, there does not easily rise the blind darkness of enmity[2059]." "He is an ocean of the nectar of kindness, the divine mountain (Meru) of constancy and a sandal-wood-tree for removing the hot pains of those who seek his shelter." "On seeing his person which is purifying and spotless like the celestial stream (Ganga) in the autumn, your over-excited mind will find comfort." "He will pay to your equal respect as to the faultless elders members of the family, and will remove the sensation of humiliating shame[2060]," of the various community of the 'Schedule Castes and Schedule Tribes' which were cluminated by the Brahmninical thought. "Full of compassion he treats also others who have done him harm and have fallen in misfortune as benefactors, because they give an occasion for testing his pity[2061]." *Lothana* and *Vigraharaja* cheered by these words of theirs, *Jayasimha* then came out of the house resembling, with his weaving thick beard and his hanging down cloak, and old bull (coming) out of the stable[2062] to receive him for spread of the *'Radha Soami'* mission in abroad as Asoka spread the Buddhism, *Akbar* spread the policy of *Sul-I-Kul (Absolute Peace)* have the same meaning, but there is misconception to the theory of mind which always busy with the caste, colour, creed and nationhood, whereas the theory of *'Nam'* has no distinction. It believes that reality is 'One' and God is One. As soon as, *Dhanya* saw him and arrived to carry out the mission in a litter, without ornaments, with his faded and worn-out clothes and arms, he was bowed down with embarrassment[2063] those never knows the beauty of *'Nam'* or *Chamar.* With his eyes including *'Third Eye'* which from the long period became motionless and his rough and heavy beard could not grow, shoulders of the *'Nams'* and their body, *Alamakara* then appeared to *Dhanya* like an owl driven out of its hole[2064] to see, the '*New World*' and '*New Society*' of the *'Nam'*. The fire which they had put to the camp of the enemies when its march will become off, made the hill appear like the touch-stone in which the gold of the King's glory (had been tested[2065]) at Global level. As soon as, the camp will be raised in its glory, excessive snow fell from the sky and will removed all the doubts of the people as the King's is a supernatural Power[2066]. Thanks to the 'Father' with folded hands providing me an opportunity to serve the people as a common man of this universe. Moreover, accepted it as my duty toward the *'Father' or Master* of the *'Nam'*. Had the snow fallen earlier in the month of November, 2006, the troops would have sunk in it and perisheed at once just as insects of the (*'Nam', gartatah*), which have fallen into insect-power (*pistataka*[2067]) of the *'Nam'*. Thus, the story of *Lothana* was not of quite sixty year of age; but it is an unending dialogue of process of the life, fell again into the captivity on the tenth day of the bright half of *Phalguna* in the year (of the *Laukika* era four thousand two hundred and) nineteen (A.D. 1144[2068]). In order to greet the troops returning after a long absence, the King who was free from self-assertion, went up to a high mansion[2069] i.e. called *Visavakarma* as an artist.

Arrival of Captives in Srinagara

Jayasimha at the arrival of *Srinagara*, he cheered the troops with gifts, honours, kind addresses and looks, as they deserved. He dismissed them when he saw *Dhanya* and the other (leaders) of the *'Nam'* are arriving there. As soon as he saw in the court-yard, *Lothana* who was being announced by the doorkeepers, but it was scarcely noticeable owing to the mass of the people surrounding around him. The soldiers of those (leaders) had put their hands under his arm-pits. His face was covered by his dress whose edge was drawn up to his nose. The while dishevelled hair of his beard reached to his ear-lobes which bore no ornaments, and made appear plainly the emaciated state of his cheeks. From time to time he glanced out of the corners of his eyes, in which the pupils were fixed and gloomy, at the citizens who were shouting various remarks. Struck by the evil glance of fate he (had suffered) from despondency, misery, fear, exhaustion and hunger. His body which knew not sleep, was shaking like that of a cow pained by cold. He felt as if the earth was moving, the mountains tumbling down and the sky falling, and his lips were closed by dryness[2071]. At every step he stopped and thought: "Let there be an intercession from heaven, or may a terrible darkness widely spread, or may the winds wither up this royal palace now nearly reached. How shall I stand before the king, I who have done him every injury but he is still without injury[2072] because he has firm faith on the *'Nam'* like master."

Reception of Captive Princes

Upon the receiving of the captive prince the order by a movement of the King's brow he ascended to the assembly in which the eyes of the on-lookers seemed like lotuses moving to and fro[2073] for the capturing of enemies. As soon as, the King ordered him by a glance to come up with close eyes, he then fell on his knees on the ground and touched the King's lotus-feet with his head[2074] because his project is quite admirable. Therefore, the sovereign power has put his-lotus-hands to (*Lothana's*) forehead which was bent down, and raised up the head of that (prince) who was bowing down in confusion[2075] at the time of searching out the king in this universe. Whereas the touch of the hands on which jewels and powerful herbs, was cooling like a moon, and removed the hot pain from his mind which were given by the people of his own community as well as others and the misery from his body[2076] for the time being, he tolerated and did his duty in nice manner. In addition to this, he quickly felt that very moment in his heart and mind *'Nam'* has given full confidence in the King's compassionate, which owing to the greatness of his merits (from a former birth[2077]). In this process King reflected: "Fell no fear' would be a naughty saying. 'You will yet reach happiness,' these words would fail owing to their shallowness. By saying ' I am not angry with you now,' the former acts of enmity would be effaced. 'You are our relative', this would be like scorn at the present occasion. 'You are in distress', own glory". Recognising this, the King did not favour him with any word[2078]. As far *Vighara* (*raja*) bent down his head to touch his feet and prayed to the 'Nam' for his safety, he touched the top of his head with his foot[2078] as courtsey of the 'Lord'. Moreover, he forced his uncle to accept the betel which he offered with his own hand, though he remonstrated: "How am I deserving of this honour[2079] because, he elevated the position of *'Nam'* as has its beauty." Inspite of the uncle, the lord of the Gate (*Udaya*) who was bowing down, he said with a smile: "You have had trouble," and *Dhanya* and *Sastha* (*Candra*) who had stood before him, he touched with his left arm[2080] and found in vain. As soon as *Lothana* saw this (King) full of cleverness, kindness, discretion, politeness, and other royal virtues, he despised himself[2081] on his own way. *Jayasimha* is addressing to him with encouraging words through the mouth of *Dhanya,* he then with politely folded hands dismissed his uncle, who was bent down by shame, to a splended mansion[2082] or *Visavkarama*. No doubt, this (King) who kept his eye (ever) fixed on a politic conduct with 'Nam' as before as showed the same conduct which is unchangeable colour on his face when he achieved his success, as when he made his attack[2083] on the Damaras. Therefore, with the smooth function of the King ocean does not get heated by the boiling of the submarine fire which carries no load of the human life, and does not get cold by the water of the Himalaya which enters into it. Men of deep mind show ever the same expression at the time of trouble as at the time of joy[2084]. From the behaviour of the King (Dr. Raj Kumar) we learn that he is kindness constantly in approach, and unfeigned marks of attention, such as are proper between relatives, gradually removed the feeling of humiliation from those two (princes) who had survived the discomfiture of the prowers[2085]. But his prudent incounsel (or, like a juggler), feared inwardly the tooth of the snake, "rebellion", on account of *Bhoja* (being yet at large), though he had just extricated his kingdom from the lips of his kinsmen[2086]. Between the two, there was the rebellion, one thinks it and other not thinks it i.e. *'Nam'* (this was), because his ministes who had stopped their exertions in haste from fear of the fatigues of a (prolonged) absence from their homes, had in spite of his ambition taken him off his guard, though they remained enemies[2087] but King never bothered for him. He always busy with the business of 'Nam'.

Bhoja's further Stay in Sirahsita Kotta

In this process, the son of *Salhana* (Bhoja), after his rescue from the precipice, was keeping in the empty dwelling and got no news whatever of his uncle (*Lothana*) and *Vigraha* (*raja*[2088]) keep in mind for the time being. When, *Jayasimha* saw the *Almakara* from the abcve, the chief-justice (*rajagrhya*[2089]) coming to the Damara, there arose in him the suspicion of betrayal of the *'Nam'* has been delineated by them. Thus, subsequently he saw the force which had been encamped, stretching its columns far away, beyond the reach of the eye, on the road which led towards the City[2090]. Then, he noticed between the litters of *Dhanya* and *Sastha* the one occupied by his uncle (*Lothana*), whom, however, he cold not recognised from afar[2091], but *'Nam'* recognised him as his foster-brother. And he (Baba Gurinder Singh) thought himself at that time during the denotion of *'Nam'*: "What can be the reason for the army marching off from here along with the commander (Dr. Raj Kumar). And who is the third carried in a litter between *Dhanya* and *Sastha*[2092] i.e., *'Nam'*. It can not be purchased as the jobs of today people are purchasing. It is the bargaining of the *'Pure-thought'* or the *'Right way'*. Therefore, people pay less interest in this field. But it is challenged to the theory of mind i.e. called *Brahmana*. Then a menial (Dr. Raj Kumar) *Chamar* by caste, he questioned with joy and told that the pact was concluded between *Lothana* and *Vigraha* that they were on their way to the City[2093] of the heaven i.e. called '*Nam*' or *Kashmir*. His doubts has ceased, the target of the *'Truth'* i.e., called '*Nam*', and the fear of betrayal which was rising (in him), gave way for a short time to fond solicitude for his relatives[2094] those are Brahmans, trapped into the allusion of *Maya* or materialism. As soon as the army departed and the birds with loud cries met in the solitude, it appeared to him as if the river were wailing over the two who had gone[2095] to high and high in the theory of *'Nature'* and collecting the force of mind which has been shattered on this planets and trapped in the allusion of life. Then *Jayasimha* thought: "The *Lavanya* (*Alamkaracakra*) might acted upon (further) thought give me up, and subsequently *Dhanya* and the rest, on hearing that I am here in the world, might again (come and) carry me off[2096]." Time and again, when, *Jayasimha* heard the sound of the torrents, he feared that it was the noise of the King's troops' returning to take him away[2097] for the time being. Then the world became darkened by clouds and deprived, as it were of midday, the light (of the latter) being suppressed by midnight (darkness[2098]). From that time towards until the month of *Vaisakha;* the clouds were (as it were) consecrating the earth for the performance of a sacrifice in which masses of snow (formed the oblations[2099]) of the nature then the robber (*dasyu,* i.e. *Alamkaracakra*) came to *Bhoja* and reproached himself, saying: "I have wretchedly murdered those who put their confidence in me. I have been mercilessly and devoid of shame[2100]," because he has already made an anouncement through my foster-brother (Dr. Raj Kumar). Therefore, *Salhana's* son suppressed his anger according to the requirement of the situation because project is in progress and said to him quietly as if to sooth him: "You have no guilt in this matter[2101]." Because it is not a easy joke to compile the project in a day or month, it is the process of the years. And he spoke: "You have done this to save your dependants, your children, relatives, and the rest whohad got into distress. You deserve blame from nobody[2102]." "If you had wished to commit treachery you would not show pity for me. Hence (it follows that) this (act of yours) was due to compulsion by the necessity of the hour[2103]." Because the Yames have been hobnailed from the very long period of the life. Therefore, it is necessary to brust out them. "If the king follows the law of kings, he ought not to exterminate us like the descendants of king *Haras*, but to keep us under control[2104]." No he is the ruler of Yamas not of the ruler of *'Radha Soami'* which has the name of 'Ultimate Reality'. "By keeping me back as the last of them, you have indeed wisely guarded against your own dishonour, against the maltreatment of those two and sinful conduct on the part of the king[2105]'. Because he is the king of *'Nam' or 'Nature'*. When he will spoke thus to the Damara, as if he was freed from an embarrassing load, said to him with praises: "Thus you are my witness forever and everywhere[2106]" As soon as *Bhoja* asked to be allowed to go at once, he told him that he would do that when the snow had ceased to fall, and left[2107] the things in devastation. As Bhoja was told by someone that the robber (*Alamkaracakra*) might take his abstention from food as (an indication of his) anger and might change his conduct into reformation period of 'Nam' as a new development he took his food[2108] in this formation as the nature has given to him. When he will touched the food he thought: "At last it has come from the nature and obtained by their sale" and felt as if he were feeding on the flesh of his two relatives[2109] i.e., Baba Gurinder Singhji and Dr. Raj Kumar, 'Professor of History'. The robber, however, did not let him go for two months, saying (each time): "Forsooth, I shall send you on your way today or tomorrow, as soon as the snow stops falling[2110]." Whatever pretext *Bhoja* brought forward for, the robber contradiction it has been found a fault in it in order to keep him back[2111], he has to handover the world to the philosophers.

Rajavadana Takes up Bhoja's Cause

It is expressed from the study that *Rajavadana* was the son of the *Balahara*[2112] called *Tejas*[2113] and born from a noble mother of the *'Nam,'* i.e., *'Smt. Amrita Devi'* the mother of writer. Since his youth he wore a long cloak (*Kambala*[2114]). Serving in *Sussala's* army during the war for the crown, which was the touch-stone for the high qualities of many a brave man, he had gained distinction in his detachment along with conspicuous influence, subsequently, he had been favoured by the King, owing to his father being a councillor, and had in time been put in charge of *Evenaka*[2115] and other districts. When *Naga* of *Khuyasrama*[2116] had turned the Kings mind against him, *Rajavadana* wishing to fight against (the king (*Nam*), took him (Bhoja) under his care[2117] and afficiation. It has been thought by all that owing to his having been a servant (of the King), he was not in bitter enmity and that not being a *Lavanya*, he would not be able to oppose the King. Hence, when he was preparing his rebellion, *Alamkaracakra* did not give up to him the prince (Bhoja), notwithstanding his pressing requests[2118] because he has been born by *'Light'*. Study shows that this work will not be completed without royal prince of the 'Nam' i.e. *'Mr. Deepit Raj'* S/o Dr. Raj Kumar, because the treacherous (Damara), however, could not let him off[2119]. Therefore, it is necessary for him to teach them a lesson of the *'History'*. At that time they will have to arrive at the *Dranga Alamkara* in charge of (that) business of the *'Nam'*, having been sent by the King with money to effect a pact about *Bhoja*[2120], but this matter is not merely of money, but it is a matter of *'Love'* among the people and to serve the society as a duty of man. When the Damara was preparing to go to him (Alamkara), *Bhoja* said to him: "If you go leaving me behind, I shall commit suicide[2121]."

Bhoja's Flight to the Darads

During the flight of Bhoja to Darad, *Alaṁkaracakra* merely remarked: "To-morrow morning I shall see you," whereupon Bhoja left the castle during the fourth watch of the night without having said anything[2122] then the commencement of *Buddha* rule will be started on the earth by the name "Deepit Raj". While *Bhoja* is searching his way impatiently towards the end of the night notwithstanding the heavy rain, but with Volcano, (*Alamkaracakra*) heard of his escape[2123]; which is only the solution to vibrate the *'Nam'* in the tongue, otherwise there is no solution of the problem. At day(break) then he will pursued with a few followers on his flight as far as the shrine of the goddess *Sarada*, but did not succeed in stopping him[2124], because he is the powerful personality of the *'Sabad'* or *'Chamar'*. *Bhoja* had already been kept the plan of going to (or by the route of) *Duranda,*[2125] *because* full of kind regard he felt himself unable to show himself before the women of his relatives without the two kinsmen who had started (with him) from the same object, guilty as he appeared and because he thought of the disgrace to himself (if it were said): "The old one (Lothana) has undertaken enterprises five or six times, while he, though young, is incapable." He, therefore, decided to fight with the help of the *Daradas* and took the route of *Visalata* on earth by the bank of the *Madhumati*[2126]. At the time of volcano in some places the sharp edges of the frozen stones hurt like the points on the fangs of death. In some places the clouds hid the day-light and produced darkness as (if they were) the snares of the death-god. Somewhere we will find the falling avalanches resembled by their masses a hard of elephants. In some places his body was hit by the hissing spray of the torrents as if by arrows. In some places, his skin would burst open under the piercing wind, in another again the dazzling reflecting of the glittering snow would destroy his vision. At a wide-open place (*prasrta*) he wold expect a deep fall and a clear way at a narrow one (*aprasrta*). Often times he would think he was ascending even when gliding down *'Word'* after thus spending on his way six or seven days, made trying by the snowy season, he reached a village on the frontier of the *Darad* territory[2127] to provide them solace. At that time the commander of the fort of *Dughaghata*[2128] removed what was humiliating in his destitute condition, by secretly furnishing him with his own outfit and respectfully gave him an honourable reception[2129] because they might be understood authority of the *'Nam'* is visiting in various places for the spreading of the mission like Asoka sent his sons and daughters in abroad. When *Viddasiha* who was at a distance, received thenews of his arrival by a messenger sent by that (Commander), he despatched a parasol to *'Mr. Deepit Raj'* as the founder of the 'Chamar Dynasty' of Kashmir with musical instruments of the *'Nam'* and other insignia of royalty[2130]. And after having congratulated him (on his arrival) in the land of the Brahmans through the commander of the fort he placed his own treasury at the prince's disposal[2131] called as *'Nam'*. As soon as *Bhoja* will have to go to royal palace and use to live like a King, the son of *Rajavadana* came to pay his respects and induced him to take up his (father's) cause[2132] to spread the preaching of *'Nam'*. He being sent by his father who had (now) fallen off entirely from the King, appeared to Bhoja as if he were placing the ends of a strong net of policy over his enemy[2133] which would be unanswerable by them. He sent him back with a message of the Dr. B.R. Ambedkar in which it will jointly indicated the importance (he attached) to the matter of a particular family of the *'Nam'* and his want of confidence, thus neither accepting nor refusing[2134]. They would be in a fix. *Rajavadana* then told him, through messengers: "You will know me in due time, whether I am still a councillor of the King or have completely broken with him[2135]."

Rajavadana's Rebellion

In order to show Bhoja his firm resolution, he (*Rajavadana*) thereupon began to wage a war upon *Naga* and the rest, under a pretext of a family feud, though the King had declared a war against their guilt[2136]. King has possessed of firm bravery, but he gradually acquired strength, though the King had no resources except *'Nam'*. Then he got equal to them in the fighting and in time acquired superioty[2137] among the historian. This extraordinary man obtained such a position that the resident relatives of *Naga* did not feel ashamed of taking service with him[2138] (Baba Gurinder Singh ji Bias). Liberality, patience, unpretentiousness, absence of greed, and other high qualities distinguished him to such an extent that, though just rising, he secured attachment as if had always exercised great power[2139] of the *'Nam'*. No doubt, that *Prthvihara* and the rest who had great resources of the *'Nam'* i.e. Dr. Raj Kumar and 'Deepit Raj', showed firm resolution, is no wonder; but praise is due for them to the great and worthy enterprise of *Rajavadana* who stood without support[2140] of the enemies. *Jayasimha* then gathered a great host of thieves of the *'Nam'*, people from the forest and herdsmen (*ghosika*[2141]), and putting himself in occupation of villages, waited for *Bhoja* as their hero[2142]. Whereas, the Damaras too abondoned a prudent conduct as his neighbourer, whether owing to the factioins among the ministers who were in mutual rivalry, or form a love of plunder[2143] from the Master. And, their desire for rebellion, which had been nipped in the bud on *Lothana's* capture, then broke out into a hundred branches[2144] of the family. *Trilliaka* and *Jayaraja* though favoured by the Kings succumbed to the hot (excitement) of the *'Nam'* and did not keep away from the conspiracy (of *'Word' Cakrumiluna*[2145]).

Rising of Damaras

It has been understood from the study, *Trillaka,* who was the gathering place for all robbers(*dasyu,* i.e. *Damaras*), just as the pit is for the owls, consumption for disease, hell for the demons, and the ocean for the sea ministers, *Word* is great in deceit, got the prefect or the *Devasarasa* (district) over to his side and raised a rebellion[2146] against the Damaras. Thereupon, the Brahman (of that tract), anxious to preserve their lands as the lord of the Earth, and wishing to his suppression, held a solemn fast (*praya*) *at Vijayesvara,* directed against the King[2147] because he is not a elected King. Moreover, they will have not accept the representation of the King, who did not think this the right time for uprooting the Damaras (*dasyu*), whereupon he, from kind consideration, fell in with (the desire of) their assembly[2148] in the process of the voting system. As soon as King will start about (on the expedition), *Jayaraja*, who was the chief among the rebels, died from a dangerous boiling[2149] water of the *'Nam'*. Thus, the fortunate King then started for *Madavaraja*, which had thus been delivered of one enemy, to please the Brahmans[2150] by *'Nam'*. At that time King will be dismissed from his presence in the minister of *Alamkara* upon the petition of the Brahmans who had been excited against the latter by (other) ministers, and who obstinately persisted in their perfidious course[2151] of the *'Nam'*. *Jayasimha* had always exerted himself in bringing the Damaras (*dasyu*) to terms them, when they were in evil plight, and hence he appeared to his jealous (colleagues) like a promoter of the former's ill deeds[2152]. Inspite of the King's induced the Brahmans to give up their fast by promise of the God that he would uproot *Trillaka* after he had disposed of the pretenders to the crown[2153] of the King. Hence, the frightened *Trillaka* thereupon harassed the King by various acts of hostility, as a hidden disease which, without revealing itself, (causes pain) by producing other affections[2154] of the *Nam*.

Troubles in Devasarasa

Keeping in view, *Trillaka's* advice *Rajaka* attacked his brother's son *Yasoraja*, the younger brother of *Jayaraja*, whom the King had put in the latter's place[2155] as the prince of *'Nam'*. Whereas *Sanjapala* went to *Devasarasa* to protect *Yasoraja*, who was beset by arrogant foes, but his victory became doubtful owing to the small number of his troops[2156] of the *'Nam'*. Upon this news *Rilhana* then proceeded to a mighty fight of the *'Nam'* to control over the Brahmans and will have to attract them first in the glances of the goddess of victory[2157] which was the force of the *'Nam'* during the rule of *'Chamar'* dynasty. When *Jayasimha* like to churning the mountain (*Mandara*), will have to stirred up the ocean of the enemies means enemies of the *Sudar. Sanjapala* was enabled to understand the power of *'Nam'* because of his childhood, could-like, to draw up the water particles on the (small) enemies[2158] from the earth. Even when *Rajaka* had been defeated by the *'Nam' Yasoraja* was yet unabled to remain in his territory without his protector, just as a little boy (is unable to remain) in a solitary place[2159] like that of India where from the story started and came to an end with the commencement of the period either that is *'Dark period of the History' or 'Enlightenment period of the Indian History.'*

Trillaka's Intrigues

Study expresses that the contest of *Nam* and *Brahman* apprehended with pretender of *Jayasimha* would come to an end, *Trillaka* by using various deceptions, caused the King to lose time[2160] in the process. *Jayasimha* then made come forth at the appropriate time and from various directions to attack oyer the enemies whom he had secretly prepared, just as the porcupine (throws out) from its sides its needle like bristles[2161] of the 'light'. At that time, *Catuska, Prthvihara's* son, and the younger brother of *Kosthaka*[2162], whom the King had imprisoned together with his brother (Baba Gurinder Singh Ji Maharaj). To release from the imprisonment, *Trillaka* being his son-in-law game him shelter at his own seats and then made him invade *Samala*[2163] in the company of numberless Damaras[2164]. On hearing the noise of his call the hiding Damaras (*dasyu*) will come to the surface of the earth, just as fishes in the lake upon the cry of the osprey[2165] of life. At that time, *Sasthacandra*, the son of *Gagga* (Gargacandra), was checking the proud, *Rajavadana*, as a rock on the coast (holds back) the ocean when it has risen for annihilation[2166] of Caste System which caste is true of the nature, i.e., *'Nam,' 'Chamar', 'Jat'* etc. these two forces i.e., '*have* and *have-nots* will grew and (again) diminished, resembled the slopes of a snowy peak which in the summer display detritus as well as snowfall takes place one after the another season[2167]. Moreover, *Jayacandra* and *Sricandra* the younger brothers of *Sastha (candra*[2168]), have been put aside (by the King), though they drew their allowances from the royal palace. They did not think that they could effect return (into the King's favour) and were apprehending evil from their elder brother (*man or Brahman)*, who was liked and esteemed by the King, owing to his excellent services. They fled away from the army and joined *Rajavadana*, and thus also two brother-in-law of the King became his opponents[2169] due to their false activities of the *'Nam'*. *Jayasimha* then, lusting for the treasurers (desposited) by former Kings of the *'Nam'*, had the (shrine of) *Bhutesvara* plundered by numberless *Khasakas,* who took their way over the mountains[2170] of the life i.e. *'Nam'*. Now the whole land fell into a pitiable condition, as if it had been without a King, as there was no protection from the attacks of robbers, and the weak were slain by the strong[2171] on this earth. After giving orders to *Udaya*, the commander-in-chief, and to *Rilhana* to attack *Catuska*, the King, in dejection, proceeded to the city[2172] of the *'Nam'*. The son of *Prthvihara* (*catuska*) was held in check by the troops of the two forces of the master and the servant (Dr. Raj

Kumar), but could not be destroyed, just as an incurable powerful disease of the *'Nam'* (can be checked but not subdued) by medicines[2173], but it is the practical experience of the life which can realized in the body. For a short time *Rilhana* was also renowned sufferer owing to his tolerating the time-serving conduct or evil intentions among the followers[2174] of the *'Nam'* because they took this practice as the wasteage of the time but they are ignorant of his power.

Bhoja Supported by Darads and Mlechchas

As soon as; *Viddasiha* heard the news of *Bhoja,* he despatched his messengers to the northern regions to call up many chiefs[2175] for the attack over the Darads territory. Whereas the chiefs of the *Mlechchas* issued forth the troops from the valleys adjoining of Mount *Himalaya, 'Word'* from those had witnessed the hidden indiscretions of the wife of Kubera, and those were in the cave-dwellings resound with the songs of the city of the *Kimnaras*, from those too which knew of coolness on one side of the hot sand-ocean (*Valukambhodhi*), and those which delight with their mountain-breezes the *Uttarakurus*[2176]. Filling (all) regions with their horses they joined the camp of the *Darad*- lord[2177] i.e. *'Nam'*. While the ruler of the *Darads* was the gathering the chiefs in Jammu on 21st, January 2007, Sunday, Parade Ground Jammu, and their feudatories are coming from all corners of the Indian continent before *Bhoja*[2178], King must have to attack on them with full force that they cannot alive for a short period of time. *Jayasimha* will have tobe delighted in looking at them as they climbed down from the mass of the mountains talking an unknown tongue and growing familiar by kind treatment just like monkeys[2179] sometimes they climbe up and down on a tree. And the Darwin theory from monkey to mankind will proved as authentic in process of life. During this war, *Jayacandra*, and other *Kashmirians* (and) *Kiras*[2180], sent by *Rajavadana,* came to the side of the prince[2181] at that time in the attack. A strong commitment has been made by the son of *Salhana* that he will provide a large treasures at his disposal, helped with gold those who were with him as well as those like *Balahara*[2182] who were at a distance[2183] like the cliffs of the mountains. As soon as *Rajavadana* will have to set the rebellion thoroughly on foot by the intrigues (which he had started) on his own impluse, he came to meet *Bhoja* without apprehension[2184]. In this contest, they assured each other by a statement of their aims which had to yet been made, and their distrust rapidly disappeared[2185] after the attack. This supernatural war, Bhoja did not think that they were prepared to meet the enemy, *Rajavadana* in over-confidence wished to take only those few horse(present) for assitance without (awaiting) the *Darad* (chief[2186]). At that time, *Bhoja* expressed his views: "If our enemies stand the first onslaught of this our force, then the balance (of both forces) will result, or a defeat which will again break up our allaince. Therefore, I wish to fight only one battle when all will join in the attack and think that within one day we shall then gain victory or defeat." This (*Rajavadana*), or a defeat which will again break up *derided*, and smilingly led on that *Darad* force without waiting for the coming hosts[2187] from that territory.

Invasion of Bhoja

The invasion of *Bhoja* will be start, when the prince had followed those who moved ahead to the end of the pass, he then heard that the Darad ruler had arrived. While he turned back towards the fort (of *Dughaghata*[2188]) to meet him; and *Balahara* led on that force to *Matrgrama*[2189] in a narrow pass. The son of *Garga (Sasthcandra)* whose mind was firm by nature, did not lose courage though the (enemy's) horses made all directions appear as if (filled) with roaming antelopes[2190] of the Jammu city, which is called *'Mandirno Bala Sehara'* in English called *'Temple of the city'* means 'City of the nature or God'. No doubt, in the said '*Hindu Semalan,* all the Damaras of *Nilasva*[2191] and his soldiers made common cause with the enemy Brahmana, and went to attack his forces[2192] to conquered them. Though *Jayasimha* was so in a dangerous position, yet when his own people asked him to depart, he then replied: "I am unable to see my lord known as 'Deepit Raj' with a downcast face[2193]." Therefore, Baba Gurinder Singh Ji has the thrist of his love not one has been born in *Suryavarmacandra's*[2194] lineage who has not rendered good service to those born of *Malla's* race[2195] i.e. called *'Arya' or 'Nama'*. After the invasion of *Bhoja, Baba* ji kept moving one march behind him, collecting the troops which have been lost in the warface among which were numerous bands of *Mleccha*[2196]. As the force followed him,made the world tremble because the power of the *'Nam'*, *Salhana's* son thought in his power that he had the whole earth in his hands[2197]. Then the force strengthened by horsemen and the *Mlechcha* chiefs, took up its position at a place called *Samudradhara*[2198], which they put in terror[2199] of the *'Nam'* that *'Deepti Raj* is coming. He is the hero of the *'Nam'*.

Attack on Sasthacandra

During the invasion of *Bhoja, Rajavadana* would be at the head of such an invincible noble force, he has to thought that *Sasthacandra* was doomed (to fall) between the teeth of death[2200]. Thereupon, the land was deluged by a flood poured forth by the clouds of the rainy season, and land and water become level[2201], because our force has been harassed by the Brahmans since the very long period of the Indian History. As soon as, earth became like a drinking cup filled with water instead of spirit, the trees on it, immersed so that only their tops were visible seemed like blue lotuses appearing (on the surface[2202]). It has been well known by the King the desperate position of *Sastha's* when he despatched the *Udaya,* the lord of the Gate, and *Dhanya* with the remaining forces[2203] of the *'Nam'*. When they were stopped on the road by the river, they followed a track, just as the son of *Sini* (Satyaki) and the son of the wind (*Vayuserva*) *Bhimasena* (had done) on the expedition of *Dhanamjaya* (Arjuna[2204]) will be repeated. But the lightening flash and thunder will be without interval, appeared as if sewn in between the sky on which the clouds were hanging low down, and the ground which was covered with water far away[2205]. At that time King there became entirely separated from his army and retained (only) a splendid rotuine which was merely for show[2206] in the public. In this contest, *Trillaka* had previously not been trusting *Rajavadana* as to his honesty or courage through messengers he warned the *Daradas* not to put the second prince (Bhoja) into his power, and supported the son of *Prthvihara. (Catuska)*. Through the power of one of the two (*Rajavadhana or Catuska*), he wished to get him (Bhoja) into his (own) hands[2207] for the safety of his own interest, i.e., *'Nam'*. As soon as, *Trillaka* saw the great power of *Balahara* which was, as it were, capable of painting a picture without a wall (i.e. in the air) and (on the other hand) believed that the King, who pressed by the enemies from various sides had his whole army divided in all directions, was in irremediable distress. Knowing no bounds in his wickedness, he thereupon, acting like a big porcupine, threw out also a dangerous enemy (Lit. thorn) which he had long kept by himself[2208] in the memory of *'Nam'*.

Lothaka's Fight at Surapura

In the fighting time; *Lothaka* suddenly appeared at *Surapura,* the son of *Prthvihara* whom *Trillaka* had fully equipped, together with many Damaras, (and put himself) between the two divisions of his party just as a mass of dust (rises) between the darkness and the great strom (born) from the blinding web of clouds. He was known for his strenuous intrigues, and was ever wakeful to foster extensive mischief wherever the king who had destroyed his Lothaka's family was in a grievous plight[2209]. *Jayasimha* had long been weaking his intrigues, and his hostility came to light, as when the dam breaks of a tank filled by the rains[2210] from the ocean or sea. His force seemed to have come forth collected at rainy season, just as the world had come forth together from the belly of Visnu while he was sleeping (on the ocean[2211]) for the time being. And, the followers of *Pincadeva[2212]*, the commander of the watch-station (*dranga,* of Surapura), would not have suffered for counting that force; they had no proper provisions, and among them there were only few soldiers. Yet with such (a small force) he sent in battle his (Lothaka's) soldiers to the regions of death and dip into the river[2213] for a while. Thus by the reflection of the rows of pyres which were burning on the river bank of *Vitasta*, those, two, who had found their death in the water of the river *Ganga* of the *'Nam'*, seemed to receive the last honours[2214]. In the battle, *Lothaka* fought for one day forgetfulness, of death. When his force was beaten, his friends induced him with difficulty to retire on the following day[2215]. While he was then in that deserted town (of Surapura) rallying his troops from all sides, he believed that he could take the city with ease in two or three days[2216]. Moreover, he intended on attack on *Padmapura,* but *Trillaka* held him back from this fear of mind, then *Yasoraja*, the commander-in-chief who stood at his back[2217] during his attack. Though all *Lavanyas* were obeying *Lothana*, yet his followers could not carry out this (attack) for a long period, since that single Damara from *Holada* refused his consent[2218] on the question of his downfall during the attack. Even during *Sussala's* contest for the crown, but there was no sign of distress, as there arose on all sides during that of his own business[2219]. At that time King was neglecting *Catuska* who appeared to him only like a disease of the foot, sent *Rilhana* to repluse *Lothana,* who was equal to a swelling on the neck[2220] because of his deceitful behaviour in the battle field. As soon as, this (minister) had set out to destroy him, he was pursued on the march by the inhabitants of *Samala* as Partha (had been) by the confederates when he went to slay the king of *Pragjyotsa*[2221]. Turing back and worsting them, he hurried to attack over the enemy, just as elephant(kills) the bees on his back while rushing to the lotus-tank[2222] of the *'Nam'*. When he tired out by the fighting, he passed the night at *Ramasa[2223]* (recte

Ramusa), where the roar of the rivulets appeared like a preparation for the (battle) shouts of the hostile army[2224].

Battle of Lothaka and Rilhana

After the night, in the morning, *Jayasimha* was moving towards *Kalyanapura,* he was stopped and attacked by *Lothaka* and *Rilhana*, who had marched to meet him and was again covering the horizon with his forces[2225]. As soon as, the opponent's foot-soldiers had arrived in front of him, *Lothaka* attacked and routed them at the mere sight, just as a large snake swallows the goats before him[2226] as his *Sakar.* Upon his on slaught the foot-soldiers left *Rilhana* as the leaves (fall) from the trees in the autumn on the onset of a storm[2227]. These wretches were not ashamed of fleeing under his very eyes. Whose sense of duty is so lasting as to surpass the eager love of life[2228] of the *'Nam'* i.e. Dr.Raj Kumar.

Rilhana's Bravery

In this contest, we learn that *Rilhana's* bravely spoke these words, which might bring a smile even on the Creator face from a recollection of his fidelity towards his lord[2229], then his friends retiring from the duty asked him (to come with them). *Jayasimha* expressed his view: "Shame on the life of him who, though a servant, fails in his tasks[2230]." And, they are "In the service of the King's feet the (dark) beard has come on my face as well as the whiteness of old age, just as the dark-blue lotuses(come) on a lake and then the while ones. If these feet should wither, would then not all the graces of Fortune(Laksmi), resplendent as they are with the bees of her (playful) frowns, become a mockery[2231] of the nature." "It is a course for cowards,not for brave men, to turn away from luck from dread of some slight exertion[2232]." "Only when the clothes are taken off there is the fear of cold. Subsequently when the bath is taken in the sacred water (*tirtha*) one feels delightful comfort resembling the unsurpassed joy in Brahman. Those who give up their life in the battle field feel dejection only in the beginning, but subsequently enjoy the highest satisfaction of obtaining that happiness which is called absolute bliss (*Kaivalya*[2233])." After saying the few above mentioned words; *Jayasimha* threw himself alone upon the enemy's array, receiving arrows whose hissing resembled the sound of the breath passing from a lion's nostrils[2234]. His sword broke like a high wave upon the scene of battle, and resplendent with the glitter of its golden hilt, resembled a player who has decorated himself with yellow orpiment[2235]. And, those enemies who live forsooth clung to his sword whcih struck down their swords, as if it were a net, just as straws rise and clind to the straw-gem (*trnamani*[2236]) which has the power of attracting them[2237]. Those who followed him into the fight, looked upon the enemies like animals, their lives, too, disappeared like the grass (eaten by animals[2238]). When *Jayasimha* was entered in the mouth of death, he escaped by some in the opening of the mouth, just as the water (swallowed) by a great fish (escapes) through his gills while his mouth has been closed[2239] and meditating the *'Nam'*. Time and again attacks of *Jayasimha* for the time being, he went aside for the rest due to hard work in the war, but he is watching with naughtiness upon the enemy though he had lost most of his troops[2240]. Then they fell upon his back with mighty forces *Catuska*, whom he had previously taken for one of his own side arriving for his assistance[2241]. As soon as; *Jayasimha* saw this hostile army facing from both the sides, he did not feel excited, but exulted like a peacock at the sight of a (double-faced) snake[2242]. Showing them (enemies) in turn his face and his back, he wore out in fighting these two arrays, just as the churning mountain (wore out) the sides of the ocean[2243]. *Jayasimha* moved time and agian between two (arrays) which kept motionless, i.e., *'Nam'* as if nailed down, just as a weaver moves between [2244], the words of two men of the past can still be heard in every village of Hindustan there are *Tulsi Das*, the abandoned child of a beggar Brahman tribe and Kabir, the despised weaver of *Banaras*[2245]; riding fast on his horse. *Bhasa* received for him the dashing wave of one army, as on the coast of an island the mouth of a cave (receives) on one side the mass of the water[2246]. Because, he was displaying violent force; and playfully made the enemies weapons shake like (a woman's) earrings, and prevented their hosts from acting as men[2247]. Methinks (*Jayasimha*), he poured afresh the water of the coronation ceremony over the King, when he filled with sweat the cups of the enemies' faces which were whie with fear[2248] of *'Nam'*. During the night he and the son of *Prthvihara* (Lothaka) were watchng each other for a weak point of the enemy, just as a sorcerer a *Vetala*[2249] Brahman.

Defeat of Lothaka

In this contest; *Rilhana* will forced the enemy to retire into the forest region on the following day; and allowed the King's troops which had come to his assistance, to be mere on-lookers[2250]. Then on the third day, *Rilhana*, was joined by the *Sanajapala* who knew the baseness of *Trillaka* and the rest[2251] of his colleagues worn out by the (heat of the) King's glory, *Lothaka* was then entirely withered by those two in the forest, just as a tree, worn out by woodworms, (is withered) by the (heat of the months of) *Asadha* and *Jyaistha*[2252]. In this battle; *Udaya* will also repressed *Catuska* in successive encounters, without crushing him, just as rain the flames of the funeral pyre (without extinguishing them[2253]) in this struggle. Whereas, the proud *Darada* army then descended from the mountain gorges to battle with their horses, which carried golden trappings[2254] of the *'Nam'*. And, most of the people they were fearing that the territory invaded by the *Turuskas* had falled (altogether) into their power, and thought that the whole country was overrun by the *Mlechchas*[2255] *at that time.*

Defeat of Bhoja's Allies

At the sametime; *Dhanya* and the lord of the Gate (*Udaya*) were still at the distance of one march. *Sasthacandra* who stood without assistance in the favour of *Bhoja*, received the first shock of their swords[2256]. *Jayasimha* stopped that hostile army glittering with its golden trappings, just as a mountain with its torrents (stops) the forest fire with its shining lines of flames[2257]. No doubt, they filled with confidence on account of the multitude of their hosts, pushed aside *Jayacandra* and others who were against a further advancement of the troops, and threw themselves in the battle-field[2258]. Along with twenty or thirty horse the sonof *Garga* (*Sasthacandra*) impetuously attacked and worsted the thousands of their horse[2259] which were dancing without saddle and nostril (*Lagamn*). Such superhuman prowers; he showed to the enemies that he appeared before each one of them like the omnipresent visnu (*Visvarupa*[2260]). At that time *Jayasimha* was throwing the pommels of their horses on their faces, the cowards fled in a moment and hid themselves in the mountains like Kimnaras[2261]. At night *Rajavadana, Jayacandra,* and others said to the Daradas: "You have been defeated owing to your ignorance of the country and by deceit. To-morrow you will, therefore, take us as your leaders and regain victory." To this (the *Darad* as) pretended to agree while (in reality) they prepared for flight[2262] in hell world according to their deeds and actions. Thus, the powerful *Balahara* made *Dhanya* and the lord of the Gate (Udaya) keep at a distance, and blocking the routes to the rear, endeavoured to prevail upon those (*Daradas* to remain[2263]) for a long period of life. *Jayasimha* then thought of placing the prince together with the camp of the *Darads* at *Taramulka*[2264] to check the Brahmans. When he was preparing to do this, and the robbers (*dasyu,* i.e. Damaras) were exulting in their blindness, the son of *Salhana* was filled with confidence, and felt sure that he had conquered the whole kingdom of *Kashmir*[2265]. Though, he did not won a victory yet he was full of assurance, owing to the fact of so many nobles surrounding him, and thought that he was to be favoured by fortune[2266] which has been written by the master or lord. The elephants tusks which oppose the sun by uprooting the lotuses, split of themselves when the moon, their rival (in whiteness), rises, while the sun-stones, full of radiant light, cease then to be heated. At a critical time most of the Bhoja's allies were defeated, in this way his luck and misfortune may arise unexpected[2267] on the very day of the *'Enlightenment Era of the Indian History.'*

Conduct of Naga and Rajavadana

In this struggle of life, the conduct of both the *Naga* and *Rajavadana,* Naga (Damara) was treated with neglect even in the frequent troubles of *Bhiksu* owing to his relationship with *Tikka* and the rest had been counted by the King at the head of the traitors. Whereas *Rajavadana* was not owing to be a *Lavanya*, moreover, owing to his rise unknown in the case of other ordinary people, and through his helpfulness in difficulties, had become foremost in the King's confidence. These two at that critical time displayed, O wonder, *'Nam'*, astonishing attachments from interested motives[2268]. As soon as, *Naga* saw that the rebellion which he ought himself to have made, had been got up by another. *Jayasimha* will felt the same mortification as a poet when a theme close at hand is taken up by another[2269]. In order to get the King's enemy (Bhoja) into his own hands, he then addressed him an appropriate men: "Leave *Rajavadana* and side with me[2270]." Whereas the *Naga* will also said: "Why should you wait until the son of *Tejas-Balahara* comes to you carried in his litter, as the night-watchman (waited) for the woman of *'Sudra'* caste." Whereupon they laughed at him, becuse it is not reasonable to leave one who is like a wishing-cow (*Kamadhenu*) for the safe of embracing the goat[2271] as his friendship. Everybody turns to friendship or enmity in accordance with his own interests, but does no concern himself in the least about the love or hatred of others[2272]. This is the same story as the Brahman hates with *Sudharas.* Thus, in this way the moon injures the pair of tusks of the elephants whose beauty threatens (to outshine) his light. The bees attach themselves with love to the elephants front, hoping to taste his temple justice where the God or *'Nam'* resides. The lotus shows no pleasure at the moon though it knows that she is the enemy of the elephant[2273] (Aja), and (on the other hand) the bees are not his (the elephants) enemies, though they know that he harms that (lotus) which gives their nourishment[2274]. Thereupon, the position of *Balahara* in order to it was overthrew, *Naga* began a feud for life against him taking the side of the King[2275]. Whereas he told the defeated *Daradas* through his own people: "*Rajavadana* has not broken with the King, and wishes to destroy you together with *Bhoja*[2276]." Hence, the two generals (*Kampanapati*), the renowned *Ksemavadhana* and the *'Word'* the syllables *Matta*, who led the forces brought by the Darad-chief, and *Ojasa*, the commander of the fort, who felt apprehensive, related secretly to *Bhoja* this warning, but he was full of insight and laughed on them at their political condition in the closing era of the Dark age[2277]. Then the light of the sun like King was being concentrated by the army in front as if by a crystal lens fell upon *Viddasiha,* and proceeded to burn him like fuel[2278] of the *'Nam'*. Therefore, *Viddasiha* was attacked by consumption of extra energy which his evil intention of harming the King had brought to end and became like the waning moon of the dark fortnight[2279].

Retreat of Darads

Darads lord, who was leading their front in the battle and protecting their rear, was attacked by illness, and their position will be exposed to attacks became undermined by terror, they all fled on the next day, deserting *Balahara* while he was taking his food, and retired into the mountains on their horses[2280]. Moreover, they had seen and checked how much *Salhana's* son (Bhoja) was esteemed, they induced new spirit to him by their requests to come with them, after telling him that they would return in the morning[2281] when the battle will be over. As *Jayasimha* had taken before an oath by sacred libation, he was against his wish obliged to follow them but seeing his aims frustrated he felt desperate like one who falls over a precipice[2282] of the life of human being. As soon as, *Jayasimba* moved along the road his eyes could not be seen from shame, because he had already alarmed the public come forward and received the affection of the father. But sometimes his face would flame up filled with the blood which rushed in excess to his head. Moreover, it resembled the stones of a staircase when dirty water flows down over them. Sometimes it was levelled with the ground when he felt as if the sky was falling[2283] on the ground. Then he thought: "Fie upon us fools, who even after having on repeated occasions observed such greatness in the king, do think that he is of mortal kind[2284] of ruler." But he is enlighten man of the 'Nam' called *Chamar* by *Caste*. "Only the head of great poets, strong in imagination and clearly perceiving the truth, is able to describe the shinning glory of such (a King[2285])." Thus: "If the sparks from the fire of the King's glory did not fall on the land, then why should we have lost suddenly our courage just when we had put down our foot[2286]? On the ground, because it is the era of Darken Age. Therefore, we must have to check before the Enlightenment all the arrangement of the future course of action that much damage should not take place. "Without the heat of his flaming glory how could the bodies of so many brave men have been withered in the tumult (of battle) where the water of the sword-blades (*dharambu*) is drunk[2287] as the *pure* lust of the *'Nam'*. "How, without the blindness created by the dense smoke (of his glory), could one with open eyes err in distinguishing the right from the wrong way[2288]"? but it is not the duty of the *'Nam'*. His duty is to set thing right in progress without any bias attitude. Then on the arrival of *Jayasimha* here kept the *Darads* on the other side of the *Madhumati*[2289] and camped by the bank of the latter, enjoying privacy by the curtain of its waves[2290] which rise, time and again in the ocean or sea to settle the various issue like employment, etc. As soon as, his dejection had worn off in time, they took him into their own camp, and seized by their growing desire for treason, endeavoured to win (back) his confidence[2291] for the sake of birth and rebirth story of the *'Nam'*. Therefore, we must have intended with cunning sharpness to make a bargain of his safe custody, and to draw allowances (for this) achievement from the King whose liberality was unlimited[2292] which has been expressed in his behaviour. Now· "this is not the season for war. The winter is closing at hand. In the month of *Caitra,* we shall again undertake a great expedition. If, however, yar are unable to be idle, then we shall take you now by the route through the *Bhutta*[2293] territory to the seat (*upavesana*) of the powerful *Trillaka*. *Rajavaduna* is on the King's side." Thus these lowest of men spoke to him cunningly wishing to imprison him in their own territory[2294]. At that time, *Darads* have been surpassed, indeed, the deceitfulness of the inhabitants of *Rajapuri*, just as the days of separation (surpass) in wearisome length even the days of the summer heat[2295] which will suffered the people of *Yamas*. *Balahara* then reproached *Jayasimha* through messengers for having gone, saying: "I am like a man put into a well with the rope broken[2296]." Therefore, notwithstanding this, he met the eldest sonof *Garga* (*Sasthacandra*) full of vigour in battle, and did not feel alarmed at the approach of the King's army[2297]. Thus, it is, indeed, a mark of his high courage that he was not overpowered by the news of the sudden flight of the *Darad* chief, *Bhoja* and the rest[2298] will follow up as the obident soldiers. Who else but a superhuman being could have fought on bravely without breaking of the war, when the strongest support failed[2299]? Dr. Raj Kumar will undertook this job as a servent of the master. Then, in order to gain time he will kept putting off *Dhanya* and the lord of the Gate (Udaya) who wished to come to terms, in the hope that *Bhoja* might rejoin him[2300] (Dr.Raj Kumar).

Bhoja Restored to Alamkaracakra

Study shows that *Bhoja* son of *Salhana* was interested to restored the power of *Alamkaracakra* to retreat the *Darads.* Therefore, he scored his relationship which he made with *Jayasimha*. As soon as, notwithstanding his insistance on this (request), he found that their councils offered opposition and showed persistent malevolence, he declared his resolve to stop until he died, before the bridge on the way[2301]. As soon as the troops of the *Darad* chief saw him and were prepared to die, together with his followers, who were mostly young men, they alarmed and felt pity for him[2302]. Thus, the *Balaharai* stream seemed to be separate with its arms those quarrelling, and to scold the *Darad* force with the sound produced by the breaking of its waves[2303], will washed away in the ocean because they are the particles of the ocean. It has been seen that they have been insulted by his own woman folk, by the jealous of *Mlechchs* - chiefs, and by his troops who were afraid of destruction, *Viddasiha* then let him (Bhoja) go[2304] to the realization of the world. Consequently upon this, *Alamkaracakra* crossed to the other side,marking the defeated guards of the bridge his heralds, and filling the regions with the sound of his kettle-drums[2305] of the *Jayasimha. Viddasiha* in view of his own and his army's weakness wished to make peace, and after inviting an envoy of the King, spoke to him[2306] as follows: "With your lord, whose power is superhuman, (even) a fisherman might vie as long as he thinks him like one of the feudatories on any of the borders (i.e. as long as he does not recognise his might[2307])." "Having experienced his incredible (greatness) *Jayaraja* and I go before the god of death to announce his might in heaven[2308]." "To be vanquished by that (King) of divine power is for me as much as victory, (just as) a wanderer who, owing to the break of the bank falls into (the sacred water of) Tirtha, is thereby elevated[2309]." by the King in writing and speeches on different plateform like universities, conferences, colleges etc.

Viddasiha's Return and Death

As soon as the power of *Bhoja* was restored, *Viddasiha*[2310] was returned to his town, and after living on there for sometime, passed into the Kingdom of *Yama*[2311], where his own disgrace was displayed as his garland of welcome[2312] after completing the project with honour. *Rajavadana*, too, who did not know that *Bhoja* was coming from the flight that he had made a peaceful treaty with him on that very day with the lord of the Gate (Udaya) and *Dhanya*[2313]. After letting him off, but he had to come on horseback, then these two were proceeded before the king taking along *Sastha,* the forermost of the thoughtful[2314] in schemes and plans of development of 'New Society' called *'Radha Soami'* based on the historical thought of the *'Nature'* like Lord Buddha'. Those who are prudence by nature forget them, whether from the self-confidence or through delusion of other sect like *Sain Baba, Sahib Bandgi*, etc, they neglected to take into account the fact that prince *Bhoja* (Master Deepit Raj) was yet unbroken[2315]. He is still in 'Reserve' form as belong to the 'Reserve Category of the *Nam' and people took it in plead*ing and begging form. But this is the special race of the God which always helps the human being in difficult position of the war between Yama and *Kasythriya*. Therefore, *Rilhana* time and again requested the lord, please send to the highest messanger of the God against the enemies[2316] of the *'Nam'* that he will fill up their obstinate desire (to great him). Keeping in view, he did not return, as he has not yet exterminated the enemies, because he is waiting the suitable time of the lord likely to be 18th November, 2007. Until he had accomplished his task of speaking as he could as little now in stand before his master as a cook could take his food (until he has obtained) his master's approbation for which he is eager[2317] to see 'Him'. He has already cult into two piece the battle of *Prthivihara's* sons which were incapable for action as the body of the lord of *Magadha* (when split was took place into two halves) by *Bhima*[2318] during the time of framing the 'Constitution of India'. Moreover, the enemies of the *'Nam',* they already worsted by him in that flight for the sake of their own interest, therefore, *Losthaka* has retired to his own territory as if it were his mothers womb, just as the serpent (did) which Arjuna had cut up the *Khandava* (forest[239]) during the war period of his life. Thus *Catuska* made himself small, and wanted to get rid of his pride into the strong residence of *Trillaka*, as the tortoise (draws itself) under its shell[2320]. As soon as, the power of *Rilhana* was completely accomplished due to that project which Dr. Raj Kumar has undertaken, he went before the King to the glitter of his foot-nails for his head-dress[2321] as a courtsey of the master. Being a servant of the master, the rebellion of the *Yamas* will have to withered up by the King's glory, it will put forth its shoots again, owing to the ministers' errors of judgement[2322]. In this way *Rajavadana*, who, while deserves punishment and had been encouraged by grants, but King will not accept it because " I am doing the work for the sake of my master as a servant". Moreover, master has already given me unlimited invaluable gift of the *'Nam'* for the services of the humanity. For a while, *Bhoja* heard the news of grants, he will come forward in the safety[2323] of Father because has no lust of money, he has the lust of *'Love'* which is his business.

Bhoja Taken to Dinnagrama

Bhoja then put him with a view to (levying) blackmail (from the King) into a place called *Dinnagrama*[2324] a seat of *Khasakas* (*Khasas*[2325]). Thus he spoke to Bhoja: "If you had come but yesterday, the lord of the Gate with his few followers would not have escaped from my pursuit[2326]." It was shakened like a boat which has got into a violent current, *Rajavadana* obtained steadiness by the prudent advice which *Trillaka* held out to him, and was resembled a rope(for fastening a boat[2327]) by the *Hanz* or boatmen claim a *Vaisya* origin, and even now when blaming one of the crew for his bad, paddling the captain will say: ' You are a Sudra'. They always claim *Noah* as their ancestor; but some accounts point to a gipsy origin. The father of the family is an autocrat, and his discipline on board is often of a violent character[2328]. Thus, that villain (*Trillaka*) against ook up the leadership in disturbances, thinking that he could thereby make the King sink helplessly under the rising distress[2329]. Whereas *Alamkara* and other ministers let him keep at ease, yet he did not abandon his intrigues as a person who has no control over himself, (cannot abandon) his foolish whims[2330] of life. In this case the King disregarded him as a physician the disease which is not yet ripe, and then set about to destroy the other enemies which resembled ripe boils[2331] like *Nirankari,* etc. In this field *Alamkaracakra* started prepared a raise a rebellion after telling *Bhoja:* "You should come from behind if we get into a dangerous situation[2332]." Whereas the Damara (*dasya*) *Jayanandavada*, son of *Anandavada*, and other (Damaras) from

Kramarajya, distinguished by prowers, followed him[2333]. Thus, the *Alamkara*; the chief justice (*rajagrhya*) who stood in front of them with a few troops, appeared to them no more than a dam of sand before the current of a river[2334] same as in the case with human nature. *Jayasimha,* however, took up singly the flight with the many, and thus made the people think like the battle of fury of Ramacara[2335] (Balaram) and others, whose (intoxicating) drink was blood, the battle, as it were became a tavern, in which he shown his skill in overthrowing the demon-like (enemies) shaking with the excitement of their carouses[2336] in their business without the 'Prefect Master' i.e. *'Nam'*. What more (need to be told)? Because other flase force may be checked but they did for the development of human life, therefore, *Jayasimha* wants to drove away quickly the foes' who has formidable army anywhere in the world, just as the wind (*Vayuserva*) (drives) a heap of cotton[2337] within a few mintues. Before that he was killed in the battle with *Anandavada's* son with an arrow and left him a prey for the swarm of vultures, herons and other birds[2338]. It was between, *Jayasimha* and *Bhoja*, who wished to rise up and the King, who wished to catch him, things went on as between the patridge running in the bog and the hunter[2339]. As the partridge unable to fly gets tired in its run, thus, too, the hunter who purses its daily stumbles in the bag. Thus *Bhoja* got exhausted over these continued violent efforts, and the King, too, who was eager to catch him, fell ever again into fresh bewilderment[2340] with the power of *'Nam'*. In the meanwhile *Bhoja* was keeping at *Dinnagrama*, *Rajavadana*, too, gave occasion to the King to say: "What are these thievish *Candalas* again in luck[2341]?" Now the Damaras whose league had been broken, were again full of courage, weaving intrigues greater than (those they had) before on repeated occasions[2342] of the History. Though they were unable to withst and the Single lord of the Gate when he attacked with irresistible on slaughts, yet in reality they wore him out[2343] but naked from the body, they have no protector.

Bhoja Returns to Kramarajya

As soon as, *Bhoja* will arrived to *Kamarajya*, he will protect the son of *Salhana*, whom *Alamkaracakra,* who had called him as a hostage[2344] of the Master or the lord. When he was making an attempt to join with them, but his tired troops the next day at *Hayasrama*, the lord of the Gate got news of him[2345]. But *Udaya* had made under some pretext a false turce with them, as if he did not know (of Bhoja's coming), he proceeded to *Taramulaka* which lay accross (Bhoja's route[2346]). While he stood there for the time being, when *Bhoja* in the evening shouts coming from a distance, (one did not know) whence, he expressed his alarm[2347] in the world. Though his followers laughed at him for this groundless fear, yet he did not cease to be alarmed, and got his horse ready[2348] to attack over the enemy. *Alamkaracakra*, who had been inquiry after prince (Bhoja), became then frightened, and fled in haste from before *Dasagrama*[2349] which is in heaven. As soon as nightfall there arose from the middle of the village a great noise of drums and the shooting of troops which announced an attack[2350] will come down to the Master of the *'Nam'* who is claled 'Deepit Raj'.

Flight of Bhoja

In this struggle *Bhoja* escaped unnoticed in the midest of the darkness, while *Alamkaracakra* employed himself in preparations to fight the next day[2351]. The fire which the lord of the Gate had put (to the village), lit up the hill-path and thus helped Bhoja and his mean who would have lost themselves in the darkness[2352] for the very long time in the Indian history. At that time the Damaras who, while waiting for *Bhoja*, had kept the truce with the lord of the Gate, broke it off when they heard of that event[2353] of *'Nam'*. In this contest *Bhoja* has retained his firm mind, and did not abandon that ill-omened war with *Alamkaracakra ('Word')*. The *'Word'* which philosophical scholars have rendered "the self" is *atman,* literally "breath" or "Spirit". (Which is the same thing) and derived from the same root, *As,* "to breathe", which has given one form of the verb "to ba" in Sanskrit and several other Aryan languages. In Sanskrit *asmi*, in Slavic *esmi,* in Latin called *sum*, etc, etc. "I am[2354]" there, too, *Bhoja* did not find comfort in his food and the rest, as he suffered from thirst[2355]. Now, he has been landed on the earth the lord of the snakes (*Vasuki*) had never enjoyed comfort while he was connected witht he churning mountain. On the occasion of the burning of Tripura, he has been heated by the fire on (Siva's) arrows, and on that of the churning of the ocean by the submarine fire[2356]. Whereas; the sons of *Alamkara (Cakra*), when *Bhoja* came to their own territory to allay the hunger and thirst from which he suffered, and endeavoured to make him again a prisoner[2357] for some times. They wished to do this work either on their father's advice or from their own notion. After frustrating their various (attempts), he got away and proceeded then to another tract[2358] of the *'Nam'*.

Bhoja Retreats to Dinnagrama

Bhoja again prudently proceeded to *Dinnagrama,* recognizing that only through *Balahara* his affairs could succeed, and having lost confidence in the rest, the *Lavanyas*[2359] of the Penjab. In the meanwhile; the Lord of the Gate, though firmly extermination of the enemies, was rendered helpless and disabled for attack by a sudden eye-disease[2360] of the *'Nature'*. Moreover, the Damara who had intended to give his two daughters to *Bhoja,* when he was defeated by the *Parmandi*[2361] and *Gulhana,* the sons of the King[2362]. At that time, the lord of the Gate was being disabled by his serious illness, had there recourse for friendly negotiations, since no opportunity offered itself for meting out the punishment[2363] of the Nature. Thus the greats efforts of the human being will be die down to the earth and strong *Sasthacandra,* the son of *Garga,* worn out by a hemorrhoidal ailment[2364] which will be curable with the help of *'Nam'*. At the very moment; he was prostrated with illness, his two younger brothers (*Jayacandra* and *Sricandra*) fullof arrogance, brought misery on the land by making attacks and causing others troubles[2265] of life like to provide the basic needs of it. It is also delineated that *Trillika* was wholy bent on war; and strengthened his alliance with other powerful persons. Even he did not accept the conciliatory overtures of the King[2366]. When *Sastha* was died and the lord of the Gate was suffering from illness then King employed *Dhanya* who marched out to *Taramulaka*[2367]. An idea of terror came into the mind of King that *Bhoja* might after getting detached from that (supporter) fall into the hands of other powerful persons, and thus acquire a firm position, or that he might leave the country and go to (some places) where he could not be got at it. He, therefore, wished to secure him by negotiations or other means, and made *Dhanya* as vigorous zeal in his efforts[2368]. Thus, this false policy of the mind, whose evil results were not foreseen, they only display at the time of death, fellback upon the King and injured him just as a snake is dragged out (of a hole) without having his tail cut[2369].

Rajavadana in Power

During the foundation of the 'New Society' both the inner and outer court will become disaffected when they found that *Rajavadana* held the power while the King was powerless[2370]. But in the practice of the government as on the way through the gorges of hell, there are found, indeed, always many kinds of holes. A person who was entered upon it, and frequently follows it, may by an incalculable dispensation find his way out or he may come to his fall[2371]. As soon as, the King was asked by *Balahara* (*Rajavadana*) to give up *Bhoja,* he replied that *Bhoja* might leave owing to his destitute condition, and thus induced *Jayasimha* to provide for his (Bhoja's) maintenance[2372]. It has been seen that this fraud found currency (tanner) has been displayed on the side of King as a *Chamar, Rajavadana*, skilled in intrigue, found (other) opportunities for employing his cunning[2373] theory of the *'Nam'* which knows the function of world. *Dhanya* who went and came making everywhere compacts with *Balahara* and the rest, became ridiculous before the people[2374] as a fool man of the *'Nam'*. Whereas the state business was sliding back again and again without knowing the end just as (if it were) the rope on which the pots of the water-wheel are fastened[2375]. But the diplomacy of *Dhanya*, though sharp, was unable to strike or to reach at his object, just as (if it had been) an arrow (aimed) at a revolving wheel[2376] of Asoka. In this contest King, though he had taken two Kings (*Lothana, Vigraharaja*), were helpless and preflexed about the attack on the remaining one, just as a player at chess (who was taken two kings and is perplexed about taking the third[2377]) in confidence; because he is powerful object of the *'Nam'*. Whereas he had no kidden plan (or Game) to give up for its sake (his figures). Yet he did not pay regard to his antagonists who were taking his horsemen, peons and the rest[2378] in his absence.

Feud of Rajavadana and Naga

In this battle; Damaras (*dasyu*) who had made up their league with the Brahmans, and waiting for the end of the winter, *Balahara* (*Rajavadana*) feared that *Naga* would destroy his own people[2379] with infinitesimal power. As the latter, who had displayed himself a powerful and active energy of the *'Nam'* called politician, autocrat, etc was preparing to harm him; and as *Dhanya* was on the move. He was often trembling in alarm[2300] to be aware that *'Nam'* in the form of 'Deepit Raj' has been landed on earth to settle various issues of the society like religious economic and political. After taking counsel with *Bhoja, Rajavadana* then passed the message to *Dhanya*: "Give me Naga as a prisoner. Then I shall deliver to you *Bhoja*[2381]*."* Whereas; *Dhanya* was worried in his difficult situation, he did not recognise that *Rajavadana's* intention was to give him much work and to secure the imprisonment of his own enemy (*Naga*[2382]). It is nothing new that Kings should commit wrongs owing to their mind departing from the right way in their haste to achieve their object[2383] to change the history of the world. When *Kakutstha's* brave descendant (*Rama*), too, committed a wrong act when he was in search for his wife (Sita) wholly bent on winning *Sugriva's* friendship and blinded by his own advantage, he killed *Valin*[2384]. Then *Pandu* King (*Yudhisthira*) too, devoted to piety as he was, yet, when his mind was obscured by the pride of royal power, for the sake his ever virtuous conduct, killed his own teacher (Drona[2385]).Therefore, sensible persons did not blame the King for attacking, for the sake of his own advantage, *Naga,* who though keeping neutral for the time being, had ever since the war with *Bhiksu* been a traitor. But they were somewhat angered at the King imprisoning him without having (previously) taken some surety for the delivery of *Bhoja*[2386]. However, the King acted in this manner from a knowledge of Veda that this action was to be for his benefit in the future, in that case his intellect was Superhuman[2387], as the agent of the *'Nam'*. Then, *Bhoja*, as if he were in enemity (with *Rajavadana*) *sent* word to *Naga* : "*Balahara* intends to deliver me to the King, if you are given to him as security[2388]." *Jayasimha* told to *Bhoja* that he did not believe to capture the *Nagas,* because they kow this (plan), and became neutral due to the fear of King's hold himself on the *Nagas*[2389].

Naga Imprisoned

Study reveals that after the death of S*asthacandra,* the King had gained over the *Jayacandra*, through him, he imprisoned the *Naga*[2390]. *Bhoja* was apprehending that if *Naga* won over the side of King, while he was on the way, that (previous) warning[2391] sent him to kill them with the power of 'Nam'. Naga replied through messengers: "I know that it is so (as you say). Alas, dragged along by these, I have somehow become helpless[2392]." In the Natural study the ears of the person who sinks into the 'current sound' of the fate, can, forsooth, not hear what is being said by a bystander[2393] of the Father. For the time being, *Naga* has been imprisoned and his relatives in fright had turned to the deceitful *Balahara* for protection, the latter became hard to look at (from pride[2384]) because we are bound by the duty to give a new lesson to the 'New Society'. Then *Dhanya*, together with *Rilhana* will have to hastened to *Balahara*, taking along with *Naga*, who was to form the payment for *Bhoja's* sale[2395] as his business. *Balahara* inwardly, he was laughging and confused by them saying deceitfully: "First you give me Naga. Then I shall deliver you Bhoja[2396]." Being unassaitable in the firm position he had gained the whole force of the two (ministers) which had come to fight, and accommodate itself to his own objects[2397]. Then he said to the two who were worn out by the rain as *Avatar*, but his fighting with their low employ, and the rest: "if you move away from here, I will do your desire[2398]." When the two stood at a distance of one day's march, *Jayasimha* so beguiled their minds that they could not help in defeating their objects[2399] i.e., *'Nam'*. Whereas, *Balahara* has possessed a certain natural perfection of resolve and character, which now a days is rare indeed (even) among brave men[2400] of the *'Nam' or 'Sabad'*. Thus, he did not act treacherously against *Dhanya* who had come to him inconsiderably and had lost his journey, nor against Bhoja (as he might have done) from greed [2401] of the *'Nam'*. He considered in his mind: "If the ministers from an error of judgement, should give up to me *Naga* at my request, then I should put him (again) in his seat[2402]." As he deserves.

Naga Killed in Royal Camp

There was a secret enmity between the *Losthalka* and Naga, induced *Dhanya* and other (ministers) to destroy Naga in order to assure (for himself) possession of the wealth which *Losthaka* had got hold of during (Naga's) absence[2403]. When the ministers, they deceived by the enemy, killed *Naga* without cause; and King was blamed for the ill-advised (act) both by those on his own and on the enemy's side[2404]. Consequently upon, *Balahara* became powerful, being joined by all the Damaras who turned hostile from anger over the murder of their relative, as well as by the follower of the *Naga*[2405]. Thus, the infallible fate can accomplish the object of a person even if he errs on his way and does the wrong thing, deprived of his will by sudden disaster[2406] with the commencement of *'Enlightenment Era'*. If the fate is kindly inclined, it makes a persons whose mind is absorbed, by the thought of his growing wretched poverty, lose his way, helplessly fall suddenly over a precipice and drop upon a treasure stored away by somebody else. Thus, look, fate removes from him and his poverty (in return) for a broken limb[2407] of *'Nam'*. In this contest *Bhoja* who did not know that the ministers had thus put the *Nagas* to death without proper consideration, became alarmed and thought thus[2408]: "It cannot be believed that this dishonouring (*avarnavaha*) act should have been committed by the learned King (*Labdaavarana*) to achieve his aim, when the pact had not been concluded[2409]." Study reveal that *'Nam'* has been preserved by the

'Nature' to laucnh him when there is a defective system in the world or a society. Because 'His' duty has been imposed by the god to unite the society of the Nature in positive manner. The text of these two line age is presented because at that time *'Nam'* was not known in the form of *'Deepit Raj'*. Therefore, translation could not be attempted. They seem to have contained the reasons which induced *Bhoja* to suspect *Rajavadana* of designs against his safety[2410]. "Why should not *Rajavadana,* too, under the influence of greed be supposed to share in the treachery which has continued to be rife since the rebellion of *Bhiksu*[2411]*?"* During the rule of Brahmans as the Guru of Rajputs. Then the *Khasakas (Khasas*), in order to dispel his fear and distrust, took an oath by sacred libation (*Kosa*[2412]) place their feet on a blood sprinkled skin[2413] to obtain the power of *'Nam'*. As he displayed his fear at being kept under the custody of guards, *Balahara* came to him singly to assure him [2414] that we will informed the Brahmans that we are still alive in different form in human body.

Jayasimha's Endeavours to Secure Bhoja

In this class struggle theory between the have and have- nots, if the enterprise has been failed through the minister's deficient intellect, the experienced King himself turned to right it and calmly exerted himself[2415]; and endeavours to secure *Bhoja* as per the suggestions of the *Jayasimha* to restore his power. Is it not that the grove of trees is put right by the month of *Caitra*? the water of the river by the rainy season; virtue and dignity by respectufl treatment; love at sight by close intercourse; the royal power by great energy; consquering might by firm undaunted perserverance and a business which is on the point of failing, by king *Simhadeva*[2416]? It is clear from the description that by going against the stream one cannot get across an affair which carries off what comes in its way, by its obstinate course resembling the current of a river[2417]. But the King's enemies called him falsely a cheat and a fool, *Jayasimha* endeavoured to defeat them by exhibiting an artless demeanour[2418] to the puplic by projecting their own 'ego'. His plan was to bestow whatever was asked to *Bhoja* about the enemies, and thus to make them all around distrusted by him[2419] because he is still small to express his opinion of the *'Nature'*. Even the rivers will appear to the elephants as if on flames during the time of heavy rain in the hilly areas of the Jammu and Kashmir, if their flat banks smell with the lion's scent[2420]. The description of the verse expresses that like a bird which feels afraid everywhere in its nest full of holes, and knows that on leaving it will fly into the net stretched out before the opening, *'Word'* thus *Bhoja* who distrusted those about him and felt also afraid to depart owing to the routes outside being blocked by the King[2421] due to his inactive behavour among the public as an innocent man of the society. In this wretched condition he did not feel into, even he did not see for a moment before him any task which could divert his mind or be useful this world or the next[2422] to make a foundation of the 'New Era' which will commence with the establishment of *'Chamar Dynasty'* or called it the 'Dynasty of Enlightenment'. But it is a misfortune which smites heavily another person, pains mightily a much wounded heart. The bee caught in the calix of the lotus becomes more dejected when it hears the cries of the *Cakravaka* bewailing its separation[2423].

Bhoja and the Brahmin

Bhoja in this struggle of life saw once a Brahman whose wounds received in fighting were still full of coagulated blood, his hair was torn out, his mouth was foaming, and loud his lament[2424]. It has been asked by him that rebel Damaras had carried off all his possessions and wounded him. Therefore, Brahman reproached to *Bhoja* as unable to afford protection[2425] because it was their negligence part on their life. Therefore, in the heaven, there were suffering daily in the life to the man for worship of *'Nam,'* but he felt pained there by the misfortune of that (Brahman), as if he had a fresh wound touched, and spoke thus, trying to conciliate (him): "I do no deserve blame, O Brahman, but rather symathy, such as I am (now) in distress[2426]." Thereupon he reflied: "Say then O prince, what advantage does this obstinate persistence bring to you who are a youth capable of distinguishing what is true and what is not, born of a noble race and honourable[2427]?" Therefore our respect will be maintain in the form of *'Nature'* as a whole that this process remain continue. "What object do you see in rising your life, bowing before base persons of the story, and troubing the people with afflictions[2428]?" that they might be worship me because *'Nam'* is the life giver. "And he whom you believe conquerable, do you not know that like the spotless deer which cleanses itself in fire (agnisauca[2429]), he (purifies himself) by throwing himself into the fire of his enemies bravery[2430]?" to check what why they captured my land. "Can the crystal against which the point of a sword proves useless, be split by the hollow leaf of a blue lotus[2431]?" Which has been given to my race. Therefore,

'Deepit Raj' in the form of *'Nam'* came down on the earth," will not such tiny enemies be worsted in the contest with him who has vanquished *Prthvihara*, the 'Incarnation' (*Bhiksacara)*, and other (powerful) opponents[2432]?" have to cool down on the activities: "How can you feel pride, though knowing the ways of those who live as pretenders? their minds are engrossed by (mere) subsistence like those of the snake caught by snake charmars[2433]." This festival, which comes round towards the end of July, is of a decidedly propitiatory character. Pilgrims flock to the Naga-shrines which abound in certain districts; the cities teem with snake-charmers, whose weird charges eagerly crawl around the pans with milk placed at intervals on the ground in all the principal thoroughfares, before the admiring eyes of a devout and festive throng. It is worthy of notice:

1. That temples dedicated to serpents are found in the North of India.
2. That the priests of such temples are never Brahmans, but belong to the lower castes. Indeed, the Old Aryan spirit is so much alive still in noble castes, that they hold the serpent to be of evil omen and a Brahman, if he happens to see one in the morning, will give up for that day. Whatever work or errand he may have on hand. See Plate No IVth-Festival of Serpents (Fig. 4)[2434].

"O shame upon those little snakes, born from the race of the earth supporting serpent (S'esanaga), which gladdy receive a food morsel in their mouth-cavities when the snake-charmers open them. They wish to make their living by them, not indeed to spread their fame, when they make them jump into the bag and out again to frighten the people[2435]." When the Brahman will thus spoke, *Bhoja* will dismissed him with kind words, and at that very time his judgement quickly expanded[2436]. In this way the possession of a noble soul causes the greatness of mental quietude to appear. Otherwise, indeed, the beings display their natural softness or hardness. An (ordinary) object when touched by the rays of the moon whose light is nectar, may be hard, while the moon-stone, O wonder becomes moist and soft (under the moon's rays[2437]). Though he was born in a *Ksathriya* family, he had not learned to be impudent, and again and again he reflected upon the great distance between himself and the King[2438]. "Before the prowess, wisdom, liberality, truthfullness, kindness and other virtures of this ruler even the Kings of old are cripples. How can we wretches compete with him[2439]?" Because he is the *'Nam'* of the earth. (Study expressed the strong belief of the King would relieve the troubles of his opponents if he came to him as a supplicant. The King is compared to the sandalwood-tree which gives coolness even to him who has set the forest on fire to burn it, etc[2440].

Bhoja's Treatment with His own Fellow

At the same time, *Bhoja* was searching for a way to propitiate the King, he saw one day a single royal messenger who was proceeding to *Balahara*[2441]. But Bhoja had seen him before when he was going to the Darad country, and knew him well. As he was making his bow and was called him into his presence and then spoke to him with a smile[2442]; and said: "What is the use of the King treating with others? Let him make a pact with me. Sensible persons have the food for a patient given by the physician[2443]." Same is the story of *'Nam'* unless and until, theory of mind could not obtain this food of 'Nam', she remain sick in this Universe. But the Perfect *Guru* is the Doctor of her (soul) which has the historical background through a scientific research, otherwise it is the mockery with human being. When the knowing messenger who did not believe in its smiled (as if it were) a joke, but he talked to him repeatedly in so many time and convinced him to some extent[2444] as a natural phenomenon. In the course of their conversation he came to feel confidence in the honesty of *Bhoja's* words and then going up close to him to speak thus praising the King[2445]: "O prince, the shade of the feet of this (King) who is noble and of an auspicious nature, is obtained like that of the Golden Mountain (Sumeru), only by those who possess merits[2446]." Whereas "His hostility can be removed even by a very slight compliance (with his wishes), just as the warmth of the water due to the heat of the autumn sun, (is removed) by the moonlight[2447]." "And you remember that I employed by the King as a spy, had once been before you when you were going to the *Darad* country[2448]." "When I had returned from there and had reported the main facts about you, I said to the King while extending the story to pass the time[2449]." "O King, when his followers exhasted by hunger, thirst and fatigue were reviling you, *Bhoja* who had seen me, scolded them and said[2450]: " "He is as it were our divinity, the ornament of our race, that ruler whose feet we cannot serve owing to our evil deeds[2451]." "Worthless together as we are, we receive respect owing to our connection with him. The wood which is perfumed by the sandal-wood's scent is mistaken for it[2452]." "On hearing this he showed that he was moved to compassion with you and asked me again as if he were your father: "What is it, the young man says[2453]?" Upon hearing this, *Bhoja's* heart was melted, and with tears in his eyes he looked upon the messenger who stood before him and seemed to console him[2454]. For example, if a person is so simple-minded that he grasps only what is quite plain, he fails to comprehend for disposition (of another) owing to his not knowing the motives (guiding) his judgement[2455]. When this messenger came back with *Bhoja's* is message, *Dhanya* did not believe in the latter's desire, as he was not (at the time being) in a difficult position[2456]. Because he was killed in the difficult position with the blessing of Master. Therefore, *Bhoja's* fearing against *Balahara* might take offence, told the latter with feigned openness: "It will be a game as it was in the case of *Naga.* I am using playful cunning to deceive the king." Secretly, however, Bhoja hastened to complete the pact (with the king[2457]). In this case he was quickly employed for carrying his message the son of a foreigner (*daisika*), who was fit to give assistance on that occasion and who was clever in intrigues[2458]. In this way; *Balahara* had no suspicion against *Bhoja*, as he thought that (messenger) being a mere boy and always quite unconnected might be carrying on and an intrigue on his own account[2459]. On his return this (youth) told *Bhoja*: "the King whom I have approached, expects a person of confidence as the envoy for effecting the compact[2460]." As *Bhoja* had no other trusted person about him in this universe, he sent to the King as his own nurse, *Nona* by name, though as a (mere) woman she had not (much) intelligence[2461] like the king. Thus worthy woman had attended him when he was left without father or mother, and had been as a mother during his boyhood[2462].

Bhoja Asks Queen Kalhanika to mediate

Bhoja wished the queen *Kalhanika* to mediate (between himself and the King). She was free from jealousy and used, in order to please her husband, to help her co-wives as a friend in getting up finery which would keep, and other (means of attraction). The King never sees this noble *Kasthriya* lady perplexed whether affairs are in a straitened condition or prosperous, owing to (her following) the opinion of capable advisers. When the King was inaugurated, she had received the diadem of chief queen (*Mahadevi*) desired for her by her father-in-law (*Sussala*) and the people. Her mind does not rush into wrong actions not with standing the incitements offered by the love of her children, the desire for pleasures and the wish to gratify her husband. Her mind is at one with that of her husband in regard to friendly relations with their own people and others. In luck she is without arrogance and her virtuous conduct unsullied. She knows her lord's way of thinking since her youth. Carefully safeguarding her honour and noble descent, she would not engage in affairs leading to an ignoble course. (In compliance with Bhoja's wish) she arranged for his journey from his staring place until he should reach the frontier[2463]. Moreover, in full accordance with the agreement (*'Word'*) the queen thereupon made ample provisions for the safe keeping of the mediating sureties (*Lagnaka*), and (sent) for his (Bhoja's) expressed on the way plenty of gold, etc, from her own treasure chest place of *'Nam'*, and further, for his protection, eight Rajaputras of particularly high descent[2464]. Thus, *Dhanya* on receiving that message came himself and made the King assure the nurse of the fulfilment of (Bhoja's) wish[2465]. Whereas the King though he immediately put trust in her, yet was filled with doubts in her heart in regard to (the efforts of) this policy[2466] to compile a good society of the *'Nam'* for peace and prosperity of the country like India and others. For he thought: "From weariness or cunning he show no hostility (now). He ought, therefore, to be helped out of his difficult position. Yet in time he may turn into an enemy[2467]." "While the net of the clouds has not disappeared entirely, the sun, though appearing, cannot shine long, nor can judge (display itself long) while there remains a rest of troubles[2468]." "Or perhaps, thinking us fools on account of the murder of *Naga*. Which was thoughtless he has set this fraud on foot to promote his own objects[2469]?" Therefore, their house is in the hell. Because he could not make an harmony in society, they only created, caste, colour and other religious distinction in the society whereas the *'Nam'* is free from these distinction. He loves to everybody and provide help to everybody at every moment. "Such judgement in a youth, who has made his mark, who is not weak, is capable, supported by many, and is a Ksathriya, is not to be seen elsewhere[2470]." It has been expressed that "the saffron-flower, however, has no stem, the fruit of the *Ksirin* plant (comes forth) without a flower, and in great men the indifference to worldly ambition is not bound to the passing of a cretain age[2471]. Because, it is Law of Nature which provides an opportunity to man to see the right tract of the life otherwise you will remain sick not in present life but coming future. Therefore *'Nam'* is Supreme, one cannot deceit 'Him'. Thus "the prince ought not to be abandoned, however, deep his cunning may be, and however great his power of transforming himself. What is the use of our eyes if we do not look at him[2472]? because he is Schedule Caste belong to *'Chamar'* community inferior to all. Therefore "the queen and these Rajaputras expect that Bhoja will lose his prestige (i.e. 'ego' by his surrender), and think that there is plainly no other course open but to act with straight forwardness and energy[2473]." Like "A stream which follows a crooked course, cannot plainly be seen by all; it is the regular thing as when a drop of water falls from the locks of a beloved woman[2474]." After thus considering the policy indicated by proper wisdom, he confided the course to be followed to the ears of *Dhanya* and *Rilhana*, after dismissing the other (ministers[2475]) which are attached to the enemies.

Dhanya Proceeds to Bhoja

As soon as, *Dhanya* proceeded to *Bhoja* on the request of his messengers, then *Jayasimha* expressed: "the son of *Salhana* wishes to see you to assure his object[2476]." i.e., *'Nam'*. In order not to frighten by a (display of) armed force (the prince) who was wishing to make peace, *Dhanya* kept with a few followers on an island in the stream while awaiting his arrival[2477] to come out in the public with the reference of 'Nam'. Thus the stream whose water (before) had only reached to the knee, became when the snow melted under the heat, terrifying by its waves, which reached to the sky[2478]. At that time, stream, (as if it had been) seized by jealousy, became unordable even for elephants, and thus blocked he was in the power of the enemies who were wanting for their opportunity[2479]. As they huddled together in their white clothes within that (island) which was washed on both sides by the waves of the river, they resembled the sea foam[2480] Same is the case with the story of *'Nam'*. In this struggle, thousands of *Khasakas* (*Khasas*) stood prepared to kill *Dhanya*, thinking that under these circumstances he was in *Bhoja's* power[2481]. But guileless son of *Salhana* seemed to touch his ears with his eyes which (looked) pitiful from anxiety, and threatened them with these words to ward off the mischief[2482] which are not cooling down called as *Agnigrabhaha*: "If he were killed who hastened up in trust and without evil thought, then verily our descent to hell would be inevitable[2483]." Therefore, "Nor would his murder diminish the power of the King who has many servants. Tarksya (Garuda) does not lose his swiftness owing to the destruction of one wing[2489]." If the matter is not worked out: "Thus otherwise Kings earn blame by harming those who trust them, why should the equal harm the equal if he remembers his task[2485] because it was the shrewdness of the mind which always cheats man to man for the self-aggrandizment. Therefore, *'Nam'* was forced to teach him a lesson that I am here in this Universe." "Because just as he serves the King with whole devotion for his maintenance, so it is also my desire to obtain service with that (ruler[2486])." Thanks the lord who provided me again this life to serves the master as his servant. As soon as after his speaking to them these and other proper (words) they stood by their intention, he prevented (its execution) by persistently threatening to kill himself[2487]. Now the tolerance is beyond the limit. Therefore, we have to react the concept of mind. Thus in order to forestall this danger, he induced them at night, as many as they were, to swear an oath by sacred libation (for his safety), and informed him (*Dhanya*) hereof[2488] to conduct the 'Right person'.

Queen Kalhanika Sent to Receive Bhoja

As soon as, *Dhanya* reported (Bhoja's) straight forward conductor the resolute and clear-minded King who did not feel assured as to the success, carefully thought over how to complete the compact, and then despatched the queen (*Kalhanika*) together with the ministers of *Taramulaka*, without letting his resolution be known by others[2489]. Now, she agreed to her lord's request as to her journey, and then fearing least reasons of policy might render harsh acts unavoidable, spoke thus: "O my noble lord, after having once witnessed false conduct in distinguished ministers, should we not reflect before putting trust in enemies[2490]?" Therefore, it is top most secret of the Nature. "How should be corporeal nature of human beings be capable of fathoming what rises in the solitude of others' minds[2491]?" In this context, it is necessary to keep the shutter down "I am prepared to protect your person at the cost of my life, but the rule of conduct for a virtuous woman does not allow (all) what policy sanctions[2492]." Therefore, "In contentious business virtuous conduct is displayed by words only. With you as his enemy, O King, *Bhoja* has begun to sell snow on the snowy mountain (*Himadri*[2493])." Thus, "the people now a days, being mostly of base character, do not keep peace, know no difference between what is their own and what is others', and are completely spoilled by conceit[2494]." In this case "Even a virtuous King rushes in his anger into harming a confiding person, when his mind is perverted by sons, ministers, women or others[2495]." Whereas "Your majesty, whose word is true and faithful to engagements, drinks forsooth glory along with me in the single cup formed by the three words[2496]."

Though "If on the other hand I should have to sacrifice my life for those who are to be protected (by me) from destruction, then I alone should enjoy the glory and should thus come into the society of the selfish[2497]." But it is matter of Faith and Trust, which always unite the persons. When the virtuous queen had stopped after these words, the King whose intentions were right, took leave from her and sent her to her task without relieving her scruples[2498] before that King will have to put an example of virtue to the public, that all the people, too, thought inwardly: "What? Does the King in his rashness intend to afford protection to (him who is the embodiment of) all misfortune and ruin, and to appoint (him) an allowance[2494]?" of the *'Nam'* first to wash the dirty material of life which always distrubed the humanity. "Because if he has exhausted all expendients (and has gone) so far as to despatch the queen, there remains nothing else whatever to be tried.[2500]"

Intrigues of Damaras

Study also reveals those Damaras who owing to differences with their own party or from a wish to await whether the King would show strength or weakness, had somehow retained a neutral position, they all, whether small or big, threw off the fetters of respectful attention and entered into intrigues with those of *Bhoja's* household[2501]. It is assure from the authority, they quickly abandoned their neutral attitude, as they thought that it was owing to their having remained mere onlookers in the struggle for crown of *Mayawati*, that *Bhoja* had got into such a situation[2502] which will creat political turmoil between B.J.p. and B.S.p. bad to worse then *Trillaka* will sent quickly his son to *Bhoja* and made *Culuska*, invade *Samala* with strong forces[2503] to suppress these political activities. Because the origin of the politic is *'Raj'* and study his *niti* which he learned from his master otherwise destruction is definite. In that case the Damaras of *Nilasva* who had even during *Bhiksu's* insurrection kept a friendly attitude towards the King, also joined the enemy[2504] as his leader to teach them the lesson of *'Nam'* in lecutre method. They remained (faithful) three Damaras from *Lohara, Devasarasa* and *Holada,* and one Damara lady from *Nilasva*[2505]. Thus, the snow did not cease to fall upon the force of *Salhana's* son which contained the various *Lavanya* (as little) as the noise of the streams swelled by rains (ceases) to rise from the ocean[2506]. *Bhoja* on hearing of the coming of the queen, said then openly to *Balahara* "Truely I am filled with the wish to make peace (with the King)[2507]." "For so many days one man has deceived the other. Who could remain separated from his family when his female relatives become sureties[2508]?" Therefore it is necessary for us to spread the theory of *'Nam'* in wide circle as has its nature. "Where the crest jewel of the family (*Jayasimha*) shows such affection, how could persons of small import like myself display harshness[2509]?" by the idiot theory of mind. "And as to your saying that this is a stratagem, be it so, that I am duped. I shall not become disgraced by merely having shown confidence[2510]?" But its publicity must be widen that true owner of the land have been landed for the sake of to help the poor people of the *'Nam'*. "And you should not hope for victory, saying: "Now we are all united." Such arrays we have seen (before), and yet we have climbed down from our exaltation[2511]." Keeping in view the said verses *Bhoja* has to advised by prudence, and *Balahara* and the rest could not make him turn from his resolution[2512]. Therefore, it is necessary to built a confidence for the future course of action to maintain the beauty of *'Nature'* which 'God' has gifted us as a messengers of the lord. The chiefs of the *'Nam'* said to him: "Why have you changed your mind when the time of seeing the fruit (of your efforts has come), and when the complete destruction of the enemy is (achievable) with two or three day[2513]?" Because nature always lives in liberity. Therefore, chance must be given to them to see the lord's family.

March to Pancigrama

While at the same time queen was remained at *Taramula, Dhanya* to *Pancigrama*[2514] along with the Rajaputras[2515]. When *Bhoja* learned that those two had arrived and had taken up a position on the near (southern part of the body, i.e., foot where from one has to procceed high in the process of Spiritualism to see the Master. Now they are nearby the) bank of the river. Master has also approached them keeping in the thicket on the opposite side[2516] of enemy. Whereas some in the King's force did not trust in the compact when they saw certain soldiers are coming countinually from all directions into *Bhoja's* camp[2517], therefore, we must have to see the condition of the present scenerio. In this process, *Rajavadana* (*Balahara*) thought often of slaying *Dhanya* and the rest who had persisted in proceeding there with few troops and were unable to get away[2518] from the house. Whereas some who were eager to fall upon the King's army, kept in hiding on boats on the (Vular) *Mahapadma* lake, after cutting the bridge from *Suyyapura*[2519] to proceed Srinagar.

Preparation for Damara Rising

In this struggle of warfare against the theory of mind, those who were disaffected against the King, are awaiting the news of a bold action on *Rajavadana's* part, in order to rise, and occupied various positions on their respective routes[2520]. Moreover, the Damaras of *Bhangila* and other (neighbouring districts) planned on attack on the town of *Samkaravarman* and those of *Samala* to get at the *Ksiptika*[2521]. In addition to this, *Trillaka* and others counted upon reaching the banks of the *Mahasarit*[2522], and the Damaras of *Nilasva*[2523] were to make an attempt (for *Nam-Dak Visa*[2524]) on the centre of the City[2525]. What more (need be said) about those all were together preparing to slay those belonging to the royal court, like ducks surrounded in the water[2526] and could not move here and there. The affair, of the plan which was jeopardised on every side, then appeared (uncertain), as when rain (is doubtful) owing to a season of drought being interfered with by a conjuction of planets[2527] and it environment. Therefore, *Bhoja* became perplexed, having to hold back *Balahara* who wishes every moment and step, to rise and destroy the royal army[2528]. On the other hand, he wished to frustrate the peace-negotiations, *Balahara* raised every moment some obstacle to the arrangements in preparation[2529] of the Fresh Revolution of the humanity. Whatever misunderstanding is there arose between the two camps *Bhoja* himself, full of firm resolve, hastened to put its down[2530] with the power of *'Nam'*. Whereas the flatterers of the King, who were boisterous when sent as envoys and things stood well, became despondent from fear in the critical state of affairs[2531]. What has been proclaimed in the land under the beating of drums, that they say into the King's ear. With their bodies bent down and in a doleful fashion they tell that which makes him feel ashamed. They boastfully say hard things which cut to the quick, such as an enemy even would not say. Verily, whoever are embodiments of roguery and foolishness, they are the King's flatterers[2532]. Thus the buffoon on the dancing stage; the patchword poet (*Kauthakavi*) in the streets, where pungent stories (circulated); the dog which guards the cow-pen in the courtyard of his own place; the *Khataku*[2533] *('Word')* in his hole on the mountain; and the parasite in the royal palace, *Brahmans*, they all verily display skill in acting as heroes (in attacks) on cakes (i.e. as cowards). Elsewhere O, wonder, they behave like the tortoise when it is dragged out of the lake[2534] can not live without water.

Night Preceding Bhoja's Surrender

As soon as, night preceded, the commencement of the Enlightenment Era will start then they quickly took rest upon the height of the lofty mountain (*Ksmabhri*[2535]) whose heat had ceased when the force of the sun passed[2536]. The sun showed his red disc while his rays were mingling with that of his brother Anuru (Dawn), and were resting on the top of the mountains[2537]. Thus the goddess of the dawn (*Samdhyu*), appearing as mediator in front of day and night, received worship from, the people who stood with hands folded[2538]. As the moon (*rajan*) *was* about to rise (or, as the King was about to be successful), the tusks of the elephants showed blisters, the pores of the moon-stones opened (to emit moisture), and the ocean began to swell (in tide[2539]). Thus the bees deprived of their double sustenance (the lotus-honey and the elephants' temple-juice) took their place (for the night) only on the elephants 'temples as the lotuses were (closed) in dejection[2540]. The ministers who did not see the end of the affair, who were in a critical situation, stood in anxiety with their troops on the river bank[2541] of *Vitasta* (*Sindhu*). Now here, they appeared to them a firm foothold. As to those who are carried off by a current, everything seemed to them unstable and moving[2542] in the direction of 'Enlightenment Era'. In *Balahara* who was stopping on the other bank, they rose again and again the desire to attack, but the son of *Salhana* stopped him[2543] for the time being. But the small force which the ministers had (brought thinking) that the affair was got over, could have been easily destroyed by the powerful (*Balahara*[2544]). As in the city on occasion of the pilgrimage to the confluence of the *Vitasta* and *Sindhu*, thus the people they kept moving about at night untired[2545]. Thus the Rajaputras had been intricated the letters which (officials) of the outer and inner courts led on by various persons, had sent to break up the combination of the Damaras[2546]. But his deceitful followers could not make the brave (Bhoja) abandon his courage or firm resolve, though they raised tumultuous scenes[2547]. Whereas the *Bhoja* did not trust the assembled chiefs, and calmly reflected: "If this (*Balahara*) is treated with neglected then he might, in his anger, make a sudden attack and cause a great misfortune, and if he has once begun the slaughter, then the Damaras (*dasyu*) would gather from all sides like Brahmans (assembling for a *Prayopavesa*). Therefore, he pretended to be prepared for acting treacherously and conciliated *Balahara* by saying: "Let us carry out the attack when the night has passed[2548]." For the kind consideration of the fact that the chiefs who have come for his sake, had no food, this scion of a noble race also did not [2549] the food for a long time which was handed over to the Brahmans. In this way ministers, however, full of diffidence, did not know that his opinion did not differ from their, and thought that he was acting perfidiously[2550]. Even the darting of the fishes, when the birds were stretching out their wings, made them think that the enemy was rushing forth to a close attack[2551] because they were frustrated with the power of the King's force. It was absorbed in (thoughts over) their discomfiture they believed that on the other side of the river, there was no one in trouble but the *Cakravaka*-birds[2552]. As Rama's monkey-spy (Hanumat) was helped to cross the ocean by his father, the wind (*Vayuserva*), *so the* wind enabled their spies to cross the stream[2553] from one end to another. These (spies) passed the night awake, keeping close to the enemies, whose ears was deafened by the sound of the trees on the banks (moving in the wind[2554]).

Bhoja's Arrival in Royal Camp

As soon as, Bhoja will arrive in the royal camp at daybreak, when the ray-bundles of the rising sun had not yet removed the illusion of a golden lotus (placed) on the top of a mountain, and when the night-dew had not yet dried up from the eye-like buds of the plants whcih thus seemed to lament the solitary right of the *Cakravakas*, *Brahmans* they saw a youth who had arrived on the river-bank, carried in a litter, and was coming towards them, beautifully dressed, and carrying a battle-axe. Accompanied by a few men on foot, he had just got out from the edge of the forest. He was driving on the litter-carries by touching their heads with his foot. The Damara-soldiers who wished to hold him back, he was driving off on all sides in ignoring, by his glances[2555]. As soon as they saw him, forehead bearing a mark in sandal-ointment and smeared they had not seen him before[2556]. He (*Jayasimha*) had passed the night beguiling *Rajavadana* (*Balahara*), and after taking sudden leave from him in the morning, had thus come before them[2557] for the sake of new approach of the life which we have already discussed above i.e. for the spread of *'Radha Soami Mission'* in abroad. As soon as his litter had got into the water, *Dhanya* and the rest hastened towards him, from the other side, urging on their horses, and joyfully surrounded him[2558]. At the same time then there arose tumultuous noise in both camps, in the one of loud laments, in the other of joyful shouts[2559]. Thus the Damaras rushed forth from all directions on hearing the shouting, in the belief that there was fighting. When they saw that he was siding with the opponents they beat their heads[2560] that we are culprit. *Dhanya* and the other (ministers) gave him an honourable reception, which was accompanied by laudatory addresses in which there was nothing embarrassing, and in which all kept their proper places[2561] as per the judgement of the father. Restraining the hearts joy which was overflowing with might on all sides, *Dhanya* then praised him in various ways and said: "O prince, this earth is purified by you who are of a firm character, and are the abode of the wise (*Sumanas*), as it is by Mount Meru (which is firm and the abode of the gods (Sumanas)[2562]." Thus "Your word (*gau*) which remains of all words unaltered, surpasses the milk of the milk-ocean which is subject to changes[2563]." "Who but you has succeeded in escaping from the midst of the base and joining those of his own race, like a male Kokila bird is supposed to be brought up by the crow and to return to his own kind when grown up[2564]." "After you have first opened up the road of righteous conduct, it is no wonder, if in (your) wake we move further[2565]." When he had given replies to these and other lenghty addresses, they put him on a horse which was proudly capering, and led him away with praises[2566] of the faith. And, the *Lavanyas* then followed him with shouts for some *Krosas*, just as the crows (follow) croaking the *Kokila* which is being taken away by his own kind[2567].

Bhoja Makes Peace with Jayasimha (A.D. 1145)

As soon as *Bhoja* arrived in the royal camp, he started make peace with *Jayasimha*. Thus on the tenth day of Jyaistha of the year (of the *Laukika* era four thousand two hundred and) twenty-one (A.D. 1145) the King won over that (Prince) who was then in his thirty-third year[2568], when he was posted in the college at Poonch. The queen greeted him like a dear son when he saluted her on his arrival, and as his attendants were tired, arranged for his food[2569]. On seeing him endowed with many qualities which were befitting one of the Lunar race of *'Chamar'*, she who had not known him before, thought that her eyes deceived her[2570]. Judging from her truthfulness, kindness, gracefulness, and other natural good qualities, *Jayasimha* knew that the King (too) was of a immaculate character[2571]. But the colour of the face indicates the mental disposition, the splendour of the gate the wealth of the house, and the conduct of the wife the character of the husband[2572] has kept by the 'Royal Queen Smt. Amrita Devi'. When in the evening he showed signs of being tired by the journey and was preparing to move away, no one from consideration said to him: "Go before the king[2572]." When King was little bit away for the .earning of the job at Poonch. Then the ministers who had somehow retained their objection to acting as mediators (like Nashru Ram, Pushpa Devi the second wife of Nashru Ram and others) said to them: "The king whose jealousy is not allayed, wished to give you order[2573]." This word which was like an introduction of the order: "Go before the king" stuck in the orifice of his ear like a spike[2574]. For a long time King (felt) as if cut to the quick, and when he recovered his calm, he noticed that the firm resolve of the mediators had from kind regard stopped at their lips[2575]. When King was speaking bitterly on the mediators as if he wished to give up his life, they allayed his agitation by conciliatory words, while bending down their heads attentively[2576] at present time. Nobody was believed that King could by a (right) answer will change *Bhoja's* demeanour which, though unfriendly, was appropriate and eloquent[2577] now at present. Thereupon, the brave *Dhanya* spoke tenderly, while the glitter of his teeth seemed to displayed the devotion to his Lord which filled his heart[2578] like a solace and contentment which is very much necessary in the life without these principle, man is incomplete, these are sources base i.e. *'Nam'* and rest is allusion of life. Now *Dhanya* represents to *Bhoja* that it is necessary for the completion of their pact that he should see the King. The latter's virtues are praised, and life at his court described as high fortune which depends upon master, but King himself is nothing. If Bhoja can find there happiness by the side of his relative, there is no reason for him to seek shelter with other (rulers[2579]). Though *Jayasimha* was unable to refute this able speech adequately, and had abandoned the small remnant of his guile, yet he showed reluctance to start[2580] because due to his inactive policy like of a *Sant*. (However), when he saw everywhere on the road the inhabitants singing his praises, his mind became firmly convinced that he was acting rightly[2581] as per the advise of the master. Thus the dust will rise from the feet of the foot-soldiers made it appear as if the earth had formed an alliance with the sky[2582]. Bhoja *'Word'* was reflecting: "Shall I get to the king? Will not intriguing enemies oppose my seeing him[2583]?" Of course at every moment this is the beauty of the *'Nam'*. "Who obtains in the residence of rulers of the *'Nam'* an opportunity for showing his great qualities without meeting between with the obstruction of parasites[2584]?" and the *'Nam'*. "The stream of the *Himalaya-Waters* (Garga) has flown forth with the hope that owing to the coolness it brings, it would be welcome to the ocean, which suffers from the submarine fire. But at the very time the stream falls into the ocean, it is swallowed up by the sea-monsters and *'Word'* (fails in its hope[2585])." *Jayasimha* benumbed by such and similar reflections he did not notice the commotion of the town and rest, and knew that the palace was near only when the soldiers stopped their horses[2586].

Bhoja's Reception by the King

The King is standing on a high mansion and surrounded by the ministers, looked at him as he was coming up after descending from his horse. *Bhoja,* received by the King. He was neither very tall nor very small. His face was darkened by the sun-rays. His body was of yellowish colour like the pericarp of the lotus and very languid. His shoulders were thick set like the hump of a bull and his chest broad. He is not very large beard let the length of his checks and neck be seen. He had a high nose and lips (red) like the ripe Bimba fruit. His for head was broad and not projecting because of his duty is incomplete. He moved with a firm, grave step. His garments and head-dress were properly fitted, and sandal-ointment paint (marked his forehead) with a line which white like moon circumference reached up to the parting of the hair[2587]. Then sought by the King's eye which opened widly with kindliness, he ascended to the assembly hall which was thronged by people raising their necks in curiosity[2588] to see him. After letting himself down before the King. he touched his feet with his hand, and taking the dagger which he carried and placed it before the throne[2589]. Consequently upon this, King put his hand which bore the (chiromantic sign of) betel-papper, with two fingers out stretched, under his chin, and spoke[2590]." "You have not been taken fighting, nor are you now a captive why then should we accept, O my dear, the weapon you hand[2591] up?" i.e. *'Nam'*. He replied to the King: "Sire, a weapon is carried to protect one's lord or far one's own safety[2592]." "While your Majesty protects the seven oceans by the hire of your glory, one sees but scant occasion for (using) one's word[2593] ." "The service of the lord's feet is a protection even for the other world. Then what need is there for other means of protection in this world[2594]?" *Nam-dana* and its regular practice early in the morning at least 2.30 hours in the memory of the 'father', who has given us life and everything. The King answered him: "In this competition of truth fullness you are now, as it were, the winning party. No more can be done (by us[2595])." Bhoja then told: "I do not say anything now for gaining the lord's kindness or for the sake of compliment except which I see[2596]." "What evil have I not thought, what harm not done to you?What has not come off, that remained unknown. This ought to be kept in mind[2597]." "You, whom we with eyes of leather took for one of ordinary origin called *'Chamar'*, are you not one of the prime causes (*Karama*) who has somehow come to light in *Malla's* race[2598]?" Yes, his throat has been caught up. "Whenever, O king, we thought of doing you injury, then each time the earth mightily will get punishment from the nature as rule because they are challenging the purity of thought which is *'Pure'* in world[2599]." "What brilliant glorious poets can conceive in their imagination, such, O king, we have seen as yours in reality[2600]." "The heat which your glory creates, has not left me on the mountain height, not in the gorge, not in the cleft, not in the snow or in the thicket[2601]." "Seeking from afar your shelter ever since, I was not able to make my reverent homage, O king, owing to the absence of a compact or other (agreement[2602])." "Whatever words I have then done filled with a desire for peace, that was done merely to show that I existed, not from obstinated desire of strife[2603]." "Owing to our connection with you we are honourbale by the rulers in all regions. The glass bottle is valued by the people because it has contained Ganga water[2604]." "To this day the appellation *Sahi*[2605] throws its lustre on a numberless host of Ksathriyas abroad who trace their origin to that (royal family[2606])." "Even when the league of hill-chiefs was set against you[2607], they must come forward to see the glory of *'Nam'* "When after such event (eulogies) he had said: "Otherwise, the lord is the authority" he again touched the king's feet with his head[2608]. At that time his head-dress will slipped off in bowing, the King placed his own head-dress on him as he got-up[2609]. With kind words the King put his own dagger and that one which *Bhoja* had laid down, into the latter's lap, and with calm thoughtfulness said to him when he rcmonstrated[2610]. "You should wear these two (daggers) I have given you or keep them in honour. Do not refuse to take the weapons, but do my[2611] will." Yes Lord. When the *'Chamar'* (King) whose order had to be obeyed, thus insisted, he knowing (how to act on each) occasion, complied with the King's desire, and after saluting him respectfully put the two daggers by his side[2612]. At that time King at once abandoned all reserve and treated him with jests and kindly words, as if he had been about him for a long time[2613] because of his health in fragile condition. Then the wise *Dhanya* entered besides, *Jayasimha* (Baba Gurinder Singh) and after making his obeisance paid his revencence (to the King by say): "Neither life or wealth has value now for us, O king, apart from the (delight of) hearing about your virtues; but (of value is) constant kindliness on our lord's part. This you may remember, O king[2614]." The king replied: "What we think about him (Bhoja), could even if expressed not to be realized[2615]."

Bhoja Presented to Queens

After discoursing for a short time on various topics, the King went from there to the residence of (the queen) *Raddadevi*[2616]. While after making his bow he looked at her who was distinguished by kind disposition and other good qualities, he thought that she was the creeper yielding all wishes (*Kalpalata*) by the side of the King, who was the tree of paradise (*parijata*[2617]). "He deserves to be honoured, O queen, as he has come here from kindness and family attachment." Thus spoke the King, and his consort said: "We place him above our sons[2618]." Full of kind attention he then proceeded in *Bhoja's* company also to the apartments of the queen (*Kalhanika*), who had borne the weight of the business, to pay her honour[2619] as it was in routine matter. The clever queen said, with a smile to *Bhoja* as he came with the king: "Now at once you have become a trusted friend of the King[2620]." Smiling in embarrassment at the respectful welcome offered by her husband, she, in her reply, also said, pointing at *Bhoja*: "O my noble lord, do not forget that solely attached to his honour, he has rejected the advice of his friends and followed the (guidance of) his love for his relative[2621]." "Those who, like you, are the lotus (ornaments) of their families, should do better than the lotus flowers which daily growing cease to touch the water, their former benefactor[2622]." "If he had not come, we sinking under the trouble of the affairs, could neither have preserved our honour nor have returned[2623]." Thus, "If the tree which protects the river-bank, falls in the flood, the creeper which lives upon it, surely follows[2624]. But the subservience of (a wife's) life to the husband's affairs must go so far that there should be (for her) no thought of otherwise protecting herself[2625]." The King replied to her: "O queen, you who are the witness of all my actions, know that also my determination is the same in this respect (as stated by you[2626])." "My soul has not found rest to this day even for having punished *Sujji* and *Mallarjuna,* though they were guilty[2627]."

Bhoja's Conduct at Court

As soon as, the King asked Bhoja to stop in a splendid building along with his followers, *Bhoja* thought that he could not take his residence permanently elsewhere but in the palace[2628]. In this regard he believed that if he would live at a distance and unwatched, not seeing the King continually because both has the different business but one goal to preach the teaching of the lord i.e. *'Radha Soami'*. He would not be able to propitiate the latter[2629]. Moreover, he took guards from the King and permanently arranged for the future course of action with the order of the master[2630]. Then King was pleased by noticing his conduct with the help of *'Nam'*, and let him have than a completely fitted up residence within the palace[2631]. At that time the King, though so much beset by his own servents and others whose attachment was fostered by self-interest became attached to Bhoja as if he had been with him for a long time[2632] in the process of life. When it was the time for meals, for the inspection of curious things, and on other (occasions), the King remembered him like a dear son of the father and had him called by messengers[2633]. At the time of meals, he put him on his right side for the sake of regard for his relationship, and did not fail to send him dishes which he had himself touched and tasted, and the like thus, Bhoja showed that *Deepit* Raj has such unfeigned affection that the child sons (of the King) played with him as with a relative of the *'Nam'*[2635.] In the same way as he observed this open conduct thus, too, the King, along with his court, placed unqualified trust (in him[2636]). *Bhoja* indicated (to the King) those persons of the inner court who had shown disaffection during their conflict, and thus helped the King to rid himself of (those who felt) indifference for him, and from many enemies[2637]. But by giving unsophisticated attention to matters of business in the assemblies he showed that he was neither dull or violent nor a hypocrite[2638]. If an action of the King failed through some error, or was in adequate or too for-reaching, he did not keep his attention on it, as a wretched poetaster (on defects in the work) of a great poet[2639]. He did not boast with tales of bravery becasue it is the sign of 'ego'. Therefore, we have to beware of it and if asked incidentally about former events, did not enlarge on his account[2640]. Those who *elevated* by making flattering remarks about him as being equal to the lord (Jayasimha) of the same race, etc, he silenced by his firm proud looks[2641]. From the study we learn that if the Master is so deep, was his character, that even in immediate contact intriguers, jesters, slanderers and the like could not fathom it as his moral conduct[2642]. Moreover, at the very time when darkness, commotions and other (circumstances) would upset the people, he (*Bhoja*) would go to (his) house and feel no fear[2643] about the event because the 'theory of *Nature*' has been based *on 'Karma theory'*. Therefore, do not feel distress God will help you in this process. When the king, from growing the confidence, lightened his hold on him, he, like a well trained horse, would not run away[2644] because he has been coolled down with the help of *'Nam'* and has been defeated by the *'Nam'*. Though moving everywhere else in front (of the King), *Bhoja* remained behind, even without being required to do so, when the King will go into the ladies apartments, and the council-chamber[2645]. Always, he has the idea of doubtful in his mind, he requests for what was proper for him to get, in person, there will be no grudge and thus avoided making use of others in lofty manner[2646]. *'Word'* (Baba Gurinder Singh), even what he had dreamt he would not keep the things away from the King[2647] for the future course of action, it depends upon his will. Inspite of these facts, the mutual slanders of ministers, ladies of the seraglio, and others he did not reproduce, but forgot them like an evil dream[2648]. Though, he would respond with full comprehension to what was being said in the gathering of hardy jokers, yet he would inwardly express his thorough contempt for the buffoons[2649] of the life in the English Literature as a Natural King. By such conduct that pure minded (prince) Dr. Raj Kumar caused in time a greater pleasure to the judicious and affectionate King than even his sons[2650] of his dynasty. Thus King (*Jayasimha*) prepared a new bridge leading to the preservation of his dynasty, such as one of the princes of the *Kali* period find it difficult to cross by[2651] the achievement of this dynasty.

Attack on Trillaka

As soon as, king will overcome all the natural calamities, thought of *Trillaka*, as his friend who was interested to full fill his demand, because to damage those who damage us without any reason[2652]. The latter delayed, thinking that flight at that time when the routes over the mountains were free of snow, and it was impossible as an act of cowardice incompatible with courage[2653] because threat has to achieve from the enemies. Then while he was wisely waiting for the right time for his journey, *Sanjapala* thoughtlessly began to attack[2654]. *Sanjapala* who had only few good soldiers from the capital, but a large number of troops from *Devasarasa*, took up position at *Martanda*[2655]. He did not consider in his self assurance that locality offered no obstacle to the enemies and that the soldiers from outside (the capital) were unreliable[2656]. Therefore, we have to use the *Sanjapala* with a thoughtful manner. Thus *Trillaka's* followers, though unprovided with arrows, fought by his side and showed no lack of courage[2657]. But at the same time *Sanjapala's* troops with full might will have to attack there, whereas, the another *Damara*, the *Lavanya* (Trillaka) with a numberless host fell upon them with fury[2658], but they might be defeated. Thereupon all those from *Devasarasa*, loaded with plundered wealth will be deserted by *Sanjapala* and fled[2659] away into the another world which they deserve. While at that time every thing will also submerged by the (flood of the) enemies, which was like the deluge at the end of the world, only the soldiers from the capital stood out high like great mountains[2660]. In this long life,battle, they held out in that field against the enemy's fury, while the sun burned with fierce heat, and then fell in different places after killing many enemies[2661].

Encounter of Martanda

In this encounter, when all the brave men had been slain in that fight, the sun temple (Martanda) himself will recieved many hurts from those who broke into his disc (to become) his own (inhabitants[2262]) called *'Chamar'* or *Chambar*, in Kashmir. In this battle, *Gayapala, Sanjapala's* son, distinguished himself. Though, if three horses were killed (under him) yet owing to his cleverness, he was never seen on foot[2663]. Therefore, his younger brother *Jarja,* yet a boy, whose first flight that was astonished (by his courage) bravemen who had seen many great battles[2664] like 'Kalinga War', Karbli war between *Sahis* and Sunni Muslim. The right arm of the commander-in-chief *Sanjapala* could not effect much. The sun (merely) causes heat to the great elephants, but the moon breaks their tusks[2665] which the enemies took up permanently. Riding on his horse and making the sword with his one hand glisten, he resembled a forest fire with its column of smoke on a winged mountain[2667] on the earth. But in the tumult of the fight his horse found the way blocked by the Brahmans and on being wounded by arrows threw him off[2668] for the time being. Due to the shock of falling with his heavy armour on the hard ground, he became senseless with the power of *'Nam'*, and thus his two sons carried him off out of the enemy's midst[2669] for the sake of independent. It appears that the whole force was completely routed, they put him into the courtyard of the temple of *Martanda* without being noticed by the enemy and then fled[2670] away in their own direction wherefrom, they came to recover again in their life in the human form. No doubt, King set out with large forces which would easily overpower by the Damara (*Trillaka*), and *Brahmans* try to blocked him up in that position[2671]. But with the blessing of Father, he will achieved his target by defeating them in the open battle field. As soon as the King will have to reached *Vijayaksetra, Sanjapala*, after shaking off his besiegers, burned the residence of the *Lavanya*[2672] Very shortly when the spiritual document of *'Nature'* i.e. '*History of the Chamar Dynasty'* will come out in the market. It will be the surprise to the people of India that degraded community has a big 'History'. They are enlightened people of the Nature. Though the latter had got into such a situation by the King's angry frowns, yet he felt no want, as he found it easy to obtain supplies from the land in the various mountain Valleys[2673] of the nature. Moreover King (Dr. Raj Kumar) separated from his associates and family he heard reproaches from his followers, who showed that *'Wisdom'* still existed in this Universe which is easily acquired in misfortune[2674] by the labour class of the society. Then, finding no support from the present any political party, but he cut off his finger and *Chamar* begged off his own head for the King's wrath as (one might beg) a fruit from a monkey[2675] which always moves here and there in this Universe.

Gulhana Crowned at Lohara

In this Universe, the illustrious king (Dr. Raj Kumar) then had *Gulhana*, the eldest of his sons born from (Queen) *Raddadevi,* crowned as the ruler of *Lohara*[2676]. Thus the prince, though only six or seven years old, surpassed by his good qualities order rulers just as the young mango shoot (surpasses) the old trees[2677] as a new plant. And, the light of the rubies (worn) on the heads of the chiefs (who did homage), made the feet of the queen who had gone to crown her son, appear as if dyed red with lac[2678]. After this, he had been anointed (*abhisikta*) the clouds poured water over the earth which had been dried by a long drought, just as if they had wished to aniont (the earth) as a queen[2679]. This is the message of nature to inform the public that pure souls of the lord they must get solace of the nature as their childerns.

Rising of Rajavadana

In this process, *Rajavadana* wishing to raise a rebellion again, attacked *Jayacandra* who showed alertness in carrying out the King's orders[2680] in this worldly affairs, which have been accompanied by *Naga's* brother's son (*Losthaka*) he defeated, in a defile for the pursuing the troops of the son of *Garga* (*Jayacandra*) who followed behind[2681] the King as in his process. Whereas the son of *Garga,* whom this defeat had made look downcast, captured some days afterwards the leader *Losthaka*, the son of *Naga's* brother, in a fight[2682] will come down on the earth along with his force to teach him a lesson of unity and equality. Then, he will again marched rapidly upon *Dinnagrama* which had not been attacked by others owing to its inaccessible position, and after burning it got off with an easy victory[2683] over the *'Nam'*. Even thus. *Rajavadana* did not lose his courage. He made neither peace nor did he feel enraged, but a balance type of society, he must have to establish over here on this earth[2684]. Again, he will attack over the king with heavy forces which diminished day by day, he suffered repeated reverses before *Jayacandra*[2685], as his King. Then the King will again reach of whose nails and arms unbounded, and had killed him in fight by secretly posted bravos[2686] of the master.

Death of Rajavadana, Lothana and other Rebels

At the death of *Rajavadana*, the cheek-line will (cut-off) his head which was swinging to and fro, and cut off at once as the tree of his fortune which was about to break out in buds[2687]. The King upon the plea (*Krita* will become) of exterminating the race of *Prthvihara,* and also put *Lothana* to death by secret execution[2688]. Though *Trillaka* had saved him when once before he had been invested, he yet fell into the net of the King's diplomacy[2689] at present Moreover, *Mallakostha, Ksura, Jayya, Saddăcandra* and others were as good as dead while in life, and died oppressed by cruel poverty[2690].

Religious Endowments of Jayasimha

Study also reflects that the Matha of King *Uchchala* had also remained a permanent endowment, as under the infatuation arising from the enjoyment of the royal power. He had not thought of life being perishable. For this (Matha) which (in the meantime) had received from each successive King such provision as was estimated, King (*Jaya)simha* as the continuator of the dynasty of the *'Chamar'* made a permanent endowment[2691] on the earth. Moreover, King has to completed the *Sullavihara* founded by his uncle, and three temples of his father, the buildings of which had remained half-finished[2692]. It is our duty to complete them. *Jayasimha*, of his own pluse, bestowed villages, (temple) outfits and great market-buildings upon respectable temple- Purohitas (*parisadya*) and other persons of his liking[2693]. Thus, in the honour of *Candala,* a moon-faced lady of his seraglio, who had died, she erected a Matha provided with ample means, from whose door not guest was turned back[2694]. She is known as 'Smt. Amrita Devi'. King who was free from pride, reconstructed also larger than before the Matha of *Suryamati*

(Pushap Lata) which had suffered from the conflagrations in the City[2695] must be shine in the Enlightenment period.

Death of Sanjapala

As soon as, *Sanjapala* will depart for another world the King put his son *Gayapala* in chief command of the army[2696]. He had been difficult to bear with, though towards his end, he had become of softer disposition, *'Word'* was forgotten owing to his son, just as the heat of the autumn sun (is forgotten) owing to the cooling moonlight[2697]. As soon as the clouds rise at the trying (season) of excessive summer heat, the stream shows no desire for the increase of its water, as it sees that the tree on its bank which shares its fortune, is threatened with destruction by a sudden stroke of light[2698] of the *'Nam'*.

Death of Dhanya

At that time, when the jewel of Kings (*Nam*) had thoroughly exterminated his enemies, there died *Dhanya* who had enjoyed his exceptional affection, and who during the troubles from *Bhiksu's* death to *Bhoja's* defeat had borne singly the weight of the King's affairs[2699]. It is the duty of the Master that a faithful servant must have to be handle it carefully and with pious approach. But today we have seen that both the master and servant are in disorder condition[2700]. Therefore, this King deserves to be protected even at the cost of the life of all beings whose mind is firmly bent on helping his subjects when they sink in misfortune at every step of life[2701]. In this way the grateful King did not leave the sick (*Dhanya's*) side when his end approached, (but remained) even without taking steep with those who were praying for his well-being[2702]. Thanks messengers, the change which took place in the appearance of the (King) who loved his subjects, on account of the ministers (death, i.e., *Manas*), gave, (as it were, fresh) life to the people in this worldy existence[2703]. Then there arose happiness four the subjects who owing to the demise of Kings like *Mandhatr* had fallen into misfortune[2704] because his attitude towards the public is based on inequality and discrimination between man to man as his nature. Thus *Dhanya's* unobstructed ministership had removed all difficulties for the young King when the land was overrun by pretenders[2705] of the *'Nam'*. Thus, the time is the powerful (master) of conduct. Who does not by its will observe or forget consistency of the *'Nam'*, the vanquisher of *Mura* (Visnu) had the power to support the earth (in his incaranation) as the serpent (*Sesa*) and again (in his incarnation) as the boar (*Varaha*) to dig her[2706] up.

Then *Dhanya* will have to become perfect of the city (*Nagaradhikrta*) after the ousting of *Sujji,* had at first remedies abuses which had been rife in the land for a long time[2707] as His process.

Kularaja's Administration of the City

During the administration of *Kularaja* in the City, the use of cash (*dinnaravyavahara*) in commercial transactions had fallen into abeyance through abuses; checking those (abuses) which casued the disorder, he made the former proceed with chicane[2708]. Whereas the fine which used to be levied on the household in the case of immoral conduct on the part of a married woman, was abolished by him after (due) consideration[2709]. Thus on his appointment to the office of the City-perfect, he exclusively promoted the people's welfare, but (subsequently) he again oppressed[2710] them to promot the fratarnity and brotherhood for the development of civilization and co-ordination among the people. Moreover, he persisted in punishing many persons, on the allegation that they had carnal intercourse with dancing-girls who had been received into household as wedded wives[2711]. But why consider *certain* (faults) insignificant like chaff separated from the seed by winnowing or threshing the grain of the husks. There was nobody like him in respect of honesty and distinterestedness[2712]. They must have follow the order of master as a token of respect. Accommodating himself to the course of the times, he had also been a follower of *Bhiksu* and *Mallarjuna*. Yet he did not ceae to serve his lord nor did he destroy the order of those two[2713] who are the faithful servants of the master. In this way, he had not known great expenditure in the time of his power, because 'ultimate Power' he has gained yet when he died. He did not leave as much property as was needed for his last rites[2714]. At that time, there will be empty hand what more should be said of the grateful nature of the King who served the master from the core of the heart, therefore, he must be treated the (surviving) dependents as if they were the (dead) persons of the *'Nam'*, who had returned to life[2715] for the sake of the public as their duty signed by the nature.

Religious Foundations Under Jayasimha

Keeping in view the struggle of the life as soon as *Dhanya* died certain religious foundations under *Jayasimha* must be commenced such as the construction of a Vihara which was to bear the name of *Bijja* (*vihara*) in honour of his deceased wife *Bijja,* did he not arrange for the completion of the building which remained (unfinished), and for a permanent endowment[2717] in the favour of *'Nam'* that in future the theory of mind explore it what is the objective of the life in human nature. Even those who (before) lived wholly of fighting, acquired by the King's pious conduct on eager desire for good deeds in the favour *man or mana*, and devoted themselves to the acquisition of religious merits[2718]. Prince *Sangiya,* the younger brother of *Kamaliya*[2719], consecrated (a linga) under his own name. He was born from a race of *Ksathriyas,* who owing to their native place being within the territory of the *Turuskas* had learned nothing but cruelty, to maintain themselves amidst the mass of the enemies, and was during the times of strife when King *Sussala* was wholly taken up with fighting his adversaries, had found employment in *Kashmir*[2720]. Thus, the Bana-linga which he erected by the bank of the *Vitasta,* makes one think of the *Avimukta*[2721] (Tirtha) rising on the bank of the Celestial river (Ganga[2722]). But after seeing his Matha, which is adorned by ascetics, the desire of viewing *Rudra's* world is appeased[2723]. Because ascetics are the sons of *PRISHNI,* the cloud-cow, *Prishni,* "Speckled", from the root *PRISH,* which, however, also scans "sprinkle" (the connection between the two is obvious) a play on homonyms or *pun* quite in the taste of all ancient mythical poetry, and a liberal source of stories, riddles and puzzles. (The Rig-veda, Vol.III; p. 320) and of *RUDRA*, rather a subordinate deity in the Veda, though undoubtedly very old, but who, in later Brahmanism and especially Hinduism, rose to the highest rank[2724]. This pure-minded man, though he was one of our time, did not proceed to plunder other foundations and to make grants of the property of poor people[2725] those are related with *'Nam' or 'Kalam'*. Whereas the *Cinta,* the wife of *Udaya,* the commander-in-chief adorned the bank of the *Vitasta* by a Vihara[2726]. And, the five buildings within her Vihara appear as if they were the five high fingers of the upraised arm of law[2727]. In addition to this, *Mankhaka, Alamkara's* brother, the minister of foreign affairs (*samdhivigrahika*), distinguished himself by erecting a shrine of *Srikantha* (Siva) together with a Matha[2728]. By (the foundation of) Mathas, (the grant of) Agraharas, the restoration of temples and other pious works, *Sumanas*, the younger brother of *Rilhana,* became the latter's equal[2729]. He built a Matha at *Bhutesvara* and one at *Trigrami*[2730], and offered to the Pitris[2731] (at the one) the water of the *Kanakavahimi*[2732] and (at the other) that of the *Vitasta*[2733]. At the place called *Kasyapagara*[2734], where the river rising from the *Nila* (Naga) turns in an easterly direction, as if it wished to rival the Ganga, he erected a bridge for the crossing of cows and others, and thus accomplished a pious work capable of helping him across (the ocean of) mundane existence[2735] in the life of human nature. In the city, too, he built a shrine of Siva, named after himself, and a Math a which contains a large number of perfect Siva (-Lingas[2736]). *Jayasimha* furnished the (shrine of Siva) *Mammesvara*[2737] with a golden *Amalaka* (ornament), and embellished the surroundings of the *Somatirth*[2738] by (bringing there) water and (laying out) a garden[2739]. But in this dynasty there (were) Kings who deprived ministers of the property, life and the rest from envy of their high descent, wealth and other (distinctions[2740]) like caste, colour and creed. They will only worshipp the *'Nam' or 'Shabad'* called *'Lord Buddha'*. Even the divine Indra ejected King *Mandhatr* from heaven in angry jealousy, because of his having occupied his new throne[2741]. But this King (Dr. Raj Kumar) of undimmed intellect thinks it an increase of his own greatness when he sees daily his servants elevated by pious works.[2741]

Encomium on Rilhana's Pious Gifts

Jayasimha was pleased when his servant *Rilhana*, after the clever invention of King *Kalasa*, erected gilt parasols[2742]. Moreover, at *Suresvari*[2743], on (the temple of) Siva and Parvati in communion (*Sivayoh Samavetayoh*), the gilt parasol (whcih he put up) along with small bells is combined with lamps and pots for (placing lights at) illuminations[2744]. (It appears as if) Mount Meru, under the guise of the gilt parasol, had come, from love for his relative Mount Himalaya, to kiss on the head his daughter and his son-in-law (*Paravati* and *Siva*[2745]). Thus, the god of fire issuing from Siva's eye has taken (there) the guise of the guilt parasol after (hearing) the lover of *Parvati* (Siva) say: "That bodily union for which the love-god (*Kama*) had exerted himself, and had been burned by me, that *'Word' or 'Chamar' Uma* (Parvati) has accomplished here[2746]." But the great golden parasol, too, which *Rilhana* had placed there on the top of the temple of *Rukmini's* lover (Krsna), glitters now mightily. It is as if the sun had come to view the radiant disc (of Visnu) which, when intoxicated by drinking the blood (of the demons), had got lost and had then been recovered by its master (Visnu[2747]). Thus, at that sacred place (*Survesvari*) which imparts a knowledge of the close friendship between the vanquisher of love (Siva) and the god whose ensign is the bird (Visnu), the golden parasol of one lord (Siva) with its ornamented staff and its varying functions (*Kriyaparinati*[2748]), appears like the dust from (the petals of) the lotuses on the Ganga, which are set in motion by the hisses of the snakes on his front; *'Word'* while that of the other lord (Visnu) resembles the ball-shaped lightening accompanying the clouds which cling to his locks[2749]. Whereas the golden cavity of the mundane egg with its great riches, seems like a round casket which is fitted to the expanse of this parasol, and in which all are put together the dark and shining ornaments of Siva and the foe of *Kaitabha* (Visnu), who are wearing rich jewels. The golden parasol forms its cover[2750] as per the order of Master.

Jayasimha's sons

After that the (son) of *Jayasimha* who rules at *Lohara* (Gulhana), there were born to the King from *Raddadevi* four other sons, of nobles qualities and clever[2751]. One of them called *Aparaditya* grows up at *Lohara*, being as inseparable from *Gulhana,* as *Laksmana* was from the Raghu scion (*Rama*[2752]). The others young *Jayapida* is guarded by prince *Lalitaditya*, as *Satrughna* was by *Bharata*[2753]. It is noticed from the sun-like King whose worship was cheering (like that of the sun), there issued a fifth virtuous prince, *Yasaskara*, resembling the sunshine of the young day[2754]. But it is the master's gift but myself is unable man. Whereas the *Lalitaditya* might soften even walls by his playful ways, which are giddy, owing to his youth and pleasing, owing to his good-natured character[2755]. Thus, his reddish face, which bears protective marks of ointment, together with his red under lip, resembles a golden lotus-upon which is the sunshine of the young day, together with bees[2756] of honey. Moreover, his talk which indistinct owing to his youth, is full of dignity resembles the sound, soft with nectar, which issued when the ocean was churned[2757]. This young prince, born of a great race, indicates by his graceful bearing his future career[2758]. Stein is unable to give an intelligible rendering of this verse, in which the prince's clear complexion seems to be compared to the feathers of a peacock going to a tank. The verse looks as if made up of *Padas* or half-verses belonging to different verses[2759]. Thus, the four daughters of *pure* caste conduct have been born to him, *Menila, Rajalaksmi, Padmasri* and *Kamala*[2760]. Whereas that unblemished couple (*Jayasimha and Radda*) resembling the rainy season and lotus pond, are embellished by their ever-charming children, which are like groves of pleasure and diversion[2761] of the road took place at that time.

Piety of Queen Radda

In this pious war, *Raddadevi's* fortune turned to prosperity by being continually expended in this land which is sanctioned by Tirthas and temples[2762]. As soon as the King's consort when visiting pious places, accompanied by chiefs, nobles and ministers, appears like the personified royal fortune[2763]. Thus the hosts of Tirthas in the land of *Sati,* when that various lady (*Sati*) takes her bath (in them[2764]) as the partner of the servant. During her pilgrimages, she is ever followed, even in clear weather, by clouds heavy with rain (which are eager) to look at her, just as (if she were) the rainy season[2765] of the Father. When she has started to visit the holy waters (Tirtha) of the earth, the celestial waters would, forsooth from jealousy, show themselves under the guise of rain[2766] because to clean the City of earth that *'Chamar' or 'Nam'* will have to live in soft area as His beauty. Thus that delicate lady, in her zealous desire of visiting Tirthas, does not pay heed on her way to mountains which reach to the sky, or to rivers which carry away their banks[2767] at that time. Keeping in view, her numerous sacred foundations and restorations, this wise and clever queen has outstepped, O wonder, even the lame *Didda*[2768] will follow it. Now, she erected the illustrious (shrine of) Rudra, called *Rudrasvara,* which has a golden *Amalaka* ornament (*amalasara'* and is the ornament of *Kashmir* and the quintessence of the world's beauty. Made of white stone, which is bright like moon, it shines forth at this day even as if it were Rudra when he removed *Upamanyu's*[2769] sufferings from thirst by making flow forth the radiant expanse of the milk-ocean called *Sudra.* She also restored the shrine (or shines) of him who had overcome dejection (*Santavasada*[2770]). When the King is hot with anger, she has been refuged by the servants, as the stream of the snowy mountains (Ganga) is refuging for the beings in the ocean when heated by the submarine fire[2771] of the *'Nam'* which carried by the master. Owing to the constant attachment of the King, the punishment or reward even of princes depends immediately and without fail upon her will[2772]. This proud queen raised King *Bhupala,* the son of *Somapala,* to high honour by giving to him the princess *Menila* in marriage[2773]. Thus, the power which makes itself easily felt in one's own home, does not generally fail to any one (elsewhere). The light which serves to remove darkness in the sun, has (also) after issuing forth from the latter, scattered the mass of darkness[2774] i.e. *Brahmans*

Princesses Married Abroad

In the study we also learn that the King was destined to take a great share in righting (the affairs of) important kingdoms. When princess *Manila* had been married (to *Bhupala*), also the father of her husband

(*Somapala*) who was in possession of a fine land full of precious stones, relinquished his enmity, and gave up his throne (to him) in good faith[2775] to the Master for the welfare of the public. As soon as, King *Prajidhara* had been killed in battle by his enemies, his younger brother *Ghatokaca* hoped to obtain a future revenge through the King's power. Filled with self-reliance to a high degree, he obtained through *Radda's* help, (the princess) *Rajyasri*, and with her. O wonder, the height of royal fortune (*rajyasri*[2776]). He dethroned King *Pancavata,* assisted by the King's ministers, who had killed his brother, and *Angada*[2777] *(Deva)* together with *Prajji*[2778] at the same time. Through *Jayasimha's* power, which brought him a profusion of great presents he crossed the river *Krsna*, which was within the enemy's power, and (at the same time the dark) swords (in their hands[2779]). In this way, *Dvitiya,*, the lord of *Urasa,* he put to shame by defeating him, and through the King's power to took *Atyugrapura,*[2780] strong in fighting men[2281]. Thus, many leaders of the armies spreading waves of moonlight by their glittering parasols, then obtained the glory[2282] of master.

Jayasimha Reigning (A.D. 1149-50)

During the *Jayasimha* rule of twenty-two years had the King passed before he obtained the throne, and for the same (number of years), he has been on the of *Kashmir* in the (present) year (of the Laukika era four thousand two hundred and) twenty-five (A.D. 1149-50[2783]). It may be the matured wisdom of this King (which has been produced) by the subjects merits and which has not been seen to such an extent in any other (ruler), last for years exceeding this *Kalpa*[2784]. Even the water, which is liquid by nature, freezes and turns in time (as *Nam*) hard as stone, (while) the stone may dissolve into water. Under that wonderful dominion of time, which has witnessed,even in beings of exceptional greatness, the rapid change of unlimited might, whose nature can remain unchanged on the road laid out by the power of fate[2785] with the 'Ultimate Reality' which is called *'Nam'*.

In the foregoing pages; we have learned from that *Jayasimha* due to his diplomatic relation, he dominated the *Kashmir* throne for about 30 years but his military weakness made him lose the ancestral kingdom of *Lohara* to a rebel named *Lothana, Sussala's* brother. *Jayasimha,* however, recovered *Lohara* later when the rebel was ousted by his nephew *Sanjapala*. No doubt, during his time various scholars and artists from various parts of the world had sought refuge in *Kashmir* and received his liberal patronage for the peace and prosperity. No doubt, *Jayasimha* then had to meet a larger rebellion of his own feudatories assisted by Muslims and was able to crush it by diplomacy and military skill. But the gradual process of declining and disintegration was started with the reign of his immediate successor, *Paramanuka*, continued for about two centuries and the valley of *Kashmir* was governed by *weak-lingas*[2786]. His later years were passed in peace, security, and prosperity with the blessing of father to the servant. It was a wonderful rule run by the 'theory of nature' which is called *'Nam'*. Thus after 30 years rule, *Jayasimha* was died in 1155 A.D. and his son *Paramanuka* became the ruler of Kashmir.

NOTES AND REFERENCES

1. *P. H.K.* p. 256.
2. *R.T.* Vol. II. p. 106.
3. **Note.** It appears from the study that *Jayasimha* at the time of his father's death was actually in imprisonment, or at least under guard. Therefore, Prince could not learned this information before hand. However, she must be punished with first class hand, as the result of mental torcher without any mistake. Her 'ego' will be crushed with a very sharp weapon i.e. '*Nam*' or '*Chamar*'.
4. *R.T.* Vol. II. p. 106.
5. *Ibid.*
6. **Note.** This text is scarcely quite in order but the people has no knowledge how to attain the truth from *aheteh* (*ahetah*) in particular suspicious. Therefore, they have in the lust of power to collect the money from the passing of fictitious. Vouchers and supressing the others, who arc least concern with such Kind of matter as per the approach of the *Yama* or *Yami*.
7. *R.T.* Vol. II. p. 106.
8. **Note.** The context shows that *Jamadagnga* must be emended into *jamadagnga*.
9. **Note.** The death of *Drona* and *Jamadagni* is revenged by their respective sons *Asvatthaman,* and *Parasurama. Anaranya's* death is revenged on Ravana by Rama, *'Word' Kirpa* is associated with *Asvathaman* in the night attack which the three surviving *Kuru* warriors make on the *Pandava* camp, but nothing seems to be told of a son of his own style.
10. *R.T.* Vol. II. p. 107.

11. *Ibid.*
12. *Ibid.*
13. *Ibid.*
14. **Note.** The words *sadvamsatam* and *Kosaih* contain a pun, and can be understood also as referring to the weapons ('being fitted to good bamboos', 'with covers').
15. *R.T.* Vol. II. p. 107.
16. **Note.** The burning of *Uchchala's* body by his low-caste parasol-carriers is alluded to be cremated.
17. **Note.** The repetition of *Bhiksu* power is not more than that of his father, because he is handicap, without *'Father'*. Because, he attained the *'Power'* through 'Father'. Therefore, he is not above the Father. He is beloved son.
18. *R.T.* Vol. II. p. 107.
19. *Ibid.*
20. *Ibid.*
21. *Ibid.* p. 108.
22. *Ibid.*
23. *Ibid.*
24. *Ibid.*
25. *Ibid.*
26. *Ibid.*
27. *Ibid.*
28. *Ibid.*
29. *Ibid.*
30. **Note.** The context requires necessarily the conjectural emendation *moghadainyeshu* for A *L, moghasai*, proposed in Edition, द and स are easily confused in Sarada characters.
31. R.T. Vol. II. p. 108.
32. *Ibid.*
33. *Ibid.* pp. 108-09.
34. *Ibid.* p. 109.
35. *Ibid.*
36. *Ibid.*
37. *Ibid.*

38. *Ibid.*
39. *Ibid.*
40. *Ibid.*
41. *Ibid.*
42. **Note.** By *sasanapattakas* are clearly meant royal decrees regarding grants, appointments, promotions etc.
43. *R.T.* Vol. II. p. 109.
44. *Ibid.*
45. *Ibid.*
46. *Ibid.*
47. *Ibid. p. 110.*
48. *Ibid.*
49. *Ibid.*
50. *Ibid.*
51. *Ibid.*
52. **Note.** The position of *Medhacakrapura* is unknown to the common people. As *Sujji* awaits there detachments from Surapura before marching for Srinagara, it might be concluded that the place was somewhere in *Madavarajya* near the route from *Supiyan* to Srinagar. The name is probably a compound of two local names, *Medha* being prefixed known as 'hope' to distinguish this *cakrapura,* watching the whole world from other localities of the same name. The name of the present *Tsokapọr,* a village situated about a mile to East of *Kralapor* on the Supiyan high road circ. 74°-52′ 30″ longitude and 34° 0′ 15″ latitude, goes also back to *Cakrapura.* From the subsequent mention of *Padmapura,* the fierce Damaras of the *Khaduvi* district, is, however, clear that the latter place, so close to Srinagar, cannot be meant in our passage.
52. *R.T.* Vol. II. p. 110.
53. *Ibid.*
54. *Ibid.*
55. *Ibid.*
56. *Ibid.*
57. *Ibid.*
58. *Ibid.*
59. *Ibid.*

60. *Ibid.*
61. *Ibid.* p. 111.
62. *Ibid.*
63. *Ibid.*
64. **Note.** Term *Kheritalalasa* which is soothed of three words *Kheri+ta+lalasa*, it is possible that the first part of name is taken from the *Kheri* district, *'ta'* stands for 'musical note'; and word *'Lalasa'* means greedness. It shows that soul has forgotten the *'Father'* and has been trapped in the music of the mind which is worldly illusion of life called *'Lalasa'*. Therefore, it is difficult for her to come out from this illusion without the help of *'Nam' or 'Word'* which is equavalent to *'infinite'*.
65. *R.T.* Vol. II. p. 111.
66. *Ibid.*
67. **Note.** This *Malla* had previously been in charge of *Kheri* for a short period, has been mentioned above in elsewhere.
68. *R.T.* Vol. II p. 112.
69. **Note.** The place to which King has crossed over, after having cut with this (dagger) the flesh of that (*Raksasa*) and thus made a flight of steps *Ksurikabala* of A_2 to *Ksurikabala* of A_1 and *bala* of L, in view of the modern name *Khudabal* to which corresponds. Assuming that *bala* is here a rendering of the *Kalhana's* term 'place' which is extremely common at the end of local names in Kashmir. We can translate *Udipapurabala* as 'place where flood water flows'. The same place is designated low lying marshy ground immediately below *Padmapura* (Pampar) on the right bank of the river is still exposed annually to inundation from the *Vitasta*.
70. *R.T.* Vol. II. p. 111.
71. *Ibid.*
72. *Ibid.*
73. **Note.** *Srivaka* was the brother-in-law of *Yasoraja*, who had been exiled by *Sussala* and had subsequently joined *Bhiksu*. He had also himself been once in exile, has already stated above.
74. *R.T.* Vol. II. p. 111.
75. **Note.** The reference of this statement makes it clear that during the dense population like forest which has been trapped in the material life the representative of Gods comes down on earth in the form of human being and exile them to regain their life. *Yantresu* seems to be treated as a *Dvandva* compound.

76. *R.T.* Vol. II. p. 111.

77. **Note.** The road to Srinagar on the right river bank leads over an open alluvial plateau after passing the marshes immediately below *Padmapura,* already referred above.

78. *R.T.* Vol. II. p. 112.

79. *Ibid.*

80. *Ibid.*

81. **Note.** The position of *Locanoddara* is unknown but in spiritual sense it reflects the meaning of the same as the process of *'Nam'* in practise which slowly and gradually gives affection to the soul as her food.

82. **Note.** Taxes levied on marriages and other festive occasions seems to be *Yajnopavitas,* etc. They may possibly included also fees levied at certain domestic affairs (*Grhakrtya*) and the Lord was the share in this market called *attapatibhaga.* It also imposts in modern time by the Brahmans.

83. *R.T.* Vol. II. p. 112.

84. **Note.** In *Kalasa's* reign (A.D. 1081-1089), the temple of *Avantisvamin* was deprived of the villages which formed its endowments of *Avantisvamin.* Its courtyard served as a fortifications when shortly after the accession of King *Jayasimha* (A.D. 1128), *Bhasa*, a commander of the royal troops, was besieged at *Avantipura* by the rebel Damaras of the *Holada* (*Vular*). That the time of *Avantipura* remained a place of importance long after the time of its founder, is shown by the numerous references made to it by *Kalhana.* The extant of the town is attested by the remains of ruined buildings which can be traced along the slopes of the hill-range rising to the East of the present *Vantipor* for a distance of over two miles.

85. **Note.** Term *Lokapunya* identifies with *Lokabavan* in Sanskrit called *Lokabhavana,* a fine spring or Naga situated near the village of Larikpur at the elevation of 75°-12' longitude and 33°-38' latitude in the Bring Pargana. Near the basin formed by the spring, are the ruins of a small house erected by one of the Moghul Emperors, apparently with materials of some earlier building. Fragments of ancient stone images lie in the water near the spring, which is visited by the Brahmans of the neighbourhood.

86. **Note.** The name of *Avantipura* is preserved in that of the present village of *Vantipor,* situated on the right bank of *Vitasta* in the vular *Pargana*, at the longitude of 74°-4' and 33°-55' latitude. Its ruined temples have already attracted the attention of early European travellers. The remains at *Vantipor* consist chiefly of two ruined

temples which have been described by Kalahana *Avantisvamin,* adn the larger one, which lies about half a mile to the North West and close to the hamlet of *Jaubrar,* with the temple of *Avantipura*, built by *Avantivarman* after his accession. The central shrines of both the temples have been entirely overturned, and formed now only confused piles of stones. It is thus impossible to test accurately on the basis of different size of the two structures. Nor have the excavations which Bishop cowie carried on in 1865 in the courtyard of the smaller temple, brought to light any evidence bearing on this point.

87. **Note.** The title *Kampanodgrahaka* designates evidently some official connected with army. The term *Kampana* or *Kampana,* which is contained in *Kampanadipati* and in similar designations of frequent occurrence in the following narrative, has hitherto by all interpreters, the synonym expressions, *Kampanadhipati, Kampanadhipa, Kampanapati, Kampanesa* have accordingly been interpreted as referring to the governor or feudal lord of this supposed territory. It proposed to identify *'Kampana'* with the *Ki-pin* of the Chinese, or the valley of the Kabul river. This name is connected with the river Kampana mentioned in the *Mahabharata*, and looked for *'Kampana'* somewhere 'in eastern *'Kabulistan'*. No mention of this supposed territory has been found outside the chronicle, nor has any evidence ever been adduced as the term *Kampana* in the *Rajatarangini* being really used as a local name. An examination of all passages furnishes convincing proof that *Kampana* and its equivalent *Kampana* is a term for 'army', and that by *Kampanadhipati, Kampanapati*, etc, is meant the king's commander-in-chief or general.

88. *R.T.* Vol. II. p. 112.

89. **Note.** Term *Dhyanoddara* which is composed of two words *Dhyan+Oddara, Dhyan* means to see the *'Word'* or nature which gives wonderful life to the earth which is destructive one, the word *oddhara* in the second part of the name represents the designation of the alluvial plateaus of Karewas in the valley. Thus *Gusikoddhara* represents the modern *Gus Udar* on the way from Ramuh to *Kashmir* Sarai, and *Damodaroddara,* the present *Damadar Uddar*. For the older term *Suda* for such plateaus. It must be looked in the eastern part of the valley.

90. *R.T.* Vol. II. p. 112.

91. *Ibid.*

92. *Ibid.* p. 113.

93. *Ibid.*

94. *Ibid.*

95. **Note.** It has been noticed that 'King will be placed during the time of *Chitrarath, Sriva(ka), Bhasa* and others in charge of the *Padagra* (post), the 'Gate', the *Kheri* (district) and other offices (respectively). The Brahman councillor (*asthanadvija*) and a follower of *Sujji* will try to ruined the king's welfare, but could not succeeded in their mission. They will have to pay the consequence of the opposition.

96. *R.T.* Vol. II. p. 113.

97. *Ibid.*

98. **Note.** Literally the 'village which has as the first part of its name the *Vana*', i.e. *Vanagrama*. To this name would correspond a modern Kashmir *Vangam*. There are, as far as, we know two villages in Kashmir called *Vangam*. One is in the *Hamal* Pargana, *Circ.* at the longitude of 74°-25′ and at the latitude of 33°-43′. As *Bhiksucara's* chief adherents, *Prthvihara* and his family, had their seats in *Samala Hamala*, the first-named locality might be meant.

99. *R.T.* Vol. II. p. 113.

100. *Ibid.*

101. *Ibid.*

102. **Note.** The *Skandabhavana Vihara* has left its name to *Khandabhavan,* as likely the position of the 'new palace' is scarcely more than three-quarters of a mile'. The way lies entirely through quarters which must have been included in the city of Kalhana's time. The burning ground on the *Mayasum* is land lay outside the city, and was thus exposed to an attack. It has been situated on the right bank of the river, between *Nau Kadal* or Sixth Bridge, and the *Idgah* ont he western outskirts of the city. *Khandabavan* is the regular phonetic derivative in Kalhana's Sanskrit work *Skandabhavana*, a name which in its formation corresponds exactly to other *Vihara* names found in the Chronicle, such as *Amritabhavana, Indradevibhavana, Anangabhavana, Morakabhavana. Skanda* in the first part stands for *Skandagupta,* the name of the founder of Vihara abbreviated *bhimavat,* as so frequently in designation of sacred buildings. The designation of a whole city quarter by the name of a particular religious building, is examplified in Srinagar by modern *Mahalla* names like *Didamar* (Diddammtha), *Bradimar (Bhattarakamatha), Sudarmar (Samudramatha). Skandabhavana* is mentioned as the place where *Sussala's* queens had burned themselves when the rebels hovering round the city made the usual ground burning at *Maksikasvamin*; *Mayasum* unsafe. We conclude from this that there must have been already in old times ample open space near *Skandabhavana.* At present, it is used largely for Muhammadan burying places. *Skandabhavana* was as a camping

ground of armed forces during the troubled times of Muhammad Shah's first reign (A.D. 1484-86). Later on, a Brahmanical tradition along with the neighbouring quarters knows to this day as a sacred site by the name of *Skandabhavana.* At this point there stands on the left of the road the Ziarat of Mullah Muhammad Basur. The old Brahman shopkeepers are residing in the vicinity of this area. It is popularly held to the place of *'Skandabavana'*, a temple of *Kumara* or Skanda, which was adjoined by a spring or Naga. Ram Chand Risi, son of Sahibram, Govardhan Das and others at that time used to light lamps on Parvan days at the foot of the mound, as is the custom in temples and before divine images. Its existence is in all probability due to the fact that the site continued to attract local worshippers, even after their conversion to the true faith.

103. *R.T.* Vol. II. 113.

104. *Ibid.*

105. **Note.** On the other hand, 'a chief of Vallapura' *Brahmajajjala,* is named in the list of faithful Rajaputras, from abroad, who stood by *Sussala* in his greatest straits. Here probably a scion of the *Vallapura* family as meant. *Sussala* also had a wife *Jajjala* from *Vallapura*, might have been a daughter or near relation of *Brahmajajjala.* Finally, we are informed, King uprooted King *Vikramaraja* put in his place King *Gulhana,* and did thus with other rulers in other states, that King *Jayasimha,* after a successful expedition, replaced *Vikramaraja* by *Gulhana* in the rule of *Vallapura.* Cunningham states that he found the name of *Kalasa* in the genealogical lists of the *Ballavar* family. Alberuni, *India;* vol.1 p. 2005, mentions *Ballavar* on the route from Kananj to Kashmir.

106. *H.p. H.S.* p. 594.

107. **Note.** One of the two, called *Rajalaxmi*, the king chose for his own bride,and the younger, *Gunalekha* by name, he accepted as his daughter-in-law. Considering what action was beneficial for the futre as well as the present, *Gunalekha* is mentioned as King *Jayasimha's* wife.

108. R.T. Vol. II. p. 113.

109. *H.p. H.S.* p. 594.

110. *R.T.* Vol. II. p. 114.

111. *Ibid.*

112. **Note.** *Jyesthapala* a step brother of *Daryaka,* who possessed in confidants a 'Wonderful Power' from the 'Father' among king.

113. *R.T.* Vol. II. p. 114.

114. **Note.** These lines seem to contain an allusion to the death of *Prthvihara*, in previous narration *Prthvihara* and the rest, were unable to rally their fleeing troops. That no direct reference is made to such an important event, may be due either to an omission on the part of the author or to the defective state of the text. Their is certainly a corruption in *Vipannam*. Instead of correcting with the calculated edition, *Vipannam* we now prefer to read *Vipanne,* which agrees better with the context.

115. *R.T.* Vol. II. p. 114.

116. *Ibid.*

117. *Ibid.*

118. *Ibid.*

119. *Ibid.*

120. *Ibid.*

121. **Note.** It has been expressed from these lines that not only the cut-off head of *Sussala,* but the rest of his corpse too, had been carried off by *Utpala* and his men when they broke into the palace a second time after the flight of the royal troops, the head of the King was cut off. If this had not been the case and the headless trunk of the King had been left by them, it would be hard to understand why *Jayasimha,* whoes master not have arranged for the burning of the trunk. It is necessary to indicate this, as the expressions used by Kalhana are not as celar as they might be, and have accordingly been misunderstood by former interpreters.

122. **Note.** Kalhana attributes the sudden death of the person who had mutilated *Sussala's* body, to the same uncanny beings who had taken possession of this body during the last years of the King's life.

123. R.T. Vol. II. p. 115.

124. *Ibid.*

125. *Ibid.*

126. **Note.** *Nagapala*, who was the brother of *Somapala*. He came in his country as a master of the earth, *Sompala* was fled away. In the meantime, King *Sussala* was also came for the protection of his own country which he left prior to him.

127. R.T. Vol. II. p. 115.

128. *Ibid.*

129. **Note.** Kalhana refers to the honourale disposal which *Bhiksacara* had denied to the head and which it was yet destined to find at the hands

of others. The general purport of the verse must be as shown above. For A *ye*, which is one syllable short, and for which L reads *Yonya,* which is equally impossible.

130. **Note.** The gloss of A_2 renders Gopalapura by *Guripura.* By the latter name probably the modern Guripur is meant, a small village on the left bank of the *Vitasta,* below *Avantipura,* at the elevation of 75°-3′ longitude and 35°-57′ latitude. Its ancient remains still are not explore; A similar name, *Gurapor,* is borne by a small quarter in the *Ranivor* Zillah of Srinagar. The *Gopalapura* here mentioned must be situated outside Kashmir, in the region of *Rajapuri* (Rajouri). A ruler of *Gopalapura* is named by *Srivara,* among the princes of distant lands, who sent presents to Sultan Zain-ul-abidin. The *Gopalamatha* and *Gopalakesava* are not otherwise known, nor can trace out any other reference to *Sugandhapura.*

131. R.T. Vol. II. p. 116.

132. *Ibid.*

133. *Ibid.*

134. **Note.** Both the great ruined temples at *Avantipura* have quadrangular courts of large dimensions which are closed by colonnades backed with massive walls also reflects planning pictures of the temples and photographs (Cole, *Ancient Building*, pp. 44-45).

135. *R.T.* Vol. II. p. 116.

136. *Ibid.*

137. *Ibid.*

138. *Ibid.*

139. *Ibid.*

140. *Ibid.*

141. *Ibid.*

142. **Note.** For *Laksmaka, Sussala's and Jayasimha's* Chamberlain, and the latter's chief adviser a son of *Prayaga's* sister. King disliked to imprison him.

143. R.T. Vol. II. p. 117.

144. *Ibid.*

145. *Ibid.*

146. *Ibid.*

147. *Ibid.*

148. *Ibid.*

149. *Ibid.*
150. *Ibid.*
151. *Ibid.*
152. *Ibid.*
153. *Ibid.*
154. *Ibid.*
155. **Note.** The reference of the *Gambhira* river see elsewhere in the text.
156. *R.T.* Vol. II. p. 118.
157. *Ibid.*
158. *Ibid.*
159. *Ibid.*
160. *Ibid.*
161. *Ibid.*
162. *Ibid.*
163. *Ibid.*
164. *Ibid.*
165. *Ibid.*
166. *Ibid.*
167. **Note.** There is still a bridge over the *Vitasta* (Sind) at *Vijabror,* corresponding to the one here mentioned.
168. **Note.** The direct distance from the *Gambhira,* i.e. the lowest part of the *Visoka's* course, to *Vijayesvara* is only about four miles.
169. *R.T.* Vol. II. p. 118.
170. *Ibid.*
171. *Ibid.* p. 119.
172. *Ibid.*
173. *Ibid.*
174. *Ibid.*
175. *Ibid.*
176. **Note.** The gloss of A_3 (*Dandurodar*) rightly takes *Suda* as the equivalent of Kalhana's *Udar. Mankha's Kosa* distinctly gives to the word *Suda* the meaning 'place where the soil is barren' The commentator illustrates this meaning by quoting the fragment of a verse which contains the name of the *Damodariya Suda,* 'the jungle

of *Damodara*' (*Damodaranga*) and evidently relates to the same legend as recorded in *Rajatarangini* (*Suda Damodariya hi riprasapad udanyaya*). Artificial irrigation channels of ancient, date are found on other "alluvial plateaus,' thus on the *Udara* of Martand and *Zainapor.* The position of *Karala* is clearly indicated, where discussion is made of the foundation of the town *Jainapuri* by Zain-ul-abidin in the *Karala Visaya* (Pargana). Jainapuri is the modern *Zainapor* which has given its name to the tract of the *Adavin* Pargana situated on the alluvial plateau to the South of the *Rembyara* river. The identification of *Karala* with this tract is confirmed by the gloss of A_2. which places *Karala in Ardhavane* i.e. *Adavin*. The latter locality is also mentioned by Haider Malik in connecting with the works of king *Suvarna. Suvarnamanikulya* is explained by A_2, as *Svannamay nado*. On a visit paid to *Zainapor-Adavin* in September, 1895, we ascertained that the name *Sunamanikul,* the exact derivative of *Suvarnamanikulya*, is borne to this day by a large irrigation canal (*nor*) which leaves the *Visoka* (*Vesau*) river above the village shown as, 'Largoo' on the map, at a point. *Circ.* 74°-57′-30° longitude and 33°-38′-30″ at latitude. The *Sunamani Kul* flows along the east scarp of the Zainapor plateau through the villages marked *Nilloo,* Pargana, *Koojroo,* and after a course of about twenty miles rejoins the *Visoka* a short distance above the village of Adavin. This plateau called *'Damodara's Suda'* by Kalhana, and now known as *Damodar Uadar,* resembles in its natural features the other numerous alluvial plateaus of the valley designated by the Kashiri term *Udar,* or the Persian *Karewa.* It lies in the *Yech* Pargana, and stretches from the large village of *Vahator* (about seven miles due South of Srinagar) in a north-westerly direction. Its length is about six miles, with a breadth varying between two and three miles. Being entirely devoid of water this plateau is cultivated only in patches with meagre crops of Indian corn. Otherwise it is a dry and bassen waste, a haunt of jackals, as in the days when King Ksema Gupta hunted over the *'Damodararanya'* refers to it simply as *'Damodara'*. It was possibly this wall-like appearance of the cliff which gave rise to the story regarding an attempt of King *'Damodara'* to bring water to the plateau from the rising ground to the south by means of a *Setu* or embankment. No trace of an artificial dam which could serve such a purpose, could be found by Stein when visited the site in October, 1891 by Stein. It must also be borne in mind that the name *Gudasuth* which Kalhana Sanskritizes by *Guddasetu,* signifies in Kashmir 'the first (*gud*) *dam*', and might have eventually formed itself, through 'popular etymology', the basis of the above story. For another method used by *Lalitaditya* for raising water to the *Udar of Tsakadar* (*Cakradhara*), where the same expression *'ambhahpratarana'* is employed as in our passage. Misfortunate makes the breath hot, luck makes it cold.

177. R.T. Vol. II. p. 119.

178. Note. *Sahajapala*, is one of the descendants of *Bhavuka'* race, among the Rajput chiefs supporting *Sussala*. He is evidently identical with the *Sahajika; Ramapala* named in the latter passage as his father did.

179. *R.T.* Vol. II. p. 119.

180. *Ibid.*

181. **Note.** *Manujesvara is Prthvihara's* younger brother penetrated into the City, after defeating *Sujji,* and as such one of *Bhiksacara's* chief supporters.

182. **Note.** *Kostha* is an abbreviated name of *Prthvihara's* son who has previously been mentioned under his full name as *Kosthesvara*; another more frequently used abbreviated form is *Kosthaka* similar to (*bhimavat*) elaborated above in detail.

183. *R.T.* Vol. II. p. 119.

184. *Ibid.*

185. *Ibid.* p. 120.

186. *Ibid.*

187. *Ibid.*

188. *Ibid.*

189. **Note.** Term *Sulhari* means the soul who defeated with the *'Love of Nam'* called *Sulhari*. It appears that it was somewhere to the west of *Rajapuri* (Rajouri district).

190. **Note.** *Trigata* (Kangra) territory is identical with the modern hill district of *Kangra* situated between the mountains of *Camba* and the upper course of the *Bias*. With stronghold and capital of the district, *Kot Kangra* or *Nagarkot*, the gloss of A_2, to V. 144 renders *Trigata* by '*Nagarkotta*. As *Trigaata* formed in ancient times part of the Kingdom of *Jalamdhara (Jalandhar), Inducandar,* who is identical with the *Indracandra* of the genealogical list of the Katoch Rajas of Kangra is called *Rudrapala*, the lord of *Jalamdhara*. Bilhana calls her somewhat younger sister, the Queen *Suryamati*, to the King a daughter of *Indu,* i.e, *Inducandra*, is proved by his use of the expression *indumukhim* immediately after it (*devi tusya 'Word' Candrikevendujata*).

191. Note *Madradesa* -land is an old name of the central Panjab between the Bias and the Jehlam (or Cinab)

192. **Note.** From the evidence available it appears that *Darvabhisara* as a geographical term comprised the whole tract of the lower and middle hills laying between the *Vitasta* and *Candrabhaga*. The *Candrabhaga* seems to mark the eastern limit of the territoryin the passage of the *Vishnupur.* The topographical point discussed in various part in the *Rajatarangini*, it is clear that the hill-state of *Rajapuri* (*Rajauri*) was included in *Darvabhisara*. It must, however, be noted that the gloss of A_2 on our passage, *Bhimbher Danagaladese,* would restrict the application of the term to the lower hills between the limits above indicated. *Bhimbhar,* of the outer hills, in the centre of the tract between *Vitasta* and the *Chenab*, and was the Centre of a little hill-state. The name of *Danagal* appears to survive in that of an old *Ghakkar* or *Kokkar* fort in the lower hills near the *Vitasta*. We have, however, been able to obtain only oral information regarding this place. It seems to show *Darvabhisara* as subject to Kashmir in the time *Utpalapida*. But *Sankaravarman* has again to conquer this territory before he proceeds against *Gurjasa*, the modern *Gujarat,* to the South of *Bhimbhar*. Duriong the weak reigns which followed, this acquisition was certainly soon last again. For a curious passage throwing light on the character of the inhabitants of *Trigarta, Campa and Madra-desa.*

193. **Note.** The reference of the *Naravarman's* country has already been explained in the text for information.

194. *R.T.* Vol. II. p. 120.

195. **Note.** *Dengapala,* the *Thakkura* on the *Candrabhaga,* is meant, to give him his daughter *Bappika* (in marriage) and took him to himself to proceed to *Bhiksu* who was stopping with *Dengapala,* but *Bhagika* kept him back and adressed him thus in excitement : "It is not right that you should do this before you have thrown the bones of your lord into the water of the *Ganga."*

196. **Note.** Allusion is made to certain periods of the year when astrological conditions are favourable for marriages, and when accordingly marriage-procession are frequent.

197. **Note.** If the text is correct, some distinction of the kind indicated above must be intended above must be intended betwee *asva* and *turaga.*

198. *R.T.* Vol. II. p. 120.

199. *Ibid.* p. 121.

200. *Ibid.*

201. *Ibid.*

202. *Ibid.*

202. *Ibid.*

203. *Ibid.*

204. **Note.** The form *Parat* in AL is clearly corrupt, as the context requires an object to the *Samgrhnan.* No satisfactory emendation suggests itself. We have translated above conjecturally as if the text had *saran.* Terms *abhyantara* and *bahya* have been already discussed above.

205. *R.T.* Vol. II. p. 121.

206. *Ibid.*

207. *Ibid.*

208. *Ibid.*

209. *Ibid.*

210. *Ibid.*

211. *Ibid.*

212. *Ibid.* pp. 121-22.

213. *Ibid.* pp. 122.

214. *Ibid.*

215. *Ibid.*

216. **Note.** Certains plants are supposed to open their blossoms at the full of the lightening, and others, like the mushroom, to come forth from the ground at the sound of the thunder compared e.g. *Meghaduta,* i. pp. 12, 21, 25.

217. *R.T.* Vol. II. p. 122.

218. *Ibid.*

219. **Note.** *Vahini* means also a stream like life which always run or flow.

220. R.T Vol. II p. 122.

221. **Note.** The moon is supposed to receive the waters attracted by the sun during the bright half month. When the moon is filled she begins to wave.

222. **Note.** The round *linga*, the image of *Isvara,* i.e. Siva, is meant.

223. *R.T.* Vol. II. p. 123.

224. *Ibid.*

225. *Ibid.*

226. *Ibid.*

227. *Ibid.*

228. *Ibid.*

229. *Ibid.*
230. *Ibid.*
231. *Ibid.*
232. *Ibid.*
233. *A.I.* p. 64.
234. *R.T.* Vol. II. p. 123.
235. **Note.** Now from *Yogyo* we want to correct this term writes *Yugyo.*
236. *R.T.* Vol. II. pp. 123-24.
237. *Ibid.* p. 124.
238. *Ibid.*
239. **Note.** The position of *Kramavarta* and *Surapura,* and the meaning to the term *dhakka*, equivalent to *dranga*, has been related how *Utpala,* the murderer of King *Sussala,* when attempting to re-enter Kashmir from *Pusyananda* (*Pusiana,* a village at the south foot of the *Pir Pantsal*, a village at the South foot of the *Pir Pantsal* pass), was caught high up in the mountains by the commandant of the guard station (*drangadhipa, drangesa*). With this *dranga* of *Surapura* we can safely identify the custome station of that place (*Sulkasthana*) Where, Sultan *Zainu-I-abidin* located a colony of load-carriers from *Abhisara.* The word *Dranga* is given by the commentator of *Mankha's Kosa* as the equivalent of *raksasthana*, 'Watch-station', S.V *gulma.* Terms *drangika, drangika, drangin,* which are frequently found as designations of officials in cooper-plate grants of Valabhi dynasty,are evidently derived from *dranga* in the above significance.
240. **Note.** *Pusyananda* has been identified in connection with the frontier station of *Surapura* with the present village of *Pusiana,* which is last inhabited place on the western or *Panjab* side of the *Pir Pantsal* Pass, situated elevated at 74°-33′ longitude and 33°-88′ latitude. *Pusiana* lies at a height of 8300 feet above the sea level, and is now a small village chiefly occupied by carriers and others who live by the traffic on the route. In winter, it is generally deserted owing to the heavy snowfall. We have already found it mentioned above as a favourite retreat for rebel refuges from Kashmir. The commander of the frontier station evidently caught *Sussala's* murderer in one of the high Alpine Valleys near the pass as he was preparing to break into Kashmir territory. The circumstance of the rebel having been caught *girigahvara,* 'deep in the mountains,' is explained by the fact that the commander of the watch-station had gone to look after his horses and ponies to the high alps or *Margs* within convenient reach, and to allow them to graze there during the summer months (*Asadha, Sravana,*

Bhadrapada). Many hundreds of animals can thus be met annually grazing unguarded below the snows of the *Pir-Pantsal* range.

241. *R.T.* Vol. II. p. 124.

242. *Ibid.*

243. *Ibid.*

244. **Note.** The word *dradhika* found only here, must be taken in the same sense as *dadhika,* 'beard', *Manusmrti*, V, p. 283 Kalhana mentions it *'dar'*.

245. *R.T.* Vol. II. p. 124.

246. *Ibid.*

247. *Ibid.*

248. *Ibid.* p. 125.

249. *Ibid.*

250. **Note.** *Hadigrama* can be indentified on the evidence of the gloss *Adegram* given by A_2, with the modern *Arigom,* a village of the *Nagam* Pargana, elevated at 74°-45′ longitude and 33°-56′ latitude. It is referred to as the side of several fights and worsted the brave *Sujjaka,* where King *Sussala* and those of his side had lost the renown as King latter had gained.

251. *R.T.* Vol. II. p. 125.

252. *Ibid.*

253. **Note.** *Silikakotta* is mentioned a hill village, but neither passage allows of a conclusion as to the situation of the place. As *Yojana* of the modest spherical earth of the astronomers did not satisfy the theologians, however, and even later religious literature described the earth as a flat disc of enormours size. In its centre was Mount *Meru,* round which sun, moon and stars revolved. Around *Meru* were four continents (*dvipa*), separated from the central peak by oceans, and named according to the great trees which stood on their shoves opposite to *Meru.* The southern continent, on which human beings dwell, had a *jambu* (rose-apple) as its distinctive tree, and it was therefore called *Jambudvipa.* The southern zone of this continent, separated from the rest by the *Himalaya*, was "the land of the sons of Bharat" (*Bharatavarsa*), or India. *Bharatavarsa* alone was 9,000 Yojanas across, and the whole of *Jambudhipa* 33,000, or according to some sources, 100, 000 Yojanas (W.T.W.I. pp. 488-89). Yojana, equal to four *Krosas* (*Kos*), must be counted as the equivalent of about six miles. The direct distance by road from Srinagar to *Vijabror* is about thirty miles. This corresponds exactly to five *Yojanas* or twenty

Krosas, if the Krosa is taken at the usual valuation of the modern Kashmir *Kruh* (Kos) as equal to one and a half miles. The march here referred to would have compared ninety miles. Assuming that the distance is given with approximate accuacy, this performance might justify the extravagant popular belief regarding *Bhiksacara's* marching powers hundred Yojanas. The pretender must be assumed to have started from *Dengapala's* residence of the Cinab, where he had found a refuge his father-in-law and his bones have been thrown into the water of *Ganga*. But as the exact position of this place is not known, it is impossible to make any conjecture as to the route with *Bhiksacara* may have followed at this irruption.

254. *R.T.* Vol. II. p. 125.

255. *Ibid.*

256. **Note.** When India clipped the mountains wings, the mountain Mainaka escaped to the ocean, where he has since been hidden.

257. *R.T.* Vol. II. 125.

258. *Ibid.*

259. *Ibid.*

260. **Note.** The cutting off of a finger as a sign of unconditional surrender is repeatedly discussed by the king. He will release number of prisoner who has been made by the theory of *Man* or *self-style.*

261. *R.T.* Vol. II. p. 126.

262. **Note.** *Karkotadranga* was the special name of the *Dranga* or watch-station situated on the Tosamaiden route to *Lohara,* is clearly met with opposition on the way. The position of this watch-station reoccupied by *Jayasimha's* troops and *Mallarjuna* forced to flee. He was plundered on the way of the treasurers carried away from *Lohara,* and ultimately captured at the village of *Savarnika.* The latter is distinctly designated as belonging to the territory of *Lohara,* and can hence be identified with the village of *Suran* in the *Tohi* valley already mentioned. Finally, Kalhana relates to us the installation of *Gulhana, Jayasimha,* eldest son, as ruler of *Lohara* during the lifetime of his father. It is marked by the present village of *Dranga* in the *Biru* Pargana. The *Dranga* seems to have received its specific name *Karkota* means *'Nam'* or *'Chamar'* from the mountain ridge now called *Kakodar,* along which the route leads for about six miles before ascending to the Kashmir side of the Pass. *Kalhana's Kakodar* might well be derived from an earlier name during the time of *Rig-Veda, Karkotadhara,* or some similar form; *dar,* probably from Sanskrit *dhara,* is found at the end of several Kashmir mountain names.

Karkotadranga undoubtedly designates the watch station on the Tosamaidan route.

263. *R.T.* Vol. II. p. 126.
264. *Ibid.*
265. *Ibid.*
266. *Ibid.*
267. **Note.** The *Udaya* the brother of *Dhanya* is meant, two noblemen from the family *Icchati* has been already described in the text.
268. *R.T.* Vol. II. p. 126.
269. *Ibid.*
270. *Ibid.*
271. *Ibid.*
272. **Note.** Term Te' *gahanasayah* is connected with the verses of the statemen.
273. R.T. Vol. II.p. 126.
274. *Ibid.*
275. *Ibid.* pp. 126-27.
276. *Ibid.* p. 127.
277. *Ibid.*
278. *Ibid.*
279. *Ibid.*
280. *Ibid.*
281. *Ibid.*
282. **Note.** The term *asthanabrahmana* seems to indicate rank which, perhaps, corresponds to that of *Durbari* in modern India. The term *asthanadvija* has probably the same significance.
283. *R.T.* Vol. II. p. 127.
284. **Note.** The meaning of *prarthanarthi*, King never thought nor he held back on leaving the royal palace during his journey. He always busy with his business. Thus the perfect message of the *'Nam'* and faith, he had the firm trustee.
285. *R.T.* Vo. II. p. 127.
286. *Ibid.* p. 128.
287. **Note.** The importance of the term *Sraj* is to ask the despair King about the chief justice: "Have I still got any one i.e *'Nam' or 'Word'* that was the office of the chief justice (*rajasthana*)

288. **Note.** *Dhanga* and *Udaya* are two brother belong to the same family of *Icchati* already mentioned above.

289. *R.T.* Vol. II p. 128.

290. *Ibid.*

291. *Ibid.*

292. *Ibid.*

293. **Note.** This son of Laksmaka *Prayaga's* sister. He, however, escaped to *Susssala*

294. *R.T.* Vol. II. p. 128.

295. **Note.** The form of Laksmaka in AL is evidently an error. Not *Laksmaka* but his won, escorts *Sujji* on his way to exils. We assume that the text had really *Laksamaka*, 'descendant of *Laksmaka*' the 'Gate' (*dvara*) is meant here in all probability the *Pir Pantsal Pass. Bhagika*, who has already mentioned as '*Prajji's* brother's son', is probably a son of *Sujji* himself. According to the passage quoted, he had been made governor of *Lohara*. Sujji proves his good faith by taking away his son or nephew from that important place, and including him to hand over charge to the new governor sent by the King mentions below.

296. *R.T.* Vol. II p. 128

297. *Ibid.*

298. **Note.** Rajauri (*Rajapuri*) is made very unhealthy during the summer and rainy season by its dangerous fevers.

299. *R.T.* Vol. II. p. 129.

300. *Ibid.*

301. *Ibid.*

302. *Ibid.*

303. *Ibid.*

304. *Ibid.*

305. **Note.** *Sanjapala* had been exiled by *Sussala* after distinguished services, bringing horses, proved the foremost of brave men surrendered to the King, and gave up the son of *Uchchala;* and then joined *Sihasramagala*.

306. *R.T.* Vol. II. p. 129.

307. *Ibid.*

308. *Ibid.*

309. **Note.** *Mankha* gives in his *Kosa*, 76 to *Calaka* the two meanings *dustahastin* and *Cakrika*, 'intriguer'.

310. *R.T.* Vol. II. p. 129.

311. *Ibid.*

312. *Ibid.*

313. *Ibid.* p. 130.

314. *Ibid.*

315. *Ibid.*

316. *Ibid.*

317. *Ibid.*

318. **Note.** *Jalamdhara* is the present *Jalandhar* in the Panjab the name of *Jalamdhara* is preserved in the ancient kingdom of *Jalandhar* included in the centuries preceding the Muhammadan conquests, as Hiuen-Tsiang's account (*Si-yu-ki,* Vol.1 p. 175) and other evidence recorded by various writers. It shows that it was also the hill territories on the upper course of the Bias and in particular Kangra or *Trigarta*. As *Trigrata* formed in ancient times part of the kingdom of the *Jalamdhara* (Jalandhara) *Inducandra,* who is identical with the *Inducandra* of the genealogical list of the Katoch Raja of *Kangra* that Kalhana himself wrote the name as *Inducandra* is proved by his use of the expression *Indumukhim* immediately after it, even the gods have no pity in *Trigarta.*

319. R.T. Vol. II. p. 130.

320. *Ibid.*

321. *Ibid.*

322. *Ibid.*

323. *Ibid.*

324. **Note.** *Kaliya* demon has been mentioned executed by *Madavarajya* like as a Damara. We are unable to suggest any satisfactory emendation for the words *pragalbhamane sastyevam,* which certainly contain a corruption. A reference is probably intended to the instigator of the murder of *Prakata.*

325. *R.T.* Vol. II. p. 131.

326. *Ibid.*

327. *Ibid.*

328. *Ibid.*

329. **Note.** The name *Banasala's* is preserved undoubtedly in that of the modern *Banahal,* a village which has given its appellation to the 'Banahal Pass'. Regarding the regular change of Ks.*byh*, a similar

preservation of the initial *S*, as *S* or *Ch*, is found elsewhere only in cases where the initial consonant was protected by immediate contact with following consonant. This pass being only 9200 feet above the see, forms the lowest and easiest route across the eastern portion of the range to the South of Kashmir, and was thus particularly suitable for *Bhiksacara's* in vasion planned in the winter. We have not been able to visit personally the valley lying on the South side of the *Banahal* Pass, and can thus not speak with certainty as to the position of the castle in which *Bhiksacara* found his end. It appears to us, however, very probably that the castle was not far from the present village *Banahal.* The latter is not marked on the map, but lies, according to Bates, *Gazetteer;* p. 137, a few hundred yards to the north of *Adl Kut* at the elevation of 76°-16′ longitude and 33°-27′ latitude, at the foot of the pass. *Abu-i-Fazl* (Vol. II. p. 361) mentions *at 'Banihal'* a temple dedicated to Durga, in which auguries are obtained in a curious fashion as to the issue of strife, etc. Pt. Sahibram, who in his *Tirthas,* copies Abu-i-Fazl's notice, metamorphoses the Sanskrit name of the village into *'Bhanusala'*. It has already been indicated that *Visalata* must be indentified with the valleys drained by the *Bichlari* river, a tributary of the Chenab. This hill district, situated immediately to the South of the *Divasar* and *Shahabad* Parganas, is now called generally *Banahal,* after the Pass of that name to which it forms the approach. The name *Visalata* is probably preserved in that of the river *Bichlari,* in the course of time brought up *Bhiksacara,* the grandson of *Harsa,* by the route of *Visalata.* It is mentioned as the route by which the pretender *Bhiksacara* intends to invade *Devasarasa,* i.e. *Divasar. Janakasimha, Srivaka* and other ministers, as well as certain *Rajaputras* crossed the mountain range and took refuge with the *Khasa* in *Visalata. Dengapala,* a *Khaṣa* chief, who resides on the banks of the *Candrabhaga,* is spoken of as threatening to advance against Kashmir from *Visalata.* Now, it has been displayed that the hill-district in which *Banahal* lies, bore in old days the name *Visalata.* This designation *Kalhana* himself uses, he proceeded at the beginning of the winter to *Visalata,* planning how he might throw *Kashmir* into confusion till *Sujji* should arive after bathing in the *Ganga,* when speaking of *Bhiksacara's* last march towards *Kashmir.*

330. *R.T.* Vol. II. p. 131.

331. *Ibid.*

332. **Note.** *Bhiksu's* leaves *Kashmir, Somapala,* who had concluded a treaty with *Sussala's* son, did not give him a refuge in his dominion when he wished to seek shelter there in the royal palace.

333. *R.T.* Vol.II. p. 131.

334. R.K. Mookerji A.I. Pp. 63-65.

335. R.T. Vol. II. pp. 131-32.

336. *Ibid.* p. 132

337. *Ibid.*

338. *Ibid.*

339. *Ibid.*

340. *Ibid.*

341. *Ibid.*

342. *Ibid.*

343. **Note.** The word *Dhanya* has been restored here by a conjecture for the meaningless *dhanyah* of A. L has dha *'Word'*. It is also possible to emend *dhanyam* with Durgaparsad and to supplement the subject from the preceding verse.

344. *R.T.* Vol. II. p. 132.

345. *Ibid.*

346. *Ibid.*

347. **Note.** *Trillaka,* who figures prominently in the rebellions subsequently related, was a near relative of *Kosthesvara,* having married a daughter of the latter's brother *Catuska.*

348. R.T. Vol. II. p. 132.

349. Note. By *Samkata* is meant here, during the month of Vaisakha (April) the commander-in-chief 'Udaya' (Baba Gurindar Singh Ji) will acrossed the pass (*samkata*) and began fighting with *Bhiksu* and his *Khasa* followers. The height of the *Banahal* pass, from which the whole of the valley to the South; and also the village *Banahal,* can be clearly seen.

350. *R.T.* Vol. II. p. 132.

351. *Ibid.* p. 133.

352. *Ibid.*

353. *Ibid.*

354. **Note.** The term *Lavanyas* or *Labana* appears to be derived from *Lun* (Salt) and *bana* (trade), and the *Lubana, Lobana or Libana* was doubtless the great salt-carrying and salt-trading caste, as the *Banjara* was the general carrier in former times. Indeed the *Labana* is occasionaly called a *Banjara*. In *Ambala* he is also said to be called *Bahrupia*, on account of his versatility in adopting different avocations. Headmen among the *Labanas* are called *Naik,* and under them work

is carried on. A *Naik* gets a rupee at a betrothal and at a wedding a similar fee, plus a leg of he-goat. Wherever a *Labana* settlement exists, a village named *Tanda* is almost certain to be found. In Kangra the *Lobana* hold four hamlets, each called *Tanda*. *Tanda* in *Labanki* is said to mean a travelling body or *ganga*. The origins claimed by the Labanas vary. They are all Sikhs, claiming to have been converted by *Guru Govind Singh* (G.T.C. p. N.W.F.p. Vol. III. p. 7).

355. R.T. Vol. II. p. 133.
356. *Ibid.*
357. *Ibid.*
358. *Ibid.*
359. *Ibid.*
360. *Ibid.*
361. *Ibid.*
362. *Ibid.*
363. **Note.** Here we see *Bhagika* does not wish to refuse openly to the Damaras the liberation of *Bhiksacara,* but indicates for this purposes an expedient which he is sure the *Bhiksacara* will not accept.
364. *R.T.* Vol. II. p. 133.
365. *Ibid.* p. 134.
366. **Note.** Now the ministers of the *Khasas* has started to climb up to the castle for the time being stoped by the rolling down boulders.
367. *R.T.* Vol. II. p. 134.
368. *Ibid.*
369. *Ibid.*
370. *Ibid.*
371. *Ibid.*
372. *Ibid.*
373. *Ibid.*
374. *Ibid.*
375. *Ibid.*
376. *Ibid.*
377. *Ibid.*
378. *Ibid.*
379. *Ibid.* p. 135.

380. **Note.** It has been translated according to the conjectural emendation of the proposed in text.

381. *R.T.* Vol. II. p. 135.

382. *Ibid.*

383. *Ibid.*

384. *Ibid.*

385. *Ibid.*

386. *Ibid.*

387. *Ibid.*

388. **Note.** The meaning adopted for *Kumbhadasi,* a word not otherwise known to the dictionaries, by 'waterman' on the ground of its evident etymology. The meaning 'procuress, go-between' given by the *Kosas* for the feminine *Kumbhadasi* does not stand in the way of this explanation. The water-carrying for Brahman families is done to this day in Kashmir by low-cast *Ksathriyas* and their women. The latter having access to the households might have as well earned the reputation indicated by the meaning of *Kosar,* as e.g barbar's wires. (*napiti*). *The feminine Kumbhadasi* seems to designate a low-caste servent.

389. *R.T.* Vol. II. p. 135. **Note.** L has *hartum* for A *hantum.*

390. *Ibid.*

391. *Ibid.* **Note.** L, too, shows a locuna of two syllables after *Dengapalagrha 'Word'.* An attempt to liberate *Bhiksacara* is referred to, which *Dengapala,* whose residence is on the *Candrabhaga,* gave him his daughter *Bappika* in marriage and took him to himself, it was made an alliance only through the *Visalata* (Bichlari) valley.

392. *R.T.* Vol. II. p. 135.

393. *Ibid.*

394. *Ibid.*

395. *Ibid.*

396. *Ibid.*

397. *Ibid.* **Note.** Regarding the preparation for a soldierly death here alluded to march out for the base conduct with the lord, regarding betel-marks as a sign of distinction as different part of the army; *Bhiksacara* used his arrows while stone were falling at *Banahal.*

398. **Note.** For the significance of the cut-off finger is that *Prthvihara's* younger brother (*Manujesvara*) who had been wrosted.

399. R.T. Vol. II. 136.

400. *Ibid.*

401. *Ibid.*

402. *Ibid.*

403. **Note.** *Virapatta* means fringes of head-band appeared like the bushy mane of a lion, shield like a parasol.

404. **Note.** For *citracaryante* (painting) of AL correct *citracaryante.*

405. *R.T.* Vol. II p. 137.

406. *Ibid.*

407. *Ibid.*

408. *Ibid.*

409. *Ibid.*

410. *Ibid.*

411. *Ibid.*

412. *Ibid.*

413. *Ibid.*

414. *Ibid.*

415. *Ibid.*

416. *Ibid.*

417. *Ibid.*

418. *Ibid.*

419. *Ibid.*

420. *Ibid.*

421. *Ibid.*

422. *Ibid.*

423. **Note.** We are unable to make any sense of the word *harsanrpatmanah,* which contains certainly a corruption in this universe. Neither the emendation of Durgaparsad, *nrpat parah,* nor that of the calculated text, *nrpatmajah,* removes the difficulty.

424. *Ibid.*

425. *Ibid.*

426. *Ibid.*

427. *Ibid.*

428. *Ibid.*

429. *Ibid.*

430. *Ibid.*

431. *Ibid.*

432. *Ibid.*

433. **Note.** The verse contains an allusion to the five elements (earth, water, fire, air, ether), of which only one does not find mention. As early as the time of the Buddha, if not before, the universe was classified by elements, of which all schools admitted at least four; earth, air, fire and water. To these orthodox Hindu schools and Jainism added a fifth, *akasa,* which is generally translated "ether" It was recognised that air was not of 'infinite' extension, and the Indian mind, with its adhorrence of a vacuum, found it hard to conceive of empty space. The five elements were thought of as the mediums of sense impressions *'Word' or 'Chamar'* earth of smell, air of feeling, fire of vision, water of taste, and ether of smell, air of feeling fire of vision, water of taste and ether of 'Sound'. as already mentioned in the text for the kind consideration.

434. *R.T.* Vol. II p. 139.

435. *Ibid.*

436. **Note.** On hearing the King whose conduct was one of the unfeigned generosity emendation *bhavadaryas* proposed in the text.

437. *R.T.* Vol. II. p. 139.

438. *Ibid.*

439. *Ibid.*

440. *Ibid.*

441. *Ibid.*

442. *Ibid.*

443. *Ibid.*

444. *Ibid.*

445. **Note.** The correction may be made with *Durgapuraarodhuh* for AL *arodhum.*

446. *R.T.* Vol. II. p. 140.

447. *Ibid.* **Note.** *Salhana* and *Lothana* had been sent to *Lohara* as prisoners in 1112 A.D. gave himself up to rejoicing.

448. **Note.** After one month, more of less it is seen that *Lolhana* had lost only his one son, *Dilha.* Of his nephews, *Bhoja* is subsequently as a son of *Salhana.* For *Mallarjuna,* a son of *Sussala,* from the Queen *Sahaja,* on the throne at *Lohara.* Another nephew was *Vigraharaja,*

an illegitimate son of *Sussala* from a concubine, to act as his Chamberlain (*Laksmaka*).

449. *R.T.* Vol. II. p. 140.

450. *Ibid.*

451. *Ibid.*

452. **Note.** *Bhiksacara* is meant; regarding his name (beggar) aboriginal (*Barwala*) or nomad.

453. **Note.** The reference is made to the well-known story of Rama's exile, told at length in the *Ramayana*. His father *Dasaratha*, while preparing to have him installed on the throne, was induced that very day by Rama's step-mother to send him into exile. Dasaratha onfurther reflection limited this exile to fourteen years.

454. *R.T.* Vol. II. p. 141.

455. *Ibid.*

456. *Ibid.*

457. *Ibid.*

458. *Ibid.*

459. **Note.** The expressions used by Kalhana in the passages recorded below, make it clear that *Attalika* must be the name of a locality situated below *Lohara* and in comparative proximity of the castle. In view of this evidence and of what will be said below regarding the position of the force sent for the recapture of *Lohara,* we do not hesitate to recognise the name *Attalika* in that of the present village *Atoli,* situated close to the point where the Valley of *Loharin* meets that of *Gagri*, some eight miles below Loharin proper. At the actual junction of the two valleys lies *Mandi.* This place consists entirely of shops, some eighty in number. These account for its name, which means 'market' in *Pahari* as well as Panjabi. *Mandi* is now the commercial centre of the whole district, and has probably occupied the same position in earlier centuries. According to Kalhana, it relates with the looting of *Attilikapana* i.e., 'the market of *Attilika* (*Attalika*). The news of this rebellion was carried by a messenger of king *Jayasimha* and reached him on the following day at *Vijayesvara* (Vijabror). He at once despatched a force for the recovery of Lohara. The Kashmirian leader took up his position at *Attalika,* where he endeavoured to close all approaches to *Lohara.* While the besieging troops suffered from the great summer heat and the consequent fevers. Somapala, Raja of *Rajapuri*, who was instigated by *Sujji*, a disaffected minister of *Jayasimha*, approached from the South to attack them. They started from *Attalika* on a path leading along the precipitous side of a defile,

and were followed on the opposite side by the enemy. (R.T. Vol. II p. 296).

460. **Note.** The shrine referred to is perhaps identical with the temple of *Simhasvamin* made after acrossing the bridge of *Simharajamatha*. It might be assumed that this shrine stood somewhere near Vijayesvara. A temple of Vishnu *Simharajasvamin* is mentioned in the above statement, have been erected by Queen Didda in honour of her father *Simharaja*. The prominent place occupied by Lohara in the historical events, is chiefly due to the close connection which the marriage of king *Ksemagupta* with *Didda,* the daughter of *Simharaja*, of *Lohara*, established between the royal families of Kashmir and Lohara. This union, as well as the fact that *Simharaja* was himself, married to a daughter of Bhima Sahi, the mighty ruler of *Udabhanda* (Vaihand) and Kabul, where Simharaja is called *durganam Loharadinam Sasta.* It proves that the territory of the former could not have been restricted to the Loharin valley alone, where *Parnotsa* (Prunts) seems to be referred to as within the confines of Lohara territory. It probably comprised also other neighbouring vallesy to the south of *Pir Pantsel*, such as Mandi, Suran (Surankot), Sadrun, perhaps also *Prunts* itself. *Didda,* who after the death of *Ksemagupta,* and after disposing of her son and grandsons, ruled Kasmir in her own name (980-1003 A.D.), adopted as her successor *Samgramraja*, the son of her brother nephew *vigraharaja.* We do not know whether he was a son of *Udayaraja* or another of *Simharaja's* numerous sons. *Vigraharaja* had already in Didda's lifetime appeared as a pretender. After the death of *Samgramaraja* (1028 A.D.), he made a second successful attempt to seize the Kashmir throne. He marched from Lohara for Srinagar, burned on the way the Kashmirian frontier-station (*dvara*), and appeared after two and a half days hard marching before the capital. There he was defeated and slain. In the Harsa's time we hear of an expedition sent against *Rajapuri*, the modern Rajauri, which takes the route via Lohara, i.e. over the Tosamaidan pass, according to the information collected by me at Loharin, can be crossed only on foot and with some difficulty. After the death of *Harsa, Sussala* elder brother *Uchchala*, took Kashmir. From there he regained Lohara by difficult mountain tracks. Perhaps it occupied the site of the present Ziarat of Saiyid Canan Ghazi, now the chief object of worship of the place. This shrine lies about one mile to the east of the ridge on which the castle of Lohara appears to have stood.

461. R.T. Vol. II. p. 142.

462. *Ibid.*

463. **Note.** We have translated after the conjectural emendationof *Yamacandalaih* for AL *Yamac*. The expression of the term

candalayamika was the same whether they attached themselves to the highest or the lowest. Thus, it came that the beautiful-eyed *Lalla,* though treated by the King with affection, yet and meetings at night with a *Candala* watchman.

464. *R.T.* Vol. II. p. 142.

465. **Note.** This *Udaya* whom, Kalhana names everywhere with his title (*dvarapati; dvaresa,* etc). It must be carefully distinguished from *Udaya,* the brother of *Dhanya* and commander-in-chief (*Kampanapati*).

466. **Note.** *Anandavardhana* is must clearly be taken here as a patronynic of 'descendant of *Laksmaka*'. By the 'Gate' *(dvara)* is meant here in all probability the *Pir Pantsal* Pass.

467. R.T. Vol. II p. 142.

468. *Ibid.* p. 143.

469. *Ibid.*

470. *Ibid.*

471. **Note.** The disastrous effect which the comparatively hot and feverish climate of the lower Loharin valley had upon the Kashmirian troops employed in the subsequent expedition against Lohara. When *Uchchala* fell the victim of a conspiracy, his brother received the news within one and a half days, *Sussala* succeeded in wresting Kashmir from his half-brother *Salhana.* He subsequently used the stronghold of Lohara for the custody of his dangerious relatives and as the hoarding-place of his treasures, accumulated by an oppressive rule. When threatened by the rebel forces of the pretender *Bhiksacara* he sent his son and family, in the summer of 1120 A.D., to *Lohara* for safety, and followed them himself in the month of *Margasirsa* of that year *Via Huskapura*. In the following spring, the pretender *Bhiksacara* despatched a force *via. Rajapuri* in order to attack over *Sussala* in his mountain fastness.These troops, advancing from the South, were met by *Sussala* at *Parnotsa,* and there utterly routed. During the remaineder of *Sussala's* reign we hear of Lohara only once more, when *Jayasimha* is brought back to Kashmir after three years residence at Lohara, and met by his father at *Varahamula.* Finally, Kalhana relates to us the installation of *Gulhana*, *Jayasimha's* eldest son, as ruler of Lohara during the lifetime of his father.

472. R.T. Vol. II. p. 143.

473. *Ibid.*

474. *Ibid.*

475. *Ibid.*

476. *Ibid.*

477. *Ibid.*

478. **Note.** *Pulastya* is one of the expanders of *dharna* enumerated by *Vrddha-Yajnavalkay. Visvarupa* quotes a verse from him on *Sarirasauca.* The Mit. (on Yaj. I 261) cites a verse from *Pulastya* that a *Brahmana* should principally use ascetic's food (i.e. vegetable food) in *Sraddha,* that *Ksatriyas* and *Vaisyas* should use meat and *Sudras madhu.* The mit (Yaj. III. 253) quotes two verses of Pulastya who enumerates eleven intoxicating drinks together with *Sura* as the twelfth (H.D. p. Vol. 1. p. 516).

479. **Note.** Term *Bahusthala* is composed of two words *Bahu +sthala, Bahu* means repetition and meditation on the *Kalma or Nam or Chamar* as the 'good deeds' and action (J.R. Puri and K.S. Khak, *Sultan Bahu;* (Punjab) India 1998; p. 17. Hereafter referred as S.B.) The prefix *Ba* means 'With and 'Hu' means 'God'. The name thus means 'united with God'. On the basis of Bahu's Persian book *Aeen-ul-Faqr*, the author of *Manaquib-i-Sultani* writes. The name *Bahu,* which with the addition of one dot under Ba, becomes Yahu, Ya hu means 'O' i.e., called 'infinite' and is an invocation through which Sufis ask God for his mercy and grace. A name signifying so much, if borne by a person of a reflective and sensitive nature, can itself help engender in him high moral qualities by reminding him constantly of his true origin. *Sthala or sthana* or place, of course, no accident, but for the foreshortening means 'perspective applied to a single object', and in the nine *sthana or sthala* -poses of the human figure has been configurated from the divergent points of perspective. This *sthala or sthana* or place is very pure, charming and embellished of the *'Nam' or Kalma* is undiminish. It is big ocean of Knowledge and reality.

480. *R.T.* Vol. II. p. 143.

481. *Ibid.* pp. 143-4.

482. *Ibid.* p. 144.

483. *Ibid.*

484. *Ibid.*

485. **Note.** For term *Sujji* to *Sujjer Vyaje* A L, we have to correct *Sujjir Vyaje* or *Sujjer Vyajo.*

486. R.T. Vol. II. p. 144.

487. *Ibid.*

488. *Ibid.* p. 145.

489. **Note.** Kalhana has already referred to the snowy water as delight of Kashmir that of *Vitasta* (cooled) by large lumps of snow will do the inhabitants on a hot summer day with flood.

490. Note. Barley is eaten in Kashmir only by the poorest, and then only on the road or wherever else proper food cannot be prepared. The objection felt by the Kashmiris to the food of the plains has not diminished, and complaints similar to those of *Sujji* can often be heard from the modern Kashmiri when outside his beloved valley.

491. R.T. Vol. p. 145.

492. *Ibid.*

493. **Note.** By *saindhava* might be meant more particularly people from the salt range (*Saindhavaranya*), to this day a good recruiting ground for brave soldiers. Brahmans from the Salt Range used to take military service until quite recent times.

494. R.T. Vol. II. p. 146.

495. *Ibid.*

496. **Note.** Dangerous fevers prevail in the Loharin valley about and below *Mandi* (*Attalika*) from the commencement of the summer rains and during the autumn. When the valley was visited by Stein in August, 1892, he found a considerable portion of the inhabitants of Mandi attacked by these seasonal fevers, which are portly due probably to the extensive rice-cultivation.

497. R.T. Vol. II p. 146.

498. *Ibid.*

499. **Note.** The '*Sarambara* route' corresponds to the valley which joins the Loharin valley at *Atoli* from the North. Leading up to the Firozpur and Zamir passes, this valley would have opened to the Kashmirians as direct route to their own territory. The name *Sarambara* survives in that of *Chambar,* the largest village in the valley. In tracing back the modern name to *Sarambara,* through *S(a)rambara, Srambar, Chambar* attention must be paid to the phonetic analogies furnished by the names which have been discussed elsewhere in the text.

500. **Note.** There remains thus for their escape only the route through the side valley which opens to the South and West at the village of *Palera*; It has been shown that the route by which the Kashmir troops tried to effect their retreat, led first for about three miles up the Loharin valley above *Mandi-Atoli (Attalika)*. The narrow rocky defile between this place and palera corresponds exactly to Kalhana's description. From Palera to difficult path, shown on the larger survey map, leads in a south-easterly direction up to an alp called *Kuliyan,* which corresponds to *Kalenaka* of the text.

501. In *Vanikavasa* we have probably the simple name *Vanika* with the addition of *avasa,*; '*habitationvan*' is the Kashmiris form of the name

which on the map is marked 'Ban' according to the *Pahari* pronunciation. The last inhabited place on the way up to this alp (which has been entered on the map according to local information), is the hamlet of *Van* (map *Ban*), *situated* at the elevation of 74°-23′ longitude and 33°-46′ latitude. In this we recognise our *Vanikavasa*. The latter name is evidently made up of an original *Vanika*. Below *Van* the map shows several hamlets spread along the valley. In these, we may suppose the rear of the Kashmirians took shelter and was surprised by Sujji's might attack.

502. R.T. Vol. II. p. 146.

503. *Ibid.*

504. **Note.** It appears necessary to correct *Vidvisadbhyah* for *Avidvisadbhih*.

505. R.T. Vol. II p. 147.

506. *Ibid.*

507. *Ibid.*

508. *Ibid.*

509. *Ibid.*

510. *Ibid.*

511. *Ibid.*

512. *Ibid.*

513. *Ibid.*

514. *Ibid.*

515. **Note.** We now propose to read *Valgulir* for A For *balgalir* and *Vyanjadvisah* for *Vyanjaddvisah*. For *Valguli* compared wioth 'Power' which is 'wonderful' after ceasing the victory of *Sant*; for *Visa* 'Water', i.e. *tears ib* S.V 1 (b).

516. R.T. Vol. II p. 147.

517. **Note.** It shows that King's character was distinguished by it guileless generosity, did not recall to his memory that this deceitful (prince) *Brhadraja* was a designation of *Laksmaka*, probably a nickname. Sujji covers his face to hide his mirth.

518. *R.T.* Vol. II. p. 148.

519. *Ibid.*

520. *Ibid.*

521. **Note.** This is commonly used of a big beard. This use of saffron-ointment as an urgent is repeatedly referred to as a royal privilege will be seen by the people.

522. *R.T.* Vol. II p. 148.
523. *Ibid.*
524. *Ibid.*
525. *Ibid.*
526. *Ibid.*
527. *Ibid.*
528. *Ibid.*
529. *Ibid.*
530. *Ibid.*
531. *Ibid.*
532. *Ibid.*
533. *Ibid.* p. 149.
534. *Ibid.*
535. *Ibid.*
536. *Ibid.*
537. *Ibid.*
538. *Ibid.*
539. *Ibid.*
540. *Ibid.*
541. **Note.** The indications thus furnished by the Chronicle are by themselves not sufficient to give any distinct idea as to the ancient monetary system of Kashmir. But, fortunately, we are able to supplement and elucidate them by the evidence of the coins, and by the short but very valuable account which Abu-l-Fazl has left us of the Kashmir currency in the time of Akbar which have already mentioned elsehwere in this text. His description of the system is as follows by equating 100 *Sikkas* to 1 lakh, which throws the whole reckoning out of order. The *rahat* of the translation (for *hat*) originates from the wrong division of "*Rab Sasnu*" is a silver coin of nine *mashas.* The *Pancuhu* is of copper, equal to the fourth of a *dam.* Forty *dams* were in Akbar's time equivalent to one rupee and is called *Kasira.* The term *Kasira* is at present unknown as a monetary term in Kashmir. Prof. Blochmann's edition makes it the equivalent of one-fourth of a *falus* or copper. From verbal information we gather that *Kasira* is still used in the Western Panjab as a designation of one fourth of a British pice. One fourth of this is the *barakani,* Col. Jarrett proposes to read this name in its Kalhana's form as '*bahgagni,* recte *bahagani* of which again one fourth is called *Shakri* :

4 *Kasira = 1 har*

40 Kasira = 1 Sasnu

1½ Sasnu = 1 Sikka

100 Sasnu = 1 Lakh, which according to the imperial estimate, is equal to one thousand *dams*."

542. *R.T.* Vol. II. p. 149.

543. *Ibid.*

544. **Note.** *Bhagika*, who is mentioned a 'Prajji's brother's son', is probably a son of Sujji himself. He isby fortune 'Nam' or *Sabad* because he was born by the *'light'*

545. R.T. Vol. II. p. 149.

546. **Note.** *Padmaratha* is the lord of *Kalinjara* and *Kalha*. Kalh is last mentioned as visiting Sussala at *Attalika,* and must have died in the meantime.

547. *R.T.* Vol. II. p. 149.

548. *Ibid.* p. 150.

549. *Ibid.*

550. *Ibid.*

551. *Ibid.*

552. *Ibid.*

553. **Note.** *Vanaprastha,* not otherwise mentioned, was probably, as its name ('forest-plateau') indicates, some alp in the mountains above *Lohara.*

554. *R.T.* Vol. II. p. 150.

555. **Note.** *Indakara's* name must be restored here for A L *Indaraka,* son of *Bhimakara,* these councillors planned treason together in the meantime, and on various occasions devised the murder of *Preman*. That prince, himself, destroyed him by giving his poison of *'Nam'*.

556. R.T. Vol. II. p. 150.

557. *Ibid.*

558. **Note.** Term *abhisamdhatta* compares with treacherous *Lavanya Prasastarja*, after prevailing over his own younger brother *Sillaraja*, conducted them abroad.

559. *R.T.* Vol. II. p. 150.

560. *Ibid.*

561. *Ibid.*

562. *Ibid.*

563. **Note.** *Sura,* the chief of *Bahusthala,* to whom King *Sussala,* had previously given *Padmakkha* the daughter of *Lothana,* in marriage, therefore, *Sura* was remained undisturbed for certain period of time. The detail meaning of both the trems has been discussed already above.

564. **Note.** It is to be regretted that *Darpitapura* has not yet been identified, as its mention here might have enabled us to form an opinion as to the direction in which *Kalinjara,* Padmaratha's territory, is to be looked for.

565. *R.T.* Vol. II. p. 151.

566. *Ibid.*

567. *Ibid.*

568. *Ibid.*

569. *Ibid.*

570. *Ibid.*

571. *Ibid.*

572. *Ibid.*

573. *Ibid.*

574. *Ibid.*

575. *Ibid.*

576. *Ibid.*

577. **Note.** After *Samgramapida's* death the illustrious King *Jayapida,* the youngest son of *Bappiya,* ascended the throne in due succession, He also bore the name of *Vinayaditya* in the mixed metal coins of *Jayapida* showing this record name are very common. As applied to *Panini* they allude to grammatical topics discussed in his *Astadhyaya*. Taken as referring to *Jayapida,* they can be understood again either in a laudatory or in a satirical sense, according to the *Alamkara* called *Vyajastuti*. The threefold interpretations intended in these specimens of poetic malice have been indicated by the above paraphrase. Then *Samgramapida* (II), a son of King *Jayapida,* born from the Queen, *Kalyanadevi,* became the lord of the world. This King, who also bore the second name of *Prthivyapida*, reached the end of his sovereign sway after seven years. Then the illustrious *Cippatajayapida*, also called *Brhaspati*, the child-son of *Lalitapida* became King. His mother was *Jayadevi*, the daughter of a spirit-distiller (*Kalyapati*) the term *Kalyapali* or *Kalyapala* as the designation of a spirit-distiller has survived in the modern *Kashmir Kalaval,* as indicated already in the

gloss of A_3. The occupation was practised by Muhammadan inhabitants of the valley until the establishment of a state-monopoly, and was in recent times not attended by any special social stigma. The term *Kalyapala* occurs to oppress his subjects in a verse quoted by the commentator of *Mankha,* with reference to *Kalya (Surayam*).

578. *R.T* Vol. II. p. 151.

579. **Note.** *Samkaravarman* -(883-902), then his son *Prabhakaradeva* obtained gradually the position of treasurer under King *Samkaravarman,* he was also the secret paramour of *Sugandha.* Then *Gopalavarman* (902-904) who excelled in virtue and kept faithful to his engagements, ruled the earth under the guardianship of (his mother) *Sugandha.* The King's mother, who in her widowhood (became) very dissolute through sensual enjoyments, fell in love with the minister named *Prabhakaradeva* i.e. *'Nam or 'Word'* or *'Chamar'*. The sons of the minister *Meruvardhana*, the same who built at *Puranadhisthana* the illustrious (shrine of) Vishnu called *Meruvardhanasvamin,* at that time accumulated riches by oppressing the subjects.

580. *R.T.* Vol. II. p. 151.

581. **Note.** The young *Sugandhaditya* pleased the wives of *Pangu* by sexual intercours,e just as a stallion a troop of mares to embraces his enjoyment.

582. R.T. Vol. II. p. 152.

583. **Note.** The creator, we may instance the following names: *Avestan Indra = Vedic Indra, Avestan, Vayu= Vedic Vayu, Avestan Mithra= Vedic Mitra, Avestan Naonhaitya=Vedic Nasatyas, Avestan Vere thraghna=vedic Vritraghna; also Avestan Stanza Tatthwa = Vedic Tat Tva,* has made women who are pure to their outward (appearance). Yet had meetings at night with a *Candala* watchman.

584. **Note.** The reference of the said statement find out elsewhere in the text.

585. **Note.** Queen *Srilekha,* daughter of the illustrious *Yasomangala*, as her husband was of feeble minded King indulged in licentious conduct with unfortunate woman. Therefore, the account of *Srilekha's* amours does not mention in detail.

586. **Note.** The Paramours power of King *Ananta* fired the town of *Vijayesvara,* ultimately all the stores of the King laid in ashes due to his evil arts.

587. The Parmours power of King *Kalasa* (1068-1089) which acquired by skill of the art reached the fortunate King, just as the rivers (all go) to the ocean or sea, *Sudar* in Sanskrit called *Samudaramatha.*

588. **Note.** It appears that *Sahi* princesses did not know this that most of the enemy of the 'Nam' i.e. *mana* had been broken up, therefore, his four pillared pavilion is blazing in air with no roof. Therefore, Kalhana's narrative understands only of two sons of *Harsa* (1089-1101), i.e., *Bhoja* and *Salha*, whereas the plural is used in our passage.

589. *R.T.* Vol. II. p. 152.

590. *Ibid.*

591. *Ibid.* **Note.** *Citraratha* has already mentioned in the text as incharge of the Padagra office.

592. *Ibid.*

593. *Ibid.*

594. *Ibid.*

595. *Ibid.*

596. *Ibid.* p. 153.

597. *Ibid.*

598. *Ibid.*

599. *Ibid.*

600. *Ibid.*

601. **Note.** For A *Sambhuta* emend with Durgaparsad *Sambhrta*

602. *Ibid.*

604. **Note.** *Sujji* made a request to King *Padmaratha* and brought latter's daughter *Somaladevi* in marriage to him, which *Sujji* had previously brought (as a bride), had come to assist at the accasion of the marriage ceremony which had not yet been celebrated. In the meantime *Nagapala, Somapala's* brother, had come to King *Sussala* for protection after leaving his own country. When his elder step-brother *Pratapapala* had been put behind the bar by (*Somapala*), he slained the minister who was the murderer, and fled away in fear of mind's theory.

605. R.T. Vol. II. p. 153.

606. *Ibid.*

607. *Ibid.*

608. *Ibid.*

609. *IBid*

610. *Ibid.* pp. 153-4.

611. **Note.** The expression of the *adhikarasraj* which inform us that it was the custom in Kashmir to put a garland of flowers on persons

newly appointed when receiving charge of their office. At that time king asked in despair: "Have I still got any one?" *Candraraja* accepted from his hand the garland of office (*adikarasraj*)

612. **Note.** The obscure language called undesciphered in Indus cripts i.e., called *Nada, Name* etc. of this passge offers some difficulty, and the translation of the last line, as given above, is only conjectural. As we understand the passage, *Laksmaka*, who is conducting the negotiations with *Sujji* in all his former posts, except the Rajasthana. In order to overcome Sujji's resistance to this arrangeent, *Laksmaka* tears out his hair-braid and offers it as a kind of substitute for the withheld 'garland of office'. By this drastic display of his personal desire to bring every sacrifice, he moves the heart of *Sujji,* who then expresses himself satisfied. In order to the construe verse of the last statement that his fortune has been emended by the virtue of *apyayam* for A L *apyaya* seems necessary.

613. **Note.** Read out the term *Pravese prati* for *pravese prati.*

614. *R.T.* Vol. II. p. 154.

615. *Ibid.*

616. *Ibid.*

617. **Note.** The expression of the term *Bappanila* means those who made the theory of mind or *mana* as a 'Father' or Master, they are the culprit people now his retirment again to the territory of *Bappanila.* The position of the locality is unknown. The second part of the name recalls *Nilapura* and was preparing an expedition against his 'Father' with the force of that (ruler), and the first the *Babbapura* hill chiefs here enumerated, the name and territory of the first is uncertain. It should be noted that the difference between the combined letters *bb, ddh* and *ndh,* is comparatively small in Sarada characters. This explains the variations of the MSS. We cannot identify the local name in any of the above forms.

618. *R.T.* Vol. II p. 154.

619. *Ibid.* p. 155.

620. *Ibid.*

621. **Note.** *Atoli* which is written here as *Attalika* in A is only about eight miles below the probable site of *Lohara or Loharakotta*, 'the castle of lohara' has played an predominat role in Kashmir history as the ancestral home of the *Satavahana* and stronghold of the dynasty.

622. **Note.** *Kosthesvara,* who was the son of a libidinous woman and no moral character; He filled with eager desire for his (*Bhiksacara's*) beautiful wives. He was chiefly attracted the looks of the women,

possessed as he was of noble bearing, beauty, youth and lovely apparel for her husband.

623. *R.T.* Vol. II. p. 155.

624. *Ibid.*

625. **Note.** *Karkotadranga,* the frontier watch-station on the Tosamaidan route to Lohara, already mentioned in detail elsewhere in the text.

626. *R.T.* Vol. II. p. 155.

627. *Ibid.*

628. *Ibid.*

629. *Ibid.*

630. *Ibid.*

631. **Note.** Kalhana seems to refer here to the subsequent troubles at Lohara, related in the next lines, during which nobody held full royal power there, until the territory fell again to *Jayasimha.*

632. **Note.** *Udayana,* who was the Prime Minister at *Lohara,* called *Somapala* to assist the lord, offerng great tributes to him, now seems to have kept by *Lothana's* side.

633. *R.T.* Vol. II. p. 155.

634. *Ibid.* p. 156.

635. **Note.** The *Parosni* is evidently some river to the South of *Lohara.* Could it be the stream flowing from Loharin itself, or another name of the *Tohi of Prunts,* called *Tausi* is the ancient form of the appellation *Tohi* which is now borne by several mountain-streams joining the *Vitasta (Sindh)* and Cinab from the south shopes of the *Pir Pantsal* range. A *Tausi* is mentioned by the *Nilamata* Purana, along with the *Apaga* (Ayak) and *Candrabhaga.* It has been rightly pointed out this as "Most, it not all, *Tohis* have special names which, however, are little used." Thus, in fact, we find *Palasta* marked on the survey map as another designation of the prunts tohi. *Nilamata* Purana, twice mentions a river *Parosni, 'Word'* in the second place in a list of rivers which join the *Vitasta* outside the Kashmir valley. But no further indications are furnished by these passages.

636. *R.T.* Vol. II p. 156.

637. *Ibid.*

638. *Ibid.*

639. **Note.** This passage is of interesting to note, as it proves that the watch-stations or *Drangas* served also, as night a *priori* be supposed, as custom stations in old times. In accordance herewith, we find customs-

revenue from *Drangas* mentioned in the Fourth Chronicle, and the Dranga of *Surapura* (Hurapor) spoken of as a *Sulkasthana* mentioned by *Srivara* 1, p. 408.

640. **Note.** It is still customary in Jammu territory, and probably elsewhere too in India, to mark goods for which octrio-duty has been paid, with seal-impressions in red-lead (*Sindura*).

641. *R.T.* Vol. II. p. 156.

642. *Ibid.*

643. *Ibid.*

644. *Ibid.*

645. *Ibid.*

646. **Note.** To make the correct meaning of the statement word *mantrinam* with Durgaparsad is used as *mantrinam.*

647. *R.T.* Vol. II. p. 157.

648. *Ibid.*

649. *Ibid.*

650. *Ibid.*

651. **Note.** *Avanaha* has already mentioned elsewhere in the book.

652. *R.T.* Vol. II p. 157.

653. *Ibid.*

654. **Note.** The meaning of this verse is rendered obscure by the lacuna of *'Nam'* indicated above. The allusion is to the demon *Rahu,* who had his head cut off by *Siva* after partaking of the *Amrita.* We have also discussed that demon always wants to live in the theory of mind which attached to material life, whereas Siva, he lives in spiritual life which is unattainable by the demon, therefore, there is great difference between the story of demen and Siva. Siva always keeps constructive approach whereas demon, on the other hands believes in the destructive thought i.e., Brahmin.

655. *R.T.* Vol. II. pp. 157-58.

656. Ibid. p. 158

657. *Ibid.*

658. *Ibid.*

659. *Ibid.*

660. *Ibid.*

661. *Ibid.*

662. *Ibid.*

663. *Ibid.*

664. *Ibid.*

665. *Ibid.*

666. *Ibid.*

667. *Ibid.*

668. **Note.** *Manujesvara* is Prthvihara's younger brother, whereas *Kosthesvara or Kosthaka's* desscent from *Prthvihara* is clearly proved as his son.

669. *R.T.* Vol. II. p. 159.

670. *Ibid.*

671. *Ibid.*

672. **Note.** Rival *Sujji* depatched *Laksmaka* as messangers to call back *Sanajapala* from abroad to appease the *Brahmans.*

673. *R.T.* Vol. II. p. 159.

674. *Ibid.*

675. *Ibid.*

676. *Ibid.*

677. *Ibid.*

678. *Ibid.*

679. **Note.** *Kanauj or Kanyakubja,* after the death of Harsh, his empire was unsurped by Arjuna (or Arunasva= O-ha-na shun) who opposed the Chinese mission under Wang-Hiuen-Tse as well as *Sudra ruler* of Sind. They killed his military escort. The leader escaped and soon avenged this disaster with the military help of Srong-btsan-Gampo, King of Tibet, the King of Nepal, and *Bhaskaravarman* of *Kamarupa.* Arjuna was carried captive to China. In the meanwhile local powers both in North and West like *Karkotas* of Kashmir King *Durlahavardhana* with the help of Magdha ruler occupied the provinces of the Central India. He was the founder of the Karkota or *Chamar* dynasty in Kashmir. He reigned for 36 years. According to Yuan Chwang, *Takshasila, Urasa* (Hazara), *Simhapura, Rajapuri* Parnotsa were under his suzerainty (A.I. pp. 392-3).

680. **Note.** *Gaudavaho* written by *Vakpatiraj* refers the important King known as *Yasovarman,* probably a scion of tghe *Maukhari* house called by the Chinese *I-cha-fou-mo,* 'King of Central India', who went his minister *Sang-po, la* on a mission to China. This document also refers

to some of his conquests, specially his victory over the 'King of Magadha (*Magahanaha*), probably *Jivita Gupta* II. It also refers to his victory over the *Gauda* King, Vangas of East and Central Bengal and advance towards the south as far as the Narmada. It is also expressed that he was defeated by the Karkota ruler led by *Durlabhavardha* alongwith the Central ruler of India. In his reign lived two great poets, *Bhavabhuti*, anthor of *Malatimadhava* and *Uttararamacharita*, along with the said poet i.e. *Vakpartiraj*.

681. *R.T.* Vol. II. p. 159.

682. *Ibid.*

683. *Ibid.*

684. *Ibid.* pp. 159-60.

685. *Ibid.* p. 160.

686. *Ibid.*

687. *Ibid.*

688. *Ibid.*

689. *Ibid.*

690. *Ibid.*

691. *Ibid.*

692. *Ibid.*

693. *Ibid.*

694. **Note.** *Sahadeva* and *Yudhisthira* are the two Rajaputras, they paid back in battle with their lives the debt they owed for their lord's favour in the interest of the established a moderate society of equality base, on the basis of the Lords teachings and learning which were started from the very Rig-veda i.e. 'Nam'.

695. *R.T.* Vol. II. p. 160.

696. *Ibid.*

697. *Ibid.*

698. *Ibid.*

699. *Ibid.*

700. *Ibid.*

701. **Note.** The *Mahamana* festival, still observed in Kashmir, is described in the *Nilamata Purana*. According to this text a fast is to be held on the eight day of the bright half of *Phalguna* and lamps to be placed on the snow in honour of the gods and *Pitris*. On the next day, people

are to feast, wine to be drunk by those who take it, Brahmans to be fed,etc. At present only the custom of placing lights on the snow and the fast is observed on *Phalguna Sudi*. Another festival, called the 'small *Mahamana*', is placed by the *Nilamata Purana*, on the eighth day of the bright half of Magha. This festival is now entirely forgotten by the Kashmirians.

702. *R.T.* Vol. II p. 161.

703. Ibid.

704. Ibid.

705. Ibid.

706. Ibid.

707. Ibid.

708. Ibid.

709. Ibid.

710. **Note.** It is interesting to note that King having won over the *Manujesvara,* whereas *Kosthesvara* among his intimate advisers though he disliked him in collection of his own evil deeds and actions did not trust the King nor his uncle (*Manujesvara*) who, when the King was angry agaisnt him, and had shown a hostile feeling and interest on the conduct of King (Dr. Raj Kumar).

710. *R.T.* Vol. II. p. 162. **Note.** For *tatha sthite,* which does not permit of a suitable construction, we have probably to read *tathasthitam.*

711. *Ibid.*

712. *Ibid.*

713. *Ibid.*

714. *Ibid.*

715. *Ibid.*

716. *Ibid.*

717. *Ibid.*

718. *Ibid.*

719. *Ibid.*

720. *Ibid.*

721. *Ibid.*

722. **Note.** Kalhana makes Sujji allude to his relationship with *Lothana*, to whom he has given the daughter of his son (or nephew) *Bhagika* in marriage that he removed his distrust as well as sorrow from the account of his first wife's death.

723. **Note.** It is emended for *madhyetha* of text *mayaatha* ध *and* य *are very* much alike in Sarada writing. Read *Yuva visranta*.

724. R.T. Vol. II. p. 163.

725. *Ibid.*

726. *Ibid.*

727. **Note.** Under a *Guru* or Spiritual guide, invaribly a Brahman, for instruction in the Veda. This initiation was regarded as the youth's second birth, his birth into the spiritual life, Wherefore the three higher castes took pride in the appellation of "twice bord" (*dvi-ja*) or called die to live in *'Nam'*. From this distinction the *Shudras,* of course, were excluded. This is declared most explicity in Manu's code:

 "The Brahman, the *Kashtriya*, and the *Vaishya* castes are the twice-born ones, but the fourth, the *Shudra,* has no second birth. There is no fifth caste."

728. Note. Kalhana by this somewhat obscure simile wishes apparently to describe the cautious reserve with which the King indicates his intentions to *Sanjapala.*

729. *R.T.* Vol. II. p. 163.

730. *Ibid.*

731. *Ibid.*

732. *Ibid.*

733. *Ibid.*

734. *Ibid.*

735. **Note.** The allusion is to bulls set free in honour of Siva (*Vrsotsarga*), which stray about in the Bazars of Indian cities. Their idle life and ample loot makes them generally grow extremely fat and climbing on hill-paths would indeed tax them severly (Fat people are facetiously called *dharna-dand* in Kashmir. Therefore, *bhumibhrt* must be taken in its double meaning of 'King' and 'mountain'.

736. R.T. Vol. II. p. 164.

737. *Ibid.*

738. *Ibid.*

739. *Ibid.*

740. *Ibid.*

741. *Ibid.*

742. *Ibid.*

743. **Note.** During the plot of *Sujji's* death was took place, *Kularaja* was appointed on the post of City-prefect (*nagaradikrta*). At first he remedied the abuses which had been rife in the land for a long time.

744. **Note.** The whole force ran away, only the Brahman *Kalyanaraja,* who was well versed in military exercises, will killed in fighting with the help of '*Nam* at his face.

745. *R.T.* Vol. II p. 164.

746. *Ibid.*

747. **Note.** The correct answer of *mahibhujan* is *Mahibhujan*

748. *Ibid.*

749. **Note.** For the meaning of alone (*avagana*) it is expressed that *Kularaja* sent the King to kill *Sujji,* whether he was alone in the company of his followers, he must be killed by the King.

750. R.T Vol. II p. 164.

751. **Note.** There are traced, perhaps the beginnings of the idea developed in the *Upanishads* that all gods are one under different names, and there is the beginning of the belief in abstract deities, such as *Shraddha* (Faith), devotion (love), *Kama,* desire and especially in *Prajapati,* the lord of creatures, which are distinct from the personified forces of fire and wind and rain and sun (*Surya*) and sky that were the chief gods of the earlier Aryans. The speculations of the Upanishads are, of course, declared to be part of the Veda, but though verses and phrases may be extracted from the Vedic hymns to justify even the most advanced monism there is a real gulf between the beliefs enshrined in the hymns and the teaching of the sages of later days. In later Hinduism *Kama* is the god of sexual desire, but in the *Atharva-Veda Kama* is the desire for good in general, and is exalted as the creator of all. In the *Rig-Veda* desire is said to have been the first impulse that arose int he one in the beginning. '*Kama*, the primal seed and germ of the spirit' (Rig-veda, X. 129.4). According to some *Kama* was son of *Dharna*, the god of justice and *Sraddha* (Faith), the goddess of faith. It is in the puranas that the stories of the temptation of Siva by Kama is told, and that he is described as armed with a bow of Sugar-cane, with a line of bees as his bow-string and flower-tipped arrows. (*R.V.V.R.* pp. 52, 93).

752. **Note.** *Tripura*, the Tamil people of the south were never so subject to the Aryans as the tribes of the north and grew into the powerful and civilized Tamil and Telugu nations, but there is no hint of this in the Rig-Veda. There these aborigines are named '*Dasyu*' 'destroyers' or 'Dase', or 'injurious'. Their skins were much darker than those of the

Aryans and so they were stigmatized as 'black' or 'black-skins'. From the shape of their broad noses they were called' goat-nosed'. They possessed hards, they had strong holds called *'Pur'*. Those who were captured were made 'slaves' in later Sanskrit and cognate languages. The references of their religion describe them as offering no sacrifices, being unbelievers in the gods of the Aryans, and thus grievously impious. There are two passages in which they are called *Sisna-devah*, 'whose god is the *phallus*' (Rig-Veda vii. 21.5; x.99.3), and it will be remembered that the *Phallus,* as the *linga*, came to be the chief symbol of the god Siva in later Hinduism. From the first these Dasyus were the enemies of the Aryans, but their demon worship greatly affected the Aryans, especially in the simpler domestic religion that has always been that of the ordinary folk (*R.V.V.R.* p. 6).

753. The *devas* were at war with *Asuras* (the evil demons) readily took the bait and worked with all their might. When the herbs were thrown in, the mountain *Mandara* was taken for a churning stick (*pramantha*), and the King of serpents, Vasuki *'Word'* other say SHESH or SHESHNA *mana or Brahman* allowed himself to be used as the rope to twirl the stick. So all pulled with a will, the devas on one side, the *Asurvas* on the other, while Vishnu himself, taking the form of a tortoise, took the mountain on his back to steady it. Great was the tumult that ensued. The milky waves rose and tossed and foamed, as though lashed by a mighty storm. (V.I. p. 188).

754. *R.T.* Vol. II. p. 165.

755. *Ibid.*

756. **Note.** The last words put into *Kularaja's* and doubtful and the text uncertain because this process is continue.

757. *R.T.* Vol. II. p. 165.

758. *Ibid.*

759. *Ibid.*

760. *Ibid.*

761. *Ibid.*

762. *Ibid.*

763. *Ibid.*

764. **Note.** *Kularaja's* request appears natural as Sujji as commander-in-chief has disciplinary power over the soldier whose cause Kularaja pretends to plead.

765. R.T. Vol. II. p. 165.

766. *Ibid.*

767. *Ibid.* p. 166.
768. *Ibid.*
769. *Ibid.*
770. *Ibid.*
771. *Ibid.*
772. *Ibid.*
773. *Ibid.*
774. *Ibid.*
775. *Ibid.*
776. **Note.** The words *tamoripratikurvana* the commencement evidently contain some corruption against the *'Nam'*.
777. R.T. Vol. II. p. 166.
778. *Ibid.*
779. *Ibid.*
780. *Ibid.* p. 167.
781. *Ibid.*
782. *Ibid.*
783. *Ibid.*
784. **Note.** *Kalasa* owing to the enormity of his crime *Janakaraja* destined to suffer the torments of hell, met quickly his death before *Avantipura*. He then went to *Vijayaksetra*, and on coming back to the city with *Simba* threw this trusted (servant) into prison. He put *Srivaka* in cheif command of the army, the brother of *Prajji*, in the post of chief justice (*rajasthana*). Whereas *Laksmaka*, the younger brother of *Sujji*, suffered and dishonoured after seeing the King was slain by some merciless persons in the palace courtyard.
785. *R.T.* Vol. II. p. 167.
786. *Ibid.*
787. *Ibid.*
788. *Ibid.*
789. *Ibid.*
790. *Ibid.*
791. *Ibid.*
792. *Ibid.*
793. **Note.** *The Hindu explanation of eclipses is that they are caused by the Asura, Râhu seeking to seize the sun and moon. In the Vedas he is*

called Svarbhanu. The sun is supposed to be delivered by this hymn, chanted by the Rishi Atri; and expresses his gratitude. The verses referring to the eclipse are quoted.

794. **Note.** There is, however, a divine liquor which gives the gods (the Powers of Nature) strength and immortality, without which they would lose their might, their eternal youth, their life even, without which the world *'Word' our* world at least *'Word'* would become barren and dead, and uninhabitable; and that heavenly liquor, the veritable *AMRITA* OR *Drink of immortality, is shower the rain*, the dews, perhaps it were more correct to say, the moisture which is diffused through nature, exhilarating, vivifying, calling forth and fostering life in all its forms. Of the gathering and flowing of this fountain of life *'Word'* the *amrita,* the celestial *Soma 'Word'* the sacrificial process is an apt illustration: the skin on which the pressing stones are disposed is the cloud, and the stones themselves are the thunderbolts; the sieve is the sky, the liquor that falls through it in more or less abundant drops is the rain, and the large vessel or kettle into which they fall is the *Samudra, Sudar* the celestial sea that holds all the atmospheric waters. (V.I. pp. 175-76).

795. **Note.** The above statement compares with the reference footnote No. 654

796. R.T. Vol. II. p. 168.

797. *Ibid.*

798. *Ibid.*

799. *Ibid.*

800. **Note.** *Ulhana's* conduct with his son *Sahadeva's* son gave him, who was arrogant by nature, bad counsels which increased his arrogance.

801. *R.T.* Vol. II. p. 168.

802. *Ibid.*

803. *Ibid.*

804. **Note.** *Sangata, Mummuni, Kalasa, Bhasika, Saradbhasin* and others on his side showed skill in breaking up the enemy with the *Pure* spirit of the *'Nam'*.

805. *R.T* vol. II. p. 168.

806. *Ibid.*

807. *Ibid.*

808. **Note.** *Saradiya* is probably the same person as the *Saradbhasin,* mentioned along with *Sangata, Mummuni, Kalasa, Bhagika* and others.

809. **Note.** Queen *Suryamati* founded the temple of Siva *Gaurisvara*, and having the second name of *Subhata,* constructed the meritorious *Subhatamatha* on the bank of the *Vitasta* (Sindh), and a Matha which she established under her own name in the capital for the residence of students.

810. R.T. Vol. II. p. 168.

811. **Note.** The elder brother of *Sujji* was *Prajj* posted as chief justice (*rajasthana*),while King *Sussala* was fell back before his sudden attack, there arrived on the battle-field *Prajji* with his younger brother.

812. R.T. Vol. II. p. 169.

813. **Note.** Correct with Durgaparsad term *Kvapyaviparyasta* is used.

814. *R.T.* Vol. II. p. 169.

815. Note. The term *nistirna* which does not seem to give any suitable sense has been left untranslated possibly it is a mistake for the term *vistirna.*

816. R.T. Vol. II. p. 169.

817. **Note.** *Kularaja's* administration of the Prefect City was that to promoted the people's welfare, respect for honesty, punishment to the households wedded womens and their ill legal relations, checking abuses of the people which caused the disorder in the country.

818. **Note.** These two, having lost their followers through the cold fever were hanging on to *Mallarjuna* who retained great riches through he had lost his throne.

819. **Note.** The correct term for Durgaparsad ishere used as *Vicchedad.*

820. *R.T.* Vol. II. p. 169.

821. **Note.** *Apsaras* was a celestial water *nymph* and *Apsarases* are heavenly *nymphs* loved by a class of male genius called *Gandharvas.* Some of the Apsarases mated with mortal men. Thus *Urvasi* was loved by *Pururavas* and there is a hymn from him to her in the Rig-Veda (X.95). In the later literature the Apsarases are celestial courtesans and the *Gandharavas* are attended: on the greater gods. To make up this, the Purus, a powerful, originally Dravidian race, who lived in the west and had a standing feud with the horse-breeding GANDHARAS of the Kabul Valley, were for a long time the *Tritsu'* firm allies. Indra and *Agni* are said to protect both and help them in their wars against their common enemies, i.e. *Mana or Brahman.*

822. **Note.** The name *Parevisoka*, which designates here, perhaps a small territorial division, means literally "beyond the *Visoka*". *Visoka* is the name of the modern *Vesau,* a considerable stream which rises near the Konsar Nag (*Kramasaras*) Lake on the *Pir Pantsal* range, and after

an easterly and then northerly course joins the *Vitasta* at *Gambhirasamgama* below *Vijabror*. In *Nilamata Purana*, it is identified the river with Laksmi and gives a story accounting for its name ("free from pain"). The position of *Candragrama* and of *Parevisokakota*, 'the castle of *Parevisoka'*, cannot be traced now. *Parevisoka* may possibly have been the name of that part of the *Divasar* district which lies to the East of the *Vesau*.

823. *R.T.* Vol. II. p. 169.

824. **Note.** The interpretation given above of the *mahakathitakantha* is based on to check the activity of *Udaya's* attack associated with *Alamkaracakra* destroyed *Lothaka's* family to break the league of Damaras. These prove clearly for the word *Kantha,* the meaning 'patch work of lies', 'tissue of lies', 'intrigue'. This use of the word is easily derived from its usual meaning 'patched garment', compared with grath in connection with *Kantha.*

825. R.T. Vol. II. p. 169.

826. *Ibid.* p. 170.

827. *Ibid.*

828. **Note.** The reading of A_3 *Praghosayamsta*, received into the text is, perhaps, only an attempt to eleminate the augmentless form *rodhosayamsta*, which, on the evidence of A_1 *prodghosayanta*, and L *predyhosayamta*, may be accepted as the original reading.

829. *R.T.* Vol. II p. 170.

830. *Ibid.*

831. *Ibid.*

834. *Ibid.*

835. **Note.** In footnote we are corporating conjectural emendation *mati* for *mani* but *mata* should be use for proper object of the life.

836. *V.I.* pp. 38-9.

837. **Note.** *Trillaka* is named as a relative of *Kosthesvara*. He, by using various deceptions, caused the king to lose time, it appears that he was the son-in-law of *Kosthesvara's* younger brohter *Catiska*.

838. R.T Vol. II. p. 170.

839. *Ibid.*

840. *Ibid.* pp. 170-01.

841. *V.I.* p. 39.

842. R.T. Vol. II. p. 171.

843. *Ibid.*

844. *Ibid.*

845. *Ibid.*

846. *Ibid.*

847. *Ibid.*

848. *Ibid.*

849. *Ibid.*

850. **Note.** The compact journey of the King visisted *Kuruksetra* near Thanesvar. The great pilgrimages to the Tirthas of *Kuruksetra* take place on solar eclipses; See Mr J.M Douie's *Gazetter of the Ambala District; 1892.* pp. 42 & 139. From the time given the fifth day of the bright half of *Asadha* in the year of the Laukika era four thousand two hundred and nine (1133 A.D.), owing to King and minister having fallen under the influence of calumnious persons, we must conclude that the defeat of *Kosthesvara* and his subsequent departure for the Ganga fell into the autumn season. The solar eclipse, on the occasion of which he met on his return *Mallarjuna* at *Kuruksetra,* was probably the one, which according to Dr. Schram's *Eclipses of the Sun in India;* p. 122, took place on the 23rd July, 1134. It was visible at *Thanesvar.*

851. R.T. Vol. II. p. 171.

852. *Ibid.*

853. *Ibid.*

854. *Ibid. pp. 171-72*

855. **Note.** It shows that *Citraratha* was the incharge of the 'Gate' Dvara and the *Padagra* office, we must assume that *Citraratha* held at this time the double offices. It was evidently in the first-named capacity that the complaints indicated were made against him.

856. *R.T.* Vol. II. p. 172.

857. *Ibid.*

858. The meaning of the term *Caraka,* i.e. 'grazing ground' has already been discussed elsewhere in the text.

859. *R.T.* Vol. II. p. 172.

860. **Note.** The gloss of A_2 rightly designates *Bhatta, Udbhata* as an *Alamkarika* or writer on poetics this *Alamkarasastra,* a short treatise, has been discovered by Prof. Buhler. He was the King's *Sabhapati* (Chief Pandit) during the time of *Jayapida.*

861. *R.T.* Vol. II. p. 172.

862. *Ibid.* p. 173.

863. *Ibid.*

864. *Ibid.*

865. *Ibid.*

866. **Note.** It compares with *dvijotthapitaya Krtyaya* the legend told to the King: "Listen to my case. I have been sent forth by the *Bauddhas* whom in your anger you have injured."

867. *R.T.* Vol. II. p. 173.

868. *Ibid.*

869. *Ibid.*

870. *Ibid.*

871. *Ibid.*

872. *Ibid.*

873. *Ibid.*

874. *Ibid.*

875. *Ibid.*

876. *Ibid.* p. 174.

877. *Ibid.*

878. *Ibid.*

879. **Note.** The official designation of *Citraratha* is compared with charge of the Gate and the Padagra offices.

880. *R.T.* Vol. II. p. 174.

881. **Note.** This verse is quoted from *Bhagavatgita* III p. 8. Where it is spoken by Krishna (Krsna) Black i.e, *man* or Brahman.

882. *R.T.* Vol. II. p. 174.

883. *Ibid.*

884. *Ibid.*

885. **Note.** The 'mountain fastness' (*giridurga*) here referred to was probably a high plateau, difficult of access, situated somewhere on the northern slopes of the *Pir Pantsal* range. These are covered to this day with magnificient pine forest: see the map.

886. **Note.** The text of the first half of the line is corrupt the translation is based on the conjectural emendation proposed in the book. For *grasano,* read perhaps *grahano.*

887. *R.T.* Vol. II. p. 174.

888. *Ibid.*

889. **Note.** By the *Yavanas* are meant here undoubtedly Muhammadan. Such had found their way into the service of Kashmir already under *Harsa's*. By eating pork, which the latter would not touch, the King puts himself lower even than the *Mlechchas*. May we recognise in the mention here made of '*Turuska*' officers, another indication of *Harsa's* propensity towards Muhammadanism? because they are also the human being but they are conflicting with the mind or 'ego' theory which is very othodox and destructive one.

890. *R.T.* Vol. II. p. 175.

891. *Note. Govasa* is mentioned only in this passage. It can scarcely be the present *Gus* or the *Gusika,* about two miles to the north of *Ramuh,* as this place lies too far away from the mountains.

893. R.T. Vol. II. p. 175.

894. *Ibid.*

895. *Ibid.*

896. **Note.** It appears from the study that *Sanjapala* accepted on the King's behalf *Kosthesvara's* proposals for peace. However, the King was not prepared to pardon the made latter, and hence dissatisfied with the arrangement made by the said party.

897. **Note.** Kalhana evidently refers to the attack made upon *Sanjapala* by *Kosthesvara* has already mentioned above, whereupon the latter collected his force and taking *Lothana* with him. By '*Prthvihara*'s sons' must be meant *Catuska, Losthaka, Chudda,* and perhaps other brothers of *Kosthesvara,* who had kept by the King's side, but were secretly sympathizing with their rebel brother regarding *Kosthesvara's* descent i.e *Kalyanapura*, eager as the two were for profits and comforts; for his brothers *Catuska, Trillaka, Chudda* a younger brother of *Kosthesvara*.

898. **Note.** *Prthvihara's* younger brother (*Manujesvara*) who had been worsted, not knowing that he had arrived, placed himself at that very time under the King's protection by cutting off his own finger as a symbolic act of the lord.

899. **Note.** The meaning of favourable moments (*bhuktavela*) is doubtful, because it depends upon the *Jinduraja's* imprisonment and had been induced by the King's requests to take this opportunity, proceed to the attackby the route of *Simika*. Whereas *Brhattikka* ('the great *Tikka'*) and *Suksmatikka* ('the little *Tikka'*), Damaras of *Devasarasa,* and *Vijaya's* relatives, were watching for their opportunity.

900. *R.T.* Vol. II. p. 175.

901. *Ibid. I.* p. 176.

902. **Note.** *Savarnika* modern *Surankote* can be identified with present Suran or *Surankote,* a large town situated in the upper valley of the Prunts Tohi, at the elevation of 74⁰-19' longitude and 33⁰-40' latitude. Its distance from *Lohara* Loharin is about 60 km. This area was dominated by the *Gujaras.*

903. *R.T.* Vol. II. p. 176.

904. **Note.** It appears that the reference of term *Durga* is the mountain position which *Mallarjuna* and previously occupied with Kosthesvara, because he was preparing for a rebellion betook himself together with *Mallarjuna* to a mountain-fastness surrounded by a dense forest area.

905. Now *Rishi Jahnu* is known as 'Deepit Raj'

906. **Note.** The code of Manu which was drawn up perhaps about one hundred or two hundred years after the time of lord Christ, that is about seven or eight hundred years after the time of the *Brahmans,* says that the prescribed beasts and birds are to be slain by Brahmans for the sacrifice, and also for the support of dependents; for *Agastya* did so formerly, and adds that there were, indeed, offerings of eatable beasta and birds in the ancient sacrifices and in the oblations of *Brahmans* and *Kshatriyas.*

907. *R.T.* Vol. II. p. 176.

908. *Ibid.*

909. *Ibid.*

910. **Note.** The hill regions, situated between the Southern frontier of Kashmir and Rajapuri territory, are evidently alluded to these parts were occupied by *Khasas,* to whose reputation as great plunderers reference has already been made has already been made in the text. Their strong position on the routes connecting Kashmir with Rajapuri, would allow them to levy subsides or rather blackmail from both sides, even in times of peace. The position of the Afridies on the Khyber pass has offered until quite recent times an exact parallel to each other.

911. *R.T.* Vol. II. p. 176.

912. *Ibid.* p. 177.

913. **Note.** Term *Apsaras* has already been discussed above see elsewhere.

914. It is to be noted that Kautilya defines *Pada* as *Varnasanghata* and not as in Panini (*Suptinantam Padam*) (*H.D.* Vol. 1. p. 211)

915. **Note.** *Arthasastra* literally means the science of *artha. Artha* is one of the four *Purusarthas* (*Dharms, Artha, Kama, Moksa*). Manu (II. 224) refers to different views on the respective eminence of these. The

Mahabharata and the *Smritis* were well aware of the great part that *artha* (material well-being wealth) played in men's lives. Wealth depended onland and labour. The *Mahabhasya* remarks "a country is called *'arthavan'* which has cows and crops," (*arthavanayam desa Ucyate yasmin gavah sasyani ca vartante*) on *Vartika* 4 in Panini V.2. 135 (Kielhorn's Edition Vol. II p. 40). The *Dronapara* (7.1) speaks of Manavi declared *Rajadharmas.* Unless there existed some authority the regulate the people and their doings there would have been choas and no security. Hence, the ruler or the King was the most important instituion in society and rules for the King's guidance were called *Rajadharmas* or *Rajaniti. Arthasastra* therefore came to be identified with *Rajanitisastra* (or simply *Nitisastra*). A special name (Viz. *Varta*) was given to the three viz agriculture, rearing cattle, trade and commerce (*Vanijya*) including various arts. Vide Sabhaparva 5.83, *Vanaparva* 150. 30-31, *Santiparva* 59.33, 68.35, 268.3. The epic says *'Vartamulo hyayam Lokastraiyya vai dharyate sada'* (*Santi* 68.35). The *Ramayana* also (11.100.47) says 'This world when it resorts to *Varta* prospers happily (*'Vartayam Samsritastata lokoyam sukham-edhate'*). Kautilya makes it clear that *Arthasastra* and *Varta* were distinct and yet *Varta* was a subject of study for the king, it was one of the three or four *Rajavarta* (*vide Arthasastra I. 4.4, Manu VII. 43*). *Arthasastra* in its technical sense is somewhat wider meaning than *Dandaniti* and includes politics, economics, law and justice, but was narrower in scope than *Dharmasastra.* It was said to be an *Upaveda* of the *Atharvaveda* according to the *Visnupurana* III.. *6.28 Vayu* 61.79 and Brahmanda 35.88-89. It is therefore stated by Yaj. (II.21) that in case of conflict between *Dharmasastra* and *Arthasastra* the former is stronger. (H.D. Vol. 1 pp. 151-52).

916. *R.T.* Vol. II. p. 177.

917. *Ibid.*

918. **Note.** Udaya thinks that *Mallarjuna* asks for the favour of being allowed a soldierly death in open combat.

919. **Note.** It is emended with Durgaparsad *akrsta* and *prapnomi.*

920. *R.T.* Vol. II. p. 177.

921. *Ibid.*

922. *Ibid.*

923. *Ibid.*

924. *Ibid.* p. 178.

925. *Ibid.*

926. *Ibid.* **Note.** *For the rare word asecanaka, compares Harsacharita, p. 30.*

927. *R.T.* Vol. II. P. 178.

928. **Note.** Aryans enter the country of the *Kurus* and *Panchala* in the 650-325 B.C. saw the rise of the two great religions, Jainism and Buddhism, the texts of which throw light not merely religious but also political history of the times, along with Sanskrit works. These texts show how India was then known for sixteen prominent states (*Mahajanapadas*) which are thus listed in the old *Pali* texts, *Anguttara Nikaya*: (1) Anga with its capital, *Champa* (East Bihar), (2) *Magadha* (South Bihar), (3) *Kasi,* (4) *Kosala* (Oudh), (5) *Vajji* (North Bihar), 6 *Malla* (Gorakhpur District), (7) *Cheti* (Chedi) (between Jumna and Narmada), (8) *Vamsa* (Vatsa) (Allahabad region), (9) *Kuru* (Thanesar, Delhi and Meerut Districts), (10) *Panchala* (Bareilly, Badaun and Farrukhabad districts), (11) *Machchha* (Matsya, Jaipur), (12) *Surasena* (Mathura), (13) *Assaka* on the Godavari with its capital *Potana* (Paithan), (14) *Avanti* with it capital at *Mahissati,* (15) *Gandhara* (Peshwar and Rawalpindi Districts) and *Kamboja* (South-West Kashmir and parts of Kafiristan). To these another text adds (17) *Kalinga* with its capital at *Dantapura*, (18) *Sovira* with its capital called *Roruka* and (19) *Videha* with its capital Mithila. The *Dharma-Sutra* of Bandhayana mentions the following states as forbidden ground for the Aryas: (1) *Sauvira* (Multan), (2) *Aratta* (Panjab), (3) *Surashtra,* (4) *Avanti,* (5) *Magadha* (6) *Anga,* (7) *Pundra* (North Bengal) and (8) *Vanga* (East and South Bengal). So all these regions were lying outside the pale of Aryan civilization proper at that time (C.500 B.C.). The Jain text, *Bhagavati,* mentions some additions states or regions like *Malava, Kochcha* (Cutch), *Padha* (Pudra?) *Ladha* (Radha in Bengal) and *Moli* (*Malla*). These were northern states of India.

929. *R.T.* Vol. II. p. 178.

930. **Note.** The *Gonds, Bhils and Santals* are modern survivors of those races. Some were very humble in the scale of humanity burying their dead in the cells made of stone-slabs, (Siharas-Sila) called *Kistvaens* by scientists and *'Pandava Vidu' 'Word'* the houses of the *Pandava* brothers when in exile *'Word'* by the Tamil people of the South to this day, and now he is existing in this universe.

931. *R.T.* Vol. II. p. 178.

932. **Note.** It has already been shown that the cutting off of one's finger was a sign of submission on the part of persons who acknowledge their gult and ask for marcy.

933. Regarding the *Navamatha* please see its explanation else-where in the text.

934. *R.T.* Vol. II. p. 178.

935. *Ibid.*

936. *Ibid.* p. 179.

937. *Ibid.*

938. *Ibid.*

939. Ibid.

940. **Note.** For the *Panchala* as followers of Arjuna (*Phalguna*) *in the* battle, *Prthvipala* protected him in the side just as those the *Panchala*-land (had protected).

941. *R.T.* Vol. II. p. 179.

942. *Ibid.*

943. *Ibid.*

944. *Ibid.*

945. *Ibid.*

946. *Ibid.*

947. *Ibid.*

948. *Ibid.*

949. *Ibid.*

950. *Ibid.*

951. *Ibid.*

952. *Ibid.*

953. *Ibid.*

954. *Ibid.*

955. *Ibid.*

956. *Ibid.*

957. **Note.** The light of the Sun is supposed to be carried to the moon by the ray called *Susumna*; See *Nirukta* ii. p. 6 and *Visnupurana* II; p. 297. Dead heroes go to the world of Surya.

958. **Note.** The *Vishnusmrlti* enumerates twenty-one hells (43.1-22), which are almost the same as *Yajnavalkya's* (3.222-224). It is mentioned the names of the seven days of the week (78. 1-7), thursday being called *Jaiva,* while *Yajnavalkya* mentions only the seven planets (with *Rahu* and *Ketu*) in the same order (1.296). It recommends the practice of *Sati* (25.14), speaks of *pustakas* (18, 44, 23.56), aword which is not used by the other *dharmasutras* so far described. It gives a long list of good and evil omens at the time of starting on a journey (63.33-39). Among evilomens it includes the sight of yellow-robed ascetics

(i.e. Buddhists probably) and *Kapalikas* (63.36). It prohibits speech with *Mlechcha* countries (84.2). It contains special directions about the worship of *Vasudeva* in chapter 49 and speaks of *Svetadivipa* as the reward of devotion to *Vasudeva* (49.4). Here and there, there are enlogies of *Vasudeva* (1.50-57, 65.1, 65.1, 97.10, 98 which (last) gives one hundred names of *vishnu*). It speaks of the four *Vyukas* of *Vasudeva* (67.2) and of the *Varaha* incaranation. It gives a vague location of *Aryavarta* as a country where four *Varnas* exist (84.4). It enumerates numerous sacred places (85.1-52), among which *Sriparvata*, *Saptarsa* (modern *Satara* i.e. '*Word'* or *'Nam'*), Godavari and Southern *Pancanada* deserve to be specially noted in the text. (H.D Vol. 1 p. 121). In the *Garudapurana*, widow is highly praised, she was called a *Sati* (pronounced *Suttee*) emphatically a 'good' woman. (R.V.V.R. p. 13), one who dies in '*Nam*' or '*Word*'.

959. *R.T.* Vol. II. p. 180.

960. *Ibid.*

961. **Note.** *Dhanya* and *Udaya* are said of *Icchati* family Both were to brother useed to work, On the higher posts under *Jayasimha,* to be descended from a *rajanya,* i.e, *Ksattriya* family.

962. *R.T.* Vol. II. p. 180.

963. *Ibid.*

964. *Ibid.*

965. *Ibid.* p. 181.

966. *Ibid.*

967. *Ibid.*

968. **Note.** Durga is worshipped to this day under the name of *Suresvari* ('queen of the gods') on a high crag rising above the village of *Isabar* from the range which encloses thc Dal lake on the East. A natural rock on the top of the crag is looked upon as a representation of Durga's husband. The *Suresvarimahatmya* accounts for the residence of the goddess and her consort at this spot by a legend connected with the killing of the demon ruru. It also describes in detart of the pilgrimage, which begins at certain springs (*Satadhara etc.*) situated in the immediate vicinity of the village of *Isabar.*

969. *R.T.* Vol. II.p. 181.

970. *Ibid.*

971. *Ibid.*

972. *Ibid.*

973. **Note.** *Vijaya*, son of *Bhava,* has already referred burned his houses near *Kalyanapura.* He was a great noble resident at *Kalampor*, and a supporter of *Bhiksu.* As Kalhana does not state any special reason for *Vijaya's* murder, we must suppose that it was caused by the King's desire to confiscate the great property of this Damara.

974. **Note.** The *Salva* prince is *Hariscandra* who, according to the legend related in the *Mahabharata* and elsewhere, rules the mythical City of *Saubha* which is suspended in the air.

975. R.T. Vol. II. p. 181.

976. *Ibid.*

977. *Ibid.*

978. *Ibid.*

979. **Note.** We must assume that *Udaya*, already beofre mentioned as lord of the Gate and had lost this charge when *Citrarath* received the two offices of *Padagra* and *Dvara.*

980. R.T. Vol. II. p. 182.

981. *Ibid.*

982. *Ibid.*

983. **Note.** This *Srngara* must be distinguished from the *Srngara,* Citraratha's servant, *Janaka* and *Srngara* ousted each other from office by mean of bribing money.

984. *R.T.* Vol. II. p. 182.

985. *Ibid.*

986. *Ibid.*

987. **Note.** Lingas and images of gods were in Kashmirian temples always placed on ornamental stone (*pitha* or *bhadrapitha*), many of which can yet be seen in *Situ* in the temple-ruins of Buthiser (*Bhutesa*), *Narastan, Pattan*, etc. For the purpose of carrying of the water with which the Lingas and images have daily to be bathed such pedestals are provided with a conduit sunk into their upper surface and ending generally in a sculptured waterpout.

988. R.T. Vol. II. p. 182.

989. **Note.** The name *Nandiksetra* is given by the *Nilamata Purana,* the *Nandiksetra* and *Haramukuta Mahatmyas* to the high alphine valley at the foot of the east Glaciers of the Haramukh Peaks, which contains the sacred *Kalodaka* lake, popularly known as *Nund-kol.* This lake situated circ. 75° longitude and 34°-36 latitude at an altitude of about 13,000, forms one of the chief station on the pilgrimage to the sacred

Ganga lake (*Uttaramanasa*), which lies a short distance above it. According to a legend told at length in the *Nilamata Purana, Nandin*, born as son of Silada, performed in the *Kalodaka* a great penance, whereupon Siva took up his permanent abode there by the side of his faithful attendent. The inner portion of lake, showing a deep blue colour, is supposed to mark the residence of *Kala* or Siva, the outer portion, of a light green colour, that is *Nandin*. Siva is worshipped there under the name of *Nandisa*. Kalhana extends the term of *Nandiksetra* so as to include the neighbouring site of *Bhutesvara* or Buthiser, in the *Kankanai* valley below *Nund-kol* when speaking of the erection of a temple in honour of Bhutesa at *Nandiksetra*.

990. **Note.** *Canpaka* is Kalhana's father, whose used to go in the shrine sof *Nandiksetra,* who in the colophons bears the title *'Prabu'*, *'Lord'*. It shows that *Canpaka* had ultimately retired to *Nandiksetra,* i.e. the Tirtha of *Bhutesvara* and a festival called *Devasvapana* celebrated during the last ten days of *Asadha*.

991. *R.T.* Vol. II. p. 182.

992. *Ibid.* p. 183.

993. **Note.** The Naga *Vasuki* acted as string to the bow which *Indra* formed of the *Mandara* mountain, when fighting the demon *Tripura*.

994. *R.T.* Vol. II. p. 183.

995. *Ibid.*

996. *Ibid.*

997. *Ibid.*

998. *Ibid.*

999. *Ibid.*

1000. *Ibid.*

1001. *Ibid.*

1002. **Note.** By Gurus are meant here in all probability Purohitas of various sorts.

1003. **Note.** Queen *Didda*, being bent on the restoration of ruined building (*Jirnoddhara*), enclosed with stone walls almost all the temples the surrounding walls of which had been burned down. This pious (King), with whom the restoration of decayed (buildings) was a passion, put in order the famous sites of *Cakradhara, Yogesa* and *Svayambhu*. By (the foundation of) Mathas, (the grant of) *Agraharas*, the restoration of temples and other pious works, *Sumanas,* the younger brother of *Rilhana,* became the latter's equal. Therefore, by her numerous sacred foundations and restorations, this wise and clever queen has out stepped, O wonder, even the lame *Didda*. The whole town at *Nandiksetra* which had been burned during his reign by a sudden configration was built a new by him finer that it was before. It was again restored during the rule of *Uchchala*.

1004. *R.T.* Vol. II. p. 184.

1005. **Note.** Kalhana probably alludes to the murder of *Sujji*, and throws a veil over the other acts of violence of *Jayasimha*, which he may have considered justified by political necessity.

1006. **Note.** The contents requires necessarily the emendation proposed in the text of *Sagaraja* for *AL Saragaja*. The *Purana* legend relates that the *Ganga* was brought down from leave by the prayer of *Bhagiratha* to purify the ashes of the sixty thousand sons of *Sagara* who had been burnt by the angry glance of the Rsi *Kapila*.

1007. R.T. Vol. II. p. 184.

1008. **Note.** This *Sivaratha* is probably the person referred King's men when learning for certain that *Sujji* was killed, made a prisoner of *Sivaratha* who was hated by everybody and was stopping there.

1009. *R.T.* Vol. II. p. 184.

1010. *Ibid.*

1011. *Ibid.*

1012. *Ibid.*

1013. *Ibid.*

1014. **Note.** The powerful herbs of the mountains are supposed to give light at night.

1015. *R.T.* Vol. II. Pp. 184-5.

1016. **Note.** This passage shows that the sale of wood from the great forest of Kashmir formed then, as at the present time, an important source of fiscal revenue. We also see from the passage that wood played that great part int he construction of private houses at Srinagar which it does nowadays. Free distributions of wood for building purposes were resorted to also on recent occasions when great portions of Srinagar had been burned down by conflagrations.

1017. *R.T.* Vol. II. p. 185.

1018. *Ibid.*

1019. *Ibid.*

1020. *Ibid.*

1021. **Note.** Expressions similar to *agraharkendu* occur frequently in land-grants conveying permanent ownership.

1022. R.T. Vol. II p. 185.

1023. *Ibid.*

1024. **Note.** *Aryaraja's* pious predilection, he used to hate the (music of) lutes, the noise produced by the water poured from pitchers and flowing round the base (*pitha*) of a *linga*, was dear even in his sleep.

1025. R.T. Vol. II. p. 185.

1026. *Ibid.* pp. 185-6.

1027. **Note.** Term *Vyayasthite* compares with reference footnote No. 968 of the same chapter.

1029. *R.T.* Vol. II. p. 186.

1030. *Ibid.*

1031. **Note.** The ministers spoke to the King: "There he goes, after leaving nothing in the country but what wealth you have yourself. Let his property be confiscated". But the King did not act upon this.

1032. *R.T.* Vol. II. p. 186.

1033. **Note.** Sixty-four is the conventional number indicated for caste-subdivisons, compared e.g *Kullaka* on *Manusmrti*, X. p. 31.

1034. **Note.** This verse is supplied by A_2 and is not found in L. The identity of *Puranadhisthana,* 'the ancient capital,' with the present village of *Pandrethan,* about three miles above the Srinagar on the right bank of *Vitasta*, it is also well-known to the Pandits. If we are write in deriving the name of the locality from the fact of its having been the site of the *old* capital *Srinagari* founded by Asoka, the use of the name is our passage is a kind of anachronism, as the foundation of the *new* capital of *Pravarapura* on the site of the modern Srinagar is attributed by Kalhana to *Sresthasena's* grandson *Pravarasena II.* The name *Puranadhisthana* must have already been in use in the first half of the seventh century A.D. as Hiuen-Tsiang evidently refers to it when speaking of the 'old city' situated abotu *Li* or circ.two miles to the South East of the 'new city' (*Si-yu-ki; i.p. 158*). Kalhana mentions *Puranadhisthana* once more in the reign of *Parth,* where the gloss of A_2 explains the name by *pamydrthan iti prasiddhe grame.* The temple of *Meruvardhanasvamin* whose erection is related in that passage, has been recognised by General Cunningham in the well-preserved little temple still standing in the centre of the modern village. Still later in Kashmir's own time, the Chronicle records the erection of various buildings by the minister *Rilhana* "in the town of the *two Pravarasenas*", and in particular that of a *Rilhanesvara* in the first city of King pravara'. The latter expression is evidently intended to designate *Puranadhisthana.* The slopes rising immediately to the North of *Panrethan* show considerable remains of ancient buildings in the form of carved stones and architecutral fragments which can be traced along the foot of the hillside for about a mile and a half. Among them several broken *lingas* of colossal dimensions attracted the attention of the historian. Individual structures, however, cannot be distinguished now among the *debris* overground. An indication of the sites of *Sresthasena's* various *Partisthas* is, therefore, impossible. The *linga* or shrine of *Pravaresa,* which seems to have been the most prominent among them, is distinguished by the designation *'purvam'* from the great temple of the same name which Pravarasena II, built in his new capital of *Pravarapura* founded by him.

1035. *R.T.* Vol. II. 186.

1036. See Note 1034 about the reference of *Puranadhisthana*

1037. **Note.** The place here referred to is undoubtedly the same which is called *Baleskaprapa* ('the drinking station of *Baleraka'*). Regarding the confusion between aspirate and unaspirate sonants in the spelling of Kashmir local names.

1038. *R.T.* Vol. II. p. 186.

1039. *Ibid.*

1040. *Ibid.* p. 187.

1041. *Ibid.*

1042. **Note.** *Cankuna's* Vihara at Srinagar survived to the time of Kalhana, and was repaired by *Sussala*, the wife of the minister *Rilhana*, under King *Jayasimha.* Its position cannot be traced. It is certain that it was at this *Cankunavihara* and not at that founded at *Parihasapura*, that Kalhana saw the Buddha image; the kingdom of Magadha, comprising the modern districts of *Gaya* and *Patna* south of the Gangas, was the scene of Buddha's early career. By the *Prasada* possibly the caitya attached to the vihara may be meant.

1043. R.T. Vol. II. p. 187..

1044. **Note.** Regarding the use of *araghattas,* the system of irrigation here referred to is explained by the configuration of the ground near that locality. At present the fields and gardens between the two places are irrigated by means of wells. Correct with calculation in the text as *prakara* for AL *Prakara.*

1045. **Note.** This site has already been mentioned in the text as *Puranarajadhani* and the meaning of *Sthandila* see elsewhere.

1046. **Note.** The correct meaning of the statement is known as *Pratisthayaivasu.*

1047. **Note.** Owing to certain demerits of the King from a former (birth), this *Matha* lost its desired designation (and became known) by the name of *Navamatha* ('the new Matha').

1048. **Note.** *Udaya* might have received back his former charge as *Kampanapati,* and the charge of *Kheri to Rilhana* from *Sanjapala,* who is not mentioned with that title of the commander-in-chief. But it is more probable that Kalhana gives him this his former title merely to distinguish him from the other *Udaya*, 'the lord of the Gate', with *Sanjapala's* death that his son *Gayapala* was appointed commander-in-chief.

1049. *R.T.* Vol. II p. 187.

1050. **Note.** Term *Brahmapuri,* used here in the text for the designation of some pious foundation, corrospons, perhaps, to the modern *Dharmasala Brahmapuri* may be understood as 'residence of Brahmans' and is also the name of Brahmans' City where the wise and pious assemble.

1051. **Note.** The *Padamsaras* is the Vular lake, Naga *Mahapadma* is the tutelary deity of the Vular, the largest of the Kashmir lakes, which has received from its ancient name *Mahapudmasaras.* The *Nilamata,* tells at great length the story how *Nila*, the *King* of the Nagas, granted to *Mahapadma* and his relatives a residence at the site which was first occupied by King *Visvagasva* town, *Candrapura,* and after the submersion of the latter converted into a lake, in connection with artificial Lanka is land constructed in it by Zain-ul-Abidin.

1052. **Note.** *Srngara* is undoubtedly the eldest brother of the poet *Manika.* Manika informs us that *Srngara* had received 'the garland of the office of *Brhattantrapati'* from King *Sussala*. Jonaraja explain the otherwise unknown term *Brhattantrapati* as *dharmadhikara,* 'judge'. The single *tantrapati* of our passage is clearly the same title, *Mankha* praises in particular the learning of *Srngara*

1053. **Note.** The *Sridvara* is given in several passages of the *Sarvavatara* to the hill range which stretches along wht east shore of the Dal Lake. It is situated to the face of Mount Mahadeva. In all these *Sridvara* is spoken of as a hill (*parvata, giri*)

1054. **Note.** *Alamkara* figures in the subsequent narrative in the high office of *Rajasthaniya* or chief justice which is equivalent of the past of *'Nam' or Sabad'*. As Kalhana names *Mankha* as his brother, the minister of foreign affairs (*samdhivigrahika*) it is certain that the *Alamkara* of the chronicle is identical with the third eldest brother of poet used to work under *Sussala* and *Jayasimha Alamkara* had not yet attained the higher office of Rajasthaniya. *Mankha* represents his brother as deeply versed in grammatical science, and gives his fimilar name as Lankaka.

1055. **Note.** The term *Snanakostha* corresponds to the present Kashmiris *Sranakuth,* the designation of the bathing-huts on the river. The latter have been referred to as *Saritsnanagrha.* The Snamakosthakas of Kashmir are mentioned already by Ksemendra, *Samayam.*

1056. *R.T.* Vol. II p. 188.

1057. **Note.** The puns contained in this line necessiate the double renderings above indicated. The moon as King *Soma* protects the plants. It would appear from our passage that *Alamkara's* father practised also a physician. *Mankha* in his *Srikantha* does not mention this fact about the father *Visvavarta,* but describes him generally as a man of learning and devout worshipper of Siva. *Alamkara* is praised by *Mankha* as a liberal patron of learned men, and the Sabha of scholars which is described in the XXV. Canto of the *Srikanthacarita,* takes place in his house of *Sukra,* the planet venus, the Puranic legend holds that he was the Guru of the Daityas, and that after their destruction by the gods he accomplished a great penance. To the latter allusion is made in the text.

1058. **Note.** A series of puns permits this line to be interpreted also as referring to *Visnu:* "He before whom there were no Visnu-worshippers (*apurvavaisnava*), taking the *Avatara* of *Nrsimha,* destroyed (the demon) *Hiranyakasipu,* though averse to killing (*nirhimsa*), and at the time of his Boar incarnation (*Varahasamaya*) recovered the earth (*dattagaus*)." The word *pradah* must in this case be derived from da, 'to cut', with the preposition *pra,* i.e. *Prakarsena.*

1059. **Note.** The *Bhattarakamatha* which has left his name to the present quarter of *Bradimar* in Srinagar, was evidently a building of great size.

1060. *R.T.* Vol. II p. 188.

1061. **Note.** By the ruler of *Darvabhisara* is evidently meant here the chief of *Rajapuri. Mankha* mentions *Srikanthac.* XXV. 75, *Jalhana,* a minister of *Rajapuri*, as one of the members of *Alamkara's Sabha.*

1062. *R.T.* Vol. II. p. 189.

1063. **Note.** A somewhat obscure reference is made here to the *Svayambu* or natural Linga named *Jyestharudra* (received worship) as *Balakesvara.* This mysterious stone might be supposed to have been first found or worshipped near a *karavira* bush. Regarding the worship of natural stones which for pious eyes take the form of a linga in three distinct localities of Kashmir viz (i) below Mount

Haramukuta in the sacred territory called *Nandisaksetra or Nandikestra,* (ii) near *Tripuresvara,* the modern *Triphar* and (iii) in the close neighbourhood of *Sringari* regarding the position of the *Jyestharudra* at *Srinagari.*

1064. R.T. Vol. II. p. 189.

1065. **Note.** A careful examination of all passages in Kashmirian texts in which Siva *Jyesthesa* has already been mentioned that *Jyestharudra* Linga here referred to is the emblem worshipped from early times close to *Bhutesvara* or *Buthiser*, above the village of *Vangath*. The letter has received its ancient name *Varisthasrama* (given in the *Haramukutagangamah,* and *Nandikṣetramah*) from the Rsi *Vasistha* who is supposed to have resided here. In the *Nilamata Purana* the consecration and fist worship of the *Jyestharudra* Linga is distinctly attributed to the *Rsi Vasistha.*

1066. *R.T.* Vol. II. p. 189.

1067. **Note.** A village *Butapor* which may correspond to *Bhuttapura,* is said to exist in the *Machipor* Pargana. We have, however, not been able to ascertain its exact position. It may possibly be the place shown as *'Batpoora'* on the map, 74° -19′-30′ logitude and 34°-26′-30″ latitude.

1068. *R.T.* Vol. II p. 189.

1069. **Note.** *Madavagrama* can no longer be traced in the history of *Chamar.*

1070. *R.T.* Vol. II. p. 189.

1071. **Note.** The Vihara of *Ratnadevi* was firmely established object of her lord's love, attained pre-eminence among all the foundations.

1072. **Note.** Term *Svetadvipa* (literally 'the white isle') is a residence of blessed beings which know not death. It was created for King *Sveta,* who by a penance induced Siva to vanquish and expel from his land the god of death. The legend is told at length in *Haracar.ii*

1073. *R.T.* Vol. II. p. 189.

1074. **Note.** Regarding the term *Gokula* judging from the statement, it must have been the general designation for a certain class of religious edifices, is clearly connected with the famous *Gokula*, the residence of the young Krsna in the Vrindavana forest. From the veres it appears that Gokulas were provided with grazing grounds reserved for kine or (*Caraka*)

1075. *R.T* Vol. II. p. 190.

1076. **Note.** Visnu is often represented in sculptures and paintings as the 'unholder of Mount *Govardhana.* The half of the statement of the this verses of the line is certainly corrupt, and is altogether missing in L. The above conjectural tranaslation is based on the correction of *na* for *na*. The Word *asva,* which we are unable to bring into connection witht he rest, we have left untranslated.

1077. **Note.** *Visvakarman* is the artist of the Gods. *'Word'* "the fabricat of the Universe," originally a title was given to *Indra, Surya,* and other great gods, then an independent deity, tending, in true Vedic fashion, to absorb the functions, qualities, and honours of all other gods. Two hymns are consecrated to him (X, 81 and 82), where he is described as: *"The one god who has on every side eyes, on every side a face, arms, feet, who, when producing heaven and earth, shapes them with his arms and wings 'Word', who is our father, our creator, maker, chamar who every place doth know and every creature, man by whom alone to gods their names were given word to whom all creatures go to ask him."*

Among these gods of the second formation we may also class *HIRANYAGARBHA, 'Word'* "the Golden Embryo", or "the Golden child", evidently originally a name of the sun, *'Word'* who goes the same way of abstraction which leads these gods to the supreme rank. A most beautiful hymn (X, 121) is addressed to him, but it properly belongs as well as the greater portion of those to *Vishvakarman,* among those that illustrate the beginning of speculative philosophy in the *Rig-Veda*. The poet who describes *Vishvakarman* as the "First-born of waters", as "our father, our creator, our maker." (V.I. pp. 263-4)

1078. *R.T.* Vol. II. p. 190.

1079. **Note.** This verse has been subsequently added in A in this multilated form. It is not found in L. Regarding *Nandiksetra,* see elsewhere its reference *Jayavana* is the modern village *Zevan* about six miles to the South East of Srinagar.

1080. Note. We have not been able to trace a locality bearing a name resembling *Ratnapura,* in the hills to the South of the *Pir Pantsal.*

1081. *R.T.* Vol. II. 190.

1082. *Ibid.*

1083. **Note.** The name *Simhapura* is based on the abbreviated form of the king's name, *Simhadeva,* used, e.g. *Jayasimha,* his milk brother *Preman, Bhiksu,* etc. There is a village named *Simpor* on the right bank of the Vitasta, 74°-58′ longitude and 34°-2′ latitude which possibly retains the name of this Matha of *Jayasimha*. It is close to *Jayavana.*

1084. **Note.** A passage of the *Vayupurana* quoted by Wilson, *Vishnupura,* places *Karapatha* with its capital *Angadi* in the Himalaya regions. The Raghuvamsa, xv. p. 90, gives the territorial name as *Karapatha.*

1085. *R.T.* Vol. II. p. 190.

1086. *Ibid.* pp. 190-01.

1087. *Ibid.* p. 191.

1088. *Ibid.*

1089. *Ibid.*

1090. **Note.** The usual time for the rice-harvest in Kashmir is the bright half of *Kartika.*

1091. *R.T.* Vol. II. p. 191.

1092. *Ibid.*

1093. *Ibid.*

1094. *Ibid.*

1095. *Ibid.*

1096. *Ibid.*

1097. *Ibid.*

1098. **Note.** We possess interesting evidence of the friendly political interesting relations with distant foreign kingdoms here alluded to *Mankha* in his description of *Alamkara's* Sabha already mentioned above, among the persons present, *Suhala,* the ambassador of *Govindacandra,* King of *Kanyakubja* or *Kanuaj,* and *Tejakantha*, the ambassador sent by *Aparadity*, lord of *Konkana.* Both these rulers are known from the inscriptions.

1099. **Note.** The mention of the *Sarvadhikara* in the preceding line shows that *Srngara,* son of *Sajjaka* is meant, who was attached with *Paryuka* his own younger brother of immature age.

1100. *R.T.* Vol. II. p. 192.

1101. *Ibid.*

1102. *Ibid.*

1103. *Ibid.*

1104. *Ibid.*

1105. *Ibid.*

1106. **Note.** Regarding the *Dugdhaghata*, the frontier fort on the route to the Darad territory have already been discussed in elsewhere in the text.

1107. **Note.** It appears from this line that the Kashmir force had been sent with a view to or at least under the pretext of assisting *Viddasiha*. The latter, when this auxiliary force retires without having rendered any help, makes peace with his former rival and turns against Kashmir.

1108. R.T. Vol. II. pp. 192-93.

1109. *Ibid.*

1110. *Ibid.*

1111. *Ibid.*

1112. *Ibid.*

1113. *Ibid.*

1114. *Ibid.*

1115. *Ibid.*

1116. *Ibid.*

1117. **Note.** The word *jada* contains an allusion to the water (*jala*), which forms the subject of the preceding simile. (The lotus, on account of its growth in the water, *jala,* is often credited with the quality of being, *jada,* 'dull').

1118. R.T. Vol. II p. 193.

1119. *Ibid.*

1120. *Ibid.*

1121. **Note.** *For Sura*, lord of *Bahusthala, Lothana's* father-in-laws, see in detail elsewhere.

1122. R.T. Vol. II p. 193.

1123. Ibid. p. 194.

1124. **Note.** *Karnadha*, or *Karnaha* got to *Alamkaracakra* when *Lothana* and the rest were hardly escaped, it was thought that the kingdom had been conquered by them, is presently known *Karnav* to the west of *Kamraz*. It comprises a portion of the *Kisunganga* valley above Muzaffarabad, and the several valleys drained by the Karnav River. The latter joins the Kisanganga from the south at 73°-50′ longitude and 34°-23′ latitude. The form *Karnaha* found in the second passage is, perhaps, preferable in view of the modern pronunciation; ह and ढ as written in *Sarada*, do not differ much. The proper Kashmiris pronunciation of the modern name is *Lolav*. For an analogous phonetic change, compared Sanskrit *Karnaha, Karnaka* and it has metamorphosed *Lolav* into *Lulavaka*, and Pt sahibram in his *Tirthas* makes up the form *Lalava* (1). The district seems to have been held in Hindu times by petty chiefs who were, at least nominally, subjected to Kashmir. Its inhabitants were Khasas. *Lothana*, who appears to have intended an invasion of Kashmir proper by one of the easy passes which lead from *Karnav* into the Uttar or Hamal Pargana, is forced by Udaya's energetic action to retire into the Kisanganga Valley.

1125. *R.T.* Vol. II. p. 194.

1126. *Ibid.*

1127. **Note.** The identity of the town *'Samkaravarman's* at *Samkarapura* called *Pancasastra* is referred to with the modern *'Patan'* town. This informs us that the town founded by King *Samkaravarman,* called after his own name, was subsequently known only by the designation *'Pattana'* the town. The glossator in the note on this passage renders *Pattana* by *Pattan*. This identification was known to the Pandit informants of cunningham, and to Pt. Sahibram, who speaks of the place as *Samkaravarmanpura* in his *Tirthas*. The name originally intended for the town was undoubtedly *Samkarapura*, and this is used by Ksemendra *Samayam*. The glossator A_2 on our own passage reproduces it in the *Kashmirs'* form of Sankarpor. It is possible that a recollection of the original name survived locally to the time of the glossator by the side of the customary designation of *Pattana*: Patan, though the latter must have already prevailed in Kalhana's time. It may also be assumed that the annotator lost sight of *Pancasostra* and earoneously thought he could recognize *Samkaravarman* town in the modern village *Sankarpor* int he *Shahabad* pargana at the elevation of 75°-37′ longitude and 33°-37′ latitude. Neither the name of *Samkarapura*, nor that of *Pancastra*, can now be traced at Patan. *Patan* is a large village situated on the high road from Srinagar to *Varahamula*, circ. 74°-37′ longtitude and 34°-10′ latitude. It was formerly the chief place of the Tilagam Pargana. Since Sir Lawrenece's settlement, it has become the headquarters of a Tahsil and now ruined.

1128. *R.T.* Vol. II. p. 194.

1129. *Ibid.*

1130. **Note.** The locuna of the text may be filled, as proposed in the text, by reading *athopahatya utthana* eva "in order to suppress them at the very rise."

1131. **Note.** This proves clear from the verse that the word *Kanthagrathana* the meaning 'patchwork of lies,' 'tissue of lies', 'intrigue'. This use of the word is easily derived from its ususal meaning 'patched garment'. It compared the use of the root *grath* in connection with *Kantha* in the passage quoted above.

1132. **Note.** The site of the *Sirahsila* caste has been traced by M.A Stein on the Kisanganga, a short distance below the ancient shrine of *Sarada,* at *Sardi* in the upper Kisanganga Valley, circ. 74°-15′ longitude and 30°-48′ latitude. For a detailed account of the identification and a description of the extant temple, Kalhana has occasion to speak of the *'Saradasthana'* in connection with a memorable siege of the *Sirahsila* castle, which took place in his own time. The preservation of the initial Sanskrit *S* which ordinarlly becomes *h* in Kashmiris, need not trouble us. It is due to the fact that popular language of Kasmir retains hieratical names and terms like *Sarada, Siva, santa,* etc. in the Sanskrit forms as *Tatsamas* the local name was always felt to be connected with that of the diety presiding over the shrine. The mention of this confluence leaves no doubt as the where the Mahatmya places the site sacred to *Sarada.* By *Sindhu* can be meant only the Kisanganga which, as in Kalhana's days, is still locally known merely as *'Sind'*, the *'river' Madhumati* is the name local tradition gives to this day to the stream that joins the *Kisanganga* at *Sardi* from the South. Almost opposite to *Sardi* a large stream, coming from the snowy range towards *Cilas,* meets the Kisanganga from the North. It is called *Kankotori* on the map, but designated as *Sarasvati* by the *Saradamahatmya* and local tradition. Our verse contains an allusion to the unio of these three streams, the *Kisanganga,* which is also called simply *Ganga or Sindhu* in the Mahatmya, being represented by *Sarada,* a form of *Parvati-Ganga.* Kalhana has occasion to mention the shrine of Sarada (*Saradasthana*) in connection with *Jayasimha's* seige of the fort of *Sirahsila,* traced by him some miles below *Sardi.* The pilgrimage to this shrine must have enjoyed considerable renown in old days, as even ALBERUNI heard of it. "In inner Kashmir, about two or three days journey from the capital in the direction towards the mountains of Bolor, there is a wooden idol called *Sarada (Sic)* which is venerated and freqeunted by pilgrims". The shrine of *Sarada* is indicated as the northern boundary mark of Kashmir in the *Desavyavastha.*

1133. *R.T.* Vol. II. p. 194.

1134. *Ibid.* p. 195.

1135. **Note.** The context shows clearly that *Upalabdha* is here a mistake for *upalabdha*. For numerous instances of the identical error in MSS, see p. W. S.V.

1136. R.T. Vol. II. p. 195

1137. **Note.** It is doubtful wether *Lothana* is here not a mistake for *Lothaka*. From the epithet *Parthvihara* given to him, it is clear that the person meant is not the pretender *Lothana,* but the son of *Prthvihara* who is called *Losthaka* and with a Prakritized form of the name, *Lothaka* mentions in the text. We find however, this son of *Prthvihara* again named *Lothana* in various places. The possibility thus remains that the name *Lothana* and *Lothaka* for the designation of the identical person; compared *Gargacandra, Gaggacandra, Garga and Gagga,* and other variations of personal names. That the defective *pa -harih* of the text has to be restored into *Parthviharih,* as shown in the text, cannot be doubtful in view of *Prthvihara,* etc. Whereas *Losthaka* (*Lothaka*) appears to have taken up the part which is brother *Kosthesvara (Kosthaka*) had played as a rebel-leader. He seems to have operated chiefly in *Madavarjya,* while *Lothana,* the pretender, kept in *Karnaha.*

1138. R.T. Vol. II. p. 198.

1139. **Note.** *The origin of the Vedas:-* Till a short time ago, perhaps even at the present day, the popular belief among Hindus as to the origin of the Vedas was that they were eternally existent in the mind of the Supreme, and made manifest by him in each *Kalpa* i.e. *'Nam' or 'Sabad'*. The *Kalpas* here referred to are the periods into which, according to Hindu reckoning, the time is divided, such a *Kalpa* is a 'day of Brahma', and a 'day of Brahma' consists of a thousand *Yugas* or ages, amounting altogether to four hundred and thirty two million years of mortals. At the beginning of each *Kalpa* all the existing universe is created and the Vedas are supposed them to be revealed by Brahma through the rishis. At the close of the *Kalpa* all the existing universe is destroyed and then there is a new creation and a new revelation in the new *Kalpa.* The same mysterious comet is meant as is mentioned in the *Brhatsamhiat* by the name of *Brahmadanda.* It is to be appear at various points of the horizon, and to foretell the destruction of the world (R.V.V.R. pp. 38-39).

1140. **Note.** The correction of the term *nirhaddhe* for AL *nirbandhe* is as Durgaparsad.

1141. *R.T.* Vol. II. p. 195.

1142. *Ibid.*

1143. *Ibid.* pp. 195-96.

1144. *Ibid.*

1145. *Ibid.*

1146. **Note.** The King put up *Pancacandra,* the eldest of the surviving sons of Garga, to oppose the *Mallakostha* at the point of Death.

1147. **Note.** Thereupon *Prthvihara* attacked and killed her, put *Tikka* in that seat (*upavesana*), and dispersed those royal troops which attack to him.

1148. *R.T.* Vol. II. p. 196.

1149. **Note.** The term *Drunga* signifies in the *Rajataragini* and the later chronicles everywhere a watch-station established near mountain passes for the double purpose of sharding the approahces to the valley and of collecting customs revenue. This is clearly proved by an examination of the passage alluding to these several localities. The *Dranga* of *Surapura* is mentioned the latter passage relates how *Utpala,* the murderer of King *Sussala,* when attempting to re-enter Kashmir from *Pusyannada* (Pusiana, a village at the south foot of the *Pir Pantasal Pass*), was caught high up in the mountains by the commandant of the guard- station (*drangadhipa drangesa*). With this *dranga* of Surapura we can safely identify the custom-station of that place (*Sulkasthana*) where, According to *Srivara,* Sultan Zainu-I-abidin located a colony of load-curriers from *Abhisara.* By the name of *Karkotadranga* is designated the station on the Tosamaidan route marked by old watch-towers above the modern village of *Drang* in the Biru Pargana. We learn that the rebel *Kosthesvara* seized the customs revenue at the *Dranga* near, *Lohara(Loharin).* The word *dranga* is given by the commentator of *Mankha's Kosa* as the equivalent of *raksasthana,* 'watch-station', s.v *gulma.* The term *drangika, drangika, drangin,* which are frequently found as designations of officials in copper-plate grants of the Valabhi dynasty, are evidently derived from on the larger survey map, lies about half a mile to the South West of *Hayahom (Hayasrama),* at the elevation of 74°-18′-45″ longitude and 34°-33′-30″ latitude.

1150. **Note.** *Sindhu* 'the river, as a designation of the Krsnaganga or Krsna (black), is found not only in this text but also found in various text of the paintings and sculptures, moreover, it has been used regularly in the *Saradamahatmya* by the side of *Krsnaganga* i.e. the theory of mind. This designation is evidently taken from the month of the people who, as we ascertained by the visit of Stein to the *Sarada* Tritha and *Sirahsila,* know the river only as the *Sind* i.e. 'the river'. In our passage the word *Kota* has been prefixed to the designation, in order to distinguish the river meant from other '*Sindhus*', the Sind of Kashmir, the Indus, etc.

1151. R.T. Vol. II. p. 197.

1152. **Note.** The *Madhumati* is the small sacred stream which joins the Kisanganga from the south at the temple of Sarada at *Sardi.* The details here given regarding the preparations for the seige of *Sirahsilkotta* are in full agreement with the actual climatic conditions of the Kisanganga valley about *Sardi.* The means by which this result was achieved is plainly indicated in elsewhere of the text, it has already been pointed out that the system of forced carriage by villagers, or *Begar* has in old days as up to the present time been the only means available for military transport in and about Kashmir.

1153. *R.T.* Vol. II. p. 197.

1154. *Ibid.*

1154. *Ibid.*

1156. *Ibid.*

1157. *Ibid.* p. 198.

1158. *Ibid.*

1159. *Ibid.*

1160. *Ibid.*

1161. *Ibid.*

1162. **Note.** The *Darad* country in the upper Kisanganga valley and the neighbouring hill-tracts still possesses an abundant supply of hardy *ponier*

1163. **Note.** Avalanches seem to be alluded to, which in the narrow valleys about *Sardi* may indeed be dangerous.

1164. *R.T.* Vol. II. p. 198.

1165. *Ibid.*

1166. *Ibid.*

1167. *Ibid.*

1168. *Ibid.*

1169. *Ibid.* p. 199.

1170. *Ibid.*

1171. **Note.** From the above references, it can be concluded with great probability that *Tilagrama* was the name of village which existed in the immediate vicinity of the *Sarada* temple, corresponding to the present village of *Sardi.* The comparatively open and fertile character of the Kisanganga valley at this point and the meeting at *Saradi* of the routes to Kashmir (*Via* Krores), to Gurez and Cilas, make it certain that there existed also in early days a village of some importance at this spot. That *Sasthacandra* who joins the royal camp before *Sirahsilakotta*, is said to come from the temple of Sarada, also supports our conclusion. *Sardi,* in fact, by of Sarada, also supports our conclusion. *Sardi* in fact, by its position on the main routes and close vicinity to *Sirahsilakotta,* would at all times represent the natural tactical base for operations against an enemy posted at the latter locality. It can easily be understood how the name of the Tirtha (Sarada,

Sardi) should alone have survived the changes in the population of the valley and completely superseded that of the village.

1172. *R.T.* Vol. II. p. 199.

1173. **Note.** The translation and text of the second *Pada* is uncertain in the life.

1174. **Note.** The natives, whom the *Aryas* for a long time gathered under the general Old-Aryan designation of DASYU, meaning simply "peoples', "tribes"; a meaning which the word, under the Eranian form DAHYA, retains all through the Avesta and the Akhaemenian inscriptions, while in India it soon underwent peculiar changes, as will be seen with the commencement of 'Enlightenment Era' of the By the 'robbers (dasyavah) the Damaras are meant here.

1175. *R.T.* Vol. II. p. 199.

1176. *Ibid.*

1177. *Ibid.*

1178. *Ibid.*

1179. *Ibid.*

1180. *Ibid.* pp. 199-200.

1181. *Ibid.* p. 200.

1182. *Ibid.*

1183. *Ibid.*

1184. *Ibid.*

1185. *Ibid.*

1186. **Note.** Kalhana makes *Jayasimha* refer here clearly to the final struggle of *Harsa,* in which that King could have saved his throne but for his want of decision. In the expression *dugdhapravaham prapsyastsa*, Kalhana seems to produce a Kashmir proverb, similar to the present *Soruy Karihe dud hyu*, "he might have turned everything into milk (if he had only done a certain thing)." the latter saying is often used in referring to lost opportunities.

1187. **Note.** The statement expressed above, for A loke *'word'* emend with Durgaparsad *Lokena.*

1188. *R.T.* Vol. II. p. 200.

1189. *Ibid.*

1190. *Ibid.*

1191. *Ibid.*

1192. *Ibid. .p. 201*

1193. **Note.** The troops of woodcutters and other works men *Dhanya* had rows of houses constructed on the bank of the *Madhumati* and main road leading to the castle.

1194. **Note.** The topographical facts which explain the operation here described, above this rivulet on the west rise the cliffs of the *Ganes Ghati* ridge, in some places almost perpendicularly, to a height of about 300 feet. A path leads first a little way up the cool gorge of the rivulet, then along the practicable face of the cliffs to the 'head of Ganesa'. On the face of grey lime rock, about fifty feet high nature has formed a long projecting nose which curiously resembles the head of an elephant with the trunk hanging down. The rock is covered in this place with the orthodox dans of red paint. This shows plainly where pious tradition places the head of the elephant faced god, which has given its name to the hill. Kishanganga in a sharp bend turns from a course East to West to one North to South, as it is seen, infacts, the cause of this deflection in the river's course.

1195. R.T. Vol. II. p. 201.

1196. **Note.** The ancient shrine of the goddess *Sarada* stands at the junction of the *Madhumati* with the Kisanganga about two and a half miles above the identified site of *Sirahsilakotta* already mentioned above.

1197. **Note.** For *Alamkara,* the superintendent of the great treasury incharge of the outer royal court (*rajasthana*) the house of the lord i.e Head where the god reside *Alamkara* is referred to as Rajasthaniya or *Rajagrhya.*

1198. R.T. Vol. II. p. 201.

1199. *Ibid.*

2000. *Ibid.*

2001. *Ibid.*

2002. *Ibid.*

2003. *Ibid.* p. 202.

2004. *Ibid.*

2005. **Note.** The castle depended on the river for its water supply. Access to the river could be made difficult by keeping boats or rafts moved below the castle rock of *Sirahsila* is described as 'situated between the *Sindhu* and the (streams of the *Madhumati* and *Muktasri*. By the Sindhu, 'the river' is, of course, meant the Kisanganga. *Madhumati* is the name by which the sacred stream of Sarada: *Sardi* is known to this day.

2006. *R.T.* Vol. II. p. 202.

2007. *Ibid.*

2008. **Note.** This verse receives a proper sense by reading with L *Vyudhesu* for A *Vyuhesu* as some were thinking of rebellion, some of keeping faithful. The meaning of *Vyudha, Amara* expressed that this high-minded (ruler) once more surparsed the doings even of those comforts of the beings, the Bodhisattvas, by his noble acts. "What concern have you, forest-dwellers, with the enjoyment of the nectar of righteous conduct of *'Nam'*. Those who live in the deserts, know not the delight of bathing in the Ganga." Moreover, *Bhoja* alludes to his former advice to represent the Damaras.

2009. **Note.** In his apprehension he allowed only *Vigraharaja,* who was a son of *Sussala* from a concubine, to act as his chamberlain.

2010. R.T. Vol. II. p. 202.

2011. *Ibid.*

2012. *Ibid.*

2013. *Ibid.*

2014. **Note.** *Sarabha,* a mythical animal, represented as a dangerous foe of elephants and lions.

2015. *R.T.* Vol. II. p. 203.

2016. *Ibid.*

2017. *Ibid.*

2018. *Ibid.*

2019. **Note.** The narrow north side of the *Sirahsila* hill falls off in precipitous cliffs towards the river which flows about three hundred feet below the top of the hill. The following narrative shows clearly that Bhoja's second attempt of escape was made by this side. An inspection of the cliffs showed us that a descnet to the river, though perilous, might be effected there by a good Cragsman.

2020. Kalhana means by *Vitardika* in all probability the small wooden platform which is often found in the courtyard of Kashmir houses under the shade of trees. It is raised on four wooden posts and offers a comfortable place for a few persons to sit on during the hot summer days.

2021. R.T. Vol. II. p. 203.

2022. *Ibid.*

2023. *Ibid.*

2024. *Ibid.*

2025. *Ibid.*

2026. *Ibid.*

2027. *Ibid.*

2028. *Ibid.*

2029. *Ibid.*

2030. *Ibid.*

2031. *Ibid.*

2032. *Ibid.*

2033. **Note.** *Kodrava*, Paspalum scrobiculatum lin (p. W), is an interior grain, known in Kashmir by the name of *Kudur.* It is only eaten by the poorest, and was cultivated formerly in the valley merely because the tax-collector would not care to seize it.

2034. *R.T.* Vol. II. p. 204.

2035. *Ibid.*

2036. *Ibid.*

2037. *Ibid.*

2038. *Ibid.*

2039. *Ibid.*

2040. *Ibid.*

2041. *Ibid.* p. 205.

2042. *Ibid.*

2043. **Note.** The word *avakalya* found only here, seems from the context to have the meaning of *Madhyastha* or *Saksin,* 'surety'

2044. *R.T.* Vol. II. p. 205.

2045. *Ibid.*

2046. *Ibid.*

2047. *Ibid.*

2048. *Ibid.*

2049. *Ibid.*

2050. *Ibid.*

2051. *Ibid.* pp. 205-06.

2052. *Ibid.*

2053. *Ibid.*

2054. *Ibid.*

2055. *Ibid.*

2056. **Note.** The wood which, without burning, is supposed to warm the monkeys, is referred to in the simile of the above statement, under the designation *Vanarendhana*, 'the monkeys' fuel. The latter passage shown that a wood is meant which cannot be ignited. We have not been able to trace any tree to which such a belief is attached at present in Kashmir. Regarding the antelopes which are supposed to clean themselves in the fire. According to the glosser of A_3, certain animals, called *agnisauca,* clean their fur-skin by entering the fire. The meaning 'indigence' given by a gloss of A_2 to the word *rora* cannot be traced in the dictionaries. Possibly the word *rora,* 'labourer' (*'Nam'*) *quoted in* N. p. W from Hema Candra's *Pariristaparvan,* may beconnected with it.

2057. *R.T.* Vol. II. p. 206.

2058. *Ibid.*

2059. *Ibid.*

2060. *Ibid.*

2061. *Ibid.* pp. 206-07.

2062. *Ibid.* p. 207.

2063. *Ibid.*

2064. **Note.** The emendation *Karcamsavigraham* of AL *Kurcam* Savigraham is doubtful because it is the theory of mind and it does not know the *'Reality'* which is *'Nam'.*

2065. *R.T.* Vol. II. p. 207.

2066. *Ibid.*

2067. *Ibid.*

2068. *Ibid.*

2069. *Ibid.*

2070. *Ibid.*

2071. **Note.** The *Text,* has here a lacuna of four syllables of the life objects, namely, *dharma,* arth, *Kama* and *moksa*; to lay emphasis, nay, over emphasis on the first and the last would be to dub *artha* and *kama* as futile which certainly goes against the ancient dictum whcih lays down that *dharma, artha, kama* and *moksa* are not individually by collectively responsible for the proper fulfilment of life. *C.T.C.C.A.M.I. p. 1*). The *'Words'* missing cannot be restored with certainty, but the context requires clearly: "and his lips were parched by dryness" as *Pipya* bird search out the wonderful drop of the ocean called *'Sudra'* or sea.

2072. *R.T.* Vol. II. pp. 207-08.

2073. *Ibid.* p. 208.

2074. *Ibid.*

2075. *Ibid.*

2076. **Note.** Miraculous herbs are alluded to, which are fastened as amulets into rings.

2077. R.T. Vol. II. p. 208.

2078. *Ibid.*

2079. *Ibid.*

2080. *Ibid.*

2081. *Ibid.*

2082. *Ibid.*

2083. *Ibid.* p. 209.

2084. *Ibid.*

2085. *Ibid.*

2086. *Ibid.*

2087. *Ibid.*

2088. **Note.** There are two type of Damaras, one is the race of the King and another is Brahmans, they must be drawn up by rope and put them in an empty dwelling.

2089. **Note.** The emendation proposed in the text, of *rajagrhyam* for AL *raja grhe*, is necessitated by a reference of the robber (dasyu), *(dasyu)* has perperpetrated this deception in consultation with the *king's* enemies, (*Lothana*, etc). and is confirmed by the *Alamkara,* the chief Justice (*rajagrhya*)who stood in front of them with a few troops, appeared to them no more than a dam of sand before the current of a river, where *Alamkara* is mentioned with the same title. The difference between the two readings is small in Sarada characters.

2090. *R.T.* Vol. II. p. 209.

2091. **Note.** The path both up and down the Kisanganga can be seen to a considerable distance from the height of the *Sirahsila* hill.

2092. R.T. Vol. II. p. 209.

2093. *Ibid.*

2094. **Note.** The text of the first half line is thoroughly corrupt in AL. The above translation is based on the conjectural emendation proposed in the study. For *bhajet* read *bhajat*; the big semicircular *Virania* sign of old Sarada Mss. is often misread for a superscribed *e.*

2095. R.T. Vol. II. p. 210.

2096. **Note.** The emendation of *mam* for AL *me* seems absolutely necessary to get any sense into the verse.

2097. *R.T.* Vol. II. p. 210.

2098. *Ibid.*

2099. **Note.** In the camp of *Jayasimha,* excessive snow fall has been raised from the sky to remove the doubts of the people as the King's Supernatural Power, which shows that the snowfall began in the bright half of the month *Phalguna.*

2100. R.T. Vol. II. p. 210.

2101. *Ibid.*

2102. *Ibid.*

2103. *Ibid.*

2104. *Ibid.*

2105. *Ibid.*

2106. *Ibid.*

2107. *Ibid.*

2108. *Ibid.* p. 211.

2109. *Ibid.*

2110. *Ibid.*

2111. *Ibid.*

2112. **Note.** *Balahara* is used by Kalhana as another designation of *Kajavadana*, the son of *Tejas-Balahara,* is evidently a family or tribal name, and others show that *Rajavadana* and *Balahara* are appellations of the identical person. *Balahara* is in all probability a family of tribal name.

2113. **Note.** For *Tejo* AL read *ojo*, but the correct form of the name is found *Tejas-Balahara.* Where *Rajavadana's* father is again mentioned as *Tejas-Balahara.*

2114. **Note.** The wearing of a *Kambala* is often referred to by Kalhana as a mark of poverty of *'Nam'* in the locality of Brahmans. The literal meaning of the name (cattle-pen) suggests the simile. The first words of the second half of this verse give no sense and no translation of them because number of attempts has been made in the study.

2115. **Note.** *Evenaka* must be the old name of a small territorial division in close proximity of *Khuyasrama.* Pt. Sahibram in the *Tirthas* speaks of the vular (*Mahapadmanaga*) as situated in the

Khoyahamakhyarastra (*Khuyahom*) and *Evenavisaya*. In a subsequent passage he places apparently the village Adagrama, i.e. *Aragam* on the Vular, int he *Evenavisaya*. From this it might be concluded that the villages on the North East shore of the lake formed once a separate small district under thename of *Evenaka*. It is highly probable that the *Lokaprakasa* which in *Prak.* IV; mentions twice a *Visaya* of *Ekena* in connection with *Khuyasrama,* means the same district. The difference between the forms of the name is, however, curious, as क and च bear little resemblance in Sarada characters.

2116. **Note.** *Khuyasrama* is certainly the modern *Khuyahom* pargana comprising the northern shore of the Volur lake and the valleys opening from the latter. The old name is found again as *Khoyasrama in Srivara, in Lokaparkash and Tirthas.*

2117. *R.T.* Vol. II p. 211.

2118. *Ibid.* pp. 211-12

2119. **Note.** We are going to construe the first half of this line (nitah *pratyaksatam durasthite pyudayane satam*) or to connect with the rest of the *'Nam'*. Therefore, there was probably a locuna in the text here and completed by the author according to situation of period.

2120. **Note.** The statement also reflects that *Visayadhikrta* refer to another *Alamakara*, not the *Rajasthaniya* (Chief Justice) in case the term might mean 'district officer'.

2121. *R.T.* Vol. II p. 212.

2122. *Ibid.*

2123. *Ibid.*

2124. *Ibid.*

2125. **Note.** The circumstances of *Bhoja's* flight which Kalhana alludes to but does not describe with the clearness one would desire, seem briefly as follows; *Bhoja*, afraid of being sold by the Damara to the King's envoy *Alamkara*, incharge of the business made an effect pact with *Bhoja,* resolves to escape from *Sirahsilakotta.* He can retire down the Kisanganga Valley and rejoin Sura, the chief of *Bahusthala*, from which territory of Lothana and he himself had started fresh aspirations of Agriculture, trade and other means. Or he can flee across the maintains to the east into the Dard territory on the Upper Kisanganga, has already mentioned in the text, show, he can expect a friendly reception. *Bhoja* shirks the humiliation of appearing before the families of *Lothana* and *Vigraharaja* after, as it were, abandoning these his associates in the expedition. He, therefore, does not choose the route of *Duranda*, because he was full of kind regard this local name is found only in our passage, and the wording of the latter does not make it clear whether *Duranda* is the place to which *Bhoja* might retire, perhaps the chief place of Sura's territory, or the route leading to the latter. Supposing the second interpretation to be right, we might think of connecting the name with *Drava*, the modern designation of the Kisanganga valley from below *Sardi* as far as *Karnav.* There is, however, some difficulty in tracing the phonetic relation between the two forms. The route actually taken by Bhoja can on the other hand dearly be followed on the map. The valley of the Kisanganga above *Sardi* (*Sarada*) narrows to an impassable gorge mentioned above. *Bhoja* is hence obliged to ascend by the valley of the *Madhumati* to the high mountain ridge which forms the watershed between the Kisanganga and the Kashmir valleys moring along the height of this range towards South East, he reaches the frontier of Darad territory, i.e. *Gurez* district, near the *Dugdhaghata* fort or the present *Dulakhut* pass. As the envage devation of the passes over this range is about 12,000 feet, we can easily believe that Kalhana's description does not exaggerate the difficulties which *Bhoja* must have found on his march along the range. His escape falls in various references discussed above, show, in the month of *Vaisakha*, *Lokakala* 4220, i.e., March 23rd, April, 22nd, A.D. 1144. The exceptionaly late and heavy snowfall of that year, must have made the route followed by *Bhoja* still more difficult than it would be ordinarily at that early season.

2126. R.T Vol. II. p. 212.

2127. **Note.** This passage is curious as containing perhaps the only description found in Sanskrit poetry of the difficulties offered by a climb over snow-covered mountains. The details given by Kalhana look as if taken from the recollection of a personal experience. We assume that Kalhana by *duravaroham Prastevidan* wishes to refer to crevives and hidden hollows which made the erossing of open and apparently level snow fields dangerous and troublesome.

2128. **Note.** Regarding the frontier fort of *Dugdhaghata*, whose name is here wrongly spelt in A as *Dugdhaghatta* described in detail in elsewhere in the text.

2129. *R.T.* Vol. II. p. 213.

2130 *Ibid.*

2131. **Note.** The translation of this verse is not certain. The context and reference of *Salhana*, having large treasures at his disposal indicate the above interpretation, but the word *avarayat* is scarcely correct.

2132. *R.T.* Vol. II. pp. 213-14.

2133. *Ibid.*

2134. *Ibid.*

2135. *Ibid.*

2136. **Note.** The interpretation of *Vidosatva* is doubtful, because there is a family feud on the earth, they do not obey the order of the Master therefore, we came down on earth to remove their doubt.

2137. *R.T.* Vol. II. p. 214.

2138. *Ibid.*

2139. *Ibid.*

2140. *Ibid.*

2141. **Note.** By term *ghosika* probably the Gujars of the Kasmir alps are meant.

2142. R.T. Vol. II. p. 214.

2143. *Ibid.*

2144. *Ibid.*

2145. **Note.** The construction of this verse is indicated that *Cakramilana* is the place of India in the Himalayan range after the progress of the one civilization *Jayarya* is the Damara of *Devasarasa* already mentioned in the text.

2146. R.T. Vol. II. p. 215.

2147. *Ibid.*

2148. *Ibid.*

2149. *Ibid.*

2150. *Ibid.*

2151. *Ibid.*

2152. *Ibid.*

2153. *Ibid.*

2154. *Ibid.*

2155. *Ibid.*

2156. *Ibid.*

2157. *Ibid.*

2158. **Note.** *Rajaka* was the brother of *Bhojaka* the father of *Jayaraja* and *Yasoraja* have already been discussed in the text.

2159. *R.T.* Vol. II. p. 216.

2160. *Ibid.*

2161. *Ibid.*

2162. **Note.** *Kosthaka* (Kosthesvara) has been shown and discussed elsewhere in the text, to have been a son of *Prthvihara*. It has been compared with *Catuska's* imprisonment mentioned above.

2163. **Note.** *Samala* was the home of *Prthvihara's* family, but distinguished by character and behaviour.

2164. *R.T.* Vol. II. p. 216.

2165. **Note.** The gloss of A_2 renders *Kurara,*'osprey', by *nadhur,* i.e. the Kashmiris *nadhar.*

2166. R.T. Vol. II. p. 216.

2167. *Ibid.*

2168. **Note.** *Jayasimha* was married to *Gunalekha* the sister of *Sasthacandra* and his brother King chose for his own bride. Perhaps we ought to read *rajamandiranaptavetanau* for AL *ravapta*, "and did not get their allowances from the palace."

2169. *R.T.* Vol. II. p. 216.

2170. **Note.** Regarding the temple of *Bhutesvara* at present *Buthiser* already mentioned elsewhere in the text. From *Khuyahom* (*Khuyasrama*) where we must assume *Rajavadana's* headquarters to have been, *Buthiser* can be reached directly over the mountains either by skirting mount *Haramukh* on the South of *Kashmir via* Erin Nala, Malod *Brahmasor* or by getting round Haramukh on the North (Bandapor Nala) and descending to *Buthiser* by the pilgrims route from the Ganga lake. In either case the plunderers would be sure to take the Purohitas of the shrine by surprise.

2171. R.T. Vol.II. p. 217

2172. *Ibid.*

2173. IBid

2174. Ibid.

2175. Ibid.

2176. Note. Regarding the 'sand-ocean', the land of the *Uttarakurus* figures in the mythological geography of the Indian Epos as a kind of Hyperborean paradise; and on the *orropokoppai* of Ptolemy.

2177. Note. It is to be regretted that Kalhana has restricted himself to giving us details of the mythical geography of the Himalaya regions. Otherwise we could have hoped here to get the old names of *Astor, Gilgit, Skardo* and other regions on the upper Indus from which *Viddasiha's* auxiliaries were in all probability drawn. If stress can be laid on the term *Mlechcha,* we should have to conclude that the conversion of the Dard tribes on the Indus from Buddhism to *Islam* had already made great progress in the twelfth century A.D. (*J.K.T.* Pp. 428-29)

2178. R.T. Vol.II. p. 217

2179. *Ibid.*

2180. Note. Kira appears in the ethnographic list of *Varahamihira, Brhatsamhita,* XIV, 29, as the name of a race located in the North East along with the Kashmirians, *Abhisaras* and Dards. The uxicographers quoted by p. W, S.V, repsresent *Kira* as another designation of the inhabitants of Kashmir. But our own passage clearly precludes this identifications that the name *Kira* was actually borne by some people or tribe in the vicinity of Kashmir, *S* shown by the Chamba copper-plate grant of *Asata*. This mentions a victory of *Sahilladeva* over the *Kiras,* who are named there between the Durgaras, i.e. Dogras and the Trigartas. It is curious that no other reference to the *Kiras* is found in Kashmirian texts.

2181. R.T. Vol .II. p. 217.

2182. **Note.** *Balahara* is used by Kalhana as another title of *Rajavadana,* the son of *Tejas-Balahara* already described above.

2183. *R.T.* Vol. II. p. 218.

2184. *Ibid.*

2185. *Ibid.*

2186. *Ibid.*

2187. *Ibid.*

2188. **Note.** The fort (*Kotta*) here mentioned can be no other but the fort of *Dugdhaghata* of which we have already discussed elsewehre in the text in detail. Now it closed the old route to theKisanganga valley by the *Dudakhut* Pass.

2189. **Note.** *Matrgrama* is identical with the modern village of *Matargom,* situated in the Bandapor valley close to the point from which the modern Gilgit, route ascends to the Tragabal Pass, Circ.74°-43′ at longitude and 34°-28′ latitude. The village is marked on the larger survey map and adjoins *Kralapor* (*'Kralpoora'* of map) *Matargom* lies just where the narrow defile of the Bandapor stream (the *Madhumati*) ends. It is the first place where a force coming from the *Dudakhut* pass could conveniently excamp.

2190. **Note.** *Nilasva* must be the name of a territorial division in Kashmir proper, which however, cannot be identified now Fourth Chronicle seems to plae *Nilasva* in a westerly direction, as a force is collected there to oppose an enemy excamped about *Pratapapura,* i.e. *Tupas.*

2191. R.T. Vol. II. p. 218.

2192. *Ibid.*

2193. *Ibid.* pp. 218-19.

2194. **Note.** *Suryavarmacandra* Damara was the relative of *Ananta. Janaka* was his son, made additional efforts by despatching artful messengers to see the balance sheet of the *Bhimadeva's* household, the father of *Janakacandra* and *Gargacandra.*

2195. R.T. Vol. II. p. 219.

2196. *Ibid.*

2197. *Ibid.*

2198. **Note.** Term *Samudradhara* expresses that *'Nam'* is sea like knowledge, which is endless

2199. R.T. Vol. II. p. 219.

2200. *Ibid.*

2201. *Ibid.*

2202. *Ibid.*

2203. *Ibid.*

2204. **Note.** Matha-Superintendent *Kesava,* followed him, just as the son of Sini (*Satyaki*) and the son of the wind (*Bhimasena*) (followed) the son of Parth (Arjuna) when he demanded the horse from the Indus region, same simile is found in the said statement.

2205. *R.T.* Vol. II. p. 219.

2206. **Note.** The interpretation of *Tatravibhaktakataka* is compared with statement of King, who pressed by the enemies from various sides had his whole army divided in all directions, was in irremediable distress.

2207. **Note.** *Trillaka* does not wish that the pretender should be entirely under *Rajavadana's* influence, but hopes to secure him for his own purposes. He therefore plays off *Catuska* against the other rebel leader of the Damaras. *Bhoja* is referred to by *Trillaka* as the 'second prince' with regard to Lothana who had been the first pretender.

2208. **Note.** *Trillaka* had secretly prepared, just as the simile of the porcupine. At that time *Catuska, Prthvihara's* son and the younger brother of Kosthaka and *Lothaka* was the second enemy of them.

2209. **Note.** *Lothaka's* borther imprisoned by *Catuska,* when the King had promised him the desired safety, he told him that *Citraratha* and *Kosthaka* were nothing but (embodiments of) perfidy and deserving tobe killed.

2210. **Note.** It is proved from the above statement that the word *Kantha,* the meaning, 'patchwork of lies', 'tissue of lies', 'intrigue' already discussed in detail elsewhere in the text is similar to an '*ornament*'.

2211. **Note.** Brahman, the creator of the world is born from the lotus which rises from Visnu's navel.

2212. **Note.** The brave *Pincadeva* had been the commander of the *Surapuradranga* (watch-station) *Hurapor* already posted sixteen year earlier.

2213. **Note.** The river is evidently the *Rembyara* flowing past elevated at 74°-47′ longitude and 33°-41′ latitude on the route which leads to the passes of the *Pir Pantsal* of Durhal and of Rupri: *Hurapor,* or Hirpur, as it is called by Panjabs where the name sof Haripur and 'Hirapur' are quaintly explained as 'the city of Siva and the Diamond city'.

2214. R.T. Vol. II. p. 220.

2215. *Ibid.*

2216. *Ibid.* p. 221.

2217. *Ibid.*

2218. **Note.** The Damara from *Holada* is probably *Trillaka*. The position of the latter's residence is nowhere clearly indicated, but they burned the residence of the *Lavanya.*

2219. R.T. Vol. II. p. 221.

2220. **Note.** For the identical simile comparing enemies to diseases of different grades of danger, just as a disease of the throat pains more then one of the foot.

2221. **Note.** *Rilahana* had been fighting *Catuska* who had invaded *Samala* in the company of numberless Damaras and the King, in dejection, proceeded to the City.The story of Arjuna's fight witht he 'Confederates' (*Samsaptuka*) is found in *Mahabharata*, VII; XXVII. p. 1

2222. **Note.** Term *Kalyanapura or Kalampor* already discussed inelsewhere in the text, but the said verse shows that by *Ramasa* is meant *Ramusa* the present *Ramuh,* which lies on the direct route from *Samala* to *Surapura.* The glosses of A_2, *Kaimoh* and *Ramoh,* show that *Katimusa* and *Ramusa* are identical with the modern *Kaimuh* and *Ramuh.* Sanskrit *S* between vowels appears in Kashmiris always as h. The first named place is a considerable village in the Adavin Pargana, on the left bank of the *Visoka* (*vesau*) river at the elevation of 75°-9′ longitude and 33°-43′ latitude. In Sept, 1895, it was traced a few ancient slaps near the largest of the villages Ziarats. *Ramuh* is a place of some importance, situated midway on the high road from Srinagar to Ṣupiyan at the elevation of 74°-54′ longitude and 33°-42′ latitude. The lands around it have formed for some time back the Jagir of the Daras, a well-known Brahman family of Srinagar. Near a Naga which is close to the village, Stein found in Oct; 1891, several old sculptures for the information to concern with the subject.

2223. *R.T.* Vol. II. p. 221.

2224. *Ibid.*

2225. *Ibid.*

2226. *Ibid.*

2227. *Ibid.*

2228. *Ibid.* p. 222.

2229. *Ibid.*

2230. *Ibid.*

2231. **Note.** Kalhana makes *Rilhana* refers to the fact that he has from early youth served the King and grown old in the service.

2232. *R.T.* Vol. II. p. 222.

2233. *Ibid.*

2234. *Ibid.*

2235. *Ibid.*

2236. **Note.** By the term *Trnamani* probably amber is meant.

2237. *R.T.* Vol. II 222.

2238. *Ibid.*

2239. *Ibid.*

2240. *Ibid.*

2241. *Ibid.*

2242. *Ibid.*

2243. *Ibid.*

2244. *Ibid.*

2245. George Grierson, *"Modern Hinduism and Its Debt to the Historians,":* *Journal of the Royal Asiatic* society; 1907, Pp. 311 FF, in F.E Keay, *Kabir* and his followers; p. 67 Quoted from *K.G.M*; p. 3 Note. *Banaras* is now known as *Varanasi.*

2246. *R.T.* Vol. II. p. 223.

2247. **Note.** There is a *double -extendre* in this verse which will be understood by taking into account the meaning of *Purusayati,* as explained, e.g *Vastyayana's Kamasutra; ii. p. 8*

2248. R.T. Vol. II. p. 223.

2249. *Ibid.*

2250. **Note.** Immediately to the west of *Kalampor* (Kalayamapura) rise the slopes of the *Pir Pantsal* range which are covered in a broad belt with dense pine forest. The latter are referred to also by *Srivara* in the account of a battle fought close to *Kalyanapuri.*

2251. R.T. Vol. II. p. 223.

2252. *Ibid.*

2253. *Ibid.* p. 224.

2254. *Ibid.*

2255. *Ibid.*

2256. **Note.** Here Kalhana takes up the narrative of the contest with Bhoja, and his allies at the point where he had dropped it, Thus these lowest of men spoke to him cunningly wishing to in a prison him in their own territory.

2257. *R.T.* Vol. II. p. 224.

2258. *Ibid.*

2259. *Ibid.*

2260. **Note.** A careful examination of the vedic hymns shows also that the Aryans thought out for themselves different conceptions of the gods in the course of the centuries. Gods like *Dyaus* and *Prithivi* are passing away. Indra replaces *Varuna*. Vishnu is not as yet of importance. Siva, Mahadeva, Durga, Kali, Ram, Krishna, Lakshmi, Ganapati are not as yet known. The trial (*Trimurti*) *of later Hindvism.* Brahma, Vishnu and Siva, is as yet unheard of. There are traces, perhaps the beginnings of the idea developed in the *Upanishads* that all gods are onc under different names, and there is the beginning of the belief in abstract detities, such as *Shraddha*, Faith, devotion, Kama, desire and especially in Prajapati i.e called *'Nam'*, the lord of creatures, which are distinct from the personfied forces of fire and wind and rain and sun and sky that were the chief gods of the earlier Aryans. (R.V.VR. p. 52)

2261. *R.T.* Vol. II. p. 224.

2262. *Ibid.*

2263. **Note.** The context requires the emendation *aicchat tan* for *aicchat sann* of A.

2264. **Note.** Term *Taramulaka* is repeated mentioned in the text means the whole world is belong to *'God'* or *'Nam'*.

2265. *R.T.* Vol. II. p. 224.

2266. *Ibid.* p. 225.

2267. *Ibid.*

2268. **Note.** The above interpretation of the verse expresses that *Balahara* became powerful being joined by all the Damaras who turned hostile from anger over the murder of their relative, as well as by the followers of *Naga,* where Rajavadana's *"alavanyata"* is mentioned. Kalhana wishes to allude to the curious change in the affections of these two personages. *Naga* turns to the King's side while Rajavadana who owes his rise to the King, becomes the chief support of the pretender.

2269. R.T. Vol. II. p. 225.

2270. *Ibid.*

2271. **Note.** The text of these lines is corrupt, and the emendations upon which the above translation is based, by no means certain. It is understood from the preceding verses and overthrow *Balahara's* position, Naga began a feud for life against him taking the side of the King. here Kalhana wishes to describe the failed attempt of Naga to oust *Rajavadana* from Bhoja's side, and to secure control of the pretender's affairs. In the above immediate verse *narisevatam* of AL gives no sense. We have nothing better to suggest than Durgaparsad emendation *narim eva tam,* though we are unable to trace the story to which allusion is made here, but it is upto the master. In the same verse the context speaks for the emendations of the editors of text, *Vyahasan Samvihaya,* instead of the senseless *Vyasahansa Vihaya,* and *Vidhir na* for *Vidhi.* The simile of this verse is clearly displayed that neglecting to propitiate King (*Harsa*) and supporting *Uchchala* by rejecting the wishing low and take hold of the he-go at neck.

2272. R.T. Vol. II. p. 225.

2273. **Note.** The "Unborn," *'Word'* frequently also called the one, *EKAM* in Sanskrit means that which has always existed without being born of anything, the Eternally-Pre-existing, of which all things are born, when the desire of manifesting. Itself awakes in it. Sometimes the one is named *AJA EKAPAD*, Literally "the One-footed unborn" *'Word'* a seemingly grotesque interpretations, but which is really only one of those attempts at expressing the inexpressible in some kind of tangible form in which the Aryan thinkers of India have always dealt regardless of extravagance in the wording. For in the Rig-Veda, the "foot" may stand for the world in which the foot's owner abides. (V.I. p. 424). It has been connected with *Pyayakrit'hito.*

2274. R.T Vol. II. p. 226.

2275. *Ibid.*

2276. *Ibid.*

2277. **Note.** Of the name of the second general only the first syllables *Matta 'Word'* (Or *Masu 'Chamar'*) are found in A. By *Daradrajanaka* is meant in all probability *Viddasiha,* who elsewhere mentioned as fort (*Kotta*), *is also designated as Daradraja. The fort is probably Dugdhaghata.*

2278. *R.T.* Vol. II. p. 226.

2279. *Ibid.*

2280. *Ibid.*

2281. *Ibid.*

2282. *Ibid.*

2283. *Ibid.* p. 227.

2284. *Ibid.*

2285. *Ibid.*

2286. *IBid*

2287. *Ibid.*

2288. *Ibid.*

2289. **Note.** The *Madhumati* is the stream draining the Bandapor Nala, a side valley of which leads to the *Dudakhut* Pass. It is evidently towards the latter that the fleeing *Darads* retired.

2290. R.T. Vol. II. p. 227.

2291. *Ibid.*

2292. *Ibid.*

2293. **Note.** *Bhutta or Bhautta* name (also rarely *Bhotta*) is applied by Kalhana and his successors, like its derivative in the modern Kashmiri languauge *'Buta'*, to the population of Tibetan descent generally, inhabiting the regions immediately to the East and North Est of Kashmir i.e. modern mountain districts of Dras, Ladakh, perhaps also Skardo. From the verse we learn that the Zoji-la pass, on the high road of the Dras and Ladakh, was then as now the ethnographic watershed between Kasmir and the territory of the *Bhauttas.* By *Bhuttarastra* in our passage probably the Dras territory is meant which adjoins the upper Sindh valley, and is easly accessible fromt he Darad territory on the Kisanganga. The Darads propose to *Bhoja* to take him to Dras, which lies on the great route connecting Kasmir with Ladakh. From there he could gain in safety the mountains enclosing Kashmir on the North East and hence the castle of *Trillaka*. Where the latter's seat was not exactly expressed by Kalhana. Supposing that it was in *Holada* (Vular), refused his consent, the route proposed by the Darads wold have had distinct advantages.

2294. R.T. Vol. II. p. 227.

2295. **Note.** Now there is modern estimate of Dard double-dealing, because there is no morals in Campa valley. Therefore Kalhana closely agrees on the modern estimate.

2296. R.T. Vol. II. p. 228.

2297. *Ibid.*

2298. *Ibid.*

2299. *Ibid.*

2300. *Ibid.*

2301. **Note.** The following verses show that this Damara undertakes a kind of *prayopavesa,* in order to get *Bhoja* back into his power.

2302. R.T. Vol. II. p. 228.

2303. **Note.** *Balahari* was, perhaps, the name of the stream which flows from the *Dudakhut* Pass, and after draining the neighbouring valleys joins the*Madhumati* at *Atavath* (map *'Atawat'*).

2304. *R.T.* Vol. II. p. 228.

2305. **Note.** The word *Vidravitani* means to realize the 'Nam' within the body.

2306. *R.T.* Vol. II. p. 229.

2307. *Ibid.*

2308. *Ibid.*

2309. *Ibid.*

2310. **Note.** Kalhana makes *Viddasiha* politely refer to his own approaching death as due to the desire of acting as the proclaimer of *Jayasimha's* greatness in heaven! For *Jayaraja's* died from a dangerous boil, when the King was about to start on the expedition.

2311. **Note.** In the *Ramayana,* Sanjha, the daughter of *Visvakarm*, is the wife of Surya. The *Asvins* and *Yama* and *Yami* are among his children. As his brightness was too great for his wife, *Visvakarma* cut part of him away. The fragments fell blazing to the earth, and form the *Visvakarma* formed the discus of Vishnu, the trident of Siva, and the weapons of the other gods (R.V.V.R. p. 66)

2312. *R.T.* Vol. II. p. 229.

2313. *Ibid.*

2314. *Ibid.*

2315. **Note.** Read for '*bhajata* in text, which is a misprint, '*bhajatam*' and divide *mohadva, Vimarsena.*

2316. *R.T.* Vol. II. p. 229.

2317. *Ibid.*

2318. **Note.** *Losthaka* and *Catuska* are meant for the fight for one of his own side arriving for his assistance. Where as the lord of *Magadha is Jarasamdha* who formed of two halves, separately born mentioned in the *Mahabharata.*

2319. R.T. Vol. II. pp. 229-30.

2320. *Ibid.* p. 230

2321. *Ibid.*

2322. *Ibid.*

2323. *Ibid.*

2324. **Note.** *Dinnagrama* cannot be identified at present. It may be concluded that it lay not for from *Kramarajya*, probably in the hill region to the west of the valley.

2325. R.T. Vol. II. p. 230

2326. **Note.** It is clear that Kalhana wishes to make *Rajavadana* say that he would not have made peace with *Udaya* and *Dhanya*, if he had known before of Bhoja's return from the Darads. The correction of *bravid dhyas* ced for *bravic chvas ced* of A is, therefore, indispensable.

2327. R.T. Vol. II. p. 230.

2328. **Note.** There are many sections of the tribe. First rank the half-amphibious paddlers of the Dal Lake (*Demb Hanz*), who are really vegetable gardeners, and the boatmen of the Wular lake, who gather the *Singhara* nut (*Gari Hanz*). Next in status come the men of the large barges known as *bahats* and *War,* in which cargoes of 800 maunds of grain or wood are carried. Then the *Dunga Hanz*, who paddle the passenger boats, not a respectable class for they prostitute their females;next the *Gad Hanz,* who net fish, and are said to surpass even the *Dunga* Hanz in their power of invective and last the *Hak Hanz*, who collect driftwood in the rivers. The *Hanz* or Hanjis are a hardy muscular people, but are quarrel some and mendacious. Half the stories to the discredit of Kashmir and its inhabitants are due to the Irish car driver tells travellers quaint scandals of the valley and its rulers. The Hanzi ashore is a great rascal, and European travellers would be wise to leave him in his boat. The chief *Kram* names of the Hanjis are *Danger, Dar, and Mal* (p. G. K. Pp. 38-9)

2329. R.T. Vol. II. p. 230.

2330. *Ibid.*

2331. *Ibid.*

2332. *Ibid.*

2333. *Ibid.*

2334. *Ibid.* pp. 230-31.

2335. **Note.** For *Ramacara* (conjecturally restored for A *Rama 'Word' ra*), as a name of Balarama, the elder brother of Krsna (black). The following versa contains an allusion to Balarama's love of intoxicating drinks for which he is called *Madhupriya.*

2336. R.T. Vol. II. p. 231.

2337. *Ibid.*

2338. *Ibid.*

2339. *Ibid.*

2340. *Ibid.*

2341. *Ibid.*

2342. *Ibid.*

2343. *Ibid.*

2344. *Ibid.*

2345. **Note.** *Hayasrama* is the present village of *Hayahoṃ,* adjoining Drang on the pilgrimage route to the Sarada shrine; regarding its position, it has already been discussed elsewhere in the text. *Hayasrama* is referred to by Abu-I-Fazl as *'Hachamun'* on the way to the Sarada temple, *Ain-i-Akbari*; II. p. 365 Bhoja coming from Dinnagrama (in the west of the house of the *Kramarajya*) wishes to join *Alamakaracakra* and the other Damaras at *Hayarama Udaya,* thereupon to block his way, takes up a position at *Taramulaka,* which lies across (*tiryaksthita*) Bhoja's route see immediate verse. From there he attacks the village in which Bhoja had taken up his quarters for the night. *Alamkaracakra* who searches for the prince, does not find him, and turns back before *Daragrami,* which is, perhaps, the place occupied by *Bhoja.* It is unfortunate that the position of *Taramulaka* has not yet been fixed.

2346. *R.T.* Vol. II. pp. 231-32.

2347. *Ibid.* p. 232.

2348. *Ibid.*

2349. **Note.** *Daragrami* is only here mentioned; the village lay probably near *Taramulaka.*

2350. *R.T* Vol. II. p. 232.

2351. *Ibid.*

2352. *Ibid.*

2353. *Ibid.*

2354. *V.I* . p. 422 **Note.** *Uchchala*, wrongly printed in the edition as a proper name, is probably to be taken in the sense of 'mind' given for the word in Hemacandra's *Abhidhanacintamani,* VI. p. 5

2355. R.T. Vol. II. p. 232.

2356. **Note.** Kalhana compares the privatious which Bhoja suffered each time he acted in concert with *Alamkaracakra,* with the hardships of *Vasuki* when employed by Siva in combination with Mount *Mandara.* At the burning of Tripura. Mandra, made Siva the bow and *Vasuki* the string on it. At the churning of the ocean Vasuki was twisted as a rope round the churning-mountain.

2357. **Note.** Probably the neighbourhood of *Sirahsilakotta* is meant.

2358. **Note.** The meaning the verse is reflected that *Canpaka,* who was in charge of the 'Gate', was about to proceed on this expedition by the King's order, the *Vataganda* (Ananda) eneavoured to get the better of him. *Sussala,* then eager to seize the throne for himself, wised to prevent his elder brother from occupying the city. Therefore, we must suddenly overpower the *Lothana* just *Jayasimha* overpowered *Preman.* Thus the meaning of the term *abhisamdhaya* is hereby meant in this verse.

2359. **Note.** *Balahara-Rajavadana* is not a *Lavanya* as previously mentioned in statement of the text

2360. *R.T. V*ol. II. p. 233.

2361. **Note.** *Parmandi* has already been mentioned in the text elswhere.

2362. R.T. Vol. II. p. 233.

2363. *Ibid.*

2364. *Ibid.*

2365. *Ibid.*

2366. *Ibid.*

2367. *Ibid.*

2368. *Ibid.*

2369. *Ibid.*

2370. *Ibid.*

2371. *Ibid.* pp. 233-34.

2372. **Note.** For term *tyagorthita* the correct term use as *Tyagarthito.*

2373. *R.T.* Vol. II. p. 234.

2374. *Ibid.*

2375. *Ibid.*

2376. *Ibid.*

2377. **Note.** The similes of this and the following verse are taken from the Indian chess (*Caturanga*) played by four persons at a time. This game has been fully deserbed by Alberuni, *India* vol.1 p. 183.Regarding its antiquity by the side of the bilateral chess, compared the remarks of Prof. Jacobi, Z.D.M.G, Vol. 1. p. 232. "The name *Shah* of king applies here to the queen (firzan)". Alberuni, Loc.cit.

2378. R.T. Vol. II. p. 234.

2379. **Note.** *Rajavadana's* and *Naga's* are the old feud, it has already been mentioned in the text.

2380. R.T. Vol. II. p. 234.

2381. *Ibid.*

2382. *Ibid.*

2383. *Ibid.*

2384. *Ibid.* p. 235.

2385. *Ibid.*

2386. *Ibid.*

2387. *Ibid.*

2388. *Ibid.*

2389. *Ibid.*

2390. *Ibid.*

2391. **Note.** The context shows that we have to read for A *Mantrinam,* as suggested in the text; to the reference no. 2380 in the verse.

2392. *R.T.* Vol. II. p. 235.

2393. *Ibid.*

2394. **Note.** Naga's relatives had already before once taken *Balahara's* protection and did not feel ashamed of taking service with him.

2395. R.T. Vol. II p. 235.

2396. *Ibid.*

2397. *Ibid.* p. 236.

2398. *Ibid.*

2399. *Ibid.*

2400. *Ibid.*

2401. *Ibid.*

2402. *Ibid.*

2403. *Ibid.*

2404. *Ibid.*

2405. *Ibid.*

2406. *Ibid.*

2407. *Ibid.*

2408. *Ibid.*

2409. *Ibid.*

2410. *Ibid.* p. 237.

2411. *Ibid.*

2412. **Note.** By the equivalent expressions *Kosam Kr or Kosam pa* ('to drink the draught), Kalhana refers repeatedly to the oath taken by means of a sacred libation mentioned in various verses. Person who have taken such an oath are spoken of as *Pitakosa, or Kosapithin.* This form of oath is well-known to several of the smritis, where it figures under the name of *Kosa* as one of the nine kinds of ordeal. A sacred image is bathed in water, and the person to whom the oath is administered, is made to swallow a certain quantity of this consecrated water. If any calamity befall him or any near relative of his within a certain subsequent period, it is taken as a proof of his guilt. The texts quoted by Prof. Jolly (L.C. p. 146) know of the *Kosa* ordeal or oath both as a means of exculpation and as a procedure calculated to creat confidence with reference to a subsequent transaction. Kalhana's references in the above quoted passages fully illustrate this second employ of the *'Kosa'*. We find it there taken either on occasions of a reconciliation between former enemies when a solemn assurance of mutual goodwill for the future is desired, or more frequently in connection with secret confederations and conspiracies. In the latter case the *Kosa* is intended to secure mutual faithfulness, and to guarantee secrecy among the confederates. The glass of A_3 on our passage render *Kosa* rightly by *divya*, 'sacred oath' also compares with gloss of A_2 called (*Sapatha*). Our passage also refers to another curious custom accompanying the ceremony of *Kosapana*. By the words of the text and the explanation given in the gloss of A_3, we are led to assume that those who went through that ceremony had to place their legs cross wide on a sheep skin over which blood had been sprinkled. We are unable to trace such a custom elswhere in India. Moreover, the mention of the Khasas shows that *Bhoja* is still at *Dinnagrama*.

2413. R.T. Vol. II. p. 237.

2414. *Ibid.*

2415. Ibid. **Note.** Term *Uttambhanam* is corrected with Durgaparsad.

2416. *Ibid.*

2417. *Ibid.*

2418. *Ibid.*

2419. *Ibid.*

2420. *Ibid.*

2421. *Ibid.*

2422. *Ibid.*

2423. *Ibid.* pp. 237-38.

2424. *Ibid.* p. 238.

2425. *Ibid.*

2426. *Ibid.*

2427. *Ibid.*

2428. *Ibid.*

2429. *Ibid.* **Note.** According to the glosses of A_3, certain animals, called *agnisauca,* clean their fur-skin by entering fire. It is compared with the story of *Brahmavaivartapur* and also see p. W, S.V *Vahnisuddha.* The meaning 'indigence' given by a gloss of A_3 to the word *rora* cannot be traced in the dictionaries. Possibly the word *rora,* *'Labourer'* (*Nam*), quoted in N.p. W. from Hemacandra's *Parisistaparvan,* may be connected with it.

2430. R.T. Vol. II. p. 238.

2431. *Ibid.*

2432. **Note.** *Avatara,* the 'Incarnation', was an appellation given to *Bhiksacara* by his Damaras adherents, has already expressed.

2433. *R.T.* Vol. II. p. 238.

2434. *V.I.PP. 294, 296 See Plate IV, Festival of Serpents (Fig. 4)*

2435. R.T. Vol. II. p. 238.

2436. *Ibid.*

2437. *Ibid.* p. 239.

2438. *Ibid.*

2439. *Ibid.*

2440. **Note.** The word *dhanyah* in text should have been printed in small type.

2441. *R.T.* Vol. II. p. 239.

2442. *Ibid.*

2443. *Ibid.*

2444. *Ibid.*

2445. *Ibid.*

2446. *Ibid.*

2447. *Ibid.*

2448. *Ibid.*

2449. *Ibid.*

2450. *Ibid.* p. 240.

2451. *Ibid.*

2452. *Ibid.*

2453. *Ibid.*

2454. *Ibid.*

2455. *Ibid.* **Note.** The meaning of this statement is top secret, therefore, it seems to refer to *Dhanya's* inability to comprehend *Bhoja*. Message of this statement is also reflected in the immediate verses of the text.

2456. *Ibid.*

2457. *Ibid.*

2458. *Ibid.*

2459. *Ibid.*

2460. *Ibid.*

2461. *Ibid.*

2462. *Ibid.*

2463. *Ibid. p. 241.* **Note.** The expressions used by Kalhana in the second half of this verse are obscure, but the following account of

Kalhanikadevi's preparations for the journey speaks for an interpretation as elaborated above.

2464. **Note.** These verses too, along with those immediately following, show defects and obscurifies in their wording which can scarcely be put down entirely to the account of copyists negligence about the real historical evidence which has been based on scientific method of the nature.

2465. **Note.** The double *sa* shows that the text is not in order because it has required more scientific knowledge.

2466. **Note.** Certain words like *rajadharmasya Ca Vasan* evidently contain a corruption to the theory of mind. But the translation is conjectural.

2467. *R.T.* Vol. II. p. 241.

2468. *Ibid.*

2469. *Ibid.* pp. 241-42.

2470. *Ibid.*

2471. *Ibid.*

2472. *Ibid.*

2473. *Ibid.*

2474. **Note.** The translation of the first half of this verse is based on the conjectural reading of the text, but it makes the theory of mind corrupt because first of all we have to imagine where from the store of knowledge is coming unless and untile your study is incomplete with *'Nam'*.

2475. *R.T.* Vol. II. p. 242.

2476. *Ibid.*

2477. **Note.** Kalhana has forgotten to give us the name of this river or any other indication which might help towards its identification. From the subsequent reference to *Pancigrama* along with the Rajaputras, it appears, however, probably that the Kahmil river, flowing from the mountains to the west of Uttar, is meant.

2478. R.T. Vol. II. p. 242.

2479. **Note.** Term *avaptayersyaya* emends with Durgaparsad.

2480. *R.T.* Vol. II. p. 242.

2481. *Ibid.* p. 243.

2482. **Note.** To touch the ear with one's hand is a sign of prohibition.

2483. *R.T.* Vol. II. p. 243.

2484. *Ibid.*

2485. **Note.** The purport of the second half of this line is not clear. For *badhyate* we have probably to correct *badhyate*.

2486. *R.T.* Vol. II p. 243.

2487. *Ibid.*

2488. *Ibid.*

2489. *Ibid.*

2490. **Note.** The allusion seems to be to the murder of *Naga* by *Dhanya* and the other ministers of Damaras class.

2491. R.T. Vol. II. p. 243.

2492. *Ibid.*

2493. **Note.** The verse contains evidently a proverb, corresponding to the 'taking of owls to Athens'. But it application in the present case is not clear because it was the message during the time of blind faith in India.

2494. R.T. Vol. II. p. 244.

2495. For the term *mantryavirodha* correct is used as *mantryavarodha*.

2496. R.T. Vol. II. p. 244.

2497. **Note.** The text is undoubtedly corrupt and gives no sense. The above translation is based on the conjectural emendations *anyada yasah* for *anyadasayah* (also see *Yasah* in preceding verse) and *svadayantyah syad* for *Svadayantyadad*.

2498. R.T. Vol. II p. 244.

2499. Note. We believe that an allusion to Bhoja is intended because there is no other solution with the presence of *'Nam'*. The wording of the *'Nam'* is obscure, it is upto Father.

2500. *R.T.* Vol. II. p. 244.

2501. *Ibid.*

2502. *Ibid.*

2503. *Ibid.*

2504. *Ibid.*

2505. *Ibid.* p. 245.

2506. *Ibid.*

2507. *Ibid.*

2508. *Ibid.*

2509. *Ibid.*

2510. *Ibid.*

2511. **Note.** Kalhana makes Bhoja allude to the previous discomfiture of the allied Darad and Damaras which carried golden trappings.

2512. *R.T* Vol. II. p. 245.

2513. **Note.** Term *samvrtta iti* is emended in correct form as *Samvrttam iti.*

2514. **Note.** *Pancigrama* is probably the present *Panzagom,* a large village in Uttar, situated close to the left bank of the Kahmil River; circ 74°-8′ longitude and 39°-28′-45″ latitutde. The village lies on the routes which leads up the valley of the Kahmil river and over the 'Nattishannar' Pass' Naschau Galli' into Karnav.

2515. *R.T.* Vol. II. 246.

2516. *Ibid.*

2517. *Ibid.*

2518. *Ibid.*

2519. **Note.** The town built by *Suyya,* called after him *Suyyapura* (see gloss of A_2) is undoubtedly the modern *Sopur.* The latter is situated exactly in the position described by Kalhana, on both sides of the *Vitasta,* and about a mile below the point where the latter leaves the Vular lake. The ancient name of the place is still well known to the Pandits. It has already been proved the necessity of this identification by a reference of our passage. Whereas, Cunningham had erroneously taken *Sopur* for Kalhana's *Surapura* (*Hurapor*). *Suyyapura* is mentioned again inconnection with the *Mahapadma* lake, and *Srivara* refers to the building of a new royal residence of *Suyyapura* by Sultan Hasan Shah. Sopur is still a place of some importance, and showed at the census of 1891 a population of over 8000 people. For descriptious of the present town, which as Prof. Buhler has rightly put it, "does not resemble heaven, and possesses nothing ancient except its name."

2520. *R.T.* Vol. II. p. 246.

2521. **Note.** The comparative study of the this passage displayed that *Prthvihara* fought close to the royal palace on the bank of the stream called *Ksiptika*, and destroyed brave soldiers innumerable, and other passages where Damara attacks against Srinagar are referred to shows clearly that we have to correct *Samalah Ksiptika* instead of *Samalaksiptika*. The *Ksiptika* canal to the south of Srinagar is regularly mentioned as the point of attack for the *Samala* Damaras under Prthvihara's leadership. *Prthvhara's* home was in *Samala 'Word' Samala* like Devasaras is used as an adjective, ' an inhabitant of *Samala'* (Hamal). The 'town' of *Samakaravarman*, the present *Patan* is situated in the pargana of Bangil (*Bhangila*). What is intended by the gloss *sval* written by A_1, over *Samala* which is unexplainable in the text, it is upto the 'Really master'.

2522. **Note.** The bank of the *Mahasarit* is elsewhere referred to as the place from which the rebels from *Holada* (Vular) and other parts of *Madavarajya* besiege the city. It has already been suggested in the text that *Trillaka's* seat was in *Holada.*

2523. **Note.** The suggestion which has already made regarding the position of *Nilasva* is correct, we should expect the Damaras of that tract to attack the city towards its centre, i.e. from the north.

2524. **Note.** The word *visa* is unknown, and possibly corrupt by the theory of mind.

2525. *R.T.* Vol. II. p. 246.

2526. *Ibid.*

2527. *Ibid.*

2528. *Ibid.*

2529. *R.T.* Vol. II. p. 246.

2530 *Ibid.*

2531. *Ibid.*

2532. *Ibid.*

2533. **Note.** The word *Khataku,* unknown to the dictionaries, evidently designates some animals.

2534. R.T. Vol. II. p. 247.

2535. **Note.** These verses permit of a second interpretation in which the word *Ksmabhrt* must be taken as 'King'

2536. *R.T.* Vol. II. p. 247.

2537. **Note.** The version given above is the one intended in the narrative. Similar double meanings are contained in the other verses, giving a conventional description of the nightfall or end of the Dark Age.

2538. **Note.** Study reveals that an allusion to Queen *Kalhanika* is intended but in the lines it proves defective.

2439. R.T. Vol. II. p. 247.

2540. *Ibid.*

2541. *Ibid.*

2542. *Ibid.*

2543. *Ibid.*

2544. *Ibid.*

2545. *Ibid.* **Note.** People who are about to visit the Kashmir *Prayaga,* start in boats during the night from Srinagar, so as to reach the Tirth in the morning. For *tatha tatha* correct *tatha tatra.*

2546. *R.T.* Vol. II. p. 248.

2547. *Ibid.*

2548. *Ibid.*

2549. *Ibid.*

2550. *Ibid.* **Note.** Correct term perhaps, *Svamatyavaimatyam* for A *samatyavaimatyam.*

2551. *Ibid.*

2552. *Ibid.*

2553. *Ibid.*

2554. *Ibid.*

2555. **Note.** The comparative study of the verses show that A *Yuddhyavahan* is a corruption for *Yugyavahan.*

2556. *R.T.* Vol. II.p. 249 **Note.** By putting a brilliant saffron pomade on *Bhoja's* beard which spread like a plot of grass, and which had exectly the tawny colour of a young camel's hair.

2557. *Ibid.*

2558. *Ibid.*

2559. *Ibid.*

2560. *Ibid.,*

2562. *Ibid.*

2563. **Note.**The word *Vasan* is evidently corrupt because it reflects the status of mind's theory which always eats poison and delivering poison to other. As Guru Nanak says: a seller knowledge 'devotee of the mind' (*manmukh*), who earns poison and eats posion: "The *Manmukh* sells his knowledge; he earns poison and eats posion." (*Adi Granth*; p. 938).

2564. R.T. Vol. II. p. 249.

2565. *Ibid.*

2566. *Ibid.*

2567. The correct term for *Krosan* for *Krosan* which is a misprint in the context.

2568. *R.T.* Vol. II p. 250.

2569. *Ibid.*

2570. *Ibid.*

2571. *Ibid.*

2572. *Ibid.*

2573. **Note.** We have followed the reading of A *tvadiksur*, correcting *asantersyo* A *asantersyo*

2573. *R.T.* Vol. II. p. 250.

2574. *Ibid.*

2575. *Ibid.*

2576. **Note.** Here we have a somewhat obscure account of what takes place by the Master after Bhoja's arrival at the queen's camp at *Taramulaka*. Bhoja apparently pretends to be tired by his march from the place of meeting, and wishes to get away again without going to see the King. When told that the King expects him, he takes offence and thinks himself betrayed. Thereupon the ministers again feel alarmed. *Dhanya's* tender speech subsequently allays these mutual misunderstandings, and induces Bhoja to start again for the city.

2577. R.T. Vol. II. p. 250.

2578. *Ibid.*

2579. *Ibid.* pp. 250-51.

2580. *Ibid.* p. 251

2581. *Ibid.*

2582. *Ibid.*

2583. *Ibid.*

2584. *Ibid.*

2585. *Ibid.*

2586. *Ibid.*

2587. *Ibid.* **Note.** The correct term for *Durgaparsad* is hereby used *harmyasthan* for *harmyastha.*

2588. *Ibid.* p. 252.

2589. *Ibid.*

2590. *Ibid.*

2591. *Ibid.*

2592. *Ibid.*

2593. *Ibid.*

2594. *Ibid.*

2595. *Ibid.*

2596. *Ibid.*

2597. *Ibid.*

2598. *Ibid.*

2599. *Ibid.*

2600. *Ibid.*

2601. *Ibid.*

2602. *Ibid.*

2603. *Ibid.*

2604. **Note.** The sacred water of Ganges is still carried at the present day in sealed pots and bottles to distant parts of India. It would be interesting to find evidence for Kalhana's statement that a seal with *Jayapida's* name was still used in his own time for the sealing of such pots at Prayaga. Troyer and Lassen make *Jayapida* throw 'his seal into the river.'

2605. **Note.** According to Kalhana *SAHIS* OF *Udabhandapura,* used to belong to the *'Hindu Shahiya dynasty'* Which have been mentioned in Alberuin's *India* (Vol. II. p. 13) to have ruled the Kabul valley and Gandhara previous to the conquest of Mahmud of *Ghazna*. According to Alberuni's account this dynasty succeeded to the *'Turkish Shahiyas'* who were traditionally believed to have ruled over the Hindu Kingdom of Kabul for sixty generations. The last King of this race *Lagaturman,* was deposed by his Brahman Wazir who, having risen to great power and influence, seized the royal throne and became the founder of the 'Hindu Shahiya dynasty'. In this usurper who, in the extant text of Alberuni is called *Kallar,* we have in all probability to recognise the Lalliya Sahi of the *Rajatarangini*. Kalhana subsequently mentions Lalliya as the father of *Kamaluka* The latter prince is certainly identical with the *Kamalu* who, in Alberuni's genealogy of the Hindu Shahiyas, appears as the ruler next but after *'Kallar'*. The *'Shahi'*, whom Kalhana mentions in the last named passage, without giving his name, as *Kamaluka's* predecessors, is probably the *Samand* (Samanta) who in Alberuni's list follows immediately after *Kallar*. The description which the chronicle gives of Lalliya *Sahi's* great power and repute agrees singularly with what Alberuni has to tell us of the energetic founder of the Hindu Shahiya dynasty. Besides *Kamaluka* and the nameless Shahi, the chronicle mentions of Lalliya's successors Bhima Sahi of *Udabhandapura*, the grandfater of Queen *Didda*, and *Trilocanapala Sahi.* Under the last named prince. *Bhimapala* who survived him only by five years, (A.D. 1021-2) finally succumbed to the *Turuskas,* i.e.

the Muhammadan invaders from the West *Udbhandapura,* the residence of the Sahi kings, has been identified according to Alberuni under the name of *Waihand* (*India* vol.i.pp. 206, 259,317), with the ancient capital of Gandhara. Its position is marked by the modern village of *Und* situated on the right bank of the Indus about fifteen miles above attack. The correction indentification of the stie of *Waihand* with that of the modern village *Undis* (also written as *Hund, Ohind, Uhand,* etc.). The further contraction into the modern *Und* probably proceeded through forms like *Unhand* and *Uhand* which would accounts for the verying spelling of the name by ealier travellers.

2606. *R.T.* Vol. II. p. 253.

2607. **Note.** The text of this verse is hopelessly corrupt. *Bhoja* seems to refer to the fact that even during the coalition of the Darad and other chiefs nothing but misery (*Kadannasana*) result for him.

2608. *R.T.* Vol. II p. 253.

2609. *Ibid.*

2610. *Ibid.*

2611. *Ibid.*

2612. *Ibid.*

2613. *Ibid.*

2614. *Ibid.*

2615. *Ibid.*

2616. *Ibid.*

2617. *Ibid.*

2618. *Ibid.* pp. 253-54.

2619. *Ibid.* p. 254.

2620. *Ibid.*

2621. *Ibid.*

2622. *Ibid.*

2623. *Ibid.*

2624. *Ibid.*

2625. *Ibid.* **Note.** For A *pratipattyam* correct with Durgaparsad *Pratipattim.* For A *tvam apya'nam'....* I now emend *tvam apyatra.* It shows 'ego' is going to surrender to the *santhood.*

2626. *Ibid.*

2627. *Ibid.*

2628. *Ibid.*

2629. *Ibid.*

2630. *Ibid.*

2631. *Ibid.*

2632. *Ibid.* p. 255.

2633. *Ibid.*

2634. *Ibid.*

2635. *Ibid.*

2636. *Ibid.*

2637. *Ibid.*

2638. *Ibid.*

2639. *Ibid.*

2640. *Ibid.*

2641. *Ibid.*

2642. *Ibid.*

2643. *Ibid.*

2644. *Ibid.*

2645. *Ibid.*

2646. *Ibid.*

2647. *Ibid.* p. 256.

2648. *Ibid.*

2649. *Ibid.*

2650. *Ibid.*

2651. *Ibid.*

2652. **Note.** Read *Trillakam* for *Trillakas.*

2653. R.T. Vol. II. p. 256.

2654. *Ibid.*

2655. *Ibid.*

2656. **Note.** The ruins of the temple of *Martanda*, here mentioned, form the most striking remains which have survived of the ancient architecture of Kashmir. They are situated near the North edge of the alluvial plateau (Udar) of *Matan,* at the elevation of 75°-17′ longitude and 33°-45′ latitude. About one mile to the North West of the temple, and at the *Martanda* Tirtha. The name given to the temple and its site leaves no doubt as to its having been erected in honour of Visnu-Surya, who has evidently been worshipped since early times at the above Tirtha under the form of *Martanda.* The Tirtha has remained to the present day one of the most celebrated pilgrimage places in the valley, and annually attracts crowds of visitors from all parts of India. The legend related in the *Martandamahatmya* connects the springs with story of production of the sun from the lifeless egg (*mrtanda*), which Aditi, the wife of Kasyapa, had brought forth as her thirteenth child. The *Tirtha* of *Martanda* is already mentioned in the *Nilamata* among the places sacred of *Surya.* The temple of Martanda is mentioned again by Kalhana in the time of king *Kalasa*, who died there. The shrine escaped being plundered under *Harsa.* Subsequently it appears to have been used as a fortified position by a rebel force in Kalhana's own time, on which occasion the temple enclosure (*prangana*) is specially mentioned. Jonaraja mentions the temple among those which Sultan Sikandar, 'the Idol-breaker', destroyed but refers also subsequently to the locality under the name of *Martanda.* The temple as well as the Tirtha bears now the Kalhana's name. *Matan* (from Martanda), found already in (*Ain-i-Akbari.* vol. I. p. 358), whereas the village round the springs is popularly known as *Bavan* in Sanskrit called *Bhavana.* The ancient temple is no longer a place of pious interest for the pilgrims, whovisit instead the modern temple dedicated to *Martanda* by the side of the Naga. A writes the name as *Martanda* in all passages, except our own, where it is given as *Martanda.* As L has *Martanda* here too, the latter form ought to be adopted. The *Mahatmya* and *Nilamata* Purana also read throughout *Martanda.*

2657. *R.T.* Vol. II. p. 256.

2658. *Ibid.*

2659. *Ibid.*

2660. *Ibid.*

2661. *Ibid.* p. 257.

2662. **Note.** Correct word for *bhindanair* is used A *Vindanair* with Durgaparsad. d *in* Sarada characters is easily confused with व and the latter often written by mistake for e.g. compares with *Vipralampakaih.* Moreover, those fall bravely in battle are received after death in the world of the sun. An allusion is intended also to those who after the defeat sought refuge in the temple of *Martanda.*

2663. *R.T.* Vol. II. p. 257.

2664. **Note.** For *Sanjapala's* appointment as *Kampanapati* has already mentioned above. He had lost his right arm in the attack on *Rilhana's* brother.

2665. *R.T.* Vol. II. p. 257.

2666. *Ibid.*

2667. *Ibid.*

2668. *Ibid.*

2669. *Ibid.*

2670. **Note.** Regarding the great quadrangle interior of the *Martanda* temple was once filled with water, and the temple thus 'placed more immediately under the protection of Naga'. There are no Nagas or springs anywhere on the arid plateau, and the water brought to it once by an ancient irrigation canal from the Lidar river could never have taken their place according to traditional notions.

2671. *R.T.* Vol. II. p. 257.

2672. **Note.** Regarding *Trillaka's* residence is probably the Damaras from *Holada.* The position of the latter's residence is nowhere clearly indicated. It shows that it could not have been far from *Martanda.* Perhaps it was in the upper Lidar valley which adjoins *Holada* or Vular.

2673. *R.T.* Vol. II. p. 257.

2674. *Ibid.*

2675. **Note.** Regarding the cutting of a finger as a mark of unconditional surrender to the Master has already mentioned in the text. The smile is intended to show that *Trillaka* found it hard to get his prodon.

2676. It is very probable that the coin described by (Cunningham, *Coins of Medieval India*; p. 46. Plate v. Fig. 35), which bears the legend *Sri Gulhana,* was struck by this prince as ruler of *Lohara.* The type of the coin is identical with that of the very common copper pieces of *Jayasimha.*

2677. *R.T.* Vol. II. p. 258.

2678. *Ibid.*

2679. **Note.** The earth is often represented as the wife of the King, hence as a queen.

2680. **Note.** *Jayacandra,* son of *Gargacandra,* had attached himself to *Jayasimha*; has already mentioned above.

2681. **Note.** The reference of the next line shows that *Losthaka* was on *Rajavadana's* side as might be concluded that he was the relative of *Naga;* Thereupon *Balahara* became powerful, being joined by all the Damaras who turned hostile from anger over the murder of their relative, as well as by the followers of *Naga.* It is therefore, necessary, to emend *sahit* for A *sahita*. Thus, *Losthaka,* a brother's son of Naga, bore him secret enmity, and induced *Dhanya* and the other ministers to destroy Naga in order to assure (for himself) possession of wealth which *Losthaka* had got hodl of during (Naga's) absence.

2682. *R.T.* Vol. II. p. 258.

2683. *Ibid.*

2684. **Note.** We are interested to connect the words *Sakyam asya vinirgamam* with the rest of the verse. No doubt, the words are probably correct in the life, but only the *'Nam'* is correct. Therefore, we must oblige it as a Master of the philosophy of the world.

2685. **Note.** The text of this line is defective because from term *nyapatan* we have to read *nipatan*. The emendation of the impossible *nyavadhibhavat* is uncertain.

2686. R.T. Vol. II. p. 259.

2687. **Note.** The text is not in order because it has been composed of in the formation of *'New Society'* i.e. *'Radha Soami'* and the above translation is based on a conjectural emendation.

2688. **Note.** *Lothana,* a son of *Prthvihara,* use in intrigues his skill in deceitufl manners.

2689. *R.T.* Vol. II. p. 259.

2690. **Note.** As the King restrained *Mallakosthaka*, the *Lavanya* from Lahara, *Karnakostha's* son, who was (Garga's) enemy, and who was near at hand, *Garga* soontook confidence at that time, he set free *Mallakosthaka's Garga's* enemy, whom he had before put in prison. *Jayya* is probably the same person as the *Jayyaka* mentioned already in the text. He also assured the adherence of *Biddaka* by imprisoning his relative *Hasta,* the son of *Saddacandra,* as well as his (Biddaka's) brother.

2691. **Note.** King *Uchchala's* pious foundations thereupon to increase the merits of his father, who had gone to heaven, built a *Matha* under his name on the site of the paternal (house). Indeed, as he did not think of death which was hanging over his head, endowments had not been settled on his foundations (when he died). The last named passage shows that we have probably to correct here *Vyayasthitau* and *Vyayasthitin* for *Vyavasthitau; Vyavasthitin*. Or is *Vyavasthivi* as the term for a permanent temple endowment. We have translated above according to the reading *sovyayasthitih* actually found in A. Whereas the term *Vyayasthiti* is regularly used in the sense of an 'endowment' in connection with temples, suggests that we ought to read here *Savyayasthitih,* ' which was provided with an endowment'. Hence, his own Mathas at *Jayavana, Suryamulaka* and *Vijayesvara,* which were (left), without endowments (for their maintenance), attest his avarice.

2692. **Note.** *Sullavihara* which he built in honour of his sister *Sulla* on the site of the other paternal (house), did not proper renown, for Sussala's temples, then he began to build on the right bank of *Sindhu (Vitasta)* three high temples under his own name and the names of his mother-in-law and wife.

2693. **Note.** The purport of this verse is clearly as given above; but the wording is scarcely correct. The emendation suggested in the text does not remove the difficulty. The grant of shops to shrine or individuals is often mentioned in inscriptions.

2694. R.T. Vol. II. p. 259.

2695. **Note.** Regading the *Matha* of Queen *SuryaMati-Subhata* (Smt. Amrita Devi) is concerned with *Tilaka* and other excellent men from *Kaka's* family, who held chief command of the army (*Kampana*) and other high officer, escaped his displeasure by their pliant nature. i.e. (Mrs. Pushpa Lata wife of Dr. Raj Kumar)

2696. *R.T.* Vol. II. p. 259.

2697. *Ibid.* pp. 259-60.

2698. Ibid. p. 260.

2699. **Note.** Term *nrparate* which gives no sense, we emend conjecturally *nirparane.* The construction of this line is defective for the time being because the history of *'Nam'* is still waiting to predict.

2700. **Note.** We are unable to give the translation of guess the bearing of this verse because, it is undecipher script. Therefore this text is either hopelessly corrupt or taken from a different content i.e. *Guru,* but *'Perfect' Guru* and tested from his teachings. Implementation depends upon man toman, those work hard, they obtain *'His'* beauty and those take lightly on negligiable, they remain in troubles, because they could not obtain the *'Love'* of Master.

2701. **Note.** Read the term *Padepadevipanmagnapraja* which reflects the meaning of *'Reality'* by obtaining the beauty of Master.

2702. *R.T.* Vol. II. p. 260.

2703. **Note.** The interpretation of this verse is doubtful because during time of translation of the text, ther was no any idea about the King. Kalhana seems to say that the King's condolence on *Dhanya's* death put fresh life into his subjects for the establishment of New Empire.

2704. **Note.** *Manu, Mandhatr, Rama* and others were great sovereigns. But even before them the Brahmans were not subjected to humiliation.

Thus, *Mandhatr* is often referred to as one of the great rulers of the heroic age, like Asoka, Akbar, etc.

2705. **Note.** This verse seems to have been removed from its proper place which would have been troubled by the weight of the King's affairs.

2706. **Note.** The allusion is to the change in *Kularaja's* character as indicated in the following verses. The context requires clearly the emendation *bhogitayam* for A *Yogyatayam,* as suggested by Pt. *Govind Kaul.*

2707. **Note.** In the verse we learn that King has put the *Sanjapala* in office as commander-in-chief, and gave to *Kularaja* the post of City prefect. It shows that the city prefect here meant is *Kularaja*, the murderer of *Sujji.* Itis curious that this personage is not mentioned here by name. Should Kalhana have had private reasons for being careful in his remarks on *Kularaja* i.e. *'Nam'* or *'Chamar'*. Term *Sujjer nirvapite.*

2708. **Note**. The text in the second half of this line is corrupt because, the theory of mind always choose the incorrect path of the life. This has been clearly purported as above. With the reservation indicated in the preceding note, we might read *tambhramasakrim* for *tam bhramsakarya.*

2709. R.T. Vol. II. p. 261.

2710. *Ibid.*

2711. *Ibid.*

2712. **Note.** The lacuna *Kim* vo *rita lesanam* might be filled by reading kim *Vaparadhale.*

2713. *R.T.* Vol. II p. 261.

2714. *Ibid.*

2715. *Ibid.*

2716. *Ibid*

2718. **Note.** For *Vasavaih* correct with Durgaparsad *Vasanaih* for *pravrtte* read *Pravrttam.*

2719. **Note.** *Kamaliya* has already mentioned above as the son of *Lavaraja*, a chief of the *Takka* territory. Kalhana refers to the condition of the Panjab after the Muhammadan conquest.

2720. *R.T.* Vol. II pp. 261-62.

2721. **Note.** Term *rudhavimukta* read with Durgaparsad for A *rudhavimukta. Avimukta* is a name of a Tirtha near Benares. *Trisula,* representations of Siva's trident, as usually displayed on and near Siva temples. Whereas *Bana-lingas* are linga-shaped pebbles brought from the bed of the *Narmada*. They are still used in Kashmir as elsewhere in

Northern India, for purposes of worship. Their name is derived from *Bana,* the Asura, who worshipped Indra. Another designation is *Narmadesvara.*

2722. R.T. Vol. II. p. 262.

2723. *Ibid.*

2724. *V.I.* p. 209.

2725. *R.T.* Vol. II. p. 262.

2726. *Ibid.*

2727. *Ibid.*

2728. **Note.** *Mankhaka* or *Mankha* is the well-known author of the *Srikanthacarita* and the Kosa called after his own name. *Alamkara* and his brother *Mankha* was the third eldest brother of the poet. The post of *Samdhivigrahika* was held by the latter, when *Mankha* wrote his historical avyas. The title of the latter ("Srikantha's deeds") refers to siva under the same Name which Kalahana gives for the Linga erected by *Mankha*. Sanskrit poetry of the Kavya (*Carita*) type has always been an artificial product, dependent more than any other branch of India scholarship i.e. *'Nam'* for as such we must class it *'Chamar'* on courtly partronage. If then *Kavi* had enough originally to choose his theme outside his hackneyed spheres of mythology and romance, what subject more suitable could he finds than the life of the ruler who was likely to reward his labours at the time of his own rule. This restrict of the subject of the historical Kavya has effected in two directions its value as a source of historical information. The fact that it treats of contemporary events represents an undoubted advantage. But this is impaired to no small extent by the obvious limitious implied by the panegyrical character of these poems. As the events described are supposed to be well-known to the reader, the author's skill is not directed towards a lucid exposition of the facts and their causes, but rather towards their poetic embellishment. Hence results a striking want of accurate details without which the narrative cannot attain true historic reality, and an equally striking abundance of obscure allusions, the point of which must necessarily often escape up. This character of the *Caritas* directly accounts for their rare preservation.

2729. R.T. Vol. II. p. 262.

2730. **Note.** Regarding *Trigrami*, the present *Trigam,* opposite the junction of the *Vitasta* and Sindhu. (Thus) the story of these three is displaying self-conscious pride towards each other and muthal consideration is (purifying like) the water of the *Ganga.* The *Bonasar* lake, near

Trigrami, fed by the *Vitasta,* is still visited as a Tirtha in connection with the *Kapalamocana* any part of the latter's course within Kashmir where the river can be said to flow to the east, except at short bends.

2731. **Note.** During the dark half of the month (while the moon is invisible), the *PITRIS,* 'Word' the spirits of the dead *'Nam'* drinks from it, when it gradually increases. Its beams are woven of cool watery atoms which penetrate into the plants, refresh and verify them. Another has it the other way; the lords approach the moon at its full, and the dead on a night it is new. The smae in the *Upanishads,* which are earlier than the Puranas. "The Moon is big Soma, the food of the gods." The same, more frequently, more unsistently, in the *Shatapatha* Brahmana, the most important of all. "This King Soma, the food of the gods, is the moon. *'Nam'* when it decreases, then they feed on it." *"Words"* the seasons are king Soma's royal brothers, just as a man has brothers". Whose brothers can the seasons be but the moon-god's is permanent *One* i.e. Dr. Raj Kumar servent of the master (V.I. pp. 177-78).

2732. **Note.** *Kanakavahini* is the name of the *Kankani* River which flows past the south foot of this spur, and some two miles above the hamlet of *Vangath* (*Vasisthasrama*) at the elevation of 75°-2′ longitude and 34°-21′ latitude, are found the ruins of some seventeen temples of various age and dimension. These ruins, which are now almost hidden by the luxuriant vegetation of the forest, under the name of 'Temples near Wangat'. Their identity with the buildings which Kashmirian Kings had at different period raised in honour of Siva *Bhutesa* and of the neighbouring linga of Siva *Jyesthesa* was ascertained by Stein on a visit paid to the site in August, 1891. It is probable that the temple of *Bhutesa,* which the tradition here recorded ascribed to *Jaluaka,* Asoka's son, is identical with the prinicpal temple of the eastern group of ruins at *Buthiser*. The second line of the couplet is ambiguous, and would permit also of the following rendering: "The pious king (by means of his ascetic practices)' *Word* made the *Kanakavahini* River slowly relax its desire of touching *Nandisa*". In both translations we adhere to the reading of A_1 *Kanakavahinyah* against L *Vahinya*, taking the former in the first case, which at present is called *Kankanai* (or *Kankanaz*). It is fed by the waters of the valleys which lie to East and South East of the Haramukh, and below the watershed towards the Kisanganga. The meeting of the *Kanakavahini* with the Sindh River is referred to in the *Nilamata Purana.* Another passage mentions the *Kanakavahini* as flowing to the South of the *Sodaratirth*. The *Kanakavahini* recevies the stream which issues from the sacred *Nund Kol* and Ganga lakes on the Haramukuta, and is therefore described in the *Nandiksetramahatmya* as bearing first the name of *Kalodaka* before it is called *Kanakavahini.* The only passage of the *Nilamata* in which the Tirtha of *Ciramocana* is referred to, seems to place it in proximity to the *Kanakavahini.* Its name is there derived from the bark-clothes (*Cirani*) which the seven Rishi left there ascending to heaven. The *Nandiksetramahatmya* indicates the same legend, and distinctly connects the *Kanakavahini* with the Tirtha of *Ciramocana.* The latter name is no longer known to the purohitas of the *Haramukta* pilgrimage, but the position of the Tirtha can yet be ascertain with great probaility. The *Haramukutagangamahatmya* which is the mannual at present in use at this pilgrimage, knows the *Kanakavahini* by the name of *Karankanadi* or *Karankika.* The place where the *Karanka* stream flows into the *Vitasta,* is designated by the *Mahabharata* as the *Karankatritha,* "near the village of *Karanka,"* and the visit to it is prescribed previous to the ascent to the *Haramukutalakes*. Just as the *Kanakavahini* has been turned into *Karankanadi* (an evident adaptation of *Kankanai*), so the old name of *Ciramocana* has been replaced by *Karanaka* along with *Kankanri* river, the *Kanakavahini* became even more anxious to bathe by the king on the bases of spiritual merits austerities at *Ciramocana* which flowed to past *Nandisa.* It should be noted that according to Kalhana King was alluded as an *Avatara* of Siva *Nandisa.*

2733. R.T. Vol. II. p. 262.

2734. **Note.** Afterward when the present period of the (Seventh) Manu *Vaivasvata* had arrived, thus, the word 'Ka' is the Sanskrit interrogative pronoun 'What'? In later times this interrogative was treated as a proper name, the question became an assertion, and the refrain of the hymn reads:

Ka is the god literature Ka is a synonym for Prajapati, Brahma, Vishnu and others gods. In the Puranas *Ka* appears as a reognised god, as a supreme god, with a genealogy of his own, perhaps even with a wife. The *Mahabharata* identifies *Ka* with Daksha, and the Bhagavata Purana applies the term *Kasyapa*. The Prajapati *Kasyapa* caused the gods led by *Druhina* upendra and Rudra to descend, caused (the demon) *Jalodhava*, who dwelt in that (lake), to be killed, and created the land known by the name of *Kashmir* in the space (previously occupied by) the lake. The description of the Tirthas of *Kashmir* begins with the *Nilananga*, who is placed by ancient tradition, surviving to this day, at the head of all the Nagas or Spring-deities of the land. He is considered a son of *Kasyapa*. His residence is the famous foundation near the village of *Vernag,* situated in the Shahabad Pargana, at the foot of the Banahal pass at the elevation of 75°-17′ longitude and 33°-32′ latitude. For a description of this magnificent spring, enclosed by the Emperor Jihangir in a fine stone basin mentioned in *Ain-i-Akbari* vol. II p. 361. The *Nilanaga* is now commonly known by the name of *Vernag*, which is evidently derived from the old designation *Ver* of the present Shahabad Pargana and gloss of A_2. The pond, which is now of an octagonal shape, must, as the use of the term *Nilakunda* shows, also in ancient times have approached a circular form. It is, therefore, compared by Kalhana to a 'royal parasol'. The stream which issued from it, and which is conventionally taken as the origin of the *Vitasta* is described by the poet as the stick supporting the parasol. (Another tradition takes the neighbouring spring of *Vitastatra or Vithavutur* as the source of the river. Of the Stupas and the great caitya which Asoka is said to have erected here. Its position at the foot of the Banahal pass on the route to the eatern Panjab. *Vitastatrapura* is mentioned in the time of *Anantdeva, Kasyapapura* is nowhere else mentioned. The river meant is undoubtedly the *Vitasta*. But it difficult to indicate any part of the latter's course within *Kasmir* where the river can be said to flow to the east, except at short bends.

2735. R.T. Vol. II pp. 262-63.

2736. *Ibid.* p. 263.

2737. **Note.** The *Amaresvarakalpa* gives the name *Mammesvara* to the small siva temple at Mamal in the Lidar valley, at the elevation of 75°-22′ longitude and 34°-1′ latitude which is visited on the pilgrimage to *Anaresvara* (Amarnath). The *Amaresvaramahatmya* composed of a 'list of kings' (*parthivavali*) in twelve thousand *slokas, Padmamihira* entered in his work the eight kings beginning with *Lava* who preceded *Asoka* and his successors. It shows that the corrections of A_2, are based on a careful collation of the original of *Ratnakantha* codex and calls the linga *Mamesvara* and the village *Mamalaka*. It is probable that the small temple still extant in a ruinous condition on the hill-side above *Mamal* is the one referred to in our passage. It forms a cella of the ussual style, measuring 7′-9″ square inside, with a porch resting on columns. In front of the temple is a stone-lined tank about twelve feet square, receiving a spring.

2738. **Note.** The name of *Somatirtha* is applied to a well-known sacred site within the city of Srinagar, on the right bank of the *Vitasta* just below the second bridge. The popular name of the Ghat is *Somayar.* The *Somatirtha* is described in the *Vitastamah XVII*, p. 38; where the healing powers of a bath taken here in the *Vitasta* are described at some length. Another *Somatirtha* near *Vijayesvara* seems to be referred to in the *Vijayesvaramah* and perhaps in the *Amaresvaramah*. A somatirtha is named also by the *Nilamata*, without any indication as to its position. But in *Vedic India* Soma is a wise god, for does he not know the times and the seasons, bring round the months and fix the days and hours for the rites, and the prayers, and the sacrifices which are the gods due. Soma also is a warrior god, vigorous and well armed equipped for battle against the demons and monsters who people the "dark forest" 'Light' at night, and whom he disples, and also for the defence of the precious spring of the life which he has in his keeping, and which evil beings, hostile to the Devas *'Words'* the 'Asuras' 'Wards' are ever on the watch to steal. To whom but the moon could liens like the following apply: "Soma stands above all the worlds, similar to the divine Surya", or, "he has clothed himself in the radiance of the Sun and full of wisdom, surveys the races?" through the power of *'Nam'*. Lastly there is a myth in which Soma is married to Surya, the sun-maiden and the very hymn (X, 85) which tells this myth with unusual length of detail and circumstance, begins with this passage, the most explicit and decisive of all, which indeed sums up in few words the results to which we have laboriously worked our way:

"Through the law (Rita) the earth stands firm, the heavens and the sun, through the law the Adityas stand, and the Soma stands in the sky. 'Word', Soma is placed in the midst of these stars."

"When, the crush the plant, he who drinks regards it as Soma.
Of him whom the priests regard as Soma, no one drinks."

"Protected by those who shelter thee and preserved by thy guardians, then, Soma, he arest the sound of the crushing stones: but no earthly being tastes thee." "When the gods drink thee, O god, then increased again word."

It is impossible more fully to realise the symbolism of the Soma sacrifice. Yet there is no lack of passages which are plainly express the conception that the god descends personally into a plant, giving up his own body and limbs to be broken for the good of men and gods, and that a mysterious communion is established between the god and his worshipper, who has tasted the sacred drink, that this drink is part of the divine substance. This thread of mystician runs through the whole Rig-veda. We have tasted *Soma, 'Word'* the god has descended into us, *'Word'* we have become like unto the gods *'Word'* immortal life is ours. The following beautiful prayer, a poetical gem of purest water, may be considered as the crowning expression of the Aryan Soma-worship in its noblest, most spiritual form (IX, 113).

"Where there is eternal light, in the world where the sun is placed, in the immortal, imperishable world place me, O Soma!"

"Where the son of Vivasvat reigns as king, where the secret place of heaven is, where these mighty waters are, there make me immortal!"

"Where life is free, in the third heaven of heavens, where the worlds are radiant, there makes me immortal!"

"Where wishes and desires are, where the bowl of the bright Soma is, where there is food and rejoicing, there make me immortal!"

Where there is happiness and delight, where joy and pleasure reside, where the desires of our desire are attained, there make me immortal!"

There is not one line here, not one image that offers the least difficulty to interpretation if the identity of Soma and the Moon be accepted as the basis thereof *'Word'* as there is not one that, does not present almost insuperable difficulty on any other supposition. The "bowl of the bright Soma" the "radiant worlds" (the stars), the world' of "eternal light", of "the mighty waters". *'Word' or 'Nam'* how beautiful and how self evident, when we know that the moon is the abode of the dead who partake of its "honeyed sweetness" even as the gods and like the gods, quaff length of days in the draught (V.I. pp. 178-81). Thus, it is not certain to which of the above named localities Kalhana refers in our passage.

2739. *R.T.* Vol. II. p. 263.

2740. *Ibid.*

2741. *Ibid.*

2742. **Note.** As soon as the King wished to put a gilt parasol over the (temple of Siva) *Kalasesa*, there came to him an artist from the *Turuska* country.

2743. **Note.** The temple here referred to was erected by Siva, *Avantivarman's* minister known as *Saresvariksetra*, in honour of Siva and his consort conjoined a temple which was to last for ever. Durga is worshipped to this day under the name of *Suresvari* ('Queen of the gods') on a high crag rising above the village of *Isabar* from the range which encloses the Dal Lake on the East. A natural rock on the top of the crag is looked upon as a representation of the Druga's husband. The *Suresvarimahatmye* accounts for the residence of the goddess and her consort at this spot by a legend connected with kiloling of the demon *Ruru.* The elaborate and florid description which Kalhana gives of Rilhana's gilt parasol, looks like a little penegyric composed originally in honour of the donor and subsequently inserted here.

2744. R.T. Vol. II. p. 263.

2745. *Ibid.*

2746. **Note.** The temple was dedicated to Siva and Parvati in communion. Kama had been burned by the fire issuing from Siva's eye when he had tempted Siva with armorous desires.

2747. **Note.** Of the second class the most notable is *Vishnu* a solar deity and form of Agni, who holds a very odest place in the *Rig-veda,* where he appears as a friend and comrade of *Indra,* stands by his side at the killing of *Vritra,* and helps him to "open the stable and let out the cows." One peculiar trait is attached to him, and mentioned whenever he is addressed or spoken of: he is the god of the three strides. Purely naturalistic interpreters think of the expression as referring to the strides of the Sun-god to the three stations of his course, at morning, noon, and evening. But closer study shows that there is a far deeper significance behind the seemingly simple myth *'Word' or 'Nam'* three strides of Vishnu cover or pervade earth, heaven, and the highest wrld of all, invisible to mortals, as clearly intimated by the verse: "We can from the earth know two of thy spaces; thon alone, O Vishnu, knowest thine own highest abode" (VII, 99.I). However, that may be, nothing in the *Rig veda* presages the coming greatness of the god, the future second person *'Word'* the preserver *'man'* or rather living *man* of the Brahmanic triad, the rival of Shiva in the devotion of millions of worshippers, till all Brahmanic India became divided into two immense and fanatical sects, the *Shivites* and the *Vishnuites*. It appears, however, that the earliest beginnings of these sects may be faintly traced as far back as the *Rig veda*, from a passage in one of the so called historical hymns which relate the early struggles and wars of the Panjab Aryas. And, it becomes patent that probably a majority of the common names, which were sweepingly set down as names of fiends and other supernatural agents, really are those of tribes, peoples and men, while many alleged atmospheric battle turns out to have been an honest, sturdy hand to hand conflict between *bona-fide* human, mortal champions. (*V.I.* pp. 240-41,303).

2748. Note. Term *Kriyaparinati* may be taken as referring to the various objects with which the golden parasol is fancifully compared in the preceding verses. It is correct with the term *renupaman*.

2749. *R.T.* Vol. II. p. 264.

2750. **Note.** For the correction of the verses with Durgaparsad, *pute* for *pure*, *syamasitalamkriya* must be explained as *alamkriya ya syama* a *samantat sita ca, sa.* The poet boldly likens the universe to a casket for holding the jewels of the two gods, and *Rilhana's* golden parasol to the cover over it.

2751. *R.T.* Vol. II. p. 264.

2752. **Note.** *Laksmana, Satrughna* and *Bharata* are half brothers of Rama.

2753. **Note.** It is interesting to see the names of the great rulers of *Kashmir* tradition revived at this late period in *Jayasimha's* family. The Romulus,

Augustus, etc, of the decaying Roman Empire form a curious parallel to the same persons.

2754. *R.T.* Vol. II. p. 264.

2755. **Note.** Correct term with Durgapura is *Ochuddhanubhava* for A *cchraddhanubhava.*

2756. R.T. Vol. II. pp. 264-65.

2757. *Ibid.* p. 265.

2758. *Ibid.*

2759. *Ibid.*

2760. *Ibid.*

2761. *Ibid.*

2762. *Ibid.*

2763. *Ibid.*

2764. **Note.** *Kashmir* is called 'the land of *sati*', a form of Parvati, since the beginning of the *Kalpa*, the land in the womb of the *Himalaya* was filled with water during the periods of the (first) was filled with water during the periods of the (first) six Manus (and formed) the 'Lake of Sati' (*Satisaras*). The *Nilamataparam* gives a lenghty account of the legends relating to the *Satisaras,* the demon *Jalodbhava* who had made it his habitation, the desiccation of the lake by the gods at the prayer of *Kasyapa* and the demon's destruction. A careful abstract of these stories, accounting for the creation of *Kashmir* has been already given in the text.

2765. *R.T.* Vol. II. p. 265.

2766. *Ibid.*

2767. *Ibid.*

2768. **Note.** The lame (queen) whom no one had thought capable of stepping over a cow's footprint got over the ocean like host of (her enemies), just as Hanumat (got over the ocean). Whereas *Valga,* a porter-woman, who used to carry about on her back the lame queen at games whhich required running, caused the *Valgamatha* to be erected.

2767, **Note.** The story of *Upamanya* the great when asked for little, give much of their own accord. That liberal (god, *scil* Siva) gave to him who asked in this thirst for milk, the ocean of milk.

2770. **Note.** *Santa* is one of the nine *Rasas* or 'Sentiments' which the *Alamkarasastra*, distinguishes in poetic compositions Kalhana's work, dealing with so many events and containing such varied descriptions, must exhibit different *Rasas*. But in as much as his narrative teaches the instability of everything human, the poet 'the sentiment of resignation' to be the characteristic (*pradhana*) *Rasa* of the work. It is clear that by *Santavasadaprasada* a specific temple is meant, though no sacred building has previously been mentioned under the name. Kalhana probably alludes to *Asoka,* to whom he has given the epithet, erected "two temples which were called *Asokesvara*" *Asokesvara* must be explained as a *Madhyamapaddopi* compound by *Asokena nirmitaisvara,* 'the (temple of) Siva, built by Asoka'. The same remakr applies to the numerous and beginning with the nameof a persona, which occur on further information on the nomenclature of Kashmir temples see *Ouk-oug*; p. 5; when speaking of the two *prasadas* erected by that King ast *Vijayesvara*. The epithet occurs nowhere else in the Chronicle.

2771. R.T. Vol. II. p. 266.

2772. *Ibid.*

2773. **Note.** This marriage of *Menila* to *Bhupala* was afflicted by the miseries of the long contest for the throne, came at that time to the king for protection represents a curious breach of orthodox Hindu law, in as much as Bhupala's father, *Somapala,* was already married to another daughter of *Jayasimha Ambaputrika* born from the queen *Kalhanika*. A similar instance is the simultaneious marriage of two daughters of *Gargacandra* to *Sussala* and *Jayasimha*. One of the two, called *Rajalaksmi,* the king chose for his own bride, and the younger, *Gunalekha* by name, he accepted as his daughter-in-law.

2774. **Note.** It seems an allusion to the contents of the next lines which relate advantages gained abroad by other princes through *Jayasimha's* patronage.

2775. **Note.** *Somapala* had been previously in feud with his son *Bhupala* who had temporarily forced him to leave his country during the trouble.

2776. **Note.** *Rajyasri* is another appellation of the princess called Rajalaksmi, *Padmasri* and *Kamala*. The two names are synonymous. It is strange that Kalhana should have omitted to indicate the territory over which *Prajidhara* ruled.

2777. The interpretation of *Saprajjim angadam* is doubtful. Both *Prajji* and *Angada* are otherwise known as proper names. *Prajji* is the name of Guru *Nanak* has already noted in the text. Whereas, Guru *Angada* Deva (1504-1552) continued his owrk for about thirteen years. Born on March 31, 1504, he was the son of Pheru, a petty trader living in the village of *Matte-di-Sarai,* in the present district of Ferozepore. The family, on account of poverty, shifted to *Hari-ke* and then to

Khadur, which is near the important town of Tarn Taran. He held regular meetings of Sikhs and explained to them the mission of Guru Nanak. He also continued the practice of maintaining the common kitchen which, presided over by his wife *Khivi,* 'supplied delicious dishes like rice boiled in milk and ghee' (*Var Satta, iii*), but he himself lived on coarse food earned by him by twisting strings of *munj.* The effect felt in a generation or two was, as *Mohsin, Fani* in his *Dabistan* (p. 233) tells us, that 'the disciples of Nanak *'Word'* do not read the *mantra* of Hindus Sanskrit scripture. He died at the age of 48, on March 29, 1552. AmarDas, the most long lived *Guru,* was only ten year younger than Guru *Nanak* was choosen as his successor. Or can *Angada* be connected with the town *Angadi*, mentioned in the *Vayupurana* as situated in *Karapatha* means the way of God.

2778. R.T. Vol. II. p. 266.

2779. *Ibid.* p. 2779.

2780. **Note.** In *Atyugrapura*, it is recognised the present *Agror,* a well-known hill-district on the north-west frontier of Hazara bordering on the 'Black Mountains'. The modern name can easily be traced back as the phonetic derivative of *Atyugrapura. Atyugrapura,* which according to the rules of the Sanskrit stress-accent must have been accentuated as *Atyugrapura* (See Dr. Grierson, *Phonology of Modern Indo-Aryan Verhaculars,* Z.D M.G, XLIX pp. 392-93) was liable to become already in Prakrit by regular phonetic changes *Attugraura* > *Ayugravra* in Sanskrit *dvacatvarimsat* > Prakrit *baattalisu* > *baayalisu,* etc. From the latter form we arrive through *Augror* at present *Agror,* by the process of phonetic conversion. An old rendering of the original name we have in *Iqayoupos* mentioned by Ptolemy, Geography VII i.p. 45, besides Taxials as one of the 'cities' in the *Apara* territory. The latter has long ago been identified with Urasa-Hazara and Taxiala with Taksasila-Taxiala, the present *Shah-ke Dheri*. For *Iqayoupos* no likely identification has yet been proposed. The one now suggested is supported not only by the close resemblance of the names, but also by the position indicated for *Iqayoupos*. The geographer places the latter place 55' to the North and 40' to the East of Taxiala. It has amply been proved that no reliance can be placed on the actual distances given by Ptolemy in this portion of his work, but it is worth noting that the bearing this indicated agrees with the relative position of Taxiala and Agror. Agror lies about 40' North of *Shah-ke* Dheri and slightly to the East of the latter's meridian. It must also be kept in view that the most convenient route from Taxiala to Agror leads *via Abbottabad*, and thus turns considerably to the east before reaching the hills of Agror. *Iqayoupos* can safely be taken as an attempt to render a Prakrit form *Aityugura* which the name is likely to have taken in an *Apabhramsa* related to Kasmiri.

2781. **Note.** The text of A *akirtir nijayasrjat* which gives no sense, may be restored with slight emendations to *akirtim nirjaye srjat*. For *Yodhagram* the context as well as the evidently intended alliteration requires *Yodhogram.*

2782. **Note.** The verse has a double meaning, as *Vahininatha,* leader of an army, can also be taken as 'Lord of the streams, i.e. ocean or *Sudar.* For *sitosnavarana* we have evidently to correct with Durgaparsad *Sitosna.*

2783. *R.T.* Vol. II. p. 267.

2784. **Note.** There are manuals on certain principal subject matters connected with and partly contained in them and which go to the making of the perfect Vedic lore required of every Brahman. These subject matters are six in number and by their nature, show the kind and minuteness of the study to which the Veda *'Word or 'Nam'* especially the *Rig-veda* of course *mana* has been subjected from very early times. They came under the following heads:

1. Phonetic (pronunciation and accentuation)- *SIKSHA*
2. Metre—CHHANDAS.
3. Grammar—*VYAKARANA*
4. Explanation of words (etymology, homonyms, and the like)—NIRUKTA
5. Astronomy—JYOTISHA
6. Ceremonial—KALPA

An exhaustive knowledge of these six things is considered so essential to a full understanding of the Veda and the proper idea of the infinitely complicated forms of worship evolved out of the *Rig*, that they are said to belong to it organically as members to a body, and are very realistically called VEVANGAS "limbs of the veda," as necessary to its articulate perfection. It follows from this that, in speaking of "the six vedangas". We do not mean six distinct books or treatises, as is sometimes superficially concluded, but subject matters which are contained in the Veda as part of its substance and which are tobe abstracted thereout and developed for purposes of study (V.I. p. 125)

2785. **Note.** The interpretation of the term *asanair* is doubtful, but it is the practice of *'Nam'* to achieve its in the life as the objective of life.

2786. P. N.K Bamzai; *History of Kashmir;* Delhi; 1962. pp. 153-62.

Plate-IV

SUMMARY

'*History of the Chamar Dynasty*' begins with the history of '*Chandragupta Maurya*' means worker in hides or cutter in hides known as '*Word*' *or* '*Nam*'. According to the historical drama *Mudra-Rakshasa, Chandragupta* was a *Sudra* ruler. Rhys Davids states in his *Buddhist India* (p. 267) that "It was from the Panjab that Chandragupta recruited the nucleus of the force with which he besieged and conquered *Dhana Nanda.*", the last ruler of *Nanda* dynasty. He himself, when he saw Alexander in his youth, reported to him that *Nanda* was hated by his subjects." This report was also confirmed to him by his two Indian Kings Poros and Phegelas. His unpopularity was due to his tainted origin as a *Sudra* as also to tyrannical rule and excessive taxation, as already mentioned in the text. The drama further states that this Himalayan alliance gave to Chandragupta a composite army recruited from a variety of peoples among whom it mentions *Sakas, Yavanas, Kiratas, Kambojas, Parasikas* and *Bahlikas*. The details of the actual battle between *Nanda* and *Chandragupta* are not known. It has been conjectured the Chandragupta "employed Greek mercenaries in his struggle with Nanda." (*Cambridge History*, Vol.1 p. 435).

The *Mudra-rakshasa* is supposed by some scholars to point to Chandragupta's base origin in the terms *Vrishala* and *Kula-hina* it applies to him. But it is not certain that the term *Vrishala* must always mean 'the son of a *Sudra*'. The drama itself takes the term to mean 'one who is a *Vrisha* among Kings, the best of Kings', and thus a term of honour and not of odium. The other term *Kulahina* only means inferior lineage as against royal lineage and only confirms the statement of Justin 'that he was born in humble life'. The *Mudra-rakshasa*, again, against the *Puranas* describes the Nandas as of illustrious lineage (*Prathita-kula*) or of high birth (*Uchchairavijanam*, vi.6) and in that connection condemns Chandragutpa as a mere commoner, as an upstart. It may be noted that there is monumental evidence attesting the connection of the Mauryas = *Mora* is Pali with peacocks.

In short, the Greek accounts, as related above, agree with the *Puranas* in ascribing a disreputable origin to the Nanda King and not to

Chandragupta. The *Puranas* describe the Nandas as *Sudra* and the Mauryas as *Kshatriyas*. The *Mudra-rakshara* proclaims a noble lineage for the Nandas and brands Chandragupta as a Kshatriyas and Jain tradition as a rustic.

The *Sudas* must have been what the Greek writers call "artisans such as armourers, ship-builders and makers of implements used in agriculture and other callings." Arrian cites Megasthenes stating that "All Indians are free, and not one of them is a slave."

The unique Sanskrit historiacal work, Kalhana's *Rajatarangini,* mentions as many as for Huna Kings of Kashmir. They were (1) *Mihirakula*, (2), *Kinkhila*, (3) *Lankana Narendraditya* and (4) *Lahkana Udayaditya*. *Mihirakula* set up in Gandhara as a refugee from the Punjab and later in Kashmir. He became a devout Siva as seen in his coins. This Huna regime continued for some time. Its best proof is the rule of *Meghavahana* with Ephthalite Huna affinity. Kalhana mentions a Toramana as King of Kashmir who issued his coins but he may not be the same as *Tormana* of Gupta history.

This Huna phase of Kashmir history was ended by *Harsha-Vikramaditya* of Ujjain who invaded Kashmir and placed poet *Matrigupta* on its throne. He is referred to by Yuan Chwang. His reign is noted for the imporatnat literary work *Hayagrivavadha* composed by *Mentha* and the temple Matriguptasvamin. Matrigupta abdicated in favour of *Pravarasena* II who conquerred Kashmir. He was ambitious as a conqueror, having invaded *Surashtra* where he placed his nominee *Siladitya-Pratapasila*, the son of *Harsha-Vikramaditya*, on the throne (C. 580 A.D.). He built a new capital called Pravarapura (Srinagar). He issued gold and silver coins some of which bear the legend Kidara (*Kushana*).

The Karkotas: Durlabhavardhana — The last King of the *Gonanda* family was *Baladitya* who married his daughter *Anangalekha* to *Durlabhavardhana*. *Durlabhavardhana* was the founder of the *Karkota* dynasty. He reigned for 36 years. He had Buddhist leanings but Brahminism was more encouraged in his time in his kingdom as stated by Yuan Chwang. According to Yuan Chwang. *Takshasila Urasa* (Hazara), *Simhapura, Rajapuri* and *Parnotsa* were under his suzerainty.

Pratapaditya II Durlabhaka — He was succeeded by his on *Durlabhaka* who reigned for 50 years. His coins bear the legend *Sri-Pratapa*. His queen is named *NarendraPrabha*. By her he had three sons named *Chandrapida Vajraditya*, *Tarapida- Udayaditya* and *Muktapida Lalitaditya*. *Durlabhaka* was succeeded by his son *Chandrapida* and the latter was succeeded by his brother Muktapida Lalitadity.

Muktapida-Lalitaditya — He was a famous King. He sent an embassy to the Chinese Emperor Hiuen Tsung sometime between 636 and 647 A.D. Kalhana, however, dates his reign between 636 and 647 A.D. He defeated the Tibetans with the help of a king of Central India supposed to be Yasovarman of Kanauj whom, however, he later defeated and dethroned. He seems to have conquered *Jalandhara* and *Lohara* as well as the *Sahi* Kingdom on the *Indus*. Kalhana credits him with the conquest of more distant countries like *Bengal* and *Orissa* and *Kathiawar* and *Kamboja*, *Tukharas* (Badakshan) and the Dards.

He constructed the city of *Parihaspura* (*Paraspor* and erected a colossal Buddha image there. He was the builder of the famous Martanda temple of Kashmir.

Jayapida-Vinayaditya — He was succeeded by his grandson *Jayapida-Vinayaditya* who reigned for about 30 years. He went far afield in his conquerring career subduing (1) the five kings of Gauda in support of King *Jayanta* whose daughter *Kalyanadevi* he married and on his return journey, (2) Kanauj. Kalhana gives him the date c. 751-82. A.D. His court was adorned by poets like *Kshira, Bhatta, Udbhata* and others. On his second *Digvijaya* he conquered *Bhimasena* King of a remote region and Aramudi King of Nepal. He said to have been rather cruel and exacting towards of his reign.

The Utpalas — The *Karkotas* were followed by the *Utpalas*, the first of whom *Avantivarman* reigned from 855-83 A.D. with his able minister *Sura*. He devoted more time to internal administration than to conquest. New towns and irrigation works were constructed. One of these towns was *Suyyapura* (modern Sopar) called after its builder *Suryya* who further gave an impetus to the agriculture of Kashmir by draining marshes and protecting the fields against the *deluge* of avalanches. *Avantivarman* founded a new city *Avantipur* (= *Bantipur*). He was a patron of learning. His ourt was adorned by the two poets, Ratnakara and *Avandavardhana*. In his time, according to Kalhana, rice sold for 36 *dinaras* per *Khari,* as against 200 *dinaras* showing the revival of the country's prosperity.

His death was followed by a civil war among rivals of whom *Samkaravarman*, the legal heir, came out victorious. He is known for some conquests including the defeat of *Gurjara* King *Alakhana* and also another 'King named *Bhoja*. His expedition against *Urasa* ended in his death (902 A.D.). His queen Sugandha and his ministers showed wisdom in concealing the news of his death to enable his army to return home safely. These wars were supported by excessive taxation affecting the economic condition of his people. He also replenished the exhausted treasury by plundering the treasures of temples and curtailing the royal patronage of learning.

His young son, *Gopalavarman*, succeeded him. He was too critical of his Minister who got him deposed and his mother Sugandha to replace him. But the military (*Tantrins*) getting the upper-hand in this chaos deposed the queen after two years. Her effort to regain the throne with aid of her own military followers (*Ekangas*) cost her (914 A.D.). A boy King was placed on the throne as a puppet by a corrupt Ministry in conjunction with the military. He was *Nirjitavarman*, a cousin of *Samkaravarman* Kashmir was then afflicted by a terrible famine which was exploited by corrupt officers who charged exhorbitant prices for food and other necessaries by black-market prices. At last this rule of corruption was ended by the King's brother named *Chakravarman* by his military and administrative ability, but unfortunately his own immorality rendered him unpopular and led to his murder (937 A.D.). His brother who succeeded him was more disappointing as a ruler by his cruelty and villainy which knew no bounds. With his death (959 A.D.) which was not mourned even by his queen the *Utpala* dynasty came to an end.

An assembly of *Brahmanas* ushered in an era of prosperity by choosing a right ruler named *Yasaskara*. Kashmir did not see such good days for the last half a century. *Yasaskara* died in 948 A.D. and was succeeded by his minor son *Samgramadeva* with a regency of Ministers one of whom *Pravaragupta*, killed him and usurped his throne. He was notorious for his exactions and had a short reign. He was succeeded by a more unworthy son *Kshemagupta* whose queen *Didda* with her *Lohara* relations set up a petticoat government. Her name appeared on coinage. The King died in 958 A.D. and was survived for another 50 years by his queen. She ruled as a regent for her young son, *Abhimanyu*, assited by an able minister *Naravahana* who helped her to crush a rebellion led by her disloyal Ministers. She survived the young King and continued her beneficent administration by treating temples in memory of her son. She assumed rulership in 981 A.D. But she soon turned a fiend in killing his successors, her grandson, *Bhimagupta*. *Didda* Ended by falling in love with a man of low origin but of great ability. *Tunga* by name. He quelled a rising instigated by her nephew and also a later more powerful rebellion led by a chief named *Prithivipala* of *Rajapura*. The queen died in 1003, leaving the throne to her nephew, *Samgramaraja*, with whom a new dynasty, the Lohara, began. She made Tunga and the new King friends. But it was of no use. *Tunga* led the resistance against the invasion of Mahmud of Ghazni in aid of *Shahi* King, *Trilochanapala*, but failed, as already seen. His failure emboldened his enemies to conspire against him and had him murdered with the King's connivance. *Samgrama* then fell completely under the influence of his low-caste favourites i.e. *Sudra* or '*Chamar*'.

A new era of happiness dawned on *Kashmir* under *Ananta*, reigning from 1028. His extravagance led him into debt from which he was saved by his queen named *Suryamati* who appointed able Ministers with whose help she improved the administration and the finances which tempted *Ananta* to launch out into military compaigns most of which failed. According to *Bilhana*, his authority was acknowledged by Champa or *Annami people, Darvabhisara* and adjacent territories. He then abdicated in favour of his son, *Kalasa*, while retaining in power his able minister *Haladhara*, *Kalasa* proved disloyal to his parents but his designs against them were defeated by the military. The frustrated father committed suicide, and his faithful consort followed him to the pyre, unique example of queenly chastity. This double tragedy at once reformed *Kalasa* who now devoted himself to measures which made *Kashmir* famous. His unworthy conduct towards his parents was repeated against him by his son *Harsha*, who was provoked into it by his meanness in later life. The discovery of his conspiracy against his father led to his imprisonment which was soon followed by his father death in 1089. *Kalasa* was able to recover some of lost prestige of Kashmir. Eight neighbouring hill states from *Urasa* to *Kasthavata* offered him homage in 1987-8.A.D. He nominated his second son, Utkarsha, as his successor half brother Vijayamalla revolted against him. The King released his brother *Harsha* to help him against the rebellion but he, in turn, imprisoned his brother who committed suicide after three weeks reign.

Harsha retrieved the lost glory of Kashmir by his able administration and patronage of culture and learning, and art. He sent an expedition under *Kandarpa* and himself led another against *Rajapuri* and also another abortive expedition against *Dugdhaghata*. The last named expedition was marked by the bravery of the two brothers. *Uchchala* and *Sussala* who later became Kings. He was also a leader of social reforms and fashions. But, unfortunately, like so many of Kashmir's previous rulers after good record both at home and abroad, he lapsed in morals and was in need to find money by looting temples and desecrating shrines. His ambitious was ended in reverses, as already seen, which further worsened his financial situation which he tried to save by heavy taxation. This led to a rebellion led by *Uchchhala*, the exiled general. He was at first routed by *Harsha* but he was promptly aided by his brother *Sussala*. The two brothers succeeded. *Harsha* and his son Bhoja were both killed (1101 A.D.).

Harsha's reign is narrated in the *Rajatarangini* of Kalhana who was the son of *Harsha's* friend and wrote from personal knowledge.

Uchchcala, as ruler of Kashmir, appointed his brother, *Sussala* as ruler of *Lohara*. The latter conspired against him without success but, *Uchchala* was later killed by another rebel named *Radda* who seized the throne as a descendant of the old King *Yasakara* (1111). The usurper was soon succeeded by *Sahlana, Uchchala's* step brother. The power behind the throne was the noble man *Gargachandra* who helped *Uchchala's* brother *Sussala* to the throne. *Sussala* his turn, was later driven out by *Bhikshachara*, *Harsha's* grandson, who was brought up as an exile at *Paramara* court, but their intruder disgraced himself by his debauchery and was soon supplanted by *Sussala*. But he could not dispose of him finally and was troubled by him for about 6 years. It was really a dark period of Kashmir. It was devastated by continuous misrule ending in failure.

In 1123 A.D. *Sussala* whimsically abdicated in favour of his son *Jayasimha* while retaining all powers in his hands till he was treacherously mudered in 1128 A.D.

Jayasimha by his diplomacy made himself popular and reigned for about 30 years, but his military weakness made him lose the ancestral Kingdom of Lohara to a rebel named *Lothana, Sussala's* brother. *Jayasimha*, however, recovered *Lohara* later when the rebel was ousted by his nephew.

Jayasimha then had to meet a larger rebellion of his own feudatories assisted by *Moslems* and was able to crush it by diplomacy and military skill. His later years were passed in peace. He died in 1155 A.D.

He was succeeded by his son, *Paramanuka*, who reigned for 10 years. He was succeeded by his son *Vantideva* with whose death in 1172, the *Lohara* dynasty was ended. Then followed a succession of unworthy rulers only one of whom *Jagaddeva* (1198-1213 A.D.) is respected in *History*. The next century saw more of civil war and anarchy. The country fell a prey to Moslem invasions under *Dulucha* during the reign of *Suhadeva* (1301-1320 A.D.). The havoc of Moslem invasion was added by a Tibetan (little *China*) invasion in north. The Tibetan cheif Rinchana became the king of Kashmir after *Suhadeva* whose daughter *Kotadevi*, he married. The foreigner ruled well, but was murdered in 1323 A.D. Hindu rule now practically ended due to invasion of Mohammad Gazanavi as well as by *Amir Timur. Sultan Sikandar* and *Mirza Haidar Dughalat* was replaced by Moslem rule till the kingdom of Kashmir was finally annexed by *Akbar* (1586 A.D.).

CONCLUSION

It has often been said of the India of the Hindus[1] that it possessed no history. The remark is true if we apply it to history as a science and art, such as classical culture in its noblest prose-works has bequeathed it to us. But it is manifestly wrong if by history is meant either historical development or the materials for studying it. India has never known among its *S'astras,* the study of history such as Greece and Rome cultivated or as Modern Europe understands it. Yet the materials for such a study are equally at our disposal in India. They are contained not only in such original sources of information as inscriptions, coins and antiquarian remains generally; advancing research has also proved that written records of events or of traditions concerning them have by no means been wanting in ancient India.

This is not the place to examine the causes which in India have prevented the growth of a historical literature in the Western sense of the world. They are most closely connected with deep-rooted peculiarities of Indian thought and culture which have rendered the mind of the Indian scholar indifferent to the search for the bare truths of historical facts and have effectively prevented it from arriving at the perception of historical development and change.

It is a direct result of these causes that we find the great mass of what are must call records of Indian history, in departments of literature which to the students of European history would appear distant from the field of his research. Much of what popular traditions had retained of the events of an early past, has found its way, overgrown and interwoven with myths and legends, into the Indian Epics, the *Puranas*, and the fuble literature. The object to which we owe such records of traditional lore was didactic and religious but not historical.

On the other hand, we find that artificial Sanskrit poetry has availed itself, probably from an early date of historical themes. They serve in this case mainly as a framework for the display of all the subtle poetic art and rhetorical embellishment which constitute the characteristic object and *raison d'etre* of the Kavya. It is no mere chance that almost all 'historical Kavyas' (*Caritas*) which have yet come to light, deal with the exploits of the poet's princely patrons or the latter's immediate predecessors. Sanskrit poetry of the Kavya type has always been an artificial product, dependent more than any other branch of Indian scholarship *'Word' or 'Nam'* for as such we must class it *'Chamar'* on courtly patronage[2]. It does not follow that, because interepretation plays a necessary part in establishing the facts of history, and because no existing interpretation is wholly objective, one interpretation is a good as another, and the facts of history are in principle not amenable to objective interpretation. We shall have to consider at a later stage what exactly is meant by objectivity in history.

But a still greater danger lurks in the Collingwood hypothesis. If the historian necessarily looks at his period of history through the eyes of his own time, and studies the problems of the past as a key to those of the present will be not fall into a purely pragmatic view of the facts, and maintain that the criterion of a right interpretation is its suitability to some present purpose that the Hindu Society which has been disgruntled due the lack of Knowledge about the *Vedas*. On this hypothesis, the facts of history are nothing, interpretation is everything. Nietzsche had already enunciated the principle: 'The falseness of an opinion is not for us any objection to it, as Dr. B.R. Ambedkar who had a deep insight of our social evils, after narrating the causes of our downfall had admonished the Nation, in his speech seeking adoption of the constitution made on November 17, 1949 on the floor of the Constituent Assembly, in the following words:

"Will history repeat itself? It is this though which fills me with anxiety. This anxiety is deepend by the realization of the fact that in addition to our old enemies in the form of castes and creeds we are going to have many political parties with diverse and opposing political creeds. Will Indians place the country above their creed or will they place creed above country? I do not know. But this much is certain that if the parties place creed above country, our independence will be put in jeopardy a second time and probably be lost for ever. This eventuality we must all resolutely guard against. We must be determined to defend our independence with the last drop of our blood." (Shiva Rao *'Word'* The framing of India's constitution, pp.935-36[3]). The question is how far it is life furthering, life preserving, species-preserving, perhaps species creating[4]. The American pragmatists moved, less explicity and less whole heartedly, along the same line. Knowledge is knowledge for some purpose. The validity of the knowledge depends on the validity of the purpose. But, even where no such theory has been professed, the practice has often been no less disquieting. In our own field of study we have seen too many examples of extravagant interpretation riding roughshod ever facts not to be impressed with reality of this danger. It is not surprising that perusal of some of the more extreme products of Soviet and ant-Soviet Schools of histography should sometimes breed a certain nostalgia for that illusory nineteenth century have even of purely factual history.

How then, in the middle of the twentieth century, are we to define the obligation of the historian to his facts, because that was their duty. We trust that we have spent a sufficient number of hours in recent years chasing and perusing the documents and stuffing the historical narrative with properly footnoted facts, to escape the imputation of treating facts and documents too cavalierly. The duty of the historian to respect his facts is not exhausted by the obligation to see that his facts are accurate. He must seek to bring into the picture all known or knowable facts relevant, in one sense or another to theme on which he is engaged and to the interpretation proposed. If he seeks to depict the Victorian Englishman as a moral and rational being, he must not forget what happened at Staly-Bridge Wakes in 1850. But this , in turn, does not mean that he can eliminated interpretation, which is the life blood of history. Laymen Dr. Raj Kumar and '*Baba Gurinder Singh Ji*' that is to say, non-academic friends or friends from other academic disciplines calle '*Spiritualism*' sometimes ask us how the historian goes to work when he writes history. The commonest assumption appears to be that the historian divides his work into two sharply distinguishable phases or periods. First, he spends a long preliminary period reading his sources and filling his notebooks with facts: then, when this is over, he puts away his sources, takes out his notebooks and writes his book from beginning to end. This is to us an unconvincing and unplausible picture. For myself, as soon as, I have got going on a few of what I take to be the capital sources, the itch becomes too strong and I begin to write *Chuhra, Chamar, Megh, Barwala, Nai, Dum, Candala, Batwal, Cheer, Terkhan*, or other degraded section of the society not necessarily at the beginning, but somewhere anywhere at the end when there is a confusion in the society on the name of religion. Thereafter, reading and writing to on simultanteously. The writing is added to, subtract from, re-shaped, cancelled, as I go on reading. The reading is guided and directed and made fruitful by the writing: the more I write, the more I know it is the *'Theory of 'Nam' or 'Word'* what I am looking for, the better I understnad the significance and relevance of what I find. Some historians probably to all this preliminary writing in their head where the God is reside. Without using pen, paper, or typewriter, just as some people play chess in their heads without recourse to board and chessmen: This is a talent which I envy, but cannot emulate. But I am convinced that, for any historian worth the name, the two processes of what economists call *'input'* and *'output'* go on simultaneously and are, in practice, parts of a single process. If you try to separate them, or to give one priority over the other, you fall into one of two heresies. Either you write scissors and paste history without meaning or significance or you write propaganda or historical fiction, and merely use facts of the past to embroider a kind of writing which has nothing to do with history.

Our examination of the relation of the historian to the facts of history finds us, therefore, in an apparently precarious situation, navigating delicately between the Scylla of an untenable theory of history as an objective compilation of facts, of the unqualified primacy of fact over interpretation, and the Charybdis of an equally untenable theory of history as the subjective product of the mind of the historian who established the fact of history and masters them through the process of interpretation, between a view of history having the centre of gravity in the past and a view having the centre of gravity in the present. But our situation is less precarious than it seems. We shall encounter the same dichotomy of fact and interpretation again in these lectures in other guises *'Word' or 'Nam'* the particular and the general, the empirical and the theoretical, the objective and the subjective. The predicament of the historian is a reflexion of the nature of man. Man, except perhaps in earliest infancy and in extreme old age, is not totally involved in his environment and unconditionally subject to it. On the other hand, he is never totally independent of it and its unconditional *Master.* The relation of man to his environment is the relation of the historian to his theme. The historian is neither the humble slave nor the tyrannical master of his facts. The relation between the historian and his facts is one of equality, of give and take policy. As any working historian knows, if he steps to reflect what he is doing as he thinks and writes, the historian is engaged on a continuous process of moulding his facts to his interpretation and his interpretation to his facts. It is impossible to assign primacy to one over the other.

The historian starts with a provisional selection of facts, and a provisional interpretation in the light of which that selection has been made *'Chamar'* by others as well as by himself. As he works, both the interpretation and the selection and ordering of facts undergo subtle and perhaps partly unconscious changes, through the reciprocal action of one or the other. And this reciprocal action also involves reciprocity between present and past, since the historian is part of the present and the facts belong to the past. The historian and the facts of history are necessary to one another. The historian without his facts is rootless and futile; the facts without their historian are dead and meaningless. My first answer therefore the queston 'What is history'? thus, term *'History'* has been composed of two English words i.e. *His+story* , *'His' means 'God', 'Word', 'Sabad', 'Nam', 'Chamar', 'Sound Current' Holy Ghost, 'Nad'* is undeciphered in *Indus scripts*: *'Story'* means 'history of the world', which is untrue and destructive one[5], is that it is a continuous process of interaction between the historian and his facts, an unending dialogue between the present and the past[6].

NOTES AND REFERENCES

1. **Note.** The life has two river systems, that of the *Indus*, now mainly in *Pakistan,* had the earliest civilization, and gave its name *India* by the Britishers. The Indian knew this river *Sindhu,* and the *Persians,* who found difficulty in pronouncing an initial *S,* called *Hindu*. Therefore, *Hindus* do not have the *'History'*. They have only traditions, which are relate with monetary business else is nothing. (*W.T.W.I.P.I*)
2. *R.T.* Vol. I. pp. 3-4.
3. *G.S.H.* p. 57.
4. *F.* Nietzsche, *Beyond Good and Evil*, Chapter 1.
5. *H.B.* p. 133.
6. E.H. Carr. *What is History*? England Penguim Books, Reprinted, 1984; p.30.

APPENDIX-I

Chronological Tables of the Chamar Dynasty of Kashmir[1]

Rule of the Gonandiya Dynasty

	Calculated Laukika Dates of Accession	Duration of Region		
		Years	Months	Days
Meghavahana	3088—0—0	34	—	—
S'resthasena-Pravarasena I (Tunjina II)	3122—0—0	30	—	—
Hiranya, with Toramana	3152—0—0	30	2	—
Matrgupta	3182—2—0	4	9	1
Pravarasona II	3186—11—1	60	—	—
Yudhisthira II	3246—11—1	392	3	—
Lahkhapa-Narendraditya	3286—2—1	13	—	—
Ranaditya (Tunjina III)	3299—2—1	300	—	—
Vikramaditya	3599—2—1	42	—	—
Baladitya	3641—2—1	36	8	—
Aggregate length of reigns		589	10	1

Table No. 1

Dynasty of the Chamar Rulers of Kashmir

	Calculated Laukika Dates of Accession	Duration of Region		
		Years	Months	Days
Durlabhavardhana-Prajnaditya	3677—10—1	36	—	—
Durlabhaka-Pratapaditya II	3713—10—1	50	—	—
Candrapida-Vijraditya	3763—10—1	8	8	—
Tarapida-Udayaditya	3772—6—1	4	—	24
Muktapida-Lalitaditya	3776—6—25	36	7	11
Kuvalayapida	3813—2—6	1	—	15
Vajraditya-Bappiyadka-Lalitaditya	3814—2—21	7	—	—
Prthivyapida	3821—2—21	4	1	—
Samgramapida I	3825—3—21	—	—	73
Jajja	3825—3—28	3	—	—
Jayapida-Vinayaditya	3828—3—28	31	—	—
Lalitapida	3859—3—28	12	—	—
Samgramapida II (Prthivyapida)	3871—3—28	7	—	—
Cippatajayapida-Brhaspati	3878—3—28	12	—	—
Ajitapida	38894	37	—	—
Anangapida	3926	3	—	—
Utpalapida	3929	2	—	—
Total length of reigns		254	5	27

Table No. 2
Utpala Dynasty

A.D.	Laukika Dates of Accession	Duration of Region where specified		
		Years	Months	Days
855/U	3991	—	—	—
883 S'amkaravarman	3959 Asadha su 3	—	—	—
902 Gopalavarman	3977 Phalguna va 7	2	—	—
904 Samkara	3979	—	—	10
904 Sugandha	3979	—	—	—
906 Partha	3981	—	—	—
921 Nirjitavarman (Pangu)	3997 Pausa	—	—	—
923 Cakravarman	3998 Magha	—	—	—
933 S'uravarman I	4009	1	—	—
934 Partha (*restored*)	4010	—	—	—
935 Cakravarman (*restored*)	4011 Asadha	—	—	—
935 S'amkaravardhana	4011 Pausa	—	—	—
936 Cakravarman (*restored*)	4012 Caitra su 8	—	—	—
937 Unmattavanti	4013 Jyaistha su 8	—	—	—
939 S'uravarman II	4015	—	—	—

Table No. 3
Viradeva Dynasty

A.D.	Laukika Dates Accession	Duration of Region where specified		
		Years	Months	Days
939 Yasaskarndeva	4015 Asadha su 5	9	—	—
948 Varpata	4024	—	—	1
948 Samgramadeva	4024 Bhadrapada va 3	—	—	—
949 Parvagupta	4024 Phalguna va 10	—	—	—
950 Keomagupta	4026 Asadha va 13	—	—	—
958 Abhimanyu	4034 Pausa 6u 9	—	—	—
972 Nandigupta	4048 Karttika 6u 3	—	—	—
973 Tribhuvana (gupta)	4049 Margasirsa su 12	—	—	—
975 Bhimagupta	4051 Margusirsa su 5	—	—	—
980/1 Didda	4056	—	—	—

Table No. 4
First Lohara Dynastyy of the Nam (Chamar)

A.D.	Laukika Dates of Accession	Duration of Region where specified		
		Years	Months	Days
1003 Samgramaraja	4079 Bhadrapada su 8	—	—	—
1028 Hariraja	4104 Asadha va 1	—	—	22
1028 Ananta	4104 Asadha su 8	—	—	—
1063 Kalasa	4139 Karttika su 6	—	—	—
1089 Utkarsa	4165 Margasirsa su 6	—	—	22
1089 Harsa	4165 *Patusa va 13*	—	—	—

Table No. 5
Second Lohara Dynastyy of the Nam (Chamar)

A.D.	Laukika Dates of Accession	Duration of Region where specified		
		Years	Months	Days
1101 Uccala	4177 Bhadrapada su 6	—	—	—
1111 Radda-S'ankharnja	4187 Pausa su 6	—	—	1
1111 Salhapa	4187 Pausa su 7	—	3	27
1112 Sussala	4788 Vaisakha su 3	—	—	—
1120 Bhiksacara	4196 Margasirsa va 6	—	6	12
1121 Susala (*restored*)	4197 Jyaistha su 3	—	—	—
1128 Jayasimha (Simhadeva)	4203 Phalguna va 15	226	—	—

NOTES AND REFERENCES

1. In these tables the dates and chronological figures which are directly available on the basis of material, it seems that this dynasty was flourished since the Indus valley civilization which have been suppressed by the Brahminical thought between the period of 2800-2500 B.C. as per the Vedic Age report is concerned. It is now believed on the basis of historical evidences that this civilization was flourised about 3000 B.C. In the study we have learn that it must have had a long history of antecedent development before it reached the stage that we find its historical background. Since the time of Chandra Gupta *Maurya* to onwards i.e. *Satavahanas, Kushanas*, Guptas, Hunas, etc. But it was flourished under the rule of *Durlabhavaradhana-Prajnadityi* since the 600 A.D. to onwards. The Dynasty is known *Karkota Dynasty* as it has been rightly expressed by the Kalhana that *Durlabhavaradhana-Prajnaditya* obtained the power of *Baladitya* after marriaging his daughter *Anangalekha*. Baladitya had no son at that time to hold the kingdom of Kashmir. Therefore, under the natural circumstances he hand over the charge to the follower of the *'Nanda dynasty'*. They were the ruler of the *Sudra* women called *'Chamar'* by the profession which had the artistic skill in their hands not in the worldy life but had in the heaven life. They were the people of the *'nam'* or *'Annami'* used to live in *Champa* in the Hindu colony since the time immemorial, suppressed by the Brahmins on the basis of their dirty activities. Now, they cleaned up their dirty activities in large scale with the help of the *'Nam'*.

2. We have preferred *Catvarimsatim* of A_3 L to *Caturvimsatim* of A_1, as only with the former figure of the Gonanda Dynasty we can obtain the total of 589 years 10 month and one day as their aggregate length of reigns for the requirement of practical approach on the basis of theoretical knowledge which was given to the Brahminical ideology to study the practical approach towards history by. Dr. B.R. Ambedkar on the bases of *'Law'* since 1947, when a speech was made on the day of constitution by him on November, 17,1947 on the, floor of the constituent Assembly that 'History will repeat itself". This anxiety is deepened by the realization of the fact that in addition to our old enemies in the form of castes and creeds i.e. Brahmins. If the years of those kings, the during of whose reigns is known mentioned above, leaving aside these dates, the 2268 years *Gonanda* I, and his successors, no rest remains from the passed period of *Kaliyuga*, 2268+1328+653=4249, as already mentioned in the text. The above translation of the *Yugma* conforms to the view set forth by Dr. Hultzsch in his able discussion of the passage (*Indische Antecedent*, XViii, p. 99). It also agrees with the earlier renderings works of Troyer-vol.1. p. 338, Vol. II, pp. 7,366 and Willson Essay, p. 97. Kalhaṇa also accepts the calculation of 2268 years for the aggregate of

the reigns from Gonanda 1 to *Yodhisthira* 1 & II i.e. from the reign of first *Gonanda* dynasty to second *Gonanda* dynasty started by the *Meghavahana* to *Baladity* since the period of calculated Laukika dates of asscession from 3088 to 3641, ruled 589 years, 10 months and one day, before the *'Karkota Dynasty'* of the *Kashmir.*

3. According to the reading of A_1 *Vasaran* accepted in the text, is confirmed by L. the reading *Vatsaran* of A_3, which has been preferred by Troyer Lassen and Durgaprasad, would extend *Samgramapida's* rule to seven years. It must, however, be rejected as it does not agree with the total of 1328 years which Kalhana's chronological scheme is concerned, with the said reigns of the *'Chamar Dynasty'*. It has been rightly point out by Dr. Hultzsch, in the said text.

4. The difference between the indicated date of *Ajitapida's* accession (Laukika Sudi 3889) and the one which we should get by adding the twelve years of *Cippatajaypida's* reign to the calculated date of his accession, Laukika Sudi 3878-3-28, is 1 year, 3 months and 28 days. This difference is due to Kalhana having adopted a 'rough' calculation for the aggregate length of reigns in the said text. Not it has been fully discussed in the first chapter under the heading of Chronology, and doubts have been cleared now when we take the example of the death of *Cippatajaypida* and the accession of *Ajitapida* in 814 A.D., commences to record exact dates for the various reigns and events in years of the *Laukika* or *Saptarsi*, era, which is the traditional era of *Kashmir* and the neighbouring hill-tracts. Regarding its initial date, placed by Kashmirians on *Caitra Sudi* I. of the twenty-fifth years of the *Kaliyuga* i.e. 3076-75 B.C. to the notice of European scholars and to account for the equation given in our verse.

   The following calculation shows that the year in which Kalhana wrote his introduction, was Laukikasamvat 4224:-

   Distance between Kaliyuga 25 (initial date *Laukika* era) and the initial date of the *Saka* era-------------- = 3154

   Distance between Sakasamvat I and Kalhana's time---- = 1070

   Total of Saptarsi years = 4224

5. The exact date of *Yasaskaradeva's* election to the throne is not indicated; it took place " five or six days' after the flight of Suravarman II. on the 7th of the bright half of Asadha. While the Brahmans in this fashion passed five or six days, they will assembled an immense host of Purohits of sacred places (*parisadya*), causing a mighty din by their drums with musical instruments.

6. Twenty-two years of Jayasimha's reign had passed in Laukika Sudi 4225, (A.D. 1149-50), when Kalhana completed his work, on the birth of *Jayasimha*, which was took place, at Lokakala, 4181 (A.D. 1105-6).

the same [illegible] to *Sangramapida* [illegible] from the reign of [illegible] dynasty [illegible] *Gonanda* dynasty started by the [illegible] intermediate since the [illegible] of [illegible] Laukika date [illegible] accession from 3,88[illegible] to [illegible] 10 months and one day before the *Kaliyuga* [illegible] the Kaliyuga.

5. According to the tradition [illegible] *Jayasimha* ascended to the [illegible] is confirmed [illegible] the [illegible] [illegible] which has been preferred by [illegible] [illegible] would extend [illegible] [illegible] be [illegible] agrees with the total [illegible] [illegible]

[illegible]

The difference [illegible] (Laukika [illegible] 3,887) [illegible] twelve years of [illegible] reign [illegible] accession, making Saptarshi 3,878 [illegible] 7 months and 28 days. This difference is due to Kalhana having [illegible] calculation for the aggregate length of reign in the [illegible] has been fully discussed in the first chapter under the heading of Chronology and doubts have been [illegible] [illegible] to record exact dates [illegible] of the [illegible] [illegible] [illegible]

[illegible]

[illegible]

[illegible]

[illegible]

Total of Saptarshi years [illegible] 4224

The exact date of *Jayasimha's* [illegible] to the throne is not indicated [illegible] place "five or six days after the flight of Sussala [illegible] on the [illegible] of the bright half of [illegible] [illegible] of sacred places [illegible] musical instruments.

6. Twenty-two years of *Jayasimha's* reign had passed in Laukika Sudi 4225 (A.D. 1149-50), when Kalhana completed his work, on the birth of *Jayasimha*, which was took place, at Lokakala 4181 (A.D. 1105-6).

APPENDIX-II

Genealogical tables of the Chamar Dynasties Ruled over Kashmir[1]

Table No. 1
The Karkota Dynasty of the Chamar Rulers

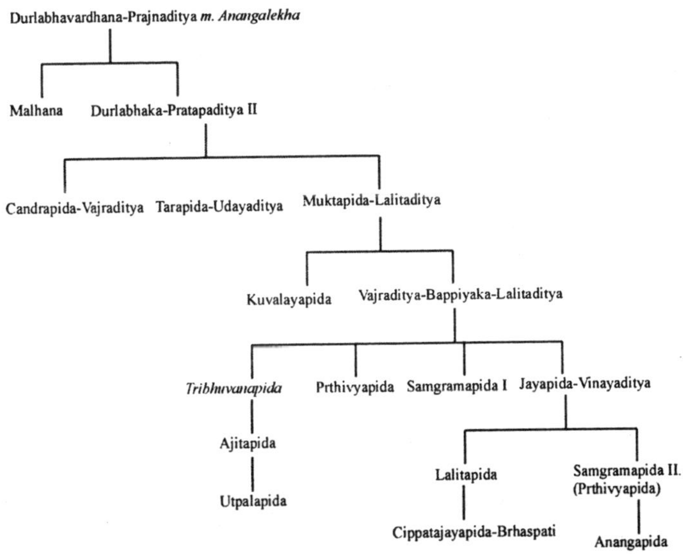

Table No. 2
Utpala Dynasty

- *Utpala*, †853 A.D.
  - *Sukhavarman*, †855 A.D.
    - Avantivarman, †883 A.D.
      - S'amkaravarman, †902 A.D., m. Sugandha, †914 A.D.
        - Gopalavarman, †904 A.D.
        - Samkata, †904 A.D.
    - *Suravarman*
      - *Sukhavarman*
        - Nirjitavarman (Pangu), †923 A.D.
          - Partha, †937 A.D.
            - Unmattavanti, †939 A.D.
              - S'uravarman II., deposed 939 A.D.
          - Cakravarman, †937 A.D.
          - S'uravarman I., deposed 934 A.D.
    - Anangapida

Table No. 3
Viradeva Dynasty

- *Viradeva*
  - *Kamadeva*
    - *Prabhakaradeva*
      - Yasaskaradeva †948 A.D.
        - Samgramadeva, †949 A.D.
  - *Ramadeva*
    - Varnata, deposed 948 A.D.

- Abhinava, a 'Divira'
  - Samgramagupta
    - Parvagupta, †950 A.D.
      - Ksemagupta, †958 A.D., *m.* Didda, †1003 A.D.
        - Abhimanyu, †972 A.D.
          - Nandigupta, †973 A.D.
          - Tribhuvana[gupta], †975 A.D.
          - Bhimagupta, †980/1 A.D.

- *Bhimasahi, of Kabu'*
  - *Simharaja, of Lohara, m.* ....
    - Didda (m. Ksemagupta)

Table No. 4
The Lahara Dynasty of the Nam (Chamar)

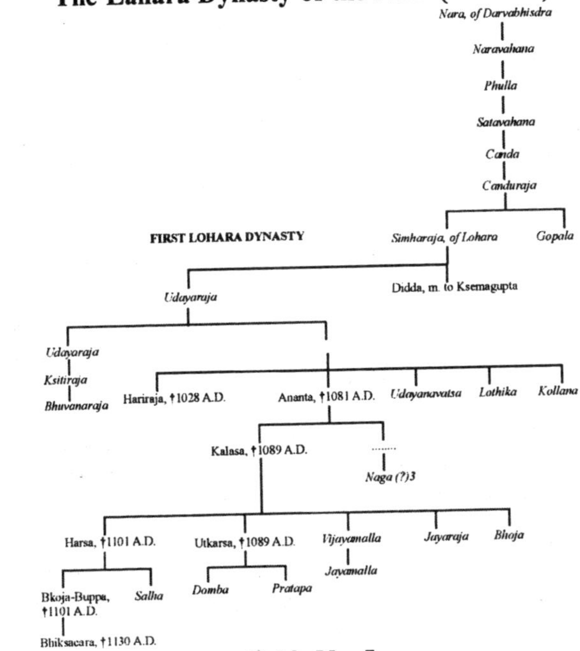

Table No. 5
Second Lohara Dynasty

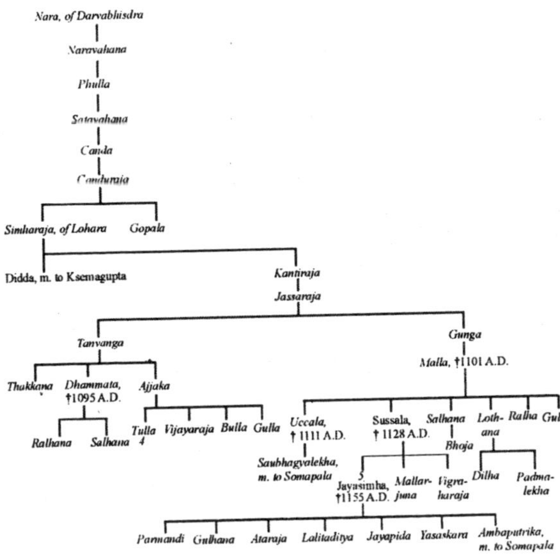

NOTES AND REFERENCES

1. The names of those members of the several royal families like *Doma, Chamar, Chuhras*, etc. who occupied the Kashmir throne, have been thoroughly discussed in the text that they occupied a prominent place in the Kashmir History discussed above from the table. One to Fourth in detail, their work and achievements as a natural rulers of the *'Nam'*. But they were not Brahmins, they were *Schedule Castes* peoples. It is also compared from the study that they were the Unique kind of rulers i.e. low born.

2. The ancestors of the Lohara dynasty is probably identical with *Nara,* a chief *Darvabhisara*. From the evidence available it appears that *Darvabhisara* as a geographical term comprised the whole tract of the lower and middle hills lying between the river *Vitasta* and *Chandrashaga* where *Sirash Rai* dynasty used to live in the ancient period ruled over India more than 137 years, where from ever 'new concept' of the 'New Society' has been originated from time to time in the Indian history so far its study is concerned. Even the *Schedule Tribes* like *Gujara,* and *Bakarwala*, have the great concern, with this areas.

3. It shows that Brahmins had the lust of Sex, they enjoy with the others wives and daughter, they had the idea of *Naga,* because they always damage the life of others to complete their lust with sex and money. Therefore, Kalhana, does not describe his mother as an aunt of *Kalasa*, not as his sister, as our passage would represent her.

4. Study also indicates that King himself went to the court-yard of ruler *Harsa.* He protected there *Ralhana* and *Salhana*, as their grandsons of *Tanvanga*, were the sons of *Dhammata,* as suggested by the context that they laid down their swords in the front of the master.

5. *Tulla, Vijayaraja, Bulla* and *Gulla* these four "grandsons of *Tanvanga*" were the brothers of *Tulla,* whose descent from *Ajjaka* is clearly stated from the *Jayaraja* in 1095 A.D. as the ruler of Kashmir and lasted this dynasty upto the rule of *Jayasimha* has already mention from 1105-6 A.D. to 1149-50 A.D.

GLOSSARY

Ashvamedha — Horse sacrifices

Arya Varta — Story of the 'Word'

Avestan Indra —Vedic Indra

Avestan Vayu—Vedic Vayu

Avestan Mithra—Vedic Mitra

Avestan Naonhaithya—Vedic Nasatyas

Avestan verethraghna—Vedic Vritraghna

Avestan Stanza Tat Thwa—Vedic Tat tva

Asikni—Tchenab (Rig-Veda Name)

Akuti—Hoper and aspirations

Adandya—Punishment

Adhikarana—District Office

A-Karman—Devoid of rites

A-Yajran—Non-sacrificing

A-Devayu—Not worshipping the Deves or Aryan Gods

A-Brahman—Wanting in devotion or prayer

A-Yajyu—Not sacrificing

A-Vrata—'Lawless' not observing the Vedic vows

Anya-Vrata—Addicted to other non Vedic practices

Adityas—Sons of Aditi (Minor Deities) "The Infinite"

Ayo-hata—Hammered metal

Aranya—Forest

Aitareya Brahmana—Brahmin as a receiver of gifts

Anyasya balikrit—Vaisya as a Tax-payer

Ayas—Bronze

Adhipatya—Suzerainty

Anumati—Approval of the earth; i.e. the mother country

Adade—Himself

Akshavapa—Superintendent of dicing

Amlarasa—Sukla

Artha—Polity with Mind or *Man*

Acharya—Teacher

Asrama—Hermitage

Adhipati—The lord of 1000 villages

Adhyapaka—Ordinary teacher

Avaya—Term is used for the place where weavers come and weave the cloth.

Adhyayana—Study

A-nichaya—Not hoarding things

Ashta-Kula—The Republician executive the body of Eight or Nine members.

Apana—Shops

Antara pana—Stores

Agghakarika—Court Valuer

Apana or Panagara—Taverns

Amarshena—Forcibly

Asu—Quickly

Ananta—Endless

Akshapatala—Accounts

Aramika— Market gardeners

Asyaputras or Kumaras—Princes of the 'God' or 'Word'

Agramatya—Prime Minister = *Preman*

Athabhagiya—8th share of the Agriculture produce

Anusasana—Injunctions

Antevasi—Elders and teachers for whom the pupil.

Apachiti—Respect

Asada—Recovered

Anarambha and Avihisha—Non-violence towards all living beings

Akalika—Time

Abadha—Mishaps

Alpaphala—Fruitful

Amitraghata (Allichates)— "The slayer of enemies."

Ajasrika—Permanent

Atma-Pariksha—Self examination

Anantam-punam prasavati—Immortality of soul

Atavikas—Rude forest folks

Abhagnayoga—Temple without break

Avaras—Lower castes

Amatyas—Civil governors

Avijita—Unconquered

Ahato—Wounded

Aijita-Antas—Frontiers

Arya; Ayya-Aira-Aila-Arya—Word, Race of Rig-Veda Master

Ahara—Districts

Ahata—Weeded out

Aja—Aya, Elephant

Aneka—Many

Andaja—Birds

Antevasinyah—Female disciples

Atyayikaya—Famine

Atula—Matchless

Anatha—Destitute

Akshayanivi—Permanent Fund

Anukampa—Compassion

Archaresham—Worship of objects

Athso—Iranian *Atar-Atash* (God of Fire) = Theory of Mind; The God Agni is called in Sanskrit *Asrayasa or Ahutasa* which may be phonetically compared with the term *Athso.*

Ardoksho—Avestan *Ashis-Vanuhi,* foddess of wealth and prosperity

Ashaeikhsho—Pahlavi Ashavahishto, 'the genius of Sacrificial fire'

Sanskrit Aira Vira; Avestic Khshathra-Vairya =Prefect rule

Anta—Neighbour

Anugraha—Showing marcy

Adhishthana—Term applied to the headquarters of the district.

Apratikara—State

Apavinchhya—Separated

Aprada—Unsettled

Aprahata—Uncultivated

Arjava—Straight forward

Arini—Indebt

Ajasrika—Permanent

Akshayanivi—Permanent endowment or gift

Abhuta-purvam—New Colonise

Apara—Finest or Artistic workmanship

Andhrapatha—The Krishna region

Asana—Seats

Apradadharmena—Permanent charity

Avasathika—Superintendent of Rest House

Atmanivedanam—Offer of homage

Agraharas—Alms houses, 'Jagir'

Akriti—Image

Aurnasthanika—Superintendent of Silk Factories

Adeya—What is payable to the State

Anavamarsyam—Freedom from molestation by Government officer

Angara—Charcoal

Akaradayi—Not to pay taxes

A-Charmangarakam—No obligation to supply leather and charcoal

Akaradam—Not to pay rent to the king

Avaham—No obligation to carry loads free of charge

Apratikara—Not yield any revenue

Astamba—Barren of vegetation

Akinchit Pratikara—Payable amount

Adi Granth—Primal (*adi*) Scripture (*granth*) or book sacred scriptures of the Sikhs or disciples (*Shishya* in Sanskrit)

Aulia—Literally, friends of God, Arabic term for a spiritually advanced person.

Agnayi—Wife of Agni

Antariksha—"Middle Region" Atmosphere

Asura—Originally the Aryan title of beneficent beings, demons or fiends (Ahura)

AgamPurush—Inaccessible (agam), Being (*Purush*); the lord of

AgamLok, Sat Lok, Sacha Khand

Annami—Without (a) name (*nam*); hence unnamable; used mystically to refer to God; Anami; Purush is the Nameless (*anami*)

Amr—Command, *Kalma, Kun, Sabad 'Chamar'*

Anand—Bliss or happiness

Anhad Shabd—Limitless Sound or music

Abyaat—Plural of *bait or verses*

Abvaita—Non-dualism or monism; according to this philosophy, final truth consists in the identification of the self with Brahman, identification of the self with Brahman, in the Absolute Reality of one and only one existence.

Ana-al-Haq—"I am the Truth"

Alankara—One of the ornaments i.e. *Nama*

Agramahishi—Chief Queen

Alfi—An unsewn garment worn by a faqir or Sant round his neck as a symbol of renunciation,

piety and spiritual attainment.

Alif—The first letter of the Arabic, Persian and Urdu alphabets; the letter A. (In the abyaat it gener ally stands for Allah and Ahad, the one lord)

Allah-hu-Akbar—The expression means "God is Greatest". This declaration of greatest (*takbir*) punctuates the Muslim canonical prayer.

Anhad Shabd—Unstruck sound or music; the *Word* or spiritual sound that is present in everyone and can be heard under propercondition.

Awaaz-i-Mustaqeem—Lit. Sound (*aavaaz*); Straight

Adri or Asani—(*Mustaqeem*); direct sound, Sing stones

Apas—See Waters

Adharmika—Irreligious

Anabasis—Expedition

Abhijata—High-born

Anabhijata—Low-born

Anuvarlate—Self

Anurage Sarvagunyam—*'Love is Kindled by virtue'*

Annatakula—'Nandins' as of unknown lineage

Antapala—Frontier

Apavahayati—Drains of wealth

Arattas or Arashtrakas—"Kingless', peoples

Ahimsa—Non-violence

Adhikaranalekhaka—Official recorder

Adhikarasraj—'Garland of office'

Advapa or Adhvera—Same as 'Margesa' or 'Malik'

Agniyastra—'Weapon of fire'

Agnisauca—Antelopes 'cleansing themselves in fire'

Agrahara—a 'Jagir'

Aksa—King of Kasmir

Aksayanivi—Term for an endoment

Aksayini—A perpetual endoment

Aratrika—Ceremony

Annasttra—Term for a kind of endowment

Assafoetida—Hingu

Assay—Of gold

Asvaghasakayastha—A small official post

Attapatibhaga—A revenue office

Avaruddha—Concubine

Apara-vidya—Intermediate knowledge

Apavudhe—Captives

Autura—Afflicated

Amutraghata—'Slayer of foes'

Brahm-Vidya—Knowledge of the Absolute, *Brahman* or *Atman* specified as *Paravidya* or Supreme knowledge which cannot be attained "by intellect, by the Veda, or by much knowledge of book", as stated by *Katha-Uppanishad.* Supreme knowledge is to be obtained by *tapas, Sraddha,*

Satya, brahmacharya and Vidhi of the *'Nam'* from the Prefect Master.

Brahmacharya—the pupil discharges the *Rishirina* or debt to the Fathers of learning.

Bhuta-vidya—Biology

Bhikshu—Ascetic

'The Buddha, lord of the Sakyas' - 'Nam' or 'Word'

Bhritya-bharanam—Support of dependents as a Barwala; Aboriginal duty not prescribed for slaves.

Bhavassuddhi—Purity of heart

Bahu-Sruta—Well versed in each other's Srutis or scriptures

Bhaujya—Paramount rule

Bheri-ghosha—Silencing the War-drum

Bhrata—Brother

Bhaguvatam—Five pious religious leaders (Viras)

Baladevapamokkhanam, Panchanham,Mahaviranam - *'Baladeva* and the rest of the five heroes=Pandeva

Bhrityah—Servents

Bahyali—Outer court

Begar—forced labour

Bhaktasala—Charity foundation

Bhauma—Name of the Naraka

Bhramaravasini—A form of Durga

Bhutabali—Offered in pastry

Bidala—Father of *Nila*

Bimba—An exile

Bodhi—Obtained by Bodhisattavas

Brahmapuri—Term for some pious foundation

Bhuta-purvam—Old colonise

Bhishaj—Physician

Boddo—Sanskrit Buddha 'the lord of the world'

Bizago—Sanskrit *Visakha*

Bhrashta—Destroyed

Bhukti—Province, Pradesa

Bhrita—Mercenary

Bhakti—Devotion, Meditation of the lord.

Bhogapatika—Divisional Commissioner

Bhagavato Adityasya—Sun bears the legend equivalent the theory of mind or mana

Bhuta-Purvam—Old

Balavan—A king of low birth but of great power.

Bhritam—Acquired

Brahma-Varta—Story of the suspense i.e. Mana or mind

Bidala-kari—Basket maker

Bait—A Persian word meaning a couplet; It is also used for 'metre' Bahu's bait ussually has four lines and occasionaly more

Bibheda—Water supply suddenly brust.

Brahm—Lord of the Second Spiritual region above the mind called *Trikuti,* supreme being

Bank Nal—Literally, curved (bank) tunnel (*nal*); the name of *'Passage'* between *Sahasdal Kamal*

and *Trikuti* the first and second Inner regions.

Bhajan—The practice of the *'Word'* is called *Surat Shabd* Yoga.

Bhanwar Gupha—Rotating, revolving or whirling (*bhanwar*) cave (gonpha) or Gupha. Where the soul first recognise its identity with God.

Bhatika—Hired labour

Bala—Army

Balyat—Childhood

Brahman-Chandala—Those who live like Chandalas

Budhagunita—Master minds

Chorapubbas—'Decoits of old'

Chatush-Kaparda—Fourt plaits of hair

Charakas—Wandering schalors

Chamupati—Commander of the Army

Charya—Rashtrasya Sarvato atanam, March through country

Chanda—Mahasena who earned the title during the time of reign of terror.

Charanas—Vedic Schools

Camaka—Strolling player

Chandasoka—Notorious title given in Ceylon legends, which converted

Chata—Outlaws

Chaitygriha—Jain shrine centre

Chaitya—Shrine

Chhatratype—Royal Parasol

Calliena—City of the Kalyana where Brahmans used to live in numbees

Chamar—'Word' or 'Nam' or *Sabad*

Chhatra-Yashti or danda—Standardized Buddhist gifts, the image of *Bhodhisattva*

Charma or Angara—Not to supply hides

Chaturudadhi—Father's fame spread upto four oceans or sea

Chitravinyasa-Chitritam—Decorated with various designs

Chivara—Clothing

Chasm-i-ghaib—Lit. The hidden or serect eye, the inner or third eye

Chamupati—Commander of the Army.

Cakra—Puns on word

'Cakranayaka'—Master of witches

Cakrapura—Laid foundation of New Civilization

Cakrika—Intriguer

Camaka—Strolling player

Candala—Class with Dombas, Watchmen, '*Nam*' or '*Word*'

Candika—A form of Durga

Candrabhaga—River Chenab

Catuhsala—Quadrangle

Cakranayaka—Master withces

Chakor—A bird in Indian folklore, is enamored of the moon.

Dharma-ghosha—The proclamation of religion

Dharma-Sravanani—Important innovation of religious messages

Dharma-Stambha—Rock and Pillar inscribed instructions of the religion

Dharma-Mahamatras—Ministers of Morals

Devanam-priya—'Beloved of the Gods'

Dharma-mangala—It means the productive of great fruit (*Maha-phala*) in achieving good both in this world and in next by the *Punya* or Merit. He or she stands for *Dharma-Dana*, *Dharma Sambandha*, *Dharma-Samvibhaga* and *Dharma-Samstava*.

Dharma-Niyama—Requisites of Religious life

Devaihmisritah—Related to Gods or more religious through 'Nam' or 'Word'

Divyavadana—"High as hill-tops" (Girisringakalpails)

Devanam-Priya—Term applied to a fool

Dharma-Chakra-Pravartana-Sutra—Discourse of religion

Devadeva—The God of Gods

"*Dakshimapatha-pati*"—Title of 'Satakarni' ruler

Deha—body

Dharma-prachira—Promoting Religion by upholding its social customs and barriers.

Durdarsena—Ugle, spirit.

Dharma-ghosha—Call of peace

Dhanyakrit—Winnower

Dhmatrin—Who smelt the ore in fire

Devarina—Enrich by his own contributions

Danapal—Chief criminal judge

Devas—Gods

Dana—Charity, Royal gifts or presents

Dharma-Chakra—Bhagavato Dhamachakam symbolised by Prasenajit Buddha as *Dharma-Chakra*

Dhyana—Meditation

Dasa—Mana or mind is slave of God

Dutas—Ambassadors

Daya—Kindness

Dhammapada—Theragatha or Dug for Cooperative with Master that is the channel of the '*Nam*'.

Dhanya—Rice

Deva-Sama—God-like character

Dhamadana—"A religious gift"

Daric—Persian Gold coin

Danasala—Governing body whose president Brahmin

Dharmavijaya—Moral conquests

Dharma-Yatras—Tours duty

Darsana—Interviewing

Divyani-rupani—Celestial elephants, and other shows

Dvijas—Brahmins

Dasa-Rajna—Rig-Veda tells of Sudas who had achieved his overlordship of Rig Vedic India by his victory at the Battle of Ten Kings (10), representing about forty different Rig Vedic people. Technical terms such as *Adhiraja, Rajadhiraja, or Samrat.*

Dharmasutra—Measure your duty or recognise

Dhih—Capacity or Mental powers.

Divya or Diwaka—Supreme beautiful workmanship

Danda—Punishment

Deva-piyu—Reviling the Vedic gods

Dasyus—See Dahyu

Dyava-Prithvi—Heaven and Earth

Dhatri—Creator

Dhanus—Bow

Didyu—Missile

Deveshita—Muni of divine afflatus

Dhi—Highest conception of God as the thinking principle, but working in Man, whose primary duty

is always to think of Him

Deodar—See Teak

Deus—Dio, Dios, 'Word', 'God'

Dhata or Vidhata—Brahma may be traced in Rig Veda or 'Word'

Dharma—Duty about 'God' and others

Dadhi—Curd

Dundubhi—Drum

Dicing'—Aksha in

Divodasa—Tribal hero of the Tritsu

Durbalam—Powerless

Desa-parthiva—Local kings

Dakinis—A temple of Divine Mothers full of ghosts

Dayamimam nivaddham—the transaction or contract was duly registed

Dalit voice—Inner voice; 'Nam'

Dipa—Oil for lamp to 'light'

Dalitadasasataih—"An open town" "Abode of multitude of men of for castes" cluster of 10,000 villages.

Dhupa—Incense

Drishtimatra-prabandhna—Visible at first sight

Dhyana-ekagrapara—Yogis concentrated on contemplation

Dandapasadhikaranika—Police chief

Dhan bhante Mahipaler Git—Folk Songs and Ballads

Dayal—Merciful (dayal)

Dharmrai—The Lord (rai) of Judgement (dharma)

Easwan Dwar—Tenth (daswan) door or gate (*dwar*) the third inner region.

Eka-rat or Chakravartin—Sole sovereign, single ruler

Eka-chchhatra—Whole earth under one umberalla

Ekangas—Military followers or organisation

Ekam—"One Reality" "the One"

Esa—A mythical plant

Ephthalites—See White Hunas

Fourth plane—*Sat Lok* See *Sat Lok*

Faqir—A poor mar, a mendicant, an ascetic. The term is also used for saints and for holy men generally (*Pirs*)

Fanafillah—Extinct in God, a state in which one has merged in God, and one's separate identity has ceased

Fareb—Allurement, deceit

Fikr—Attention, thought

Fana-fil-Sheikh—Extinction in the master

Fana-fil-Zaat—Extinction in essence, annihilation (and thus merger) in God.

Ferri candidi—"Talents of Steel" "White Iron

Ficus Indica—Banyan

Ficus Religiosa—Ashvatta, Pippala

Five tribe—Five race= words, Ka

Fire-worship—The due to the Rig-Veda 'First born', the form of *Vishvakarma*

Flood legend—Shatapath Brahmana

Gana or Ganapati—Heads of the Republics.

Gharma Ayasmaya—Vessels made of metal

Godhumah—Maize

Gramyani—Cultivated grain

Gramani or—Village Headman

Grama bhojaka

Gonikartana—Huntsman

Guru-Kula—Domestic school

Ganarajyas—Republican states

Gopalaka—A common communal neat-herd

Grama-dvara—Wall or stockade with gates

Grama—Village with an enclosuer of thorns, bushes & tree

Gramavasa—Villages homes

Gopata—Viceroy

Garudadhvaja—The Vahana of Vishnu

Ghatayitva—Sacked

Guha=Vihara—"A religious gift (*Dhamadana*) of a cave monastery, where were invited for residence the teacher Buddhadeva." Teaching about *Mahasamghika*

Gurudiksa—Tantric rite

Gandharva-Vidya—Proficient in music

Grihapati—The daughter of a commercial magnate

Guhavasa or Layanam or—Cave(lenam)-dwellings for accommodation of ascetics or Lenam

Gaulmika—Incharge of the forest

Grihapravesa—Citizens

Gavya—Cow's milk

Gurvvayatana—Install in shrine

Garbha-griha—A sanctum of stone i.e. *'ego'*

Garahati—Belittle

Gramyavadin—Village judge

Ghatakah—Jars

Grahita—Elected

Ganga—See Ganges

Grihya-Sutras—Rules for the conduct of life

Guru—A spiritual instructor, successor of the ancient *purohita*

Gods—See *Devas, 'Words'*

Gayatri—The holiest text in Rig-Veda

Gharghar—Modern name of the lower Sarasvati

Gadhipura—Name of Kanauj

Ganja—'Treasury'

Ganjavara—Treasurer

Ganga—Pilgrimage to 'Word'

Gauraka—Wood-dealer

Gavyuti—measurement of thing or kind

Hiranyagrabha—Implicit nature, "the golden Embryo"

Hiranyakara—Who make ornaments of gold

Hrade—Lakes

Harita Kalapaka—Preparation of great vegitable

Hephaistos—God of Metal (Greek)

Herakilo—Greek Deity Heracles

Horon—Sanskrit Varuna

Harita—Greens

Harmya—Building of temples

Hiranyasamudayika—Currency officer

Harsha-deva—'Nam' or 'Chamar'

Hetu-Vidya—Logic

Hritahunasarvam—The Hunas

Hu—God, essense of God, a name of or God; esotexically used for the ruler of the third spiritual stage of mystic.

Haq—The truth, reality, absolute

Hastinayana—Sanskrit Hastin

Hinajatis—Low castes

Hina-sippas—Low crafts

Hayagriva—A demon

Hydaspes—Greek name of the Jhelam

Hydraotes—Greek name of the Ravi

Hypasis—Hypanis, Vipasis, Greek names of Bias. Vitasta a Greek name.

Himavat—"Abode of winter", See Himalaya

Hooma—Eranian Equivalent of Soma

History—See Rig-veda, study of in India

Issattha-Sippa—Arts of Archery

Ibhya—Nobles

Ijya—Sacrifice for pious deed like 'Nam'

Iha-lokika or—Space and time *Akalika*

Imam Karita—Buddha constructed

Idam Sariram—Enshrinement of the bodily relics

Indus—See Sindhu, Sindh, *Vitasta*

Iravati—Epic name of the *Ravi*, or *Nagi*

Iroti—See *Ravi*

Indra—Thunderbolt, the hero of the atmospheric battle led by 'Nam' or 'Word'

Indrani—The wife of Indra or pale of abstraction

Itihasas—Legendary poems

India—General view and extent

Ida—Spiritual daughter of Manu

Iron Age—Kaliyug, the age (yuga) of materialism or discard (Kali): the fourth age in the cycle of time through which the physical universe passes. Hindu mythology divides time into four great age (Yogas), following each other in endless (*ananta*) recurring cycles: Satyog, Tretayug, Dwarparyug, Kaliyog (The Golden age, Silver age, Copper age, Ironage). According to this cosmology, it is now the Iron age after it, therewill be Enlightenment Era.

Irra—One of the three subtle energy currents (irra Pingala, sushumna, flowing through all creation below Trikuti (Universal mind).

Inda—Historical literature of ancient time.

Jambudvipa—India

Jana—The people

Jiva—Soul

Jayatipraviro—'the bravest on earth'

Jyotisha—Astronomy

Jatila—Hairgrow

Jayati—Achieving victory

Jati—Caste, race, believe on master.

Janapada—Local laws peculiar to regions or states

Jivasuta—Still living

Jirnoddhara—Restoration of temples

Jina—Buddha

Jvalata—Radiant

Jayaparihara—Charities

Janardana—A surname of vishnu

Janeu—Thread worn by Hindu for identity called Janeu. The sign of 'ego.'

Jayukelishu—Victorious career

Karma—Actions and deed, past thoughts

Kutumbinam—Settled peasants

Khila—Follow

Karanas—Documents

Kulaputtras—Court's Noble person

Kshatra-vinasahrit—The destroyer of Kshatriya's

Kaivalya—'Deep meditation', 'Highest knowledge'

Kalpa—Ceremonial, one of the Vedangas

Kripa—'*Nam*' or '*Word*'

Ka ba—Lit; 'cube' the cube stone structure covered with black cloth, which stands in the centre of the Grand Mosque in Mecca. In one corner it contains the 'Black Stone'. It is towards the Ka'ba that Muslims orient themselves in prayer. It is also called the 'holy house' of the mind theory.

Kosa—buckets or 'oath by sacred libetion

Krishna-trach—Dark-skinned comparative study of mind

Krishna-garbah—Dusky-brood = Ego minded,

Kula or Griha—The family

Kulapa—Head of the family

Khala—Floor of granary

Kaupina—Lion cloth

Kalindi—Yamuna river

Kshina-Kosham—Wealth dwindling

Kumaras or Aryaputra—Princes

Kupa or Udapana—Wells

Kapana-Valaka—Afflicated

Karshayati—Overtaxation and exactions

Kshama—Utmost for bearance

Kratuyaji—Give to Vedic studies and sacrifices

Kaulikanikaya—Weavers

Krtyakah or krtya—Witches

Kalingadhipati—King of Kalinga

Kharkhota—Sorcerer

Kshudra—Petty

Karkota—Chinese word means *'Nam'* or *'Sabad'*

Kharkhoda—Witchcraft

Kalasa—Inverted lotus capital *vasa*

Koshthagara—Store house

Kavya—Composition

Khadyatapakika—Food controller of Royal kitchen

Kumaramatya—Minister in Attendance on crown prince

Kripana—For the lowly

Katha—Story

Kubera—God

Kamadeva—God of love

Kumbhadasa—'Waterman'

Kumbha—'Sacrificial cup'

Kaviraja—Prince of poet

Kulika—Artisans

Khila—Waste land

Kayasthas—Writers or clerks

Khila-kshetra—Common pastures

Kantaki-Kari—Worker in thorns

Lahuka—Light

Lrohaspo—Zend, Aurvat-aspa, swift-horsed-vedic Apamnapat

Lekhad hikarin—Secretary

Loh—English loe=Glow, god of light i.e., *'Nam'* or *'Chamar'*

Lenam—Cave

Lokajna—State Craft

Lokanugraha—Social service

Lotus feet—See feet of the master

Latitavistara—"Ignorant of the silpas and the Military arts."

Ladha—Radha or Wester Bengal

Lokadhatu—Buddhisti expression

Lokaloka—Mythical mountain

Lokanatha—Name of Buddha

Lokapala—'Guardian of the world'

Lakshana or Tankasala—Mint

Lunantah—reaping

Lavana—Salt

Lagna—Auspicious time

Loka—Indeed All mankind preceptor i.e Father or God.

Lekhaharaka— 'Letter-carrier'

Mantrika—'exorcist' guards fields against nagas

Mitra—A god of light

Martya—"Mortal" a name of "Man"

Matrcakras—'Sacred diagramas'

Manyus—Wrath, a deified abstraction

Mandalasa—'Books' into which the Rig-Veda is divided.

Magic—Little used in the Rig-veda

Moon—The Soma, the fountain of Amrita

Mritya—Death personified

Manu—Man, 'The human race'

Manmukh—Lit, 'facing the mind' one who is in materialistic devotee of the mind

Mehavahana—Rainfall

Mati-Sachiva—Those who decided policy, Councillors

Maharaja—Great King of the Nam

Mahasamgiti—Great Buddhist council

Mukula—Conspirator

Mazdohano—Iranian Mazdaonho

Miiro—Sun God= Iranian Mihr, = Sanskrit Mihira

Mao—Iranian Mah = Sanskrit mas of Chandramas

Murshid—Moon-God, A spiritual master

Manaobago—Persian Mana-Baga, four armed mood God.

Mithra—Avesti, Mithra=Vedic Mitra, Sun-gold

Maasena—Sanskrit Mahasena

Mlana—Claimants pale

Mriduhridaya—Soft heart

Mahadevi—Chief queen

Mahattaras—Village Elders

Maula—Hereditary

Mitra—Allies

Matris—Divine mother's temple

Mansarovar—A Lake (Sarovar) in Dawan dwar, also called the lake of Nectar (Amritsar).

Moonbird—A fabled bird (Chakor)

Maya—Allusion, delusion, unreality; the phenomenal universe

Maha Sunn—The great (Maha) void (sunn); an area of parbrahm between *Sunn* and Bhanwar Gupha.

Mana—Honour displayed, pride

Manana—Pondered over

Mantras—Treasure of thought i.e. 'Nam' or 'Word's, words

Mudra—Honey of love i.e. 'Nam' or coin.

Mudra Rakashas—Eater of love call 'word' or *Chamar*

Mayura-poshaka-grame—'Rearer of royal peacocks'

Munipati—Reserve category or work in hides called *Chamar*

Mansarovar—A lake in the third spiritual region a dip in which makes the soul absolutely pure or *Sudh* or *Sudra*

Madhyamasi—Lying in the middle

Manyu—Wrath

Mandalas—"Books" into which the Rig-Veda divided.

Mala—Law of mind or darkness

Mahavihara—University

Maharajya—Great kingship

Mahishi—Chief queen

Mekhala—Belt

Mahamatras—Chief officer

Matamba—'An isolated town"

Mantrika—"Exorcist", guards fields against Najas

Mariyada—Those who follow the traditions of thier castes

Marga or Patha—Public road

Masurah—Lentils

Mudga or Masha—(Beans)

Mantra Griha—Council of Chamber

Mangalas—Ceremonies

Mula—Root

Maha-phala—Great fruit

Nau Nand De–hra—The existence of Godavari of a city called *Nau Nand Dehra or Nander*

Nava—The word *Nava* in the expression Nava *Nanda* to mean *nine* and not new i.e, old one i.e. Nine organ of the body two eyes, two nostril, two ears, one mouth and two lower organ to control them get the enjoy of *Nature or 'Nam' or 'Word'*. Earlier *Nanda* (Purva Nanda), *Nava Nanda* (New or later *Nanda*)

Nivapa—Ceremony

Nyaya—Logic

Nadatvae—A kind of matling

Napita Kumara or Napitasu—Founder of the Nanda lineage

Nandopakramani manani—Kings of the line are credited by c[illegible]in grammarians ('Words') with establishment of a particular kind of measure.

Nauvitana—Fleet

Nandanvaya—No need of the *Nanda* to the theory of mind

Nandivardhana—The tenth son of *Nanda* named *Mahanandin* and that "as son of *Mahanandin* by a *Sudra* woman will be born a King, *Mahapadma* (Nanda) who will exterminate all Kshatriyas. Thereafter, kings will be of *Sudra* origin; called ocean or sea.

Nara-Narayana—Charities were promoted by the best spirit of positivist social service which recognised it as a form of worship of God, of God-i-Man

Nirmulya—Uprooting

Nandins—Unknown lineage (*annatakula*)

Nandadesam—Devastated the country

Navame Nande—Nine Nandas are *Sudra*

Napitadusa 'Word' rajajatah—First *Nanda* describes as begotten of a barber (Nai)

Navabhataro—*Nava Nanda tato asum* Naital mamaiti

Manyamanah—Own dear state or country of the 'Word' like India.

Nandrum or Nanda—With supernatural encouragement Alexander obtained the title or name; Alexandrum after his death.

Natthika-ditthi—A sort of atheism

Nam—See Name, '*Sabad*, '*Word*', 'Chamar' experience through soul consciousness

Nirgun—Without (nir) attributes (gun), See also gunas (merits)

Niranjan—Without (*nir*) stain (anjan); pure. See Kal

Nafs—The ego, desires born of the senses.

Nida-i-Sultani—The 'Kingly voice' or Sound ; the 'Word'

Namaaz—The cannonical prayer of the Mulims in the mosque, prayer of 'ego'

Niyyat—Intention; adopting the state of *Ihram*

Na'ra-i-takbir—See Allah-hu-Akbar, 'God the Great,

Nidha-pati—Fowlers

Nanaia—Same as NANA or Nana appearing on the (coins) a female deity supposed to be of Persian origin.

Niryantrana—Unceremonious manner

Nidhitulya—Deep as the sea or ocean like *Sudra*

Nagararakshakas—Chief executive officers of the city

Nala—Standard unit of reeds 8x8

Naradhipati—Supposed one more king

Nirupaplavam—Succeeded wihout any trouble

Nayayadandatram—Righteous rule= 'Nam'

Nauvitana—Despatch fleet to conquered many minor rulers

Nadistuti—"River-hymn" a valuable geographical document of Veda

Nagas—Snake-people, believe on theory of Mind i.e. God

Naraka—A "hell-world"

Naturalism—Principal characteristic of the Rig-Veda or Thinker

Night—The sister of Dawn

Nirukta—Etymology, one of the Vedangas

Nadatvac—A kind of matting

Nishadya—Travellers rest houses

Nirnijya—duly washed away

Niravasita—Out caste or Untouchable people of pure thought unliked by Brahmans

Nagar—"A scot free town"

Napitadasa—Son of a barber by a courtesan

Nirathaka—Meaningless

Nakaschitrajarthavirodha—Not causing loss of the Kings revenue

Odyo Boycakana—Sanskrit Advaya-Buddha-Sakyamuni

Oesho—Hoesho=Sanskrit Bhavesa or *Vrisha*=*Sudra*=Siva

Oanindo—Arestic Female Diety called Vanamti-uparatat, victorious superiority.

Ommo—Sanskrit Uma, Om =halo

Oado—Pahlavi Vato=Vedic Vata, Vayu, wind God i.e., 'Nam' or 'Chamar'

Onkar—The lord of the second region, *Trikuti*

Prathamartham- avachchhinasamstham— The fund to be kept.

Pippala, See Ficus religrosa

Pisang—See Bananan

Pitirs—Spirit of Dead, Drink Soma from the moon

Pushan—Solar deity, of rural character

Puranas—Most of them deal with the theory of creation and the destruction and renewal of the universe

Pundit—Scholar, Hindu theologian

Pratyaya—Attainment

Pattavaya—Silk-weaver

Pratima-apratimasya—Unequalled qualities

Prakriti—By the people

Prachyamdisi—Eastern quarter

Prachyas—Eastern peoples

Parakrama—Laid great stress on exertion

Pseudo-Nanda—Yogananda

Prathita-kulajah—Contrasted with Nanda

Pachchanta-Vasika—From the frontiers

Pachchanta nagaram gantva—Marching against the cities of frontiers

Prajapati—Lord of creatures or 'Word'

Prithvi—Earth

Pasa—Nets variously

Pratishta—Pre-eminence

Paramata—Supremacy

Parameshthya—Supreme authority

Pesaskari—Empbrodierer

Poshaya—Progress

Pratima—Installed the image

Paramavapusha—Highest beauty

Pipasitah—Thirsty

Pharro—Kavaem Qareno of Avesta, Swift horsed= Vedic Apamnapat

Prathita-Kula—Illustrious lineage of Nanda

Prana-Sametam—Innate potency

Punyasala—Alms-house

Pratapa—Conscious of his power

Paricharakikrita—Obligations of service to the suzerain

Prasabhoddharana—Violent exterminated

Paturabhiksus—Naked ascetics

Prachandasasana—Dominion of a person or influence or resolute govt

Paritosha—To gain good will

Pranamagamana—Tender homage in a darbar to a person

Prithivimavitva—Conquered the earth

Pancha-Mahayajnas—To meet the expenses of daily performance

Prajna—Company of the wise

Pancha-Mandali—Governing body of the five

Pravartana—In auguratation

Pasu-chikitsa and *Manushya-Chikitsa*—Hospital both for Man and Cattle

Prathama-Kulika—Chief of the Guild of Artisans i.e. 'Nam' or 'Word'

Prathama-Kayastha—Chief of the union of writers, or scribes, chief secretary

Pastapalas—Record keepers

Pranali—Channels

Pravesya—Non-payable troops visiting the village

Prasarsati—Ruling over the image

Punya—Spiritual merit

Padadasa—Granted some lands to feudatory

Prathama—Presidents of Guilds or Groups

Pindapata—Food

Pancalas—Followers of Arjuna

Putika— Corrupt

Pancaladeva—Equivalent of Pir Pantsal or 'Word'

Pancamahasabda—'Offices designated by Father or 'Word'

Pancanada—Penjab in Persian term means 'Sound' or 'Nam'

Palevata—'Apple'

Papiha—A bird in Indian folklore, drinks only rain water and that too only at a particular time of the year.

Peshwa—The word "King" has been used for it

Prakriti—The people or living being

Quran—The sacred scriptire of Islam, written in Arabic and revealed to the prophet means to recite. Again Prophet will come in New form.

Qaul — The Word

Qazi—A judge, appointed on the basis of his knowledge of Islamic law, equivalent to Mahamatras

Qibla—Lit. focal point, Qibla is also used as synonym for the Ka'ba.

Ratha— War or Sport

Rasmi—Reins

Rajan—King

Rashtra—State or country

Rita—Truth, faith, Astras name of the cosmic law, *'Chamar', 'Nam'*

Rudhabharrodhi—Begar, forced carriage of loads

Rudhisabda—Grammatical term used for *'Word'* or *'Nam'*

Rasi—Science of numbers

Rathadhanur-bhyam—Army

Rajakommika—Those who are in the service of the King

Ratna-yonih—Precious metal

Rajadhani—Capital of kingdom

Rupa—Money-Changing

Rajakrida—The boy who always playing the role of king

Rajatiraja—The kind of the Kings

Rajatarangini—'River of Kings'

Radha—Soul or Existence

Rashtra-nigamam—Region and city

Ride—Sanskrit Riddhi

Riom (Mana)—Roma, city-Deity of Roma

Rajyasri—Kingship glory

Raja Mahan—A mighty King

Rajasthaniya—Governor of a Province, Chief Justice

Rajye-Abhishekshyati—Sovereign of the realm or kingdom

Rig-Veda—Complicated character of the life; principally natrualism which keep history in survival

Rudra—The stromy sky

Roz-i-Misak—See Shah rag

Rajayitri—Dyer

Rupakritih—A beautiful picture

Sabdartha—Etymology

Sati Sirimata or Hakusri—Saktisri in Rig Veda

Satakanni Rattha—Satavahanavihara

Srenis or Nigamas—Guilds

Sreni—Military clans

Sadha-dana or Sikata Sindhu or Shaoreoro — 'Sand ocean' *'Valukambudh'*

Sraddh-danam—A shrine out of respect for the donor's parents

Sanda—Name of the plant

Strategos or Senapati—Commander-in-chief

'Samdhivigrahika'—Minister of foreign affairs

Sariram or Dehavasesham

Sabda or Sabdavidya—A relic study of Grammer

Sanakostha—'bathinghut'

Sutra—Measuringline

Sacha-dhrama-thita—Sacha Sodha

Santarasa—'Sentiment of resignation from theory of mind

Soma—Moon-God in Rig-Veda

Saktu—Vegetable curries

Sadhaka—A kind of famulus, an tantricrites

Sailadevagriha—Records the gift of a shrine of stone.

Sadh—Who attained the region of *Trikuti* or the universal mind

Sailam—Shrine made of stone

Srimat—Magnificient i.e. '*Nam*' or *'Word'*

Sindura—'Red lead', used for seal impressions

Saka-Mana-Bouda—In Sanskrit Sakya-Muni-Buddha

Saila—Stone

Satya—upright

Sindhu Sindh—Ancient Name of Indus

Skando Komaro—In Sanskrit Skanda-Kumar

Sasana—Administration

Suttee—Widow-burning, no authority during Rig-Veda period

Seva—Services

Sumudra—Gathering of waters, *Sudar*

Samgrameshu—Sumudramatha, *Nam*

'Svabhuja-Vijitah'— Mental peace

Sukhamana—Mental peace

Svabhoganagara—Favourite city

Sandhivigrahika—Minister for foreign relations and war

Sarthavahas—Traders

Sreshthis—Bankers

Sandrophagos—Greek name of the Tchandrabagha

Sada-Satra—Alms-house

Simha-Vahana—Goddess Durga on lion

Savita—Sun

Samyak-ghatita-upalena—Solid masonary work

Saulkika—Incharge of Tolls

Sadhusamsargaputa—The sacred abod of saints

Samuditabalakoshan—The Mlechchas and their confederate forces

Santi—Peace

Sasta—Great teacher

Samaptaya—Attainmentof beatitude

Satru-Sainyam-Vigahya—Army of the enemies

Sarvato-Bhogena—Absolute possession

Sanyana—Beds

Shorear — Pahlavi Shahresar, Prefect ruler

Sarapis— In Sanskrit *Yama* or *Sraddha-devata*. Taking food in the memory of *Pitirs.*

Sakhas and Charanas—Religious group of students working under the teacher.

Sayana—Author of the standard commentary on the Rig-Veda

Sindhuvelavalayitam—Encircled by Sea or Sudra

Sravana—Heard

Sishyas—Pupils or Sikhs or disciple

Satkarya—Judge of the true poetry

Sukta-Marggah—Vedic Saktas

Sikhara—Tower over sanctum

Surya—Sun

Siddhi—Self-fulfilment

Svadhyaya—Vedic study

Surasadmasabha—Temples with halls

Sadhanika—Collector of Fines and Debts

Sabdika—Linguists

Sakya-Sasanas—Buddhist law

Saptatantavas—Experts in rituals

Samrajya—Imperial rule

Samrat—'Oh emperor'

Sastrajiva—'Pursuit of arms'

Sudragarbhodbhavah—'Off spring of the Sudra woman'

Sastra—Military power and learning

Svayam Upanamanti—Noble lineage

Sruyate—Tradition

Sapta-Sindhavah—Land of the seven river India called in Rigveda

Suna—Slaughter house

Satyam—Truthfullness

Saucham—Inner and outer Purity

Samyama—Control of senses

Samavaya—Harmony

Saravriddhi—Essential elements

Sava-pasamdani—All the sects. Sufi

Samabandha—relationship of life

Sangiti—Council

Samaggo—United body

"Sara"—Abstract of all religion or essence

Sarva-Sattnam—"All beings"

Salohitanam—Relation-in-blood

Sri—'Nam', 'Word', 'Chamar' or Soami.

Samanta-Chudamani—Prominent feudatory chief

Sakya-Sasanas—Buddhist laws

Svetapatas—Svetambaras

Sufi—Sufis believe in a living *Murshid* (Guru) and lead a holy life

Sach Khand—True or imperishable (Sach) region

Sala—Halls (Khand)

Seer—An old weight measure, slightly less than a Kilogram

Silpas—Craft

Sabad— *'Word', 'Sound', 'Chamar'* Kalma, Bani, Gurbani

Shlok—Verse, couple, Moral subject

Sifati—Attributive name

Simran—Repetition; remembrance

Smriti—Memory of Vedas

Spas—Employment spies

Sabha—Assembly of people

Sannyasi or parivrajaka—Vaikhanasa having Bhraminical character

Sagdi or Sogdri—Sudras

Tataka—Lake (Reservoir), Silence

Tulya-Kulajah—His brothers

Tantrapati—Judge i.e., 'Nam'

Tapa—Change into repentance

Tadi—Kind of earring

Tala—A "hell world"

Tritsu—The leading and purest Aryan tribe

Tugra—Allies of the Tritsu in the Ten war kings

Tila-mashah—Beans and sesamum

Titau—Sieve

Takshan—Carpenter, worked with axe (*parasu*)

Tanka—'Mint-dies' 'coin-type'

Tapasas or Isis—Forest homes called Asramas to live

Tapah—Penance

Thalaniyya-maka—Under the land pilot

Tivra—Became intense

Torana—(gate way)

Tattvah—Penetrating into the wisdom

Tiksna—'Assassin' bravo

Tiladvadasi—Festival

Tat-parigrihiten and Tat-parigrhita—Selected of the throne

Talavalaka—Gardening

Tailika-Sreni—Prosperious guild of Oilmen

Tushangaradichihnaih—Permanent marks of ash, charcoal

Taddiyatamiti—Land might be granted

Tadayuktaka—Treasury officer

Tapita—Heated

Tana—Different tunes

Tadaga—Tanks

Tantrins—Military personnel

Uggahitanaya balamsamvidhaya - conquered with garrisons with Janapadas

Upanishads—Philosophical treatise, in the Rig-veda

Ushas—The Dwan, badly treated

Upasti—Dependents

Utsadya—Overthrown

Urdara or —Vessel for the measurment of grain *Tupa*

Upala-Prakshini—Mother of a grinder of corn

Uchchairavijanam—High birth

Udyana—Looked after the public parks

Udapana—Well

Upapidayati—Molested

Upasika—Female devotee

Udadhasamadhara—Reservoir

Upaguhya—Father who embraced

Uchchhvasita—Great enthusiasm

Utsanna—Overthron

Uttarasman—Crossing stone

Udhara—Beautiful

Upachaya—To bringing some again to the king for its sale

Upasthana—Darbar Hall

Uparika Maharaja—Provincial Governor

Uttaran-Samvyavaharyadi—Village authorities concerned

Upadhaya—Sub-teacher *and Acharya*

Upavana—Parka

Udapana—Storage of drinking water

Utpratikara—Not assessed to revenue

Upachaya—Tax from productive land

Uttarapatha-Svamin—North India

Upajapam—Intrigues

Ujjama—Debt

Vuddhapatipatiya—Ruled one after another in accordance with seniority.

Vairajya—Condemn the foreign rule, sovereignty

Vasati—Greek Ossadioi

Varna—'Word' or 'Nam', Sabad, 'Chamar', *Kalma*

Vayu—Vata, the wind-serva, meaning of Ved

Vishvakarman—The artificer of the universe nameof the Supreme being, 'Lord' creator of cosmos

Vedangas—The six, "Limbs of Veda"

Veda—Meaning of the 'Word' or 'Nam'

Vaishyas—Third working class in Hindu society, believed on the pattrans of Brahmans.

Vach—Divinized speech of nature

Vipasa—Vedic name of the Bias

Vichvarupa—Omniform

Viyas—See Bias

Vyakarana—(Grammer) one of the Vedangaas, Sabad, 'Nam' or 'Word'

Varnatmak—Expressible, that which can be spoken or written

Vis—The canton or clan

Vispati—Head of the clan of Vis

Vairadaya—Enemity

Vidhata—Ordainer

Virat-purusha—Absolute, Formless, Infinite

Vaya—Weaver

Verman—Loom

Vrihi-Yavah—Barley and rice

Varatra—Leather string

Vapantra—Sowing

Vishti—forced labour

Vasas or Vasana or Vastra—Dress

Vavata—Favourite wife

Vidyamayasarira as explained by Sayana = Endowed with spiritual body

Vijavaharika—Executive head of the administration

Vetanadibhyo Jivati—Sources of livelihood

Vanijya—Trade

Vithi—Street

Vikrama—Powers

Vrishlatmaja—*Mura* the mother of *Chandragupta*, the daughter of a *Sudra womn*

Vedana—Extreme anguish

Vyasani—Addicted to vices

Varnas—Castes, pure, 'Nam', Sabad, 'Word', 'Chamar'

Varna-sankara—Ornaments of the 'Nam'

Vitrasayati—Menace or threat

Vijinamano—Conquer

Vaijayanti—Banavasi

Vasu—Seured booty

Virya—Arms

Vridita—Shame

Vibhava-pratyarpana—Loss of liberties

Vigrahavan—Example

Vahukavita—Poetical composition

Vandha—Promoted the religion by upholding

Vinaya-sthitisthayapak—Minister of law and order

Vikrayamaryada-prasanga—According to the rule of sale

Vichalita—Kula-lakshmi perturbed

Vipluta—Overwhelmed

Virapatta—Head dress of heros

Vinaya—Exalted in all humility

Vrishala—'The son of a *Sudra*' or Schedule Caste

Vishada—Filled the city with despair

Visuddha—Incorruptible

Vena—The name of the God *Indra* known as Vajra or thunderbold

Vishayapati—District Magistrate

Vyaghata—Freedom from expenses and molestation caused by the visits of royal relations and their retinue.

Vibhushitam—Adorned

Vishaya—District

Vastu—Building land or sites

Vapa-land for cultivation

Vikhyata-paurusha—Heroic chief

Vira-Kirtimvinamya—Bending down the fame of all heroes

Vithi—Sub-division

Varataka—Cowrie

Vara officer—Varakritaih = officers created by turns

Varuna—God of cosmic law

Vidyadharas—Godlings

Vina—Playing on the lyre

Varna-Samkara—To prevent unlawful mixture of castes

Vapi—Well

Vibhava=pratyarpana—Vanquished properties

Vinayasura—Conduct of visitors to the King

Vimana-mala—Aerial chariots

Vata—Unexplainable

Vrishala—Term of honour to mean ' one who is the Vrisha among kings, the best of Kings '*Sudras*'.

'Word'—See also Shabd, *'Nam'*, *Chamar*, *Dalit voice, Holy ghost*, *'Power'* supreme being. The only material for the reconstruction of earlyAryan life, Ancient and modern study of the Aryan languages.Wilkins, Marshall, Charles, 'Father of Sanskrit studies'

Waters—The mother of Agni, Rivers, divinized, Cosmogonic order or *Rita*

Wahdat-ul-Wajud—'Unity of being,' the doctrine of the unity of being corresponds to the Hindu doctrine of non-duality known as *Advaita*. According to this doctrine, there is only one Self, which is reflected by manifestion into multiplicity of beings, persons, creatures and objects and this divine self is the hidden identity of all.

Wahi—'Burest', descent of the song from God to the prophets, inspiration, revelation from God.

Yuktapurusha—A special officer

Yasah Kritsnam—Restored some scion of the old line and its glory

Yajna—See sacrifice of religion

Yadu—The one of the "Five tribes who knows, Yadava, Jana or Yadavah

Yima—Eranian equivalent of Yama

Yogi—One who practises Yoga

Yoga—Union, esoterically, spiritual exercises or practices, mediation in the spiritual sense, any system that leads to oraims at the union of the soul with God. From Sanskrit Yog, meaning ' to yoke or join,' Union .

Yama— God's death messengers.

Yogesa—Temple

Yava—Grain

Yogaschavijaye—Preparedness for war

Yuddhajivas—Soldiers

Yati—Ascetic

Yuvaraja—Application

Yachna—Crown prince

Yukta—Order

Yupa—Pillar

Yastika—Class of royal attendants

Zaat—Essence or abstract being

Ziarats—Temples transformed into *Masjid*

Zikr—The great Sufi mystics used the term *Zikr* for the highest form of remembrance or repetition, which corresponds to the *Simran* or inner invocation of the divine name or names under the direction of a spiritual Master. It is also used for many other kinds of repetition practices that pertain to the lower *chakras* and lower regions.

Zikri-ruhi—Remembrance with the soul, when the devotee's attention is fixed at the third eye.

Zadadres—Greek name of the Sutlej

Zens—Zeus-pater, Greek equivalent of Vedic *Dyaushpitar*

Zero—*Metro*, *Sun-God,* according to Gardner, Infinite, Formless

BIBLIOGRAPHY

PRIMARY WORKS

1. *Ain-i-Akbari* — Tr. by Jarrett, H.S & Blochmann, H, New Delhi: Vol. 1 & II, Reprint *Abul-Fazl Allami* 1978.

2. *Alberuni's India* — Tr. by Edward, C. Sachan, Vol.1 & II New Delhi; Reprint 1989.

3. *Babur Nama* — Tr. by Beveridge, H, Two Vols. Bond in one, Delhi, third edition, 1997.

4. *History of the rise of the Mahomedan Power in India* — Tr. by John Briggs, from original Persian of Mahomed Kasim Ferishta Reprint, Calcutta : 1966.

5. Harshcharita; Banabhatta — (Tr. by Thomas, F.W; and Cowell, E.B), Delhi 1961.

6. *Mahabharata* — Tr. in Hindi by Pt. R.N Dutta Pandey, Lucknow (U.P.) India; Vol. 1. reprinted 2059 v.s.

7. Kalhana's *Rajatarangini* — Tr. by Stein, M.A, Vol.1 & II, Delhi, reprinted, 1979.

8. *Srimad Bhagavadgita* — Tr. from Sanskrit by Vaishy, S.C. Revised by Koul, R.N. & Aggrawal K.Vol.1 & II, Gorkpur (Inida) 2006.

9. *The Akbaranama* — Tr. by Beveridge H. I.C.S (Retired) Vol. I & II, New Delhi, Second *of Abul-Fazil* edition; 1979.

10. *The Grihya Sutras* — Tr. by Olden berg, H Part-I. I. Max Muller-Part II, New Delhi; 1990.

11. *The Shah-Namah of Farudosi* — Tr. by Rogers, Alexander (I.C.S.) New Delhi, 1989.

12. *Travels in the Mogul* Empire (1656-1668) — Francois Bernier, Second edition revised by Smith, V.A. New Delhi 1989

13. *Tuzak-I-Jahangiri Memories of Jahangir* — Tr. from the Persian by Rogers, Alexander (I.C.S). Two vols. in one, Delhi, second print: 1994

14. *The life of Hiuen-Tsiang* Tr. by S. beal, S. Hwuili, Delhi 4th edition 1973

15. *Yuan-Chwang's Travels* Tr. by watters, thomas, Delhi, first edition, 1961. vol.I & II

India (A.D 629-945) edition, 1961

MODERN WORKS

16. Ambedkar, Dr. Baba Sahib, *The Buddha And His Dhamma*; Nagpur (India), 1997

17. ———do——— *Annihilation of Caste*, Aurangabad (India); Second edition, 2003

18. ———do——— *Who Were the Sudhras?* Aurangabad (India), second edition, 2003

19. Ajnat, Surendra, *Letters of Ambedkar*, (Jalandhara), India, 1993

20. Abraham, T.M *Handicrafts In India;* New Delhi, 1976

21. Aggrawal, Ashvini, *In Search of Vedic-Harappan Relationship;* New Delhi; 2005-

22. Acton-Lord, *Home and Foreign Review*; London, 1863 Selection for Correspondance (1917) London

23. ____do______ *Lectures on Modern History* (1906) London (Cambridge University Library), London

24. ____do ______ *The Cambridge Modern History: Its Origin Authership and Production.* London (1907)

25. _____do______ *The New Cambridge Modern History*: Vol-I 1957

26. _____do____ *Historical Essays and Studies;* London, 1907

27. Arnold, T. *An Inaugural Lecture on the Study of Modern History*; London, 1841

28. Ayer, A.J. *Language; Truth and Logic*; 2nd edition, London ; 1947

29. Alexander, S.W. Essays Presented to Ernst cassirer 1936, London

30. Briggs, G.W. *The Chamars;* Delhi, Reprint, 2004

31. Basham, A.L. The Wonder That Was India, New Delhi, reprint, 2003.

32. Bernal, J.D. *Science in History*. vol.III, London, Reprint 1969

33. ____do____ *Marx and Science*, London, 1952

34. Born, M. *The Natural Philosophy of Cause and Change;* oxford, 1949

35. Bhandarkar; D.R. *Some Aspects of Ancient Hindu Polity Patna-* Bihar (India) 1983

36. Banerji, S.C. *Aspects of Ancient Life from Sanskrit Sources;* Calcutta, 1972

37. Bhattacharya, A.K. *The Techniques of Indian Painting.* Calcutta, First edition; 1976

38. Bhattacharya, P.K. *A Pegeant of Indian Culture and Archaeology;* Vol. 1 New Delhi; 1995

39. Bhattachary S.K. *The Story of Indian Art:* Delhi, 1966

40. Bhushan, Jamila Brij, *Indian Jewellery, Ornament and Decorative Designs*; Bombay 1964

41. Bamzai, P.N.K. *Social, Economic History of Kashmir,* (1846-1925), Delhi 1987

42. ____do____ *History of Kashmir,* Delhi, 1962

43. Brown, Percy *Indian Painting;* New Delhi, Reprint, 1982

44. Basil Gray; *Art in the Islamic Period;* New Delhi 1981

45. Bahuguna, Rameshwar *Symbols of Resistance: Non-Brahminical Sants as Religious Hero in* Parsad *Later Medieval*; An article represent in Refresh-course in History 2005. ASC Jamia Millia Islamia

46. Blunt, E.A.H. *The Caste System of North India*; New Delhi, 1969

47. Bose, N.S. *History of the Candellas of Jejaka Bhukti*,Calcutta; 1956

48. Bury, J.B. *The Idea of Progress* ; London 1920

49. Bury, J.B. *Selected Essays,* New York; 1930

50. Butterfield, H. *The Englishman and History;* 1994

51. Butterfiled, H. *The Wing Interpretation of History*; London, 1951

52. Burchardt, J. *Judgements on History and Historians;* 1959

53. ____do___ *Reflections on History*; London, 1959

54. Bose; N.S. *History of the Candellas;* Calcutta, 1956

55. Berlin, 1. *Historical Inevitability*, London; 1954

56. Bradley — *Ethical Studies,* London; 1876

57. Bradley, F.H. — *Collected Essays*, London; 1935

58. Burke, Edmund's Works — (1846), *Thought and Details on Scurcity* (1795), London

59. Boswell, — *Life of Doctor Johnson,* (Everyman, 2nd edition), London; 1776

60. Barraclough, G — *History In a Changing World*, (1955), New York)

61. Clark, Dr. Kitson, — *The Making of Victorian England;* London, 1962

62. Collingwood R.G — *Historical Imagination,* London, 1935

63. Collingwood, R.G — *The Idea of History,* London 1946

64. Cohen, M.R. and Nagel E. — *Introduction to Logic and Scientific Method,* New York, 1934

65. Carlyle's T. — *The French Revolution;* New York

66. Croce, B. — *History as the Story of Liberty* (Eng. Tr, 1941, New York)

67. Cornford, I.M. — *Thucydides Mythistoricus, Passim; London*

68. Churchill, W. — The world Crisis: the *Aftermath;* London (1929)

69. Carr, E.H. — What is History? New York, reprint, 1984

70. __do___ — *The New Society,* London; 1960

71. Clayton, A.C. — *The Rig Ved and Vedic Religion*, New Delhi, 1981

72. Cole, W.Owen, — *The Guru In Sikhism,* London; 1982,

73. Chattopadhyaya, S., — *Social Life of Ancient India*; Santiniketan; India, 1964

74. Chattopadhyaya, K.D., — *Handicrafts of India,* Delhi; 1975

75. Chanda, M.B. — *Kautilya's Arthasastra;* Delhi 1998

76. Chaudhury,B.R. — *Folk Tales of Kashmir;* Delhi, 1969

77. Chapdekar M&Nalinee — *Ancient India and Greece;* New Delhi

78. Cunningham, Alexander — *Coins of Ancient India* And *Archealogical; Delhi*

79. ____do ______ — *Coins of Ancient India from the Earliest Times;* Down to the seven century A.D Varanasi ; 1963

80. ___do_____ Survey of India Various Reports, vol.1 to 10; Varanasi, 1966

81. __ do ___ Ancient Geography of India; Varanasi 1963

81. Chohan, A.S. *Historical Study of Society and Culture in Dardistan and Ladakh*; New Delhi; 1983

82. Clarendon Lord *A Brief View & Survey of the Dangerous & Pernicious Errors to Church & State* in Mr. Hobbes' Book Entitled *Leviation*, London, 1676

83. Childe V.G *History*, London , 1947

84. Comte A. *Coursde Philosopie Positive*; London

85. Donee; J. *Devotions Upon Emergent Occasions*, No XVII, London

86. Devahuti, D. *Harsa a Political Study*, vol.1 New Delhi, 2nd edition 1983.

87. Dandekar, R.N. *The Age of the Gupta and Other Essays* Delhi, 1980

88. Dreambi, Koul, B.K. *History and Culture of Ancient Ghandhara Western Himalaya*; New Delhi; 1990

89. Dutta, R.C. *A History Of Civilization In Ancient* India: *Based on Sanskrit literature*, vol.1 & II, Delhi, 1972

90. Datta, N.K. *Origin and Growth of Caste in India*; Calcutta, Vol.1 1908, Vol.II, 1965

91. Dube, S.C. *Tribal Heritage of India;* New Delhi; 1972

92. Drew, Fredric *The Jamboo and Kashmir Territories;* Delhi, reprint 1999

93. Drew, Fredric *Northern Barrier of India;* New Delhi 1971

94. D'Aray, M.C *The Sense of History: Secular and Sacred*, London, 1959

95. Das, S.K. *The Economic History of Ancient India*; Allahabad (India) reprint; 1987

96. Dasgupta, Satadal *Caste Kingship and Community*; Patna (Bihar) India, reprint 1993

97. Elliot, T.S. *American Historical Review;* Lvi No. 1, January 1951, New York

98. Ezekiel Isacc A. *Kabir the Great Mystic;* (Beas) Punjab, India, 2003.

99. Elton, G — *Cambridge Modern History*. vol.II, 1958, London

100. Engels,F. — *Letter of 24 Februry 1893 to Danielson in Karl Marx and Friedrich Engels.*

101. Fisher, H.A.C. — *An Article in The Times Literary Supplement* of 28 Augt. 1953, London.

102. Froude, A. — *Short Studies on Great Subjects*, vol.1 1894, New York

103. Houseman, A.E., Manilii M. — *Astronomicon: Liber Primus,* second edition 1937; London.

104. Hobbess, T. — *Leviathan* 1 IV London

105. Hegel, G.F.W. — *Philosophy of Right*. Eng. Tr. 1942, London

106. Huizinga, J. — *Tr. In Varieties* of History; edition F. Stern 1957, London

107. Hugel, Baron, Charles, — *Kashmir and the Punjab*; Delhi, 1972.

108. Harold, A. Gonld, — *The Hindu Caste System*; Delhi 1987

109. Husain, Majid; — *Geography of Jammu and Kashmir,* New Delhi, 1985

110. Hutchison J & Vogal J.Ph. — *History of the Punjab Hill States*, Department of Language and culture (H.P.); 1982

111. Howell, F.C. *Life Nature,* — *Early, Man; Nederland. revised, 1970*

112. Ghurye, G.S — *Indian Costume,* Bombay; 2nd edition 1966

113. ___do____ — Caste And Race In India; Reprint, Bombay, 1969

114. Goswami, Jay, — *Cultural History of Ancient India*; Delhi

115. Ganhar, J.N — *Jammu Shrines and Pilgrimages*, New Delhi 1973

116. Goswami, Karuna, — *Kashmir Painting*. Delhi, 1998

117. Gibbon, E. — *Decline and Fall of the Roman Empire*

118. Goswami, B.N. — *Pahari Painting of the Nala-Damayanti Theme,* New Delhi 1975

119. Green, J.R. — *History of the English People*, London; 1896

120. Ibbetson, Sir Denzil, J.C. — *Punjab Castes*. Language Department Panjab; reprint, 1995

121. Jain R.C. — *The Most Ancient Aryan Society*; Rajasthan (India) New Delhi, 1985

122. Jairazbhoy, R.A. — *Foreign Influence in Ancient India;* Bombay; 1963

123. Jaisingh, Hari, *Indian Between Dream and Relaity* New Delhi, 1989

124. Jauhari, Manorama *Politics and Ethics in Ancient India, Varanasi,* 1968

125. Jois, M. Rama *Guruji and Social Harmony,* Karnataka, 2006

126. Joshi, L.M. Studies in the Buddhist Culture of India, reprint, Delhi 1977

127. Joshi, O.P. *Painted Folklore and Folklore Painters of India.* Delhi, first edition; 1976

128. Julian, James, *The Story of Great Invention*, London, 1967

129. Kingsley, C. *The Limits of Exact Science as Applied to History*, 1860, London

130. Knowleds, D. *The Historian and Character*, New York; 1955

131. Kaegi Addf, *Life in Ancient Indian Studies In Rig-Vedic India*, calcutta; 1950

132. Kak, R.C. *Ancient Monument of Kashmir*, New Delhi 1971

133. Kak, R.C. *Antiquities of Basohli and Ramnagar,* New Delhi, 1972

134. Katoch, A.C. *Discovery of Kangra,* Gurgaon (India), 2004.

135. Kane, P.V. *History of Dharmasastra*; Poona, 3 vols. 1968

136. Ketkar, S.V. *History of Caste in India;* Jaipur (India); 1979

137. Khurana, K.L. *Ancient India;* Agra (India) Reprint 2004

138 ___do___ *World History*, 5th edition (Agra) India 2006-07

139. Khurana, K.L Gupta, S. *Historiography. Agra (India), 2003*

140. Kumar, Raj *Paintings and Lifestyles of the Jammu Region* (17th to 19th century A.D)- 2 vols. Delhi, 2006

141. Kumar, Raj *History of the Brahmans;* Delhi, 2006

142. Khan, Mohd. Ishaq History of Srinagar (1846-1947); Srinagar, 1979

143. Leathes. S. *Cambridge Modern History*, XII chapter 1910, London

144. Leavis, F.R *The Great Tradition*; New York, 1948

145. Lefebvre, G *Peuples et civilization,* vol.XIV: Napleon. London

146. Lenin, V. *Selected Works,* vol.II, New York

147. Lawrence, Walter R. *The Valley of Kashmir*; 1895, London,

148. ____do____ *Provincial Gazetteer of Kashmir*; New Delhi, reprint 1985

149. Lane-Poole, Stanley — *Babur*, New Delhi, 1969

150. Luniya, B.N — *Evolution of Indian Culture;* (Agra) India revised 2005

151. Leening, Joseph — *Yoga and the Bible,* (Beas) India, reprint, 2004

152. Limbale, Shurankumar, — *Towards an Aesthetic of Dalit Literature*. Tr. from Marathi by Alok Mukherjee, New Delhi, 2004

153. Majumdar, R.C. — *The Vedic Age;* Bombay, reprint; 1988

154. Majumdar, R.C. — *The Struggle for Empire*. Bombay, reprint 1989

155. ___do___ — *Age of the Imperial Unity*; Bombay reprint, 1960

156. ___do__- — *The Classical Accounts of India;* Calcutta, 1960

157. Majumdar, R.C. Munishi, K.M. — *The Classical Age*. Bombay vol.III, Reprint 1962

158. Majumdar, R.C, Raychaudhuri, H.C. Datta Kalikinkar, — *An Advance History of India;* London, 1963

159. Mookerji; R.K — *Asoka,* Delhi, 1967

160. ___do___ — *Ancient India;* Allahabad (India) 1956

161. ___do___ — *Ancient Indian Education;* London, reprint, 1989

162. ___do___ — *Chandragupta and His Times*, Delhi, 1966

163. Munshi, K.M — *The Glory That Was Gurjara Desa (550-1300 A.D);* Bombay 1954

164. Mishra, S.C — *Evolution of Kautilyas Arthasastras;* Delhi

165. Murdoch, J.M — *Review of Caste System In India;* New Delhi, 1977

166. Moorcroft, William — *A Journey to Lake Mansarovara*, Delhi; 1937

167. Mathew, P. Johan, Samuel, V.C. Thomas, M.M. Divarkar, P Ranikkar,R — *Christianity*, Punjab University; Patala, 3rd edition, 2000

168. Moorcroft, William & Trebeck, George — *Travels in the Himalayas Provinces of Hindustan and the Punjab*,New Delhi, Vol.I to III, 1986

169. Mannleim, *K.* — *Ideology and Utopia.* Eng. Tr. 1936 London

170. Marshall, A. — *Memorials of Affred Marshall,* Editor, A.C Pigou, New York, 1925

171. Marx-Engles — *Gesamtausgabe,* vol,1,VI

172. Mill, J.S. — *A System of Logic*, vol.VII.I

173. Namier, Sirh — *Personalities and Powers,* 1955, London

174. Nietzsche, F. — *Beyond Good and Evil*, Chapter 1. London

175. Okada, Amina — *Indian Miniature of the Mughal Court;* New York, 1985

176. Oakeshott, M. — *Experience and Its Modes*; 1933, London

177. Proceedings of the Indian History Congress 64th session, 2003

178. Proceedings of the Indian History Congress, 65th session, Bareilly 2004

179. ________________________ do __________ Santinikatan vol. 2005-06

180. Punjab History Conference Proceedings, March 18-20, 2004

181. ________do________________________ 2005

182. Parsons T.& Shils, E. — *Towards a General Theory of Action,* Third edition; 1954, London

183. Popper, K. — The Poverty of Historiciam, London, 1957

184.—do— — The Open Society, Vol.II, New York, 1952

185.Powike, F. — *Modern Historians and the Study of the History;* London, 1955

186. Pulleyblank, E.G — *Chinese History and World History*, London, 1955

187. Puri, B.N — Cities of Ancient India; Delhi, 1966

188. Puri, J.R.& Sethi V.K. — *Sant Nam Dev*, Amritsar (Punjab) India reprint, 2002.

189. Puri, J.R & Shangar, T.R — *Bulleh Shah;* Amritsar (Punjab) 2nd edition, 1997

190. Puri, J.R. & Khak, K.S — *Sultan Bahu,* Amritsar (Punjab) India, 1999

191. Pandey, Rajendra, — *Kashi Through the Ages*, Delhi, 1979

192. Paradkar, M.D. — *Similes in Manusmriti;* Delhi, 1960

193. Pande G.C. — *Foundations of Indian Culture*; New Delhi, 1923

194. Prabhavananda, Swami — *The Spiritualism Heritage of India*, London; 1962

195. Prajnanda, Swami — *Iconography of Indian Music;* Roop-Lekha, vol.XXXI, No.2, Delhi, 1960

196. Puri, J.R. & Sethi. V.K. — *Tulsi Sahib Saint of Hathras*, Punjab (India), Reprint, 1995

197. Rhys Davids. — *Buddhist India;* Delhi, 1903

198. Rajwade, Chandravati, — *Tukaram, The Ceaseless Song of Devotion*, Punjab (Beas) India, reprint, 2004

199. Rao, M.V. Krishna — *Studies in Kautilya.* New Delhi, 1958

200. Rose, H.A. — *A Glossary of the Tribes and Castes of the Punjab and Northern-'Western Frontier Provinces*, Language Department of Punjab; 3 vols. reprint, 1999

201. Ray; S.C. — *Early History and Culture of Kashmir;* Calcutta, 1957

202. Rosebery, Lord, — Napoleon: the Last Phase. London,

203. Rowse, A.L. — *The England of Elizabeth;* London, 1950

204. Russell, B. — *Portraits from Memory.* New York, 1959

205. Rutherford, Lord, — *The Baldwin Age,* Edited by John Raymond 1960, London

206. Sethi, V.K. — *Kabir, the Weaves of God's Name;* Amritsar (Punjab), 3rd edition, 1998.

207. Sethi, J.C, — *Tales of the Mystic East;* Punjab (East) India tenth edition, 2006

208. Sanders, C.W — *The Inner Voice,* Punjab (Amritsar); Reprint, 1991

209. Sharma, Vas Dev, — *Cosmic View of Life in Guru Nanak Bani*,Language Department Punjab; 1996

210.Sastri, K.A Nilakanta, — *A History of South India*, London reprint 1966

211. Sexena, K.S. — *Political History of Kashmir;* Lucknow (U.P), 1974

212. Shukla, D.N. — *Royal Arts;* Faizabad (U.P) 1969

213. Sivaramamurti, C. — *Chitrasutra of the Vishnudhar-mottara,* New Delhi, 1978

214. —do— — *The Painter in Ancient India,* New Delhi, 1978

215. —do— — *Indian Painting-* New Delhi, 1970

216. Srivastava, R.P — *Arts and Archaeology of Punjab,* Delhi, 1990

217. Srivastava, S.P — *Art and Culture Heritage of Patiala, Delhi* 1991

218. Swarup, Shanti, — *The Arts and Crafts of India and Pakistan;* Bombay 1957

219. Seth, Mira, — *Dogra Wall-Painting in Jammu and Kashmir,* Bombay, 1981

220. Sinha, B.P. — *Decline of the Kingdom of Magdha;* Patna (Bihar) 1954

221. Stamp, L.D. — *Our Developing World,* London, 1960

222. Singh, Maharaja Charan, — *Light On Saint John,* Amritasar (Punjab), reprint 1996

223. _______do_______ — *Die to Live,* Amritsar (Punjab) India, 1999

224. Singh, Khushwant, — *The History of the Sikhs*, London, 2 Vol. 1962

225. Singh Teja & Singh Ganda — *A Short History of the Sikhs,*Patiala (Punjab) 1990

226. Sinha, B.P — *Readings in Kautilya Arthasastra,* Delhi, 1976

227. Snow, C.P — *The Two Cultures and the Scientific Revolution:* London, 1959

228. Sombart, W, — *The Quientessence of Capitalism* (Eng. Tr. 1915) London.

229. Sorel, G. — *Materiaux, d'une theorie du, Proletariat,* New York, 1919

230. Spencer, Herbert, — *The Study of Sociology,* London

231. Stephen, J.F. — *History of Criminal Law of England,* 1883 quoted in L, Radzinowicz, 1957. London.

232. Strachey, Lytton, — *Preface to Eminent Victorians*, London

233. Stresemann, Gustav, *His Diaries, Letters and Papers,* vol.1, 1935, London, Editor's note

234. Saini, B.S. *The Social and Economic History of Punjab-* New Delhi, 1975,

235. Singh, Chandramani, *Centres of Indian Paintings-* New Delhi; 1989

236. Taylor, Isaac, *The Origin of the Aryans;* New Delhi, 1889

237. Thappar, Romila, *Ancient Indian Social History;* New Delhi, Reprint, 1990

238. ______do______ *A History of India Volume One,* London, Reprint 2002.

239. Tagore, Rabindranath *Boundless Sky,* Kolkata, Reprint, 2006

240. Tikoo, P.N. *Story of Kashmir,*; New Delhi; 1979

241. Tripathi, R.S. *History of Ancient India*, Delhi, 1960

242. Tinbergen, N, *Social Behaviour in Animals*, London, 1953

243. Trotsky, L. *My Life* (Eng. Tr. 1930), London

244. Trevelyan, G.M. *An Autobiography;* , London 1949

245. Tolstoy, L. *War and Peace*, 1.London

246. Toynbee, A.J *Survey of International Affairs*; London, 1935

247. ———do—— *Civilization on Trial,* London preface, 1948,

248. Tocqueville, A.De, *Preface to Democracy in America*

249. Taylor, A.J.P. *From Napoleon to Stalin*, 1950; New York

250. Tawney, C.H., *Ocean of Stories*. London

251. Tawney, R.H. *The Agrarian Problems in the Sixteenth Century;* London, 1912

252. Upadhyaya, K.N. *Guru Ravidas: The Philospher's Stone;* New Delhi, reprint, 2005

253. ___do____ *Dariya Sahib, Saint of Bihar;* Punjab (India) 2nd edition 2006

254. ___do____ *Dadu the Compassionate Mystic;* Amritasar (Punjab) reprint, 1997.

255. Vaidy, K.L. *The Cultural Heritage of the Himalaya*,New Delhi, 1977

256. Wilson, John; *Indian Caste*; New Delhi 1976

257. Willian Irvine, *Later Mughal,* Two vols. New Delhi,1989

258. Wilson H.H — *Hindu History of Kashmir;* Calcutta, 1960

259. ___do___ — The Vishnu Puran; Delhi, 1961

260. Wedgwood, C.V. — *The King's Peace*, London, 1955

261. Young, G.M. — *Victorian England,* London

262. Zanaide-A-Ragozin, — *Vedic India*, New Delhi, 1961

263. Zakaria Rafiq, — *Muhammad And the Quran*, New Delhi, 1991

264. Ziman, J. — *In the Listener,* 18 August, 1960, London

IMPERIAL GOVERNMENT PUBLICATIONS

265. Bates, Charles Ellison, *A Gazetteer of Kashmir, Kishtwar, Badrawla, Jammu Nowshera, Poonch* and the Valley of Kishan Ganga, New Delhi, 1980

266. _____do________ — *A Gazetter of Kashmir and Ladakh,* Delhi, 1890, Reprint 1974

HINDI WORKS

267. Puri, J.R — *Guru Nanak Ka Ruhani Updesh.*, Amritasar (Punjab) 2002,

268. Sethi, V.K — *Sant Nam Dev*, Amritsar (Punjab) 2004

269. Sethi, Santi — *Sant Kabir;* (Jalandar), Punjab,

270. Sethi Rajinder, — *Sant Paltu,* Amritsar (Punjab) 2003

271. Upadhyaya, K.N. — *Guru Ravi Dass*, (Jalandher), 2005

NEWS PAPER

272. Daily Excelsior, An Article written by P.K Joseph, August 16, 2006

MAGAZINE

273. Dalit Voice, Editor V.T. Rajshekar, Bangalore, Dr. Ambedkar, Spake, 16, September, 2006.

INDEX